A Gentle Madness

A Gentle Madness

*Bibliophiles, Bibliomanes,
and the Eternal Passion for Books*

NICHOLAS A. BASBANES

Henry Holt and Company
New York

Henry Holt and Company, Inc.
Publishers since 1866
115 West 18th Street
New York, New York 10011

Henry Holt® is a registered
trademark of Henry Holt and Company, Inc.

Library of Congress Cataloging-in-Publication Data
Basbanes, Nicholas A.
A gentle madness: bibliophiles, bibliomanes, and the
eternal passion for books / Nicholas A. Basbanes—1st ed.
p.   cm.
ISBN 0-8050-3653-9
1. Book collecting.   2. Bibliomania.   I. Title.
Z992.B34   1995   94-33931
002'.075—dc20   CIP

Henry Holt books are available for special
promotions and premiums. For details contact:
Director, Special Markets.

First Edition—1995

Designed by Paula R. Szafranski

Printed in the United States of America
All first editions are printed on acid-free paper.∞

3   5   7   9   10   8   6   4

Grateful acknowledgment is made to the following institutions for permission to quote from previously unpublished material: American Antiquarian Society, Worcester, Massachusetts; William L. Clements Library, University of Michigan, Ann Arbor; Columbia University Oral History Research Office, New York City; The Huntington Library, San Marino, California; The Newberry Library, Chicago; and The Rosenbach Museum and Library, Philadelphia. Endpaper illustrations from *Bibliophily in Caricature* (1934).

For
Constance V. Basbanes

Contents

List of Illustrations

Acknowledgments

Roger E. Stoddard, curator of rare books at the Houghton Library, Harvard University, listened, offered wise counsel, and read substantial portions of the manuscript.

For courtesies too numerous to enumerate: Bart Auerbach, bookseller, New York City; Sidney E. Berger, director of special collections, the University of California, Riverside; George B. Griffin, journalist, Douglas, Mass.; Priscilla Juvelis, bookseller, Cambridge, Mass.; and the late William A. Moffett, librarian of the Huntington Library, 1990 to 1995.

For showing me the treasures: Nicolas Barker and Mirjam M. Foot, the British Library; William R. Cagle and Joel Silver, the Lilly Library, Indiana University; John Dann, the Clements Library, University of Michigan; Raymond W. Daum, Kathleen G. Hjerter, and Dave Oliphant, the Harry Ransom Humanities Research Center, University of Texas; Florence de Lussy, the Bibliothèque Nationale; Catherine Denning, the John Hay Library, Brown University; Kimball Higgs and

Martin Antonetti, the Grolier Club; Norman Fiering and Susan L. Danforth, the John Carter Brown Library; H. George Fletcher and Elizabeth Poole-Wilson, the Pierpont Morgan Library; Paul Gehl, Newberry Library; William L. Joyce, Firestone Library, Princeton University; Alan Jutzi and John Rhodehamel, Henry E. Huntington Library; Barbara Kuck, Johnson & Wales University; Thomas Kren, J. Paul Getty Museum; John Lannon, Boston Athenæum; Richard Luckett, Pepys Library, Magdalene College, Cambridge University; Marcus A. McCorison and Georgia B. Barnhill, American Antiquarian Society; Bernard McTigue, New York Public Library; Laura V. Monti, Boston Public Library; Leslie A. Morris, Elizabeth E. Fuller, and Ellen S. Dunlap, Rosenbach Museum and Library; Stephen Parks, Christa Sammons, Archibald Hanna, and Marie Devine, Yale University libraries; Stephen T. Riley, Massachusetts Historical Society; Julian Roberts, Bodleian Library, Oxford University; Rita Smith, the University of Florida; William P. Stoneman, Scheide Library, Princeton, New Jersey; Sem Sutter, Joseph Regenstein Library, University of Chicago; John Van Horn, Library Company of Philadelphia; Peter M. Van Wingen, Library of Congress; Elizabeth Walsh, Folger Shakespeare Library; and David Zeidberg, University of California, Los Angeles.

I am indebted to colleagues at newspapers throughout the United States who combed their clips and files in response to my questions, with particular thanks to: Lita Solis-Cohen, *Maine Antique Digest*; Doug Cumming and Rebecca McCarthy, the *Atlanta Journal* and *Atlanta Constitution*; Michael Lichtenstein, the *New York Times*; Carlin Romano, the *Philadelphia Inquirer*; Jack Miles, the *Los Angeles Times*; Mike Reynolds, *Inside Media*; and Clifford Endres, free-lance journalist, Austin, Texas.

For help in securing public documents: Mary Allison Foster, Dutchess County Registry of Deeds, Poughkeepsie, New York; James R. Vosburgh, attorney, Washington, North Carolina; Mary Elizabeth Hugeback, clerk's office, United States District Court, Des Moines, Iowa; and Glenn V. Longacre, National Archives, Chicago depository.

Robert and Christine Liska, owners of Colophon Books in Exeter, New Hampshire, and Robert Fleck, owner of Oak Knoll Books in New Castle, Delaware, found the old and out-of-print titles I had to have. Thanks as well to Donald C. Dickinson, Mary Ann Kraus Folter,

Stephen T. Massey, Nina Musinsky, David W. Redden, Justin G. Schiller, Barbara Sloan, and Michael Zinman for providing various research materials. I am grateful, too, to Caroline Birenbaum at Swann Galleries, Susan Britman at Christie's, and Matthew Weigman at Sotheby's for keeping me current on various auctions.

Appreciation to Phyllis Button Whitten for her translations; Joan Paulson Gage for her sharp eye; Andrea Braver for her assistance in California, Ray Cornell for his help in Iowa; Annette Rebovich for transcribing tapes; Kenneth J. Botty and William T. Clew, consummate newspapermen; Dolores Courtemanche for watching the store while I was on the road; Bonnie Tobias for the creative travel arrangements; Elaine J. Newton, who was always nearby to help; George J. Basbanes for legal advice; Brian A. Higgins for riding shotgun on all those day trips to New York City; and Everett M. Skehan for his friendship and unwavering encouragement.

This book would have been impossible without the cooperation of the collectors, librarians, and booksellers who shared their knowledge and experiences with me, and whose names are listed in the "Author's Interviews" section of the bibliography. I regret being unable to get everything they told me into the book, but I profited enormously from everyone I talked to.

I can't thank Tom Disch enough for putting me in contact with Glen Hartley and Lynn Chu, my literary agents, who were champions from the beginning and who made significant contributions to the book that emerged. The careful reading I received from production editor Jenna Dolan and copy editor Katherine L. Scott was nothing less than heroic. Thanks as well to Jennifer Unter at Henry Holt for helping make the process go so smoothly.

To have Allen H. Peacock, friend and bibliophile, as my editor is a blessing of consequence; he is a man of intelligence, integrity, and unshakable good will.

I wish to record profound gratitude to my parents, John and Georgia Basbanes of Lowell, Massachusetts, and to my father-in-law, Louis G. Valentzas of Pompano Beach, Florida.

My thoughts go out to the memory of four fine and wonderful people who also believed in me and in my work: Stella Valentzas, Stella Koumoutseas, Raymond Morin, and E. Nelson Hayes.

My daughters, Barbara Georgia Basbanes and Nicole Stella Basbanes, have given me their love and their patience and inspired me to do my best.

For Constance V. Basbanes, my wife, reader of first resort, and most demanding critic, words, for once, fail me. She has my love, respect, and deepest admiration.

O blessed Letters, that combine in one
All ages past, and make one live with all:
By you we doe conferre with who are gone,
And the dead-living unto councell call:
By you th' unborne shall have communion
Of what we feele, and what doth us befall.

—SAMUEL DANIEL,
Musophilus, 1599

I cannot live without books.

—THOMAS JEFFERSON,
Letter to John Adams, 1815

In nature the bird who gets up earliest catches the most
worms, but in book-collecting the prizes fall to birds
who know worms when they see them.

—MICHAEL SADLEIR,
The Colophon, Number 3, 1930

Anything can be anywhere.

—ZACK JENKS,
Cadillac Jack, by Larry McMurtry

Prologue

A brisk wind Midwestern farmers call the Alberta Clipper swept through the frozen cornfields of Iowa one January morning, creating a windchill factor many degrees below zero. The old Cadillac bucked whenever a gust struck, but Stephen Blumberg maintained control. A million miles of pavement had passed beneath this self-described "rescuer of the past" over the previous twenty-five years, so it was not surprising to learn that he had always found the road a tonic for his anxiety. On this particular Saturday, Blumberg and I were headed southeast on Highway 163 for Ottumwa, the scene, in a sense, of his crime. With a verdict in his Des Moines trial still four days away, and with court in recess for the weekend, he had agreed to talk to me candidly about his life as the most enterprising biblioklept of the twentieth century. The red-brick Victorian house we were going to visit would be empty of books, of course—government agents had removed the rarities he stole from 268 libraries throughout North America and placed them in a secret

1

Nebraska warehouse—but Blumberg was buoyed nonetheless by the prospect of seeing his home for the first time in ten months.

Ottumwa is a community of 25,000 best known, perhaps, as the hometown of Radar O'Reilly, the popular television character from *M*A*S*H*. It was also the childhood home of Edna Ferber, who in a 1939 autobiography recalled with outrage an anti-Semitic episode suffered by her family in the city just before the turn of the century. The noted author of *Show Boat* and *Giant* held Ottumwa "accountable for anything in me that is hostile toward the world in which I live," and made a declaration that easily could have applied to Stephen Blumberg fifty years later: "Whatever Ottumwa means in the Indian language, it meant only bad luck for the Ferbers."

Once inside the city limits, we stopped for fuel at a Texaco station. As I paid for the gasoline and Blumberg waited in the car, the clerk said to me, in a flat monotone: "Stephen Blumberg." He nodded toward the self-service pumps near the idling Cadillac, and then jabbed at a photograph on the front page of that morning's Ottumwa *Courier;* it pictured a smiling man with a thick mustache, unruly hair, and wide, bulging eyes. "That's the guy with the library on Jefferson Street." I left quickly, but the point had been made; the house on Jefferson Street was the place where the wiry man outside had gathered an astonishing cache of contraband books.

Extensive press reports had suggested that Blumberg's haul was worth up to $20 million, a figure that had made him a minor celebrity in the criminal world. He told me that while undergoing a pretrial psychiatric evaluation at a federal medical facility in Missouri, he received what amounted to a royal summons from a Mafia don. Paramount on the mobster's mind was why a thief with such impressive "inside talent" as Blumberg obviously had would "waste" his skills on books instead of "things that are more liquid" like gold and diamonds. "I never took the books to sell," Blumberg explained to the man. "The idea was to keep them." Hearing that stunning admission, the mobster abruptly ended the meeting. "He decided I was really crazy," Blumberg said.

We both laughed, but the discussion suddenly turned serious when Blumberg asked with unmistakable urgency: "Nick, do *you* think I'm crazy?" Stephen Carrie Blumberg stood accused in United States District Court in Des Moines of transporting stolen property into Iowa. His lawyers freely acknowledged that he had plundered libraries on a massive scale, so the central issue was not stolen books, but the state of his mind. The following week, twelve jurors would decide whether or not he should be sent to prison or found not guilty by reason of insanity.

By the time of my trip to Iowa, I already had spent close to three years interviewing collectors, booksellers, and librarians throughout the United States in an attempt to understand the phenomenon of book collecting. I had browsed through countless second hand bookstores, stopped at flea markets, gossiped at antiquarian fairs, attended important auctions in New York, and conducted hours of research in the stacks and archives of many institutions. Abroad, I had visited the Bodleian Library at Oxford, the Pepys Library at Cambridge, the British Library in London, and the Bibliothèque Nationale in Paris. Applying the techniques of investigative journalism, I had been studying a number of intriguing book stories that insiders had talked about openly, but that few could document. I had even found a title for my work-in-progress, one based on a description once used by Benjamin Franklin Thomas to characterize his grandfather Isaiah Thomas as a person "touched early by the gentlest of infirmities, bibliomania."

To provide a context for this "gentlest of infirmities," I wanted to weave the material I had gathered into a series of related narratives. As a connecting theme, I wanted to show that however bizarre and zealous collectors have been through the ages, so much of what we know about history, literature, and culture would be lost forever if not for the passion and dedication of these driven souls.

Using the rich resources of Harvard University's Widener Library as a base of operations, I read everything on book collecting that I could find, from the earliest derisive accounts written many centuries ago by Lucian and Seneca to the most current articles in that essential English quarterly, *The Book Collector.* Fresh insights on such notables as John Carter Brown, George Brinley, Henry Huntington, Estelle Doheny, and Frank Hogan were possible through examination of letters and papers on file at the Grolier Club in New York City, the Rosenbach Museum and Library in Philadelphia, the Huntington Library in California, the American Antiquarian Society and the Boston Athenæum in Massachusetts, the John Carter Brown Library in Providence, the Newberry Library in Chicago, the Watkinson Library in Hartford, and from oral histories maintained at the University of California at Los Angeles and Columbia University in New York. This information provided the structure for part 1, which was by no means intended to be an encyclopedic discussion of "book passion," but a series of illustrative accounts.

"What is Past is Prologue," proclaims the inscription on the pediment of the National Archives in Washington, D.C., a quote from Shakespeare's *The Tempest*. Using this rich precept as both framework and guide, I was determined to travel across the United States and find today's collectors, to talk about their craving for books, and try to grasp what impels them to acquire with such determination. Their stories are told in part 2.

My journey brought me in contact with a breathtaking variety of riches. At the Huntington Library, I saw 5,300 fifteenth-century books, known as incunabula, stored two floors below ground level in an area called the outer vault. Behind a two-foot-thick steel door, in the inner vault, I handled the manuscript of Benjamin Franklin's *Autobiography*, a presentation copy of John Smith's *History of Virginia*, and a copy of *Alice's Adventures in Wonderland* given by the illustrator, John Tenniel, to the engraver, with comments by Lewis Carroll (Charles Dodgson) written inside. On various shelves were boxes of holograph writings by Abraham Lincoln, George Washington, Thomas Jefferson, Henry David Thoreau, Robert Burns, Charles Lamb, and many others. Before leaving, I opened a large 1472 copy of the first printed edition of Dante's epic poem, *The Divine Comedy*.

In a dazzling corner of the Folger Shakespeare Library in Washington, D.C., I saw seventy-nine First Folios of Shakespeare's plays, all lying flat, one shelf on top of another, like so many bars of gold bullion, and opened the copy numbered 1 to the title page signed in 1623 by the London printer Isaac Jaggard. A few hours later, when Peter Van Wingen took me into a small room at the Library of Congress where Thomas Jefferson's books are kept, there was a reverential pause. "This is the Holy of Holies," he said quietly. "For us, it begins with these books."

Everywhere I went, the dizzying cavalcade continued, and in each instance there was a tactile experience to savor and remember. At the Houghton Library in Cambridge, Massachusetts, I held a double ele-

phant folio of Audubon's *Birds of America*. A few miles away, at the
Boston Public Library, I opened one of the very first books printed in
North America, a little volume known as the Bay Psalm Book. While
doing research at the Newberry Library in Chicago, I picked up and
admired several books printed in the fifteenth century by William Caxton, England's first printer. Several months later, a California collector
allowed me to do the same with his copy of Edgar Allan Poe's *Tamerlane and Other Poems*. On the same West Coast trip, the curator of
manuscripts at the J. Paul Getty Museum brought forth several exquisite tenth-century illuminated manuscripts from the Ludwig Collection
and allowed me to turn the pages. At the Library Company of Philadelphia, I removed from a shelf the first copy of Newton's *Principia Mathematica* to be brought to North America; at Cambridge University's
Magdalene College, I admired a volume of Samuel Pepys's monumental diary; from the rare book stacks at the Lilly Library in Bloomington, Indiana, came Herman Melville's annotated copy of *King Lear*
and the Confederate president Jefferson Davis's personal copy of the
U.S. Constitution. When the third-generation book collector William
Scheide placed his copy of Johann Gutenberg's Bible in front of me and
invited me to touch where movable type had bitten into paper for the
first time, I became lightheaded. A year later, a bookseller unable to
attend a major sale in New York asked if I would handle her bids.
Priscilla Juvelis authorized me to spend a quarter of a million dollars at
Sotheby's; I was successful in eight of the contests.

About halfway into my research on this book came the first press
reports of a sensational arrest in Iowa involving thousands of stolen
books. While my intention has never been to write a diagnostic textbook about what Nicolas Barker of the British Library would teasingly
call my interest in "bibliomedicine," I nevertheless decided that an
extraordinary illustration of excess could be instructive. Without question, Blumberg was a thief, but was he "*just* a thief," as Assistant United
States Attorney Linda R. Reade would assert repeatedly at his trial? I
wanted to find out.

Right after World War II, Lawrence C. Wroth, the librarian of the
John Carter Brown Library in Providence, Rhode Island, wrote, "The
instinct to collect, like the process of fermentation, cannot be put out

of existence by legislation nor can it be deprived of its vitality by the frowns of those who are insensitive to its urge. As long as people collect and as long as there are books there will be book collectors."

> The question the historian of this and the last century will ask himself when he considers the libraries of the United States will not be "What has the book collector done for these libraries?" but "What would these libraries have been without the book collector?" He would perceive after some scrutiny of their foundations and growth that in their composition was mingled the almost indefinable quality of "distinction," bringing at least a score of them close to the level of the best of their kind in Europe. In these American libraries this quality could not have been attained with restricted public or institutional funds in so short a period of time. It was given them through the zeal and knowledge and rash expenditure of the private collector.

The title of Wroth's essay was "The Chief End of Book Madness."

Part
One

1

Touching the Hand

With thought, patience, and discrimination, book passion becomes the signature of a person's character. When out of control and indulged to excess, it lets loose a fury of bizarre behavior. "The bibliophile is the master of his books, the bibliomaniac their slave," the German bibliographer Hanns Bohatta steadfastly maintained, though the dividing line can be too blurry to discern. Whatever the involvement, however, every collector inevitably faces the same harsh reality. After years spent in determined pursuit, a moment arrives when the precious volumes must pass to other shelves. Some accept the parting with calm and foresight; others ignore it entirely. Some erect grand repositories as monuments to their taste; others release their treasures with the whispered hope that they reach safe harbor in the next generation. "A great library cannot be constructed—it is the growth of ages," John Hill Burton observed more than a century ago, an axiom that would apply to most private collections as well if not for limitations imposed by the certainty of death.

The attitudes of three nineteenth-century French bibliophiles suggest the different ways that this dilemma has been dealt with throughout history.

In most matters, Silvestre de Sacy (1758–1838) was judged a sensible and analytical scholar, a brilliant man who served from 1833 to his death as keeper of Oriental manuscripts at the Bibliothèque Nationale in Paris. But when this sober perfectionist considered the fate of his own library, his composure was tested. "O my darling books," he cried. "A day will come when you will be laid out on the salesroom table, and others will buy and possess you—persons, perhaps, less worthy of you than your old master. Yet how dear to me are they all! For have I not chosen them one by one, gathered them in with the sweat of my brow? I do love you all! It seems as if, by long and sweet companionship, you had become part of myself. But in this world, nothing is secure." He died in 1838; five years later, his books were "laid out on the salesroom table" and dispersed in a series of successful auctions.

Half a century later, Edmond de Goncourt (1822–1896)—he and his brother Jules achieved widespread fame as collaborative artists and novelists of French manners—made this stipulation in his will: "My wish is that my drawings, my prints, my curiosities, my books—in a word, these things of art which have been the joy of my life—shall not be consigned to the cold tomb of a museum, and subjected to the stupid glance of the careless passer-by; but I require that they shall all be dispersed under the hammer of the Auctioneer, so that the pleasure which the acquiring of each one of them has given me shall be given again, in each case, to some inheritor of my own tastes." When his library, known as the Bibliothèque de Goncourt, was offered for sale in 1897 in Paris, the collector's bold declaration was displayed in an epigraph to the elegant catalogue. Edmond also provided for the establishment of the Académie Goncourt to promote excellence in fiction. France's most prestigious literary prize, the Prix Goncourt, was created as a result.

A different tack was taken by Xavier Marmier (1809–1892), a member of the Académie Française who bequeathed his books to the public library in Pontarlier, his native town, with the understanding that they serve future generations of readers. With the matter of disposition safely resolved, the lifelong bachelor reflected on how much joy the collection had given him, and when his will was read in 1892, an unusually thoughtful gesture was made public. "In memory of the happy moments I have passed among the bookstall-keepers on the quays of the Left Bank—moments which I reckon among the pleasantest of my life—I leave to these worthy stall-keepers a sum of 1,000 francs. I desire that this amount shall be expended by these good and honest dealers, who number fifty or thereabouts, in paying for a jolly dinner in conviviality and in thinking of me. This will be my acknowledgment for the many hours I have lived intellectually in my almost daily walks on the quays between the Pont Royal and the Pont Saint-Michel."

In the days that followed, Marmier was widely praised as a man of generosity and "perfect politeness." The author Anatole France, the proud son of a Left Bank bookseller and himself a formidable bibliophile, described Marmier's library as one "made in his own image," an "honest, good-humored Babel, in which, in all the languages of the world, there was no talk but of sweet poetry and popular tales and the varied manners and customs of men." In a charming reflection of French book lore published just a year after Marmier's death, Octave Uzanne wrote that for the academician book hunting was "such a serious function" that he wore a "special costume for the purpose; he could stow away bundles of books in his pockets, which were numerous and as deep as sacks." Yet for all his enthusiasm, he "never forgot after a bargain to offer the stall-keeper a cigarette, or, if the stall-keeper were of the feminine gender, to take a sweetmeat-box from his pocket and beg her to accept a chocolate pastille."

On November 20, 1892, ninety-five bookstall keepers and their escorts gathered in Le Grand Véfour—then, as now, one of the more fashionable restaurants in Paris. A sumptuous nine-course dinner featuring *poulets à la chasseur* and *quartier de chevreuil à la sauce poivrade* as entrées, was served with vintage wines, followed by champagne *frappé* and fine cognac. Afterward, the senior stall keeper present, A. Choppin d'Arnouville, began his formal remarks by comparing Marmier's writings with his personal life. "I will permit myself to offer no academic opinion; but what I know well is that in the words of M. Marmier, which amount to nearly eighty volumes, you will find no bad book, no unhealthy page, no ill-natured line." He spoke warmly of the collector's "ever-ready kindness, the charm of his conversation, and the invariable and poetic gentleness he showed in all things." As for Marmier's library, d'Arnouville said it "seemed he wished it never to be dispersed. It was his custom at night to have his bachelor's bed laid among his beloved books, and over there in the depths of Franche-Comté it is still near his books that he sleeps his last sleep."

D'Arnouville took note of Marmier's fondness for world travel, and stressed that in spite of his far-flung journeys, there was one place that he found most stimulating: "Neither the most attractive landscapes, nor the mountains of his native place, nor even the tall pines he loved so much that he called them his cousins, were as much to him as the quays of the Left Bank. Every day he went along them, past the Louvre and Notre Dame and the Sainte Chapelle, giving a glance, perhaps, at the popular statue of the good king, but it was not that horizon which drew him out on that daily and uniform promenade; it was with you that he had to do, with your stalls, your boxes. He wanted to look them over once more, seeking spoil for his knowledge, opening all your books, old or new—and so happy at every find! And every day he thus enriched his library to his memory."

After the senior stall keeper concluded his remarks, a resolution that the memory of Xavier Marmier "always be kept green" was approved by acclamation, and the formal program ended with "a little dance" to celebrate the beloved book hunter's name. The joyous "festival," which the press would call "the Banquet of the Bookstall Men," then "terminated in all correctness," Octave Uzanne reported, "without a single drunkard being observable" among the guests, "thus doing honor to the absolute temperance, often doubted, of the Paris bookstall men."

If there is a lesson to be learned from Silvestre de Sacy, Edmond de Goncourt, and Xavier Marmier, it is that each contributed in different but equally essential ways to the cycle of books among collectors, libraries, and dealers. Regardless of the destinations the collectors chose for their books, steps were taken to ensure proper passage.

On May 17, 1904, a four-year-old boy stood quietly at the dedication of a library his late father had decreed should be built and turned over to Brown University in Providence, Rhode Island. "A child bearing the name of his honored father has presented to you the keys of this build-

ing," Robert Hale Ives Goddard declared on the youngster's behalf.
"No words of mine can add to the dignity or to the pathos with which
this simple ceremony is invested. Enclosed within these walls is a
matchless collection—the harvest of centuries of learning and of historical research. The books which here have their abiding home will be
an enduring monument to the patience, the scholarship and the enthusiasm for historical study of John Carter Brown and John Nicholas
Brown—father and son. To the venerable University over which you
preside, we entrust the treasures garnered around us."

The John Carter Brown Library was endowed by Rhode Island's
most prominent family, though a lot more than solid Yankee money
was required to make it possible, as Frederick Jackson Turner emphasized in his dedication address. "No one but the collector who sends his
agents far and wide with eager eye for the spoils of famous libraries
brought to the auction-block and for stray wanderers in old shops, and
who knows how keen and sharp was the contest for possession of each
of these gems, can appreciate what it meant to bring together into such
a noble assembly this elite of the original sources with all the dignity
upon them."

At the same time that the John Carter Brown Library was rising on
College Hill in Providence, and barely a block away, a much smaller
variation on this theme was being devised by Rush C. Hawkins, a
retired Union Army brigadier general and, since 1855, an avid collector of books produced during the incunabula, or "cradle period," of
Western printing, before 1501. At first, Hawkins had wanted a traditional library to house his paintings and his books, but when Annmary
Brown Hawkins, his wife of forty-three years and a cousin of John
Nicholas Brown's, died in 1903, he moved the location from New York
to Providence as a tribute to her, and modified the design to include a
mausoleum. The Annmary Brown Memorial Library opened in 1907.

Thirteen years later, at the age of eighty-nine, the colorful cavalry
officer who had led a regiment of volunteers in the Civil War known as
"Hawkins's Zouaves" died after being struck by an automobile on
Fifth Avenue in Manhattan. The general was not buried among other
departed heroes in Arlington National Cemetery, however, but in the
tomb next to Mrs. Hawkins, where he confidently had predicted that
his presence would become an "anchor" for their precious artifacts.

"They may some day want to move my books, they may want to move my paintings," Hawkins explained once to a friend, "but they will think twice before they move me." That day came in October of 1990 when all of the books and some of the paintings were moved to more secure quarters in the John Hay Library on campus. But in keeping with the general's wishes, the books are shelved in their own room as a distinct collection. The mausoleum, described in 1942 by its trustees as "A Booklover's Shrine," remains open to visitors.

When the famous English physician and author Sir Thomas Browne died on his seventy-fifth birthday in 1682, it was learned that he had made this stipulation in his will: "On my coffin when in the grave I desire may be deposited in its leather case or coffin my Elsevier's Horace," a volume so dear, he explained, since it had been "worn out with and by me." Similarly, Eugene Field, the nineteenth-century American author and collector, declared in a memoir, "I have given my friends to understand that when I am done with this earth certain of my books shall be buried with me. The list of these books will be found in the left-hand upper drawer of the old mahogany secretary in the front spare room."

Once the millionaire entrepreneur Henry E. Huntington (1850–1927) was satisfied that the library he built on the grounds of an old orange grove in San Marino, at the foot of the San Gabriel Mountains in southern California, was esteemed among the finest in the world, he set about erecting a mausoleum for his wife and himself. He selected the highest vista on his property, a gentle rise set among eucalyptus and oak trees, and retained John Russell Pope, the designer of the National Gallery of Art in Washington, D.C., as architect. Pope later used the graceful marble structure he created in San Marino—a domed, circular temple supported by two inner colonnades—as the prototype for a memorial built on the banks of the Potomac River that honors another bibliophile of distinction, Thomas Jefferson of Virginia.

The ashes of Henry Clay Folger and his wife, Emily, assemblers of the world's preeminent collection of material devoted to William Shakespeare and his era, rest in a small alcove of the great library they established in Washington, D.C. The stone marker nearby bears this inscription: "To the glory of William Shakespeare, and to the greater glory of God." A private joke among staff members runs "God gets the greater glory, but Shakespeare gets top billing."

When Elizabeth Eleanor Siddal Rossetti died in February 1862 at the age of twenty-nine, the young Englishwoman's grieving husband placed a sheaf of his unpublished poems at her side and committed both his wife and his poems to the grave. Dante Gabriel Rossetti's touching homage to an invalid wife who died from an overdose of laudanum seemed sincere enough at the time, but seven years later the emotional wounds apparently had healed, and the artist-poet furtively authorized a London dandy named Charles Augustus Howell to exhume "Lizzie's" coffin and retrieve the buried manuscript. "I should have to beg *absolute* secrecy to *everyone,* as the matter ought really not to be talked about," Rossetti cautioned in an August 16, 1869, letter to Howell, but then dangled an incentive for success. "If I recover the book I will give you the swellest drawing conceivable."

As time passed, Rossetti's anxiety mounted. "The matter occupies my mind," he wrote eighteen days later. The grave at Highgate Cemetery, he told Howell hopefully, "can be found at once by enquiry at the lodge." Another two weeks went by, and he wrote again. "An aunt of mine died two or three years ago and is, I find, buried in Highgate Cemetery, but whether in the same family grave or not I do not know— however I fancy not." He then raised the matter of literary identification. "The book in question is bound in rough grey calf and has I am almost sure red edges to the leaves. This will distinguish it from the Bible also there as I told you."

Since only the correspondence to Howell was saved, no firsthand details of the recovery survive, though Rossetti did discuss it in a letter to his brother. "All in the coffin was found quite perfect," he reported jubilantly on October 13, 1869, even though the book was "soaked through and through and had to be still further saturated with disinfectants. It is now in the hands of the medical man who was associated with Howell in the disinterment and who is carefully drying it leaf by leaf." Rossetti confided how he "begged Howell to hold his tongue for the future," though he conceded that "the truth must ooze out in time." For the present, however, there was art to consider, and no time to waste; a volume of his verses—including several reclaimed from Lizzie's grave at Highgate—was published in 1870 under the simple title *Poems.*

Twenty years later, Charles Augustus Howell was found in a ditch outside a public house in Chelsea with his throat slashed and a ten-shilling piece wedged between his teeth; an embarrassing inquest was averted when death was certified to have been caused by pneumonic phthisis. Recovered in the dead man's house were carefully maintained albums of letters from a variety of well-placed people, Dante Gabriel Rossetti among them. As a result, details of the retrieval ultimately did "ooze out." The original sheaf of poems, meanwhile, has since made its way to the Houghton Library of Harvard University.

What undoubtedly qualifies as one of history's most dramatic book exhumations involves a manuscript copy of the Gospel of St. John that was buried in the year 687 with the body of St. Cuthbert, the venerated bishop of a Benedictine monastery near Lindisfarne off the northeast coast of England. Two hundred years later, Danish invaders sacked the holy compound and the monks fled, carrying with them the remains of their patron saint. After wandering about for several years, they finally established a new monastery in Durham. When a magnificent shrine was dedicated in 1104, the carved wooden casket at last was opened, and beneath the head of St. Cuthbert's remarkably "uncorrupted" body was found the Gospel of St. John, a manuscript written in uncial (a script used in Greek and Latin manuscripts of the fourth to eighth centuries) and perfectly preserved. For the next four centuries, the gospel lay on the high altar of Durham Cathedral, where it is said to have occasioned numerous miracles. About 1540, when the priory was suppressed by agents of King Henry VIII, the volume once again was removed and passed through a succession of private owners. In 1773, a chaplain of the Earl of Lichfield presented it to the Society of Jesus. Known today as the Stonyhurst Gospel for the Jesuit college in Blackburn that owns it, the volume is now displayed in the British Library on long-term loan, still encased after thirteen centuries in its original binding of red decorated goatskin over thin limewood boards.

In an erudite examination of the quirky "disposition to possess books" first published in 1862, John Hill Burton identified a basic trait common to most collectors: "It is, as you will observe, the general ambition of the class to find value where there seems to be none, and this develops a certain skill and subtlety, enabling the operator, in the midst of a heap of rubbish, to put his finger on those things which have in them the latent capacity to become valuable and curious." Burton explained how the culling of important items from piles of refuse benefits society. "In such manner is it that books are saved from annihilation, and that their preservers become the feeders of the great collections in which, after their value is established, they find refuge; and herein it is that the class to whom our attention is at present devoted perform an inestimable service to literature."

Speaking at dedication ceremonies of the James Ford Bell Collection of voyages, travels, and early commerce at the University of Minnesota in 1953, Theodore C. Blegen surveyed the treasures newly installed around him and echoed those sentiments almost precisely: "For all time these courts will attest [to] the zeal and knowledge of private collectors who, looking to horizons beyond the rewarding personal satisfactions of collecting, have made contributions of inestimable value to scholarship."

The late Dr. A. S. W. Rosenbach of Philadelphia, the twentieth century's best-known bookseller, described the symbiosis that exists between libraries and bibliophiles. "It is a wonderful and magnificent thing that the gathering of books in this country is in the hands of leaders of her industries, the so-called business kings, and not in the hands of college professors and great scholars," he wrote during the height of the golden age of American collecting from 1870 to 1930. "It is paradoxical, but true, that not a single great library in the world has been formed by a great scholar."

While preservation and the service of scholarship are happy products of collecting, they by no means are the only compelling forces. "I am not exaggerating when I say that to a true collector the acquisition of an old book is a rebirth," the German critic Walter Benjamin wrote. "This is the childlike element which in a collector mingles with the element of old age." What is evident in the exercise—and it has been apparent for centuries—is that the closer people get to the source, the closer they feel the wonders of creativity. Storytellers, philosophers, scientists, adventurers, artists, economists, politicians, diplomats, theologians, even evil despots like Adolf Hitler, articulate their thoughts between hard covers. To see and handle a first edition of Darwin's *Origin of Species* or Newton's *Principia Mathematica* is to touch ideas that changed the way people live. To own a book inscribed by William

Faulkner or a letter written by George Washington, to have the manuscripts of literary works in variant drafts is all the more meaningful because they bring people that much nearer to the generative process. "I have known men to hazard their fortunes, go long journeys halfway about the world, forget friendships, even lie, cheat, and steal, all for the gain of a book," Dr. Rosenbach noted. Book collectors, he stated categorically—and he was including himself—"are buzzards who stretch their wings in anticipation as they wait patiently for a colleague's demise; then they swoop down and ghoulishly grab some long-coveted treasure from the dear departed's trove."

When Seymour Adelman, another Philadelphia bibliophile, was urged by friends to allow private publication of some diverting talks he had given over the years on his love for literary arcania, the affable bachelor agreed, but with reservations. "My main anxiety is that I am now in danger of losing my franchise as a collector," he wrote in an author's note to *The Moving Pageant,* published in 1977. "I was put on this earth to collect books, not to write them. It has taken me fifty years to gather my collection, now forever happily in residence at Bryn Mawr College, and I would like to add to its shelves from time to time. Hence my concern. If, because of this book, my integrity as a collector is sullied by authorship, who knows what dire consequences will follow. Will any self-respecting rare-book dealer ever let me into his shop again? Will I be permitted to attend auction sales? Will I be expelled from the Philobiblon Club?"

In a 1950 speech to the Bibliographical Society of America, Clifton Waller Barrett, builder of an extraordinary collection of American literature now housed at the University of Virginia in Charlottesville, described the temperament of what he called the genus *Collector:* "First of all, he must be distinguished by his rapacity. If he does not covet and is not prepared to seize and fight for every binding, every issue and every state of every book that falls even remotely within the range of his particular bibliomania, treat him as the lawful fisherman treats a nine-inch bass; throw him back—he is only an insignificant and colorless offshoot of the true parent stock." Robert H. Taylor, whose exceptional collection of English literature was given to Princeton University, offered this observation at a meeting of the same organization four years later: "It must be clearly understood that, generally speak-

ing, the collector is sentimental, illogical, selfish, romantic, extravagant, capricious." Citing an example from his own experience, Taylor
recalled a heated argument he once had with a bookseller over some
long-since-forgotten matter. "The trouble with you," the dealer finally
shouted in frustration, "is that you're like every other God-damned
collector," an assessment that needed no further elaboration, and
which Taylor accepted as a compliment: "I don't ask for any better
tribute."

Praise of a more formal sort issued forth at the dedication, on June
15, 1923, of the William L. Clements Library of American History on
the Ann Arbor campus of the University of Michigan. The donor, a Bay
City industrialist who had competed on the open market with Henry E.
Huntington and J. Pierpont Morgan for some of his most cherished
acquisitions, expressed no maudlin wish about being buried alongside
his books or having any statue erected to his memory. What mattered
most to him was maintaining "the integrity of this library" and keeping it "carefully guarded" from those who have "no sentimental or aesthetic interest" whatsoever in rare books. "This day and hour mark the
conclusion of a book collector's career," Clements said in his remarks,
and then placed on the record his pointed expectation that students
"who have not exhausted the facilities of the General Library" be
denied access to his treasures. "May we use with the greatest care these
materials which can never be replaced! Let those who have no valid
right to examine or handle, be content with a look; and for those who
would make the examination, may not facsimiles serve the purpose?"

By contrast, a comprehensive collection of English and Continental
literature, Bibles, Americana, incunabula, and science formally given to
Williams College in western Massachusetts just two weeks later was
assembled from the outset with vigorous undergraduate use in mind.
Alfred C. Chapin, a devoted Williams alumnus, was a lawyer, financier,
and political power broker who served as speaker of the New York
State Assembly and as the last mayor of Brooklyn, New York. In 1915
he began buying such highspots as an Eliot Indian Bible in its original
binding and a perfect 1465 copy of Cicero's *De Oratore,* but he never
regarded these purchases as his own property. Instead of sending the
books directly on to Williams immediately, he kept them in a Manhattan vault for eight years until assured that the college had a suitable

building in place to receive them. By the time he died in 1936, some twelve thousand rare volumes had been given to his alma mater. "Every item was purchased directly for Williams," the Chapin Library's first custodian, Lucy E. Osborne, wrote, "and behind every item was Mr. Chapin's personal choice."

The late Philip Hofer once recalled a trip he made to Japan in 1956 on behalf of Harvard College, where he is regarded as the greatest book donor in the long history of the institution. On the customs bill of lading for the items he had bought was written, in Japanese: "With no disrespect to the gentleman making this declaration, with an apparent sincerity, the Imperial Customs Service cannot see how he can use, or understand, so many books he cannot read. Will the Japanese consul in Boston please take notice, and if he sets up shop in America please ask for the usual Japanese export tax." Hofer then told how he often enjoyed asking groups of collectors which man was happier, "he that hath a library with well nigh unto all the world's classics, or he that hath thirteen daughters?" The happier man, he would then answer, is the man with thirteen daughters, "because he knoweth that he hath enough," while the compulsive collector, whose days are marked by "happy, as well as greedy moments," is never satisfied. "At other times he suffers agonies of jealousy, frustration, and humiliation. He would not be a true collector if he didn't."

Seymour Adelman, Clifton Waller Barrett, Robert H. Taylor, William L. Clements, Alfred C. Chapin, and Philip Hofer were "true collectors" in every respect, but nobody ever accused them of being hopelessly out of control. On the other hand, the University of Kansas readily admits that its finest natural history collections exist solely because of the "galloping bibliomania" that consumed the two men who formed them. The Ralph N. Ellis Collection of Ornithology, which includes unparalleled holdings of material executed by the British ornithologist and artist John Gould (1804–1881), "stands out for the impassioned, almost violent haste of its creation," according to Robert Vosper, who for many years was the director of libraries at the University of Kansas; the other collection, a massive concentration of books on botany and related sciences, was gathered by Thomas Jefferson Fitzpatrick, a man whose craving became "so cancerous that he could hardly forgo anything with print on it."

Born to wealth and social station in 1908, Ralph Ellis, Jr., began collecting birds' eggs and nests at the age of twelve and ornithological books at fifteen. He continued with a dedication so furious that in 1940 his mother had him committed to a California sanitarium out of fear that his activity would totally deplete the family fortune. Diagnosed as "mentally ill but not insane," Ellis finally secured his release and resumed the hunt with even greater energy. Sometime in 1944, he began casting about for an institution willing to provide permanent quarters for his collection. Frustrated by these efforts—and uneasy about staying in California any longer than necessary—Ellis orchestrated a dramatic departure. In February 1945, two freight cars were hastily loaded with his 65,000 books, pamphlets, manuscripts, plates, and illustrations, and were hauled out of Berkeley, California, on a train bound for New York, his native state.

While the boxcars were rolling east, Ellis received an "offer of hospitality" for the collection from a boyhood mentor who by then was director of the Museum of Natural History at the University of Kansas. Immediately won over, Ellis had railroad officials wire an urgent message to their engineer: Stop the train in Lawrence, Kansas, and leave the cargo there. The only compensation Ellis insisted on in return for his donation was a proper home for his beloved bird books and an office for himself. The University of Kansas happily complied. Six months later, Ellis died of pneumonia at the age of thirty-seven, alone in a hotel room. "Thus finally Ralph Ellis's shattering life has come into peaceful concentration and focus," Vosper wrote in 1961. "Only a touch of genius, I believe, and an obsessive touch of the madness of books could have produced so extensive and so well integrated a library within so brief and chaotic a lifetime."

Unlike Ellis, Thomas Jefferson Fitzpatrick collected quietly and without fanfare for more than half a century. A native of Centerville, Iowa, he served as official "field collector" for the Iowa State Historical Society from 1903 to 1907, an assignment that gave professional discipline to what eventually became his driving preoccupation. In 1913, Fitzpatrick accepted a teaching position in the botany department at the University of Nebraska and moved to Lincoln, where he lived for the rest of his life. Because he never earned a Ph.D., the highest rank he ever achieved was assistant professor, and the most he ever earned was $1,800 a year. Still, his acquisitions proceeded with determination. To generate additional income, he sold duplicate copies in his collection to numerous institutions. He also wrote scientific articles and monographs, which were published in various technical journals.

In November 1950, the eighty-two-year-old bibliomane had a brush with the law when city officials cited him for violating local building codes in his house. The maximum permissible load limit for multilevel dwellings was forty pounds per square foot; an inspector had estimated that Fitzpatrick's house was supporting more than eight times that weight—about ninety tons altogether, most of it in books. The action was later dismissed on grounds that the collector's "rights of privacy" had been invaded.

On March 28, 1952, five days shy of his eighty-fourth birthday, Fitzpatrick died in his kitchen on an army cot that he used as a bed, "surrounded by a clutter of books and papers, nestled against a potbelly stove." His immense library was turned over to a secondhand dealer for dispersal; by a stroke of luck, Robert Vosper heard about it and went to Nebraska for a viewing. "The house was full of books, packed with books, all thirteen rooms," he recalled. "Books were stacked under tables, piled up on beds, heaped in bundles on both sides of the stairways, pressed three and four deep in bookcases and onto ceiling-height shelving that lined every room and all hallways. Every room was awash with teetering piles of books, tied bundles of pamphlets, and stacks of magazines, so that we had to inch our way along trails hacked into a bookman's jungle."

The university limited its selection to ten thousand books, pamphlets, and periodicals dealing specifically with botany and the history of science, which were some of the best-represented subjects—especially Carolus Linnaeus and the eighteenth-century American naturalist C. S. Rafinesque. Other collections dealing with Americana, the Midwest, the Mormon church, and American travel went to the Kansas City Public Library; what remained was sold piecemeal. Even though Fitzpatrick's activity as a collector had been restricted by his modest means, he was a "persistent searcher and a shrewd judge of a bargain," according to Vosper. And his "foresight in collecting unpopular subjects" gave him a decided edge on the competition. Indeed,

Fitzpatrick's interest in local history and American science "antedates by a generation the widespread popular and academic concern with those same fields of collecting."

Wilmarth Sheldon Lewis was once described in a 1949 *New Yorker* profile as an American country squire "with chiseled features, English clothes, an authoritative air, an inquiring, skeptical eye, a cultivated and witty conversational style, a collector's mania, a flawless worldly charm, independent means, and a strong sense of scholarship." For all these admirable qualities, it was the "independent means" that enabled "Lefty" Lewis to devote his adult life to securing every available scrap of material and artifact related to the eighteenth-century writer Horace Walpole (1717–1797), youngest son of Sir Robert Walpole and the author of thousands of diverting letters. Lewis acquired with such single-mindedness that once he outbid his own agent at an auction. Ultimately, he claimed ownership of 2,500 letters written by Horace Walpole.

Lewis assimilated his subject so completely that he named his house in Farmington, Connecticut, the Lewis Walpole Library and furnished it with tableware, lamps, artwork, and jewelry that once graced Strawberry Hill, his hero's home in England. He also underwrote and edited the Yale University Press edition of *Horace Walpole's Correspondence,* a mammoth project that consumed forty-seven years of his life and filled forty-eight volumes. When Lewis died in 1979, his large Colonial home was given to Yale University with the stipulation that his library be maintained there intact.

In books with such titles as *Collector's Progress, One Man's Education,* and *Horace Walpole's Library,* Lewis wrote about his obsession, yet his most penetrating statement of purpose came in a passage he wrote for a speech that was never delivered. It is preserved among his papers and includes this observation: "The loyalty of collectors draws them to each other; they are a fraternity joined by bonds stronger than their vows, the bonds of shared vanity and the ridicule of non-collectors. Collectors appear to non-collectors as selfish, rapacious, and half-mad, which is what collectors frequently are, but they may also be enlightened, generous, and benefactors of society, which is the way they like to see themselves. Mad or sane, they salvage civilization."

There is no question that Wilmarth Lewis salvaged Horace Walpole from literary oblivion and gave him what amounted to a new life. Other instances of a collector causing renewed scholarly interest in a forgotten figure are rare, but by no means unknown. Probably the most striking examples of recent years involve one British bibliophile, the late Michael Sadleir, who began collecting first editions of the works of nineteenth-century English and American writers of fiction at a time when "he had hardly any serious rival," according to the London bookseller Percy Muir. "To mention only two very outstanding, but very different authors, Melville and Trollope were very nearly forgotten by both readers and collectors," Muir writes, and it was Sadleir's "enthusiasm that was almost entirely responsible for the beginning of the revival of interest in them."

In a 1951 essay titled "Passages from the Autobiography of a Bibliomaniac," Sadleir told how a 1922 book of his, *Excursions in Victorian Bibliography,* emerged from an "examination of my captures," which he further explained were the otherwise "un-sought-for and therefore cheaply priced" books he was able to acquire with little competition.

> After the publication of *Excursions,* I settled to the writing of a biography of Anthony Trollope and his mother. This was the first full-length application of a principle which had from the beginning influenced my book-collecting policy and was to become an integral part of it. I have never undertaken the intensive collection of any author or movement without the intention of ultimately writing the material collected into biography, bibliography or fiction.

Sadleir's writing over the next thirty-five years included such influential books as *Anthony Trollope: A Commentary* (1927), *Trollope: A Bibliography* (1928), *Things Past* (1944), and *XIX Century Fiction: A Bibliographical Record Based on His Own Collection* (1951), as well as a number of dated and largely forgotten novels. After his death in 1957, Sadleir's collection of nineteenth-century fiction was sold en bloc to the University of California at Los Angeles.

◆ ◆ ◆

Centuries before Sigmund Freud gave scope and substance to the study of the mysteries of the mind, people had been mad about books, yet it was not until 1809 that a name for this curious malady came into widespread use. That year, the Reverend Thomas Frognall Dibdin (1776–1847) popularized the word *bibliomania* when he published a lighthearted "bibliographical romance" he titled *The Bibliomania; or, Book-Madness; containing some account of the History, Symptoms, and Cure of This Fatal Disease.* Although Dibdin became the faithful book scout and chief cataloguer for George John, second earl of Spencer, the man who created what the noted French bibliographer A. A. Renouard called "the finest and most beautiful private library in Europe," he is remembered best as the unrepentant eavesdropper who chronicled with hyperbole and delight the Heroic Age of Book Collecting, the first half of the nineteenth century.

"It has raged chiefly in palaces, castles, halls, and gay mansions," Dibdin wrote in *The Bibliomania,* "and those things which in general are supposed not to be inimical to health, such as cleanliness, spaciousness, and splendour, are only so many inducements toward the introduction and propagation of the BIBLIOMANIA! What renders it particularly formidable is that it rages in all seasons of the year, and at all periods of human existence."

What gives Dibdin's treatise an extra measure of charm is that it cited a legitimate medical authority as source for the designation of the illness. A few months before his book was released, a respected Manchester physician, Dr. John Ferriar, published a satirical poem with the same title and addressed it as an "epistle" to his good friend Richard Heber, a collector who filled eight houses in four countries with upwards of 200,000 books. An active member of his city's Literary and Philosophical Society, Dr. Ferriar wrote a number of learned studies on many subjects, medical as well as literary. His last published work, "An Essay Towards a Theory of Apparitions," is said to contain "ingenious views on mental hallucinations." But the "diagnosis" he offered for bibliomania was all in fun:

What wild desires, what restless torments seize
The hapless man, who feels the book-disease. . . .

In later verses, Dr. Ferriar described how those afflicted display a manic interest in bibliographical features that have nothing to do with literary content:

> *The Bibliomane exclaims, with haggard eye,*
> *"No Margin!" turns in haste, and scorns to buy. . . .*
> *At ev'ry auction, bent on fresh supplies,*
> *He cons his Catalogue with anxious eyes:*
> *Where'er the slim Italics mark the page,*
> *"Curious and rare" his ardent mind engage.*

A year after Dibdin released his treatise, a pseudonymously published pamphlet titled *Bibliosophia; or, Book-Wisdom* appeared in England that proposed an alternative name. The amusing work extolled the "pride, pleasure, and privileges of that glorious vocation, book-collecting," and was addressed directly to the good pastor himself. "Bibliomania, Mr. D.!—and is *this* the softest title which you can afford to the noble passion for literary accumulation—*that* passion, to which, throughout the very book in which it is thus stigmatized, you almost avow that you are, yourself, a voluntary, if not an exulting Victim?" The author—whom William A. Jackson, Harvard's Houghton librarian, identified in his definitive Dibdin bibliography as one James Beresford—proposed his coinage as a suitable corrective: "BIBLIOSOPHIA,—which I would define—an appetite for COLLECTING Books,—carefully distinguished from, wholly unconnected with, nay absolutely repugnant to, all idea of READING them."

The Oxford English Dictionary lists more than twenty *biblio*-words in the English language: *biblioclasm, bibliognost, bibliolatry, bibliogony, bibliomancy, bibliopegy, bibliophobia, bibliopoesy, bibliotaph, bibliophagist, bibliopole,* and *bibliomania* among them—but no *bibliosophia*. Bibliomania it was and bibliomania it would remain. It is worth adding that neither Dibdin nor Dr. Ferriar gets credit for the first recorded use of the word in English. This distinction goes to Philip Dormer Stanhope, fourth earl of Chesterfield, the respected statesman, orator, wit, man of letters, and good friend of Samuel Johnson, Jonathan Swift, and Alexander Pope. Lord Chesterfield is remembered most for the erudite correspondence he maintained for thirty years with his son, also Philip Stanhope, his illegitimate child with a Frenchwoman.

Lord Chesterfield took profound interest in young Philip's welfare, and his letters invariably included nuggets of advice on a variety of concerns. "Do you take care to walk, sit, stand, and present yourself gracefully?" he asked on March 19, 1750, when the lad was sixteen years old. "Are you sufficiently upon your guard against awkward attitudes, and illiberal, ill-bred, and disgusting habits, such as scratching yourself, putting your fingers in your mouth, nose and ears?" In the same letter, the concerned father also responded to reports that Philip was developing a taste for rare books. "Buy good books, and read them; the best books are the commonest, and the last editions are always the best, if the editors are not blockheads, for they may profit from the former. But take care not to understand editions and title-pages too well. It always smells of pedantry, and always of learning. What curious books I have, they are indeed but few, shall be at your service." He concluded the lecture with a succinct warning: "Beware of the *Bibliomanie.*"

Lord Chesterfield died in 1773 at the age of seventy-eight; the following year, the correspondence he had maintained so faithfully with his son was sold for £1,575 and published in two volumes. By 1800, *The Letters of the Earl of Chesterfield to His Son* had gone through eleven editions, and the peer's wry counsel was well known in the circles frequented by Dr. Ferriar and Reverend Dibdin.

In a 1966 essay prepared for a psychiatric journal, the psychoanalyst Dr. Norman S. Weiner of Philadelphia described the bibliomaniac as a person with an "inordinate desire" for books who will "pursue a volume in an active or seductive way; he will use intrigue and stealth; he will hazard his fortune and he will journey around the world, or even marry for the gain of a coveted book." On the basis of the evidence he had gathered, Dr. Weiner suggested that bibliomania is "a problem-solving complex of activity that relieves anxiety or directly gratifies certain instinctual drives."

In the "literature on bibliomania," he continued, "mention is made that the book functions as a talisman for its owner but it is a temporary and fleeting passion." A further curiosity is that the bibliomaniac invariably must then

> set out on another quest for a great book as soon as his anxiety returns. The quality of the boasting, the constant search for new conquests, and the delight in recounting the tales of acquisition and success brings to mind the activities of the hypersexual male hysteric who must constantly reassure himself that he has not been castrated. It seems germane to this point that Casanova, after his many amatory adventures, settled down as a librarian in the castle of Count Waldstein at Dux, in Bohemia.

The psychoanalyst's conclusion—that some collectors use books as a "fetish" to provide "gratification of oral, anal, and phallic strivings"—involves "castration anxiety" and applies strictly to men. To support this position, he relied heavily on Eugene Field's sweeping assertion of a century ago: "It has never been explained to my satisfaction why women as a class are the enemies of books and are particularly hostile to bibliomania." By accepting the validity of this dictum, psychiatrist-psychoanalyst Dr. Weiner was able to confine his "symptomology" to men.

Of course, women too have collected throughout history. Rosenbach devoted a chapter of *A Book Hunter's Holiday* to "Mighty Women Book Hunters," paying particular attention to the female companions of several French monarchs. "It speaks rather well, I think, for the kings of France that they chose for friends beautiful ladies who loved beautiful books," he wrote. Gabrielle d'Estrées, Madame de Pompadour, and Catherine de' Médicis all had notable collections. Diane de Poitiers, the mistress of Henri II, had the exquisitely bound books she kept at Château d'Anet embossed with the interlaced initials H and D. In 1558 she lobbied successfully for passage of an ordinance that required French publishers to present copies of every book they issued to the libraries of Blois and Fontainebleau; this "copy tax" quickly added eight hundred volumes to the national collections. Catherine de Médicis was less subtle; when one of her kinsmen, Marshal Strozzi, died while in French service, she simply ordered the confiscation of his library. "Let us forgive her," Rosenbach suggested. "She was a genuine bibliophile."

Among history's more dogged collectors was Christina, the daughter of King Gustavus II and queen of Sweden from 1644 to 1654. Shortly after assuming power at the age of eighteen, she dedicated herself to forming a strong national library and began by consolidating the books her generals had seized from conquered cities during the Thirty Years' War. She then authorized the purchase of precious manuscripts and acquired the libraries of several private collectors, the French theologian Denys Petau, the Dutch jurist Hugo Grotius, and the Dutch theologian Gerhard Vossius among them. She also brought to Stockholm Gabriel Naudé, the former librarian to Cardinal Mazarin, to supervise the installation of her books.

In 1649, Christina invited René Descartes to visit Sweden and be her tutor. The famous philosopher quickly found the queen's petulance disagreeable, especially her insistence that lessons begin promptly at five o'clock in the morning. The Scandinavian winter was characteristically harsh, and he died in February 1650 after coming down with a fever. The queen continued to forge alliances with other authors, among them Blaise Pascal, who forwarded for her inspection a model of his calculating machine.

Two years before her abdication in 1654, Christina wrote to one of her Dutch agents, Nicholas Heinsius, who was then locating books for her in Italy: "Continue to send me lists of all that is beautiful and rare; but do not embark in any purchase: as long as I know of the rarities, I will manage the rest." According to one early biographer, Christina's great library in Stockholm "was arranged in four great halls, in which besides a multitude of printed books, were at least eight thousand manuscripts in Latin, Greek, Arabic, and Hebrew."

After leaving Sweden, Christina converted to Catholicism and stayed in Antwerp for a while before settling in Rome. Traveling with two hundred attendants, she led a spectacular cavalcade of book-bearing wagons into the Eternal City. There, she founded two academies and allowed scholars the use of her books. At Christina's death in 1689, her library, known as the Bibliotheca Alessandrina (she considered herself a female Alexander the Great), was transferred to the Vatican Library, where it was installed in an ornate room added by Pope Alexander VIII.

In his study Dr. Weiner made no mention of these women, and he ignored entirely Estelle Doheny, the California heiress whose great library earned $37.4 million for the Archdiocese of Los Angeles at a series of Christie's sales in the 1980s, the most lucrative book auction in history. He also had nothing to say about Amy Lowell (1874–1925), which is surprising, since the eminent Boston collector's fondness for large cigars might have made an unusually tempting target for a probing psychoanalyst. But such an attack would have opened the way for an interesting rebuttal, as Peter Gay made clear in his biography of Sigmund Freud, the father of psychoanalysis: "If Freud's helpless love for cigars attests to the survival of primitive oral needs, his collecting of antiquities reveals residues in adult life of no less primitive anal enjoyments." Freud, as it happened, admitted to his own doctor that the collecting of old objects, including books, was for him "an addiction second in intensity" only to nicotine.

Dr. Rosenbach, at any rate, considered Amy Lowell the greatest of all American women collectors. "Miss Lowell had a well-defined plan in the formation of her library," the Philadelphia bookseller wrote.

> She wanted unpublished [John] Keats material first and foremost, and the Keats manuscripts in her collection speak more eloquently of her successful endeavors than anything I can say of her. If she desired a particular item, she would not rest until she secured it. It was not unusual for her to call me from Boston at any hour of the night to learn if I had purchased something for her at one of the auction sales. The cost was nothing, the book everything.

Today, the Amy Lowell Collection is housed in its own room on the second floor of the Houghton Library at Harvard University, a tribute suggested by the donor of the building, Arthur A. Houghton, Jr., whose own Keats items are there with hers. The collection that Lowell gave in 1925 includes holographic manuscripts for "On First Looking into Chapman's Homer," "The Eve of St. Agnes," and "To Autumn," and was gathered initially as primary research material for her two-volume biography of the Romantic poet. But her collection also included the manuscript copy of Charles Lamb's *Grace Before Meat* and Samuel Johnson's signed personal copy of *Rasselas,* along with handwritten manuscripts by Walt Whitman, Ludwig van Beethoven, and George Eliot.

Regrettably, visitors to the Pierpont Morgan Library in New York will not find a room named for Brooklyn's Abbie Ellen Hanscom Pope, but several titles gathered by her during the late nineteenth century are esteemed among the finest in the building, including the only perfect copy known of Thomas Malory's *Le Morte d'Arthur*, printed at Westminster, London, in 1485 by William Caxton. She acquired the prize in 1885 after outbidding the British Museum; she was twenty-seven years old at the time. After Mrs. Pope's unexpected death in 1894, the man regarded by many as America's greatest book collector, Robert Hoe III, bought her choicest items for the then unheard-of sum of $250,000. On Hoe's death in 1909, her books were among the fourteen thousand lots sold at his landmark sale.

In the spring of 1990, the Grolier Club mounted an exhibition in New York called "Fifteen Women Book Collectors," which honored the accomplishments of woman book collectors through five centuries, from Diane de Poitiers to Frances Hooper. Hooper was a Chicago journalist and advertising executive who built several distinguished collections that are now owned by various institutions. To open the exhibition, Mary Hyde Eccles, one of the world's great living collectors, gave an address that began with a tribute to the "origin of a new species," female bibliophiles: "The fascinating question raised by all this is *why*, in five centuries, in six countries, do there seem to have been so *few* women book collectors? The answer is obvious: a serious collector on any scale must have three advantages: considerable resources, education, and freedom. Until recently, only a handful of women have had all three, but times are changing!"

Starting in 1940, Mary Hyde Eccles and her first husband, the late Donald Hyde, built a monumental collection of primary materials relating to Samuel Johnson and his circle at Four Oaks Farm, their home in New Jersey. Respected everywhere, the collection has been the subject of numerous scholarly studies. Eccles's talk that night recalled their "greatest collecting coup," the acquisition in 1948 of the finest Johnson collection "on either side of the Atlantic." Assembled over two generations by Robert B. Adam and his nephew and heir, Robert B. Adam II, owners of a department store in Buffalo, New York, the materials were placed on the market three days after the Crash of 1929.

Despite the undisputed importance of the material and the concerted efforts of Dr. A. S. W. Rosenbach to sell it for the Adams, few serious offers were made. In 1936, the New York State Banking Authority ordered that the collection, which included several hundred letters, many pages of manuscripts, and numerous translations, be placed at the University of Rochester as security for a bank loan for the Adams. There they remained, until finally, in 1948, a deal was struck with Donald and Mary Hyde. She told what happened next:

> On December 16, 1948—more than nineteen years after the Adam Library was first offered for sale—the collection arrived at the Gladstone, New Jersey, railway station in a blinding snowstorm. Fifty packing cases and two trunks were lifted into farm trucks and driven to Four Oaks Farm. Johnson in enormous bulk had come to live with us. One thing was immediately apparent: he needed a room of his own.

With the death of Donald Hyde in 1966, Mrs. Eccles acknowledged that she "lost a great deal of heart in the library," but slowly, deliberately, she "returned to collecting as a way of life." As the years passed, a combination of mutual interests—book friends, books, and libraries—occasioned her marriage to David Eccles of Great Britain. Now embarked on editing a new volume of Johnson's letters, she put her talk in sharp perspective: "Oh, how I wish I could find just one more Johnson letter—any scrap whatsoever. That is still the . . . *unending pursuit.*"

The therapeutic nature of books is a story heard often, sometimes in a few poignant sentences. On May 20, 1994, John F. Kennedy, Jr., informed a massed press corps that his mother, Jacqueline Bouvier Kennedy Onassis, had died the previous evening one day after returning home to her Fifth Avenue apartment from a New York hospital. Advised that nothing further could be done to stop the spread of cancer through her body, the former First Lady chose for final comfort the one place that had provided her with so much peace and satisfaction during three decades of unremitting public attention. "My mother died surrounded by her friends and her family and her books and the people and the things that she loved," Kennedy said. "She did it in her own way and in her own terms, and we all feel lucky for that."

◆ ◆ ◆

With the development of bibliomania, "the friendly, warming flame of a hobby becomes a devastating, raging wildfire, a tempest of loosened and vehement passions," the writer Max Sander wrote in a 1943 essay for professional criminologists. He characterized bibliomaniacs as people who suffer from a "pathological, irresistible mental compulsion," an inexplicable urging "which has produced more than one crime interesting enough to be remembered."

Foremost among history's biblio-criminals is Don Vincente, a former Spanish monk whose consuming fascination for books led him to commit no fewer than eight murders during the 1830s. His fixation is said to have developed at a Cistercian monastery near Tarragona, in northeast Spain, where he served as keeper of the library. One night the monastery was robbed by unknown intruders who daringly made off with huge quantities of gold, silver, and irreplaceable books. Don Vincente abruptly left the order and turned up shortly thereafter as owner of a rare-book store in Barcelona, where he gained attention as a man who bought more books than he sold and who refused to part willingly with anything of value. In 1836, a consortium of competing book-sellers was formed to secure at auction what was believed to be the only surviving copy of *Furs e Ordinations de Valencia*, "Edicts and Ordinances for Valencia," printed in 1482 by Spain's first printer, Lambert Palmart. With the backing of his colleagues, Augustino Patxot, a rival bookseller, easily secured the prize. Three days later, Patxot's shop burned to the ground, and he was found dead inside. Soon, other bodies were discovered around Barcelona, each one the corpse of a substantial man—a priest, an alderman, a poet, a judge among them—and each identified with books and learning.

The rage Don Vincente had displayed after being outbid at the auction made him an obvious suspect, and during a search of his home a damning piece of evidence—the only known copy of *Furs e Ordinations*—was found hidden in a top shelf. Further investigation turned up additional books that once had belonged to the other victims. Protesting his innocence at first, Don Vincente finally confessed when he was assured that his library was safe and that it would be protected regardless of what punishment he might receive.

In court, the presiding justice asked the killer why he had never taken any money from his victims. "I am not a thief," Don Vincente answered smugly. But was he sorry, at least, for having murdered so many people? "Every man must die sooner or later, but good books must be conserved," he replied. The defense attorney argued that his client obviously was insane, and added that in any event the evidence was circumstantial at best. But there is the Lambert Palmart book, the prosecutor countered: it is unique. Not so, the lawyer answered, and thereupon presented dramatic proof of another copy in France. When he heard this startling disclosure, Don Vincente lost control. "My copy is not unique," he shouted in disbelief, a lament he kept muttering up to the day of his execution.

Details of this shocking crime traveled quickly, reaching France when fifteen-year-old Gustave Flaubert was writing his first short stories. One of the emerging author's earliest tales, written in 1836, the very year of Don Vincente's execution, was titled "Bibliomania." It tells of a Barcelona bookseller named Giacomo who "scarcely knew how to read" but was happy "seated among all these books, letting his eyes roam over the lettered backs, the worn pages, the yellowed parchment," a man "entirely absorbed" by his passion. "He scarcely ate, he no longer slept, but he dreamed whole days and nights of his fixed idea: books."

Most of the narrative is familiar: Giacomo, a former monk, becomes furious when he fails to acquire a unique book at auction and kills Baptisto, the rival bookseller, in order to get it. Other murders follow, there is a trial, and a second copy of the book is produced, but it is here that Flaubert demonstrates the difference between imitation and a fertile imagination. Alone with his lawyer, Giacomo asks to hold the newly discovered copy, which has been brought to Barcelona for his defense. After hugging it and dropping "some tears on the leaves," the condemned man rips the volume apart page by page. "You have lied about it . . . ! I told you truly that it was the only copy in Spain."

While cases of murder in pursuit of books are rare, book theft is far more common. Lawrence S. Thompson, an FBI special agent during World War II who later taught classics at the University of Kentucky, outlined some of history's more unusual cases in a 1947 essay, "Notes on Bibliokleptomania." Early collections in Rome, Thompson explained, were built with material taken from Greece by conquering generals. And the reason books were tethered to shelves in medieval times was to make sure they stayed where they were. The most widely employed deterrent in the Middle Ages, however, was not the chain but the curse. One monastery threatened prospective thieves with damnation alongside Judas, Ananias, Caiaphas, and Pilate, while others invoked anathema, the most solemn ecclesiastical curse, leading to excommunication. A colorful example, from the monastery of San Pedro in Barcelona, goes like this:

> For him that stealeth, or borroweth and returneth not, this book from its owner, let it change into a serpent in his hand and rend him. Let him be struck with palsy, and all his members blasted. Let him languish in pain crying aloud for mercy, and let there be no surcease to this agony till he sing in dissolution. Let bookworms gnaw his entrails . . . and when at last he goeth to his final punishment, let the flames of Hell consume him forever.

Historians agree that one of the most egregious episodes of book plunder in recent times occurred in France during the 1840s and involved the methodical removal of valuable materials from various national collections. Remembered today as *l'affaire Libri,* the thefts were carried out by an Italian count who moved to France as a young man and achieved widespread renown as an academic. By the time Count Guglielmo Libri-Carucci (1803–1869) was thirty, he was teaching mathematics at the Sorbonne and before long was serving as editor of *Journal des Savants,* a respected scholarly publication. In 1841, Count Libri was named secretary of a newly formed commission charged with cataloguing historical manuscripts deposited in the nation's public libraries. But instead of conducting a responsible inventory of the documents entrusted to his care, he spent the next six years systematically stealing them.

The man's motive, it appears, was pure greed. In 1847 Libri anonymously placed some stolen books in a Paris auction. Later, in a private transaction across the English Channel, he sold 1,923 ancient manuscripts to Lord Bertram Ashburnham for £8,000. When French officials finally became suspicious, the dapper count fled to England in 1848, taking with him another cache of contraband, which he sold in a series of controversial auctions. In 1850, a French court sentenced him to ten years solitary confinement in absentia. Libri opted to spend the rest of his life in Italy, where he died in 1869.

Throughout history books have been the source of great joy, great passion, and also great pain for their owners. Emil Bessels, a celebrated nineteenth-century naturalist and explorer, lost many books and manuscripts in a shipwreck, followed quickly by a house fire that destroyed what remained of his library. "He could not be consoled for this double blow, and took his own life" in 1888, the French historian Albert Cim wrote earlier in this century in a lively essay about the "victims of books." In another case, an American expatriate, a Mr. Bryan, gave a small but superb collection of 150 books to the Bibliothèque de l'Arsenal in Paris. One day in 1903, an old and shabby-looking man visited the library. It was Mr. Bryan, who said simply, "I wish to see my books again." After looking through them one by one, the man quietly left. Two days later, he was found dead, an apparent suicide.

After his return from a French expedition to Spain in 1824, Count Henri de la Bédoyère devoted his leisure time to assembling a collection of books and prints about the French Revolution. Twenty years later he put the collection up for sale. Within days he was seized with such remorse that he began buying back his entire collection. When he died in 1861, his second library, "more complete than the first," was sold to the Bibliothèque Impériale (now the Bibliothèque Nationale).

Abraham-Hyacinthe Anquetil-Duperron, a famous eighteenth-century orientalist who translated the Zend-Avesta and a pioneer of Asiatic studies in Europe, had no heat in his apartment, no mattress or bedclothes, and lived only on bread and milk. What the scholar did have in abundance was books. On the rare occasions he went outside, he was so miserably dressed that he was often taken for a beggar and offered alms.

Oblivious to personal needs, the nineteenth-century philosopher Jean Baptiste Bordas-Demoulins preferred to spend the little money he earned on books. One day he left his attic apartment intending to spend his last *sous* on a modest meal when he noticed an interesting item in a bookseller's window. The choice was between the pamphlet or food. "He hesitated not one instant," according to Cim, and returned "peacefully to his attic, from which he was not to leave except to go to the hospital and die."

The nineteenth-century French pianist and composer Charles Henri Valentin Morhange, known to his contemporaries as Alkan, was regarded as a virtuoso while still in his teens, and for a while moved in the same artistic circles as George Sand and Victor Hugo. As time passed and his reputation receded, the musician retreated into seclusion, contenting himself with the company of his books. Accounts of how he died vary, but one asserts that on March 22, 1888, while the seventy-five-year-old Alkan was reaching for a Hebrew text, an overloaded bookshelf collapsed and the man once known as the "Berlioz of the piano" was crushed to death.

Professor Theodor Mommsen, winner of the Nobel Prize for Literature in 1902, wrote a thousand learned essays and books, and *Römische Geschichte,* a five-volume history of Rome produced over several decades, was considered his masterpiece. The German scholar's devotion to literature was legendary. Once, Mommsen, the father of twelve, was a passenger on a "horse car" bound for Berlin and was deeply immersed in a book. Annoyed at the wailing of a young boy sitting nearby, he demanded that the noisy child identify himself so that he could be reprimanded by name. "Why, Papa, don't you know me?" the boy cried. "I'm your little Heinrich." On January 26, 1903, Mommsen was similarly absorbed in another book he had just climbed a ladder to get from the topmost shelf of his library. While peering at the volume, the eighty-five-year-old historian held a candle too close to his head and set his long white locks on fire. He alertly threw the skirts of his study gown over his head and smothered the flames, but his face was scorched and his hair consumed; his death ten months later was attributed in part to the freak accident.

Antonio Magliabechi, a seventeenth-century Florentine, was a book hunter so insatiable that some people called him the "glutton of books." In its Latinized form, Antonius Magliabechius, his name can be rearranged as an anagram for *Is unus bibliotheca magna*—"He is in himself a great library."

Magliabechi lived well into his eighty-second year, but is not known ever to have gone outside Florence. Fully half of his life was spent as a virtual recluse among piles upon piles of books. Born in 1633 to parents of "low and mean rank," he worked at various menial jobs until a neighborhood bookseller took him in as an apprentice. Soon, the lad achieved widespread recognition for his bibliographical skills. In 1673 the grand duke of Tuscany, Cosimo III, put him in charge of the palace library, and it was here that Magliabechi for the next forty-one years "revelled without cessation in the luxury of his book-learning."

His memory was prodigious, and his knowledge of other collections formidable. The grand duke is said to have asked once whether a certain scarce title could be acquired. "No, sir," Magliabechi answered. "The only copy of this work is at Constantinople, in the Sultan's library, the seventh volume in the second book-case, on the right as you go in." Even more impressive was that everything he knew about books outside of Florence he knew only through the detailed correspondence he faithfully carried out with every important collector, librarian, and bookseller of the period. Disdaining the private living quarters that were offered to him in the palace, he chose instead to sleep in a wooden cradle that he slung between the library shelves, surrounded by mounds of books. He was a man, some scoffed, who "lived on titles and indexes, and whose very pillow was a folio."

By maintaining strict control over access to the books he was responsible for, Magliabechi became something of an intellectual tyrant. The historian Eric Cochrane has pointed out that an "indispensable condition of all scholarly activity" during the late seventeenth and early eighteenth centuries was "submission to that incarnate encyclopedia of scholarship," the librarian to Cosimo III. "Magliabechi did not have to give proof of his learning by writing books: the scores of authors who applied to him for information kept his name prominently displayed in the dedications and acknowledgments of half the books published in his lifetime."

Magliabechi was found dead in 1714, seated in a cane chair, a book open in his lap, "dirty, ragged, and as happy as a king." In his will he directed that the thirty thousand books he had acquired for himself be turned over to the city of Florence, with the condition that they should always be free to the public. For more than a century the collection was known as the Biblioteca Magliabechiana. In 1860 it merged with the Biblioteca Palatina to form the Biblioteca Nazionale Centrale, where it remains to this day, monitored silently by a jaunty, smiling bust of the man who was "in himself a great library."

Harry B. Smith, a writer of popular Broadway musicals in the early decades of this century, gathered an exceptional collection of presentation copies, manuscripts, drawings, and books formerly owned by famous writers. Among his treasures were love letters from John Keats to Fanny Brawne, proof sheets of Robert Browning's *The Ring and the Book,* and a letter written by Charles Dickens the day before he died. "If I were the owner of the copy of Keats's *Poems* which Shelley had in his pocket when he was drowned, and which Trelawney threw upon the funeral pyre, I confess I should never read it, though I might keep it in a little shrine and burn incense to it," he wrote in the catalogue of his collection, *The Sentimental Library.*

Smith sold his most precious possessions to A. S. W. Rosenbach, who was nurturing his own taste for "association" material—books once owned by someone of literary or other significance. Rosenbach sold many thousands of books during his career, but one item he kept among his most sacred relics was Nathaniel Hawthorne's personal copy of *Moby-Dick,* the novel Herman Melville dedicated to Hawthorne "in token of my admiration for his genius." It is preserved in the permanent collection of the Rosenbach Museum and Library in Philadelphia.

Thomas J. Wise (1859–1937) is best known for the forgeries of nineteenth-century pamphlets he cleverly produced and sold to unsuspecting wealthy collectors, though he retains credit for helping influence fundamental changes in literary taste. "I here refer not to his more nefarious and notorious activities," the London bookseller Percy Muir said in a series of lectures given in the winter of 1948–49,

> but to his quiet, revolutionary discovery that English literature
> did not die with Shakespeare or Swift, nor even with Shelley or
> Keats, but was in process of creation in every age, that authors

were still living just around the corner, people with whom you could shake hands or take high tea, who were writing books worthy of the collector's attention.

Discredited and disgraced, Wise died in 1937 three years after his activities were uncovered by two young bibliographers, John Carter and Graham Pollard. Still, his collection, known as the Ashley Library, remains an essential component in the English literature collection in the British Library. In fact, Muir contended that Thomas J. Wise "almost invented the exciting business of collecting modern first editions."

The key word is *almost,* because many other collectors have had the wisdom to save the works of living writers. The auction in New York earlier this century of the library of John Quinn is especially noteworthy because it offered valuable contemporary material on an equal footing with books and manuscripts from the past. A successful New York lawyer who was committed to fostering the production of painting and literature, Quinn was a patron of the arts in the traditional sense. For instance, he readily gave money to Joseph Conrad and James Joyce, who gave him inscribed books and holograph manuscripts in return.

Dr. Rosenbach bought heavily at the Quinn sales in 1923 and 1924, spending $72,000 for Conrad's final drafts of *Victory, Chance, Almayer's Folly, Typhoon, Nostromo, The Nigger of the Narcissus, An Outcast of the Islands,* and *Lord Jim,* among others. They remain in Rosenbach's personal collection to this day, along with the unqualified bargain of the sale, the manuscript of James Joyce's *Ulysses,* which the astute Philadelphian acquired at the 1924 session for $1,950. The controversial novel had been issued in Paris just two years earlier and was still ten years away from being published in the United States. How many millions of dollars this document would fetch at auction today is anybody's guess, but its unquestioned worth validates Edwin Wolf's observation that John Quinn was "way ahead of his time" as an aggressive collector of living writers.

Other examples of the collection of materials relating to living writers go back further than Thomas J. Wise and John Quinn. Although the glory of the Pierpont Morgan Library in New York City lies in its extraordinary wealth of classic material, one item the founder acquired directly from a living writer is considered worthy of display among the

treasures of the East Room. It is a letter Mark Twain wrote in 1909 to
Pierpont Morgan, who had inquired about the possibility of obtaining
the autograph manuscript of *Pudd'nhead Wilson*. In complying with
the request, the author offered this sentiment: "One of my high ambitions is gratified—which was to have something of mine placed elbow
to elbow with that august company which you have gathered together
to remain indestructible in a perishable world."

One of the most eloquent statements of all on the collecting of contemporary material is to be found in a largely forgotten memoir written in 1894 by Mrs. James T. Fields, widow of a Boston publisher
acclaimed for the consistently high quality of work issued under his
imprint, Ticknor & Fields. Mrs. Fields's *A Shelf of Old Books* walks
readers through the couple's library of particularly loved possessions,
pausing along the way at some of the most valued items. "There is a
sacredness about the belongings of good and great men which is quite
apart from the value and significance of the things themselves," she
pointed out. "Their books become especially endeared to us; as we turn
the pages they have loved, we can see another hand point along the
lines, another head bending over the open volume."

In a corner were several shelves filled with material James Fields
acquired from Leigh Hunt during a visit to England thirty-five years
earlier, the same material, perhaps, that had heartened John Keats
when the young poet was an overnight guest in Hunt's home and slept
in the library. "Sleep and Poetry" was written as a result:

> *It was a poet's home who keeps the keys*
> *Of pleasure's temple—round about were hung*
> *The glorious features of the bards who sung*
> *In other ages—cold and sacred gusts*
> *Smiled at each other.*

"As I quote these lines," Mrs. Fields wrote,

fearful of some slip of a treacherous memory, I take a small volume of Keats from the shelf of old books. It is a battered little
copy in green cloth, with the comfortable aspect of having been
abroad with some loving companion in a summer shower. It is

the copy long used by Tennyson, and evidently worn in his pocket on many an excursion. He once handed it to Mr. Fields at parting, and it was always cherished by the latter with reverence and affection. Here, in its quiet corner, the little book now awaits the day when some new singer shall be moved to song in memory of the great poet who loved and treasured it.

Appropriately, the frontispiece to *A Shelf of Old Books* is a wood engraving of the library in the Back Bay townhouse where James T. and Annie Adams Fields shared so many precious hours. Pictured on the right are paintings and a piano. On the left are books and a fireplace, and at the far end are two tall windows that look out on the Charles River. It is here, in this space, that Mrs. Fields concluded her meditation.

> There is no Leigh Hunt now to enchant, and no Keats to be enchanted among the old books; but as we stand silent in the corner where the volumes rest together, watching the interchanging lights thrown through green branches from the shining river beyond, we remember that these causes of inspiration still abide with us, and that other book-lovers are yet to pore over these shelves and gather fresh life from the venerable volumes which stand upon them.

Mrs. Fields was nourished by her books, and while it is evident that she read them with sensitivity as well, some collectors would argue that mere possession of these artifacts is reason enough to justify their acquisition. Winston S. Churchill addressed himself to this matter in *Thoughts and Adventures,* a collection of essays published in 1932, twenty-four years before he was awarded the Nobel Prize for Literature. In "Hobbies," one of the essays, he wrote:

> "What shall I do with all my books?" was the question; and the answer, "Read them," sobered the questioner. But if you cannot read them, at any rate handle them and, as it were, fondle them. Peer into them. Let them fall open where they will. Read on from the first sentence that arrests the eye. Then turn

to another. Make a voyage of discovery, taking soundings of uncharted seas. Set them back on their shelves with your own hands. Arrange them on your own plan, so that if you do not know what is in them, you at least know where they are. If they cannot be your friends, let them at any rate be your acquaintances. If they cannot enter the circle of your life, do not deny them at least a nod of recognition.

A century earlier, the most graceful British essayist of all, Charles Lamb, divided the human species into "two distinct races," neither of them identifiable by skin color, language, geographic roots, or religious conviction. Instead, Lamb (writing as "Elia") judged people simply as *"the men who borrow, and the men who lend."* But it was not borrowing currency that provoked his displeasure. "To one like Elia, whose treasures are rather cased in leather covers than closed in iron coffers, there is a class of alienators more formidable than that which I have touched upon; I mean your *borrowers of books*—those mutilators of collections, spoilers of the symmetry of shelves, and creators of odd volumes."

As Lamb escorted readers through his "little back study" in Bloomsbury, he pointed out the "foul gap in the bottom shelf facing you, like a great eye-tooth knocked out," a cavity that once held "the tallest of my folios." Further on, he indicated evidence of other similar offenses: "Here stood *The Anatomy of Melancholy,* in sober state. There loitered *The Compleat Angler;* quiet as in life, by some stream side." A frequent visitor to his rooms, Samuel Taylor Coleridge, was singled out for special umbrage, though Lamb did concede a single compensation:

Justice I must do my friend, that if he sometimes, like the sea, sweeps away a treasure, at another time, sea-like, he throws up as rich an equivalent to match it. I have a small under-collection of this nature (my friend's gatherings in his various calls), picked up, he has forgotten at what odd places, and deposited with as little memory at mine. I take in these orphans, the twice-deserted. These proselytes of the gate are welcome as the true Hebrews. There they stand in conjunction; natives and naturalized.

◆ ◆ ◆

In the fall of 1991, the Library of Congress mounted an exhibition to observe the one hundredth anniversary of Lessing J. Rosenwald's birth. From 1943 until his death in 1979, the former chairman of Sears, Roebuck Co. had given to the nation 2,600 exquisite volumes, the greatest benefaction in the library's history. The one hundred volumes selected for the exhibition included an enormous two-volume illuminated manuscript known as the Great Bible of Mainz. Produced in 1452, the book is thought to have influenced motifs and ornamentation used in the design of Johann Gutenberg's forty-two–line Bible, which was printed in the same city in the same year. Other treasures included Ptolemy's *Cosmographia;* William Blake's *Songs of Innocence and of Experience;* the only known copy of the first edition of the English version of the Lohengrin legend, *The Knight of the Swan;* and the only illustrated book produced by Aldus Manutius—a Venetian scholar, printer, and publisher—Francesco Colonna's *Hypnerotomachia Poliphili.* Each of these books is a cornerstone of early printing and illustration, which were Rosenwald's principal interests as a collector.

In 1977, Frederick R. Goff wrote how Rosenwald had built his collection "like a great mansion, one brick at a time." In the final analysis, Goff said, "no collector or lover of books ever possesses a great book or manuscript until it possesses him." Rosenwald was not one to browse through flea markets or garage sales. He bought through dealers, and though he undoubtedly paid handsomely for his acquisitions, he did benefit by obtaining material that was not always in fashion. In his privately printed memoirs, Rosenwald gave prospective collectors six specific pieces of advice, which can be summarized as follows: know your subject; establish a theme; find a good dealer you trust; be ahead of your time; seize unusual opportunities when they develop; and always be willing to refine your taste.

In one instance, however, Rosenwald knowingly broke a few of his own rules. He not only bought something that was repugnant to him, but also instructed his agent to spare no expense in securing it. Once the loathsome item came into his possession, he sent it off into bibliographic exile, where it remained sealed for fifty years. Yet this acquisition showed Rosenwald's unshaken commitment to the proper preservation of historic texts, regardless of their content.

The chronology began one Sunday morning in December 1937 when he noticed an item in a forthcoming sale catalogue that awoke him from a comfortable lethargy:

> Prozess gegen die Juden von Trent, 1476–1478, manuscript written in gothic letters of 614 pp. with a border on folio 2 verso, in gold and colours, with the coat-of-arms of the Duke of Württemberg, for whom this account was written, old vellum folio circa 1478.

Lot 553 was the unpublished manuscript account of a notorious fifteenth-century criminal case in which eighteen members of the Jewish community of Trent, a principality in what is now northern Italy, were arrested on fabricated charges of murdering a two-year-old boy and using his blood at Passover services. Imprisoned and tortured horribly, the Jewish inhabitants of Trent finally were induced to "confess." The men were executed and the women converted to Christianity.

Convinced that the manuscript would be used to justify anti-Jewish propaganda if obtained by the German government, Rosenwald called his "advisor on all matters pertaining to books," Dr. A. S. W. Rosenbach, and "did something that I never did before or since—once in a lifetime is enough." He instructed Rosenbach to buy the manuscript at any price. Rosenwald learned afterward that during the sale, an unidentified woman loudly insisted she had made the highest offer and demanded that the bidding be reopened. The auctioneer politely told the woman she was mistaken, and refused. "Later investigation established the lady underbidder as a German agent who had been sent to the sale for the sole purpose of obtaining Lot 553."

When the bulky folio arrived at Rosenwald's estate, Alverthorpe, in Jenkintown, Pennsylvania, it was examined, repacked, and immediately shipped to the American Jewish Historical Society in Waltham, Massachusetts, which accepted the document with the understanding that it would remain sealed for fifty years. Almost to the day, fifty years later the society put the manuscript on the auction block, explaining that the content did not fall within its primary collecting focus, the history of American Jews. Bought at Sotheby's for $176,000 by Erica and Ludwig Jesselson, well-known New York patrons of Jewish culture, the document was presented to Yeshiva University in 1988 and became part of the permanent collections. Four years later, Yale University Press published *Trent 1475,* a thorough examination of the document by R. Po-Chia Hsia, a professor of European history at New York University. Rescued from obscurity, a historic document had served scholarship and, in a small but significant way, had confirmed the vision of a collector once again.

In the last decade of the fifteenth century, a German poet named Sebastian Brant was putting the final touches on a curious vessel of the imagination, *Das Narrenschiff* (*Ship of Fools*), a copy of which was included in the Rosenwald exhibition at the Library of Congress. First published in 1494, the work had taken Europe by storm, appearing in one Latin, three French, one Dutch, one Low German, and an English version within fifteen years.

"If popularity be taken as the measure of success in literary effort," the critic T. H. Jamieson wrote in 1873, *Das Narrenschiff* "must be considered one of the most successful books recorded in the whole history of literature." One reason often cited to explain Brant's far-reaching appeal was that he wrote in short chapters, mixed his "fools" skillfully, and maintained a fluid style that engaged his readers. An accessible study of human frailties, *Ship of Fools* also was the first printed book to incorporate contemporary events and living persons in its narrative.

Of the English translations, the most enduring by far is the one rendered by Alexander Barclay and printed in 1509 by Richard Pynson. What made this version popular in England was Barclay's shrewd decision to adapt the material to English life. Though his version was not a literal translation of *Das Narrenschiff,* the original's premise was retained: several shiploads of fools set sail for their native country, the "Land of Fools," and virtually every folly and vice of the age is personified, from misers and adulterers to lawyers and hypocritical churchgoers. There are 113 sections in the work, most of them devoted to a different class of fool. First to address the reader is the Book-Fool:

I am the firste foole of all the hole nauy,
To kepe the pompe, the helme and eke the sayle
For this is my mynde, this one pleasoure haue I
Of bokes to haue grete plentie and aparayle
I take no wysdome by them. . . .

Virtually every potshot taken at book collectors over the centuries is included in these lines, foremost among them that bibliophiles covet rarity more than content, and are impressed more by damask, satin, and pure velvet bindings than the wisdom printed on the pages inside. The Book-Fool is described as having traveled the world in search of new acquisitions, because "to haue plentiy it is a pleasaunt thynge," though "what they mene do I not understonde." Contributing significantly to the popularity of *Das Narrenschiff* was the series of clever woodcuts, some of which, including the one of a bespectacled Book-Fool sitting at his lectern with a feather duster held aloft, are believed to have been executed by Albrecht Dürer.

In a fanciful story titled "A Meeting in Valladolid," Anthony Burgess allowed readers to listen in on a literary summit he imagined taking place between William Shakespeare and Miguel de Cervantes. The year is 1605, and the English playwright is in Spain on a goodwill tour intended to improve relations between England and Spain, still strained from the bitter naval engagement fought in the English Channel seventeen years earlier. While no evidence exists that Shakespeare ever left England, let alone that he ever spoke with Cervantes, there is no doubt that the dramatist knew of the novelist's work. *Cardenio*, a comedy presented in 1613 by the troupe of actors called the King's Men, is believed to have been written by Shakespeare and John Fletcher, and though the play is now lost, a surviving summary clearly shows that it was inspired by a minor but amusing character in *Don Quixote*, which had appeared the previous year in a popular English edition.

On April 23, 1616, Cervantes died in Madrid at the age of sixty-eight, penniless and embittered. On that same date—because of differing calendars, it was not the same day—Shakespeare died in Stratford at fifty-two, the victim, legend has it, of a chill brought on a fortnight earlier during a robust reunion with former colleagues from the London theater. While history does not record whether either of these writers had any obsession with books, it is noteworthy that two of their most significant characters, Don Quixote and Prospero, were touched quite profoundly by the spells books cast.

It is stirring tales of chivalry, after all, that move the man of La Mancha to go off with Sancho Panza and joust with windmills:

> Be it known, therefore, that this said honest gentleman at his leisure hours, which engrossed the greatest part of the year, addicted himself to the reading of books of chivalry, which he perused with such rapture and application, that he not only forgot the pleasures of the chase, but also utterly neglected the management of his estate: nay to such a pass did his curiosity and madness, in this particular, drive him, that he sold many good acres of Terra Firma to purchase books of knight-errantry, with which he furnished his library to the utmost of his power.

As the broken knight lies dying in his bed with a burning fever, the village priest orders the offending books incinerated and the hidalgo's library sealed off with brick and mortar.

For Shakespeare, creativity was a process of working magic with fleeting images and random thoughts. A typical meditation comes in *A Midsummer Night's Dream:*

> *The poet's eye, in a fine frenzy rolling,*
> *Doth glance from heaven to earth, from earth to heaven,*
> *And as imagination bodies forth*
> *The forms of things unknown, the poet's pen*
> *Turns them to shapes, and gives to airy nothing*
> *A local habitation and a name.*

The character Shakespeare chose to say farewell to the London stage on his behalf was a magician who draws his power from books. *The Tempest* is the first play to appear in the First Folio, not because it was the first written, nor because it was the last, but in all likelihood because it was widely acknowledged to be the great bard's parting production. In a moving epilogue, Prospero is alone on the stage and seeks permission from the audience to withdraw in peace and dignity:

> *As you from crimes would pardoned be,*
> *Let your indulgence set me free.*

The Tempest is as much about the power of books as about the mysteries of magic. When Prospero tells his daughter Miranda how he was tricked out of his kingdom by his brother, he confesses some responsibility for what happened. He explains that he had been distracted by his reading, which caused him to neglect his official duties. "My library," the magician admits, "was dukedom large enough." Forced by the palace coup to seek refuge on a tropical island, he brought with him only Miranda, his wand, some bare necessities, and prized volumes from his library. Later in the play, when Caliban drunkenly plots with Stephano and Trinculo to kill Prospero, the "hag-born whelp" makes clear that before any attempt is made on his master's life, it is necessary to "seize" his books, to "possess" his books, to "burn" his books, "for without them he's but a sot as I am." Finally, after fulfilling all his objectives, Prospero breaks his wand, abjures his "potent art," and vows to "drown" his books "certain fathoms in the earth."

In the fall of 1989, a New York collector paid $2.1 million for a splendid set of the first four folios of Shakespeare's dramatic works at the Garden Ltd. sale, the most ever spent for nonillustrated printed books. (For more on the Garden Ltd. sale, see chapter 6.) At the same auction, a magnificent copy of both parts of *Don Quixote* (the novel was issued in two volumes, one in 1605, the other in 1615) was sold to an unidentified Spanish collector for $1.65 million, more than six times the amount Sotheby's had estimated in its catalogue. Only seven other sets of the novel are known to exist in the original state, and prior to this auction, there was only one in Spain, the country the book celebrates.

"Our copy isn't in as fine a condition as the one sold at the Garden sale, but at least we got ours when it was issued," Julian Roberts, the executive librarian of the Bodleian Library at Oxford University, said a few months after the New York auction. "We had an agent then who traveled to Spain on our behalf. There was a great deal of enmity between England and Spain at the time, and he was not treated very well, but he did go there and he bought five Spanish books for us; *Don Quixote* was one of them."

This would have been around the same time, about 1605, that Shakespeare was creating the role of Lear for Richard Burbage to perform at the Globe Theatre. When the playwright drafted his will in 1616, he made no mention of any library or papers, but he did leave small amounts of money to John Heminges and Henry Condell, the actors who seven years later selflessly guided his dramatic works through William and Isaac Jaggard's press to create the First Folio. None of Shakespeare's personal books or manuscripts are known to survive, with two possible exceptions: a three-page fragment of an unproduced play about Sir Thomas More believed to be in his hand, and a book in the British Library with his name written boldly on the flyleaf. Yet Heminges and Condell note on the title page of *Comedies, Histories, and Tragedies,* the seminal collection of Shakespeare's complete works that is known today simply as the First Folio, that their edition was "published according to the true original copies."

In an introductory note addressed "To the Great Variety of Readers," Heminges and Condell issued an urgent plea: "Read him, therefore, and again, and again." They also stressed, in a timeless caveat, how "the fate of all books depends upon your capacities: and not of your heads alone, but of your purses. Well, it is now public, and you will stand for privileges we know: to read and censure. Do so, but buy it first."

Because people did "buy it first," Shakespeare's works have survived through the generations. Though a number of plays exist individually in unauthorized quarto editions, fully twenty others—*Macbeth, The Tempest,* and *Antony and Cleopatra* among them—are known from no other source except the First Folio. If someone in those days had proposed that Shakespeare's handwritten drafts be deposited somewhere safe and secure—a place, perhaps, like the university library in Oxford, the town the playwright passed through often during his many journeys between Stratford and London, the institution that had the foresight to purchase in Spain a first issue of *Don Quixote*—the legacy would be richer still.

♦ ♦ ♦

Book madness has appeared from time to time as a motif in various works of fiction, most notably perhaps as the mischievous catalyst in *Don Quixote,* but just as powerfully in more recent novels. The German writer Elias Canetti, winner of the Nobel Prize for Literature in 1981, used the theme with singular power in his 1936 novel, *Die Blendung.* (*Blendung* means "mirage," "bedazzlement.") Translated into English after World War II, the book was published under the somewhat snappier title *Auto-da-fé* ("act of faith"), an expression first used during the late Middle Ages for the ceremony accompanying the pronouncement of judgment by the Spanish Inquisition. The phrase came to mean the burning of heretics at the stake. Both titles suggest the theme of fire.

In the novel, Peter Kien is a fiercely detached European scholar whose existence is centered around his great library of 25,000 volumes. When he marries an illiterate housekeeper with the idea that she will attend to his daily needs, he fails to recognize the woman's rapacity, and his destruction is assured. "She is the heaven-sent instrument for preserving my library," he reasons with sad irony. His error is quickly apparent, and the marriage becomes a mortal combat between ignorance and independence. Momentarily alone in his library, Kien apologizes to his lifelong companions for his terrible misjudgment: "Greatly daring, he glided along his shelves and softly felt the backs of his books. He forced his eyes wide and rigidly open, so that they did not close out of habit. Ecstasy seized him, the ecstasy of joy and long-awaited consummation." At the end, Kien is in his library once again, but now he is a fugitive and police officers are pounding at the bolted door. Realizing he is doomed, Kien pulls volumes from his shelves and builds a pyre in the middle of the room. He climbs to the sixth step of his library ladder and waits. "When the flames reached him at last, he laughed out loud, louder than he had ever laughed in his life."

Combustion is also the central metaphor in *Fahrenheit 451,* an unsettling novel by the science fiction writer Ray Bradbury about an intolerant future society that outlaws books and decrees their destruction; the title is the temperature at which paper bursts into flames. Similarly, fire is the instrument of deliverance from intellectual bigotry in

The Name of the Rose, Umberto Eco's apocalyptic novel of ideas that is set in the fourteenth century in a wealthy Italian abbey noted for its magnificent monastic library. William of Baskerville, a brilliant Franciscan monk, arrives to investigate a series of horrible murders. "Everything turns on the theft and possession of a book," William soon declares, and the mystery is solved when the medieval detective determines the identity of a lost text of Aristotle. But the discovery is costly, and destruction follows. "It was the greatest library in Christendom," William says as he watches the abbey burn to the ground. "Now, the Antichrist is truly at hand, because no learning will hinder him anymore."

The British author A. S. Byatt, a former instructor of American literature at University College, London, uses the intense competition so often apparent among academic institutions as the premise for *Possession,* a richly textured novel of literary detection and ideas that won the Booker Prize for Fiction in 1990. Described by the author as a contemporary "romance," its climax takes place in a country graveyard with the opposing parties trying desperately to outwit each other and retrieve a cache of important papers from a famous writer's grave. The title takes on several layers of meaning, ownership and obsession among them.

With the release of a film based on the 1910 novel *Howards End,* the writer E. M. Forster (1879–1970) has been blessed with a new generation of readers. In the climactic scene, Leonard Bast is crushed to death by a collapsing bookcase. Forster's most recent biographer has observed that falling books appear in no fewer than five of his works. What event may have inspired the image is uncertain, but Forster used it often to suggest a number of concepts. In the story "Ansell," the hero's box of books—representing his life's work and thus his identity—falls into a ravine, providing, in an odd way, a release and a freeing. The image also appears in "The Story of the Siren," "The Purple Envelope," and in the 1908 novel *A Room with a View,* when one of the characters, a writer named Miss Lavish, is described as having lost a manuscript at Amalfi after "the Grotto fell roaring onto the beach."

Because writers are so involved in the creative process, most of them find book collecting a phenomenon too remote to understand. When A. J. A. Symons was establishing the First Editions Club in London in the 1920s, he also was working on a bibliography of prominent British writers. As part of his research he interviewed George Moore, a writer of Victorian novels who had enjoyed widespread popularity many years earlier. "Moore was much flattered, like most of the other writers my brother approached, by this move towards a lifetime canonization," Julian Symons wrote in an affectionate biography of his older brother. The aging novelist agreed to inscribe A.J.A.'s copy of a book of poems and in return asked for help with a story he was then writing about a "great collector." Moore not only wanted to know how such a person would behave, but wondered what books such a collector might show to visitors. "I think he would choose, for the sake of the ladies, first editions of Shelley and Keats and writers of that period," Moore speculated. "I wish you could supply me with a dozen names and a few accidental remarks that he might make."

Conversely, the late Ian Fleming understood not only what it meant to collect but how it felt to be collected. His hugely successful James Bond novels sold millions of copies during the 1950s and 1960s, and to this day first editions of Agent 007's adventures routinely command respectable prices in dealers' catalogues. With the able counsel of the London bookseller Percy Muir, Fleming also assembled one of the finest "subject" book collections of his generation: he devised an imaginative scheme to seek out printed works that had "made things happen" over the previous century and a half. Such a focus allowed him to include Charles Darwin on evolution, James Clerk Maxwell on the electromagnetic nature of light, Marie Curie on radium, Sigmund Freud on the subconscious, Albert Einstein on relativity, Alexander Graham Bell on the telephone, Sir Francis Galton on fingerprint identification, Ivan Petrovich Pavlov on conditioned reflexes, Robert Koch on the aetiology of tuberculosis, and even Robert Baden-Powell on the Boy Scouts (Fleming's collection included Baden-Powell's influential 1908 guide, *Scouting for Boys*). About a thousand books in all entered his collection.

Fleming's activity as a bibliophile was known in antiquarian circles, particularly because of his visibility as founder and principal owner of *The Book Collector,* the distinguished quarterly based in London that continues to provide collectors, dealers, and librarians with a forum to exchange information. Yet the scope of his collecting did not become public knowledge until 1963, when organizers of "Printing and the Mind of Man," one of the most exciting book exhibitions of the twentieth century, borrowed 44 of Fleming's books for the show mounted in London at the British Library. Sixty-three libraries and individuals from around the world lent 464 books that have shaped Western culture, but only King's College, Cambridge, with 51, lent more titles than Fleming, the creator of the modern spy novel. When he died the following year, there was concern that his collection would be broken up, but after prolonged negotiations it was acquired by the Lilly Library of Indiana University, where it remains intact today.

The biographer Joseph Blotner wrote how William Faulkner once refused to sign half a dozen copies of his books that Alfred A. Knopf had brought to a dinner party at the New York apartment of Bennett Cerf, "because special signed editions are part of my stock-in-trade." This was especially embarrassing for Cerf, who was Faulkner's publisher, because Knopf had combed so many used bookstores that day looking for the out-of-print titles. "People stop me on the street and in elevators and ask me to sign books, but I can't afford to do this," Faulkner explained somewhat ingenuously. "Aside from that, I only sign books for my friends." He finally relented, though only after Cerf interceded on his colleague's behalf. "Mrs. Knopf has been very kind to me, so if you want to pick out one of them, I'll inscribe it for you," said Faulkner.

Over the years, John Updike has authorized hundreds of signed limited-edition copies of various works to be issued by small-press printers, probably more than any other writer alive or dead. As a result of this enterprise—along with the fact that first editions of his many trade books are also in great demand—Updike understands the relationships that can develop between those who collect and those who are collected.

In *Bech is Back,* Updike tells the story of the author Henry Bech as he approaches his fiftieth birthday. "He had his friends, his fans, even his collectors," most prominent among the latter being a persistent fellow from Cedar Meadows, Pennsylvania, named Marvin Federbusch. The two have never met, but for more than twenty years Federbusch has been pestering Bech with requests to sign copies of his books and return them in post-paid padded envelopes.

One day, when Bech is in central Pennsylvania with a free afternoon and a rented car at his disposal, he decides on a whim to call on his most "faithful agitator" unannounced. Once inside the man's drab house, Bech looks around and remarks, "I don't see my books." Reluctantly Federbusch leads him to a back room where he opens a door to reveal "a trove of Bechiana": Bech in many languages, "Bech anthologized, analyzed, and deluxized, Bech laid to rest. The books were not erect in rows but stacked on their sides like lumber, like dubious ingots, in this lightless closet along with—oh, treachery!—similarly exhaustive, tightly packed, and beautifully unread collections of Roth, Mailer, Barth, Capote." After signing some paperbacks, Bech leaves with the certain knowledge that he has heard the last of the collector. "How wrong he had been to poke into this burrow, how right Federbusch was to smell hurt! The greedy author, not content with adoration in two dimensions, had offered himself in a fatal third, and maimed his recording angel."

Piqued by the high prices he discovered people were asking for first editions of *In Our Time,* Ernest Hemingway's second book, the humorist Robert Benchley was moved to write an essay in 1934 in which he asked a delightfully petulant question: "Why does nobody collect me?" Benchley did not mention that Hemingway's book had been issued in a first printing of 175 copies and was a rarity almost from the beginning of its existence, but that detail seemed irrelevant in light of his other grievances:

> I am older than Hemingway, and have written more books than he has. And yet it is as much as my publishers and I can do to get people to pay even the list-price for my books, to say nothing of a supplementary sum for rare copies. One of my works, *Love Conquers All,* is even out of print, and yet nobody shows any interest in my extra copy. I have even found autographed copies of my books in secondhand book shops, along with *My Life and Times* by Buffalo Bill. Doesn't *anybody* care?

Benchley died in 1945, but if he were still alive he might be amused to learn that some people do care about his work. In fact, two of his titles are listed in *Collected Books: The Guide to Values,* an authoritative price guide of modern first editions compiled by Allen and Patricia Ahearn of Rockville, Maryland. His 1924 book, *Of All Things,* today commands $400, and his 1928 book, *20,000 Leagues Under the Sea; or David Copperfield,* sells for $300, assuming in each instance that the copies have a dustjacket and are in fine condition. Benchley still has a way to go before his "values" achieve parity with Hemingway's, however; first editions of *In Our Time* now sell for upward of $15,000.

Three years before Robert Benchley lamented the dearth of collectors of his published works, an author of travelogues, essays, and maritime adventures who was far less popular than Ernest Hemingway had his work canonized in a bibliography. William McFee, whose oeuvre included such books as *Casuals of the Sea* (1916), *Captain Macedoine's Daughter* (1920), *Swallowing the Anchor* (1925), and *Sailors of Fortune* (1929), was so delighted by the effort put forth by his good friend James T. Babb that he wrote the introduction to the bibliography, published in 1931.

"It is impossible to be a collected author and remain innocent of the irony," McFee wrote with impish delight.

> The scorn and contempt for a collected author like myself, who makes very little money, cherished by the big fellows who make six-figure incomes from serials and novels but whose work is esteemed as garbage by collectors, is one of the joys of my life. The wistful desire to be reckoned "important" by critics who earn less than their own chauffeurs saves many a successful writer from haughtiness. I confess I share, sometimes, their bewilderment. At other times, when I am reading their works, I fancy I understand. I seem to have read it all somewhere else, long ago, in other best sellers. Perhaps collectors are a cannier lot than we authors give them credit for being. If somebody did not preserve the beginnings of literature, they would be irretrievably lost. Think of the librarian who discovered Chatterton manuscripts being used to wrap up fried fish! Think of the well-to-do novelists of Chatterton's time who have no value in a collector's estimation at all, but who have turned to dust! Collectors, in short, in these days of manipulated reputations, money prizes, and book clubs, are the repositories of integrity in our profession. Theirs is a noble madness. It behooves us never to betray their confidence.

Unlike McFee, James A. Michener is in the enviable position of being widely read and widely collected at the same time. In fact, because his books are issued in printings of several hundred thousand copies, some of his fans take unusual steps to enhance the value of their first editions. "People will drive for three hundred miles and ask me to sign their books," he said one morning in a telephone interview from his home in Austin, Texas. "I've been involved in this as an affectionate watcher for many years, and I would never try to discourage it, but it remains a mystery to me. A day doesn't go by that five or six books do not come into my office, and I groan, because it happens every day of my life. About twenty years after I am dead, somebody is going to find one of my books that *isn't* autographed by me, and it will be worth a fortune."

The North Carolina author Reynolds Price was doodling on a paper placemat in a Harvard Square café one spring morning in 1992 when he told me about the copy of *Paradise Lost* he had bought for himself five years earlier after surviving extensive treatment for spinal cancer. Price said that he had always been a book collector and that he teaches a course on John Milton at Duke University, but stressed that the thin volume means considerably more to him than love of the great poet's work. "Milton was in his early forties and I was in my early fifties when we both underwent a physically devastating illness, and in both our lives the experience led to some kind of mysterious renewal of good work," he explained. "Milton wrote his best books after he lost his sight. I have written eleven books since I had cancer, and it represents some of the very best work I have ever done. My copy of *Paradise Lost* once belonged to Deborah Milton Clarke, the daughter who took Milton's dictation after he went blind. For me, it was like the apostolic succession. I was touching the hand that touched the hand that touched the Hand."

2

Balm for the Soul

Our written records carry us only a millionth of the way back to the origin of life. Our beginnings, the key events in our early development, are not readily accessible to us. No firsthand accounts have come down to us. They cannot be found in living memory or in the annals of our species. Our time-depth is pathetically, disturbingly shallow. The overwhelming majority of our ancestors are wholly unknown to us. They have no names, no faces, no foibles. No family anecdotes attach to them. They are unreclaimable, lost to us forever.

—Carl Sagan and Ann Druyan,
Shadows of Forgotten Ancestors

If it is true that language is the miracle of our species, then it follows that writing is the witness. Words that are recorded endure, whereas those merely spoken dissolve, as Shakespeare's Prospero would have it, "like an insubstantial pageant faded." From the time writing first appeared on clay tablets in Mesopotamia five thousand years ago, it has been the object of veneration. During a trip through Thebes in the last century before the birth of Christ, Diodorus Siculus described a hall outside the tomb of the Egyptian pharaoh Ramses II where sacred texts had been kept more than eleven hundred years earlier. Above the portals was inscribed "The house of healing for the soul."

As cultures developed, books became instruments of utility and enlightenment, not just guides to ritual and worship. Gradually the ability to read extended beyond wise men and priests to embrace other segments of society. Literacy was so widespread and written material so abundant during the third century B.C. that the Sicilian historian

Timaeus, driven into exile by the tyrant Agathocles of Syracuse, spent the last fifty years of his life productively engaged in archival research without ever having to leave Athens. Rome had as many as forty libraries operating during its imperial period, along with a lively book trade that kept everyone adequately supplied.

With the secularization of books came the craving to possess them, a passion that by classical times was fully developed. For all the value they placed on moderation and restraint, ancient Greeks gathered rarities just as obsessively as collectors of today. Competition was keen, the hunt relentless, and the qualities so coveted now—good condition, scarcity, and significance—were equally prized twenty-five centuries ago. Book madness was so common, in fact, that collectors became the butt of jokes for philosophers, dramatists, and social satirists.

The historian Xenophon (431–352 B.C.), who carried a box of books with him on the anabasis (the retreat of Greek mercenaries described in his *Anabasis*), writes in *Memorabilia* about Euthydemus, a pupil of Socrates who formed an extensive library of poetry and scholarship. "Pray tell me, Euthydemus, is it really true what people tell me, that you have made a large collection of the writings of 'the wise,' as they are called?" Socrates once asked the young man.

"Quite true, Socrates, and I mean to go on collecting until I possess all the books I can possibly lay hold of," Euthydemus answered.

"I admire you for wishing to possess treasures of wisdom rather than of gold and silver, which shows that you do not believe gold and silver to be the means of making men better, but that the thoughts of the wise alone enrich with virtue their possessors," Socrates said. "And what is it in which you desire to excel, Euthydemus, that you collect books?" he then wondered. The pupil offered no reply, and Socrates pressed on: a doctor perhaps, an architect, or maybe a mathematician? Euthydemus remained silent. "Then do you wish to be an astronomer? Or possibly a rhapsodist? For I am told you have the entire works of Homer in your possession."

A hundred years later, the Athenian playwright Aristophanes ruthlessly ridiculed the tragedian Euripides' celebrated appetite for books in *The Frogs*, a comedy that took first prize at the Lenaea competition in 405 B.C. In the play's climactic scene, Aeschylus and Euripides, by then both deceased, confront each other in Hades to determine which was the better playwright. Sophocles, the third member of the great dramatic triumvirate, has wisely stepped aside while his former rivals tear apart each other's language, phrasing, sentence construction, dialogue, music, characterizations, stagecraft, intellectual depth, even syllable divisions and dramatic pauses. Finally, a weary Aeschylus issues an impertinent challenge that includes snide mention of Euripides' rumored reliance on the slave Cephisophon to help him write his plays:

> *Come! no more line for line! Let him bring all,—*
> *His wife, his children, his Cephisophon,*
> *And mount the scale himself, with all his books.*
> *I shall outweigh them with two lines alone.*

Lucian of Samosata, the second-century satirist whom Lord Macaulay called "the last great master of Attic eloquence and Attic wit," titled one of his biting treatises *To an Illiterate Book-Fancier* and addressed it to an unnamed collector he accused of being interested more in fashion than in substance. Lucian even mocked the fascination for certain books that today are known as "association" copies. "You think that by buying up all the best books you can lay your hands on, you will pass for a man of literary taste," he scolded.

> You may get together the works of Demosthenes, and his eight beautiful copies of Thucydides, all in the orator's own handwriting, and all the manuscripts that Sulla sent away from Athens to Italy—and you will be no nearer to culture at the end of it, though you should sleep with them under your pillow or paste them together and wear them as a garment; an ape is still an ape, says the proverb, though his trappings be of gold. So it is with you: you have always a book in your hand, you are always reading; but what is it all about, you have not an idea; you do prick up asinine ears at the lyre's sound. Books would be precious things indeed, if the mere possession of them guaranteed culture to their owner.

Similarly, Decius Magnus Ausonius, a fourth-century Latin writer of some note who taught rhetoric at Bordeaux for thirty years, had occasion to tease an affluent friend who had filled his home with an "Instant Library." Ausonius wondered, "Because with purchased books thy library is crammed, dost thou think thyself a learned man and scholarly, Philomusus? After this sort wilt thou lay up strings, keys and lyres, and having purchased all, tomorrow thou wilt be a musician?" Seneca, the Stoic poet and philosopher who had the fatal misfortune to serve in Nero's court, found the obsessive gathering of books just as ludicrous. "Of what use are books without number and complete collections, if their owner barely finds time in the course of his life even to read their titles? Devote yourself to a few books, and do not wander here and there amongst a multitude of them." Many generations later, another bemused poet would echo the same sentiment. "Bibliophiles," A. E. Housman sniffed. "An idiotic class."

The Roman orator and statesman Marcus Tullius Cicero (106–43 B.C.) embraced a decidedly different opinion on the matter in what is arguably the finest panegyric on literature to emerge from the ancient world. Cicero's primary purpose in the eloquent speech, known as the *Pro Archia Poeta,* was to defend a Greek poet named Archias against politically motivated charges that impugned his citizenship. Most of the address, delivered before a court of inquiry in 62 B.C., is a digression that celebrates reading and the reverence for books.

> All literature, all philosophy, all history, abounds with incentives to noble action, incentives which would be buried in black darkness were the light of the written word not flashed upon them. . . . I am a votary of literature, and make the confession unashamed; shame belongs rather to the bookish recluse, who knows not how to apply his reading to the good of his fellows, or to manifest its fruits to the eyes of all. . . . [Reading] gives stimulus to our youth and diversion to our old age; this adds a charm to success, and offers a haven of consolation to failure. In the home it delights, in the world it hampers not. Through the night-watches, on all our journeying, and in our hours of country ease, it is our unfailing companion.

Cicero is known to have maintained a formidable library at his villa in Tusculum, and when Atticus, his close friend and publisher, was living in Athens, he saw an opportunity to acquire some particularly desirable Greek books. "I want you to think how you can get a library together for me," Cicero wrote in 67 B.C. "I place in your kindness all hope of the pleasure I want to have when I come to retire." Atticus wasted little time in locating the requested books; unfortunately, the cost to procure them greatly exceeded his friend's budget. When advised of the cost, Cicero pleaded for time. "I am saving up all my little incomings to provide this resource for my old age," he wrote back. A year later, Cicero released Atticus from any further obligation to him, but expressed the fervent wish that he might yet be able to buy the manuscripts: "Keep your books safe and do not give up hope of my being able to make them mine. If I succeed, I shall surpass Crassus in riches and shall look down on the estates and meadows of all other men."

Cleopatra of Egypt has been many things to many artists and writers: a model of feminine virtue to Chaucer, a tragic heroine for Shakespeare, a sex kitten for George Bernard Shaw, a siren of staggering beauty played variously by Claudette Colbert and Elizabeth Taylor. But none of these stereotypes takes into account the woman's ability to govern effectively during gravely uncertain times or her keen appreciation for knowledge. During her visit to Rome in 45 B.C., Cicero coyly asked whether he could borrow a few treasures from the fabled collection she controlled in Alexandria, which was the envy of the civilized world. Books—many thousands of them—also played a small but telling role in her well-chronicled relationships with Julius Caesar and Mark Antony.

When the daughter of King Ptolemy XII became Queen Cleopatra VII in 51 B.C. at the age of eighteen, the great library and museum in her capital city, Alexandria, had stood as a beacon of learning and discovery for almost 250 years. The library had been founded by her Macedonian ancestors on the daring premise that all the world's knowledge could be gathered under one roof, and what remains remarkable after all this time is how assiduously the task was pursued and how glorious and enriching were the results. For nine luminous centuries, from around 300 B.C. to the seventh century A.D., Alexandria was a place of inspiration, a vibrant shrine dedicated to the limitless potential of human achievement. Alexandria was by no means the first great book repository, but because it contained antiquity's most extensive collection of recorded thought, it undoubtedly was the greatest.

Not long after Alexander the Great entered Egypt and founded the city that would bear his name, he resolved to achieve cultural respectability. Around 300 B.C., a formal academy was established within the palace walls to serve the Muses; known as the Museum, it gave poets, historians, musicians, mathematicians, astronomers, and scientists an opportunity to live and work under royal patronage. The results were awesome. At Alexandria, Euclid worked out the elements of geometry; Ptolemy mapped the heavens; poet and scholar Eratosthenes determined the circumference of the earth; Theocritus drafted the first pastoral poems; the anatomist Herophilius recognized the connection between a heartbeat and a pulse and articulated the difference between arteries and veins; inventor Ctesibius designed a water-clock and built the first keyboard instrument; the mathematician Diophantus formulated the algebraic method; Archimedes refined his theory that explained the weight and displacement of liquids and gases; Callimachus developed the allusive style of poetry and introduced systematic methods of cataloguing and shelving books; Zenodotus produced authentic versions of Homer's epics by collating every known text that could be obtained.

In order for this kind of creativity to flourish, books were essential. About 295 B.C., King Ptolemy I Soter enlisted the services of the orator Demetrios Phalereus, a former governor of Athens, and empowered him, according to Flavius Josephus, to "collect, if he could, all the books in the inhabited world." To support his efforts, the king sent letters to "all the sovereigns and governors on earth" requesting that they furnish works by "poets and prose-writers, rhetoricians and sophists, doctors and soothsayers, historians, and all the others too."

Agents were sent out to scout the cities of Asia, North Africa, and Europe, and were authorized to spend whatever was necessary. Every possible source was explored, to the point that foreign vessels calling in at Alexandria were searched routinely for scrolls and manuscripts. Anything of interest found on board was confiscated and copied. Transcripts were returned in due course, but the originals always stayed in the library. A key work of Hippocrates carried by a traveling physician from Pamphylia is said to have entered the collection in this manner. These acquisitions, according to Galen, were so commonplace that they were catalogued under a special heading, "books of the ships." Galen further asserted that Ptolemy's representatives borrowed the original dramatic works of Aeschylus, Sophocles, and Euripides from the state archives in Athens by posting fifteen silver talents as a pledge against their safe return. What went back to Athens, however, were copies, the security deposit notwithstanding.

As material kept coming in, the matter of accessibility arose, and a new bibliographical craft, translation, was institutionalized. An Alexandrian Jew who called himself Aristea records that Demetrios persuaded Ptolemy to acquire an important body of Jewish laws, but before they could be put to productive use, a problem had to be resolved. "They are not written in Syriac, as is generally believed, but in Hebrew, an altogether different language," the king was told. With Ptolemy's royal backing, seventy-two scholars were recruited to produce what tradition holds to be the first translation of the Old Testament into Greek, a sacred document still known as the Septuagint.

Around 250 B.C., Timon of Philius, a Skeptic philosopher and author of barbed lampoons, wrote of Alexandria without identifying the city by name, that in the "populous land of Egypt they breed a race of bookish scribblers who spend their whole lives pecking away in the cage of the Muses."

But not everyone in the ancient world was amused. A few hundred miles away, in northwestern Asia Minor in the kingdom of Pergamum, another library took shape under the enthusiastic patronage of King Eumenes, sparking a spirited competition between the two cities' institutions. Both kingdoms enjoyed great wealth, and since questions of cost were incidental, a lucrative trade emerged in the manufacture of forgeries. In one embarrassing instance, Pergamum trumpeted its purchase of what appeared to be a richer collection of Demosthenes' works than anything previously known. The sensational find supposedly included an unrecorded speech, until an alert researcher in Alexandria determined that the "discovery" actually had been copied "to the letter" out of a book of orations by Anaximenes of Lampsacus.

Just how keenly contested the competition between the two libraries was is underscored by a story that Pliny attributes to Marcus Varro, the scholar whom Caesar wanted to build a great public library in Rome.

Since Egypt was the principal source of papyrus, King Ptolemy V Epiphanes, who was pharaoh from 205 to 185 B.C., stopped shipment of the essential product to Eumenes II, king of Pergamum from 197 to 159 B.C. Without papyrus, scrolls could not be manufactured, and without scrolls, manuscripts could not be copied. Instead of crippling the rival library, the ploy occasioned increased production of a durable writing material fabricated from the skins of sheep and goats: vellum, or parchment. Though scholars challenge Strabo's contention that the costly process was invented in Pergamum—Diodorus Siculus wrote that ancient Persians recorded their national reports on such a material, and Josephus credited the Jews with doing the same—it certainly was improved there; in fact, the term *parchment* comes from a medieval Latin phrase for "from Pergamum." In another scheme, Eumenes II persuaded Aristophanes of Byzantium to leave his post as librarian at Alexandria and assume the same position in Pergamum, but when Ptolemy Epiphanes learned of the offer, he had the scholar arrested and imprisoned.

Perhaps the rivalry can be illustrated best by the lengths to which each library went to acquire an archive that would have been the supreme acquisition of any repository, the unique personal papers of Aristotle, the ancient world's most influential thinker. In addition to the philosopher's writings, the collection may have included research material gathered for him on the orders of his student, Alexander the Great. The young king is known to have used the vast resources he controlled to supply his former teacher with exotic specimens, including wild animals from Asia and Africa. Aristotle's books are known to have passed to a favored pupil, Theophrastus, and from him to Neleus, a colleague who refused repeated offers to sell the old master's library. To appease Ptolemy, Neleus parted with a few lesser items, but the most important scrolls remained with his heirs, who buried them in a cave near their house.

The geographer Strabo (64 B.C.–A.D. 19) wrote, "At length, but not before the books had been injured by damp and worms, they were sold to Apellicontes of Teos—rather a collector than a philosopher—who, by unskillful attempts at the restoration of defective and mutilated passages in the writings of Aristotle, increased the injury by corrupting the text." Apellicontes did something that bibliographers of any era would judge unconscionable: he filled in the blanks caused by worms and mold with words that he felt Aristotle might have been inclined to write himself, a cultural counterfeit not unlike the nineteenth-century forger William Henry Ireland's attempt to write a "lost" Shakespeare play. Still, the fragments that remained were of extraordinary value, and the saga does not end with the man who was "rather a collector than a philosopher." Apellicontes took Aristotle's books home to Athens, where he displayed them as a trophy. Posidonius noted that Apellicontes' library included the works of many authors, not just of Aristotle. On at least one occasion he was accused of stealing some Attic decrees from the state archives.

Knowledge of Apellicontes' library, in any case, was certainly no secret, since Posidonius also recorded that when the Roman dictator Sulla sacked Athens in 86 B.C., one of his first targets was this collection, which was seized and carried off to Rome. There it was used by several privileged scholars, Cicero, Atticus, and Tyrannion among them. From Sulla the library passed to Faustus, his spendthrift son, who soon found himself in debt. He sold everything, at which point the books vanished forever.

For centuries the story has been told that in 47 B.C. Julius Caesar set ships in Alexandria's harbor on fire to protect his outnumbered garrison against native Macedonians who opposed his occupation, and that the conflagration that followed destroyed much of the waterfront, including the great library. However, because it continued to function for several centuries, this charge has been largely discredited. Strabo, who visited Alexandria twenty-two years later, made no mention of such a catastrophe. Caesar records nothing about it in his *Civil Wars*, and Cicero—a political rival and dedicated bibliophile who certainly would have commented on such an embarrassment—did not mention the subject in his writings.

Still, there is persuasive evidence that forty thousand papyrus scrolls stored in temporary quarters on the piers did go up in flames. While this figure is considerable, its significance decreases when it is compared to the library's total holdings of 700,000 volumes. Just what those books were, and why they were in a harbor warehouse, has aroused speculation that Caesar had made a selection of items and put them aside for shipment to Rome. It is known that Caesar commissioned Marcus Varro to create a public library in Rome at about the same time as the trip to Egypt, and the books may have been earmarked as a seed collection for this enterprise. Or, given the Roman passion for private libraries, they could have been selected for the general's own amusement. That Caesar loved Greek literature and philosophy is well established, and that he spoke Greek fluently is also documented. His dying words, according to Suetonius, were not "Et tu, Brute," as Shakespeare would have it, but the Greek *Kai su, teknon:* "Even you, my child." The Roman proclivity for plundering the relics of conquered countries is legendary, and likely would have been practiced in Alexandria, especially if an opportunity to winnow material from an unequaled collection had presented itself. The late Edward Alexander Parsons (1878–1962), a devoted collector of classical history whose fifty thousand–volume *Bibliotheca Parsoniana* is now at the University of Texas in Austin, suggested that even though the evidence for this scenario is circumstantial, it is compelling nonetheless.

Parsons imagined an evening in the grand hall of the Alexandrian Library where the proud keepers of books placed rarity after rarity before the visiting dignitary, who on this night preferred to speak not as a general, but as a formidable intellect among equals:

Caesar, for the nonce, ceased to be the statesman, the soldier, dictator of the world. With almost the enthusiasm of youth his quick mind and glittering eyes assumed a distinct facet of his wonderful personality. He was the student, the scholar, the seeker of knowledge, the lover of books. The men of the library were busy answering his keen questions, amazed at his fund of bibliophilic learning and the sincere interest he evinced. The observant Cleopatra was delighted and never for a moment changed her role: to please, at any price, her lover, the master of the world. As his enthusiasm mounted and the desire of acquisition gleamed from his eyes, the subtle adept of the masculine heart and mind knew just when to strike. Unerringly she read his thoughts and offered him some precious manuscript which he was examining. He declined with due propriety, but she insisted the books were hers, she had so many, she forced them on him, until he, feeling that he had paid sufficient respect to the proprieties, entirely gave way, and before long orders were given for the packing of hundreds of items of the great collection.

Within two years of the fire, Caesar was dead and Cleopatra was back in Alexandria trying to keep her kingdom out of Roman control. The library continued to function, and in 41 B.C., if a story repeated by Plutarch is correct, it actually became a much stronger institution by virtue of a new suitor's whimsy. Looking for an appropriate way to please the queen of Egypt, Mark Antony is said to have ordered 200,000 "distinct volumes" removed from the library at Pergamum, which city had supported Brutus and Cassius during the civil war that followed Caesar's assassination. When the republican forces were defeated at Philippi in 42 B.C., the small kingdom paid a costly tribute.

Though the great rivalry between Alexandria and Pergamum ended abruptly, book collecting continued to flourish in Rome, provoking Seneca's tirade against people who flaunt their wealth by gathering huge libraries. One old patrician is said to have expressed his love for literature in a particularly inventive manner. Instead of buying "books without number" like everyone else, he spent vast sums filling his house with learned slaves, each of whom he required to become in effect a living edition of a classic work. One servant might recite *The Iliad* or *The Aeneid;* another would chant the *Odes* of Pindar. Every standard author had a distinctive voice. One of the most prominent Roman collectors of all, the emperor Gordian II (192–238), maintained a huge library of 62,000 volumes. He also was the author of numerous learned works and the ardent keeper of twenty-two concubines, disparate interests that prompted this tart remark from Sir Edward Gibbon: "Twenty-two acknowledged concubines, and a library of sixty-two thousand volumes, attested the variety of his inclinations, and from the productions which he left behind him, it appears that the former as well as the latter were designed for use rather than ostentation." In a footnote, Gibbon offered this: "By each of his concubines the younger Gordian left three or four children. His literary productions, though less numerous, were by no means contemptible."

By the second century A.D., Rome was firmly established as headquarters of the publishing world. Books were in demand, and a plenti-
ful labor force of slaves skilled in copying made producing them
inexpensive. Because there were no printing presses, there were no setup
costs or expensive corrections to make. Works came directly into the
shops from authors and were handed over to the scribes, and copies
were produced—often, according to the poet Martial, on the same day.
The rhetorician Quintilian was so pleased with the process that he dedicated *Institutio Oratorio* to Trypho, his bookseller. Martial records
that his first book of epigrams sold very reasonably for five denari a
copy. Cicero wrote to Atticus, the most famous publisher of the day,
"You have sold my discourse on Ligarius so well that I shall entrust you
with this duty for future works." Pliny criticized his fellow citizen Reg-
ulus for mourning ostentatiously after the loss of a son. "He composes
an oration which he is not content with publicly reciting in Rome, but
must needs enrich the provinces with a thousand copies of it."

In A.D. 529 the School of Athens was closed, effectively ending Greek
domination of the continent's cultural agenda. At Monte Cassino near
Naples, however, a learned monk named Benedict established a monastery that decreed strict procedures for the copying of ancient texts.
Thus, a medieval institution essential to the preservation of knowledge,
the monastic scriptorium, was functioning when Alexandria was captured by Saracen soldiers 111 years later. "I have conquered the great
city of the West," Amr ibn-al-As (known as Amru) wrote to his ruler in
Constantinople, the caliph Omar. "The Moslems look forward impa-
tiently to enjoying the fruits of their victory." During the occupation
that followed, the commander established a friendship with a Christian
commentator on Aristotle called John Philoponus, who asked for mercy
on behalf of the books in the library. "You have taken possession of
them, but I know that you would not know how to make use of them,"
he explained.

Amru decided he needed guidance on the matter from the caliph and
sent a messenger to Constantinople. Omar's answer took the form of a
syllogism: "As for the books you mention, here is my reply. If their content is in accordance with the book of Allah, we may do without them,
for in that case the book of Allah more than suffices. If, on the other
hand, they contain matter not in accordance with the book of Allah,

there can be no need to preserve them. Proceed, then, and destroy them." There were, it was said, four thousand public baths in Alexandria, each one heated by well-stoked stoves. Ibn-al-Kifti, a thirteenth-century Arab historian, writes that enough parchment and papyrus was distributed throughout the city to keep the waters comfortable for six months.

With the fall of the Roman Empire and the flood of barbarian tribes throughout Europe, ancient literature became an irrelevant pursuit. "The study of letters has perished," Gregory of Tours declared triumphantly in the sixth century while exhorting his countrymen to "shun the lying fables of the poets." But a lifeline was maintained nonetheless. Two sixth-century Roman scholars in particular, Boethius and Cassiodorus, provided the example by which so many classical writings escaped oblivion.

Boethius (ca. 480–524) was the last learned Roman to study the language and literature of Greece, and the first to interpret the logical treatises of Aristotle for later ages. His unorthodox views led to his arrest and imprisonment. Although he served the Ostrogoth king of Italy, Theodoric, he was condemned without a hearing for purportedly advocating the liberation of Rome and was forced to abandon his famous library with its walls of ivory and glass for a dark prison cell in the tower of Pavia. As he awaited execution in 524, Boethius composed the *Consolation of Philosophy,* a dialogue of thirty-nine short poems in thirteen different meters that paid tribute to the ancient authors and philosophers. Eight hundred years later, Dante placed Boethius in the Fourth Heaven, and in 1535, as Sir Thomas More awaited his own execution in the Tower of London, the *Consolation* of Boethius provided particular comfort.

Cassiodorus was another man who served Theodoric in a variety of important positions, including quaestor (private secretary), consul, and praetorian prefect, until sometime in the 540s; subsequently he devoted himself to scholarship and the pursuit of a Christian life. He wrote extensively on the history of the Goths and the seven liberal arts, but his most enduring contribution was to formalize procedures for the copying of manuscripts. The precepts Cassiodorus laid down were adopted by Benedict, founder of the monastery at Monte Cassino and the Benedictine order, which embraced reading as an essential discipline. The scriptorium Benedict established became the model for other monasteries and provided the principal means for preserving ancient literary works.

"It was the hand of Cassiodorus which gave the literary impetus to the Benedictine Order," the historian George Haven Putnam wrote in his history of books in the Middle Ages, "and it was from his magnificent collection of manuscripts, rescued from the ruins of libraries in Italy, that was supplied material for the pens of thousands of monastic scribes." In his landmark history of classical scholarship, Sir John Edwin Sandys compared Cassiodorus and Boethius: "While the gaze of Boethius looks back on the declining day of the old classical world, that of Cassiodorus looks forward to the dawn of the Christian Middle Ages." Of lasting significance was that each helped prevent "the tradition of a great past from being overwhelmed by the storms of barbarism." While the "Dark Ages" are often characterized as a long intellectual slumber, there remained a heartbeat. In an influential nineteenth-century study titled *History of the Transmission of Ancient Books to Modern Times,* the British historian Isaac Taylor insisted that "throughout that period, reason, though often misdirected, was not sleeping: philosophy was rather bewildered than inert; and learning, although immured, was not lost."

As a fifteen-year-old student of law at the university of Montpellier in the early 1300s, Francesco di Petracco had a diverting preoccupation that caused increasing concern for his father, a notary who had been banished from Florence by the same decree that sent Dante into exile. Fearful that his son was spending too much time reading the forbidden texts of some ancient Latin authors and neglecting his studies, Pietro di Petracco decided one day to make a surprise visit on the young man. When Pietro spotted a number of suspicious volumes badly concealed in his son's small dormitory room, he threw them in the fire. Startled by the hysterical reaction that ensued, Pietro removed two scorched volumes from the embers, Virgil's *Aeneid* and Cicero's *Rhetoric.* "Take the first one as an occasional relaxation for your mind," he told his son, "and the second as an aid to your law studies."

When he described the incident many years later, Francesco di Petracco, by then known as Petrarch, recalled accepting "these restored comrades" with humble gratitude. He made the far-reaching decision to placate his family by biding his time. Petrarch dutifully studied law at Bologna, but immediately following his father's death in 1326, he abandoned the profession for the pursuits of scholarship, poetry, and life as a formidable man of letters. A fervent patriot as well, he advised monarchs and cardinals, and as the prime mover of Italian humanism he was the architect of a two-hundred-year prelude to the Renaissance known as the Revival of Learning. Petrarch has been called the first modern man. By seeking out the forgotten writings of ancient authors, he also gained fame as a great collector of monastic manuscripts.

When Petrarch began his scholarly research he came across references to classic works, only to discover that many masterpieces had disappeared. "For every illustrious name that I invoke," he wrote, "I call to mind a crime of the dark ages that followed! As if their own sterility had not been shame enough, they left the books born of the vigils of our fathers, and the fruits of their genius to perish utterly. That epoch, which produced nothing, did not fear to squander the paternal heritage."

In Avignon, which was the temporary seat of the papacy for most of his life, Petrarch secured access to many monasteries and asked others to be on the lookout for manuscripts. "Please, if you love me, find people who are educated and trustworthy and set them to scour Tuscany, to turn out the book-cases of the monks and all the other scholars, and see if anything comes to light which will serve to quench—or, shall I say, increase—my thirst," he wrote a friend sometime around the year 1346.

In the same letter, Petrarch confessed that he was fortunate to have been "largely, if not wholly, delivered of nearly every human desire by divine mercy," with the exception of "one insatiable desire which I so far have been quite unable to control." That, of course, was books; then there was the frustration of "the impossibility of getting enough" of them. "Maybe I have more than I need," he allowed,

> but it is the same with books as with everything else—success in finding them spurs one on to greed for more. There is moreover something special about books; gold and silver, jewels and purple raiment, marble halls and well-tended fields, pictures and

horses in all their trappings, and everything else of that kind
can afford only passing pleasure with nothing to say, whereas
books can warm the heart with friendly words and counsel,
entering into a close relationship with us which is articulate and
alive.

Petrarch traveled to Milan, Padua, Mantua, Ferrara, Parma, and
Venice, where he probed ancient buildings and ruins, then moved on.
He told how the sight of some remote monastery always induced giddy
anticipation. "I would make my way towards it, always hoping to find
some of the works for which I was greedily searching."

At the top of his want list were the lost writings of Cicero, and in
1333, after traveling through Paris, the Low Countries, and parts of
Germany, he found at Liege two of Cicero's speeches, one of them the
Pro Archia Poeta. While book hunting in Verona he came across a
large manuscript containing Cicero's *Letters to Atticus,* as well as other
correspondence to the orator's brother Quintus and to Brutus. The
codex (the traditional form of the Western book, with folded and cut
sheets sewn together in a series of gatherings and enclosed by a binding, as opposed to scrolls) was in a decayed state when Petrarch discovered it buried in an "unexpected place"; and the copy he made
became the only source of a revealing correspondence that, L. Paul
Wilkinson has suggested, ranks with Rousseau's *Confessions.* Petrarch
considered the large volume his most precious possession and kept it
apart from his other books. He even tripped on the awkward book
from time to time, causing painful bruises and infection to his shins. He
described how he felt about his manuscript discoveries in a series of
impassioned letters he composed to dead authors. The first was
addressed to Marcus Tullius Cicero: "Your letters I sought for long and
diligently; and finally, where I least expected it, I found them. O Marcus Tullius, saying many things, uttering many lamentations, ranging
through many places of thought and feeling, I long had known how
excellent a guide you have proved for others; at last I was to learn what
sort of guidance you gave your self."

There were other notable finds, a badly damaged Quintilian in
Arezzo and Pliny the Elder's *Natural History* in Mantua among them.
He wrote a colleague about his efforts: "Ah, the prayers I have

addressed, the money I have sent, not only to Italy, but to France, to Germany, even to Spain and England—nay, would you believe it?—to Greece!" Greece, indeed; Petrarch acquired a Greek manuscript of Homer and sixteen dialogues of Plato, even though he never mastered the language.

Giovanni Boccaccio (1313–1375) is best known today as the author of the *Decameron,* but like Petrarch he was a major force in the rescue of classical literature. The half-French son of an Italian merchant, he was raised in Florence, where he embraced the budding principles of humanism. After his father's business failed he earned extra money as a copyist. When Petrarch passed through Rome in 1350, Boccaccio greeted him at the city gates and initiated what became a lasting friendship. His discovery of an obscure religious work on the life of a saint whom Petrarch was researching brought him added esteem. With Petrarch's encouragement, Boccaccio learned Greek. One legend holds that Petrarch was found dead in his library slouched over the first Latin version of *The Iliad,* prepared especially for him by his younger friend.

When a dying monk condemned poetry as a meaningless exercise, Boccaccio seriously considered renouncing his studies, destroying his writings, giving his library to Petrarch, and taking holy orders. "Be reasonable," Petrarch wrote him. "I know of many who have attained the highest saintliness without literary culture; I don't know of any who were excluded from sanctity by culture." Every journey, he insisted, is "a blessed one," but "the way of knowledge is certainly more glorious, illumined and lofty. Hence there is no comparison between the simple piety of a rustic and the intellectual faith of a scholar. Give me an example of a saint who arose from the mass of the unlettered, and I will match him with a greater saint of the other sort."

Boccaccio compromised by swearing to write no more amusing stories, but devoted himself with renewed conviction to the recovery of ancient manuscripts, and made some stunning discoveries. In addition to locating the verses of the satirist Martial, he found the *Ibis* of Ovid and the erotic poems of the fourth-century writer Ausonius known collectively as the *Priapeia,* of which the oldest copy now extant is written in Boccaccio's own hand. He also was the first humanist to quote the works of the Roman scholar Varro (116–27 B.C.).

In his zeal to rescue ancient documents, Boccaccio may have removed several unique manuscripts from the library at Monte Cassino in 1370 without telling anyone what he was doing. He never mentioned his visit to the Benedictine monastery in his writings, yet such a trip was described in detail by one of his pupils, Benvenuto da Imola. "Boccaccio stepped up the staircase with delight," Benvenuto wrote, "only to find the treasure-house of learning destitute of door or any kind of fastening, while the grass was growing on the window-sills and the dust reposing on the books and bookshelves. Turning over the manuscripts, he found many rare and ancient works, with whole sheets torn out, or with the margins ruthlessly clipped." Boccaccio "burst into tears" and asked a monk he met in the cloister "to explain the neglect." He was told that in order to generate income, some of the monks occasionally tore out "whole handfuls of leaves and made them into psalters, which they sold to boys," and "cut off strips of parchment, which they turned into amulets, to sell to women."

What specific items Boccaccio may have acquired during this secret visit is not recorded, but later scholarship suggests that while he was there he "recovered" significant portions of both the *Annals* and *History* by Tacitus, the Roman historian admired most by Edward Gibbon in the eighteenth century, yet totally forgotten prior to this fourteenth-century find. Within a year of his visit to Monte Cassino, Boccaccio was making numerous references to Tacitus in his own writings.

Because the document that survives is written in the tiny cursive script used in the eleventh century at Monte Cassino, there is little doubt it originated there. Whether Boccaccio took it remains a mystery, because even though he is the first Renaissance scholar to quote directly from Tacitus, the original codex cannot be proved to have been in his hands. Instead, it quietly made its way into the Laurenziana Library in Florence, which was formed in 1444 by Cosimo de' Medici with books gathered by Niccolò de Niccoli, a second-generation humanist and the last known owner of the Tacitus codex. When Niccoli died in 1437, he had the greatest library in Florence, assembled, he boasted in his will, "with great industry and study, avoiding no labor from youth and sparing no expense." Niccoli left his books to a board of trustees that included Cosimo and Lorenzo de' Medici, Giovanni Poggio Bracciolini,

and Leonardo Bruni. Because Niccoli died owing the Medici bank a considerable sum of money, Cosimo was able to secure custody of the books
as part of a settlement. They soon became the centerpiece of the Medici
family library designed by Michelangelo that remains one of the most
graceful monuments of the Italian Renaissance.

As for the Tacitus codex and the Varro manuscript, Niccoli never
disclosed how he acquired them, but fifty years earlier, as an up-and-
coming young humanist, he briefly served as curator of Boccaccio's
books after the poet died. When Poggio Bracciolini borrowed the Tacitus from Niccoli in 1437, he gave cryptic assurance that the matter
would never be mentioned. Niccoli, it must be noted, earned tremendous respect for his willingness to lend books from his library to scholars, and was remembered warmly for his generosity.

So the question is: Did Niccolò Niccoli "liberate" the Tacitus and
the Varro manuscripts from Boccaccio's estate and not tell anyone? It
seems likely that he did. And had Boccaccio previously "liberated"
them from an indifferent monastic library? That seems likely as well.
As for motivation, perhaps Boccaccio's pupil Benvenuto explained his
teacher's reasoning best by citing one of his comments on the consequences of the neglect and decay he witnessed in 1370 at Monte
Cassino: " 'So then, O man of study, go to and rack your brains; make
books, that you may come to this!' "

Petrarch and Boccaccio died within a year of each other, prompting
Coluccio Salutati, a humanist writer and the chancellor of the Florentine *signorie,* to declare that "both of the luminaries of the new eloquence" had been extinguished. Salutati was a great collector of Latin
manuscripts in his own right who located additional letters of Cicero,
which he added to Petrarch's material. He successfully conducted
explorations for lost works of Livy and Catullus, and was the first to
possess a copy of Cato's *De Agricultura,* the elegies of Maximianus, the
Aratea of Germanicus, and the commentary of Pompeius on the *Ars
maior* of Donatus. One of his most prescient acts was to arrange for the
Greek scholar Manuel Chrysoloras (1353–1415) to leave Constantinople and teach Greek in Florence for four years. His student Leonardo
Bruni said he was able to learn a language that no Italian had understood "for the last seven centuries." Another consequence was that
new expeditions mounted outside Italy now targeted Greek classics,

and the most aggressive new collector to come along was yet another student of Chrysoloras, Poggio Bracciolini.

Born in 1380, Poggio started out as an ambitious young scribe whose exceptional skills attracted the attention of Salutati, who taught him how to make accurate copies of old texts, fired his enthusiasm for the hunt, and encouraged him to study Greek. By the early 1400s, Poggio was writing accomplished apostolic letters for the papal Curia; he was elevated to the position of papal secretary in 1414, which permitted him to travel widely for close to half a century and undertake the systematic recovery of material in Italy, France, Germany, and Switzerland. His most spectacular accomplishments came while he was an aide at the Council of Constance in southern Germany from 1414 to 1418, a church summit called to settle the Great Schism—in which three men claimed to be pope—and confirm a single new pope. With few duties to perform, Poggio was able to go off on numerous scouting trips. In 1416, he traveled through twenty miles of narrow paths up a series of steep slopes to St. Gall in Switzerland, a monastery founded by Irish monks in the seventh century and well known as a repository of many books and manuscripts. There, he made a number of discoveries, most notably a complete manuscript of the *Institutio oratoria* ("education of an orator"), by Marcus Fabius Quintilian, a famous teacher of rhetoric at Rome. Poggio described the recovery in a lengthy letter to a friend, one of more than six hundred he wrote over a thirty-year period that give an unequaled window into the soul of a Renaissance bookman:

> I verily believe that, if we had not come to the rescue, he [Quintilian] must speedily have perished; for it cannot be imagined that a man magnificent, polished, elegant, urbane, and witty could much longer have endured the squalor of the prison house in which I found him, the savagery of his jailers, the forlorn filth of the place. . . . In the middle of a well-stocked library, too large to catalogue at present, we discovered Quintilian, safe as yet sound, though covered with dust and filthy with neglect and age. The books, you must know, were not housed according to their worth, but were lying in a most foul and obscure dungeon at the very bottom of a tower, a place into which condemned criminals would hardly have been thrust.

♦ ♦ ♦

In 1453, while Pope Nicholas V was establishing the Vatican Library
in Rome, an obscure visionary in the German city of Mainz was refin-
ing an invention that would forever relieve monastic scribes of the burden of preserving words on vellum and paper. The first forty-two-line
Bibles printed by Johann Gutenberg were produced between 1450 and
1455, several years before Poggio Bracciolini's death in 1459. Whether
Bracciolini, who spent his adult life as a master copyist, ever handled a
printed book is not recorded, though the possibility that he did is
remote.

The first volumes known to have been printed in Italy were produced seven years after Poggio's death by Conrad Sweynheym and
Arnold Pannartz, two Germans who briefly operated a shop in Subiaco
before setting up permanent quarters in Rome. The event was noted in
a work about the reigning pope by Gaspare da Verona, who wrote that
the two craftsmen arrived in Italy "and in a single month" published
three different titles, and quickly followed that feat by "making 200
such books every month" thereafter, "all of which they sold at a very
low price." Gaspare explained how difficult it would be "to give an
account of their craft, which was the invention of great genius, if many
did not know the whole truth," and added: "They are intending to produce other books in the same way."

One portent of how times were changing is illustrated by the rapid
evolution of new commercial functions. In one instance, a man who
began his working life as a scribe found success later as the first modern bookseller. Vespasiano dè Bisticci (1421–1498) alertly applied his
superior knowledge of Greek, Latin, and Hebrew manuscripts to the
needs of a changing society. When Cosimo de' Medici wanted to establish a library for the monks of San Lorenzo, Vespasiano arranged for
forty-five copyists to produce two hundred manuscripts, a chore that
took two years to complete. When Tommaso Parentucelli, later known
as Pope Nicholas V, was assembling a manuscript collection at the Vatican, Vespasiano, now a bookseller in Florence, became his principal
assistant.

Most telling of all is the work Vespasiano performed for Federico
Montefeltro (1422–1482), duke of Urbino, a collector of exquisite

manuscripts whose exacting tastes separated him from the seismic changes then afoot in Europe. The bookseller spent fourteen years building a collection of all the Greek and Latin authors who had recently been discovered and had them all bound in crimson and silver. The duke insisted that each be in perfect condition and that each be unique. None of the printed books then coming into fashion was allowed in his library. All of his books had to be "written with the pen," Vespasiano recalled years later; anything else would have made the collector feel "ashamed." Florentine bibliophiles were fiercely proud of their calligraphic traditions, and did not warm immediately to the idea of books that were mass-produced.

Printing came to Florence in 1472, but in the meantime, Venice had firmly established itself as capital of the publishing industry. By 1474, an overworked scribe would complain that the city already was "stuffed with books." By 1480, presses were operating in more than one hundred other cities throughout Europe, forty-seven of them in Italy. By the close of the fifteenth century—when the "cradle" period of the printed book came to an end—about 150 Venetian presses had manufactured more than four thousand editions, approximately twice as many as in Paris, the city's closest competitor, and about an eighth of Europe's entire production during this pivotal period.

At first publishers saturated the bookstalls with new editions of Latin classics, resulting in a temporary glut that prompted the emerging industry to evaluate the dictates of the market. Conferences and book fairs were held, trends were surveyed, and sales strategies were developed. The first known author's copyright was issued to Marcantonio Sabellico in 1486, and though classic texts of widely varying quality remained popular, other works printed in vernacular languages were produced for a voracious new readership. Publishers experimented during the 1490s with books that included maps, music scores, and Oriental languages.

As a consequence, printers and publishers attracted attention to themselves. The Venetian diarist and bibliophile Marino Sanudo used a single word to describe Nicholas Jenson, the most famous printer of the 1470s: *richissimo*. The historian Marcantonio Sabellico described a fanciful walk through Venice's busy bookselling quarter in a 1493 work. One of the strollers, a visitor to the city, was left alone by his companion among aggressive merchants who offered every sort of title for sale. Several hours later, the man had not left his original position, though a massive variety of volumes was stacked high on the ground around him.

A harsh critic of the Venetian press was the Dominican friar and poet Filippo di Strata, who accused the city's printers and publishers not only of "vulgarizing intellectual life," but also of being nothing more than vagabonds and idlers who shamelessly thrust armfuls of printed trash at unsuspecting people on the street "like cats in a bag." Fra Filippo also complained that because the texts were hastily prepared by "ignorant oafs," they were hopelessly inaccurate, and because they were inexpensive, they tempted uneducated fools to "give themselves the airs of learned doctors."

About 1490, a forty-year-old Roman scholar and teacher with no previous background in printing moved to Venice and set up an operation that would demonstrate convincingly that commerce and excellence could be combined in a single enterprise. Aldus Manutius (1449–1515) spent several years as tutor to the sons of the prince of Capri, one of whom later expressed his gratitude by underwriting the new venture. Beginning with the idea of creating a Greek press in Italy, Aldus brought with him a number of craftsmen from Crete. His earliest project was the printing of ancient Greek classics that had remained unpublished and the issuing of revised texts of works that had appeared in corrupted versions. From 1494 to 1515, when he died, his Aldine Press printed no fewer than twenty-seven *editiones princeps* of Greek authors and works of reference. (An editio princeps is the first printed edition of a work previously circulated in manuscript form, before printing became common.) He also published books in Latin, Italian, and Hebrew. As a printer's mark he used the familiar symbol of a crossed anchor and dolphin to indicate both speed and stability, which is usually identified with the Renaissance motto "Make haste slowly."

Aldus also produced the first italic type, a cursive form based on chancery script and modeled on the handwriting of Petrarch. Up until that time the German "gothic" typeface was in common use. The immediate result was a more condensed letter, which allowed for the production of a more compact format, known as *octavos,* that might "more conveniently be held in the hand and learned by heart." Books became even more accessible and affordable. Aldus's business relationship with Desiderius Erasmus of Rotterdam, the most famous European scholar of the period and the first person actually to make a living as a writer, enhanced his status ever further. Aldus's son, Paulus, eventually took over the management of the Aldine Press.

Printed texts, meanwhile, began to achieve the kind of stature enjoyed before only by manuscripts. In 1512 one German collector wrote to a friend, "I shall buy my Hebrew books in Italy, where Aldus has printed them in beautiful texts," and noted that his own country, where the printing craft had been invented just six decades earlier, "owes a great debt to Aldus." A half century later, John Dee, the English mathematician, book collector, and astrologer to Queen Elizabeth I, pointedly kept the "Aldines" in his library apart from all the other volumes he had gathered.

Aldus also did business with Jean Grolier de Servières (1479–1565), the French nobleman whose dedication to beautiful books and bindings qualify him to be considered the first modern bibliophile. Grolier spent considerable time in Italy on diplomatic missions and acquired a number of volumes for his library which were so distinctively bound that they continue to be associated with his name. Of the 350 or so surviving books known to have been Grolier's, about half are Aldines, forty-two produced during the lifetime of Aldus Manutius the Elder. (A grandson had the same name.) Grolier also bought many copies on vellum, and often had illuminations added at additional expense. The quality of work done for him is similar to that executed for the Venetian nobility, prompting the historian Martin Lowry to suggest the "real possibility that special orders were prepared for him in the Aldine workshop itself." The Grolier Club in New York was named in the French bibliophile's honor, and a fanciful painting in the lobby pictures a visit of its namesake to the shop of Aldus Manutius.

In his seven-volume history of the Italian Renaissance, John Addington Symonds put the rediscovered passion for collecting and the new art of printing in perspective. "All subsequent achievements in the field of scholarship sink into insignificance beside the labours of these men," he declared, and pointed out that the first publishers "needed

genius, enthusiasm, and the sympathy of Europe for the accomplishment of their titanic task. Virgil was printed in 1470, Homer in 1488,
Aristotle in 1498, Plato in 1512. They then became the inalienable heritage of mankind." He concluded that it is to these people "we owe in
a great measure the freedom of our spirit, our stores of intellectual
enjoyment, our command of the past, our certainty of the future of
human culture."

3

Rule
Britannia

History's first great tribute to bibliomania was written by a fourteenth-century prelate so consumed with the hunt that he undoubtedly caused a sensation in the book marts of Paris, Antwerp, Flanders, and Rome. As bishop of Durham and trusted adviser to King Edward III of England, Richard de Bury (1287–1345) is said to have traveled with a colorful entourage of twenty clerks and thirty-six esquires, a clear indication that he could indulge his lifelong passion with enviable vigor. And the medieval bibliophile did not disappoint; wherever he went, he sought out "the heavenly food of the mind" which he found so essential to a meaningful life.

Born Richard Aungerville near Bury St. Edmunds in Suffolk, de Bury was the son of a knight whose Norman ancestors had helped conquer England two centuries earlier. Orphaned as a child, Richard was raised by a maternal uncle who decreed a life of piety and contemplation. While studying theology and philosophy at Oxford, he gained prominence as a scholar and attracted the attention of King Edward II, who needed a tutor for his son, the heir apparent. When the prince became sovereign in 1327, the wise mentor—by then called de Bury in honor of his birthplace—remained with his grateful pupil as counselor and confidant.

During his years at court, de Bury served variously as cofferer to the king, treasurer of the wardrobe, clerk of the privy seal, papal emissary, royal ambassador, and lord chancellor of the realm. As a powerful member of the inner circle, he had no qualms about using his influence for the things he wanted, and he was disarmingly candid about what pleased him. In the final year of his life, the bishop took quill to paper and declared in crude but serviceable Latin his devotion to the "sacred vessels of wisdom" that he had always found so enriching. Writing in his ecclesiastical manor known as Auckland, de Bury combined the Greek words for "love" and "books" to create the title of his twenty-three-chapter paean, *Philobiblon;* the work is not only a study in superlatives, but the confession of a hopelessly intoxicated spirit.

"Ye are the tree of life and the fourfold stream of Paradise, by which the human mind is fed and the arid intellect is moistened and watered," de Bury proclaimed.

> Ye are the ark of Noah and the ladder of Jacob, and the troughs in which the young of those that look therein are changed in colour. Ye are the stones of testimony, the pitchers that hold the lamps of Gideon, and the scrip of David, from which the smooth stones are taken for slaying Goliath. Ye are the golden vessels of the temple, and the arms of the soldiery of the Church, by which the darts of the most Wicked One are quenched. Ye are fruitful olives, vineyards of Engadi, fig-trees that know not barrenness, burning lamps ever to be held forth in the hand; yea, all the best of Scripture could we adapt to books did it please us to speak in figures.

De Bury described the brazen collecting techniques he came to employ—all made possible, he freely admitted, after he had attained "the notice of the King's Majesty." Along with this stroke of good fortune and high position came the power to "notably advance or hinder, promote or obstruct both the great or the small." Though he always was "delighted to hold friendly communion with men of letters and lovers of books," his newfound influence afforded "a larger opportunity of visiting wheresoever we would, and of hunting, as it were, through certain very choice preserves, to wit, the private and public libraries, both of the regulars and the seculars."

He told how "the flying rumour of our love for books now spread everywhere," and how "we were reported to be even languishing from our desire for them, chiefly for ancient books, and . . . any one could easier obtain our favour by quartos than by money." Soon, there "flowed to us in place of pledges and presents, in place of gifts or prizes, bleared quartos and decrepit books, precious alike in our sight and our affection." The bishop insisted that "justice suffered no harm" by this manipulation of the court's business, yet he admitted that if he had "loved gold and silver cups, spirited horses, or no small sums of money," he could easily have "stored up a rich treasure" for himself. "But, indeed, we preferred books to pounds, and loved parchments more than florins, and cared more for lean pamphlets than fat palfreys."

Of all his travels, de Bury cherished his trips to Paris, "the paradise of the world," where he could "open out our treasures and loosen out our purse strings" and acquire "priceless books" for little more than "dirt and sand." During one visit to Italy, he spent five thousand marks; in Rome he bought texts and manuscripts at a time when rare documents had become valuable commodities to be sold on the open market. Appalled by the steady loss of such material, Petrarch rebuked his countrymen: "Are you not ashamed that the wrecks of your ancient grandeur, spared by the inundation of the barbarians, are daily sold by your miscalculating avarice to foreigners?"

Petrarch and de Bury are known to have met at least once, yet the bishop continued collecting without interruption. Mendicant friars working abroad were more than willing to act as scouts and agents for his cause, an arrangement that gave him a decided edge over the competition. "What leveret could miss the sight of so many keen-eyed hunters? What fry could escape now their hooks and now their nets and snares?" Soon

the chests of the noblest monasteries were opened; cases were
brought forth, and caskets were unlocked, and volumes that
had slumbered long ages in their tombs awakened astonished
and those that had lain hidden in places of darkness were overwhelmed with rays of new light. Books once most dainty, but
now become corrupted and disgusting, strewn over with the
litters of mice and bored with the gnawings of worms, were
lying about almost lifeless; and those that once were clothed in
purple and fine linen, now prostrate in sackcloth and in ashes
seemed given over to oblivion as habitations of moths.

By means of these methods, the bishop was able to locate "the
object and the incitement of our love," and these "vessels of sacred wisdom came into the control of our stewardship, some by gift, others by
sale, and some by loan for a time." Items de Bury could not buy, borrow, or cajole into his collection he had reproduced "in our different
manors," where he employed "no small multitude of antiquaries, copyists, correctors, binders, illuminators, and, in general, all of those who
could serviceably labour over books."

By all accounts, Richard de Bury was a thoroughly decent person
who routinely gave money and food to the poor. Committed to peace,
he argued unsuccessfully against the king's aggressive adventures in
France. "He was a man of his age, but better than his age," Andrew
Fleming West observed in the notes to his 1889 translation of *Philobiblon.* "Without rising to the level of greatness, he is far above the
commonplace." In addition to his principal library at Auckland, de
Bury maintained several others and is usually described as always being
surrounded by books. Visitors could not walk in any room without
tripping over scattered volumes.

A key word in de Bury's vocabulary was *stewardship;* though he
acquired with gusto and pleasure, he understood that in the grand
scheme he was only a custodian. In the nineteenth chapter of *Philobiblon,* he stipulated that his books should go to Oxford University
and that students could use them at no cost. He further directed that
duplicate copies could be removed from the premises provided a pledge
was left as security. Transcriptions were to be allowed, but they had to

be made inside the building; a register was to be kept and a yearly inventory to be conducted.

There is no doubt regarding de Bury's intentions, but scholars disagree on whether or not any of his books ever reached Oxford. He left no money, and there is evidence that some volumes were sold to pay outstanding debts upon his death. Because of these questions, Humfrey, Duke of Gloucester (1391–1447), the youngest son of Henry IV and the first English layman to achieve lasting fame as a bibliophile, is credited with giving the university its first books. But de Bury's collection would not have survived much longer than two hundred years regardless of where it went. Only two of his books are known to have passed safely to the present century; the rest were lost in a cultural holocaust that victimized every ecclesiastical library in Britain—including the one at Oxford. It all had to do with Henry VIII's divorce.

Since the sixth century, libraries in Britain had been the exclusive concern of the Roman Catholic Church, a tradition that began in 596 when Pope Gregory the Great commissioned a Benedictine monk to carry Christianity across the Channel. After establishing his headquarters at Canterbury, the papal envoy, later to be canonized as Saint Augustine, deposited nine religious volumes in the new abbey to form what tradition holds to have been the island's first formal repository. As other monasteries opened, theological materials were augmented by historic chronicles and literary works. By the twelfth century, a lay book trade was in operation throughout much of the English realm, and a community of parchmenters, scribes, and illuminators flourished in Oxford. When Erasmus visited England in 1497, he wrote home in awe of what he saw: "It is incredible what a treasure of old books is found here far and wide. There is so much erudition, not of a vulgar and ordinary kind, but recondite, accurate, ancient, both Latin and Greek, that you would not seek anything in Italy, but pleasure of traveling."

In 1533, to legitimize his divorce from Catherine of Aragon and his marriage to Anne Boleyn, Henry VIII defied the Roman Catholic pope and established the Church of England, with himself at its head. He claimed authority over all clergy in England. The following year, four Carthusian monks and two priests were accused of refusing to accept the king as their holy leader; carted through London in their priestly robes and habits, the six men were hanged, drawn, and quartered in a public square. Henry raised the stakes even further by ordering the execution of John Cardinal Fisher, the bishop of Rochester and the founder of a small library at Cambridge. He then set his agents loose on the symbols of the Catholic faith. Ancient abbeys throughout the realm were ransacked and emptied, dismantled and destroyed. Roofs were torn down and stained-glass windows smashed so the lead could be extracted. The graceful spires of Glastonbury, an exquisite example of English Gothic design, were reduced to rubble and used as fill for a common causeway through the marshes. "Except for such altar-books as had bindings of precious metals or jewels, the monastic libraries were scattered unregarded," Arundell Esdaile wrote in his history of the British Library.

The same year that he severed ties with the Vatican, Henry authorized an inventory of historic properties under his control. John Leland, keeper of the king's library, was appointed king's antiquary to make what was later celebrated as a "laboryouse journey" in search of England's antiquities. His responsibilities included locating old buildings, manuscripts, and coins, preparing detailed descriptions of topographical features, and identifying the remains of Roman, Saxon, and Danish civilizations. On July 16, 1536—the year of the great suppression of the monasteries—Leland wrote a letter entreating the commissioners of enquiry to take the best books in the monasteries for the king's library. After seven or eight years of arduous research, Leland is said to have taken leave of his senses, and he never completed the assignment. His findings were published posthumously, however, and are regarded as the first bibliographical account to be produced in England.

John Bale, a strident advocate of the Reformation and author of many Protestant polemics, openly deplored the mindless destruction of books and manuscripts. In a letter addressed to King Edward VI in 1549, he wrote that in turning over the "superstitious monasteries" to the Crown, "little respect was had to their Libraries, for the safeguard of those noble and precious monuments." He cited instances where a "great number" of people had used books "to scour their candlesticks, and some to rub their boots; some they sold to the grocers and soap-sellers, and some they sent over seas to the bookbinders, not in small number but at times whole ships full, to the wondering of the foreign nations." Indeed, Bale wondered how seriously England's reputation had been sullied by the desolation. "Yea, what may bring our realm to more shame and rebuke than to have it noised abroad that we are despisers of learning? I judge this to be true, and utter it with heaviness—that neither the Britons under the Romans and Saxons, nor yet the English people under the Danes and Normans, had ever seen such damage of their learned monuments as we have seen in our times."

A modest program of preservation was undertaken by Matthew Parker (1504–1575), the second Anglican archbishop of Canterbury and a scholar of some distinction who edited works by the chroniclers Aelfric, Gildas, Asser; Matthew Paris; Walsingham; and the Welsh historian Giraldus Cambrensis. Parker maintained a skilled corps of printers, transcribers, and engravers, and his 1572 treatise, *De Antiquitate Britannicae Ecclesiae,* is believed to be the first privately printed English book. A man of controversial views, Parker gathered a pertinent archive of 433 manuscripts, which he bequeathed to Corpus Christi College at Cambridge, where he once had been master.

Possibly England's greatest debt in this period is owed Sir Robert Cotton (1571–1631), an ardent antiquarian who cared deeply for the welfare of documentary materials simply because they were irreplaceable, not for any political or theological positions they may have supported. His book collection, the Cottonian Library, became one of two major components of the British Museum (later the British Library). A visit to the main exhibition room in the British Library in London offers dramatic evidence of his contribution.

Around the perimeter of the ornate hall, in two imposing tiers, is the majestic library of King George III, a monarch maligned for losing the North American colonies to bands of resourceful rebels, but justly celebrated for his spirited gathering of great books and the access he enthusiastically gave to scholars like Samuel Johnson to use them. In the central gallery are display case after display case of national treasures, many containing the manuscripts of such luminaries as John Keats, Charles Dickens, and George Eliot; others feature the principal printed editions of Virginia Woolf, Edward Gibbon, and Jane Austen. Amid these inspiring examples of creative genius and artistic imagination, pride of place is given to the contents of a single case designated "English Literature 1." Inside, the single surviving source of *Beowulf,* England's great epic poem, lies open at a passage describing the funeral of the Danish king Scyld Scefing. The manuscript is believed to have been copied about A.D. 1000, some three or four hundred years after it was composed by an unknown Anglo-Saxon writer of considerable narrative talent. According to the description card, this most celebrated work of English medieval literature "is known only from this copy." At the bottom is this designation: "Cotton MS Vitellius A. xv."

Robert Cotton's library in Westminster contained fourteen small "presses," or bookcases, and each was capped by the bust of a different Roman emperor or empress. Thus, a manuscript that carries a Caligula "extension," or designation, means it was shelved in the Caligula press, and so on for Augustus, Julius, Tiberius, Nero, Cleopatra, Galba, Faustina, Titus, Otho, Claudius, Vespasian, Vitellius, and Domitian. Called the emperor system, the imperial pressmarks have been retained for more than three hundred years in honor of this unique collection.

In the same case with *Beowulf* is *Sir Gawain and the Green Knight,* a chivalric poem that was "copied about 1400" and owes its survival to "the present unique text." Its code is "Cotton MS Nero A. x, *ff.94b-95.*" Another item on view in this case is *The Vision of Piers Plowman,* written between 1390 and 1400 by William Langford. "Virtually all that is known of Langford is to be gleaned" from this poem, which is designated "Cotton MS Vespasian B. xvi." Five of the nine objects on display here begin with the Cotton designation. In another case nearby is a seventh-century folio on vellum with breathtaking illuminations known as the Lindisfarne Gospels. "The supreme masterpiece of early Anglo-Saxon book production," the description card asserts. "Aldred's Anglo-Saxon translation is itself of great importance as the earliest surviving version of the Gospels in any form of the English language." Its designation: "Cotton MS Nero D. iv."

Born in 1570, Robert Bruce Cotton was the eldest son of a Huntingtonshire gentleman whose family, paradoxically, profited from the dissolution of the monasteries. At Westminster School he became the protégé of William Camden, author of *Britannia,* the first English historical work to embrace the emerging tenets of Renaissance scholarship and one of the most popular books of its time. Camden's technique was to tour the kingdom and conduct primary research in the field, a pioneering approach that greatly influenced his young student. At the age of sixteen, Cotton was a founder of the Elizabethan Society of Antiquaries. From Westminster he went to Jesus College, Cambridge, and by the time he entered the Middle Temple in 1588 he had committed himself to gathering the chronicles, records, charters, and artifacts that documented his country's history.

Precisely how Cotton acquired all of his manuscripts over the next thirty years is not known in detail, though a number of contemporary records do offer some tantalizing clues. Drawing on exhaustive examination of correspondence, manuscript catalogues, book inscriptions, lists of lent material, and records of gifts, Kevin Sharpe, an English historian, constructed a revealing profile of Cotton's collecting habits. "He seems to have persuaded acquaintances and friends going abroad to keep one eye open for precious manuscripts" as well, Sharpe wrote. By 1599 his collection was so rich that he already was lending books to other Society of Antiquaries members.

Of four original copies of the Magna Carta, Cotton was able to acquire two. The Samaritan Pentateuch came to him as a gift from Archbishop James Ussher. At court, he met noblemen who traveled frequently through Europe, and he also engaged the assistance of highly placed diplomats to find material for him. European scholars furnished him with manuscripts, and he was always alert to other private libraries that might suddenly be available. The seventeenth-century antiquarian John Aubrey wrote that after the astrologer Dr. John Dee died, either in 1608 or 1609, Cotton bought a piece of property on a hunch that he had buried a cache of books on magic and "spirits." While the story lacks documentation, it has burnished Cotton's reputation as a collector who would do anything to rescue artifacts.

How much money Cotton may have spent on books is not known, though there is speculation that he spared no expense. A grandson complained that the ancestral estate had been drained to buy manuscripts, while a brother-in-law sarcastically noted that the great library had been "chargeably brought together." As a wealthy property owner, Cotton did have the means to underwrite his obsession. One of his lists was headed "Divers Manuscrits as I am promised to have gotten for me this 30 April 1621," and another, "Books I want." In 1603, the year Queen Elizabeth died, Cotton was knighted by her successor, King James I, and he used his influence at court to acquire more material.

During the late 1590s and early 1600s, Cotton lived in the Black-friars section of London in the home of his first patron, Lord Hunsdon. There he established close connections with the leading literary and theatrical figures of the day—men such as the dramatist Thomas Nashe and the poet Samuel Daniel. Ben Jonson is known to have consulted Cotton's library regularly for background information he needed for his royal masques, and William Burton received extensive help for a regional history he was preparing. Many of the writers who used his library acknowledged their debt to him in print, including Richard Knolles, a historian and author of *The Generall Historie of the Turkes,* and Thomas Milles, in *Catalogue of Honour.* With Cotton's assistance, Sir Walter Raleigh wrote his *Historie of the World* while confined to the Tower on charges of treason; Sir Francis Bacon consulted Cotton while working on *The History of Henry VII.*

These also were the years when William Shakespeare dominated the London stage with his greatest plays. Many studies have been undertaken to identify the literary and historical sources of Shakespeare's works, but precisely where the playwright may have read the books he consulted remains unanswered. That England's greatest writer might have derived some inspiration from Cotton's books is pure speculation, but not impossible. The link could have been Ben Jonson, who was friendly with both men, or Lord Hunsdon, Cotton's landlord and patron, and from 1597 to 1603, director of the Lord Chamberlain's Men, the theatrical company that included Shakespeare as actor, shareholder, and principal dramatist, and which became known as the King's Men in 1603 with the death of Queen Elizabeth and the coronation of James I.

There is also a coincidence linking Shakespeare to Dr. John Dee, the eccentric book collector, alchemist, geographer, mathematician, and astrologer to Queen Elizabeth I, who was rumored to have buried books and papers in a field that was later excavated by Robert Cotton. Known also as a sorcerer, Dee was acquitted in 1555 on charges of scheming to kill Queen Mary I with magic. In later years he was concerned with the search for a Northwest Passage to the Far East, and he dabbled in necromancy, claiming at one point to have found a potent elixir in the ruins of Glastonbury.

When Shakespeare was bidding adieu to the London stage around 1611, he conceived as the leading character in his farewell production a powerful magician who at the play's end buries the twin totems of his authority, his wand and his books, several fathoms deep in the ground. (One contemporary event known to have influenced *The Tempest* was the sensational story of Sir Thomas Gates, a traveler to North America whose shipwreck and survival on Bermuda had occasioned the publication of several pamphlets in 1609 and 1610, and undoubtedly prompted Shakespeare to give his farewell play an island setting.)

Although Geoffrey Bullough made no connection between Prospero and John Dee in his eight-volume work, *Narrative and Dramatic Sources of Shakespeare* (1960), in another context he professed "no doubt" that Shakespeare had read a certain French poem, "Traison," that he used in *Richard II,* and speculated that the playwright actually may have read it in Dee's home. Bullough pointed out that a copy of "Traison" now in Lambeth Palace bears the ownership signature of John Dee: "It is pleasant to fancy Shakespeare going to consult the manuscript at the Mortlake home of the famous mathematician and spiritualist," he wrote. It is just as pleasant to fancy this prince of poets poking among the shelves of Robert Cotton's library and hearing stories from his friends about the strange sorcerer who buried his books in the ground. A more direct connection was made by Frances Yates in *The Occult Philosophy in the Elizabethan Age.* "Dee is shadowed through Prospero in this most daring play which presents a good conjurer at a time when conjuring was a dreaded accusation." Elsewhere, Yates suggests that Dr. Dee, the philosopher to Queen Elizabeth, was "defended" by Shakespeare in the creation of Prospero, "the good and learned conjuror, who had managed to transport his valuable library to the island."

Cotton's residence, located in the heart of Westminster on a site now occupied by the House of Lords, was famous as an informal athenaeum, a Jacobean form of literary salon. Cotton's library was recognized as the most important source of factual information in the realm, an archive that was valued by his friends and feared by his enemies. In his journal Cotton recorded books "lent to his Majesty at Whitehall." Other items were lent to the master of the revels, the chancellor of the exchequer, the lord treasurer, and many other noblemen and parliamentary figures. When Sir Robert fell out of favor with the coterie that assumed power after the death of King James I, a singularly vindictive form of punishment was devised just for him.

In November 1629, Cotton was falsely charged with having circulated a seditious paper titled "The Danger wherein this Kingdom now Standeth, and the Remedy." Because the "pestilential tractate" purportedly was found among Cotton's books, King Charles I ordered the library to be sealed. Some historians feel the charges were fabricated as a pretext to deprive the king's enemies of access to information contained in Cotton's book collection. Cotton was arrested, questioned, and released pending prosecution in the Star Chamber. The birth of Prince Charles on May 29, 1630, occasioned an amnesty, and charges against him were dropped. But once the library was closed, it remained so, and the keys were kept by royal subordinates.

At first Cotton was allowed occasional access to his books, but only under close supervision of the king's council. Soon, he was denied use of his library entirely. He fell into a deep depression and his repeated pleas to regain custody were ignored. Sir Simonds d'Ewes, a fellow collector and close friend, later wrote that Cotton was "outworn in a few months with anguish and grief," and described his once "ruddy and well coloured" face to be "in a green-blackish paleness, near to the resemblance and hue of a dead visage." Early in 1631, when the end was near, Sir Robert Cotton sent a dire message: "Tell the Lord Privy Seal, and the rest of the Council, that their so long detaining my books from me has been the cause of this mortal malady." Finally Charles I dispatched the Earl of Dorset with a decree to rescind the order, but word of the decree arrived at Cotton's home on March 6, 1631, half an hour after the great collector's death.

In 1809, the Reverend Thomas Frognall Dibdin wrote that the "loss of such a character—the deprivation of such a patron—made the whole society of book collectors tremble and turn pale. Men began to look sharply into their libraries, and to cast a distrustful eye upon those who came to consult and to copy: for the spirit of Cotton, like the ghost of Hamlet's father, was seen to walk, before cock-crow, along the galleries and balconies of great collections, and to bid the owners of them 'remember and beware'!"

The Cottonian Library remained the property of Sir Robert's family, passing through several generations to his great-grandson Sir John Cotton, who turned it over to the nation in 1700. But more than half a century would pass before the books found a proper home. In the meantime, they moved around from place to place, arriving finally at Ashburnham House in Westminster, where on October 23, 1731, a fire broke out and caused extensive damage, though efforts to save the material were heroic. In some instances, entire presses with the books still in them were hastily removed. Others were broken open, and books "were thrown out of the windows" to safety. Of 958 manuscript volumes in the collection, 114 were reported by a special investigating commission to be "lost, burnt, or entirely spoiled," while another ninety-eight were "damaged so as to be defective." Extensive repairs were undertaken over the next century, and many manuscripts thought lost were partially restored.

Most catastrophic by far was the damage done to a volume known as the Cotton Genesis, a series of illuminations depicting scenes from the first book of the Bible believed executed in Alexandria between the fifth and sixth centuries. The 250 miniatures were among the few examples of classical book painting still in existence. According to one speculative account, the book had first come to England in the sixteenth century with two refugee Greek bishops from Philippi who presented the codex as a gift to King Henry VIII. The manuscript then is said to have passed to Queen Elizabeth I; she, in turn, presented it to her tutor, Sir John Fontescue, who apparently discerned its proper place in the library of Robert Cotton. In a selfless gesture of generosity, Cotton once allowed a French scholar to take the treasures to Paris for four years of study. Today, only a few charred fragments remain, a reminder of just how fragile these objects are.

There was, by contrast, the miraculous survival of the Lindisfarne Gospels. Originally encased in a binding of gold, gilded silver, and precious stones, the illuminated manuscript was produced in the seventh century by Benedictine scribes on a "holy island" two miles off the coast of Northumbria. When in the ninth century a band of Danish invaders forced the monks to flee, they took the gospels with them. As they attempted a sea crossing to Ireland, a pounding storm washed the bulky book over the side. During low tide the following day, it was found ashore, intact and undamaged. Years later the volume returned to Lindisfarne, where it was recorded in a 1367 inventory. Though shorn of its gold and jewels during the Tudor sack of the monasteries, the text at least was saved and made its way into the library of Sir

Robert Cotton, a gift to him from the clerk of the House of Commons. His heirs passed it on to the British Museum, where today it is showcased as a priceless heirloom of English culture.

If there was an unforeseen lesson to be learned from Robert Cotton's experience, it was that book collecting could be dangerous, an awareness not lost on a London bookseller who ran a shop at the sign of the Rose and Crown in St. Paul's Churchyard by day and amassed a vast assortment of fiery pamphlets and fugitive tracts by night. Unlike Cotton, who was pleased to let the world know about his collection, George Thomason took special measures to conceal the existence of what soon would become an extraordinary archive of historic material.

Starting sometime in 1640 Thomason began saving every book, pamphlet, and broadside he could find pertaining to the dispute between the Royalists and Puritans that was about to erupt in civil war. Though firmly committed to King Charles, Thomason collected on both sides of the controversy. Even after the monarchy was dissolved and the king was executed, even after Oliver Cromwell was installed as head of the commonwealth, the bookseller doggedly continued on his mission, stopping only after the monarchy had been restored in 1661 and Charles II was securely on the throne.

The scope of Thomason's accomplishment is best expressed in numbers. During twenty-two years of tireless collecting he filled 2,008 volumes with 22,255 separate items. Though the collection is outstanding for its comprehensive view of the period, an occasional gem sparkles on its own. One such example is the collector's copy of *Areopagitica*, the impassioned 1644 speech against censorship in which John Milton described books as "the precious lifeblood of a master spirit, embalmed and treasured upon purpose to a life beyond life." Thomason's copy bears the handwritten inscription "ex dono authoris"—"a gift from the author."

Aside from George Thomason, nobody saved much that was printed between 1640 and 1660, even though the output of quarto pieces exceeded anything known in England up to that time. (A *quarto*, approximately nine by twelve inches, was made from sheets of paper folded twice to make four pages.) Much of this can be attributed to the proliferation of fugitive printing shops during the upheaval, and the movement of Royalist influence away from London to Oxford. In an 1897 essay for the periodical *Bibliographica*, Falconer Madan of the British Library specified the conditions that were necessary for such an archival enterprise to succeed. "In fact, the only hope of dealing satisfactorily with the whole disturbed period of twenty years lay in the appearance of some person who should see the importance of the task, should arrange a uniform system in London of catching each little treatise as it was hawked about the streets or sold over (or under) the counter, should be successful in interesting his Royalist friends in the pursuit of the pamphlets of the king's side, should be able to keep his collection safe, and, above all, should be sagacious enough to take a note of the date on which each piece came into his net."

Little is known about Thomason, not even the year of his birth, though sometime between 1600 and 1602 is likely, since he had to be at least twenty-four years old in 1626 when he was admitted to the Stationers' Company as a printer or publisher. While the bookseller did issue a number of catalogues, there is nothing to indicate how successful he may have been in the trade. Not long after Thomason's death, his estate prepared two informational documents in the hope that the government would be persuaded to buy his civil war tracts. In the process of describing the collection, the narratives shed some light on the scheme he formulated to build it.

The first document, printed about 1680 as a broadside, begins by pointing out how "very much Money" had been spent, how "great Pains" were taken, and how "many Hazards" were run to make "an exact Collection of all the Pamphlets," which totaled "near Thirty Thousand of several sorts, and by all Parties." Every item had been precisely marked, numbered, and preserved in two thousand bound volumes. "The Method that has been observed, is Time, and such punctual Care was taken, that the very Day is written upon most of them, when they came out." The collection also included "near one Hundred" pieces of manuscript "which no man durst then venture to publish without endangering his Ruine."

Because Thomason maintained close professional ties with publishers, he could arrange for the continuous flow of printed material to his shop without arousing suspicion. Not only was he the first systematic

collector of what today is called ephemera, he implemented an astonishing code of bibliographic technique generations before any such
principles were generally established. Of singular significance was the
uniqueness of the delicate tracts he preserved, a distinction that was
recognized just fourteen years after his death by his estate: "They may
be of very great Use to any Gentleman concerned in Publick Affairs,
both for this Present, and After-Ages, there being not the like in the
World, neither is it possible to make such a Collection."

The anonymous author of this broadside also told how the collection "was so privately carried on" by Thomason "that it was never
known" that "there was such a Design in hand." Once, to "prevent the
Discovery" of the tracts while "the Army was Northwards," he
"pack'd them up in several Trunks," and "sent them to a trusty Friend
in Surry, who safely preserv'd them." And "when the Army was West-
ward, and fearing their Return," the pamphlets "were sent to London
again; but the Collector durst not keep them, but sent them into Essex,
and so according as they lay near Danger, still, by timely removing
them, at a great Charge, secur'd them" once again, all the while "per-
fecting the Work" by continually adding to it. Another time "there was
a Bargain pretended to be made with the University of Oxford, and a
Receipt of a Thousand Pounds given and acknowledg'd to be" a partial payment for the collection. The thinking was that "if the
Usurper"—the Parliamentarians who had ousted the Royalists—discovered the material, university officials would have "greater Power to
struggle for them than a private Man."

Though the second account relates the same basic history as the
first, it includes some additional insights as to just how driven Thomason was. Fearful of being discovered, he once "took great pains both
day and night" to bury the tracts in the ground. Unhappy with that
solution, he then considered shipping them to Holland "for their more
safe preservation," but the dangers of a high-seas transit caused further
anxiety. Finally he hid his treasures inside hollow wooden tables stored
in a warehouse and covered with canvas dropcloths.

Close to a century would elapse between George Thomason's death
and his collection's finding a permanent home. The 2,008 volumes
were kept for several years at Oxford University (thus escaping
destruction in the Great Fire of London in 1666), then were moved

around from custodian to custodian. Finally, in 1761, Thomas Hollis V—the same Thomas Hollis who came to the aid of Harvard College after a catastrophic fire destroyed its library in 1764—persuaded the secretary of state, Lord Bute, to buy the material for £300. The collection entered the British Museum Library in the name of George III, and was known for some time as the king's pamphlets. For 150 years or so, it more appropriately has been referred to as the Thomason Collection of Civil War Tracts.

No contemporary portrait exists of George Thomason, and according to a brief obituary published in April 1666 that noticed his passing, he died "a poore man." Yet two hundred years after this humble bookseller embarked on his daily ritual of preserving the printed matter of his day, Thomas Carlyle, who wrote a biography of Oliver Cromwell, would say that Thomason had assembled "the most valuable set of documents connected with English history: greatly preferable to all the sheepskins in the Tower and other places, for informing the English what the English were in former times." In his 1897 essay on the tracts, Falconer Madan was less impassioned than Carlyle, but just as impressed by the obscure collector's matchless deed: "His achievement is unparalleled in its kind, and it does not speak well for bibliography in England that his name is so little known."

When the incomparable journal maintained for nine and a half years by Samuel Pepys (1633–1703) during the reign of King Charles II was "discovered" in the nineteenth century, the prevailing assumption was that the diarist wrote his entries out in code because he did not want anybody to read his private thoughts. Eventually it was shown that Pepys used a form of forgotten shorthand called tachygraphy, yet the vexing question remained: Why? Did this indomitable perfectionist take steps to ensure that his candid insights into Restoration life would be read by future generations, or did he wish them to remain concealed?

Because diaries were not published in the seventeenth century, it is unlikely that Pepys envisioned a printed book emerging from the million and a quarter words he wrote between January 1, 1660, and May 31, 1669. But Pepys did insist that his journal be part of the great private library he took ingenious steps to preserve intact, leaving little doubt that the six volumes were pieces of the bequest he emphatically stated was "for the benefit of posterity."

Three centuries after it was formed, the library endures as a time capsule from another era. With seven exceptions, every book that the former secretary of the admiralty chose to include is present, and every one is shelved not only in the precise order he indicated, but in the same glazed book "presses" that had been built to his specifications by British navy shipwrights. Since 1724 the library has been housed behind a graceful courtyard at Magdalene College in Cambridge on the northeastern bank of the River Cam. There is nothing else quite like it—and presumably this was part of the collector's plan as well.

Barely a fortnight before his death on May 31, 1703, Pepys specified the future of his library in two codicils to his will. A widower for thirty-four years with no children of his own, Pepys directed that his sister's son John Jackson be given "full and sole possession of all my collection of books and papers," and that the young man enjoy full use of the library for the "terme of his natural Life." He further stipulated that "all possible provision should be made" to assure "unalterable preservation and perpetual security" of his wishes, and that upon his nephew's death, the library should "be placed and for ever settled in one of our universities and rather in that of Cambridge than Oxford."

Pepys was inclined to see the library placed in the "new building" he had helped finance at his alma mater, Magdalene College, in the 1660s, but he also mentioned Trinity College as an alternative. He insisted that the library remain "in its present form" with no "other books mixt therewith." To ensure that this would be the case, he proposed a further security arrangement that would require the two colleges to conduct "a reciprocal check upon one another." Whichever institution accepted the books would have to allow annual visitations from its counterpart, and if "any breach" in "said covenants" were discovered, the library would go over to the other school immediately. Trinity has not exercised its right of inspection within the last century, but there has been no need; the terms have been observed for more than 265 years.

Inscribed above a central arch on the west façade of the stone building are the words "Bibliotheca Pepysiana," and in smaller letters is the

collector's motto: "Mens cujusque is est quisque." As he was showing
me through the library one Saturday morning during Easter break,
Richard Luckett, the Pepys librarian, offered his translation of the
phrase. "It is a quotation from Cicero," he said. "It is very contracted
Latin, but what it means essentially is, 'The mind of each, that is what
each man is.' What that says, I believe, is that *this* is not Mr. Pepys"—
he pointed to a familiar portrait of the diarist that hangs between
Presses 2 and 3—"but *this* is"—and he pointed to a book. "And *this*,"
he quickly added, indicating another, "and *this*, and *this*, and *this*."

A heady aroma of waxed leather bindings, old printed paper, and
strips of cedar that line the inside of the bookcases pervades the Pepys
Library, making the experience of a visit there pleasant for all the
senses. Entry to the fireproof room is possible only through two steel
doors, each connected to a formidable security system. "We do not
admit casual readers," Luckett explained. "A lot of my job involves
screening the queries." A historic criticism of the library, in fact, has
been the rigid standards of access imposed by the college, prompting
William Blades in his sprightly 1880 work, *The Enemies of Books,* to
include among his villains "those bibliomaniacs and overcareful possessors, who, being unable to carry their treasures into the next world,
do all they can to hinder the usefulness in this." Blades specifically cited
"the curious library of old Samuel Pepys, the well-known diarist" as
his prime example. But others have expressed a different opinion; one
such is Henry B. Wheatley, who wrote in 1899, the "interest of this
room is unique, and no one who has been privileged to enter this quiet
retreat can ever forget his visit to the Pepysian Library."

Toward the end of his life, Pepys prepared a memorandum that
outlined his concept of collecting. He wrote that a private library
should comprehend, "in fewest books in least room," the greatest
diversity of subjects, styles, and languages that "its owner's reading
will bear." With that statement, according to Luckett, Pepys was trying to "formulate exactly what his library was," and to do that he had
to be clear about what it was not. "It was not a public library in a university, it was not the library of a professor, nothing like that. It was a
private library." It is partly for this reason, Luckett believes, that
Pepys wanted nothing added to his collection. "Requiring no subtrac-
tion is not unusual. But I know of no other major library which has

not been supplemented with something new at some point. This one is kept exactly as it was."

There were to be three thousand books in the collection, not a volume more, not a volume less, because Pepys had determined this number to be ideal for a gentleman's library. There were times during the forty years of his active collecting when books were discarded to make room for new titles, which explains why volumes with the distinctive Pepys book-plate showing his motto above a pair of crossed anchors turn up in antiquarian catalogues every so often. The shelving system is by size, so that tiny books barely a few inches high are on Shelf 1 and bulky folios are on Shelf 5. The largest volumes of all are arranged around the sides of the diarist's desk, which is in effect the twelfth and final bookcase. Volumes are numbered 1 to 3,000, from the smallest to the largest. So that they would appear of uniform size, Pepys installed a series of graded wooden stilts beneath smaller books, and each stilt was decorated appropriately to match the bindings. The first codicil to his will further mandates that book placement "as to heighth be strictly reviewed," and where found "requiring it," to be "more nicely adjusted."

Pepys's comportment in life exhibited similar neatness and exactitude. "There is where the diary lives," Luckett said, pausing at Press 1. "It is not hidden; as you can see it is right there behind the glass." He gently removed the first volume from the third shelf and passed it carefully over to me. "You will notice, of course, that he didn't just start in 1660, but on January 1, 1660." Though written in shorthand, the characters are precise, tidy, finely formed, and, like the fastidiously conceived shelves of his bookcases, "nicely adjusted."

When he began the journal, Pepys, the son of a tailor, was a twenty-six-year-old steward and man of business to Edward Montagu, the lord admiral, who was a distant cousin of his but came from a totally different social sphere. In May of 1660 he sailed with the fleet to bring Charles II back from exile in Holland. The accounts Pepys wrote of these crucial months leading up to the coronation on April 23, 1661, are without equal for the period. Meanwhile, he continued his impressive advancement within the government to become clerk of the acts to the Navy Board, a civilian office responsible for designing, building, and repairing ships of the line, managing dockyards, supplying the fleet with victuals, and providing supplies and equipment. In time he would serve Charles II and James VI as secretary to the Admiralty, and the same love of order so evident in his private life helped make him a superior civil servant. Had he never kept a diary or formed a library, he would still be remembered as the individual most responsible for creating the naval force Lord Nelson would direct to victory at Trafalgar in 1812. Socially, Pepys had an impressive circle of friends that included another great diarist of the period, John Evelyn. Pepys devoted time to his love of music, theater, and female companionship, and every night before retiring, he recorded by flickering candlelight the events of the day in his diary.

On July 23, 1666, Pepys brought over to his London apartment a master joiner from the Deptford and Woolwich dockyards named Thomas Sympson, and together "with great pains" they set about "contriving presses to put my books up in; they now growing numerous and lying one upon another on my chairs, I lose the use, to avoid the trouble of removing them when I would open a book." The press Sympson built to Pepys's exacting specifications was of gorgeous carved oak and fitted with facing doors inlaid with small rectangles of glass, believed to be the first glazed bookcase ever crafted. Sympson returned the following month "to set up my other new presse for my books."

Luckett noted that iron handles were fastened on the earlier presses, brass on the last ones. "The bookcases come apart and these are carrying handles. In fact this is how they were all brought up from London in 1724. There are other subtle differences as well. Number One has adjustable shelves, whereas Number Twelve has never been adjustable; those shelves are fixed. What that suggests is that Pepys started with a practical domestic bookcase, one in which he could adjust the shelves. Eventually he saw that in order to get the maximum number of books into the smallest place, he would arrange them by height."

Pepys's book presses are notable also for the intricate carvings that appear on the cornices at the top and the plinths at the bottom. "It's very much like the carvings you have on the stern galleries of ships," Luckett said. "The choice of wood is consistent with this as well. Walnut would have been more fashionable for furniture at the time, but oak was the wood that you got in dockyards. I believe this to be the most considered library that has ever come from one man."

Because book placement was determined by size, not content, Pepys devised a detailed scheme to help him locate specific works. Two catalogues, one listing titles by number, the other by alphabet, are supplemented by a subject index called "Appendix Classica" that is keyed to a chart that pinpoints press and shelf locations. The constant addition of new books mandated the periodic reordering of placement, a process Pepys called an "adjustment" that provides other useful information about acquisitions. "You can roughly determine how long a book has been in the collection by how many different shelf numbers it has had," Luckett said.

Today Pepys would be considered a connoisseur, though the concept used three centuries ago to describe him would have been *virtuoso*—an experimenter or investigator. He collected contemporary books widely, including popular romances he called "vulgaria," but he also sought out medieval manuscripts, early printed books, and material dealing with seafaring in general and the Royal Navy in particular, as well as a wide variety of special interests that intrigued him, such as music, chess, magic, science, and herbal cures. Since Pepys sent his books out to be bound, his library is the finest collection of seventeenth-century English bindings in existence.

The Pepys Library includes among two hundred early books printed up to 1558 seven titles produced by William Caxton, eight by Wynkyn de Worde, and eight by Richard Pynson. Of the incunabula, twenty-five in the collection are considered unique, among them Caxton's *Reynard the Fox*. The library also has the only known copy of Stephen Hawes's *The Example of Virtue,* printed by Wynkyn de Worde in 1510. The library's copy of Sir Isaac Newton's *Principia Mathematica* is particularly interesting because Pepys's name appears on the imprimatur as president of the Royal Society, which sponsored the work in 1687. The only book Pepys himself wrote and saw through the press, *Memoires Relating to the State of the Royal Navy,* printed in 1690, is present in a large paper copy. Early editions of Racine, Molière, Pascal, and Descartes are represented as well.

A particularly striking item is an illustrated armament roll of Henry VIII's navy that contains the only known contemporary drawing of the *Mary Rose,* a huge ship of the line that sank off Portsmouth in 1545; recently salvaged, the vessel is on display in Portsmouth. Presented to

Pepys by Charles II, the roll was prepared in 1546 by Anthony Anthony, an officer of ordnance. Pepys cut up the roll ship by ship, mounted the individual drawings on vellum, and had them bound in an ornate volume. Another significant item is the victualer's book of the Spanish Armada, which lists every ship that sailed for England in 1588 and itemizes its stores. Pepys also acquired a nautical almanac that bears the ownership signature of Sir Francis Drake.

In addition to the books and manuscripts are some 10,500 prints contained in a score of large albums, including remarkable specimens by Rembrandt and Dürer. Some 1,750 broadsheet ballads are pasted in five large albums, and about 850 of these can be found nowhere else. There also is an enormous archive of maps and nautical charts and a collection of ephemera that includes chapbooks sold at fairs by vendors for the popular market.

On May 31, 1669, Pepys began the final paragraph of the concluding volume of his diary with the frightening admission that he was going blind: "I doubt I shall ever be able to do with my own eyes in the keeping of my journall, I being not able to do it any longer, having done now so long as to undo my eyes almost every time that I take a pen in my hand." Even though Pepys regained his sight and lived another thirty-four years, his nightly musings were done. For modern critics, the journal has a finished literary quality to it, a work that begins dramatically, proceeds forcefully, and concludes poignantly. As a social document, the diary provides as remarkable a window into the daily life of Restoration England as George Thomason's tracts do for the turbulent era that immediately preceded it. "None of Pepys's other personal papers are here," Luckett said. "Most of them ended up in the Bodleian Library at Oxford. But the diary was quite deliberately placed in his library, and was regarded as a book rather than a private document for a long, long time."

Pepys never lost his enthusiasm for books, and he drew on many sources to satisfy his hunger, including auctions, which became popular in England during his peak years of acquisition. The Leiden publishing house of Elzevier, founded in about 1580, is credited with holding Europe's first book auction in 1604; this clever innovation reached England in 1676, seven years after Pepys made his final journal entry. About a hundred such sales were held in Great Britain from 1676 to

1700, dispersing 350,000 titles and realizing £250,000. Whether Pepys attended the first London sale is not known, though he did buy at others. In his diary, John Evelyn deplored how this "epidemical" form of library disposal had become so rampant, and he expressed hope that Pepys had taken steps to "secure" his books "from the sad dispersions many noble libraries and cabinets have suffered in these later times," especially in light of the "cost and industry" his good friend had invested in them.

Joseph Addison took caustic aim at this curiously popular form of book exchange in an essay he wrote on April 13, 1710, for *The Tatler* about a "learned idiot" he called Tom Folio: "There is not a sale of books begins until Tom Folio is seen at the door. There is not an auction where his name is not heard, and that too in the very nick of time, in the critical moment, before the last decisive stroke of the hammer. There is not a subscription goes forward in which Tom is not privy to the first rough draught of the proposals; nor a catalogue printed, that doth not come to him wet from the press. He is a universal scholar, so far as the title page of all authors: he knows the manuscripts in which they were discovered, the editions through which they have passed, with the praises or censures which they have received from the several members of the learned world."

Though Magdalene College has been doggedly faithful to Pepys's wishes, there has been a single modification to the library. By making explicitly clear that the "new" item is not a formal addition to the library, but simply displayed there on long-term loan from its actual owner, officials feel they have not violated the diarist's will. "What is important to grasp is our conviction that Pepys undoubtedly would approve," Luckett said, and it is a story that illustrates as well as any other the cross-currents of collecting through the centuries.

On March 12, 1688, Pepys acquired at a London auction the manuscript copy of William Caxton's translation of Books 10–15 of Ovid's *Metamorphoses,* and it always has been a valued component of the library. Scholars had believed for centuries that Books 1–9 either were lost or never existed, but in 1965 the missing document was discovered lying buried among the "residue" of material left by the book collector Sir Thomas Phillipps at his death in 1872. The manuscript was bought for $252,000 at a Sotheby's auction by the New York dealer Lew

David Feldman in 1966, but the prospect of the 272-page document leaving Great Britain ignited a spirited controversy, which was averted only when Eugene Power of Ann Arbor, Michigan, bought the book from Feldman and presented it to Magdalene College. "It was always assumed that the part Pepys had acquired was the only one that survived, so in this, we are certain, he would have approved," Luckett said. After many centuries of separation, the two parts are now kept together in a display case apart from the twelve presses. "My delight is in the neatness of everything," Pepys had boasted, and with this satisfying denouement, it is hard to imagine the old virtuoso calling out from his grave for inspectors to investigate reports that covenants had been breached at Magdalene College.

Pepys also had an abiding wish to document all forms of calligraphy. "He was engaged in a scientific study of writing," Luckett said. "He wanted to get an example of every known script over a thousand-year period. It was an exploration, and as such it was the first attempt to put handwriting into chronological order." The fragments he gathered and pasted into three albums were turned over to a young paleographer named Humfrey Wanley, who wrote a learned commentary for each of the calligraphic illustrations that had been assembled.

In 1715, twelve years after Pepys died, the bookman Humfrey Wanley (1672–1726) began keeping a diary. Its purpose was not to set down insightful commentary on the events of the day, but to record his professional activities as librarian, cataloguer, and chief book scout for Robert Harley, the first earl of Oxford, an influential politician who achieved great power during the reign of Queen Anne and was set on acquiring the papers and books of important figures. Harley did not himself collect; he generally commissioned others to do so on his behalf. When it became apparent that he needed assistance, the most qualified person in the realm was Humfrey Wanley, and his diary is as important a record on the growth of British book collecting as is the *Philobiblon* of more than 250 years earlier.

Wanley exhibited an early interest in old books and manuscripts. He became involved in the Pepys project while engaged as an assistant librarian at the Bodleian Library from 1695 to 1700 and assumed numerous other assignments of lasting significance. The catalogue of Anglo-Saxon manuscripts that Wanley prepared for the scholar George Hickes in 1701 earned him a personal recommendation to Robert Harley. He was described as having "the best skill in ancient hands and MSS of any man not only of this, but, I believe, of any former age, and I wish for the sake of the public, that he might meet with the same encouragement here, that he would have met in France, Holland, or Sweden, had he been born in any of those countries."

Shortly after going to work for Robert Harley, Wanley acquired the library of Sir Simonds D'Ewes, the collector who recorded the "anguish and grief" suffered by Sir Robert Cotton twenty-two years earlier. By 1708 Wanley was on the job full time, and seven years later he began his diary. With the death of the first earl of Oxford in 1724, the library passed on to Edward Harley, the second earl of Oxford, an amiable dilettante and patron of the arts who retained Wanley's services and added more rare books and manuscripts.

Unlike his father, Edward Harley enjoyed his collection and often allowed his good friends Alexander Pope and Jonathan Swift to use it as well. Edward Harley left no male heir on his death in 1740, and since his widow, the dowager countess, had no interest in her husband's library, immediate plans were made for its dispersal. The government haggled over the extremely reasonable asking price of £20,000 for the manuscripts, and finally secured them for half that figure. In 1753, the Harleian manuscripts, along with the Cottonian Library, the Sir Hans Sloane Library, and the Royal Library, formed the core collections of the newly formed British Museum Library, and they share prominence to this day among the nation's irreplaceable artifacts.

Meanwhile, Harley's printed books were sold to the London bookseller Thomas Osborne II, who paid £13,000 for the fifty thousand volumes, some £5,000 less than the Harley family had spent to have them bound. But Osborne did not reap immediate riches from the shrewd purchase. It had taken more than forty years for the Harleys to build their library, and the sudden availability of so many books meant that the market was inundated. Twenty years later much of the stock remained unsold, partly because Osborne refused to lower his prices. Some of the titles were listed in subsequent catalogues as coming from the libraries of other "collectors" later discovered to be fictitious. Today, books bound in

red morocco with gold-tooled borders surrounding lozenge-shaped decorations—Harleian bindings—can be found in libraries all over the world.

Even though the reverend Thomas Frognall Dibdin declared
Thomas Osborne to be "the most celebrated bookseller of his day," he
was the object of widespread derision. Alexander Pope lampooned him
in *The Dunciad* as the losing participant in a urinating contest who had
to walk home in defeat with a chamberpot on his head. He was generally judged to be an unusually coarse man who enjoyed bragging over
wine about his many successes. "Young man," he would say, "I have
been in business more than forty years, and am now worth more than
forty thousand pounds. Attend to your business, and you will be as rich
as I am." One undocumented bit of gossip claims that Osborne once
commissioned a translation into English of an epic poem he had come
across that was printed in French; the bookseller was unaware, the
story goes, that John Milton's *Paradise Lost* was already available in
his native tongue.

Other dealers were annoyed by Osborne's insistence on charging
five shillings for each of the first two Harley catalogues, an "avaricious
innovation" on his part, according to some. He also was accused of
pricing his books too high, a charge that led him to publish a haughty
rebuttal in his preface to the third volume of the catalogue. "If I have
set a high value upon books, if I have vainly imagined literature to be
more fashionable than it really is, or idly hoped to revive a taste well-
nigh extinguished, I know not why I should be persecuted with clamor
and invective, since I shall only suffer by my mistake, and be obliged to
keep the books I was in the hope of selling."

As a young man, Samuel Johnson did some bibliographic work for
Osborne. Because Osborne was not respected for his intellectual acuity,
most observers are convinced that Johnson, who was only thirty-one at
the time of the Harley purchase, prepared this eloquent reply for him.
Johnson is known to have written in Latin the first two volumes of *Cat-
alogus Bibliothecae Harleianae*, Osborne's five-volume catalogue of
the collection, and to have worked like a "lion in harness" writing
descriptive entries for the others, which appeared in English. He also
performed numerous other jobs for the bookseller, one of which led to
an incident that has become the stuff of legend. Annoyed by the
"unnecessary delay" Johnson apparently was taking to finish editing a

"work of some consequence," Osborne one day foolishly "abused" the young scholar with a salvo of criticism given "in a most illiberal manner." After listening to the man rant on for "some time unmoved," Johnson "seized a huge folio he was at that time consulting, and, aiming a blow at the bookseller's head," sent his employer "sprawling on the floor." Rising quickly from his chair, Johnson clapped a foot on the terrified man's breast and declared: "Lie there, thou son of dulness, ignorance and obscurity."

For all the "clamor and invective" directed at Osborne by his colleagues, however, nobody suggested that the objects he acquired were worthless. Instead, the prevailing complaint was that he priced his books too high and refused to accept less than he felt they were worth. There can be little doubt that Osborne's willingness to invest heavily in a library that would take years to return a profit must have bred jealousy among other dealers, but what all the grousing demonstrates most dramatically is how competitive book collecting had become among Britain's affluent elite by the middle of the eighteenth century. Dibdin's *Bibliomania* was published and the word found its way into general usage. Dibdin later served as librarian and cataloguer for George John, the second earl of Spencer (1758–1834), the man frequently cited as the greatest collector of incunabula and early printed books that the world has ever seen.

Dibdin's signature work followed by a matter of weeks the appearance of Dr. John Ferriar's satiric poem, also titled "Bibliomania," which was published as an "Epistle to Richard Heber, Esq." Both works appeared in 1809, when Heber was thirty-five years old and already famous for his unbridled book passion. The son of a wealthy rector, Heber (1773–1833) is remembered today as the man who left eight houses, four in England and one each at Ghent, Paris, Brussels, and Antwerp, all filled with books. A. N. L. Munby, the esteemed biographer of Sir Thomas Phillipps, conservatively estimated the total holdings at 150,000 volumes. The respected Paris bookseller and bibliographer Seymour de Ricci's guess was between 200,000 and 300,000, but he added that whatever the specific number, "It is doubtful whether any private individual has ever owned so large a library."

An affable man often praised for his kindness and generosity, Heber purportedly said that no gentleman "can comfortably do without *three* copies of a book. One he must have for his show copy, and he will probably keep it at his country house. Another he will require for his own use and reference; and unless he is inclined to part with this, which is very inconvenient, or risk the injury of his best copy, he must needs have a third at the service of his friends." Heber had a full range of literary and historic interests, and his collections of foreign-language books, particularly works in French, Portuguese, Spanish, Greek, and Latin were superior. But the real strength of his library was early English literature, especially poetry and drama. From 1800 to 1830 he and his agents bought heavily at every major London auction, and he was an ardent practitioner of the en bloc purchase. "His name occurs as a buyer in every priced sale-catalogue of that period," de Ricci wrote. Though it can be argued that Heber was out of control, he was not an indiscriminate hoarder. "He studied his books carefully," de Ricci wrote, and "on several occasions started to catalogue them."

Though Heber's accomplishment is renowned, his "awakening bibliomania" remained largely unexamined until A. N. L. Munby probed the collector's formative years in an essay completed shortly before his death in 1976. "Father and Son" drew on family letters now in the Bodleian Library that were written when Heber was a student at an exclusive boarding school in Greenford, and his tolerant father was rector of Malpas in Cheshire. Munby noted that Reverend Reginald Heber was a man of "simplicity and sweetness of disposition" who became alarmed when he discerned "a rapidly growing tendency" in his son that augured "pernicious consequences."

A frail and delicate child who was unable to compete in outdoor games, Richard demonstrated a "precocious gravity and interest in learning" at an early age. By the time he was ten years old, the boy already was gathering large numbers of books. In one early letter from school, he asked his father to attend a sale on his behalf where "the best editions of the classics of all sizes" were being offered. A few months later, he asked his father to help him buy 109 volumes of poetry, for which he already had saved eight guineas.

By the time Richard was twelve, his father was becoming increasingly concerned about the bills he was getting from booksellers. "I must not allow dear Richard to be so extravagant," Reverend Heber wrote his sister Elizabeth in London on February 27, 1786, instructing

her to pay one outstanding obligation to a dealer, "but tell Dicky I will
have no more debts contracted with booksellers or bookbinders."
Eleven months later, the father was writing again, this time directly to
his son: "There is no end, my Dear, of the *expence* of buying *superfluous* books."

Oblivious to these pleas, Richard soon was writing his father about
the exciting news that an important library was being shipped from
Italy to be sold at auction in London. "I cannot say I rejoice," Reverend Heber wrote back on April 15, 1789. "Of multiplying books, my
dear Richard, there is neither end nor use." The time had come for the
rector to advance some sound moral advice:

> It is an itch which grows by indulgence and should be nipt in
> the bud. All extravagance originates in the lust of acquiring
> superfluities which are ruinous, superfluous Servants, superflu-
> ous Horses, superfluous Carriages, superfluous Pictures, super-
> fluous Libraries are the daily source of misery and beggary. A
> small collection of well chosen books is sufficient for the enter-
> tainment and instruction of any man, and all else are useless
> Lumber.

Three months later the father's tone took on a much sharper edge.
"After my repeated Commands and your repeated promises not to order
any more Books without my previous knowledge and approbation, I am
hurt to find that you pay so little regard either to your own word or my
injunctions. Your Booksellers' Bills within these two last years amount to
the sum of £70, and I am determin'd to put a stop to this extravagance."
He thereupon announced he was instructing school officials to monitor
his son's activities more closely. "In short I will not pay for another Book
that you buy without my previous knowledge and approbation."

The anxiety brought on by excessive book purchases receded somewhat, though not entirely, once Richard was admitted to Brasenose
College, his father's alma mater at Oxford. Reginald Heber died in
1804, passing the family manors of Marston in Yorkshire and Hodnet
in Shropshire on to his son, along with the wherewithal to amass a private library of printed books that would have no equal in the world.
Among the thousands of manuscripts Heber owned was the holograph

copy of Sir Walter Scott's *The Monastery.* Sir Walter was a friend who not only dedicated the sixth canto of *Marmion* to the collector, but made reference to his library:

> *Thy volumes, open as thy heart,*
> *Delight, amusement, science, art,*
> *To every ear and eye impart;*
> *Yet who, of all who thus employ them,*
> *Can like the owner's self enjoy them?—*
> *But, hark! I hear the distant drum!*
> *The day of Flodden Field is come.—*
> *Adieu, dear Heber! Life and health,*
> *And store of literary wealth.*

Heber's homosexual relationship with a young protégé caused a scandal in the 1820s, yet sexual preference did not stop him from proposing marriage to Richardson Currer (1785–1861) of Eshton Hall, Craven, regarded by some as England's first great female bibliophile. Heber is said to have particularly coveted her copy of *The Book of St. Albans,* a volume of essays on hawking, hunting, coat-armor, and blazoning of arms first published in 1486. Currer kept her books to herself and never married; her library was sold at auction in 1862 and realized nearly £6,000. Heber died alone on October 4, 1833, surrounded by books. "Poor man," the Reverend Mr. Dyce wrote to his friend Sir Samuel Egerton Brydges, "he expired at Pimlico, in the midst of his rare property, without a friend to close his eyes, and from all I have heard I am led to believe he died broken-hearted: he had been ailing for some time, but took no care of himself, and seemed indeed to court death. Yet his ruling passion was strong to the last."

In his *Reminiscences of a Literary Life* (1836), Dibdin described his first look at Heber's library, a visit he was able to arrange only after the voracious collector had died.

> I looked round me with amazement. I had never seen rooms, cupboards, passages, and corridors, so choked, so suffocated with books. Treble rows were there, double rows were there. Hundreds of slim quartos—several upon each other—were

longitudinally placed over thin and stunted duodecimos, reaching from one extremity of shelf to another. Up to the very ceiling the piles of *volumes* extended; while the floor was strewed with them, in loose and numerous heaps.

Because Heber left no testamentary instructions, his heirs wasted little time authorizing a series of sixteen sales in London, Paris, and Ghent, which began in 1834 and continued for five years. "The market was absolutely glutted and there were practically no new buyers," de Ricci wrote; receipts in London totaled £56,774 "for books which had cost their late owner a good deal over £100,000."

Heber was just one of many nineteenth-century collectors who suffered from what Dibdin lightheartedly diagnosed as a "fatal disease." In one twelve-month period alone—from November 1806 to November 1807—no fewer than 149,200 volumes were sold in London auctions by three different firms. But the era's defining moment came in a three-way contest for the right to own a single book at the Roxburghe sale. (Dibdin was a founding member of the bibliophiles' Roxburghe Club in 1812.) Dibdin would write about the fray in his *Bibliographical Decameron,* a three-volume work that loosely took the form of Boccaccio's comic poem. Because a good deal of Dibdin's writings were serious attempts at bibliography—and because a good deal of his bibliography is seriously flawed—it has been fashionable to dismiss the man as a dilettante; this is a pity, since he did chronicle a pivotal period in book collecting with spunk, elan, and a splash of excitement that retains freshness to this day.

When Dibdin wrote about "the far-famed Roxburghe Fight" in 1817, memories of the sale of the Roxburghe collection were fresh and passions were still hot. The collector John Ker, the duke of Roxburghe, was, like his good friend King George III, an ardent bibliophile, and among his treasures were rarities printed by Caxton, Pynson, Wynkyn de Worde, and Julian Notary. There were superb editions of French romances, and a strong collection of Elizabethan and Jacobean dramatic works. Of special interest was a 1471 copy of Boccaccio's *Decameron,* printed in Venice by Christopher Valdarfer. The dispersal of Roxburghe's books began eight years after his death, on May 18, 1812. When it closed triumphantly on July 4, 1814, £23,397, ten shillings, and six pence had been spent on 9,353 lots.

Dibdin wrote that anticipation for the sale was great, and added with an impertinence that was typical of him that the publication of a certain earlier work—his own *Bibliomania*—had "probably stirred up the mettle and hardened the sinews of the contending Book-Knights." The duke's house in St. James's Square was so crowded that nothing but "standing upon a contiguous bench" saved Dibdin "from suffocation." But he would not have missed the action for anything.

> For *two and forty* successive days—with the exception only of Sundays—was the voice and the hammer of Mr. Evans heard, with equal efficacy, in the dining-room of the late Duke—which had been appropriated to the vendition of the books: and within that same space (some thirty-five feet by twenty) were such deeds of valour performed, and such feats of book-heroism achieved, as had never been previously beheld: and of "the like" will probably never be seen again. The shouts of the victors, and the groans of the vanquished stunned and appalled you as you entered. The throng and the press, both of idle spectators and determined bidders, was unprecedented.

Dibdin implied that the emperor Napoleon was represented at the sale by an unidentified agent. France and England were at diplomatic variance at the time, but this didn't faze the French emperor: the Valdarfer Boccaccio was thought to be a unique book, and Napoleon was an ardent bibliophile. Nevertheless, the battle over the Boccaccio that developed was waged by three Englishmen: George Spencer, the marquis of Blandford; William Cavendish, the duke of Devonshire; and Dibdin's patron, George John, the second earl of Spencer (Viscount Althorp). As the climactic moment drew near, Mr. Evans, the auctioneer, called for silence. Dibdin described the action that followed:

> On his right hand, leaning against the wall, stood Earl Spencer; a little lower down, and standing at right angles with his Lordship, appeared the Marquis of Blandford. The Duke, I believe, was not then present; but my Lord Althorp stood a little backward to the right of his father, Earl Spencer. Such was "the ground taken up" by the adverse hosts. The honor of firing the

first shot was due to a gentleman of Shropshire, unused to this species of warfare, and who seemed to recoil from the reverberation of the report himself had made!—"One hundred guineas," he exclaimed. Again a pause ensued; but anon the biddings rose rapidly to 500 guineas. Hitherto, however, it was evident the firing was but masked and desultory. At length all random shots ceased; and the champions before named stood gallantly up to each other resolving not to flinch from a trial of their respective strengths.

Lord Spencer bid a thousand guineas, to which the marquis of Blandford added his customary advance of ten. "You might have heard a pin drop," Dibdin reported. "All eyes were turned—all breathing well nigh stopped," and from that point the contest was between Lord Spencer and Blandford. " 'Two thousand pounds are offered by the Marquis,' " Evans declared, and Lord Spencer paused for fifteen seconds before upping the figure by £250. Blandford added another ten, which abruptly ended the contest. "The echo of that fallen hammer was heard in the libraries of Rome, of Milan, and St. Mark," Dibdin concluded. "Boccaccio himself startled from his slumber of five hundred years."

The price paid for the Valdarfer Boccaccio stood as the largest sum paid for a printed book until 1884, when J. Pierpont Morgan bought a 1459 Mainz Psalter for $24,750. Lord Spencer was gracious in defeat, perhaps because he had an idea that time was on his side. Within seven years, the marquis of Blandford was forced to sell his library, and the book once again was on the market. This time competition was tepid, and Spencer added the Boccaccio to his Althorp Library for £918.15s.

The Roxburghe sale was the watershed event in what Dibdin proclaimed to be "the grand era of Bibliomania," but book passion remained intense for many decades, as the response to another auction twenty-eight years later demonstrates. In the summer of 1840, prominent collectors and booksellers on both sides of the English Channel began receiving in the mail a fourteen-page catalogue that announced the forthcoming dispersal of a private library gathered over four decades by a certain Jean-Nepomucene-Auguste Pichaud, a reclusive Belgian nobleman further identified as Count Fortsas. Though only fifty-two items were listed, intense interest was aroused by virtue of the accompanying claim that the collector "admitted upon his shelves only works unknown to bibliographers and cataloguists"—works that were known nowhere else. "It was his invariable rule, a rule from which he never departed," a preface to the catalogue explained.

> With such a system, it is easy to conceive that the collection formed by him—although during forty years he devoted considerable sums to it—could not be very numerous. But what it will be difficult to believe is, that he pitilessly expelled from his shelves books for which he had paid their weight in gold—volumes which would have been the pride of the most fastidious amateurs—as soon as he learned that a work, up to that time unknown, had been noticed in any catalogue.

The preface described what had happened when Count Fortsas learned from a bibliography that a number of the items he thought were unique actually existed elsewhere. "It made him *lose* at once the third of his cherished library. After that he seemed disgusted with books and with life; he did not make a single further acquisition," resulting in a "severe blow for our bibliomaniac" that "contributed to hastening his end." Count Fortsas was said to have died at the age of sixty-nine on September 1, 1839, at the Château de Fortsas, the place of his birth, near the remote Belgian village of Binche in Hainaut.

Accordingly, the fifty-two remaining items were to be sold on August 10, 1840, to the highest bidders. Payment would be in cash, with a 10 percent premium added to the hammer price. Under no circumstances could books be returned after the auction; those unable to attend were invited to "send their bids with every confidence to M Em. Hoyois, Printer and Bookseller, rue de Nimy, at Mons, and he will deal with them. A deposit is required from persons with whom he has not previously done business. Letters must be stamped." Count Fortsas had inventoried his library in a "pell-mell" fashion, and it was further decided that items would be listed in the same haphazard manner he had utilized, and without following any systematic bibliographical system: "For a collection so small, a classification would have been, in fact, a useless matter. The interruption in the series of numbers is caused by the works from time to time expelled from his shelves." As a final tease, excerpts from the count's own notes for each item were appended to each description.

We know now that this was the clever prank of Renier Chalons of Brussels, the impish president of the Société des Bibliophiles Belges, so we can smile at many of the items listed and described in the catalogue. At the time, however, the announcement was received with utmost seriousness. The genius of the scheme lay in the tantalizing catalogue entries. None of these books existed, but they were described in a way that made them irresistible. Supporting information, moreover, was authentic and painstakingly documented. There was a plausibility to everything. Perhaps it was a hoax, but what if it were authentic? Decisions had to be made, and many collectors and curators decided it was better to be safe than sorry.

The details of what followed were gathered by William Blades, an authority on printing history and the author of a splendid rumination on the fragility of literary artifacts, *The Enemies of Books*. His lively essay, "Count de Fortsas's Library," and his invaluable translation of the catalogue, were published in the April 1863 issue of a short-lived New York periodical, *The Philobiblon*, with additional material furnished in the November 1863 issue. Blades was fifteen years old when the hoax was perpetrated and was therefore able to gather information while many of the principals were still alive.

As the sale approached, commissions authorizing purchases were sent off to Belgium. A gentleman of Lille was interested in a pamphlet purportedly relating to the Belgian Revolution of 1814–1815 and printed in an edition of two thousand copies, but "entirely suppressed" prior to release. "A friend saved this copy for me," Count Fortsas had written in his notes. "I consider it unique." When the princesse de Ligne read a description of Lot 48, she immediately decided she had to acquire the book, purportedly bound in "green chagrin, with a lock of silver gilt." The supposed author, her grandfather, was known to have kept company with many influential women. His "memoir" was cryptically titled *My Campaigns in the Low Countries, with the List, Day by Day, of the Fortresses That I Have Lifted to the White Arm,* and was additionally described as having been "Printed by Me Alone, for Me Alone, in One Sole Copy, and for a Reason." The princess did not want this embarrassment to fall into indiscreet hands, as the letter to her agent made clear: "Buy, I conjure you, at any price the foolishness of that scamp, my grandfather."

The baron de Reiffenberg, director of the Royal Library of Brussels, was authorized to buy several items at the sale. M. F. M. Crozet of Paris sent commissions for two lots; the Belgian minister submitted orders for nine items, and stressed that his commission was without limit. Octave Delepierre, a bibliographer well known in England, wrote Hoyois with commissions for five books and imposed no limitations on price. One of the five, Number 47, had this identification: "Philosophical Disputation, in Which the Anonymous Author Attempts to Show That Man before Sin Did Not Have Sex. Cologne, 1607. 4to."

Certainly one of the most curious titles was Number 43, "The Aftermaths of Pleasure or the Discomfiture of the Great King in the Low Countries. At Ponent (Holland), 1686, 12mo." (A 12mo, twelvemo, or duodecimo is a book, approximately 5 by 7½ inches, where each leaf is one twelfth of a whole sheet.) It was further described by the count as a "libel of disgusting cynicism on the occasion of the fistula of Louis XIV. One of the plates represents the 'royal behind' under the form of a sun surrounded with rays with the famous motto: *Nec pluribus impar.*"

As the auction drew near, dealers and collectors quietly began to converge on the town of Binche, a number of them meeting unexpectedly in the same coach. The Roxburghe Club sent a representative from London. On August 9, 1840, the day before the sale was scheduled to go forward, the Brussels newspapers carried a short notice; the Count Fortsas library would not be sold after all. In a last-minute move, the citizens of Binche reportedly had bought the collection en bloc, and would deposit it in the public library as a memorial to the town's native son. A quick look around the tiny town disclosed that no such repository existed, and further inquiries revealed there was neither a Château Fortsas nor a Count Fortsas.

Fifteen years later, Renier Chalons acknowledged his hand in the prank when he enjoined the production of a facsimile by the man who had printed the catalogue for him, M Hoyois, arguing that further embarrassment should be avoided. Hoyois lost the case but went ahead and published a transcript of the court proceedings, along with related facts still in his possession, including letters and absentee bids that he had received from prospective buyers. The disagreement ended what had been a close friendship between the two men, and was the only sour note in an otherwise ingenious hoax.

In England, meanwhile, Sir Thomas Phillipps (1792–1872), the forty-eight-year-old illegitimate son of a textile manufacturer, was not quite halfway into his own frenzied quest to preserve every scrap of paper and vellum fragment he could locate. "I wish to have one copy of every book in the world," the antiquary and collector wrote toward the end of his life, and it was not an idle wish. Though he had inherited a sizable estate, virtually every shilling was spent to acquire manuscripts. The life and obsessions of Sir Thomas Phillipps were richly documented in a five-volume study prepared by his biographer, A. N. L. Munby, later abridged into a single volume by Nicolas Barker (see General Bibliography). Both works contend that Sir Thomas was the greatest collector of manuscripts the world has ever known, and the first true collector of the modern era.

The preface to an early catalogue Phillipps wrote in longhand outlined his sense of purpose, and is perhaps the most significant explanation of his lifelong quest: "In amassing my collection, I commenced with purchasing everything that lay within my reach, to which I was instigated by reading various accounts of the destruction of valuable manuscripts." Because at first he lacked the skill to "judge unerringly" which items were worth saving and which were not, Phillipps made the simple decision to take no chances: "I had not the ability to select, nor the resolution to let anything escape because it was of trifling value." His passion for manuscripts on vellum "arose from witnessing the unceasing destruction of them" by "goldbeaters," crass salvagers who extracted precious metals that had been inlaid centuries earlier by medieval illuminators—and also, of course, from the manuscripts' uniqueness.

Sir Thomas coined a word to distinguish his passion for vellum from the more common kind of bibliomania then being celebrated by Dibdin, an acquaintance who repeatedly sought permission to visit the Phillipps estate at Thirlestaine House, Cheltenham.

As I advanced, the ardour of the pursuit increased until at last I became a perfect vello-maniac, and I gave any price that was asked. Nor do I regret it, for my object was not only to secure good manuscripts for myself but also to raise the public estimation of them, so that their value might be more generally known, and consequently more manuscripts preserved. For nothing tends to the preservation of anything so much as making it bear a high price.

Sir Thomas admitted to having models that he tried to emulate. "The examples I always kept in view were Sir Robert Cotton and Sir Robert Harley. They had the advantage of me in living a century or two before, and although their collections were so immense, that some thought there was nothing to be gleaned after them, yet I foresaw that there must be vast treasures upon the Continent in consequence of the dispersion of Monastic libraries by the French Revolution." Because this preface was never published during Phillipps's lifetime, its date of composition can only be estimated. Munby placed it around 1828, when the collector was thirty-six years old, though Seymour de Ricci put it at 1837, when the first catalogue of the collection was printed privately; it contained 23,837 entries. In either case, the "vello-maniac" was still a relatively young man with many years ahead of him.

Munby conceded that Phillipps was "vain, selfish, dogmatic, obstinate, litigious and bigoted," but added that "some of his unparalleled success as a collector can be ascribed" to these nasty traits. "To amass so many and so valuable manuscripts that great scholars were forced to visit his library was the ambition of a vain man, though to say that is not to minimize his veneration for scholarship and his solicitude for the preservation of records." For all Phillipps's faults, Munby concluded that "his achievement must be judged as heroic in conception and execution."

Phillipps proposed turning his collection over to the British government, and exchanged letters to that effect with Benjamin Disraeli, then chancellor of the exchequer. Because Phillipps demanded what amounted to total control, nothing proceeded beyond the discussion stage. "Altho' I greatly sympathize with your intentions," Disraeli wrote, "I cannot hold out any prospect of my being able to induce Parliament to cooperate with you in the plan as, at present, proposed." When Phillipps died in 1872, he was confused, bitter, and unable to secure the future of his treasures in a way that would keep them together. Instead, he drafted an impossible will that assured their ultimate sale. Among his stipulations were that the books should remain forever in Thirlestaine House, that no bookseller or stranger should ever be allowed to rearrange them, and that no Roman Catholic should ever be admitted into the library. He also decreed that one of his daughters, Henrietta, and her husband, James Orchard Halliwell, should never be allowed among the collections either; he had opposed their marriage and suspected Halliwell of manuscript theft. Moreover, the funds he allowed for maintenance and upkeep were totally inadequate for the task. The man "pleased no one in life," the Reverend John Fenwick, a favored son-in-law, observed, "and I expect he has managed to displease everybody in death as well."

The collection Sir Thomas Phillipps left was so enormous that a full century of inventories, private sales, and auctions was necessary to sort it out. The bad news, for the British Museum at least, was that the man did not have it in him to give his collection to the nation outright; the nation's error was its failure to make a reasonable offer. But collectors serve civilization in many ways. The irreplaceable material Phillipps rescued can be found today in institutions all over the world where they serve scholarship. This was not his intention, but it is his legacy. Once the Court of Chancery declared in 1885 that his will was too restrictive, dispersal was possible.

Like Samuel Pepys before him, Phillipps was served honorably in death by a relative, in this case a grandson, Thomas FitzRoy Fenwick, who spent the better part of fifty years supervising the sale of the collection. In 1887, the Royal Library in Berlin acquired for £14,000 621 manuscripts that Phillipps had acquired at the 1824 sale in The Hague of superior material gathered over two generations by Gerard Meerman (1722–1771), author of *Origines Typographicae,* and his son, Jean Meerman (1753–1815). A number of papers pertinent to Welsh history went to Cardiff, important Belgian manuscripts were sold to the Bibliothèque Royale in Brussels, Dutch material was bought by the Provincial Archives in Utrecht, and other documents were acquired for archival collections at Metz, Bordeaux, and Paris. During the early years of this century, exceptional items began crossing the Atlantic to the United States, where they entered collections then being assembled by J. Pierpont Morgan and Henry E. Huntington.

When Seymour de Ricci gave a series of lectures at Cambridge University on "English Collectors of Books and Manuscripts" in 1929, he noted that six decades after the brooding collector's death, thirty thousand items still remained in crates and boxes in Thirlestaine House. What soon became known as the "residue" of the Phillipps collection would be sold in 1946 for £100,000 to two third-generation London booksellers, the brothers Philip and Lionel Robinson. Though the deal would ultimately be judged an unqualified bargain, the Robinsons took a tremendous risk because 90 percent of the library was unlisted and unexamined at the time of the purchase. The brothers bought largely on faith in the value of the holdings, but to protect themselves against possible disaster, they privately gave Harvard University an opportunity to buy the collection for £110,000. William A. Jackson, Harvard's Houghton librarian, made a noble effort to raise the money, but during a crucial moment in the negotiations he had to depart on a State Department mission to South America and could not be consulted. In his absence, and with no information on what the contents were other than assurances that they had to be splendid, Harvard officials sadly cabled regrets. Repeating an error made several decades earlier, the British Library turned down a similar offer.

Within a few months, the Robinsons were thanking their lucky stars that their entreaties had been declined. A sale of thirty-four manuscripts at Sotheby's on July 1, 1946, realized £55,190. Among the newly discovered treasures sold that day was a fourteenth-century volume of Provençal songs decorated with miniature portraits, bought by Dr. A. S. W. Rosenbach of Philadelphia for £7,500. Maggs Brothers of London paid £6,200 for a 1480 Aesop's *Fables* illuminated in Italy with 135 exquisite miniatures (it is now in the collection of the New York Public Library). Three months later, the Robinsons made back another £19,740 off their investment with the sale of 165 lots of autograph letters and historical papers, including a collection of Colonial material of particular interest to the state of Georgia. Items bought by the National Maritime Museum in Greenwich, England, and Yale University brought in another £35,875.

The Robinsons continued selling material through 1956, when they retired from active business but retained ownership of the "residue." When A. N. L. Munby published the fifth and concluding volume of his *Phillipps Studies* four years later, "many thousands of manuscripts and documents" still remained to be examined. "The formation and dispersal of the collection has so far covered nearly a century and a half," he wrote, "over a third of the period during which private libraries have been formed in England."

But the saga of Sir Thomas Phillipps went on. In 1964, Lew David Feldman of New York offered the Robinsons $10 million for what remained, sight unseen, on behalf of the University of Texas. Before a deal could be signed, President Lyndon Baines Johnson announced that he would place his papers on the Austin campus of the University of Texas, and money earmarked for the Phillipps collection was used instead to build the LBJ Library. A few months later a bin filled with wastepaper was found to contain William Caxton's manuscript translation of the first part of Ovid's *Metamorphoses,* the document thought lost for more than four hundred years and now reunited with the second part at the Pepys Library at Magdalene College in Cambridge. In 1977, all the remaining Phillipps manuscripts were purchased by Hans P. Kraus, a New York bookseller. Many sales had been consummated during the previous ninety years, yet the collection still included two thousand volumes of material. "I am confident that many discoveries will reward my venture," Kraus wrote in his 1979 autobiography.

Later that year, Kraus issued *Bibliotheca Phillippica,* a handsome catalogue of treasures he had culled from the residue. "I am sitting, figuratively, on a huge heap of manuscripts and printed books which arrived in hundreds of cartons," he wrote in the foreword. "It is still like Christmas, and scarcely a week passes without the discovery of something important." The 106 items he selected for sale in the catalogue embraced nine hundred years, from the ninth to the eighteenth centuries. Many of them were decorated with gorgeous illuminations. After Kraus died in 1988 at the age of eighty-one, his daughter, Mary Ann Folter, and her mother, Hanni Kraus, assumed control of the company and continued to sell Phillipps material well into the 1990s. "We've placed manuscripts in collections all over the world," Mary Ann Folter said in October 1994. "But all the yummy stuff is pretty much gone."

On a broader scale, the migration of these materials to the United States continued a pattern that began in earnest during Sir Thomas's lifetime and became more apparent in the years afterward. Alarms were raised by concerned British curators and scholars, but serious money was being tendered by well-heeled Americans, and the sales went on. In one dramatic instance, however, the private collection considered the most spectacular of them all—the forty thousand–volume Althorp Library assembled by Dibdin's patron, the second earl of Spencer—was saved from the "disaster of dispersion" by a widow's wish to honor her beloved husband.

Enriqueta Augustina Tennant Rylands's commitment to place a magnificent library in the industrial city of Manchester surprised the people who had known her husband, a textile manufacturer and benefactor of many charities who left an estate of close to £3 million at his death in 1888. John Rylands (1801–1888) was remembered as a pleasant man who enjoyed giving books to poor preachers, but he was not an ardent bibliophile by any means, and he left no specific instructions for the bequest that ultimately would bear his name.

But in 1890, Mrs. Rylands set about erecting an ornate gothic structure in the Deansgate section of the city, though she had only a vague idea of what specific treasures should go inside. Indeed, while the building was rising from the ground, "few people were aware that a great library was in process of formation," according to Henry Guppy, the institution's first director. But two years after construction began, Mrs. Rylands learned that "the most famous of all private collections" was about to be sold by Sotheby's on behalf of Lord Spencer's financially strapped heirs. Recognizing instantly that this collection would be "the crowning glory of her design," she wasted little time. Her bid of £210,000 beat by a matter of minutes an offer of £300,000 that would have sent the collection to the New York Public Library.

When the announcement was made, "a great sigh of relief went up" throughout England, Guppy wrote. "The nation was relieved to know that so many of its priceless literary treasures were to be secured for all time against the risk of transportation, and the public spirit which Mrs.

Rylands had manifested, was greeted with a chorus of grateful approbation." On October 6, 1899, the twenty-fourth anniversary of her
wedding day, Mrs. Rylands formally gave the building and its contents
to the nation. In his dedication address, the Reverend Dr. Fairbairn,
principal of Mansfield College, Oxford University, allowed as how
Basil Champneys, the architect, had "proved himself a genius" with the
design. And while the building alone would have been contribution
enough, he made clear that it is books that make a library, not vaulted
stone ceilings, leaded glass windows, gunmetal railings, or polished
oak floors.

"The library will be entitled to take its place among the deathless
creations of love," Dr. Fairbairn declared.

> To multitudes it will be simply the John Rylands Library, built
> by the munificence of his widow. But to the few, and those the
> few who know, it will forever remain the most marvelous thing
> in history, as the tribute of a wife's admiration of her husband,
> and her devotion to his memory. All citizens who desire to see
> England illumined, reasonable, right, will rejoice that there
> came into the heart of one who inherited the wealth of this
> great Manchester merchant, the desire to create for him so
> seemly a monument as this. It stands here fitly in a city where
> wealth is made, to help to promote the culture, to enlarge the
> liberty, to confirm the faith, to illumine the way of its citizens,
> small and great.

Two years later, Mrs. Rylands pledged another £155,000 for an
exceptional collection of manuscripts assembled by the earl of Crawford.
At her death in 1908, she had augmented the holdings to 200,000
printed books and 7,000 manuscripts. In 1972, administration of the
Rylands Library was turned over to Manchester University, and the
Rylands and university collections were merged. People who visit the elegant repository continue to be moved by the building's majestic beauty,
but the one image that lingers is of two marble statues that face each
other at either end of the Grand Hall. John and Enriqueta Rylands preside over a gift that kept the nation's finest private library inside the
United Kingdom.

4

America, Americans, Americana

As he lay dying with consumption in 1638, a thirty-one-year-old Puritan clergyman directed that half his estate and all of his books, four hundred volumes comprising 329 titles, be given to a college then being built on a one-acre cow yard in Newtowne, across the Charles River from Boston. Whatever good works the Reverend John Harvard performed during his brief ministry to the New World were not recorded for posterity, but this thoughtful gift, made on his deathbed, endowed the first library to be formed in British North America. In tribute, the General Court of the Massachusetts Bay Colony ordered that the college take the minister's name, and honored the city of Cambridge, England, where Harvard had been educated, by declaring that Newtowne thenceforth be known as Cambridge.

In similar fashion, the establishment in 1701 of the Collegiate School of the Colony of Connecticut was formalized by the gift of "forty volumes in folio" by ten Congregational ministers gathered in the home of Samuel Russell. Several years later, the institution was named for Governor Elihu Yale, whose copy of *Speculum humanae salvationis* (pseudo-Bonaventura, *Meditations de passione Christi*, England, early fifteenth century) in 1714 is believed to be the first illuminated manuscript given to an American academic library. Nineteen years after that, Bishop George Berkeley gave the school 880 volumes he had brought over from England, "the finest Collection of Books that ever came together at one Time into America," according to Yale's second president, Thomas Clap.

"Books were scarce in the New England colonies," Marjorie G. Wynne, a retired Yale librarian, emphasized in a lecture at Columbia University, yet they were "essential equipment" nonetheless. Just how dearly the colonists treasured their books was made clear in 1779, when British troops raided the Connecticut coast and advanced toward New Haven. As word of looting spread, Yale's three thousand volumes were distributed among several nearby villages for safekeeping and remained hidden until hostilities were concluded in 1782. Of course, one reason books were especially precious then is that they were so difficult to acquire. There was not even a press operating in the British colonies until 1639, when the locksmith Stephen Daye set up a shop in Cambridge and began work on *The Whole Booke of Psalmes,* a psalter commonly known as the Bay Psalm Book and prized today as the oldest surviving object printed in what is now the United States.

As other printing shops opened, the primary order of business was job work for local governments, not the production of literature. As long as European sources provided ample reading material, there was no need for duplication in America. "It was inevitable that in a new land, faced with the immediate necessity of building a state and drawing a living from farm, forest, and sea, of adapting old traditions and theories to fresh conditions, the thinking of these people should have been at first utilitarian in character, and that in consequence their writing and publishing should have been of the same nature," the historian Lawrence C. Wroth has written.

The first "great" book printed in the colonies—and the first American book immediately recognized as "collectible" in Europe—appeared in 1661 under the title *Wusku Wuttestamentum nul-lordumun Jesus Christ Nuppoquohwussuaeneumun.* Obviously, this version of the New Testament could not be prepared in England; it had to be done "in the field," as it were. Cotton Mather could barely restrain his enthusiasm for the Reverend John Eliot and the "Indian Bible" he had prepared in the Algonquin language. "Behold, ye Americans, the greatest honor that ever you were partakers of," he declared. "The Bible was printed here at our Cambridge, and is the only Bible that ever was printed in all America, from the very foundation of the world." In Europe, Eliot became known as "the Augustine of New England" and "the Apostle of the Indians" for his achievement. The first "Eliot Indian Bible" off Stephen Green's press was sent to England and presented to the dedicatee, King Charles II. Others were given to the lord high chancellor and the universities of Oxford and Cambridge. A copy at Brown University contains the annotations of Roger Williams. Another at Yale bears the signature of John Winthrop. None of these people could read this book, but they valued it as an important artifact nonetheless.

The copy now at the Library Company of Philadelphia, a subscription library founded in 1731 by Benjamin Franklin and his friends, on the other hand, first belonged to a British subject who dealt with Indians regularly and even entertained them in his home. In a bicentennial history of the Library Company of Philadelphia, Austin K. Gray told how a European scholar was discovered one day "slapping and pinching himself" among some old mathematical and astronomical books gathered two centuries earlier by a man named James Logan. "Some of these books are unprocurable today," the visitor marveled. "I have hunted for them in vain in many libraries in Europe. And here they are altogether in America, and here they have been apparently for over two hundred years. Who was this man Logan and how did he know where to look?"

James Logan (1674–1751), it turns out, spent a good deal of his life looking for books, and he found them under the most daunting conditions. Esteemed by contemporaries on both sides of the Atlantic for his keen mind, Logan was a resourceful man who excelled as a scholar, scientist, entrepreneur, and public figure. Though not the first American collector of consequence—that distinction probably belongs to William Byrd II (1674–1744) of Westover, Virginia—he is certainly the most interesting, and his library has survived largely intact to this day.

Born to Scottish Quaker parents in 1674, Logan pursued several opportunities in business and teaching before accepting an attractive offer to serve as confidential agent for William Penn, the prudent

Quaker who founded a settlement in America's Delaware Valley that continues to bear his family name. "Books are my disease," Logan wrote many years later, and that lifelong affliction must have caused unbearable agony when he left England a month shy of his twenty-fifth birthday for a frontier on the outskirts of civilization. Shortly before setting sail on the *Canterbury* in 1699, Logan sold a library that he ruefully estimated years later contained up to eight hundred volumes.

In time, Logan achieved stature and fortune as a cloth merchant, land speculator, fur trader, and shipper; along the way, he served as mayor of Philadelphia, chief justice of the supreme court of Pennsylvania, lieutenant governor, and, for two years, acting governor of the province. "In many ways, James Logan was the most important and most influential public figure in the proprietary province of Pennsylvania during the first half of the eighteenth century," Edwin Wolf 2nd wrote in his definitive catalogue of this remarkable man's collection.

"I confess a Book has from my Infancy been my Diversion and serves me agreeably to spend my vacant hours," Logan wrote in 1726 to an Amsterdam merchant. In fact, he spent those "vacant hours" absorbed in self-instruction, teaching himself subjects as diverse as advanced mathematics, botany, astronomy, and linguistics, languages as challenging as Latin, Greek, Hebrew, French, Italian, Spanish, and Arabic. His alert mind required constant stimulation, and when circumstance brought him to America, the only way to satisfy his curiosity was to arrange for a steady flow of books.

Over the next fifty years Logan conducted an active correspondence with friends, family, and associates in Europe, and most of what he wrote was copied and filed in letter-books now owned by the Historical Society of Pennsylvania, an archive that offers insight into just how his library was assembled. Once settled in America, Logan's immediate responsibility was to administer Penn's varied interests, and by all accounts he served Penn (one of five proprietors of the province) admirably. By 1708 he had begun an active exchange with the leading booksellers of Europe, ordering title after title on a variety of formidable subjects. In 1709, he sent for what is believed to be the first copy of Sir Isaac Newton's *Principia Mathematica* to enter America; using it, he mastered the newly postulated principles of calculus.

In 1710 pressing provincial business required a voyage to England, allowing Logan to immerse himself for a few brief months in London's rich cultural life. He attended lectures, observed scientific demonstrations, watched Isaac Newton perform an experiment, toyed with a microscope, made a social call on the mathematician Charles Hayes, and searched the stores and stalls of the capital for challenging things to read. When he returned to Pennsylvania, he left a "Great Chest of Books" to be sent on after him (which took three years to arrive). Once back in Philadelphia, Logan took a wife, started a family, and embarked on a frenetic decade of more acquisitions.

Any bibliophile who examines Logan's long, discursive, and often crusty letters will recognize the odd rituals of a kindred spirit. He sends out want lists. He cultivates sources. He saves catalogues. He haggles over prices. He insists on good condition. He complains when his exacting standards are not met. He preens over his triumphs. He insults his inferiors. And always, when he authorizes a purchase, he waits anxiously for the treasures to make what seems an interminable crossing over three thousand miles of open ocean.

"I observe thy method of rating a Book is exceedingly different from mine," he wrote Thomas Osborne II, "for I value a book for what I can most easily learn by it, thou on ye other hand for its antiquity, its being bound in Morocco black or red and the quantity of lent Gold that's spent on it which none but ye weak can value." To Josiah Martin, for twenty-five years Logan's principal contact for books in England, Logan confided:

> I am under this great Disadvantage in this Country that I can
> but rarely meet with any uncommon Book without purchasing
> it from England and as my reading is chiefly for my own
> Amusement and entirely out of ye way of my business, I care
> not to lay out all the Money that ye Books I desire to look into
> would cost me, because it would rise to a Considerable sum and
> they would afterwards be of very little use to my family here.

Near the end of his life, Logan filed a complaint with the bookseller John Whiston in London: "Thou may therefore well excuse me for finding fault with thee as I do when thy prices are unreasonable, who have been a buyer of Books above these 50 years and am not to be put off as a common American, as thou has divers times served me, for I know a book well."

In 1723, about the same time a sixteen-year-old printer's apprentice named Benjamin Franklin was leaving Boston for Philadelphia, Logan was making a final call on England. Once again he combined business with recreation, and again he was refreshed by contact with the leading thinkers of the day. By 1728 he was building Stenton, a country mansion north of Philadelphia, where he settled two years later and where his dedication to learning took on a new intensity. His heavily annotated books, many with the signature "J. Logan" inscribed boldly in the upper-right-hand corner of the title page, reveal a vigorous intellect. Inside Andrea Argoli's *Ephemerides,* for example, he has written his own tables for latitude in Pennsylvania, along with a note about the 1639 conjunction of Venus and the sun. In John Flamsteed's celestial atlas Logan drew a number of stars he determined had been omitted by the author. He appended missing words to Arabic and Italian dictionaries. In a set of proof sheets titled *Tabulae Astronomicae,* he rebutted several theses put forward by Sir Edmund Halley regarding the motions of comets and the satellites of Saturn. On almost every page of his Greek edition of Aeschylus he wrote alternative readings, explanations, and Latin equivalents of the text.

During this time Logan also began to submit essays to learned societies in Europe. *Experimenta et Meletemata de Plantarum Generatione,* a report detailing his experiments in the cultivation of maize, was issued in Leiden in 1739; impressed, Carolus Linnaeus named the plant *Logania* in his honor. The London journal *Philosophical Transactions,* published by the Royal Society, printed two of his papers, "The Crooked and Angular Appearance of Lightning" and "The Sun and the Moon, when nearing the Horizon, appearing larger." But it was a correspondence with Johann Albrecht Fabricius, a professor in Hamburg who was an astronomer, physician, respected classicist, and author of a fourteen-volume history of Greek literature, that led to one of Logan's most satisfying achievements.

While reading the professor's notes on early astronomy, Logan had come across an assertion that the first printed version of the second-century Greek astronomer Ptolemy's *Almagest* was issued in 1538, and in Greek. He was certain the work had appeared earlier in a Latin version—such a text was among the books he had left behind in Dublin—and he raised the question in a respectful letter to the famous scholar, written entirely in Latin; translated, it begins:

"While from all sides, most learned sir, your sacred studies in promoting literature are interrupted by the sons of the muses and the priests of the mysteries, there can hardly be one or two perhaps from these American shores who claim your attention. Therefore, allow me, since what is strange and distant wins esteem not on account of its worth but because it is unusual, to address you from the wilds of Pennsylvania." As a token of respect, Logan selected a dozen superior animal skins from his warehouse and sent them along with the letter. In reply, Fabricius reaffirmed his belief that the Greek edition represented the first printing of the work; to prove it, he sent the curious American his own copy of the book.

Despite the professor's touching generosity, Logan remained unconvinced and set about to prove his contention. On January 3, 1726, he wrote Timothy Forbes, his agent in Dublin, with an urgent request. Logan explained that in 1698 he had sold his first library "to a bookseller who lived in Castle Street," and among the "considerable quantity" of books he left behind was an early edition of the Ptolemy, printed in Latin. He provided a description of the book and suggested that maybe the volume was still around: "It is not very improbable but that same book may be found among ye Rubbish." Ever the thrifty Quaker, Logan estimated a value of five shillings but quickly professed his willingness "to give considerably more" if necessary.

Because Logan's letter-books record only outgoing correspondence, there is no way of knowing where Forbes found the book, but he did find it, and the sturdy folio bound in brown calfskin was reunited with its former owner after a separation of twenty-eight years. The text, moreover, was printed in Latin, and the year of publication was 1515. Logan's letter of gratitude, dated February 6, 1727, is filled with ebullience; to cover the cost of ten shillings he sent along a half Guinea, with instructions that Forbes keep the change and use it "to melt in a bottle with ye person thou bought it of." Like so many of Logan's books, the margins of *Almagest* are replete with pertinent commentary, but in this case the title page is where the bibliophile's passion is felt most powerfully, undiminished by the passage of two and a half centuries. *Liber rarissimus,* he has written in a bold hand below his signature, "the rarest book."

When Benjamin Franklin and his friends were working out details for their new subscription library in 1731, the person they approached for advice was James Logan. The following year, when the Library Company of Philadelphia approved its first bylaws, Logan was the only nonmember allowed to borrow books. A few years earlier, Logan had expressed serious reservations about Franklin's discussion club, the Junto—he had called its members "base and lying lackeys" for their support of paper currency—but he became friends with Franklin and considered him an "ingenious" young man. Franklin, in turn, had the highest regard for Logan.

Four years after forming the Library Company, in 1735, Franklin published Logan's metrical translation of Cato's *Moral Distichs,* the first translation from the classics to be produced in North America. In 1744 Franklin brought out an elegant edition of Logan's translation of Cicero's *Cato Major,* though the old squire required the printer to issue it anonymously. In a preface, Franklin teased his readers by noting that the work "was done by a Gentleman amongst us (whose Name or Character I am strictly forbid to mention, tho' it might give some Advantage to my Edition.)"

Five years later Logan endorsed Franklin's proposal to establish an academy that ultimately became the University of Pennsylvania. In "Proposals Relating to the Education of Youth in Pennsylvania," Franklin gave a detailed description of a library "which has been many Years collecting with the greatest Care, by a Gentleman distinguish'd for his universal Knowledge, no less than his Judgment in Books." Franklin reported how a building "above 60 feet in front, is now erected in this City, at the private Expence of that Gentleman, for the Reception of this Library, where it is soon to be deposited, and remain for the publick Use, with a valuable yearly Income duly to enlarge it." This announcement appeared in 1749, Logan's fiftieth year in America, and it resolved a dilemma he had been pondering for some time: What was to become of his precious books after his death? After considering a number of proposals, he decided to create a repository "which I suppose may vie with any in America." He also had a name for it: taking Oxford's Sir Thomas Bodley and the Bodleian Library as a model, he directed that his collection be known as the Loganian Library.

On October 31, 1751, James Logan died "in a very easy manner." The old man's final words, according to a son-in-law in attendance, were mumbled instructions for another letter to a bookseller. Benjamin Franklin's obituary in *The Pennsylvania Gazette,* unsigned but undoubtedly written by that periodical's founder and part owner, concluded with words from one consummate bookman to another:

> But the most noble Monument of his Wisdom, Publick Spirit, Benevolence, and affectionate Regard to the People of Pennsylvania, is his LIBRARY; which he had been collecting these 50 Years past, with the greatest Care and Judgment, intending it a Benefaction to the Publick for the Increase of Knowledge, and for the common Use and Benefit of all Lovers of Learning. It contains the best Editions of the best Books in various Languages, Arts and Sciences, and is without Doubt the largest, and by far the most valuable Collection of the kind in this Part of the World, and will convey the name of LOGAN thro' the Ages, with Honour, to the latest Posterity.

Half a century later, an English author, John Davis, who chronicled his extensive travels through the United States between 1798 and 1802, recalled that his first order of business in Philadelphia was to pay homage to James Logan: "I here behold the portrait of a man whom I consider so great a benefactor to Literature, that he is scarcely less illustrious than its munificent patrons of *Italy;* his soul has certainly been admitted to the company of a *Cosmo* [sic] and *Lorenzo* of *Medicis.* The Greek and Roman authors forgotten on their native banks of the *Ilyssus* and *Tiber,* delight by the kindness of a *Logan* the votaries to learning on those of the *Delaware.*"

When Davis offered that tribute, Logan's two thousand books had just emerged from several decades of indifferent stewardship, caused in part by resolution of a lengthy and complicated will. The Library Company became permanent trustee of the books in 1789, not long after passing another milestone in its distinguished history. During the hot summer of 1787, when the Constitutional Convention was meeting in Philadelphia, the reading club located just two blocks from Independence Hall served as a "delegates' library" for the fifty-five men charged with writing the Constitution of the United States. Paradoxically, Benjamin Franklin, the man who had formed the Library Company of Philadelphia fifty-six years earlier—the man who worked to preserve James Logan's books as a unit—saw no merit in keeping his own exceptional collection intact.

While the Constitutional Convention deliberated in Philadelphia, a clergyman from New England, Dr. Manasseh Cutler, on July 13, 1787, visited the home of Benjamin Franklin, then eighty-one years old. "After it was dark, we went into the house, and the Doctor invited me into his library, which is likewise his study," Cutler wrote in his diary. "It is a very large chamber, and high studded. The walls were covered with bookshelves filled with books; besides there are four large alcoves, extending two-thirds of the length of the chamber, filled in the same manner. I presume this is the largest, and by far the best, private library in America."

If not the best—Thomas Jefferson's private library was outstanding—Franklin certainly did own one of the finest during the last quarter of the eighteenth century. An inventory made after his death in 1790 listed 4,276 volumes, almost as many as owned by the Library Company. In his will Franklin directed that the Philosophical Society of Philadelphia, the American Philosophical Society (the successor to the "Junto" club), and the Library Company of Philadelphia receive a few selected items, but because of one unfortunate stipulation, most volumes faced an uncertain future: "The residue and remainder of all my books, manuscripts, and papers, I do give to my grandson, William Temple Franklin."

William Temple Franklin—the illegitimate son of William Franklin, who was the illegitimate son of Benjamin Franklin—had visited England with his grandfather before the Revolution and served as his secretary for eight years in Paris during the war, from 1777 to 1785. A few months after claiming his inheritance, Temple Franklin returned to England, taking with him the manuscript of Franklin's *Autobiography* but disposing of virtually everything else. Eleven years later, in 1801, what remained of the Franklin library was offered for sale by Nicholas Gouin Dufief, a twenty-five-year-old French immigrant soon to become Philadelphia's most successful bookseller. Precisely how Dufief came by the books has never been clearly established, but in 1803 he mailed a letter to the president of the United States, Thomas Jefferson, informing him that about two thousand items were still available, "some containing marginal notes" in Franklin's hand.

"I send you the catalogue of books remaining to me from the Library of Dr. Franklin," he wrote to Jefferson on January 1, 1803. "When you have looked it over, I beg you to deliver it to the Librarian of Congress to whom I propose, in the belief that he would be authorized to make the purchase of the collection en bloc or in part." What better way for Congress to spend money, he continued, "than to use it to rescue the books of one of the founders of the American Republic and of a great man! It is not a spirit of speculation that makes me use this language for outside of the fact that these books belong in a national library, being in large part on the *politics,* the *legislation* and the affairs of *America,* I would dispose of them at a price so reasonable, that one could never accuse me of such a thing."

On February 4, 1803, Jefferson sent Dufief's proposal to the Congressional Library Committee, noting that prior dealings with the bookseller "give me assurance that his prices would be moderate. Without presuming on the answer of the committee to this proposal I have ventured to mark with a pencil a few particular books which I imagine are worthy of their acquisition if they are not already in the library." A month later, the president wrote Dufief that because of "exhausted" funds, Congress deemed it "unnecessary" to consider such a purchase. Jefferson did select several books from the Franklin catalogue for his own library, however. Dufief promptly announced an auction, issued a new list, and sold everything. Because no catalogue survives, the full contents of Franklin's library are unknown, though several attempts have been made to reconstruct it, most notably by Edwin Wolf 2nd during his long tenure as librarian at the Library Company of Philadelphia (1955–1984).

Despite the federal government's apparent lack of interest in preserving the books and documents of its founders, a new sense of national identity did bring about a fundamental change in the kinds of material Americans collected. Though he spent two thirds of his life in America, James Logan was very much a British subject, and his taste in books was decidedly European. But a more provincial focus was already taking shape in Boston, as can be seen from the pioneering efforts of a collector whose driving interest was to document his own place and time.

Born to affluent parents in the Cape Cod town of Sandwich in 1687, Thomas Prince acquired a taste for reading while a child, living with his maternal grandfather, Thomas Hinckley, the last governor of Plymouth Colony. Hinckley not only had an excellent library but also favored the youngster with frequent gifts of books. When Prince entered Harvard at the age of sixteen, he began assembling what he called his "New England Library," material that dealt with the history and culture of his native region. Later, as associate pastor of the Old South Church—an appointment he retained for forty years—Prince gathered religious material he designated the "South Church library." His bookplates for both collections state his hope that they would "remain therein forever."

In a 1728 edition of the *New England Weekly Journal,* a notice announced the sale of a one hundred–acre parcel of "choice" farmland in Leicester, Massachusetts. "Inquire of the Rev. Mr. Prince," the advertisement advised, and added slyly, almost as an afterthought, "Who also intending to Dispose of his Library desires those who have borrowed Books from Him to return them quickly." No records exist of Prince's ever parting willingly with any of his books; that same year, in fact, he declared his intention "to lay hold on every Book, Pamphlet, or Paper, both in Print, and manuscript, which was written by Persons who lived here, or that had any Tendency to enlighten our History." He had begun assembling material for a work he would title *A Chronological History of New England in the Form of Annals,* a mammoth study that appeared in two volumes between 1736 and 1756. Though it is a convoluted work that makes for ponderous reading, Prince's book is nonetheless considered the first critical evaluation of American history.

Even more significant, perhaps, is the scholarly standard its author embraced: "I would not take the least iota upon trust, if possible. I examined the original authors I could meet with. Some may think me too critical. I think the writer of facts cannot be too critical. I cite vouchers for every passage." Prince was able to provide "vouchers" for sources because he had spent years combing the countryside for such evidence. Primary materials known to have been in his possession included the seventeenth-century journal of the Massachusetts Governor John Winthrop and seven volumes of correspondence gathered by the Reverend John Mather between 1632 and 1689. Prince's most dramatic "find" may well have been Governor William Bradford's handwritten copy of his *History of Plimmoth Plantation*. On the flyleaf, Prince penned in a detailed explanation of how he came by the manuscript and carefully noted that the lawful owner, the colonial governor's grandson, had agreed that the journal should go to the New England Library. Just to avoid any ambiguity, Prince pasted in one of his own bookplates. More than a century later, in 1855, Bradford's journal was discovered among papers that had been stored for decades in London's Fulham Palace. Nobody could say how it got there, though a number of intriguing possibilities have been suggested. But Prince's inscription, next to his bookplate, was sufficient evidence for the argument that the document rightfully belonged in Boston, not Great Britain. In 1897, the manuscript—by then known as the Log of the Mayflower—was finally presented to the Governor of Massachusetts by the British ambassador to the United States.

That such a crucial historic document could disappear without a trace came as no surprise to anyone familiar with the checkered history of Prince's New England Library; what was astonishing was that it had survived at all. When Thomas Prince died in 1758, he left specific instructions that all his books should become the property of the Old South Church. Sixteen years later, on the eve of the American Revolution, the library was said by the Reverend Jeremy Belknap to be "lying in a most shamefully chaotic state." When British forces laid siege to rebellious Boston in 1775, the Old South Church—where thousands of citizens had rallied against the Stamp Act and where the Boston Tea Party had been planned—was seized and used as a riding school. During the winter that followed, the pulpit and pews were broken up to fuel the stoves. One legend holds that some books and manuscripts were hauled down from the library in the steeple and used as kindling. Other material simply vanished, and tantalizing items like Bradford's Plymouth journal kept turning up from time to time in distant places.

In an article published in *The Boston Patriot* on October 23, 1811, John Adams wrote how he recently had "mounted up to the balcony" to the steeple chamber of the Old South Church "where was assembled a collection which Mr. Prince had devoted himself" to making. Adams said, "Such a treasure never existed anywhere else and can never again be made." When the Adams library, consisting of about three thousand volumes, was given to the Boston Public Library in 1893, an inventory found that two of the second president's books had Old South Church bookplates affixed inside. "It seems probable that in one or more of his visits to this balcony, Mr. Adams borrowed these volumes and failed to return them," the cataloguer concluded.

If Adams did take a few volumes, it could well be because he was appalled by what he saw. A year after he wrote about his visit to the steeple chamber, a committee appointed by the church reported the Prince library to be in "a very ruinous situation," with some boxes "broken to pieces, others uncovered and the books partly taken out and laying about the floor, trodden over and covered with dust." After spending the next half century in various shelters, the books finally were placed on deposit in the Boston Public Library.

A catalogue prepared in 1847 showed that the Prince library had owned as many as six Bay Psalm Books—only eleven are known to exist today—and that five were in the collection at that time. Prince probably swapped the sixth for something else. When the materials finally went over to the public library in 1866, three of the others were gone as well. Earlier this century, the bibliographer Wilberforce Eames showed how those copies were sold or traded by church deacons to three collectors: Nathaniel B. Shurtleff, George Livermore, and Edward A. Crowninshield. The Shurtleff copy is now at the John Carter Brown Library in Providence, and the Livermore copy made its way to the Library of Congress. The vicissitudes of the Crowninshield copy are another matter altogether.

At Crowninshield's death in 1860, Henry Stevens of Vermont (1819–1886), the dominant bookseller of his generation, bought the book and offered it to the British Museum for £150. Getting a negative response there, he then sold the book to George Brinley of Hartford, Connecticut, for the higher price of 150 guineas. At Brinley's sale in 1879, the railroad magnate Cornelius Vanderbilt paid $1,500 for the book, and from him it passed to his daughter, Gertrude Vanderbilt Whitney. Around the turn of the century, Mrs. Whitney asked the New York bookseller Max Harzoff to estimate the value of her delicate little treasure. Before attempting an answer, Harzoff glanced thoughtfully out the window of the grande dame's Fifth Avenue apartment. "What is *that* worth, Madame?" he said finally, waving his hand at Central Park. From Mrs. Whitney's library it was sold at auction to Dr. A. S. W. Rosenbach in 1941 for $151,000, whence it found a permanent home at Yale University, the gift of Mrs. Edward S. Harkness.

Since being deposited at the Boston Public Library in 1866, the Prince collection has suffered no further erosion, though in the fall of 1991, Old South Church parishioners quietly debated whether they should sell one of their two remaining Bay Psalm Books. Coincidentally, the discussion was held while a Thomas Prince exhibition— including the two remaining copies of *The Whole Booke of Psalmes*—was on view across Boylston Street in the Boston Public Library. Because a copy has not been sold in more than fifty years, and since the prospect of another appearing on the market ever again is remote, some auctioneers feel that presale estimates would range from $1.5 million to $4 million—a lot of money for an inner-city church with many programs to support.

"The suggestion that we sell one of our Bay Psalm Books comes up periodically," the Reverend James W. Crawford said when I asked him to confirm rumors about the proposed sale. "The Prince collection is important to us, but it is not a function of the church to be a museum, and the church is not necessarily wedded to these books. So to answer your question, yes, there was a meeting of the congregation, and the matter was discussed at length. Some good questions were asked, but we reached no conclusions."

In any case, the deaccessioning of duplicates has a long tradition, and any decision the Old South Church might make to sell its second copy would not be without precedent. For instance, William A. Jackson, the Houghton librarian at Harvard, once sold an exceptional copy of Thomas Vaughan's *Silex Scintillans* to the private collector Robert H. Taylor because the Houghton Library had another copy. Henry E. Huntington's frenetic campaign earlier this century to buy up entire collections brought in hundreds of duplicates known as *surplusage,* including two copies of Poe's *Tamerlane.* One of them was sold in a series of fifteen sales specifically organized to sell off Huntington's extra material. The man many regard as the greatest book collector alive today, William H. Scheide of Princeton, New Jersey, acquired a 1457 Mainz Psalter, one of the rarest printed books in the world, by proposing a trade with the Bibliothèque Nationale, which had a second copy. Collectors, in short, not only preserve knowledge, they disseminate it. Because Thomas Prince was bent on recovering Bay Psalm Books, scholars today at the Boston Public Library, Yale University, the New York Public Library, the John Carter Brown Library, and the Library of Congress have access to this vital artifact of America's past.

Also of great significance was the example Thomas Prince set for a new generation of collectors. Jeremy Belknap, a member of the Old South Church parish, was fourteen years old when his pastor, Prince, died in 1758. Like Prince, the precocious youngster professed an "inquisitive disposition in historical matters," and like Prince he went to Harvard College and trained for the ministry. Soon after accepting a church appointment in New Hampshire, Belknap began searching for anything that would help him understand local history. He recalled spending hours on end "in the garrets and rat-holes of old houses" reading musty manuscripts. "I am willing even to scrape a dunghill, if I may find a jewel at the bottom." By enduring such unpleasantness he was able to produce his *History of New Hampshire,* a three-volume work William Cullen Bryant later accorded "the high merit of being the first to make American history attractive."

Belknap conceived an even grander plan when he returned to Boston and became pastor of what is now the Arlington Street Church. On August 26, 1790, he proposed formation of an "antiquarian society" that would "collect and communicate" American history "from the earliest times to the present day." On January 24, 1791, the Massachusetts Historical Society was formed with high purpose: "The preservation of books, pamphlets, manuscripts and records, containing

historical facts, biographical anecdotes, temporary projects, and bene-
ficial speculations" that could be used "to mark the genius, delineate
the manners, and trace the progress of society in the United States,"
thereby working "to rescue the true history of this country from the
ravages of time and the effects of ignorance and neglect."

Though the organization was named the Massachusetts Historical
Society, Belknap was interested in much more than a single state, and
for thirteen years, until formation of the New-York Historical Society
in 1804, he had a clear field. "We intend to be an *active,* not a *passive,*
literary body; not to lie waiting, like a bed of oysters, for the tide to
flow in upon us, but to *see* and *find,* to *preserve* and *communicate,* literary intelligence, especially in the historical way," Belknap wrote
Ebenezer Hazard, the first corresponding member of the society, in
February 1791. Four years later, as he anticipated the acquisition of
some major documents, he wrote again: "There is nothing like having
a *good repository,* and keeping a *lookout,* not waiting at home for
things to fall into the lap, but prowling about like a wolf for the prey."

Belknap was a relentless collector who wore people down. After
repeated requests, Paul Revere finally agreed in 1798 to write out his
recollections of the celebrated midnight ride. John Hancock decided
that after his death Belknap should have first choice in his library. The
son of Connecticut's wartime governor, Jonathan Trumbull, chose the
society as recipient of his father's papers "in preference to a Collegiate
or other Library, where they probably would soon become 'Food for
Worms.' " Belknap also drafted a "Circular Letter of the Historical
Society" that he sent throughout the United States and Europe requesting documentary material. After his death, gifts continued to come in.
One early acquisition was a manuscript copy of the Declaration of
Independence in Thomas Jefferson's hand. Another was the handwritten draft of George Washington's answer to a demand made by dis-
gruntled members of the Continental army for back pay and better
pension benefits known as the Newburgh Address. Washington delivered his response to senior officers at his winter headquarters in Newburgh, New York, on March 15, 1783. His calming words, written
neatly on both sides of six sheets of paper, are credited with averting
hostile action against the Continental Congress by the angry soldiers.

From the beginning, Belknap stressed another purpose beyond accumulation: the publication of what he had gathered. When Thomas Jefferson heard about the novel idea, he responded

> with great satisfaction that you are about committing to the Press the valuable and Historical and State Papers you have been so long collecting. Time and accident are committing daily havoc on the originals deposited in our public offices; the late war has done the work of centuries in this business; the lost cannot be recovered; but let us save what remains; not by vaults and locks, which fence them from the public eye and use in consigning them to the waste of time, but by such a multiplication of Copies as shall place them beyond the reach of accident.

Within a year, Belknap's son Joseph, a Boston printer, was issuing a weekly newspaper with a page devoted to Historical Society material. Belknap's enterprise continues to this day with a project now under way that will occupy a team of scholars well into the next century: the Adams Family Papers, the editing and publication of documents relating to four generations of Adamses. "The art of printing affords a mode of preservation more effectual than Corinthian brass or Egyptian marble," Belknap wrote two centuries ago, echoing Jefferson: "There is no sure way of preserving historical records and materials, but by *multiplying the copies.*"

As Belknap and his colleagues prowled the countryside for fresh prey, a prosperous entrepreneur forty miles away in Worcester embarked on a quixotic mission of his own. Jeremy Belknap and Thomas Jefferson touted printing as the most practical way to preserve historic material, but little suggests they saw it as anything more than a sensible means to achieve a worthwhile end. Isaiah Thomas (1749–1831), on the other hand—fiery patriot, successful printer, and able chronicler of his craft—found the printing process as inspirational as the product, a sacred operation he declared to be "the preserver of all art."

Born in poverty, Isaiah Thomas came to know the touch and smell of ink on paper when he was a child. Only nine years old in 1758, the year Thomas Prince died, young Thomas was already completing his third year of apprenticeship in the dingy Boston shop of Zechariah Fowle. While Jeremy Belknap was looking forward to his Harvard education, this son of an itinerant ne'er-do-well set type for such broadside ballads as "The Lawyer's Pedigree," an off-color ditty sung to the tune of "Our Polly Is a Sad Slut." When he later became the most successful printer and publisher in the United States—Benjamin Franklin dubbed him the Baskerville of America—Isaiah Thomas enjoyed telling friends that he knew how to set type before he was able to read.

Thomas left Fowle's shop when he was sixteen and spent five years mastering his chosen trade in Nova Scotia, New Hampshire, North Carolina, South Carolina, and Bermuda before returning to Boston in 1770. That summer, the twenty-one-year-old firebrand established *The Massachusetts Spy,* a popular but contentious newspaper that quickly led British Loyalists to mark him as a troublemaker. On April 16, 1775, heeding the urgent advice of friends, Thomas dismantled the press he would always call "Number One" and shipped it under cover of darkness by wagon to Worcester. Two nights later, he helped Paul Revere and the Committee for Public Safety warn the residents of Middlesex County that British troops were on the march. After shots were exchanged on the greens of Lexington and Concord, Thomas gathered his equipment and set up shop. The May 3, 1775, issue of his *Massachusetts Spy* carried the first newspaper report of the portentous battles under a piercing headline: "Americans!—Liberty or Death!—Join or Die!"

At war's end, Thomas stayed in Worcester and used the community as a base for what became the most successful operation of its kind in the young republic, one that counted print shops, newspapers, publishing houses, a bindery, bookstores, even a paper mill, among its holdings. "He spread his products over the entire nation, catered to every taste, and established himself in every field of printing," Clifford K. Shipton wrote in a summary of Thomas's activities. "A great part of the American people learned their letters from his primers, got their news from his papers, sang from his hymnals, ordered their lives by his almanacs, and read his novels and Bibles. It was genius as well as opportunity which made him the first American capitalist of the printing business, for some of the rivals of his youth died in their old age in little one-room shops like that in which he began."

Yet for all his success, Isaiah Thomas is remembered today not so much for what he accomplished in business as for his hobby: the history of printing. He founded the American Antiquarian Society, the first example of a peculiarly American institution, an independent research library formed through the will, the taste, the passion, and the eccentricities of a private collector. (Other examples are the Pierpont Morgan Library in New York City, the Henry E. Huntington Library in San Marino, California, and the Folger Shakespeare Library in Washington, D.C.) By 1808—the year he bought an Eliot Indian Bible for seven dollars—he was collecting in earnest. Everywhere Thomas went he procured the kinds of materials that today are called *ephemera*: ferry tickets, almanacs, pamphlets, broadsides, posters, hundreds upon hundreds of newspapers. In his diary for 1808 he mentions numerous visits to the Historical Society in Boston and the "Old South Library in the steeple."

One of his favorite ploys was to visit the offices of Colonial and Revolutionary newspapers and buy up all the back files he could find. His entry for the sixty-dollar purchase of "old papers, Boston Evening Post, nearly complete" is followed by an account of a full week spent "in search of Old Boston printed Books and in purchasing Old files of papers for them." He also took out newspaper notices asking printers to send him copies of their work.

Exactly when Isaiah Thomas decided to write a history of his profession is not certain. Published in 1810, his two-volume *History of Printing in America* earned widespread praise, and is the standard reference on the subject. Instead of concluding his search on that triumphant note, Thomas pressed on, filling his Court Hill mansion in Worcester with hundreds of additional items. In 1812, the state legislature granted his request to establish an institution to be modeled after the Society of Antiquaries of London. Duly elected first president of the American Antiquarian Society, Isaiah Thomas stated his purpose: "We cannot obtain a knowledge of those, who are to come after us, nor are we certain what will be the events of future times; as it is in our power, so it should be our duty, to bestow on posterity that, which they cannot give to us, but which they may enlarge and improve, and transmit to those who shall succeed them. It is but paying a debt we owe to our forefathers."

Thomas donated his collection—then about eight thousand books—to the Antiquarian Society, but because no building was immediately available, everything stayed in his house. With exceptional foresight, he also kept adding more material. In 1813, his diary records the purchase of 302 broadside ballads from Nathaniel Coverly, then the largest dealer of sheet music in Boston. Thomas bought copies of the full inventory not because he enjoyed bawdy songs, but "to show what articles of this kind are in Vogue with the Vulgar at this time." Bound in three large volumes, they offer uncommon insight into how people amused themselves in the early nineteenth century. "No other American library can offer anything like it for the period," Worthington C. Ford wrote of the Antiquarian Society collection, "and all other libraries combined would still hardly be able to match the contents of these volumes."

The following year Thomas scored a major coup, the purchase of fourteen hundred books owned by three generations of Mathers—Increase, Cotton, and Richard. Other notable acquisitions he turned over to the society include William Hubbard's 1677 *Narrative of the Troubles with the Indians in New-England,* a 1660 edition of *Massachusetts Laws,* and a Bay Psalm Book. Inside the front cover Thomas noted how "after advertising for another copy of this book, and making enquiry in many places in New England, I was not able to hear of another." Thomas Prince, it would seem, had already cornered the market.

A proposal to raise funds for permanent quarters by means of a state lottery was rejected by the legislature, prompting Thomas to buy a site in Worcester and erect a building with his own money. On August 16, 1820, the proud founder recorded how a crew "began to remove the American Antiquarian Society Library from my house to the New Edifice for the Library," a transfer that continued for eight more days. On June 23, 1828, his diary has a simple notation: "Cut the Grass at A.A.S. Library." He remained active in the society's affairs until his death three years later at the age of eighty-two. Thomas's grandson, Benjamin Franklin Thomas, wrote forty years later that his grandfather was "touched early by that gentlest of infirmities, bibliomania."

Beyond the directive to gather "books of every description including pamphlets and magazines, especially those which were early printed either in South or in North America," Isaiah Thomas left an even greater legacy. "He gave the society its intellectual vigor," Marcus A. McCorison, who retired in 1992 as AAS president, librarian, and director, pointed out. "He recruited people from all over the United States to collect for the society."

One early bequest in an odd way helped the society refine its focus— by *not* becoming a permanent part of the collection. In 1816, Charles Wilkins of Lexington, Kentucky, donated the remains of a "dessicated mummy" found in an Indian burial ground on his property. "For myself, I cannot perceive how the cause of science, history or antiquarianism is to be benefitted by the preservation of these dried up particles," one of the original incorporators complained in a letter to Thomas. "The best thing in my opinion which could be done with it would be to give it to some anatomical school or bury it in the cemetery." Sixty years later, the mummy was displayed at the Centennial Exhibition in Philadelphia, then was given to the Smithsonian Institution.

The legacy Isaiah Thomas left is a library of American history, not a museum that displays trinkets and curiosities, with one exception. Old "Number One," the English common press hauled into Worcester on the eve of rebellion in 1775, is still displayed prominently in the society's Antiquarian Hall.

In organizing the American Antiquarian Society at Worcester, Isaiah Thomas reasoned that an inland location would provide "better preservation from the destruction so often experienced in large cities and towns by fire, as well as from the ravages of any enemy, to which seaports in particular are so much exposed in time of war." The War of 1812 raged as he wrote those words, and barely six months later an American military column invaded York, the capital city of Upper Canada now known as Toronto, and set the Parliament building on fire, destroying the provincial archives and library. When British troops captured Washington on August 24, 1814, they retaliated by putting the United States Capitol to the torch and destroying the Library of Congress.

After reading about the disaster in newspaper accounts, Thomas Jefferson declared the loss a "triumph of vandalism over knowledge itself," and resolved to move on an idea he previously thought could wait until after his death. On September 21, 1814, the man who would later confess to John Adams that he "cannot live without books" wrote a long letter to Samuel H. Smith, an old friend who at that time was the Commissioner of Revenue. In the course of the letter, he proposed the sale of his great library, a collection he had spent "fifty years making" and had "spared no pains, opportunity or expense" to perfect. Jefferson mentioned the years he served as minister to France, recalled how he spent his afternoons "examining all the bookstores, turning over every book," and buying "everything which related to America, and indeed whatever was rare and valuable in every science." Moreover, he had issued "standing orders during the whole time" he was in Europe with the "principal book-marts, particularly Amsterdam, Frankfurt, Madrid and London, for such works relating to America as could not be found in Paris."

As he wrote on, Jefferson could not resist the temptation to crow a little about what he had assembled. It was a collection, he proclaimed, that "probably can never again be effected, because it is hardly probable that the same opportunities, the same time, industry, perseverance and expense, with the same knowledge of the bibliography of the subject would again happen to be in concurrence." Jefferson estimated the size—a bit on the high side, as it turned out—at "between nine and ten thousand volumes," with the content "chiefly valuable to science and literature generally," though extending "more particularly to whatever belongs to the American statesman." In sum, he asserted, "I do not know that it contains any branch of science which Congress would wish to exclude from their collection; there is, in fact, no subject to which a Member of Congress may not have occasion to refer." Regarding condition, "nearly the whole" were "well bound," an "abundance of them elegantly," and represented "the choicest editions existing."

Even though Jefferson was financially burdened at the time and needed money to satisfy some debts, there is nothing in his letter to indicate he was motivated by profit. In fact, on the matter of value, he proposed that Congress choose a qualified appraiser to determine a fair price, and since an expensive war was still being waged, he made clear that extended payments would be acceptable. "The Sage of Monticello," as Dumas Malone anointed him in a majestic biography, was adamant on just one point: the library could not be broken up and sold in parts. "My desire is either to place it in their hands entire, or to preserve it so here."

Jefferson enclosed a handwritten catalogue with his letter, and asked that both items be forwarded to the Joint Library Committee for consideration. Within a week the Senate endorsed a motion to purchase the books, then sent the matter on to the House of Representatives, where it encountered unexpected resistance. Positions were decidedly political—Southern Democrats supported their colleague from Virginia, Northeastern Federalists were largely opposed—but because the formal debate centered on literary merit, it is instructive nonetheless. Cyrus King of Massachusetts led the assault: "It might be inferred from the character of the man who collected it, and from France, where the collection was made, that the library contained irreligious and immoral books, the works of French philosophers, who caused and influenced the volcano of the French Revolution, which has desolated Europe and extended to this country." Jefferson's books, King declared, were "good, bad, and indifferent, old, new, and worthless, in languages which many can not read, and most ought not."

Other members expressed similar complaints. One had heard that Jefferson's library included books by French radicals, specifically Jean-Jacques Rousseau; another was scandalized by the inclusion of the works of Voltaire. Another pointedly condemned the political philosophy of John Locke, enthusiastically embraced by the nation's founders just a few decades earlier. A member from New York wondered how the business of elected representatives could possibly be served by books printed in dead tongues such as Greek and Latin. As Jefferson had anticipated, there was talk about buying the library piecemeal, a proposal that was quickly "negatived." Representative King then suggested that Congress buy all the books, and "as soon as said library shall be received at Washington, to select therefrom all books on an atheistical, irreligious, and immoral tendency, if such there be, and send the same back to Mr. Jefferson without any expense to him." But King "thought proper afterward to withdraw" the motion, and it never reached the floor of the House.

Though cost was an issue, the intrinsic worth of the collection was never in dispute. An unidentified correspondent for the *National Intelligencer and Washington Advertiser* wrote on November 16, 1814, that Jefferson's library is such as to render all valuation absurd and impossible, if valuation were admitted into literature. It is such a library as cannot be bought in the ordinary mode in which books are purchased, because many of the books that are inestimable are wholly out of print, and many in manuscript that, of course, could not be procured. I have had an opportunity, from the privilege of frequent examinations, imperfectly to discover that it is unique,—a library which, for its selection, rarity and intrinsic value, is beyond all price.

Following Jefferson's recommendation, Congress retained a Georgetown bookseller, Joseph Milligan, who appraised the collection on a flat-rate basis: ten dollars for a folio, six dollars for a quarto, three dollars for an octavo, and one dollar for a duodecimo. (A folio is approximately twelve by fifteen inches, whose leaves are made from sheets of paper folded once. An octavo is about six by nine inches.) Using that formula, Milligan arrived at a value of $23,950 for the 6,487 books found in the collection, or an average of $3.69 per volume, an unqualified bargain even then.

On January 30, 1815, after four months of angry debate, a final vote was taken in the House of Representatives. Eighty-one members were in favor of the measure and seventy-one were opposed, with most following partisan lines. Though Vermont supported the purchase, New York and the rest of New England were against it. The ten-vote margin of victory was assured when Pennsylvania, Maryland, and Delaware formed a tenuous alliance with Virginia, North Carolina, South Carolina, Georgia, Kentucky, Tennessee, and Louisiana.

In a 1939 monograph, Randolph G. Adams, at that time director of the William L. Clements Library at the University of Michigan in Ann Arbor, examined the educational backgrounds of members of the thirteenth Congress and determined that of the 49 members with college degrees, 15 voted for the library and 35 were opposed. Breaking the numbers down further, by college, 10 Harvard graduates who voted all were against acquiring the library, as were the 11 members holding degrees from Yale. Figures for other Ivy League schools were similar but less dramatic. Of the 130 members of Congress who did not graduate from any college, 30 opposed it, but 100 were in favor. "This is an interesting commentary upon Mr. Jefferson's confidence in the common man," Randolph Adams noted wryly, and concluded: "So it was the South, with its sparsely settled Piedmont and its backwoods; it was the newly admitted states beyond the mountains; and it was the state of Louisiana, which joined with Pennsylvania to save for the Library of Congress the library of a book collector President."

Still difficult to explain is why Senator Rufus King of New York, a former minister to Great Britain and noted bibliophile in his own right, or why Timothy Pitkin of Connecticut, one of the most respected historians of his day, both fought with such conviction against the library. Equally perplexing is the opposition of Christopher Gore of Massachusetts, a former president of the Massachusetts Historical Society and benefactor of the Harvard College Library. And there was Daniel Webster—a graduate of Dartmouth College and a first-term representative from New Hampshire, though "still in a provincial stage," according to Dumas Malone—who not only cast a negative vote, but delivered a speech in opposition. Then again, as Randolph Adams mused, "This Webster lived to change his mind on many subjects," a characteristic that may explain why several years later the Great Orator ordered *Birds of America* from John James Audubon but never paid the amount due—an oversight, perhaps, but one with ramifications still felt today. Failing to secure full payment, Audubon did not ship the fourth and final volume, leaving Dartmouth College—since 1965 the owner of Webster's double elephant folios of Audubon's work—with an incomplete set of the landmark books that is now worth millions of dollars.

Nevertheless, at a single stroke the Library of Congress more than doubled the holdings it had lost in the fire and took a first step toward achieving the kind of greatness that can be measured only on an international scale, against the British Library, the Bibliothèque Nationale, and the Vatican Library. Packed in the long pine boxes that the collector-president Jefferson had designed as modular cases and arranged according to his precise scheme, the books were ready for installation upon arrival. It took ten wagons to transport them from Monticello to Washington; as the final shipment was being readied for departure, Jefferson wrote another letter to Samuel Smith. "It is the choicest collection of books in the United States, and I hope it will not be without some general effect on the literature of our country." Jefferson's classification scheme was patterned on Sir Francis Bacon's concepts of the "three faculties needed to comprehend knowledge," memory, reason, and imagination, from which he derived forty-four subject divisions. His system was maintained through the end of the nineteenth century, and it not only influenced the kinds of books that were acquired, but created an institution that served the entire nation, not just politicians and bureaucrats.

Jefferson's first library, gathered while he was a law student at William and Mary College, had been destroyed by a fire at his mother's home in 1770; the Capitol fire of 1814 prompted him to sell his second collection to the nation. In 1851, yet another blaze destroyed four thousand volumes of the Jefferson collection, but by then, at least, a course had been fixed. A brilliant core had shaped the direction of the Library of Congress. According to the institution's curator of rare books, Jefferson's spirit is its soul.

Thirty-three years after the debate over the acquisition of Jefferson's collection for the Library of Congress, a similar opportunity arose, this time involving George Washington's books. Though Congress in 1834 had acquired for $20,000 a voluminous archive of important letters and documents known as the Washington Papers, the matter of books still shelved at Mount Vernon was unresolved. Many of them had been signed by the first president, many of them bore his bookplate, many of them were elegantly bound in calfskin and tooled with emblematical designs. Pressed for money, Washington's heirs offered the government first refusal, but after finding no interest, sold them in 1848 to Henry Stevens, the Vermont native who became a wealthy bookseller by skillfully working a lively trade on both sides of the Atlantic Ocean. Stevens promptly announced with characteristic swagger that he intended to sell Washington's books to the British Museum.

In his *Recollections of James Lenox*—which some readers feel is really a disguised memoir of Henry Stevens—Stevens recalled paying $3,000 for "about 300 volumes" containing Washington's autograph. When a "great hue and cry" was raised against his plan to ship Washington's books out of the country, Stevens reluctantly agreed to sell them to a "parcel of Bostonians for $5,000." After "passing that old Boston hat round for two or three months for $50 subscriptions, only $3,250 could be raised, and therefore, as I had used a few hundred dollars of the money advanced to me by the promoters and was in a tight place, I was compelled to subscribe the rest myself to make up the amount of the purchase." Stevens found it prudent not to mention the advice he received from Obadiah Rich, another American bookseller who worked out of London. "You will find eventually that you have committed a great mistake in purchasing the so-called Washington Library," Rich wrote. "I recommend you most sincerely to dispose of them in the only place where they would be properly valued," Boston or New York.

The "parcel" of seventy spirited citizens who "passed the hat" to keep George Washington's books in the United States were all members of the Boston Athenæum, a private reading society established in 1807 that by midcentury ranked among the five largest libraries in the United States. From the very beginning of its existence, the Athenæum made it a policy to keep everything that was acquired. "The idea was to get popular and interesting things for the members to read," John Lannon, the current head of acquisitions, explained. "With the passage of time, so many of the books we bought became very important. Before we knew it, we were a research library by default."

While the Mount Vernon books are certainly the Athenæum's most famous possession, undeniably its oddest is *Narrative of the life of James Allen, alias Burby Grove,* the memoirs of a dangerous highwayman finally brought to justice after he was caught robbing a stagecoach. As he lay dying in prison, Allen asked that the reflections he wrote while incarcerated be bound with his own hide and given to John Fenno, the Athenæum member who had brought about Allen's capture. Printed in 1837—and bound as directed—the grim volume was withdrawn from general display several years ago because it detracted too much from everything else in the otherwise sedate neo-Palladian building. "The fact is that the book has no literary merit whatsoever," Lannon said. "It was always the binding that made it interesting."

A society of collectors performs a number of valuable services, not least of which is sponsorship of worthwhile projects. For instance, the finest collection of imprints produced in the Confederate States of America to be found anywhere, about six thousand items, is not in Atlanta or Richmond or Austin, but in the Boston Athenæum. (*Imprint* generally means a publisher's mark, but the author uses *imprint* to mean any published item.) In June 1865, two months after the Civil War ended, Francis Parkman, the great nineteenth-century historian, decided to gather all the newspapers, books, periodicals, broadsides, sheet music, tracts, and almanacs printed in the South during the war that he could find and deposit them in a place he felt would be safe. Parkman received an initial stipend of $500 from the Athenæum's directors to help underwrite the search and was assisted in the project by William F. Poole. "We have been and still are the largest buyers in the south and our greatest competitor has been the prices we have ourselves given," Poole wrote to one Virginia woman who wanted more money than she was being offered. "We are making our collection for preservation, and not for sale or speculation: and having ample means we are disposed to give liberal prices." The woman thanked Poole for his candor, and promptly sold her copies of the Richmond *Dispatch* for $175. "Parkman was following his historian's instincts," John Lannon said. "He knew that once the war was over, these materials would be destroyed, lost, or suppressed. What is important is not that any individual item is especially rare, but that the archive is so comprehensive. This is the Confederate imprint collection by which all others are judged."

Today, nobody questions the wisdom of spending money on a run of Confederate imprints, or seventy men's passing "that old Boston hat" among themselves to acquire three hundred autographed books from George Washington's library. A reminder of how sagacious that purchase was came on January 31, 1990, when Washington's two-volume autographed copy of *The Federalist* was bought in New York for $1.65 million by an anonymous collector, who then placed it on "extended deposit" in the Chapin Library at Williams College.

Clearly, by the mid-nineteenth century collecting had begun to change in America. No longer were books just tools for scholars and historians. They had become valuable objects in their own right, though there was still a long way to go. "This country is sadly in want of books," the Reverend Luther Farnham declared in an 1855 survey of private American libraries, called *A Glance at Private Libraries*, the first study of its kind to be done in the United States. "We have not a single library with one hundred thousand volumes, while there are several in Europe with five times this number of books, and one or two with a million or more." And what America did have, he added, was "as much wanting in the quality" as in quantity.

Farnham was also concerned with public book collections. He understood, however, that a developing nation had more pressing priorities than institutional libraries. In the 1855 survey he noted that "there were many things that necessarily preceded large public collections of books. The land was to be cleared and cultivated. After bread came the church, the school-house, and the town-house, and such collections of books as might be expected in a new country of vast material resources, that began early to mature, and that are now developed with wonderful activity." He confidently predicted that "a few years more only will be needed to give us, at least, two or three collections of books of two hundred thousand volumes each; and looking forward half a century, we can see a national library of half a million or a million tomes." Farnham's survey followed by four years Charles Coffin Jewett's *Notices of Public Libraries in the United States of America*, which reported a state-by-state, city-by-city census of institutional library holdings, reinforcing Farnham's findings. By Jewett's reckoning, there were in the United States 2,201,632 volumes in 694 libraries in 1850. Only five repositories had fifty thousand or more books: Harvard University, 84,200; the Library Company of Philadelphia, 60,000; Yale College, 50,481; the Library of Congress, 50,000; and the Boston Athenæum, 50,000.

Libraries formed by private collectors filled the void in the meantime. "The few private libraries of Boston and neighborhood, that we have found the time to glance at, have revealed quite unexpected riches." Farnham identified eighty-two libraries with a total of 298,625 volumes and 12,000 pamphlets, averaging about 3,500 volumes per library. The ten largest, "by pretty careful estimate," contained a total of 92,000 volumes, and the twelve largest had more than 100,000 volumes. "It is safe to say, that we have thirty other private libraries that will give an aggregate of one hundred thousand volumes"—all in all, he felt, a "pretty good story for one little section of the country."

Among the libraries Farnham cited were those of Edward Everett, William Prescott, Franklin Haven, Rufus Choate, George Livermore, Dr. John C. Warren, and Edward A. Crowninshield, owner of "a perfect copy of the old Bay Psalm Book." Individual rarities he mentioned are Shakespeare folios and quartos, an Eliot Bible, and "quite a collection of the Greek and Latin classics." Another collector, David Sears, was "particularly rich in French literature," including Voltaire in seventy volumes and "a pretty good variety of English books." George Ticknor's library of thirteen thousand volumes was "one of the most distinguished," since it contained "the choicest collection of Spanish books" known anywhere outside of Spain. "Thus we have found three libraries on Park Street, containing about twenty thousand volumes, and if we embrace the choice library of Mr. Ticknor, we shall have thirty-three thousand on one short street, all belonging to persons, living almost in adjoining dwellings. Such another cluster cannot, we suspect, be found in this section of the country."

In his annotated edition of *A Glance at Private Libraries*, Roger E. Stoddard reports that twenty-five of the libraries identified by Farnham and containing about 71,200 volumes have since been placed with institutions. Forty more, representing 158,225 volumes, were sold. The fate of the seventeen others, some 69,200 volumes, remains unknown.

Farnham acknowledged that the United States "has produced a few authors worthy of the name" during its short history, but he quickly pointed out how the "paucity" of available source material forced America's historians to choose between conducting research "in the vast libraries of Europe" or importing books "at a very heavy expense" from abroad. Those unable to conduct research in Europe learned to rely on the expertise and enterprise of a few book hunters who recognized the need for their services. The most resourceful nineteenth-century scout of all was a Massachusetts expatriate named Obadiah Rich.

Born on Outer Cape Cod, Obadiah Rich (1783–1850) was elected to the Massachusetts Historical Society at the age of twenty-two, an honor generally bestowed on older people of proven accomplishment. The following year he helped establish the Anthology Society, which in 1807 became the Boston Athenæum. He was appointed by President James Madison to the post of American consul in Valencia in 1816, which coincided with a time of war and domestic chaos in Spain that led to the looting of many old libraries. A perceptive intellectual, Rich was quick to grasp the opportunities and snapped up old books and manuscripts that were being sold in black-market street stalls and marts, including much material relating to the Spanish colonial period in the Americas. The bibliographer Nicholas Trübner credited Rich with making Americana, publications and documents relating to the Americas, a recognized field of scholarship. In his *Bibliographical Guide to American Literature,* Trübner wrote, "[H]ad there been no buyer for them on the spot, at the moment of the dispersion of many old libraries, both ecclesiastical and civil" when Rich arrived on the scene, "it is probable that many volumes of great rarity and interest would have perished altogether as waste-paper."

By the time he took another consular position in Madrid in 1823, Rich had amassed an impressive personal collection. Three years later he was introduced to Washington Irving, who was visiting Spain to translate into English some documents relating to the voyages of Christopher Columbus. Irving stayed at Rich's home and examined his collection of Spanish manuscript material. In the preface to his *A History of the Life and Voyages of Christopher Columbus,* published in 1828, Irving explained how the biography came to be written:

> I was encouraged to undertake such a work by the great facilities which I found within my reach in Madrid. I was resident under the roof of the American Consul, O. Rich, Esq, one of the most indefatigable bibliographers in Europe, and who for several years had made particular researches after every document relative to the early history of America. In his extensive and curious library I found one of the best collections extant of Spanish colonial history, containing many documents for which I might search elsewhere in vain. This he put at my absolute command, with a frankness and unreserve seldom to be met with among the possessors of such rare and valuable works; and his library has been my main resource throughout the whole course of my labours.

In 1829, the Library of Congress decided against buying a collection of 93 manuscripts and 383 books of primary material offered to the nation by Rich. "I fear the Congress will not have the liberal spirit enough to purchase your American Library," the historian of Latin America, William H. Prescott, wrote when he heard the disappointing news from friends in Washington. "Our legislators love money more than books." Rich's reputation did not suffer by the rejection, and by 1830 he was working in the book trade in London full time, supplying American institutions, scholars, and private collectors with the materials they needed. He developed fruitful relationships with the Massachusetts orator and statesman Edward Everett (1794–1865), the librarian and bibliographer Joseph Green Cogswell (1786–1871), the noted historian George Bancroft (1800–1891), and the author and teacher George Ticknor (1791–1871).

In 1829 Prescott recommended Rich's services to his colleagues in an item he wrote for the *North American Review:* "He has uniformly executed his orders with promptness, sagacity, and great economy. His accurate bibliographical knowledge and his extensive correspondence through all the principal cities of the continent, afford such facilities for the literary acquisitions, as we hope will be improved by public institutions and private individuals." However vital Rich's contributions were—and the two men did business for twenty years without ever once meeting in person—Prescott still had occasion to protest the "extravagant, artificial prices" his European agent sometimes charged.

As indispensable as Obadiah Rich was to American scholarship, he was no match for Henry Stevens when it came to sizing up the players, securing inventory, and controlling the flow. When Stevens moved to England in 1845, he arrived with the want-lists of two American millionaires who were about to become major influences on the international book market. A well-educated man who held a bachelor of arts degree from Yale and studied law at Harvard, Stevens became enchanted with book hunting while working in Washington, D.C., and helping the printer, newspaperman, and politician Peter Force (1790–1868) collect books, pamphlets, and manuscripts for his ambitious project, *American Archives* (nine volumes published 1837–1853). The connections Stevens established later helped him secure commissions from the Library of Congress and the Smithsonian Institution. When he arrived in London, he carried with him introductions from Francis Parkman and the historian and editor Jared Sparks. Armed with "a general commission to forage" for John Carter Brown, he promptly paid Obadiah Rich £1,000 for books from the distinguished library of M. Ternaux-Compans, author of *Bibliothèque Americaine,* published in Paris in 1837. On March 3, 1846, he shipped five hundred of the most important titles to Providence.

Shortly after setting up shop, Stevens received his first commission from James Lenox of New York City, setting in motion a period when "all Europe was ransacked" for bibliographical rarities. "Those were happy days, when on a July morning one might run down a hundred brace of rare old books on America in London at as many shillings a volume as must now be paid in pounds." His gatherings "were scrambled for in Boston and New York like hot buck-wheat cakes at a College breakfast. It was hardly possible to sweep them together fast enough."

Stevens described Lenox, a lifelong bachelor, as "a man of few words and few intimate friends, but of varied information, much studious reading, extensive correspondence and many books." Like James Logan more than a century earlier, Lenox considered his library a sacred place where it was possible to commune with thinkers of earlier generations. Stevens described the reserved New Yorker as a citizen who "paid his taxes liberally, bore his share of the public burdens, pastured figuratively the widow's cow, helped the needy, but avoided all public offices and politics." Though Lenox allowed scholars access to his treasures, he did not let outsiders inside his library, not even the estimable William Prescott. His procedure was to place requested items at the Astor Library "or some similar place of safety," where they could be consulted and returned.

James Lenox (1800–1880) and John Carter Brown (1797–1874) marked the emergence of a new kind of American collector. Both men inherited huge fortunes in the same year, 1840, both began acquiring books in middle age, and both were motivated by the pure pleasure of ownership. They were willing, moreover, to contest the English bibliographic establishment on its own turf and by its own rules, setting a precedent that would be continued in the next generation.

"The truth was that from about 1845 to 1869 Mr. Lenox was actively collecting his library so rapidly, and doing all the work himself, that he had no time to catalogue or arrange his accessions," Stevens wrote. "The great bulk of his book collections was piled away in the numerous spare rooms of his large house, till they were filled to the ceiling from the further end back to the door, which was then locked and the room for the present done with." As heir to an estate that included three hundred acres of prime real estate in midtown Manhattan, Lenox certainly could afford a librarian, but he preferred to unpack and shelve the books himself. "He gave me his money and his friendship, and I sought the world over to supply him with books and manuscripts," Stevens said. "He had a mind of his own, and a fortune to back it."

Stevens readily allowed that having both Lenox and Brown as "chief correspondents" was lucrative, though occasionally he "found it very difficult to prevent their colliding," especially since both were "exceedingly sweet on everything relating to Columbus." An embarrassing conflict developed when Stevens accepted commissions from both men to bid at the first Libri sale in 1847 for the only known copy of an illustrated edition of the Columbus Letter, printed at Basel in 1493. This copy of the "letter" (Columbus actually wrote the document as a general announcement of his first Atlantic crossing) is especially significant because it contains the first known attempt to depict the landing and the first map of the West Indies.

Brown set a limit of twenty-five guineas, Lenox authorized a lower figure of £25. Stevens bought the item for £16.10, and since John Carter Brown had tendered the higher bid, the prize went to Providence. Lenox insisted that since the item came in under his limit, it belonged to him. Further unpleasantness was averted only when Brown agreed to let Lenox have the book, though he minced no words about his displeasure. "I am still of the opinion that this Book of Right belongs to me," he wrote Stevens, but added, "surely I would not have any Controversy with Mr. L., an entire stranger to me. Let me tell you frankly that you [were] the proper person to have decided to whom the Book belonged," and that just because Lenox threatened to "withdraw his business" it should have had no bearing on the proper resolution.

"I make no such threat and rather *you* should suffer in your pecuniary Interest, by the withdrawal of a good Customer." Two months later, Lenox and Brown were introduced by a mutual friend, and they began a lasting friendship. Brown later gave Lenox a copy of the first Spanish edition of Cortez's fourth letter, enabling him to complete a set.

That same year, on behalf of Lenox, Stevens outdueled Sir Thomas Phillipps for a Gutenberg Bible, though the £500 he paid was called a "mad" price in the United States. Lenox was so furious at the amount that he at first refused to pay customs duties when the book arrived in New York. It was the first Gutenberg Bible to enter the United States, and it resides today in the New York Public Library with the rest of Lenox's books. Stevens said that on most other occasions Lenox was willing to pay "unprecedentedly" high prices "for a prime rarity." Lenox once told Stevens that he could "find the five pound notes more easily than such books, but you must not tell anybody how much I have paid." Stevens found Shakespeare folios and quartos, rare Bibles, scarce editions of John Milton and Bunyan for Lenox and also sold him a Bay Psalm Book.

Lenox was the wealthier of the two collectors, and he expected first refusal on everything of importance. Brown, on the other hand, found competition distasteful, and even considered for a while giving the exercise up entirely and selling his library. But the Rhode Islander maintained his composure, and in 1873 he exacted a little revenge by securing the only known first printing of the writings of Amerigo Vespucci to appear in Dutch, a book known as the "Dutch Vespucius" and printed at Antwerp in 1506–1507. Two hours after an Amsterdam bookseller received Brown's purchase order by cable, a letter from Lenox arrived in the day's mail requesting the same item.

John Carter Brown put together the premier collection of books and manuscripts relating to the discovery, exploration, and settlement of the New World. When he died in 1874, his wife added more material before turning the library over to her son, John Nicholas Brown, who in turn augmented the holdings with great care. "Don't buy too many common books," he instructed George Parker Winship, his young librarian, in 1897. "I don't want to fill up the library with ordinary things." A year before his death, in 1900, John Nicholas Brown committed $150,000 for a building to house the collection, and another

$500,000 to administer it. By operating with its own funds and staff ever since, the John Carter Brown Library maintains the identity of the man whose name it bears. Over the front door, chiseled in stone, is a single word: *Americana*.

Though Lenox and Brown were the most notable American biblio-philes of the mid-nineteenth century, they were by no means alone in their enthusiasm for Americana. Their most prominent competitor was George Brinley (1817–1875) of Hartford, Connecticut, a collector who in time would buy a Gutenberg Bible and a Bay Psalm Book from Henry Stevens, but who actually was attracted to the drab kind of ephemeral items more likely to end up in a dump or pulping plant than in a library or museum.

The son of a Massachusetts merchant, Brinley inherited an estate dur-ing the 1850s that was sufficient to support a growing family and satisfy his appetite for collecting. Shortly after moving to Connecticut in 1845, he bought the entire library of books devoted to the history of American Indians gathered by the Boston antiquarian Samuel Gardner Drake eight days before it was to go on the auction block. The next year he bought at a sale of books gathered by Gabriel Furman, a one-time state senator, municipal court judge, and amateur historian, picking up material about the West Indies and the Pacific Northwest with the same gusto that he gathered New England imprints. "Brinley strove to rescue, to identify, to preserve and to evaluate those books which constitute our earliest, and in many cases, our ultimate sources of information about America," Randolph G. Adams wrote. "In this he seemed clearly to understand that a book printed in California in 1850 may be as important as a book printed in Massachusetts in 1650."

During the Civil War, high prices paid for scrap paper lured many dusty bundles out of old attics and cellars; Brinley worked out an arrangement with nearby Connecticut mills that enabled him to go through the discarded piles before they went off to the pulping presses. Excited by the variety of material he found—he saved an Eliot Indian Bible in this fashion—Brinley was emboldened to go directly to the sources. Filling a buggy with pots and pans, he went from door to door throughout New England, offering housewives new utensils in exchange for pamphlets and almanacs. "By pursuing this method he rescued many works, which, except for his foresight, would have certainly disappeared from the face of the earth," George Watson Cole pointed out. "This accounts for the great number of duplicates that were sold in his library and for the many items which have not reappeared in any subsequent sale." In an unpublished memoir, Charles Brinley recalled how his father once found an old psalm book in the home of a woman who "resisted all his blandishments" to buy it. "My father did not despair; he wrote every now and then to the old lady and sent her presents. She remained obdurate until, one cold winter, he had made for her a particularly handsome flannel petticoat. He received the Psalm Book with a letter of thanks."

Years later, Brinley agreed to pay Henry Stevens $1,000 for a first-issue Bay Psalm Book, "upon condition that the transaction is strictly private. I do not want my next friend to know that I possess it because the next step among Yankees is 'what did you pay for it.'" Stevens recalled another occasion when he was describing for his "old friend" a group of "nuggets" that had been rejected by both James Lenox and John Carter Brown, including a seven-page document titled *A Declaration of Former Passages and Proceedings betwixt the English and the Narrowgansetts,* known as the Narrowgansett Declaration. Brinley was astonished: "What, do you mean to say that you have a little book such as you describe, signed by John Winthrop and printed at Cambridge by Stephen Daye in 1645, that has been declined at ten guineas by both of those gentlemen after having been sent to them on inspection?"

Assured that that indeed was the case, Brinley immediately proposed buying the book at the same price offered to his competitors, but he did not want to betray his interest to Brown. Since the book was still in Rhode Island with the other items, the deal could be difficult to pull off. "If it is inquired for separately, especially for me, and they see it again, they will be sure to keep it," Brinley reasoned. So after some thought, he proposed sending a messenger to get the "big box with its entire contents" and, "without naming the destination," have the whole lot shipped by overland express at his expense to Hartford. Eight years later, Lenox paid $215 to get the book at Brinley's sale, five times the price he had passed on earlier. In 1911, Henry Huntington paid

$10,000 for Robert Hoe's copy; a few years after that, the John Carter Brown Library paid Charles Goodspeed of Boston $15,000 for the last Narrowgansett Declaration to come on the market. "That goose is now a swan," Stevens gloated.

Brinley was able to bring many other "nuggets" into his collection after Lenox and Brown turned them down. In 1873 Stevens advised Brinley that the "greatest bibliographical rarity that ever crossed the Atlantic" was being shown to Lenox, "but as he is only a millionaire and has stopped buying, he may not keep it at any price," in which case Brinley would have the next look. "I trust your chances are small," Stevens warned nevertheless. "I had the order from Mr. Lenox twenty years ago, and am only now able to execute it; but I am more than rewarded for waiting, though the price of the book has gone up, while money has gone down." The book in question was believed by some to be the dedication copy of Captain John Smith's *History of Virginia* "in the finest possible condition, bound at the time, 1624, in rich morocco tooled all over," the "most sumptuous binding, early English, I ever saw." Lenox was busy organizing the library that, he had declared three years earlier, would become a public trust and replied that he did not want any more books, so the treasure went to Brinley.

In 1874, a year before he died at the age of fifty-seven, Brinley wrote Stevens commenting on the state of the rare-book market: "I am glad to see high prices ruling. Crazy people like to see others crazier than they are." This conviction—along with the certain knowledge that his judgment had been sound and his purchases shrewd—may be why Brinley made clear that all his books should be sold. Mindful, too, that some books belonged in institutions, he made another stipulation. Five institutions—Yale, the American Antiquarian Society, the Watkinson Library of Hartford, the New-York Historical Society, and the Historical Society of Pennsylvania—were to be given a total of $24,500 in allowances to be applied toward purchases at the auction.

Held in five sales between 1879 and 1893, it was "the greatest library of Americana ever sold," Clarence S. Brigham wrote in the introduction to a landmark survey of American book auctions published in 1937. Using the credits they had received, these institutions were major buyers at the sale, with Yale alone securing more than one thousand lots. Cornelius Vanderbilt bought the Bay Psalm Book, which has since made its way to Yale. But the most active buyer of all at the first session was seventy-nine-year-old James Lenox, who spent close to $10,000 for items that he had failed to secure when they had been offered to him years earlier by Henry Stevens on a "first refusal" basis.

Brinley's memorial is the catalogue of his sale, a rarity today in its own right. In the preface to the final volume issued in 1893, Brinley's good friend J. Hammond Trumbull stressed how inadequate his words were to measure "the service rendered to the public and the cause of American history by one who, like Mr. Brinley, rescues from destruction and oblivion the literary monuments and the 'unconsidered trifles' of the infancy of our nation, and puts them in the way of preservation and usefulness to all coming time." Charles A. Brinley offered this succinct description in his unpublished memoir: "My father was a man of strong prejudices, marked characteristics and definite tastes. He was a bibliophile, and a bibliomaniac as to one class of books."

James Lenox, John Carter Brown, and George Brinley, all contemporaries, lived within 150 miles of each other—Lenox in New York, Brown in Providence, Brinley in Hartford. While they were the most prominent collectors of their generation, others were building notable libraries throughout the country. As the nation expanded, the demand for books expanded with it. Thirty-eight years after it was established as a city in 1833, Chicago suffered a fire that destroyed thousands of buildings and most of the books that had been brought by some settlers from the East. Fine libraries gathered by Ezra C. McCagg, Jonathan Young Scammon, Perry H. Smith, Mark Skinner, and Henry T. Monroe went up in flames. McCagg's losses included the first 1623 Shakespeare folio to enter Chicago, as well as rare copies of Theodor de Bry's *Great Voyages* and Thomas Jefferson's *Notes on Virginia,* some three thousand volumes in all. Scammon's superb collection of material on the Swedish mystic and theologian Emanuel Swedenborg and his teachings had been kept in a room "big and high, filled with books in every possible corner," and had been destroyed.

The richness of these collections "suggest that books quickly assumed a place in the lives and the homes of Chicago's upper crust, once wealth and position were secure," Robert Rosenthal, a former librarian of the Joseph Regenstein Library at the University of Chicago, wrote in a 1983 essay. As soon as reliable communications with the East Coast and Europe were established, "books moved to Chicago in surprising volume and sophistication." Even though Chicago lacked an antiquarian book trade, "its pioneer collectors quickly assumed places at the forefront of American collecting."

Only three collections—those assembled by John A. Rice, Edward G. Asay, and Ebenezer Lane—are known to have escaped the Great Fire of 1871 intact. Rice, Rosenthal noted, "acquired books with such rapidity and flair that for a few short years his name was linked with the great collectors of the East." A native of Northborough, Massachusetts, he moved to Chicago in 1861 and became the owner of a hotel; in 1866 he paid $14,000 for the Americana library of John F. McCoy. Two years before the fire, Rice sold his hotel for $150,000 and promptly went broke trying to corner the grain market. Pressed for funds, he offered his books to the Chicago Historical Society for $30,000. Unable to get that price, Rice put the books up for auction in New York; the $42,252.69 that was realized set a new American record.

Edward G. Asay, a native of Philadelphia, built a successful law practice and became the quintessential Chicago collector of the nineteenth century. The considerable value of his library, in fact, is what saved it from destruction: Asay was planning a trip to Europe with his family in the spring of 1871, and he shipped the books to Joseph Sabin in Brooklyn, New York, for safekeeping. When Asay learned about the Chicago disaster, he instructed Sabin to sell his books at auction. The following year he picked up where he left off and built another excellent library. A number of his rarities were sold to Theodore Irwin of Oswego, New York, in 1881, who sold his library to J. Pierpont Morgan in 1900.

The only library to survive the fire in the city limits belonged to Ebenezer Lane, who had moved to Chicago in 1856 at the age of sixty-two after a distinguished career as chief justice of the Ohio Supreme Court. He became a lawyer and the resident director of the Illinois Central Railroad, and moved into a house on South Michigan Avenue, a fashionable section of the city that was spared by the catastrophe.

Lane bought wisely in American history, and his autograph collection
was regarded as "the very finest in the West." At his death in 1866, the
collection passed on to his son, also named Ebenezer Lane, who continued adding to it. By the time of the son's death in 1892, the Lane
Library of 10,500 volumes was considered the largest in the city. In
1911 the books were acquired by the University of Chicago. "It was
thus that the Lane Library became the only collection which not only
survived the great fire," Rosenthal concluded, "but continues to be
preserved under one roof."

When the real estate entrepreneur Walter Loomis Newberry died at
sea in 1868 while traveling to meet his family in Paris, the Chicago Fire
was still three years away, and so much of the property that had earned
him a fortune was still producing income. Beginning in the 1830s he
had bought land in Chicago "by the acre and sold it by the front foot."
Though Newberry was not a bibliophile, he made a curious stipulation
in his will that led to the creation of an exceptional research library. He
directed that in the event each of his daughters should die without
issue, his estate should be used for the construction of a "free public
library" in Chicago. When his wife died in Italy seventeen years later,
this unlikely provision went into effect, because by that time Mary and
Julia Newberry, the couple's unmarried daughters, had predeceased
their mother, leaving no direct heirs to the family fortune.

A new public library had already been built by then in the city, so
instead the Newberry trustees created a private research library based
on the Astor Library in New York, established by William B. Astor
(1792–1875), and empowered it to acquire important private collections. "Certain it is that Chicago now has the prospect of being the seat
of the ideal library of the continent, and it ought to make Chicago a
great library center," the newspaper *Chicago Inter-Ocean* declared,
and predicted that the city would become "a veritable Athens in intellectual attainments." The Newberry Library opened its doors in 1893
and promptly committed its huge endowment to purchase a wide variety of research materials. So diverse are its holdings that in 1965 the
trustees adopted as its motto, "An Uncommon Collection of Uncommon Collections."

That same year, another legacy led to the creation of a second great research library in Chicago. John Crerar, a bachelor millionaire, did not say precisely what kinds of books should be collected with his money, he just had a few choice words about what should be avoided: "I desire the books and periodicals selected with a view to create and sustain a healthy moral and Christian sentiment in the community, and that all nastiness and immorality be excluded. I do not mean by this that there shall not be anything but hymn books and sermons, but I mean that dirty French novels and all skeptical trash and works of questionable moral tone shall never be found in this Library." To make sure there were no problems, organizers of the John Crerar Library, which is now maintained and operated by the University of Chicago, opted to focus on the history of science.

In the unfoldings of my fate," Hubert Howe Bancroft (1832–1918) wrote in an entertaining memoir titled *Literary Industries,* "I found myself in the year 1856 in the newly Americanized and gold-burnished country of California, in the city of San Francisco, which stands on a narrow Peninsula, about midway between either extreme of the mighty stretch of the western seaboard, beside a bay unequaled as a harbor by any along the whole seven thousand miles of shore line, and unsurpassed by any in the world."

There, in a frontier town at the limit of continental expansion alive with swaggering goldminers and jaunty clipper-ship sailors, a twenty-four-year-old clerk opened a publishing business that struggled at first but prospered along with the boom. By 1870, Bancroft needed a five-story building to house his printing presses, binding equipment, and sales force. And while he contended that he never knew himself to be obsessed by books, he began collecting Western Americana with a fury. "Bibliomaniac I was not," Bancroft maintained.

> Duplicates, fine bindings, and rare editions seemed to me of less importance than the subject-matter of the work. To collect books in an objectless, desultory manner is not profitable to either mind or purse. Book collecting without a purpose may be to some a fascinating pastime, but give it an object and you

endow it with dignity. Not half the books printed are ever read; not half the books sold are bought to be read. Least of all in the rabid bibliomaniac need we look for the well-read man.

Bancroft insisted that he began collecting books by happenstance. "Accident first drew me into it, and I continued the pastime with vague interest," but soon there was a focus. "I had a certain vague purpose at the beginning," he allowed, and it was California, the land of promise and fortune. Good businessman that he was, Bancroft knew he was not being irresponsible because "certain books I knew to be intrinsically valuable; old, rare, and valuable books would increase rather than diminish in value, and as I came upon them from time to time I thought it best to secure all there were relating to this coast." During an extended trip to England and France, he "rummaged the enormous stocks of second-hand books in the hundreds of stores," and "my eyes began to open."

When the collection reached a thousand volumes, "I fancied I had them all; when it had grown to five thousand I saw it was but begun." He traveled all over Europe, and he kept buying books.

> So far I had searched little for Mexican literature. Books on Lower California and northern Mexico I had bought, but Mexican history and archaeology proper had been passed over. Now the question arose, Where shall I draw the dividing line? The history of California dates back to the days of Cortes; or more properly, it begins with the expeditions directed north-ward by Nuno de Guzman, in 1530, and the gradual occupa-tion, during two and a quarter centuries, of Nueva Galicia, Nueva Vizcaya, and the Californias.

Veteran bibliophiles can see where the man's logic was taking him; he had to have it all. Bancroft reasoned that if he was going to "gather all the material requisite for a complete narrative of events bearing on California, it would be necessary to include a large part of the early his-tory of Mexico, since the two were so blended as to make it impossible to separate them." He spent three months in London going through booksellers' catalogues, searching for anything that related to the

Pacific Coast. He hired an assistant to prepare a bibliography. "From London I went to Paris, and searched the stalls, antiquarian warehouses, and catalogues, in the same careful manner." He repeated the procedure in Madrid, and kept on going.

> To Saragossa, Barcelona, Marseilles, Nice, Genoa, Bologna, Florence, and Rome; then to Naples, back to Venice, and through Switzerland to Paris. After resting a while I went to Holland, then up the Rhine and through Germany to Vienna; then through Germany and Switzerland again, Paris and London, and finally back to New York and Buffalo. Everywhere I found something, and seized upon it, however insignificant, for I had long since ceased to resist the malady.

At ten thousand volumes Bancroft thought he was done. "I have rifled America of its treasures; Europe I have ransacked." But soon he felt a pull, a persistent tugging from somewhere inside: "What is this inch-thick pamphlet that comes to me by mail from my agent in London?" And then, in one bulk purchase, seven thousand books arrived in his warehouse from Mexico, and suddenly a "new light broke in upon me" about what remained to be done. "I had never considered that Mexico had been printing books for three and a quarter centuries—one hundred years longer than Massachusetts—and that the earlier works were seldom floating about book-stalls and auction rooms. One would think, perhaps, that in Mexico there might be a rich harvest."

At the 1868 auction of a six thousand–volume collection in Mexico City, Bancroft bought up fully half of the lots. Eight years later he acquired heavily at the E. George Squier sale of newspapers, books, pamphlets, and manuscripts on the history of Central America. And in 1880, Henry Stevens handled his bids at the London sale of material gathered by the late Don José Fernando Ramírez, a native of Durango who at one time was head of the National Museum of Mexico. The Ramírez collection included not only works in various Indian languages and dialects, but numerous manuscripts relating to Jesuit missions in Texas, California, and South America and books produced by the first Spanish printers to set up presses in Mexico during the sixteenth century.

When Bancroft was writing *Literary Industries* in 1890, his Pacific Coast Library exceeded fifty thousand volumes, which he proudly declared to be "the largest collection in the world of books, maps, and manuscripts relating to a special territory, time, or subject." He did, however, confess one lingering anxiety. "I trembled for its safety through fear of fire," Bancroft wrote, "well knowing that once lost no power on earth could reproduce it." As a result, he moved the books from his warehouse on Market Street to a fireproof building on Valencia Street, a decision that proved farsighted. In 1905 the University of California at Berkeley bought the books for $150,000, but delayed moving them across San Francisco Bay. Before the transfer could take place, a catastrophic earthquake devastated much of San Francisco and leveled buildings up and down Market Street. Miraculously, Bancroft's library on Valencia Street escaped destruction. Today, the 65,000 books and 100,000 manuscripts he "rifled" America and "ransacked" Europe to acquire remain the cornerstone collection in the university's Bancroft Library.

Meanwhile, what Americans had been buying up and carrying across the Atlantic was not lost on the Europeans. "In fact, there is probably no country so well stocked as the States with libraries of from ten thousand to twenty thousand volumes," John Hill Burton (1809–1881) wrote just seven years after Luther Farnham offered his midcentury "glance" at private libraries. The evidence overwhelmingly suggested "that they have bought what was to be bought, and have done all that a new people can to participate in the long-hoarded treasures of literature which it is the privilege of the Old World to possess."

Many years later, Julian P. Boyd, the librarian of Princeton University, pointed out that the removal of books to North America was a "prodigious accomplishment" made possible only by a "kind of materialism that Americans would like to forget," though had it been less, the accomplishment would not have been nearly as thorough. "Conquest and warfare, let it be said, were not among the factors that produced the tidal wave of books and manuscripts that came to American shores," Boyd wrote. "Coin of the realm, willingly offered and freely accepted, often in heroic quantity, was the sovereign agency involved."

5

Brandy for Heroes

Robert Hoe III (1839–1909) is remembered today not so much for the great library he built as for causing it to be broken up and dispersed. Whenever it is asked why some people decide to dissolve their collections rather than give them to institutions, his words invariably are recalled: "If the great collections of the past had not been sold where would I have found my books?" In 1991, eighty years after the sensational sale of Hoe's library began in 1911, a Norwegian collector, Martin Shøyen, explained why he chose to put his collection of fifteenth-century printed books, known as incunabula, up for auction:

> Donating the incunables to a public institution, or forming a private foundation for them (as some other collectors have done recently), was never considered. A greater gift to future generations would be to give them the thrill of the chase, the excitement at the moment of capture, the privilege of owning

such great books, the intriguing study of their printing, decoration, binding, and provenance. The present sale may give
them this opportunity.

If the age of Dibdin, the early nineteenth century, was the Heroic
Age of Book Collecting, then the six decades that bracketed the turn of
the century was the Golden Age, particularly in the United States,
where the building of great libraries became an emblem of wisdom and
accomplishment. Even though the Brinley sale a generation earlier had
demonstrated that Americana was a worthwhile pursuit, the most
desirable items were still European classics. The Brinley sale may have
been the greatest sale of Americana ever mounted, but it was by no
means the nation's greatest book auction; that distinction belongs to
the dispersal of Hoe's library.

For fifty years, Robert Hoe assembled one of the world's finest private libraries. Like Richard de Bury five centuries earlier, Hoe combined
motivation and means with opportunity and taste. His grandfather,
who moved to New York from England in 1803, developed the first
steam-driven rotary presses to be used in the United States. Robert Hoe
III—who directed R. Hoe & Co. through its most dominant years in the
printing equipment industry—amused himself by collecting what he felt
was the ultimate expression of the family trade. In 1896, the assistant
librarian of the Astor Library in New York, O. A. Bierstadt, compiled
an overview that celebrated Hoe's achievement. "Without counting
each and every book and pamphlet, it may be roughly estimated to com-
prise about fifteen thousand volumes," he wrote.

Of early manuscripts upon vellum and paper there is an unusually large number. [The collection's] chief characteristic is its
many-sidedness, and it is as cosmopolitan as the metropolis of
America, where it has been coming to maturity during thirty
years or more. Unlike many others, this library is not dwarfed
to a single specialty, as if its creator were a bibliophilistic mole,
burrowing so long through one small section of the world of
literature that he is blind to everything else. It is a carefully

chosen collection of a large portion of the world's literary masterpieces, in the best editions and the finest possible condition
and state of preservation.

Of equal merit was that no single element obscured the whole collection. "It is not a solo upon one bibliographical string or instrument,
but it is a complete and harmonious symphony of books—a library so
nearly perfect as to make it a heaven upon earth to the bibliophile."
Certainly any institution would have been overjoyed at the prospect
of adding this "heaven upon earth" to its treasure room, but Hoe had
made clear that he would have nothing to do with bequests. His will
was quite emphatic on the point: "I specifically authorize my Executors
to sell at auction either in this country or in Europe all my furniture,
personal property, works of art and library, especially authorizing them
as to my books to take expert advice and sell the same either in London,
Paris or New York as they shall deem most advantageous to my estate."
Shortly after Hoe's death came the announcement that his books would
be offered in a series of sales mounted periodically over nineteen
months, starting in April 1911. In an introduction to the seven-volume
auction catalogue, Beverly Chew, a fellow New York bibliophile,
described a visit his friend once made to an unnamed European library
in which everything was "covered with dust, with leaves stained and
bindings broken and in every way proclaiming the effects of indifference
and neglect." Disgusted by the sight, Hoe came home convinced that
only "those who love books should have them in their custody."
    Though Robert Hoe was greatly esteemed in book circles, his passing
meant little more to the world at large than that of any other businessman who had prospered during America's Gilded Age—but his passing
affected another major dispersal. The death a year earlier of Brooklyn
bicarbonate of soda manufacturer E. Dwight Church was attended with
little fanfare as well, and when his exceptional library was sold privately
just a few weeks before the Hoe sale opened, the news coverage was not
overly revealing. In fact, the identity of the man who actually bought the
Church library, Henry E. Huntington of California, was not immediately
disclosed, and probably was concealed deliberately. The Wall Street
bookseller George D. Smith told the press that he alone had bought the

books, that he was "hopeful" of selling them "en bloc to the United States government," and that if those efforts failed, he intended to "break up the collection and dispose of it to private collectors." In fact, Smith intended to do nothing of the sort—a signed bill of sale in the Huntington Library archives demonstrates quite conclusively that Huntington had bought the books from the Church estate—but some high-stakes gamesmanship was going on, and the likely reason for it was the forthcoming Hoe sale, which had electrified the book world.

Hoe had been the founding president of the Grolier Club, the oldest and most prestigious society of book collectors in the United States. Though his fortune was not nearly equal to that of J. Pierpont Morgan (1837–1913), it was considerable nonetheless and certainly sufficient to satisfy his taste for rare books. As John Hill Burton had pointed out fifty years earlier, Americans had been using their new wealth to buy up great English libraries and bring them to the United States, but like every other commodity the world has ever known, the source was not inexhaustible. In what may well have been a modest nod of thanks to the mother country, the first journalist J. Pierpont Morgan allowed to see his New York library was not an American, but an unnamed "special correspondent" for *The Times* of London, who wrote an exultant account of his exclusive tour of the "marble palace" in midtown Manhattan. "I have entered the most carefully guarded treasure-house in the world, and nothing in it has been hidden from me," the correspondent reported in the December 4, 1908, issue of the newspaper. "Mr. J. Pierpont Morgan is probably the greatest collector of things splendid and beautiful and rare who has ever lived. There is no one with whom we can compare him except, perhaps, Lorenzo de Medici, and he surpasses even that Prince in the catholicity of his taste."

As he proceeded through "bronze gates into a lofty hall of rarest marble," the correspondent found himself "frightened by the task" of having to give "even the roughest description of some of the things I saw." Everywhere he turned, there was a mind-boggling treasure to behold. He asked the identity of a "gorgeous jewelled volume," and learned it was the Ashburnham Bible, an outstanding example of early British handicraft which Morgan had paid £10,000 to secure several years earlier. Passing by incunabula "that not even the British Museum can match," he paused at William Blake's original drawings for the

Book of Job, Phiz's illustrations for *The Pickwick Papers,* and the holograph manuscripts for *Endymion, A Christmas Carol, Vanity Fair,* and
Ivanhoe. He spotted Shelley's private notebook, and then he glanced
over handwritten documents and letters of Samuel Johnson, Charles
Dickens, Robert Burns, and Charles Lamb.

"Is it Bibles that attract you?" he asked. "There are thirty shelves of
them—two Gutenbergs . . . one on paper, the other on vellum; the
Hebrew Bible of 1482; all of the English Bibles from the Coverdale
onwards; Bibles owned by celebrated personages, such as Colbert's, in
thirty-two volumes, with the statesman's arms on the covers; Mme. de
Maintenon's, Sir Walter Scott's; Bibles in Icelandic and other strange
tongues; a set of the Gospels in ten volumes, exquisitely bound for
Padeloup." Going to the other side of "Mr. Morgan's own Library
Room," he described a similar panoply of Elizabethan and Jacobean
first editions. "Practically everything is here—Shakespeare folios and
quartos, Milton, Sidney, Spenser, Jonson, Drayton, Sir Thomas
Browne, Marvell, Waller, Burton, hundreds of others." And "all the
famous printers" were there as well, twenty-one shelves alone filled
with Aldines, another seven with Elzeviers. "Are you interested in Caxtons and Wynkyn de Wordes? Here are two score of them, including
several that are unique."

The breathtaking tour proceeded with other discoveries. "Everything
one takes from the shelves is precious, everything is the finest specimen
of its kind that could be obtained." When the visitor thought he had seen
all there was to see, he was brought into yet another room where "the
richest jewels in this marble casket" repose, including the only known
manuscript fragment to survive of John Milton's *Paradise Lost.* "This
room is not only burglar-proof and fire-proof; it is actually a safe, of the
latest pattern and with all the improvements. One enters by a thick steel
door fitted with a combination lock, and the walls of the room are of
steel, while a steel shutter protects the window at night."

Though the Englishman admitted "nothing but admiration" for
Morgan and professed great esteem for "his generosity, his love for
precious things, his enterprise in discovering them," he also had to
accept the reality that "these heirlooms of England will never go back,
and I repeat they should never have come here in the first place." Still,
in one instance he acknowledged begrudging respect for the entrepre-

neur's legendary knack for outmaneuvering his competitors. "The story of how Mr. Morgan obtained the Byron volumes reads like some record of the Humanists. He found that there were no Byron manuscripts in England, but heard a vague rumour that there were some in Greece. Forthwith he sent an agent there with carte blanche to buy, whatever the price. The result is half a score of volumes containing the manuscripts of 'Don Juan,' 'Werner,' 'Manfred,' 'Marino Faliero,' and other works." As he completed his examination, the correspondent shook his head in disbelief, and what began as a triumphant visit to a "bookman's paradise" concluded on a somber note. "I do not believe that any one in England knows how many things that ought never to have left the country are contained in these few cubic yards of space in New York," he wrote. "I do not know whether it was wonder or sorrow that I felt the more." Today, Morgan's "bookman's paradise" at 29 East Thirty-sixth Street and Madison Avenue, is open to visitors and available to scholars from all over the world. It is one of the great pilgrimages any bibliophile can make. A ten-minute walk away, at 11 East Thirty-third Street, the nine-room brownstone once occupied by Robert Hoe and his family is gone, demolished years ago to make way for an office building. It was here in 1884 that Hoe gathered with eight other New York collectors to form the Grolier Club, and here that he kept his great book collection until he died in 1909. The announcement that his library would be sold generated tremendous interest on both sides of the Atlantic, with European dealers reversing what had become their accustomed role of selling to Americans, not buying from them. The most prominent booksellers in the international market came to New York for the sale. Making the trip from England were Alfred Quaritch and Ernest Maggs; Madame Théophile Bélin came over from Paris; Dr. Ludwig Baer arrived from Frankfurt, Germany.

On April 13, 1911, eleven days before the opening session, the *New York Times* reported that "the book that is arousing the keenest speculation among collectors and dealers as to the price it will bring is the Gutenberg Bible, printed on vellum." Until then, the most anyone had ever paid for a printed book was the $24,750 J. Pierpont Morgan had paid Bernard Quaritch, London's leading antiquarian bookseller and Alfred's father, in 1884 for the Mainz Psalter, printed in 1459 , and far more scarce than the forty-two-line Bible. The next day the *New York*

Times published another feature as a huge Sunday spread, this one under the bold headline "How Americans Get Private Libraries Worth Fortunes."

The article was occasioned by the upcoming Hoe sale, yet it had very little to say about Robert Hoe. Instead, for the first time public attention was focused on the E. Dwight Church library, which had been sold a few weeks earlier for $1.3 million but had attracted no attention because the sale had been finalized entirely behind closed doors. Much of the article illuminated high spots in the Church collection, including a Bay Psalm Book and the "only copy that has come to light" of the first collection of laws printed in America, *The Book of the General Lawess and Libertyes Concerning the Inhabitants of the Massachusetts,* 1648. Church also had acquired the unique manuscript copy of Benjamin Franklin's autobiography that had been brought to France in 1791 by William Temple Franklin and returned to this country in 1867 by the U.S. Minister to France, John Bigelow. "All of these precious volumes," the *Times* article noted, "are now stored in safe deposit vaults pending decision as to where the collection's new home is to be—or homes, rather, for there is little likelihood that it will remain intact."

The article allowed that while Henry E. Huntington's name finally had been "given out" as the new owner of the Church library, a number of "book experts" had confided that the putative $1.3 million purchase price "was probably footed by a group of rich men who came to an agreement rather than compete with each other. Of this group of bibliophiles, it is said, each will keep that part of the collection which he particularly covets, whereupon the remainder will be put on the open market." Thus, on the very eve of the Hoe sale, a coterie of New York "book experts" had dismissed Henry E. Huntington as a serious player. Any suggestion that he alone had paid $1.3 million for the Church collection was deemed patently absurd, and the man whose name had been "given out" as buyer of the Church library was assumed to be nothing more than a front man for a consortium of wealthy collectors.

That perception began to change dramatically at 2:30 P.M. on Monday, April 24, 1911, however, when Robert Hoe's books finally went on the block in the Anderson Auction Company's gallery at Madison Avenue and Fortieth Street, just a few minutes away from the dead collector's townhouse. Attracting the most attention in the opening session was a copy of St. Augustine's *De Civitate Dei,* printed in 1470 by John of Speier, "richly illuminated in gold by a contemporary Venetian artist," and one of only eight copies known on vellum. The dealer George D. Smith opened at $1,000 and matched Belle da Costa Greene bid for bid until the prize was his at $2,700. Miss Greene, it was pointed out in press accounts, was representing J. Pierpont Morgan, her employer; Smith was identified only as an independent dealer.

For the second round, which began that evening at 8:15, all four hundred reserved seats in the second floor gallery were filled with the world's most important book people. A scrapbook of old news clippings kept by the Grolier Club preserves to this day a stub for seat 107H. The action moved along indifferently until a "remarkably fine copy" of the 1486 Book of Saint Albans came up in Lot 252. It too was knocked down to Smith, who prevailed over Quaritch with an offer of $12,000. Seventeen lots after that came the climactic moment of the evening, the contest to see who would win what was identified in the catalogue as Biblia Sacra Latina, the forty-two line "editio princeps of the Bible," printed on vellum at Mainz in Germany by Johann Gutenberg and Johann Fust between 1450 and 1455 and bound in two folio volumes with contemporary oak boards and pigskin. "The remarkable nature and importance of this superlatively great book are such that a discursive comment would be unnecessary," the catalogue stated, though a "few salient features" were offered anyway, not least of which was one point put forth in bold capital letters:

IT IS THEREFORE PROBABLE THAT NO OTHER OPPOR-
TUNITY WILL EVER OCCUR TO OBTAIN A VELLUM COPY
OF THIS MONUMENTAL WORK, THE FIRST IMPORTANT
BOOK PRINTED FROM MOVABLE TYPE.

After the two volumes had been placed on a center table, Sidney Hodgson, the distinguished British auctioneer brought over by Anderson Galleries to conduct the Hoe sale, addressed the anxious gathering: "What am I bid for this?"

Someone in the back of the room provoked a ripple of skittish laughter with an offer of $100. George D. Smith quickly bid $10,000, a firm statement of intent that left no further room for frivolous pretenders. Alfred Quaritch smartly raised that to $15,000, at which point the "bidding became brisker," with advances arriving so quickly "it was impossible to say where they came from." At $30,000, Quaritch abandoned whatever hope he had of bringing back to England the book his father had sold to Robert Hoe seventeen years earlier; his withdrawal prompted a wave of patriotic applause from the Americans. Thereafter the match was between Joseph E. Widener of Philadelphia and George D. Smith, the Wall Street dealer who "book experts" and dumbfounded onlookers alike finally realized "was acting as a representative of a wealthy customer."

Widener, said to be bidding for his nephew Harry Elkins Widener, answered each of Smith's bids with a thousand-dollar advance of his own. When they reached $50,000 he shook his head. "This is the last chance you will have to purchase this book," Hodgson declared in final warning. "Do I hear any advance?" With no other bids forthcoming, and with the gallery in an uproar, the Gutenberg Bible was hammered down to George D. Smith. Presently shouts came from throughout the room: "Who is the buyer? Who is the buyer?" Hodgson glanced at Smith, who nodded his approval; the auctioneer then announced the new owner to be Henry E. Huntington, and as the ovation continued, a stately man with a bushy mustache in the front row stood to acknowledge the cheers. With flash, aplomb, and high drama, the Californian had confirmed his intention to form one of the finest libraries in the world.

The next day sales continued at the same torrid pace, with prices going "to the vanishing point," according to the *New York Herald*. Figures for "both ancient and modern tomes" were so high that even the "European experts" in attendance were "astonished." George D. Smith and Belle da Costa Greene dueled gamely once again, this time for the right to claim William Blake's *Milton*, "the original edition of the rarest of all Blake's productions"; only two other copies are recorded, one in the British Museum, the other in the Lenox Library. Though Miss Greene was reported "bent upon getting the treasure," she "gave up the struggle when Mr. Smith called out $9,000." In its continuing coverage, the New York *Tribune* noted that third-day results brought the running total to just under $300,000 and that "George D. Smith made a large majority of the purchases," while "his leading patron," Henry E. Huntington, "sat beside him." Smith was not capturing all the high spots, however. Alfred Quaritch of London waged a lively duel with Dr. A. S. W. Rosenbach of Philadelphia for the A. Firmin-Didot copy of *Cleriadus et Melladice,* a French romance printed in Paris in 1495 and the only known copy on vellum. Rosenbach was an up-and-coming bookseller whose name would soon become synonymous with twentieth-century collecting. Quaritch prevailed with an $8,000 bid, though Rosenbach secured a fine copy of the 1598 London edition of George Chapman's translation of Homer for $3,000.

By the end of the first week, there were grumblings about the "absurdly high" prices being paid and the "prevailing bibliomania" in evidence. "In bidding against Mr. Smith the rest of us are practically attacking a brick wall," Walter M. Hill, a Chicago bookseller, said. "I had no less than three hundred items which are for the Newberry Library of Chicago, but not one could I obtain." Exasperated by having to go well in excess of what she had planned to spend, Théophile Bélin quipped to reporters, "Your prices are as tall as your buildings."

Two weeks after it had dismissed Huntington in one paragraph, the *New York Times* featured a major profile of him under a banner headline, "The Man Who Paid $50,000 for the Gutenberg Bible." A six-line subhead identified him further: "Henry E. Huntington Leaps Into Fame as a Book Collector by Buying the Church Library for $1,300,000, as Well as the Chief Treasure of the Hoe Collection." Large photographs of Huntington and the Beaux Arts–style "ranch" he had built in what is now San Marino, a small community eleven miles outside Los Angeles next to Pasadena, accompanied the article. "He had worked constantly and strenuously since early youth," the journalist wrote, and described what factors made Huntington decide eleven years earlier to become a book collector. "He had made himself the street railway king of the Pacific Coast. He had piled up millions of dollars. He was fifty years old." It was then, after all his hard work, that Huntington expressed a single wish: "Now I want some fun."

Just as interesting as the main story was a sidebar the *Times* published under a five-column headline, "J. P. Morgan's Librarian Says High Book Prices Are Harmful." Belle da Costa Greene did not mention Huntington by name, but she left no doubt about whom she was criticizing. The amounts being spent "are perfectly ridiculous—they are most harmful," she complained. "They establish a dangerous precedent."

In a lengthy digression, the journalist confided that for the previous two weeks "strange doings" had been taking place. "From all over the world buyers had come, many of them dealers, some private collectors, and some—poor things—agents for great libraries that wanted to fill gaps in their collections." But just a few of the prizes were going to those dealers, and outside of "one or two rich men," few were going to collectors. "The appearance of a new collector has been the surprise of the sale. Perhaps the old-fashioned lover of books might object to the use of the term collector in this connection, for the newcomer has none of the instinct of prowling around in shops and browsing among catalogues," an experience that "has always seemed to the book-loving outsider the essence of collecting, but the new man comes in with a shovel. By the time the sale was two days old his agent was said to have spent $150,000."

Miss Greene then addressed herself directly to the issue at hand: " 'The Hoe collection is being sold practically en bloc,' " she told the reporter, and opened her annotated sale catalogue to reveal the name of one dealer—George D. Smith—that "ran down in an almost unbroken column, page after page."

What Greene did not mention was that J. Pierpont Morgan had made a number of en bloc purchases of his own over the years, some of them quite spectacular. In 1899 Morgan bought the Toovey library, which included 529 Aldines, numerous French bindings, and a superb copy of the First Folio in the original calf bearing the arms of Robert Sydney, earl of Leicester. A year later he bought for $200,000 a distinguished collection of early manuscripts, incunabula, Shakespeareana, and Americana gathered by Theodore Irwin of Oswego, New York. In 1902, at a cost of £130,000, he acquired from Richard Bennett of Manchester, England, twenty-four Caxtons, the Subiaco *Lactantius* of 1465, and a copy of *The Book of St. Albans,* material formerly owned by the designer William Morris. The following year, William Blake's drawings for the Book of Job and the John Edward Kerr collection of French romances and chivalry became Morgan's property as well. If, for all that, Miss Greene was still annoyed at the impertinence of

George D. Smith to buy so aggressively, she must have forgotten the night in 1900 when she was in London to bid on fourteen Caxtons collected by the late Lord Amherst, and how a group of booksellers kiddingly asked her during dinner not to embarrass them by posting bids they could never hope to match. When a telegram arrived at the table with news that Lord Amherst's estate had accepted her private offer of $125,000, she told her colleagues, "You may now have your reply, gentlemen. I shall not bid against you tomorrow."

Miss Greene's motivation in protesting the "perfectly ridiculous" and "harmful" prices being spent at the Hoe sale is not fully apparent in the *Times* article. But the very next day, a book described in the auction catalogue as the "only perfect copy known" of Sir Thomas Malory's *Le Morte d'Arthur*, printed by William Caxton at Westminster in 1485, was going on the block; with sixty-two Caxtons already in his collection, Morgan coveted this prize for his shelves. Miss Greene opened the bidding with an offer of $5,000. George D. Smith countered immediately with $10,000. After a third call of $11,000 came $15,000, then $20,000. A rapid exchange of $1,000 bids carried the action to $24,000, and at $30,000, everyone had withdrawn except Smith and Belle Greene. The two then exchanged $500 advances to $42,000, twenty-four calls in all. From there, the stake grew by $100 increments. Finally, Smith withdrew at $42,700, and when Miss Greene affirmed $42,800, the Caxton belonged to the Morgan Library. "Her victory evoked a hearty round of applause, and a number of persons personally congratulated her," the *Times* observed, and added: "It is said that it was the book of books in the Hoe library that Mr. Morgan wanted," and had it been necessary, Miss Greene "would have gone beyond the $50,000 paid by Henry E. Huntington for the Hoe copy of the Gutenberg Bible." Indeed, two days before the lot was to be sold, Miss Greene had cabled Morgan at Aix-les-Bains: "Shall I buy at any price?" His answer: "Use your discretion. Would give seventy-five or even a hundred rather than lose."

All this came within the first two weeks of the Hoe sale, which continued periodically for another year and a half, and though Huntington emerged as the decisive victor, plenty of impressive material was spread around. Henry Clay Folger, one of John D. Rockefeller's top executives at Standard Oil, added to his collection of items relating to Shakespeare and the Elizabethan era. The Chicago industrialist Cyrus H. McCormack (1859–1936), son of the inventor of the reaper, acquired the "Italian Vespucci" of 1504 and the 1488 editio princeps, or first printed edition, of five volumes of Homer, books that ultimately went to Princeton University. William K. Bixby (1857–1931) of St. Louis bought heavily in manuscripts, which he would later sell privately to Huntington. Though the Wideners of Philadelphia did not get the Gutenberg Bible on vellum, for $24,000 they did get Hoe's other remarkably nice copy on paper, which is now the property of Harvard University.

Though only twenty-six years old when the Hoe sale began in 1911, Harry Elkins Widener was already attracting attention for the enthusiasm he was applying to the formation of his library. A. Edward Newton, a Philadelphia collector who wrote several entertaining books about the pastime earlier in this century, recalled how he attended the first sessions of the Hoe sale with this heir to a Philadelphia streetcar fortune. One night after dinner, while the two were walking on Fifth Avenue, Widener wondered how he could ever become a great bookman if all the finest treasures continued to be claimed by his older contemporaries. "I do not wish to be remembered merely as a collector of a few books, however fine they may be," the young man told Newton. "I want to be remembered in connection with a great library, and I do not see how it is going to be brought about. Mr. Huntington and Mr. Morgan are buying up all the books and Mr. Bixby is getting the manuscripts. When my time comes, if it ever does, there will be nothing left for me—everything will be gone."

Despite the fierce competition, young Harry managed to buy a few items at the Hoe sale, some scarce issues of the *Guardian* and *Tatler* and Isaac Jaggard's 1620 edition of the "English Boccaccio" among them. But as events turned out, his time came sooner than he ever might have thought, and in ways he could never have imagined. In March 1912, Widener sailed to England on the *Mauritania* with his parents, George D. and Eleanor Elkins Widener, where he viewed lots at Sotheby's for an upcoming sale of books gathered over two generations by Henry Huth and his son Alfred and shopped at various bookstores. Eager to get back to New York for part of the Hoe sale, he arranged on April 1 for Quaritch Ltd. to ship on the *Carpathia* eight books he had just acquired, but he decided to take a rare 1598 edition of Sir Francis Bacon's *Essayes* with him. Newton told the story first—and it has been repeated frequently enough ever since to become apocryphal: how Widener quipped to Quaritch, "I think I'll take that little Bacon with me in my pocket, and if I am shipwrecked it will go with me."

In a carefully documented essay published in *The Book Collector,* Arthur Freeman, a Quaritch bookseller, demonstrated that what Harry Widener actually said regarding the small duodecimo volume and when he said it were surely more poignant and consequential than "prophetic." Widener is believed to have said, "Mother, I have just placed the little Bacon in my pocket; the little Bacon goes with me!" Harry obviously did not say those words jestfully to a London bookseller on April 1; he expressed them two weeks later, in the face of doom, as he helped Eleanor Elkins Widener board a lifeboat on the foundering steamship *Titanic*.

A few hours before the "unsinkable" passenger liner struck an iceberg in the North Atlantic on April 14, 1912, Captain Edward J. Smith had joined a group of Philadelphia socialites in the first-class restaurant as dinner guests of Mr. and Mrs. Widener. Shortly after one in the morning, with cabin lights still blazing through the portholes, the pride of the White Star fleet rose sharply at the stern, taunting the 705 horrified survivors who watched from lifeboats nearby. Abruptly, the *Titanic* went dark, then slid beneath the surface, taking with it 1,522 passengers and crew. Aboard lifeboat Number 4 with Mrs. Widener and her maid were Mrs. John Jacob Astor and her maid, along with forty other women and children.

Though a casualty list was not available until the end of the week, word of the disaster reached New York just a few hours before the Hoe sale was scheduled to resume in Anderson Galleries. Rosenbach's biographers assert that he had a commission from Harry Widener to go after Caxton's edition of Gower's *Confession Amantis* that day, though once again George D. Smith had a higher limit and bought the book for Henry Huntington. On Friday, April 20, when word arrived that George and Harry Widener were among the missing, Rosenbach wired Quaritch in London to confirm the awful news. "I think if Harry

Elkins Widener had lived he would have been the greatest collector the world has ever known," Rosenbach declared fifteen years later. "Books were his life work, his recreation, his passion." Yet Harry Elkins Widener would achieve greater eminence in death than he might ever have thought possible while alive.

"All joy of living left me on April 15, 1912," Mrs. Widener wrote Dr. Rosenbach two years later. To ease her grief, she had undertaken the creation of a monument to perpetuate the name of her son at his alma mater, Harvard University, and Rosenbach was helping make the woman's gift truly outstanding. Acting on her instructions, the book dealer had commenced what Rosenbach's biographer, Edwin Wolf 2nd, called a "hurricane of buying," quietly acquiring such treasures as Blake's *Songs of Innocence and of Experience,* a presentation copy of Chapman's *Homer,* the manuscript of Sir Walter Scott's life of Swift, Cruikshank's drawings for *Oliver Twist,* and Phiz's illustrations for *Little Dorrit.* Mrs. Widener spent about $120,000 for these purchases, which she had Rosenbach discreetly add to the library already formed by her son. In addition, Peter A. B. Widener, her father-in-law, committed $6,000 for the manuscript of Tennyson's "Charge of the Light Brigade." When everything went over to Harvard, some 3,300 rarities were in the Harry Elkins Widener collection.

Once Mrs. Widener decided that the books were going to Harvard, she took immediate steps to make sure they would be housed properly. At first she wanted to give the university a "wing" where the collection could remain safely deposited forever. But at the time of Harry's death, Harvard had been groping for ways to correct what the university librarian Justin Winsor eighteen years earlier had called "the utter inadequacy" of Gore Hall, its existing library facility. "I have exhausted the language of warning and anxiety," Winsor declared in his annual report for 1894. "Each twelve months brings us nearer to a chaotic condition. The Library goes on with its natural accessions, and friends of learning give us the means to add more to our growth. We have as yet no assurance to give them that their gifts can be properly cared for and the use of their books properly regulated for the general good."

In November 1911, five months before the *Titanic* set sail from Southampton, Archibald Cary Coolidge, the recently appointed library director, informed a Harvard alumnus that all plans for a new building were "in a state of suspended animation," and that the absence of a major donor had left the university "living, however badly, from hand to mouth." Word inevitably got out that the university was looking for a wealthy benefactor. A Boston newspaper ran a lighthearted piece on the subject, with a paragraph bordered in black made to look like a classified advertisement. "WANTED—A MILLIONAIRE," it teased, and added: "Will some kind millionaire please give Harvard University a library building? Mr. Rockefeller, take notice. Mr. Carnegie, please write." The newspaper item was intended for amusement, but on January 31, 1912, Harvard's President Abbot Lawrence Lowell asked J. P. Morgan, Jr. (1861–1943), to seek Andrew Carnegie's help. Two weeks later, Morgan wrote back his feeling that "Harvard is too dignified to have a Carnegie Library." Lowell replied that he had no objection at all "to having our library called the Carnegie Library," providing the steel magnate agreed to "give us the whole of it."

On April 3, 1912, Lowell wrote Morgan once again, this time with another request: "Do you know anyone who could speak to your father about the Library? If he happened to take a real interest in it, he could do any part of it or the whole thing; although he has done so much for us that we have no right to ask him." Six years earlier, J. P. Morgan, Sr., had funded three new Harvard Medical School buildings to honor his late father, Junius Spencer Morgan, but as Lowell noted in his letter, "There is truth in the old saying that 'one good turn deserves another'; only the second is not generally done by the same person as the first." The younger Morgan replied on April 5 that his father was abroad, and that the best time to approach him with such a proposal would be later in the summer, after he returned. But as William Bentinck-Smith has pointed out, the Morgan "fishing expedition" ended dramatically ten days later, when "out of tragedy came the completely unexpected possibility of a solution to Harvard's predicament."

The university learned that it would be getting Harry's rare-book collection, but as Coolidge explained in a May 24 letter to a colleague, the Widener family had stipulated that "we should have a proper place in which to put it." Coolidge added that some newspapers were reporting the likelihood that Mrs. Widener might give a "wing," a prospect that caused him some apprehension. "It is uncertain what the phrase 'a wing' means. If it is an addition to this old building, my enthusiasm for the gift is dampened." A week later, Coolidge outlined the dilemma to J. P. Morgan, Jr., who replied hopefully: "I should not be surprised if the Wideners did the whole thing. It would be much better than having a small detached library just for Harry Widener's books. If I can put in a word—and I may have an opportunity—I shall of course do so."

It soon developed that Mrs. Widener was willing to do "the whole thing." She readily committed the $2 million it would take to see the project through, but she insisted on bringing in her own architect, Horace Trumbaur. In February 1913, a month and a half after Mrs. Widener's formal offer was ratified, seventy-two-year-old Gore Hall, a local landmark that is still featured on the city seal of Cambridge, was gone, and earth was being broken for the new structure. On June 16, 1913, Mrs. Widener, dressed and veiled in black, laid the cornerstone. On commencement day two years later, the building was dedicated. Within hours of the ceremony, books that had been crated and stored all over the campus started coming in by the truckload—for three and a half months they arrived at a rate of 46,000 volumes a week. Today, ten levels of load-bearing stacks built around two interior courtyards remain the primary repository for Harvard's vast library system, accounting for a quarter of the university's 12.8 million titles. At the center, in an elegant room of dark oak and white marble, is a collection of rarities conceived and shaped by Harry Elkins Widener, class of 1907, and completed by Eleanor Elkins Widener, his devoted mother. "When the Library is finished, I want all the books installed there," she directed Rosenbach a year before completion. "Then I will feel happier and know I have done as my dear boy wished."

About the same time the Hoe sale was getting under way, an "unremarkable but grateful" member of the class of 1896 at Yale College was repaying his gratitude for a stimulating undergraduate course with a gift of his own. Alexander Smith Cochran, heir to a Yonkers, New York, carpet manufacturing fortune estimated in 1903 to be worth $50 million, made an interesting proposal to William Lyon Phelps, the professor who taught an Elizabethan drama class he recalled with such special fondness. Though primarily interested in yachting—his schooner West-

ward was undefeated in international matches with *Shamrock, Meteor,* and *Germania* in 1910—Cochran wanted to create a small but distinguished library of dramatic works. To house the books in style, he also proposed establishing a kind of literary gathering place near the campus for undergraduates, to be known as the Elizabethan Club.

Years later, Professor Phelps admitted that all he could remember about Cochran was that he had been "shy and reticent" in class. "I had no means of knowing whether or not the course had made any impression upon him. Nor did I know anything about him personally, or that he was a millionaire in his own right." But when Phelps saw the list of books Cochran wanted to give, the educator "nearly fell out" of his chair. "He had an astounding collection, every item a rarity, and the whole worth several hundred thousand dollars—Shakespeare quartos, a copy of the first edition of the Sonnets, of Bacon's *Essays,* and so on."

Central to the proposal was Cochran's insistence that the books be placed in a clubhouse for junior and senior undergraduates, not in the university library. He committed $75,000 to buy and refurbish a charming old building on College Street for that purpose, and promised another $100,000 as the initial endowment. President Arthur Twining Hadley at first rejected the idea as "too experimental," but quickly changed his mind when he learned that Columbia University was more than willing to accommodate the yachtsman's wishes. As an added incentive, Cochran retained Quaritch of London to make the core collection even better. A few days before an important session at the Huth sale was to get under way in London, the American's preemptive offer to buy thirty-two Shakespeare quartos for £30,000 was accepted. Included in the purchase was the 1594 narrative poem *The Rape of Lucrece,* one of just three copies in existence, a set of proof sheets for the *Richard III* quarto, and an exceedingly scarce copy of the 1599 "good quarto" of *Romeo and Juliet.*

These books formed a base that other friends of the university have augmented with other Shakespearean era gifts over the years. "What makes the Elizabethan Club unique is that it has a collection of very rare books which quite specifically were given for the edification of undergraduate students," Stephen Parks, the curator of the collection, said as he unlocked the steel door to a twelve-by-twelve treasure vault. "The fact that there are twenty million dollars' worth of books in here is beside the point. Seven days a week during term, this place is full of students having cups of tea and sandwiches, and the sandwiches haven't changed in thirty years. We have tomato on Monday, cucumber on Tuesday, chicken salad on Wednesday, cinnamon toast on Thursday, tuna on Friday, date-nut bread on Saturday, and peanut butter on Sunday." Out back is a large lawn where students can play croquet in the fall and spring. "We occasionally challenge the Signet Society at Harvard to a match." And on Friday afternoons, when the mock wall is rolled back and the vault is opened, the books are displayed and the unmistakable aroma of hot English tea mingles with the fragrance of hand-made paper and fine leather bindings. In his memoirs Professor Phelps wrote, "Little did I guess when I started giving my course in the Elizabethan dramatists years ago, that it would come to this."

Yale had sparked Alexander Smith Cochran's enthusiasm for English drama, just as Harvard had worked magic on Harry Elkins Widener. In both instances, there was wisdom to be gleaned from the results, though Harvard was the first to act affirmatively upon it. Shortly after the Widener Library opened in 1915, George Parker Winship, class of 1893, accepted an offer to leave the John Carter Brown Library in Rhode Island and become his alma mater's first rare-book specialist. His first order of business was to set aside a secure area in the new library and designate it the Treasure Room. He then culled the general stacks for rarities already owned by the university and sifted through the "welcome flood of gifts" occasioned by construction of the new building. Of more far-reaching consequence was the noted bibliographer's uncanny ability to recognize future benefactors among the student body and the ingenious methods he used to cultivate their interest in beautiful books.

Once settled in his new job, Winship began teaching what curriculum catalogues of the period identify as Fine Arts 5e, a sort of "hands-on" course attended almost exclusively by the sons of wealthy families. In a short essay written for the Grolier Club, Boies Penrose, one of Winship's fortunate few, recalled how students did not simply sign up for the "celebrated" course, they "applied for membership," and competition was keen. "For, let it be said, it was no ordinary course, to be enrolled in simply by filling in a form at the beginning of term." To ensure that applicants were "properly qualified," admission was "rigorously guarded by the master himself." As a result, "5e" became known as one of "the more exclusive clubs of Harvard, although Winship's draconian screening was certainly justified in that many of his pupils became lifelong bookmen."

Not only did the "standards of admission" make the course exclusive, but the "physical setting was likewise unique." The students met in the elegant new Widener Room, home to Harry's rare-book collection, where "easy chairs and an open fire" provided "all the sybaritic comforts of a palace" and "the environment of a connoisseur." Winship would sit at the head of a long table,

> intermittently handing around illuminated manuscripts and incunabula for our inspection. Technical instruction was at a minimum; aesthetic appreciation and cultural background at a maximum. It was the book as a creation, as a work of art, as an important factor in its time and place, that he stressed, rather than the devitalizing details of pagination and collation. And he stressed these things well; so well, in truth, that most of us were carried away with enthusiasm.

Winship taught Fine Arts 5e from 1915 to 1931. Its description in course catalogues was straightforward enough, though a few revealing phrases do appear. "This course is intended for men who are interested in books as objects of art, and who desire to possess or to produce beautiful books. An important object of the course is to train the taste of book-buyers, and to cultivate a well-informed judgment of the value of rare and attractive volumes." Arthur A. Houghton, Jr., class of 1929 and heir to the Steuben Glass fortune of Corning, New York, took Fine Arts 5e. Eleven years after receiving his bachelor's degree, Houghton underwrote construction of the first library to be built by any American university exclusively for the storage of rare books. When the Houghton Library opened in 1942 it was called "the most advanced library building in the United States, if not the world."

Bayard L. Kilgour, Jr., of Cincinnati, class of 1927, another Winship student, gave the university what was regarded at the time as the pre-eminent collection of T. E. Lawrence books, letters, and manuscripts in private hands, and after turning over more than two thousand examples of eighteenth- and nineteenth-century Russian literature—considered the finest collection of its kind outside Russia—he was named honorary curator of the Slavic Collection. Kilgour had bought most of the material from a New York bookseller after it was turned down by several institutions. "Mr. Kilgour realized the importance of it as did none of the institutional libraries to which it had been offered," William A. Jackson, then librarian of the Houghton Library, wrote in the catalogue to the collection.

Stanley Marcus, Lucius Beebe, Carl Pforzheimer, Jr., and Walter Whitehill were other prominent graduates of Fine Arts 5e. When the Houghton Library opened, another Winship protégé, Philip Hofer, offered his services free of charge and remained at the university for the rest of his life. Hofer collected with consummate taste and discrimination, and his gift of illustrated books and manuscripts "qualify him to be called the greatest benefactor of the Harvard Library," according to Roger E. Stoddard, the current curator of rare books at Houghton Library. William A. Jackson, dubbed the "grand acquisitor" for the wealth of material he added to Harvard's collections during his tenure as rare-book librarian, was "obviously envious of Winship's influence" over wealthy young bibliophiles, and once asked the master how he picked the students for his course. The response came without hesitation: "Whiskey breath and club pin."

In 1924, Chauncy Brewster Tinker, Winship's distinguished counterpart at Yale, complained to Yale alumni that Harvard was "perpetually in the lead," and acknowledged how "galling" it was to accept "Yale's being always second in the race; but even that is better than fifth or sixth." Tinker performed similar miracles on a generation of Yale collectors, but as Thomas Adams, former librarian of the John Carter Brown Library, said, "Harvard was twenty-five years ahead of everyone else." Roger Stoddard agreed, noting that "just about every major benefaction to the Harvard Library from 1935 on was related in one way or another to Winship's Fine Arts course."

◆ ◆ ◆

Henry E. Huntington never went to college and never attended any seminars where he could marvel at the beauty of illuminated manuscripts or handle exquisitely tooled leather bindings. Born in Oneonta, New York, in 1850, he spent most of his adult life creating and consolidating a railroad empire with his uncle, Collis P. Huntington, at first in the South and then, most dramatically, in California. No one really knows why he decided rather late in life to commit so much energy and money to collecting. A. S. W. Rosenbach probably guessed his motives as well as anyone. Rosenbach quoted Huntington as once saying: "Men may come and men may go, but books go on forever. The ownership of a fine library is the surest and swiftest way to immortality!" Rosenbach did not say where Huntington got that idea, possibly because he did not want to pay tribute to the late George D. Smith, the only person who could challenge Rosenbach for the title of the greatest American bookseller of the twentieth century. But in an article written for a short-lived publication called the *Literary Collector,* Smith wrote: "When the rulers of kingdoms today have crumbled into the dust and their names forgotten of the people, the memory of a maker of a great collection will be a household word in the mouths of thousands. This is the real road to fame."

If building a great library was the surest and swiftest way to immortality, then it made sense that Huntington's actions would be sure and swift as well. Not surprisingly, the same bold methods that helped him build a vast transportation empire in California were brought to bear in his collecting. Huntington was sixty-two years old when the *Titanic* sank on April 15, 1912. By the time the final lot in the Hoe sale was hammered down seven months later, he had accounted for half of the $1.9 million spent. For another $1.3 million, he also acquired the entire Church collection. And that was just the beginning.

While the phrase *en bloc* did not originate with Huntington, the practice of buying the complete libraries of other collectors became his trademark. The first issue of the *Huntington Library Bulletin,* published in 1931, four years after Huntington's death, identified 112 individual collections bought largely en bloc between 1904 and 1927. "It cannot be stated too often," Professor George Sherburn of the University of Chicago wrote, "that the Huntington Library is essentially a 'library of libraries or a collection of collections.' "

A few collections are worth mentioning. In 1913, Huntington acquired Grenville Kane's collection of letters and documents written by George Washington, at least one item for each year of Washington's adult life. Then came an archive of material assembled by Ward Hill Lamon, Abraham Lincoln's former law partner. Though Huntington would never catch up to Morgan in Caxtons, he made a noble effort in 1914 when for $750,000 he secured twenty-five superior examples from the duke of Devonshire, a trove that also brought with it 7,500 early English plays and 111 volumes of playbills gathered by the celebrated British actor John Philip Kemble.

In 1915 Huntington bought the New York lawyer Frederick R. Halsey's twenty thousand–volume collection of English and American literature, which was strong in Dickens, Stevenson, Milton, Shelley, and Poe, including two copies of *Tamerlane and Other Poems*. Two years later he acquired Baron Ellesmere's Bridgewater House library of 4,400 books that included handwritten material by Chapman and Marston and twelve thousand manuscripts, most notably the exquisitely illuminated Ellesmere Chaucer displayed prominently today as a centerpiece in the Huntington Library gallery. Huntington also understood that there are times when it is more appropriate to be discreet than decisive. When he showed up one morning at the home of New York collector Beverly Chew to conclude the purchase of 1,600 English rarities, he encountered a man in anguish. "I have not slept a wink all night for thinking about parting with my books," Chew allowed.

"If that is the way you feel about parting with your books, Mr. Chew, I will not take them," Huntington replied, "but, if at any time you decide to dispose of them, I wish the first opportunity of acquiring them." Within a year, Huntington paid Chew $500,000 and got the books.

For the first ten years of his collecting, Huntington was ably represented by George D. Smith, the wily New Yorker who appreciated cigars and racetracks with as much gusto as he did a battle in the auction rooms. His swaggering performance at the Hoe sale led to his boast: "I had the satisfaction of having taught those English and Continental booksellers something about American sporting blood that they didn't forget for many a day." On September 25, 1918, Huntington wrote Smith a letter in which he bought thirty lots from a recent Huth sale and added: "I am very glad to see that you are going to sell your valuable string of horses, and I think that by so doing *you will be able to keep in the book business.* If you should have succeeded in the horse business, you would have been a wonder, for I think that there is hardly one in a hundred keeping at it who does not go 'dead broke' before they turn up their toes."

There is little doubt, however, that Smith knew how to hedge. When he sailed to England in 1916 with a group of American booksellers, each intending to bid on the first part of the Britwell Court library, he "neglected to tell his fellow passengers that he had some days earlier bought the collection en bloc by cable," Richard S. Wormser wrote in a sketch of Smith for the Grolier Club. Shrewdly, Smith maintained offices at 48 Wall Street in New York's financial district, not farther uptown where most of the other prominent dealers conducted business. "All of the great collectors of the time were among his clients," Wormser pointed out. "His famed ability and stock of important books drew them to his shop, possibly in part because they saw, in his activities, methods similar to those by which some of them had amassed their fortunes."

Had Smith lived beyond his fiftieth birthday he probably would have continued as principal agent for Huntington and other wealthy clients, but his unexpected death early in 1920 left the lucrative field open for his competitors, most prominent among them the learned doctor of philosophy from Philadelphia, Abraham Simon Wolf Rosenbach, who already was chipping away at Smith's monopoly of Huntington's business. The Rosenbach Company archives record several sales to Huntington prior to Smith's death, one in December 1916 for a collection of William Blake drawings, another two weeks later for some Americana. Clearly, Smith no longer was acting as Huntington's exclusive agent; Rosenbach already was making significant inroads.

On August 1, 1919, Rosenbach wired Huntington with news that he had just "purchased for stock" the Marsden J. Perry library, and that he was willing to offer the Californian "first offer of Shakespeare quartos not in your collection," including "three of the earliest known published in 1591 and 1592." This was a stunning announcement. The Marsden J. Perry Shakespeare collection was not known to be on the market, and it included a number of extraordinary items. Dr. Rosenbach informed Huntington that he was traveling to California in two weeks and asked whether he could stop by to discuss the matter. "Please consider Perry purchase confidential," he added. "Telegraph me at once as would like to give you first opportunity before offering elsewhere." A reply from Huntington is not in the Rosenbach Company files, but there is no question but that the two men got together in California. A one-page agreement, written in longhand and signed by Huntington on August 19, 1919, confirms the sale of eleven quartos from the Perry collection, *King John, First Part,* and *King John, Second Part,* both 1591, among them, "all for the special price of $121,000 cash," with two of the items, a 1676 *Hamlet* and a 1684 *Julius Caesar,* "to be delivered to me tomorrow."

The Marsden J. Perry coup also enabled Rosenbach to sell material to Henry C. and Emily Jordan Folger, who were building what would become an unequaled collection of Shakespeare material. By the time George D. Smith died seven months later, Rosenbach already had made his first major deal with Huntington. The reason this was possible may have been a result of Smith's arrogance toward Marsden J. Perry, the Rhode Island financier who had been collecting Shakespeare material since the 1870s.

In a 1946 essay written in honor of Dr. Rosenbach's seventieth birthday, Clarence S. Brigham told how Marsden J. Perry's chief ambition had been to acquire the duke of Devonshire's fifty-seven Shakespeare quartos:

> One day I was talking with Mr. Perry, and I said, "I saw George D. Smith yesterday and he told me that he had bought the Devonshire quartos for Mr. Huntington." Mr. Perry's face showed his disappointment, and he said, "My collection can never now achieve top rank, and I think that it's time to sell it." In 1919 he disposed of his entire Shakespearian library to Dr. Rosenbach for a price of about half a million dollars. George D. Smith was angling for the collection and fully expected to buy it, as he didn't think that any other dealer could finance so large a deal, but his judgment failed him in not counting on the acumen and enthusiasm [of Dr. Rosenbach].

Brigham did not say this, but Perry just may have picked Rosenbach as one way of letting Smith know how he felt about losing the Devonshire quartos to Huntington. In any event, the decision gave Rosenbach, then forty-three, immediate contact with some of the most important collectors of the day. On July 23, 1919, in fact—a week before he telegraphed Huntington—Rosenbach wrote Folger in Hot Springs, Virginia, acknowledging receipt of $100,000, which he applied toward the $128,500 price of material selected from the Perry library. "At this time," the doctor wrote, with the kind of embellished aside that characterizes so much of his correspondence, "I want to congratulate you upon obtaining, what I consider, the FINEST SHAKESPEAREAN VOLUME IN EXISTENCE, and upon which no price can be placed, namely the famous GWYNNE VOLUME of 1619." This collection of nine Shakespeare plays, named for the owner whose name appears stamped on the original calf cover, predates the First Folio by four years and is probably more valuable than any other single Shakespeare item. Eight years later, in an article written for *The Saturday Evening Post,* Rosenbach managed a wild guess as to its possible worth: "I do not hesitate to say that this book would bring at least $200,000 if it were sold on the block to-day."

This tendency to boast publicly about the big prices he recorded was a chronic weakness with Rosenbach, and though dazzling numbers delivered a degree of glamour, talking freely about them caused problems. After he finished selling off most of the Perry library—William Andrews Clark of Los Angeles and Joseph Widener of Philadelphia also bought some of the material—the doctor leaked details of his coup to the newspapers, prompting a rebuke from Folger, who was then the president of Standard Oil of New York. Folger testily told Rosenbach about a discussion he had with his boss, John D. Rockefeller, after the news got out. "Henry, I see from the papers that you just paid a hundred thousand dollars for a book," Rockefeller supposedly said. Folger admitted improvising an answer—he blamed the press for exaggerating the transaction's cost—which brought another unsettling response from Rockefeller. "Well, I'm glad to hear you say that, Henry. We—that is, my son and I and the board of directors—were disturbed. We wouldn't want to think that the president of one of our major companies would be the kind of man foolish enough to pay a hundred thousand dollars for a book!"

Records at the Rosenbach Museum and Library in Philadelphia show that Folger was indeed foolish enough to pay big money for books. From 1919 to 1929, he spent $1,388,990 with Rosenbach, $421,705 for material acquired at auction and the rest for selections from stock. Rosenbach seems to have been genuinely interested in helping Folger create the world's foremost collection of Shakespeareana. On June 27, 1922, he wrote Folger a letter headed "Very Confidential" to offer him "the *only unique* Shakespeare quarto play published in the 16th century," the 1598 copy of *The Tragedie of King Richard the Second,* which he had just acquired from William A. White. "I am only permitted to offer it to you and to Mr. Huntington," he advised, "and I am making you the first offer. One of the reasons that has influenced me to do this is that you are the only private collector that already possesses a unique Shakespeare quarto, the *Titus Andronicus.* Mr. Huntington has not had the good fortune to possess any." Three days later, Folger agreed to the $55,000 asking price, providing he could defer half the payment for three months, which Rosenbach allowed.

As fruitful as Rosenbach's relationship with Folger became, the principal theater of operations was still in southern California. Rosenbach may not have fully comprehended in 1919 exactly what motivated Huntington, but Huntington himself certainly knew what he was trying to accomplish. Two days after he wrote out the terms of his agreement for the Marsden Perry quartos, Huntington dictated a jubilant letter to his librarian, George Watson Cole, in New York: "It makes quite a reduction in the number of plays I have to secure to be even with the British Museum. I should like to have you send me a list of all the Shakespeare plays lacking. Place the list on my desk and send me the duplicate."

Three months earlier, Cole had informed Huntington that their collection of pre-Restoration English plays and masques totaled 909, just thirteen fewer than the number held by the British Museum Library; the Perry quartos brought the figure down to two. The man who asserted that a great library is the surest way to achieve immortality had set as his standard nothing less than the venerable British Museum Library. In some areas, at least, he was getting close. Unlike J. Pierpont Morgan, who made it a point never to outbid the British Museum, Huntington was determined to build the finest library possible, regardless of whose feelings he ruffled. As a result, the reaction in England toward Huntington was not entirely congenial. He was a willing buyer and they were willing sellers, but they were determined to make him pay dearly. While Huntington always committed whatever funds were necessary, he still personally approved every nickel that was spent and saved money at every opportunity.

This was demonstrated by the convenient way he found to acquire a superior run of pre-Restoration imprints without letting on that they were being bought for his library. Even Dr. Rosenbach, it appears, was kept in the dark about an understanding Huntington had formed with Clarence S. Brigham, the internationally respected bookman who served as librarian of the American Antiquarian Society in Worcester, Massachusetts, from 1908 to 1930 and director from 1930 to 1959.

Clarence S. Brigham (1877–1963) was a man committed to the building of American libraries, not least of which was the one he directed. As a hobby he collected examples of English printing produced before 1640, the date traditionally taken to mark the end of "early" English books. Because the Antiquarian Society only collects American material, this pastime posed no conflict of interest with his job. Sometime after he was introduced to Huntington in 1917, Brigham offered to sell the Californian items from his personal collection at cost.

In a letter dated April 17, 1920, he also proposed taking along with him on a trip to Europe that summer a checklist of material Huntington was interested in locating, material that Brigham enthused might help create "the greatest collection in English literature prior to 1640" in the world. "I am not in the book business, and am actuated chiefly by my love of the subject and my pride as an American in your Library," he stressed. "If you think well of the plan, it should not be mentioned under any condition. If anyone knew that I was buying for you, or it was understood in the trade that you had an 'agent' buying in England, it would make a great difference in prices." Huntington wrote back within the month accepting Brigham's "kind offer to get the books on your trip abroad."

Once in England, Brigham reported regularly on his adventures, which went exceedingly well. "Absolutely no one has suspected my Huntington connection," he wrote on July 27. The following month

Brigham advised Huntington that he had already spent $9,000 for books, about $4,000 of that from his own pocket. "A dealer would charge $20,000 for what I've bought," he added somewhat ingenuously. Soon after Brigham's return to Massachusetts, the books began to arrive from England: on September 20, he acknowledged receipt of $10,000 from Huntington and confided how he was "spending most of my evenings in unpacking and checking" the purchases. "I have become so much interested in the subject," he wrote, "that the pleasure of looking over these volumes is preferable to most social engagements."

As the year came to a close, Huntington's librarian, George Watson Cole, wrote to Brigham, on November 27, 1920, pleased to learn that another trip to Europe was on for the following summer. "I am delighted to know that you are going over once more in our interest. You will, of course, take up the train of 1640 books where you dropped it when you returned home last fall and I hope you will be quite as successful, if not even more so than on your previous quest." Two weeks later, on December 13, Huntington wrote Brigham the news that he would be taking a train from New York to California shortly, "and as I plan to take the books you have in my car, I hope they will be here in time to go." On January 19, 1921, Brigham informed Huntington that "you have at the present time about 6300 titles previous to 1640, which with the 1200 titles acquired by me last summer makes a total of 7500 titles. If we should be fortunate enough to acquire the Christie-Miller collection as a whole, this would add 700 titles at once, making a grand total of 8200 titles, and passing the collection at Cambridge. This is the first lap of the journey."

These were words Huntington longed to hear, as George Watson Cole implied in April 1921: "Mr. Huntington after reading your letter suggested that the books, as fast as bought for this Library, be sent directly here; but I told him that this might divulge our little game and that it would be better for you to send them on from Worcester as fast as you receive them." Probably because a "little game" admittedly was being played, all this correspondence from Huntington and Cole was sent to Brigham's home, not his office, though Brigham subsequently deposited most of the letters he received in the society's files.

"We can readily see . . . with the additions you have made to our collection that it becomes increasingly difficult for you to find new material for us," Cole wrote on June 10, 1921. "With regard to future purchases and shipments, Mr. Huntington is very desirous that you send us lists as soon as possible after purchases have been made so as to prevent duplication and that the books be sent to us so that we may receive them in as short a time as possible after they are acquired, and in a manner that will not show your hand in the transactions."

Brigham, meanwhile, outlined his thoughts on the upcoming trip in a letter to Huntington. "Because of the approaching completeness of your collection, it is now increasingly difficult to obtain titles which you lack." But he was taking Huntington's checklist with him nonetheless, because

> no opportunity should be lost to complete as far as possible [the collection]. I do not think that there will be any need of advancing any money, as I can easily finance all purchases, unless I should happen to land some very large collection. Do you know if Dr. Rosenbach visited any large private collectors in England, or made overtures in that regard? I doubt if he has, and certainly not the collections which I have in mind, and which I hope to see through the introductions of mutual friends. Of course it is very important to me in my purchasing to be assumedly purchasing for myself.

This trip also proved successful, as Brigham's letter of December 19, 1921, made clear. "The books go forward to California tomorrow," he announced. "I am sending them by express, in two cases, insured." He then asked whether Huntington wanted him "to do anything" at the Britwell Court auction. "You lack a large number of titles in this sale, and they are very important. It looks to me as if the sale would bring the same amount as the Britwell Sale of last spring. At least 25% could be saved if the purchases could be made anonymously, or rather if the English book dealers did not immediately catch on to the fact who was buying for you."

This arrangement continued for another year. It would be comforting to report it ended happily, but that was not the case. There were minor problems: some haggling over money—the fluctuating exchange rate of the pound seems to have caused periodic misunderstandings—

and the condition of some volumes was questioned by the staff at San Marino. But a major disagreement developed when Huntington learned that Brigham had lent to Yale University an imprint bought for him, so that a photocopy could be made of the title page. "I note with interest the increase in price of this volume as it appears on your invoice, over that at which it was sold in Pickering and Chatto's catalogue of May 17th 1923, as well as the fact that you have allowed the volume to be used by others when it was the property of this library," Huntington wrote testily on December 21, 1923, and then dropped a bombshell. "I think it would be well for you to discontinue your activities for this library until such time as I may authorize you to continue as our agent."

Brigham was stunned. "I have made three foreign trips, have worked day and night poring over immense book stacks, have examined many hundreds of thousands of titles in book catalogues and have given nearly all of my spare time to the research for over three years," he replied on January 7, 1924. "And yet the profit to me, over the cost, expenses and time has been negligible. I do not think that anyone else would have given his time so long for the love of the subject." He added that he lent the book in question to Yale after being asked to do so, and that he complied because "I did not think it wise to disclose the fact that I was buying for the Huntington Library."

The most painful repercussion of the "little game" came in 1931, four years after Huntington's death, when Brigham received a copy of the first number of *The Huntington Library Bulletin,* which featured two detailed essays, one about the late founder's life and accomplishments, the other a chronological summary of his numerous acquisitions. Midway through the summary, the Massachusetts librarian read that during "the years 1921–25, when Mr. Huntington's collections of English books antedating 1640 were already rich, he employed the skillful services of Mr. Brigham, Director of the American Antiquarian Society, in securing further accessions in this inviting field. As Mr. Huntington's agent, Mr. Brigham collected, mainly in England, about 2,750 items, many of them religious books."

In a confidential letter written to Max Farrand, director of the Huntington Library, Brigham protested the suggestion that he had ever been retained by the millionaire. "Mr. Huntington never 'employed' my services nor did I act as his agent," he asserted, and explained how the arrangement grew out of his offer to sell duplicates from his own collection.

> I also suggested that since I was going abroad I could take along his checklist and would try to pick up as many titles as possible in English book shops. These books I sold at cost without making any financial profit to myself. I did it as a friendly act and not in any way as agent. In fact, not an English dealer knew, or had any suspicion, that any of the books which I purchased were for Mr. Huntington. Your announcement, now made in print for the first time, will be a surprise to some of them, if they happen to see it. [The] whole transaction [was intended] to build up Mr. Huntington's collection so that it would rate numerically higher in the world's greatest collections of early English printing. It was largely due to my help, for I obtained nearly twenty-eight hundred titles, that his collection went from possibly the sixth to third place among the collections of this kind.

At this point Brigham confessed an "ulterior motive" he had in the arrangement:

> I hoped that Mr. Huntington would be so appreciative of this help that he would make a contribution to the funds of the American Antiquarian Society, either through gift or bequest, of at least $25,000. I talked with him about this matter two or three times and he really seemed interested. He certainly had it in mind and I think, in fact, I almost know, that if he had lived a little longer, he would have brought this about. Now I wish that I had charged a profit on those books, which easily could have amounted to $25,000, and then given that fund to the American Antiquarian Society.

Brigham did not demand a correction or amplification, but he did ask that any future use of the article delete the words "employed" and "agent." Fifteen years later, Brigham wrote a short essay in which he

discussed his "friendly act" once again, stressing, as he had in the letter to Farrand, that he was motivated only by a wish to help create a
great library. He did not mention, however, that when he was buying
the imprints, he did so under the pretense of acquiring them for his
own collection. In another context, Brigham confided that he once
asked Huntington how much money he had spent on his collections.
The old man doodled for a few minutes with a pencil and paper, then
said, "I think that I have spent twenty million on books, and slightly
more on art." If there were any lingering hard feelings, they were not
apparent in Brigham's concluding opinion of Huntington: "It was the
combination of will power, sagacity and money that made him the
greatest book collector in the world."

As to why Huntington allowed the Massachusetts librarian to buy
anonymously for him in the first place, the answer may well be found
elsewhere in the same issue of *The Huntington Library Bulletin* as the
account that Brigham had found so shocking. "Mr. Huntington was an
opportunist," Robert O. Schad observed in his respectful profile, and
was "ready to consider any material offered which would augment or
improve his library."

Correspondence and archival information also demonstrate that
even though Huntington employed a professional staff, he was the final
authority on which items were to be bought for his library, and how
much should be spent. Rosenbach submitted offers on items personally
to Huntington, and though a response occasionally came from a senior
staff member, it was the "old man," as George D. Smith had referred to
him, who made every important decision. On January 24, 1923, Huntington's curator, Leslie E. Bliss, relayed to Rosenbach the collector's
commissions to purchase 168 lots in a forthcoming Britwell Court sale
in London. The next day Bliss sent Rosenbach two more letters, one
listing 103 additional items, but with a warning that "we most emphatically do not want to pay fancy prices for them. However, should you
buy them and then offer them to us at what we consider reasonable figures, it is quite probable that we will take a fair percentage, and, perhaps, all of them." Rosenbach's copies of these letters show every item
checked off, and presumably purchased. In the second letter dated January 25, 1923, Bliss relayed a counterproposal from Huntington
regarding the purchase of 140 volumes of early American imprints

gathered by Simon Gratz, a Philadelphia lawyer and close friend of Rosenbach's: "You buy the collection and keep the eighteen following books (all of which we already have), and Mr. Huntington will pay you forty thousand dollars for the remainder."

Rosenbach's original proposal had been for $50,000, but he accepted the terms. Since Gratz had consigned the books with the understanding that they were to be sold en bloc, Rosenbach asked Huntington to "keep the matter confidential and state to no one that you purchased any of Mr. Gratz's collection. You see, he intended to present it, together with his Confederate Imprints to the Free Library of Philadelphia (of which Mr. Gratz and myself are trustees) so you see it will be much better if no public announcement is made of it."

Another problem that developed the following month illustrates just how closely Huntington monitored his acquisitions. It involved a 1595 first issue of Richard Barnfield's *Cynthia,* which Rosenbach had sold Huntington in 1921. Two years later, Huntington reminded Rosenbach that the copy he received contained a "rather clumsily altered" facsimile page; since the forthcoming Britwell Court sale included "a perfect copy of the issue which you sold me with the fac-similied leaf," he thought it "only right if you would bid in this copy and exchange it for the one sold me in June, 1921. How does this seem to you?" Three months later, having received no satisfaction in the matter, Huntington wrote again. "I note that you purchased *Cynthia,* but as it was not in your Britwell shipment, I am curious to know what you did about it."

When Rosenbach finally answered, he responded forthrightly by citing an earlier exchange of letters between the two of them "concerning this item before I left for Europe. At that time I stated that as Mr. Folger had in every case acceded to your wishes and would not bid against you, I thought it only right that in this one instance he should have this copy of the book considering that there was already one in your possession." Rosenbach acknowledged having turned the book over to Folger, but added, "I might say also that there were no conflicting American bids in this sale, and that every collector here was kind enough to refrain from bidding against you."

In July 1923, Rosenbach offered Huntington an opportunity to purchase 750 incunabula gathered a century earlier by Sir Thomas

Den vordantz hat man mir gelan
Dann jch on nutz vil bücher han
Die jch nit lyß/ vnd nyt verstan

Von vnnutzē buchern
Das jch sytz vornan jn dem schyff
Das hat worlich eyn sundren gryff
On vrsach ist das nit gethan
Vff myn libry ich mych verlan

The Book Fool, by Albrecht Dürer, for Sebastian Brant's
Das Narrenschiff (*The Ship of Fools*), Basel, 1494.

Sir Robert Cotton
(1571–1631), antiquary
and collector.

A page from *Beowulf*
(c. 1000), the Anglo-Saxon
epic poem that owes its
survival to the efforts of Sir
Robert Cotton.

Pepys's library in York Buildings, London, about 1693, before being moved in 1724 to Cambridge, where it remains virtually intact.

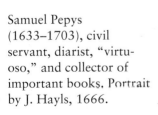

Samuel Pepys (1633–1703), civil servant, diarist, "virtuoso," and collector of important books. Portrait by J. Hayls, 1666.

Copy of *Areopagitica*, inscribed by John Milton "ex dono authoris" to George Thomason (*ante* 1602–1666), who assembled 22,255 tracts during the English civil war.

George John, second Earl Spencer (1758–1834); W. Finder after Thomas Phillipps.

The King's Library, assembled by King George III, presented to the British Museum by his son George IV in 1828 and used today as the main exhibition hall for books and manuscripts.

Sir Thomas Phillipps (1792–1872), about 1860.

Statue of John Harvard (1607–1638), the Puritan clergyman whose gift of books established the first library to be formed in British North America.

Thomas Prince
(1687–1758) of Boston,
whose acquisitions
included six Bay Psalm
Books.

James Logan (1674–1751)
of Philadelphia, who often
admitted that "books are
my disease."

Isaiah Thomas
(1749–1831), printer,
entrepreneur, chronicler
of his craft, collector,
and founder of the
American Antiquarian
Society.

Jeremy Belknap
(1744–1798), founder of
the nation's first historical
society.

*Jeremy Belknap D.D. drawn by
Cate Samuel Harris, from a painting by
Henry Sargent Esq.r in the Historical Li*

RIGHT: George Brinley (1817–1875), about 1850, at the beginning of his quarter-century effort to assemble the finest collection of American imprints ever put together.

BELOW: James Lenox (1800–1880), about 1870, whose exceptional library became a core collection of the New York Public Library.

John Carter Brown (1797–1874), whose legacy is a great library of Americana in Providence, Rhode Island.

East Room of the Pierpont Morgan Library, 1988.

John Pierpont Morgan
(1837–1913) in a 1902 Pach
Brothers photograph.

Robert Hoe III (1839–1909),
arguably America's greatest
collector.

Henry E. Huntington (1850–1927) at his San Marino, California, ranch.

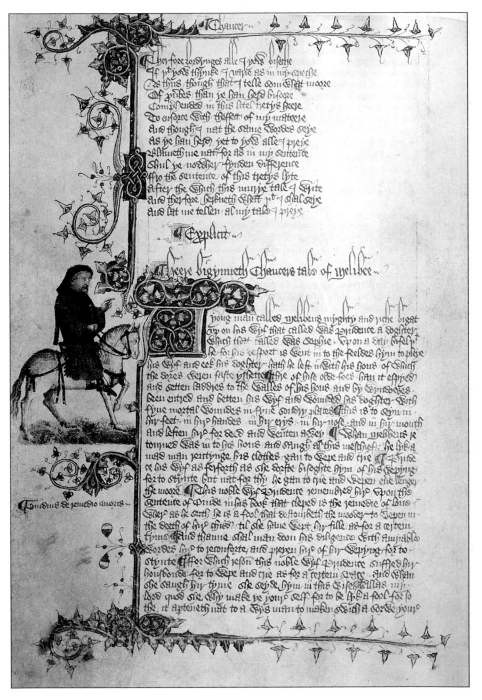

Page from the Ellesmere Manuscript of Chaucer's *Canterbury Tales*, about 1410, containing the earliest surviving portrait of the poet.

A 1907 view of the New York Public Library from Forty-second Street.

Phillipps. The transaction, one of many impressive "private treaty" agreements negotiated by Rosenbach during the 1920s, demonstrates how his spreading reputation was bringing him exclusive access to superior material. "It may interest you to know that I am the only bookseller that has ever inspected the collection," he wrote. "The only other American who has ever had access to it was Mr. J. P. Morgan, who purchased five illuminated manuscripts from it some years ago."

The volumes, all bought by Phillipps from an ancient German monastery in about 1845, "generally are in the original bindings, just as they were issued." Two paragraphs later came the ultimate teaser: "The purchaser of this collection will place his library among the very first in printed books. Sotheby's have been at Mr. Fenwick for years asking him to sell at auction, claiming that it would realize far more at public sale than by private treaty, but I have been fortunate in having it offered to me before all others." A bill of sale in the Rosenbach Company's Huntington file, dated August 3, 1923, records the purchase of 105 items from the list for $36,500. Six days later, Rosenbach offered Huntington yet another magnificent lot from the Phillipps collection, 99 folio volumes containing what are known as the Muniments of Battle Abbey, manuscripts dating from the time of William the Conqueror that are "invaluable to the student of English literature and history." By midmonth, for an additional $50,000, they belonged to Huntington. In October Rosenbach negotiated the $65,000 purchase of twelve thousand early American imprints gathered by Wilberforce Eames, for fifty years the respected librarian of the New York Public Library.

"It is unlikely that a collection so extensive and rich as that of the Huntington Library could have been brought together in so short a time by any but Mr. Huntington's method," Robert O. Schad wrote. By buying entire collections, Huntington not only acquired a tremendous volume of material, but was able to secure with single purchases what others had spent years assembling. "Each of these represented a lifetime or more of collecting," Schad pointed out. What Huntington could not possess, though, was the kind of expertise collectors gain from decades of hunting. When he finally persuaded Beverly Chew to sell his library for half a million dollars, Huntington is said to have expressed a willingness to double the price if Chew's knowledge could come along with it.

Though Huntington had occupied his new ranch in San Marino at the foot of the San Gabriel Mountains since 1910, most of the books and manuscripts he bought remained in New York for more than a decade, some at the Metropolitan Club where he maintained quarters, others in his third-floor library at Fifth Avenue and East Fifty-seventh Street, a few in bank vaults. All were waiting for a suitable repository on the West Coast. By the fall of 1920, the grand library he had been building on the grounds of his estate was ready, and the New York staff, which had grown to twelve just to process the rapidly arriving books, prepared for the big move. With this dramatic migration, California became home to a magnificent library.

The following year, a deed was drawn that made the library, ranch, artwork, and botanical gardens a public trust. As he passed his seventieth birthday, Huntington concentrated on turning the library into a permanent institution. Significantly, much of his time was now spent on developing plans for a mausoleum on the San Marino grounds "above the spot where we have laid Mrs. Huntington to rest, and where in time I expect to be," as he explained in a letter to Rosenbach, whom he wanted to come up with some suggestions for a design. Though Rosenbach's expertise was literature, not architecture, he was only too pleased to help, and his letters show an almost frantic desire to contribute something meaningful to the project.

Once Huntington started focusing on the mausoleum, it became harder and harder for Rosenbach to sell books to him. Even blunt suggestions that desirable items were being lost to rival collectors could not rekindle the old man's enthusiasm. On May 27, 1926, Rosenbach wrote Huntington directly, explaining in a lengthy letter that some recent commissions he had received from him "were not at all flexible," and that in the Anderson Galleries sale of John L. Clawson's collection of Elizabethan literature, "I was only able to obtain four out of the twenty-eight within the limits." For good measure, he added that one item "was secured by Mr. Folger for $4,000 on his unlimited bid." Huntington's limit for the lot was only $1,200. Rosenbach added that he bought a number of other important items "for stock," on which he felt "it only right and just to give you the first offer"; he was willing to sell them at cost plus the "usual commission" of 10 percent.

"You must realize that much water has passed under the bridge since the Huth Sale of 1912," Rosenbach continued, getting to the central point of the letter. "The group of new collectors, recognizing that the Clawson Sale was probably the last opportunity to secure fine English books, was willing to pay good prices for them. I really advise that you purchase this lot of the greatest rarities, as they are nearly all unique and well worth the prices at which they sold." Rosenbach stressed that he remained "always desirous of pleasing you, and I thought that even at a sacrifice of my own interests, I would purchase the lots that you desired, if the prices were at all within reason." He added that he had recently purchased some other "collections abroad of the greatest interest," one of which included the only known poem in Spenser's handwriting. Rosenbach then asked if he could come out to California the following month for a visit. Huntington's brief reply on June 4, 1926, must have been devastating. "I have received your letter of May 27th and shall be very glad to have you come towards the end of the month, though I would not expect you to bring any books with you!"

The next day, a formal letter from Leslie E. Bliss, now acting librarian, made reference to an invoice for $539.99 received from the Rosenbach Company a week earlier. "You will pardon us if we call your attention to the fact that there is an error in addition." Rosenbach's bookkeeper apparently had overcharged by ninety-nine cents. "We have corrected this to read $539.00 and for this latter amount you have been certified and remittance will be made to you in due course. Kindly reconcile your books in this connection and let us know that you have so attended to the matter, for which courtesy we thank you." Early in 1927 the bookseller's older brother, Philip Rosenbach, went to California and tried to arrange a meeting. Huntington sent him a letter at the Biltmore Hotel in Los Angeles, and apologized for not receiving him personally. "Mr. Hapgood, who expects to see you tomorrow, will tell you a bit more concerning the attitude I have taken on the question of buying books."

During the eight heady years Huntington and Rosenbach did business with each other, the California collector had authorized payments of $4,333,610 to the Rosenbach Company. Now, except for a few odds and ends, the adventure was over. On May 23, 1927, three months after Philip Rosenbach's California trip, Henry E. Huntington died of cancer in a Philadelphia hospital at the age of seventy-seven. Ten days after Huntington's death, a letter to Rosenbach from Bliss clarified the attitude of the new regime: "Two boxes are in from you today. As soon as they are checked in I will pass the bill for payment, but I cannot promise a check at once, due to changed conditions here, the fact of there being no quorum of the trustees in California at present, and various other disturbing circumstances. However, you may rest assured that your account will be settled as soon as possible."

Huntington was gone, but as Rosenbach had explained to the tycoon a year before his death, new collectors had arrived on the scene, and many of them were engaging his services. He developed fruitful relationships with William Andrews Clark of Los Angeles; Carl H. Pforzheimer of New York; John Hinsdale Scheide of Titusville, Pennsylvania; Lessing J. Rosenwald of Philadelphia; and Owen D. Young of New York, chairman of General Electric Company. Rosenbach maintained a cordial but correct relationship with all of his customers, and his correspondence with J. P. Morgan's librarian, Belle da Costa Greene—who often began her letters to him with "Dear Rosey" or "Dear Rosie"—seems especially at ease.

On March 21, 1928, Miss Greene wrote Rosenbach at the Hotel Carlton in London, asking him to acquire on her behalf, if possible, the original manuscript for Lewis Carroll's *Alice in Wonderland*. "I should like to buy it *personally* and give it to the Library as I have always wanted to present something to the Library, and it is of course a book in which the Trustees would not be interested or find of sufficient importance for them to consider its purchase. I do not doubt that it is rather silly of me to want to do this, but as you know I *am very silly!*" She asked Rosenbach to cable her with information as to its probable selling price. "It may be such an insignificant looking little thing that even I could not justify my own weakness in buying it."

Rosenbach did buy the item, but not at the "reasonable price" Miss Greene suggested, and not, as it turned out, for the Morgan Library. In a tense three-way contest at Sotheby's on April 3, 1928, Rosenbach scrupulously avoided making any advances on Bernard Quaritch Ltd., which was bidding for the British Library, but once that firm withdrew, he entered the competition and secured the prize with an astounding bid of £15,400. After his highly publicized offer to sell the nostalgic treasure to the British nation at cost was unsuccessful, he brought the manuscript home and allowed it to go on an exhibition tour of several East Coast libraries. Finally he sold the *Alice* to Eldridge R. Johnson of New Jersey, president of the Victor Talking Machine Company. Eighteen years later Johnson's estate put the manuscript up for auction, and Rosenbach bought it back for $50,000. He then organized a fundraising drive and gave the manuscript to Great Britain on behalf of the American people.

"It is now dawning upon us that we have been living in the most wonderful period of opportunity that book collectors have ever had," Rosenbach wrote in *Publishers Weekly* in 1923. "It is also clear that we are never likely to see such a period again, for the rarities that have been passing through the market have been bought mainly by book lovers and collectors, not speculators, and will largely go into great university and public libraries, never to appear again at public or private sale." On this point he was only mostly correct; much of what he had sold did stay out of circulation, but a lot became available again.

As 1928 drew to a close, the biggest rare-book event since the sale of Robert Hoe's library seventeen years earlier took shape with the news that Jerome Kern, the famous composer of such musical comedies as *The Red Petticoat* and *Very Warm for May,* would be selling his library. Among his treasures were Shelley's own annotated copy of *Queen Mab* and a letter in which Edgar Allan Poe quotes Elizabeth Barrett Browning's enthusiastic response to "The Raven." "As my collection has grown, books have not only fascinated me, they have enslaved me," Kern said in his announcement of the sale. "As rare books became rarer, I battled for them, treasured them, and so became a collector. I never captured a prize, the prize always captured me." When Mitchell Kennerley, the owner of Anderson Galleries, proposed a sale of his books, "in a flash I saw an escape from my slavery."

Unlike the Hoe sale, which featured more than 16,000 books and manuscripts and took nineteen months to complete, the Kern collection included 1,484 lots to be offered in two five-part sessions, the first to run from January 7 to 10, 1929, the second from January 21 to 24. When the first session was held on January 7, Kern's operetta, *Show Boat,* was playing to full houses on Broadway, but the most sought-after seats around town that night were at Anderson Galleries.

Dr. Rosenbach set a fast pace by spending $14,200 for five Jane Austen lots, including $3,600 for *Sense and Sensibility.* For $17,500, he acquired a fine copy of the first edition of Elizabeth Barrett Browning's earliest known published work, the poem "The Battle of Marathon" (1820). Thirty Robert Browning items promptly brought in a total of $34,085. Rosenbach's winning bid of $23,500 for an inscribed second edition of Robert Burns's *Poems, Chiefly in the Scottish Dialect,* was the most spent that night on a single item and attracted the biggest headlines the following morning.

Kern told Kennerley before the sale that he would be pleased to realize $650,000 or $700,000 for his books; by the time auctioneer Anthony Bade got halfway through the B's that first night, they had made $166,363 toward the goal. When the composer heard the figures that were being bid, he sent Kennerley a telegram: "MY GOD WHATS GOING ON." The second session brought in another $175,071.50, and Kern's $700,000 goal had been passed by the time they reached the letter *H.* When the last item was hammered down on January 24, $1,729,462.50 had been spent, a record $1,165.41-per-lot average that stood as a record for more than fifty years.

"For many of the volumes it was said that I had paid excessive prices, even ridiculously high prices," Kern said shortly after the sale. "Now it is said that the prices paid for these same volumes were high, but in a few years I believe that it will not seem so." He said there were dealers who used to say he sometimes spent too much money for books. "I can recall times when ripples of laughter went round the auction rooms [when] prices that I paid seemed too high." When the stock market crashed nine months after the sale, Kern's satisfied smile of vindication may well have become a prayerful sigh of relief.

The biggest buyer by far was Dr. Rosenbach, who spent $410,000 at the Kern sale; some of the material was earmarked for his general stock, and he spent $198,210 as agent for Owen D. Young, the chairman of General Electric. Young later paid Rosenbach an additional $175,000 for more Kern books. On October 18, 1929, eleven days before the great stockmarket crash, Kern wrote Young to find out if he had bought the *Queen Mab*. "I am obliged to confess that I lacked two things, both of which were essential—'courage and money,' " Young wrote back. "Had there been no difficulty on the second, I think I might have screwed up on the first. I find it is easier to raise the first than the second. Notwithstanding that I missed *Queen Mab* I think it must be true that I was still by all odds the largest single buyer at your sale."

Four years earlier, Young had become the proud owner of a previously unrecorded copy of Edgar Allan Poe's scarcest work, *Tamerlane and Other Poems*, through the oddest of circumstances. In the summer of 1925, Vincent Starrett wrote an article for *The Saturday Evening Post* on rare books titled, "Have you a *Tamerlane* in your attic?" An elderly widow in Worcester, Massachusetts, named Ada S. Dodd looked, and discovered that she had such an item in her possession. She wrote the Boston bookseller Charles Goodspeed, who contacted Owen Young. In return for $17,500, the work entered his collection.

Young had invested heavily in General Electric and Radio Corporation of America stock, and when the market collapsed, his collecting came to an abrupt halt. "I have made it a rule now for two years not to spend any money in the rare book field until this period of terrific personal need for food and clothes is over," he wrote a bookseller who had offered him some attractive items in 1931. "I would not feel justified in spending any money for anything, no matter how rare or how cheap just now, because such items instead of giving me pleasure in the future would always rise to curse me as a luxury purchase when luxuries should not be bought." Young kept his ten thousand books for another decade, but in light of his debts of close to $3 million, his book-hunting days were over. When conditions were at their bleakest, and the temptation to sell strongest, he wrote a memo to himself, which his daughter, Josephine Young Case, preserved:

> Many years ago I conceived the notion of collecting from time
> to time rare and valuable books. In every generation there
> should be volunteers to take such treasures and to hold them
> for a time as trustees. The trust imposes an obligation to select
> carefully, to make sure that the items are sound and true and

not impostors, to care for them not only carefully but lovingly; to make them available for use by scholars and finally to pass them on to other volunteers.

In 1941 Young found a way to satisfy his deep sense of custodianship and ease his mounting debt. A wealthy Manhattan collector, a surgeon named Dr. Albert A. Berg, agreed to pay him $375,000 for a half interest in the books, which both men then presented to the New York Public Library, where the volumes joined the great collection Dr. Berg had turned over to the institution the year before.

Thousands of letters are preserved in the Rosenbach Company archives in Philadelphia, and if one feature is apparent in most of them, it is the tremendous respect Dr. Rosenbach always expressed for books. There is nothing artificial or transparent about his enthusiasm, and in the case of one distinguished client, his ardor was matched by that of a man of grace and eloquence. At his death in 1944 at the age of sixty-seven, Frank J. Hogan was remembered by the *Washington Daily News* as "the greatest trial lawyer in the country." Among his many courtroom triumphs was the stunning acquittal of California oil baron Edward L. Doheny in the Teapot Dome scandal. "He knew his law, he was persuasive as all get-out before a jury with his wit and charming personality and his intuitive knowledge of dramatic effect. He was a fun-poker, but his wit was always kindly and everybody knew him and liked him, from elevator boys, hack drivers, traffic cops to stage, screen and radio stars and Supreme Court justices."

All these were impressive compliments for a man who dropped out of school at the age of twelve, worked in a dry-goods store for two dollars a week, went to night school, earned a scholarship to Georgetown University Law School, and graduated at the top of his class. On July 18, 1931, when he was fifty-four years old—at the top of his profession and about to leave on a business trip to California—Hogan wrote his first letter to the Rosenbach Company. He had just started to buy rare books, and the purpose of the letter was to pay for some material he had acquired the previous day. "In September, I promise myself a return visit, when once again I shall want to talk Shakespeare Folio and have the delightful sensation of handling some of your gems."

Ten days later Rosenbach wrote Hogan in Los Angeles to inform him he was following up on what must have been a suggestion from the lawyer; he was sending the oil baron's wife, Mrs. Estelle Doheny, "our four recent catalogues." He also sent Hogan an inscribed copy of *The Unpublishable Memoirs,* his collection of his own short stories published in 1917, along with an additional offer: "I note that you expect to be in Philadelphia again sometime in September and I am looking forward to this visit. I wish you would arrange to stop with me for the night at my home on DeLancey Street. My private collection is there, and knowing your appreciation of books I would be delighted to show it to you." Hogan promptly replied that only an "untimely death could possibly" stop him from accepting the invitation, "though I do think that just before I make that visit you should increase your insurance with coverage for all classes of risks." Almost overnight, a close relationship had been formed. "It *is* good to know you," Hogan wrote.

On December 30, 1931, Hogan wired the first of many telegrams he would cable over the next thirteen years to extend greetings of the season:

BEST WISHES FOR A GREAT NINETEEN THIRTY TWO STOP LET US HOPE THAT BEFORE WARM WEATHER THE WORD DEPRESSION WILL HAVE DISAPPEARED FROM DAILY CONVERSATION STOP

On January 19, 1932, Hogan scolded Rosenbach for causing him to stay awake the previous evening. "For the sleep I lost, you are responsible—or, to speak accurately, creditable. What an evening with the sixteen items from the two sales at Sotheby's! Like Nevin's 'Rosary,' 'I count them over one by one.' And I love them, every one." Hogan reminded Rosenbach that though he doubted the items could "throw you into an ecstasy," his own status as a novice warranted a bit of forgivable excitement: "I am an infant hardly more than a year old." A few weeks later, Hogan attempted to bring his account up to date: "I speak of temporarily getting out of debt: Does a book collecting addict ever get permanently out." Rosenbach responded by inviting Hogan to attend a talk he was giving at Philadelphia's Philobiblon Club, and then "come to the house afterwards and meet a few Philadelphia collectors. Do not forget, as Doctor Johnson said BRANDY FOR HEROES!!"

The friendship flourished, and, precious volume by precious volume, Frank Hogan built a magnificent collection of English and American literature. "I do not want to tempt you," Rosenbach wrote in 1932, "but I have secured the only perfect copy in existence of Meres' *Palladis Tamia,* 1598, the first book to contain a catalogue of Shakespeare's plays, and the most famous volume of Shakespeareana outside of the Folios and Quartos. Although collectors have hunted for a perfect copy for two hundred years all have been unable to obtain it." In "normal times," Dr. Rosenbach declared, the book would be worth "at least" $25,000. His offer: $9,875. "I advise you even in these difficult times to make every effort to obtain this most precious volume, and the greatest addition to any Shakespearian collection."

Hogan did buy the Meres, but not for another four years, when he bought it and a first-edition copy of the *Faerie Queene,* in which Edmund Spenser had written a sonnet to Elizabeth Boyle, for $46,000. "Well, I hope I can pay you some day," he said when agreeing to the deal, but the times had been tough for everyone. "I am as hard up as the devil and I would appreciate it more than I can say if you send me a check for $4,180 for the last auction purchases," Rosenbach wrote in 1933. Hogan replied good-naturedly, asking if he could "appropriate to myself your touching words 'I am as hard up as the devil.' You are neither alone, isolated, nor peculiar. I ask myself why I incur debts when I am, at least temporarily, as frozen as the American Ice Company's best product." He enclosed a check for $2,500 with the hope "that this will help a little and, to quote O. Henry, 'gimme just a little more time, wontcha?'" Besides, he added, "I'd hate to be entirely out of debt to you."

Barely a month had passed before Hogan was writing again, explaining in a lengthy letter that he was leaving for Los Angeles to represent Edward Doheny in a proceeding "which involves more money than there is at present in the world's rare book business," and if successful, "I will again become a factor among collectors." With that as a tempting preliminary, Hogan got directly to the point: "There is nothing I so much want as a good complete First Folio." A famous copy was coming up for sale shortly at Sotheby's in London, and he wanted Rosenbach's advice. "I would be willing to blindfold my eyes, stop up my ears, have my mouth gagged and follow *your* judgment," he wrote. "I do feel inclined to send you a bid on the First Folio even if I have to mortgage the old home to pay for it." Nonetheless, if his finances did not improve, then he promised to urge Mrs. Doheny to go after it for her own collection. "I know that I ought to have a worthwhile First Folio and I think that Mrs. Doheny also should be the owner of one. I do not want anything less than a copy the condition of which you would unhesitatingly approve." Rosenbach cabled Hogan the following month to report that he had examined the book, and found it superb: "Folger has no copy as fine." He estimated it likely would sell for $42,000 to $60,000, an "outstanding bargain" for a superior item that "in good times" would be worth at least $125,000: "Use every effort to obtain it and you will never regret it," he declared. "Pawn the crown jewels if necessary."

Hogan did not pawn any jewelry, but he did arrange payment through the Riggs National Bank in Washington, and he got not only the cherished First Folio for £14,400 sterling, but also, for an additional £2,440, a Second Folio and a Third Folio. "It gave me a real thrill when I received the cable Friday we had been able to secure the great First Folio of Shakespeare in the collection of Lord Rosebery," Rosenbach wrote on July 11, 1933. "You are right about your collection of Shakespeariana. Even today it ranks among the greatest in private hands and you have bought them at specially low prices, which is something after all. I am as proud of your collection as you are!" Bogged down in legal matters on the West Coast, Hogan found separation from his new books unbearable. "I am still thrilled beyond expression about the prospect of seeing them, holding them, owning them."

Their correspondence continued warmly over the next seven years, with Hogan frequently writing long, thoughtful, erudite letters, despite his workload. Though he began collecting late in life, Hogan immersed himself in the fraternity. When Hogan gave Rosenbach commissions on lots at auction, he included detailed explanations of why he wanted certain books and why they were important to him. His letters also show him constantly asking Rosenbach about other collectors, William

Andrews Clark, Carl Pforzheimer, and A. Edward Newton among them. "Fate, and the traveling man's activities incident to the presidency of the American Bar Association, have been keeping us apart," he wrote Arthur Houghton, Jr., in 1938, sending a carbon copy to Rosenbach. "Some day in the near future I hope we shall meet because it's contrary to nature for two so deeply interested in the same fine things as English literature not to personally know each other. I do feel that I know you, though we have not met."

It is clear, too, that Hogan was largely responsible for encouraging Estelle Doheny to assemble what in five decades would become the most expensive library ever sold at auction, $37.4 million realized in six sales conducted between 1987 and 1989 by Christie's in New York. On December 18, 1934, Hogan wrote Rosenbach to thank him for coming up with a splendid idea for the holidays: "I was just casting around (in my mind) for something appropriate to send to Mrs. Doheny for this Christmas when there came to my desk today your letter of the 17th informing me that you have a wonderful copy of the Jensen Bible in the original binding, 1476. While I hadn't intended to send a Christmas present costing as much as $785, the suggestion is such a good one that I hereby fall." Fifty-three years later, Hogan's thoughtful gift for the wife of his most important client went on the block as Lot 89 in the first Doheny sale and sold for $33,000.

Collectors have always fancied gossip, and though most is passed in conversation, some occasionally makes its way into correspondence. During the hot summer of 1934, with Hogan working in California on Doheny matters and Rosenbach taking care of business on the East Coast, letters were the only way for them to discuss what was becoming the biggest book scandal of the century. A book with the deceptively innocent title *An Enquiry Into the Nature of Certain Nineteenth Century Pamphlets* was about to be published simultaneously in the United States and England, and the weeks leading up to its release were fraught with speculation. John Carter and Graham Pollard, two young British bibliographers, had done something unprecedented: they had employed modern scientific methods to determine that a number of imprints previously thought to be authentic first editions were in fact forgeries, and the evidence pointed to the English dealer and collector Thomas J. Wise, one of the most prestigious bookmen of the age, as the perpetrator.

"I am sure you will enjoy the first published report on the Wise forgeries which will shake the literary world," Rosenbach wrote on July 2, then boldly added that "it has been an old story to me." He claimed that about fifteen years earlier, he had determined that a privately published edition of Elizabeth Barrett Browning's *Sonnets from the Portuguese* was a forgery, "and I blamed it on Mr. Thomas J. Wise." Rosenbach bolstered his contention by noting how he advised Carl H. Pforzheimer to sell his copy of the pamphlet, and that the New York collector realized $1,000 in the transaction. "The reason I never said very much about it was that Thomas J. Wise is an old friend of mine and I do not like to injure anyone's reputation." Rosenbach's offer to send Hogan an advance copy of the new exposé was accepted immediately by cable. A few weeks after sending the book, Rosenbach wrote again: "I do not think there is any doubt that Wise was the forger of the pamphlets," he declared, and wondered, "As you are a keen judge of the evidence I would like to know your opinion, not necessarily at the present time, but after I have supplied you with additional comments as they appear in the press."

A week later, the man regarded as America's finest trial lawyer sent Rosenbach his opinion: "Manifestly Pollard and Carter endeavored throughout to be ultra-conservative. I approached the reading of the book hoping they would not prove their case. I laid it down, after a most careful reading of every page, knowing that they had fully proved it. With sorrow and reluctance I came to the conclusion that the evidence overwhelmingly proved not only the forgeries but that Thomas J. Wise is the forger." Even though the information was largely circumstantial, Hogan concluded that

by a process of elimination, and an overwhelming mass of evidence, the authors pointed accusingly and unerringly to Wise in a way to leave no doubt in the mind of the careful reader, first, that Wise did the forging; and second, that Pollard and Carter knew that fact as certainly as anything can be known from a convincing chain of circumstances. Circumstantial evidence is often more convincing than is direct evidence. Witnesses often lie, circumstances seldom do.

Rosenbach replied with a three-page letter of his own. "I have known Thomas J. Wise for over twenty-five years," he wrote. "I hate to admit it but an old and dear friend is the forger." Once again, he claimed that he had been "the first to suspect him." Wise, he also explained, sold many of his bogus pamphlets to American collectors such as John H. Wrenn, John A. Spoor, Luther Livingston, and William Harris Arnold, leading Rosenbach to opine: "I do not like to think that he thought American collectors were more gullible than the English, but he did nevertheless." Though Rosenbach found it "a pity that a man of Mr. Wise's really fine attainments should have stooped so low," he thought there was room for compassion. "There is one thing about Mr. Wise, however, that will appeal to the collector's softer nature. It is his great love of books—no one loved them more than he and it was on this account I think and not a purely mercenary one that he committed these forgeries. He would go to any length to obtain a fine item that would add luster to his collection. While we do not admire his tactics we cannot but have a spark of sympathy for him!"

Hogan wrote back in agreement, and suggested that Wise's motive was not money but recognition. As long as the scheme remained undiscovered, "the possession of a complete run of these unusual 'firsts' (almost pre-firsts, if such a thing could be) would be to Mr. Wise's prestige as a collector." Then he made a character judgment: "No one can read the introductions to the separate volumes of the Ashley Catalogue without realizing that Wise gloried in adulation. To be referred to as the first of modern collectors was quite apparently the man's ambition. To be looked up to as the supreme authority, the last word, in the authenticity of rarities, was something he greatly prized." Few people outside the book world knew anything about Thomas J. Wise. "I do not know the man and of course never heard of him until I began to court bankruptcy by entering the ranks of collectors," Hogan allowed. "Some strange mental quirk led him to do a really petty thing which henceforth forever will cloud his name and make odious his memory. Few will recall that, this unexplainable deviation aside, he undoubtedly was a real lover and a great collector of books."

Toward the end of the 1930s, with another world war at hand, Hogan's collecting began to slow down, though Rosenbach kept enticing him with rarities. Hogan admitted that the mention in one letter of a *Par-*

adise Lost in its original binding gave him "a thrill. That item has eluded me successfully since I began collecting." A pristine copy of Milton's epic poem eventually entered his collection in December 1937. To the public at large, Rosenbach described "my dear friend Frank J. Hogan" in one of his magazine essays as an "energetic and unregenerate book-lover." People found out just how much the eloquent trial lawyer loved books shortly after his death on May 15, 1944, when his will was read. Hogan did not have to explain to anyone why he chose "to sell at auction in the City of New York" his magnificent library, but he did nonetheless:

> I had thought of bequeathing my valuable books and collection of autographs and literary manuscript material, including my collection of first and rare editions of English and American literature, to some institution to be permanently kept together as a collection, but this idea I have abandoned in favor of a plan that will accomplish their dispersion among those coming after me, who will experience, as I have felt, a profound happiness and satisfaction in possessing these precious monuments of human thought and progress. There is something sacred in the spiritual and intimate companionship of a book, and I do not deem it fitting that these friends of many happy hours should repose in unloved and soulless captivity. Rather, I would send them out into the world again to be the intimates of others whose loving hands and understanding hearts will fill the place left vacant by my passing.

The American Golden Age of Book Collecting effectively ended with the Crash of 1929, but collectors such as Lessing J. Rosenwald, Thomas W. Streeter, Arthur A. Houghton, Jr., Robert H. Taylor, H. Bradley Martin, Estelle Doheny, Seymour Adelman, William H. Scheide, Clifton Waller Barrett, and Donald and Mary Hyde quietly but effectively continued gathering with spirit and with taste. Some libraries returned to the marketplace, others went to institutions, and a few remained in private hands. But the cycle continued.

In 1933, when America was mired in the Great Depression, Paul Jordan-Smith, a California critic and bibliophile, advised his readers to pay attention and have faith:

This is no time for the collector to quit his books. He may have to quit his house, abandon his trip to Europe and give away his car; but his books are patiently waiting to yield their comfort and provoke him to mirth. They will tell him that banks and civilizations have smashed before; governments have been on the rocks, and men have been fools in all ages. But it is all very funny. The gods laugh to see such sport, and why should we not join them?

Part
Two

6

To Have and to Have No More

For ten years near the end of the millennium, a phenomenon known as the 1980s created unexpected opportunities for book-collecting enthusiasts and evoked stirring images of the good old days. Bolstered by a robust economy, aggressive new collectors satisfied their taste for beautiful objects with a ready willingness to acquire them, whatever the cost. In response, many established owners found temptation too enticing to resist, and rarities once thought out of circulation forever suddenly appeared on the market. Price records were broken, most dramatically in antiques and the fine arts, but just as impressively in books.

Private libraries were no longer the exclusive preserve of the few. While soaring prices made paintings too costly for most people to own, books were relatively affordable, and as antiquarian fairs gained in popularity, they were much easier to obtain. For many participants, collecting meant acquiring the first trade editions of favorite contemporary authors: proven novelists such as John Updike, Anne Tyler,

225

William Kennedy, and Toni Morrison, respected poets such as James Merrill, John Ashbery, and Amy Clampitt, or popular genre writers such as Stephen King, Ray Bradbury, and Sara Paretsky.

For all the excitement, though, what recalled the grand spirit of the Golden Age most was not the new wave of collectors, but a thrilling sequence of auctions that offered bibliophiles and dealers a few rare chances at coveted treasures. Three remarkable library sales—two occasioned by the deaths of prominent collectors, the other instigated by a mysterious partnership under a veil of intense secrecy—created terrific excitement. While the numbers are impressive enough in their own right—$37.4 million in 1987–1989 for the Estelle Doheny collection, $35.7 million in 1989–1990 for H. Bradley Martin's collection, and $16.2 million in 1989 for the Garden Ltd.—what made the auctions especially memorable was that so much superior material became available over so short a period of time.

A window of opportunity to build an exceptional library had opened, and ample "disposable income" was available for just such an enterprise. "From where I sit, a hundred million dollars is not a lot of money," David Redden, a senior vice president at Sotheby's in New York and for a number of years the executive in charge of rare books sales, said a few weeks after the results of the Garden Ltd. sale had begun to settle in. "Sixteen-point-two million dollars for the Garden collection is tremendously gratifying, but just twenty-four hours before those books went up for sale, we sold *one* painting in the same room for twenty-one million. And it was not a master painting by any means, it was by Willem de Kooning, a *living* artist. That's five million dollars more than the Garden totaled, and the Garden was one of the most successful book auctions ever."

Bart Auerbach, a veteran New York bookseller and a principal consultant for Christie's, agreed. In May of 1990, he noted, a Japanese businessman paid over $160 million in one week for two paintings, $82.5 million for Vincent van Gogh's *Portrait of Dr. Gachet* at Christie's, and $78.2 million for Pierre-Auguste Renoir's *Le Moulin de la Galette* at Sotheby's. He wondered what might have happened if Tokyo real estate tycoon Ryoei Saito's taste in collectibles had been inclined toward books instead of art.

"For what that man paid for those two paintings, he could have built one of the finest private libraries in the world," Auerbach said. And that would have included a beautiful building, a staff, and a sustaining endowment. "All he had to tell his agent was one thing—'Keep your paddle in the air'—and it would have all been his." Saito certainly acquired "two nice paintings for his walls," Auerbach acknowledged, but "for a lot less money he could have gone down as one of the great book collectors of the twentieth century."

On November 1, 1994, almost five years to the day of the Garden Ltd. sale, Bart Auerbach and I stood in Christie's Park Avenue gallery with several hundred spectators and watched as a contingent of Italian bankers attempted to bring back to their country a seventy-two-page notebook containing more than three hundred illustrations and scientific writings compiled from 1506 to 1510 by Leonardo da Vinci. The contest to acquire this landmark of creativity, called Codex Hammer since 1980 in honor of its most recent owner, the late chairman of Occidental Petroleum, Armand Hammer, provided an historic case study of just what Auerbach was talking about.

Auctioneer Stephen C. Massey opened the bidding at $5.5 million. Within fifteen seconds, the presale estimate of $10 million had been passed, and advances were being made in $1 million increments. After two-and-a-half minutes of spirited competition, Massey hammered the book down for $28 million to a private collector bidding anonymously by telephone; with a commission for the auction house added, the total price for the document was $30.8 million, a record for a book or manuscript sold at auction.

William H. Gates III, the founder and chairman of Microsoft Corporation and one of the wealthiest persons in the world, is not known as a book collector, yet his acquisition of the manuscript, announced the next day, seemed perfectly appropriate. The notebook, written in Leonardo's distinctive backward style, contains such speculations as why the sky is blue and why fossils can be found on mountaintops and predicts the invention of the submarine and the steam engine. Gates said he would display the manuscript in Italy before installing it in his 37,000-square-foot estate on the shores of Lake Washington near Seattle. "I have always had a tremendous respect for Leonardo da Vinci's intellectual coupling of science and art," the billionaire said. "It's very gratifying to share an intellectual treasure of this magnitude with the world."

When Carrie Estelle Betzold Doheny died in 1958, she left several monuments. Her three abiding passions had been the memory of her husband, a California oil baron, Edward Laurence Doheny, from whom she inherited a substantial fortune in 1935, her faith, and her books. Her faith was expressed through gifts to numerous seminaries, hospitals, and religious charities. In 1939, Pope Pius XII recognized Doheny's generosity by making her a countess of the Roman Catholic Church, the first such title granted to a Southern California woman (resulting in the nickname the Countess). The following year, she was able to pay homage to all of her interests with one sweeping gesture. Acting on the suggestion of the archbishop of Los Angeles, she commissioned the architect Wallace Neff to construct a building in Spanish mission style architecture at St. John's Seminary in Camarillo, California, to be the Edward Laurence Doheny Memorial Library.

On the ground floor was the seminary's working library; the second level was reserved for Mrs. Doheny's sixteen thousand rare books and manuscripts. Her most renowned possessions included a collection of incunabula, old Bibles, and religious manuscripts, as well as a run of English and American literature and superior material relating to the exploration and settlement of California. When she died, the entire collection passed to the diocese, with the stipulation that it be kept for at least twenty-five years after her death. In 1986, the diocese announced a consignment to Christie's in New York—the Doheny collection— with the proceeds earmarked for the education and training of priests.

While that sale was taking place, H. Bradley Martin, the heir of a New York steel fortune who started gathering books while attending Christ Church College at Oxford during the 1920s, died at the age of eighty-two. Martin had maintained two enviable libraries, one in Manhattan, the other at a Georgian estate in Virginia called Rose Hill. For years, there had been talk that he wanted his books to go to some institution. Martin's remarkable collection of ornithology alone was generally regarded as the finest anywhere, institutional or private. But his will made no such provisions, and a year after his death, on June 6, 1989, the Martin library went on the block at Sotheby's in New York. When the nine-part sale concluded in June 1990, $35.7 million had been spent for some ten thousand books and manuscripts.

Both sales were spread out over several sessions and recorded totals that had never been approached in book auctions before. Pride of place in the Doheny sale was given to the Old Testament volume of the Gutenberg Bible; top billing in the Martin dispersal was a set of Audubon's *Birds of America*. In all, twenty-six thousand books went under the hammer. Yet the Doheny and Martin averages pale when compared with those of lesser-known dispersals that took place during the same period. In fewer than twenty-four hours on November 9 and 10, 1989, $16.2 million was spent for 308 "high spots" in world literature, an average of $52,815 per lot, which exceeded by far the averages logged in either the Doheny or Martin sales ($15,967 and $11,053, respectively). This was the sale of the Garden Ltd. collection, an auction that above all others recalled the reckless abandon of the Jerome Kern sale sixty years earlier on the eve of the Crash.

Beyond the impressive numbers and the excitement it generated was the fact that the Garden Ltd. collection had been built by the most baffling book collector to come along in decades. Haven O'More was a complete unknown. Even his name was a curiosity, rumored to be an anagram, for "HAVE NO MORE."

He first attracted international attention in the fall of 1979 when he bought impressively at the London sale of an enviable collection of books gathered over a span of forty years by Arthur Houghton, Jr., the Steuben glass heir whose most enduring monument is a special collections library at Harvard University that bears his name. "Haven basically swept what he wanted at the Houghton sale," Stephen C. Massey, director of rare books at Christie's in New York, said. "That really is what made the Garden sale so thoroughly magnificent ten years later, that those Houghton copies—those books people thought were out of circulation for the remainder of their lifetimes—had come back once again."

Why Arthur Houghton suddenly decided to sell his books in three comprehensive sales between June 13, 1979 and June 12, 1980, has never been fully explained. He was a principal benefactor of the Houghton Library at Harvard University and the donor of some exceptional John Keats material to the university as well, so many people thought his personal collection one day would go to his alma mater. Instead, while still in his seventies and a full ten years before his death, Houghton not only decided to sell his books, but he chose to sell them in England.

Whatever his motivation, fabulous treasures assumed to be destined for institutions came onto the market. O'More had been buying important books for several years prior to the Houghton sale, but most of his purchases were negotiated privately through booksellers. In 1976, for instance, he quietly paid the New York bookseller Lew David Feldman $150,000 for the 1543 presentation copy of Nicolaus Copernicus's *De Revolutionibus Orbium Coelestium,* previously owned by Harrison Horblit. The Houghton sale, by contrast, was held in an international arena amid intense competition. Represented by John Fleming, O'More created a stir at the Houghton sale by paying premium prices for twenty-two magnificent items.

While O'More's activity in London represented a dramatic debut, it did not come as a complete surprise to Stephen Massey, a savvy fourth-generation bookman whose great-grandfather, grandfather, and father had all been involved in the London book trade. If anything, it confirmed an urgency the auctioneer had sensed when he met O'More for the first time in April 1978. "This elegantly dressed man arrived at our Park Avenue gallery one morning and was making a scene," Massey recalled. "Because he was demanding to see a book, I got the call to go downstairs and deal with him." As Massey approached the disturbance, O'More shouted a single sentence: "Do you *know* who I am?" Massey replied that he did not have the slightest idea. "*I* am Haven O'More," the man declared, "and I want to see this *book.*"

The book in question was nothing less than a Gutenberg Bible, a superb two-volume set of the forty-two-line masterpiece printed at Mainz in Germany in the 1450s, and consigned to Christie's for immediate sale by the General Theological Seminary of New York. Though prospective buyers were allowed to examine the lot prior to auction, there were certain rules, and since the man's behavior that April morning was rude, Massey decided to enforce them. If Haven O'More wanted to see a catalogued item, he had to make an appointment.

"I wasn't worried about losing him," Massey said, "because if the book's good enough, they will always call back—they will *crawl*—if they really *want* the book." Once O'More backed down, though, the two men shook hands and Massey showed him the Bible after all. O'More arrived at the sale a few days later with the noted San Francisco bookseller Warren Howell and was the underbidder on the Bible, finishing second to Bernard Breslauer, who paid $2.2 million in behalf of the Württembergische Landesbibliothek in Stuttgart, Germany.

Had O'More prevailed, the Gutenberg Bible would have been included in the Garden Ltd. sale eleven years later, an auction Christie's made a determined effort to secure but lost to Sotheby's "in straight combat." "I breathed a sigh of relief on that score," Massey said. "If there had been a Gutenberg Bible in there, it would have been a thirty-one-million-dollar sale. The way prices were that night? A perfect Gutenberg Bible? Who knows. I am just thankful they didn't have it, because that would have been unbearable!"

Exactly where such an impressive buyer had come from became the subject of wild rumor. Some whispered that O'More had worked for the Central Intelligence Agency during the 1950s and had been given a new identity; others said he had once been an actor. O'More, who is still alive, has claimed to some that he served on General Douglas MacArthur's staff during the Korean War, where he supposedly survived a frightful combat experience. To others he has spoken of having invented sophisticated weapons systems for the U.S. Defense Department. O'More was also purported to be a poet, an architect, and a philosopher. Some more concrete information, known by a few, was that he was president of a foundation in Massachusetts called the Institute of Traditional Science. However, a look at its organizational papers is not illuminating: the foundation is committed to the transmission of "pure knowledge." O'More has also bragged that he can read ancient manuscripts in Greek and Hebrew and is adept at several martial arts, including arcane skills once practiced by American Indian warriors in the Old West. That melodramatic pose did not seem to bother anybody much, though; what did disturb the established collectors was O'More's boast—that he was the greatest book collector alive.

Thirty-four city blocks away from Christie's, in modest offices at 104 East Twenty-fifth Street, Swann Galleries mounts about thirty auctions a year. No van Goghs or Renoirs are offered there, no Chinese porce-

lain, no exotic tapestries—but solid values in books, prints, photographs, and ephemera. "You walk into Christie's or Sotheby's this
afternoon with a fifteen-hundred-dollar book, and see what they say,"
Stephen Massey said. "Lovely book, they will say, but sorry, we can't
take it." But Swann's will be delighted to take it on consignment. "Our
bread and butter is the item that sells in the area of five hundred to two
thousand dollars," explained George S. Lowry, president of Swann's.
Partly because of this lower profile, Lowry got to see Haven O'More a
few years earlier than the fancier houses uptown.

"Haven O'More arrived like a fireball," Lowry recalled, speaking
of O'More's appearance on the book-collecting scene in the early seventies. "He absolutely lit up the sky. You pay attention when all of a
sudden some smartly dressed guy you haven't seen before is sitting in
your gallery and spending serious money on books. The man came in
with a ton of money, collected for ten years or so, and then disappeared. I'd been head of Swann three or four years when he came in
with his glamorous wife and bought up a lot of books. Nobody knew
who he was. I still don't know, but I was impressed." Lowry maintains
that in some respects, O'More actually shaped the rare-book market.
"He influenced it to the extent that people were orchestrating sales and
catalogues they thought would appeal to him. If you're in the business
like me, that scares you a little bit. You get scared because here you're
dealing with somebody and you have no idea what's going through his
head. But I have to say this about him. He always bought what he
wanted. He didn't come to shop. He came to buy."

Aside from his activity at auctions, O'More bought from booksellers like Hans P. Kraus and John Fleming of New York, and Warren
Howell of San Francisco, three deans of the book trade. O'More also
did business with Arthur Freeman of Bernard Quaritch Ltd. in London, and the bookseller Colin Franklin, near Oxford, England, both
of whom became friendly with him.

Whatever his background or his manners may have been, as soon as
it became evident that O'More was spending "serious money" on
books, dealers were pleased to serve him and even perpetuate his myth.
John Fleming, the New York bookseller who began in the trade as an
associate of Dr. A. S. W. Rosenbach during the 1930s, sold O'More
many treasures and acted as his agent at numerous auctions. Fleming

also introduced him to other important collectors, such as Arthur Houghton and William Scheide of Princeton, New Jersey. Houghton once invited Haven and Lorea O'More to spend a few days at his estate on Maryland's Eastern Shore, according to Stephen Massey. In Massachusetts, where he has lived since the late 1960s or early 1970s, O'More became a generous member of the Friends of Harvard College Library and attended dinners sponsored by Boston's venerable Club of Odd Volumes. He traveled extensively, and everywhere he went he gained access and aroused curiosity. A curator at the University of Chicago's John Crerar Library recalls that O'More once pulled a rare book on the history of science from the shelves and made a single haughty comment—that his own copy was "far superior."

For all his visibility, few felt they really knew the man, not the dealers who did business with him, not even the acquaintances who entertained him in their homes. Priscilla Juvelis, a bookseller who started working with John Fleming in 1979 and now owns her own shop in Cambridge, Massachusetts, said O'More was a total enigma. "Nobody knew anything about him," she said, not even Fleming, "who probably sold him more books than anyone else." She recalled what Fleming had ventured once about O'More's regal airs: "You have to forgive a man who loves books as much as Haven."

The New York bookseller Justin G. Schiller agrees. He talked with O'More briefly at a reception given by Bernard Quaritch Ltd. during the first Arthur Houghton sale and met him occasionally over the next ten years, once traveling to Boston to see O'More's William Blake materials. "Haven was a marvelous actor," Schiller said. "To my mind, he was a modern visionary. He tried to assemble the great books of learning. Regardless of his ego, the man loved his books. What impressed me about him was that he knew the books that he owned with an obvious degree of intimacy. But we never talked philosophy, and I knew very little of his background. Nobody did." And what was the source of the new connoisseur's wealth? Schiller had no idea. "John Fleming once told me that he would happily pay fifty thousand dollars to know where Haven got his money."

Christie's rare-book man, Stephen Massey, is one acquaintance who developed a friendship with O'More. After their first meeting in the Park Avenue lobby of Christie's in 1978, they began to see each other socially. "I would say I knew him very well," Massey said. "The truth is that I grew very fond of Haven. I used to see him whenever he came to New York at fairly frequent intervals. I'd have lunch with him on his own or with him and Lorea. I was upset when he told me he had to sell the books. He didn't tell me in so many words, but it was obvious that something was up. When he expressed some interest in the first Doheny sale, which we had in October of 1987, it was mild interest, and he didn't buy anything at all, so I knew then that something was not quite right. Soon afterward I heard he had dropped from sight."

In the summer of 1989, Massey was contacted by a Boston lawyer. "The man came to New York without identifying the name of his client at first, just saying he represented a partner in the Garden Ltd., and that they were looking for an appraisal prior to the dissolution of this partnership, which might require at some stage a sale of the Garden Ltd. This particular lawyer was exploring various angles about who should do an appraisal, and he came to us, among other people." The man accepted Massey's suggestion to assemble a team of experts that would include himself and several other specialists, and the appraisal was conducted in Boston, where the books were kept.

A terse press release announcing the sale in the fall of 1989 gave Haven O'More full credit for having "conceived and formed" the collection. However, a new player, a "private investor" named Michael Davis, was identified as the person who had "funded" it, to the great surprise of the book community. How such an unusual arrangement had come about, and what happened to break it up, remained a mystery. The right to mount the lucrative sale, moreover, was given to Sotheby's, the archrival of Christie's. Massey said this devastating turn of events came to pass because of a controversial innovation that became a major part of the auction business in the 1980s. "Sotheby's wrote a large check in advance," Massey said. "We valued the collection at nine million. That appraisal was accepted by everyone—including Sotheby's—but the lawyers for the Garden parties were lured in by a large check, a rather sizable advance of money in anticipation of the sale. I heard it was four and a half million dollars, half the appraisal."

Christie's had not offered an advance on the sale. At the time, it was against company practice. "I believe if we had been asked, we would have been prepared to do it, but we went out of the starting block advising against it, which was our policy prior to 1989. Our feeling had always been that if you have a capital involvement with the goods that you sell, it's potentially damaging to the sale. That is the argument we made. We even brought Lord Carrington over from London for this proposal. We were received by a battery of lawyers in Boston from both sides. I was shocked when Sotheby's got it."

Up to that time, Massey had never heard anything about a man named Michael Davis. "But we heard about him pretty quickly," he added. "Up to now, the Garden was Haven O'More."

Added to the mystery of the man who "conceived and formed" the Garden library were the many ironies that emerged from the auction itself. Most remarkable, perhaps, is that the only time these great books were ever united as a collection was when they were about to be sold at Sotheby's. Prior to those few exciting days, when the collection was displayed for the examination of prospective buyers, all items had been kept in two bank vaults in Boston.

Only two sentences about O'More's financing partner appear in the Garden Ltd. sale catalogue: "Michael Davis is a private investor. He is the sole limited partner of the Garden Ltd., and provided the funding for the Garden's collection of rare books and manuscripts." The three lines are printed on an otherwise blank page. Haven O'More, by contrast, submitted a lengthy statement that provides some clues about his personality, and a few facts about his life. At the top of the page set aside for his statement appears the photograph of a bronze sculpture. It is a face of Haven O'More. The eyes are closed, but not relaxed in sleep; the skin is taut, the lips are drawn down, as if the person is engaged in deep meditation. Beneath the photograph reads the following:

> Haven O'More was inspired from almost the very beginning of his life by learning history, the Bible, and that he is a direct descendant of three of the most illustrious men of all time. Early readings, even before starting to school, of Shakespeare, Milton, and the Bible, especially the New Testament in Greek with his father and mother, trained O'More to think and to feel in terms of high endeavor and noble service. His great aunt on his father's side was the family genealogist. She taught O'More as a child that he descends through his father from Haven

O'More the 4th century Celt king, poet-scholar, and warrior. Later he learned from her he also descends through his father from the saint and martyr, Sir Thomas More. Through his mother, he learned, he descends from General Thomas Jonathan ("Stonewall") Jackson.

O'More did not name his mother, his father, or the great aunt who served as family genealogist, and he did not say where any of them are from or where he was raised. He did not indicate where he went to school, though he did stress that for much of his life he had studied and mastered Yoga, a practice which he described in some detail. He also explained that in his unremitting pursuit of knowledge, he had lived, worked, and traveled throughout the United States, Europe, the Middle East, the Far East, and Mexico. He stated that he had served two tours in the United States Army, one in Europe, another in Asia, and that he not only had worked at conceptual levels in the fields of higher mathematics and the general sciences, but in the analysis of linguistic structures as well, with special attention focused on Celtic, Middle Eastern, and Far Eastern philosophical foundations. Without naming any companies or institutions, he claimed to have worked as an engineer in the aerospace industry developing sophisticated programs of advanced computer design, logic, and general systems analysis, under the auspices of the Department of Defense.

More specifically, O'More stated that he was the founder and director of research, education, and publishing for an organization called the Institute of Traditional Science, a non-profit foundation specializing in the transmission of "pure" knowledge. He also founded SADEV, a publishing company based in New York and affiliated, he stated, with the Aperture Foundation, the well-known and widely respected publisher of art and photography. O'More emphasized that he was the originator, co-founder and General Partner of the Garden Ltd. partnership. The name Garden, he added, comes from the Hebrew Et-HaGaN, meaning "The First Garden" ("The Enclosure," literally), a place where "all possibility is transcendent and equal to activity," and thus an appropriate designation for his library. O'More emphasized that from the beginning of his collecting activity he concentrated on acquiring material of the greatest rarity, in the most superb possible condition, and with the widest and most consequential influence on the endeavors of men and women everywhere, embracing noble accomplishments from the earliest civilizations to the present.

Celestial motives, O'More implied, energized his scheme from the beginning. Speaking of himself in the third person, he said he

> tried never for an instant to forget that . . . such works are imbued with life-giving forces and intelligence: being intelligent, they stand most in the future while giving form and passion to the present, and sending a living light to the past . . . For many years O'More has labored to . . . open up the way to build a new sacred city which would serve all mankind from this time forward . . . O'More's intention has always been to place the universal treasures he has collected . . . in a great research library. Haven O'More has . . . aimed that, through the library's mind-awakening holdings and activities, mankind would be newly inspired and illuminated in the necessary and all-important-way for the coming movement toward the stars.

Davis's and O'More's starkly contrasting biographical statements appear at the back of the catalogue, though O'More had his say at the front as well in the form of a ten-page prefatory essay titled "On the Mystery of the Book." There, he quoted freely from John Milton, Thomas Aquinas, Paul the Apostle, José Ortega y Gasset, John the Apostle, and Ecclesiastes. "Great or supreme works of the mind," he intoned, are the "spiritual heart pumping a life-giving blood through the veins of mankind, a higher blood before any physical blood, a spiritual blood providing purpose and continuity of meaning." Only by "touching, handling, reading, looking into, smelling—feasting on" the primary versions of these works is a person able to live and be one with the "very thing itself."

O'More proclaimed in summary that the collector of great books and manuscripts is the custodian of a family of "spiritual children," and that these blessed offspring are not merely beings of flesh and blood, but progeny conceived in the "Image of God." These cherished treasures, he declared, constitute the most precious inheritance of all mankind, as well as their "greatest hope and guide sent from the future." And how does one become such a collector? "More than anything, the collector is a lover," he concluded. "The collector is in love with reality or essence."

Apart from what one might surmise from his pomposity, his preten-
sion, and his shaky diction, these two statements, written on the eve of
the dissolution of a magnificent collection, raised in the minds of most
collectors many more questions than they answered about Haven
O'More. His "family of spiritual children," the "great love" in his life,
was being broken up; privately, he had told a number of acquaintances
that "they are forcing me to sell my children into slavery."

The morning of the sale, November 9, 1989, the late Robert L.
Nikirk, librarian of the Grolier Club, and I took a cab to Sotheby's for
a look at the books to be sold that night. As we moved through heavy
East Side traffic, Nikirk speculated about the Garden collection.
"There's something very fishy about this sale," he said. "What everyone is hearing is that Mr. Davis paid the bills but he never saw the
books. Mr. Davis paid out millions of dollars, and he was never
allowed to see his own books. How this happened nobody seems to
know, but what I hear is that he was beguiled. Have you read what Mr.
O'More says in the catalogue? That all these books were going into his
cosmic library? The man obviously is a nut, but people who are crazy
can also be very bright, and nobody denies that this man O'More has
a feeling for books. But what was it? Something religious? Hypnotism?
Brainwashing? Too many diet pills? These are the things people are
asking, and they are quite serious. Nobody knows except Sotheby's,
and they're not talking to anyone. It's unique in the history of book collecting."

Inside the huge auction house that occupies a full block between
Seventy-first and Seventy-second Streets on York Avenue, the first session was still eight hours away, yet no fewer than thirty people were
already in the third-floor exhibition hall, looking over the books.
Though everything was locked behind glass doors, prospective buyers
could ask to see certain items, and attendants would take them out for
inspection. By themselves in Case 10A were the Shakespeare folios of
1623, 1632, 1664, and 1685, described aptly in the catalogue as
"together the greatest books ever printed in English," and to be sold
that night as one lot. Elsewhere were gorgeous incunabula, breath-
taknig illuminations, and sturdy classics; the first recorded printings of
Boethius, Cicero, Euclid, and Plutarch; splendid editions of Copernicus, Ptolemy, Erasmus, Thomas à Kempis, Andreas Vesalius, John Mil-

ton, and Montaigne; the editio princeps of Plato and Dante, an exceedingly scarce first issue of Proust, a presentation copy of Thomas Jefferson's *Notes on the State of Virginia,* a "great vellum notebook" kept by
William Butler Yeats, a James Joyce manuscript, a journal kept by John
Locke, an unpublished diary maintained by Vaslav Nijinsky, and a
1522 edition of Martin Luther's "September Testament," a superb
folio bound in contemporary German pigskin and the only one to be
offered at auction in the twentieth century. Everything was there, and
it was dazzling.

David R. Godine, a Boston publisher and enthusiastic collector of
early printing, sat at a table delicately holding a fragile quarto. He had
removed his suit jacket, loosened his necktie, rolled up his shirtsleeves,
and was scribbling notes on a pad of paper with a short stubby pencil.
I caught his eye and we chatted briefly. "You know, if you haven't met
Haven, there he is over there," he said softly, and nodded toward a corner where a well-dressed man stood alone with a dark-haired woman.
I immediately went over and introduced myself. "A central thrust of
my project is to demonstrate how collectors through history have been
responsible for the preservation of knowledge," I said. "Without
Robert Cotton, there would be no *Beowulf* or Lindisfarne Gospels;
without Poggio Bracciolini there is no Quintilian."

Haven O'More looked me hard in the eyes as I spoke. "You know
about the pharaohs and their libraries?" he asked. I do indeed, I told
him; they are mentioned in my book. "The Greeks at Alexandria?" Of
course, I replied, such a study would be incomplete without them.
"Books to me are very alive, and very necessary in human existence,
and what goes *beyond* human existence," he said, and I nodded. "I
love these books very much. I have written about the collection and I
will write more. But my statement is in the catalogue."

At that point, three Sotheby's officials stepped up. They were quite
agitated. "We told the press no interviews," one of them said. "We were
clear on that." Before complying with their demand to leave the table, I
shook hands with O'More. He gave me his card and suggested that I
write him. In the weeks and months that followed I pursued him, but he
never responded, and we had no further contact. I did speak once with
his wife, who informed me that her husband had not been well and had
been undergoing therapy for an ailment she did not specify.

Later that evening, two hours before the first lot was scheduled to be sold, people began arriving for an elegant reception that Sotheby's had arranged for booksellers, preferred customers, and assorted bibliophiles, a festive event that allowed everyone to loosen up with a couple of cocktails before business got under way. "Fireworks are at hand," David Redden said confidently as the opening drew near. "There is tremendous excitement, the mood is absolutely electric. All the right people are here and we have some wonderful left bids." ("Left bids" are bids on various lots entrusted to the auctioneer by people who choose not to attend the sale or to bid anonymously by telephone; the auctioneer will make offers from the podium in their behalf up to the maximum amounts they have specified.)

A revolving dais had been set up on a small stage at the front of the gallery to showcase book lots as they were announced; above the stage an electronic tote board kept track of the bidding in seven currencies: the American dollar, the British pound, the French franc, the Japanese yen, the German mark, the Swiss franc, and the Italian lira. Several television cameras were poised to record the proceedings, and twenty-three telephones were in place to handle the outside bids.

One level above the gallery, in a cubicle that overlooked the proceedings, Haven O'More sat behind a tinted window and watched as his "family of spiritual children" was sold off. At the front of the hall, just a few yards away from chief auctioneer John Marion, a young man—Michael Davis—kept a running log of the results as they were displayed on the scoreboard.

Sotheby's had projected gross receipts of $9 million, but those giddy estimates were rendered irrelevant in fewer than sixty seconds. The very first lot that came up, an Egyptian papyrus scroll containing three chapters from *The Book of the Dead* and featuring a stunning illumination of Osirus, sold to H. P. Kraus, Inc., of New York, for $187,000, almost four times above the upper estimate; O'More had bought the three-thousand-year-old panel from Colin and Charlotte Franklin of Oxford, England, in 1982. In lot after lot, similar contests were joined, with similar results. David Redden's optimism had been justified; there was tremendous enthusiasm and the mood was electric.

The four Shakespeares were sold for $2.1 million to the New York collector Richard Manney—a million dollars above the upper estimate.

Enthusiastic rounds of applause broke out as that gavel and the one concluding the auction sounded. In each case, Michael Davis stood in the front row and led the ovation. Later that night, he celebrated by throwing a party for his friends high above Manhattan in the elegant Rainbow Room at Rockefeller Center.

Four hours after the final lot was sold at Sotheby's on November 10, 1989, the thirteenth annual Boston Antiquarian Book Fair was admitting a long line of waiting customers, a good number of them booksellers and collectors who had rushed up from New York to make the 7:30 P.M. opening. Richard Manney, the proud new owner of the Garden Shakespeare folios, was searching through various stalls for less costly finds. Booksellers Anne and David Bromer, buyers of several lots in the final Garden session, arrived at their booth with fifteen minutes to spare. "The glamour of a big sale is wonderful," James Cummins, Richard Manney's agent, said while tending his stand, "but this is the meat and potatoes of the business."

Though the gross receipts for the Garden sale were about half the numbers recorded for either Doheny or Martin, Stephen Massey considers it "by far" the "more perfect" sale. "You get it in July and you sell it in November," he explained with brisk precision. "You do it in two sessions, one at night, one the next day; in and out, one catalogue, gone. With Doheny and Martin you had thousands of lots. If you examine those catalogues, you will certainly see some extraordinary items, but added to those extraordinary items are the real cement-around-the-ankles kinds of things, tons and tons of bulk. And those tons of bulk cost time and money. Now look at the Garden. Three hundred some-odd lots. Everything the best, just giant. A magnificent collection."

Massey shrugged. "Say what you will about Haven," he said, "but he bought only the best."

Colin Franklin, a prominent publisher in London for twenty years with Routledge and Kegan Paul before deciding to become a full-time antiquarian bookseller in 1970, has written extensively on printing and fine-press works. Unlike most booksellers, he collects for his own pleasure. "Everything I sold Haven, except for one Yeats manuscript which he asked me to get for him at an auction, I had owned privately," Franklin said.

As O'More bought more and more material from him, a friendship developed. Franklin recalled that Haven and Lorea O'More were "very kind" to him and his wife, Charlotte. "We enjoyed their hospitality in Acapulco, and at their home in Arkansas." He had taken note of O'More's philosophical aspirations. "It was important to him to project that, and I have no doubt that his greatest satisfaction would have been to be accepted as a man of deep wisdom," Franklin said. "The interesting thing about him was that, as we now know, he was a man who pretended to some extent. Though I'm not dismissing him as a pretender in philosophy because I've had many talks with him—philosophical talks, if you like to use a grand phrase. I would find him stimulating but totally exhausting, and so vain as to be totally impossible and ridiculous. But of course it was very important for him not to seem ridiculous. To be taken totally seriously was very important in his life." Yet Franklin was always willing to give O'More the benefit of any doubt. "From his conversation you would imagine that he read Plato in the original with some ease, and Homer, and so on," he said. "Now, it would not surprise me at all to learn that he didn't know Greek at all. But I may be wrong," he hedged.

Though Franklin thought he knew O'More well, he too said he was surprised to learn that there was a silent partner. He had never really probed him about the source of his wealth, but O'More had given him the impression that he was a self-made man with a genius for investment. "He mentioned something he'd invested heavily in. It may have been totally fiction, or it may have been true. I have no idea. In other words, he gave the impression he was buying with his own money. And he lived fairly high, but you don't have to be rich to live fairly high."

Franklin acknowledged that when he learned at the time of the sale that O'More had been "using somebody else's money" to build the Garden collection, "it was a little disillusioning" because what had intrigued him most about the man was his attitude toward money. "The impression he gave was an interesting one; the reality turns out to be not so interesting. The impression he gave was that he was a kind of philosopher-king, a person who had the ability to think when he chose, and live the philosophical life, and then, when he chose, to turn that off, and to turn on the money-making tap. If he needed another supply of money, well, he would just tune in to that wavelength, and make what money he needed. And then he would turn it off again, and come back into the philosophical mode, and buy what books he wanted. It was an impressive scenario, and I believed in it."

O'More also led Franklin to believe that he had written a hundred or more learned manuscripts over the previous twenty to twenty-five years. Nothing seemed to be published, though. O'More had shown Franklin a slim book of poems, entitled *Sacrificial Bone Inscriptions,* and there were a few short pieces in some photography books. "It amounted to but one slender thing, really, and he showed it to me with such great pride. I think that he had considerable fear of going into print and of not being recognized as the guru he would have us think he was. And *that's* why he wouldn't go into print," Franklin speculated charitably. "Perhaps he felt that anything printed and subject to public scrutiny would show him to be the man he didn't wish to seem."

Along with the show of deep learning, Franklin noticed that it was important to O'More to project a youthful air. "One great vanity of his was that he should seem very young." Franklin said he saw through this, estimating O'More to be in his sixties during their acquaintance in the mid-1980s. "It would seem that he would have us think he was forty-five for such a long time."

Once he learned the circumstances of O'More's collecting, Franklin said he felt "let down" by the man. "I realized that there had been some deception in our relationship. This man had pretended to be something he wasn't. And I thought I was the one who cared for him." Franklin shook his head slowly. "It's always humiliating when you are exposed," he said sadly. "When you are shown to be a lesser man."

Though few people knew it at the time, the real reason for the Garden Ltd. sale was not, as one Sotheby's official had asserted, because "two collectors have decided to split up and go their separate ways." In fact, the sale had been ordered by a superior court judge in Massachusetts after hearing evidence so explosive that it later would be sealed when I sought legal access to examine it.

On the first day of the sale, three Sotheby's officials had told me that I could not talk to Haven O'More anywhere inside their auction house. Why? They would not say. When I introduced myself to Michael Davis after the last lot had been hammered down, he told me to talk to his lawyer and walked away. It was apparent that there had been a major falling-out, and the obvious place to start looking for information was in the city where each of the partners had lived.

The week after the sale, I turned up traces of a lawsuit, *Davis vs. O'More,* in the Middlesex Superior Court for the Southern District, in Cambridge, Massachusetts, but was not allowed to see any of the files. Judge Katherine Liacos Izzo was assigned to the case. When I asked to meet with her, the clerk suggested I come back in two weeks. When I did so, I was told that Judge Izzo still had the matter "under advisement." This seemed odd. When I had first walked into the courthouse two weeks earlier, I had gotten a copy of the case log known as the docket sheet, and it clearly showed that the proceeding had been discharged five months earlier, resolved to the apparent satisfaction of all parties. How could it still be under advisement?

On December 14, 1989, I formally asked the chief administrative justice of the trial court of the Commonwealth of Massachusetts to intervene and allow me to see these public documents. A month later, an attorney in Judge Arthur Mason's office informed me that "the case has been impounded and is not available for public inspection." Frustrated but intrigued, I went back to the Middlesex County Courthouse and asked to see the file once again. I was not surprised to be told the case was now sealed. I then wandered into the room where the dockets are stacked and found that the seven pages I had been allowed to copy two months earlier had been replaced with a single sheet of blank paper. The case number, 88-635, was at the top with the word "impounded" written in longhand. That was all; even the name of the proceeding, *Davis vs. O'More,* had been removed. Obviously, my poking around had prompted the parties to put the entire matter under wraps, and Judge Izzo had complied. Now, the record of whatever happened in courtroom 7A from January 29, 1988 to July 5, 1989 was forbidden material. But I still had a certified copy of the original docket sheet. And all this heavy-handed secrecy had roused my curiosity even more.

Michael Davis, the now-taboo summary sheet reveals, was the plaintiff in an action started in 1988 to dissolve a partnership. Davis brought suit against O'More, individually, and in his capacities as an officer of the Institute of Traditional Science, the Garden Ltd., and the Dolphin Realty Trust. The first order of business of Davis's suit had been to seize the estimated $10 million book collection, which was being held in the vaults of the Bank of New England and the Boston Safe Deposit Company. The court also authorized an attachment of O'More's personal property, estimated to be worth another $2 million. Nineteen motions were submitted and approved on January 29, 1988, the day the action began. Representing Michael Davis was Hale and Dorr, regarded by many as the most prestigious law firm in Boston. Five lawyers were listed as counsel for plaintiff. Haven O'More had retained Widett, Slater & Goldman, also of Boston; three lawyers were identified as appearing on his behalf. Two others were listed as counsel for the banks holding the rare books.

In addition, the receipt of an affidavit from Dr. Thomas Gordon Gutheil was recorded. Dr. Gutheil is president of the Law and Psychiatry Research Center in Brookline, Massachusetts, and director of the Program of Psychiatry and Law at Harvard University Medical School. A nationally recognized authority on forensic psychiatry, Dr. Gutheil is the coauthor of *Clinical Handbook of Psychiatry and the Law,* a standard text on the subject first published in 1982 and issued in a second edition in 1991. He is the editor of a 1991 book, *Decision Making in Psychiatry and the Law,* and has written ninety professional articles and contributed twenty-two chapters to books. He is a member of the American Academy of Psychiatry and Law and the International Academy of Law and Mental Health.

Michael Davis is the son of Leonard and Sophie Davis, who met during the 1940s as students at City College of New York. Leonard Davis became a successful businessman engaged in a variety of enterprises, including Colonial Penn Insurance Group and Play-Pix Productions, Inc., producers of stage and film dramas. He was also principal owner of National Telefilm Association, which in the early 1960s sold WNTA-TV Channel 13, a New Jersey television station. In 1972, Leonard Davis received an honorary degree from the University of Pennsylvania, a tribute frequently bestowed on major donors. On May 13, 1975, the *New York Times* reported that Leonard Davis, class of 1944, had given $2.5 million to his alma mater toward the construction of a $5 million performing arts center, to be called Aaron Davis Hall, housing the Leonard Davis Center for the Performing Arts. Another article described the gift as "the largest contribution by a living person to a unit of the college."

Michael Davis had evidently been persuaded or, more likely, pressured by his family to break his legal relations with Haven O'More by bringing the suit.

I unearthed the original Garden Ltd. partnership papers almost by accident. Since the thrust of *Davis vs. O'More* was to break a partnership, the documents had to be recorded somewhere showing that such an alliance had been formed. Curiously, none was on file in the Massachusetts Secretary of State's office, which seemed odd, since both men lived in the state and the court action took place there. But among all the records of the real estate transactions near Harvard Square of Michael Davis and Haven O'More in the Middlesex County Registry of Deeds Office, I found a scrap of legal miscellany recorded in 1985. It showed that Haven O'More, the owner of a condominium unit at 14 Concord Street in Cambridge, had granted Haven O'More, general partner of the Garden Ltd., the right to use parking space number 19, which adjoins the building. The transaction was nothing more than a routine formality, but in executing it, the Garden Ltd. was identified as "a New York limited partnership" with "a post office address of c/o Aperture, Elm Street, Millerton, New York."

Limited partnerships in New York are not recorded in Albany, the state capital, but in the various county seats. Millerton is in Dutchess County, in rural upstate New York, and maintains offices in Poughkeepsie. And there, in the county clerk's office, lies the Garden Ltd. partnership certificate. The Garden Ltd., it shows, had been established on December 9, 1983, as an association formed "primarily to write and develop new manuscripts, to rewrite, edit and publish manuscripts, and to hold and collect rare books and manuscripts." Haven O'More is listed as "sole general partner," and Michael Davis was the "sole limited partner."

Michael Davis, the certificate discloses, had contributed to the partnership "marketable, listed securities" then valued at $10.05 million, subject to bank indebtedness of $2.35 million, which the partnership assumed, and rare books valued at $6 million. Nothing in the agreement suggests that Davis was seeking a rapid return on his stake in the partnership. Davis had locked himself into the partnership "until the close of business on June 16, 2029." By then, Davis himself would be very elderly, and O'More—twenty-five years older than Davis—at 105, would probably be dead. Moreover, Davis was forbidden to "sell, assign, encumber or otherwise transfer" any part of his interest in the partnership to anyone else, and no time was set forth for the return of his contribution. Furthermore, no other general or limited partner was allowed to become involved without the consent of Lorea O'More, who was the only person permitted to become general partner and to continue the partnership in the event of the death, retirement, or insanity of Haven O'More. The partnership's bills would be paid out of the first $100,000 in dividend income earned each year; Michael Davis could have 25 percent of whatever was left over as an annual allowance.

So Davis had given O'More nearly absolute control over more than $13 million—$7.7 million in negotiable securities and $6 million that already had been spent for rare books—and had done so without even signing his name. Only one signature appears on this certificate, that of Haven O'More, who executed it "on his own behalf and as Attorney-in-Fact for the Limited Partner." On the same day the partnership was formed, Davis had granted an irrevocable power of attorney to O'More, making him his "true and lawful agent and attorney-in-fact, with full power of substitution, in his name, place and stead to make, execute, sign, acknowledge, deliver and file on behalf or in respect to the Partnership" any documents that would have any bearing on the Garden Ltd. In effect, O'More was granted total authority to handle Davis's partnership affairs for the rest of his life and beyond it as well, as it remained in force even after Davis's death.

A year later, in October of 1984, the partnership certificate was amended to allow Michael Davis's contribution to be increased from $13.7 million to $17,001,589.78, the additional money being "cash in the amount of $4,105,589.78." In return, Davis was allowed an increase in allowance; he now was permitted to withdraw up to $100,000 a year for his personal use. The only signature is that of Haven O'More, signing for himself and as attorney-in-fact for Michael Davis.

In 1983, Haven O'More had been living in Massachusetts for at least ten years. Michael Davis was then listing his legal residence as Grantham, New Hampshire, where there is no state tax, though other documents show that he also lived next door to the O'Mores in Cambridge. All the rare books they bought were being kept in Boston bank vaults. Yet the certificate of limited partnership locates their principal place of business as Millerton, New York. No telephone number for their partnership is listed in the town, nor does it appear that O'More or Davis ever actually conducted business from there. An Aperture executive acknowledged that the Garden Ltd. never had offices at the Elm Street address they cited either. So why had the Garden Ltd. used a small community more than a hundred fifty miles from where the principals lived as the legal address of their partnership?

Most states have laws requiring that certificates of partnership be announced over a period of weeks in the classified advertising pages of local newspapers. Establishing the Garden Ltd. in Cambridge would have meant publishing such a detailed declaration—including the power of attorney agreement—in a Boston publication in which the arrangement was likely to be noticed. But by "settling" in Millerton, the Garden Ltd. could satisfy these requirements with notices in the *Poughkeepsie Journal* and the *Millbrook Round Table,* regional newspapers with modest circulations that do not extend east into New England or south to New York City. Thus, nobody in the antiquarian book world—and nobody in the Davis family, for that matter—would have been likely to learn about an arrangement giving Haven O'More unrestricted use of more than $17 million of Michael Davis's money.

When the partnership was formed in 1983, some $6 million already had been spent on rare books, all of it furnished by Michael Davis. O'More and Davis had been in business together for quite some time before that, however. Nine years earlier, in September 1974, the two had established the Institute of Traditional Science, Inc., as a nonprofit, charitable corporation "to explore the knowledge and learning of ancient civilizations," and to "study the applicability, relevance and relationships of such knowledge and learning to contemporary life in its broadest scope, encompassing inter alia the contemporary areas of religion, the physical and biological sciences, medicine-nutrition, and philosophy; and to transmit this knowledge and learning and the energy stored in these ancient works to the present time period and to future generations." To these ends, the institute would "establish libraries and archives of relevant published books and materials, unpublished manuscripts and other study materials for use by researchers, students and scholars of Traditional Science." Haven O'More is listed in the incorporation papers as president, his wife as treasurer, and Davis as clerk.

At about the same time, O'More and Davis had formed yet another entity, the Dolphin Realty Trust. This entity promptly began buying up property on Concord Avenue and Garden Street in an area adjoining their homes in Cambridge known as Arsenal Square. Perhaps, as O'More asserted in the Sotheby's sale catalogue, the name of the Garden Ltd. was inspired by a Hebrew word for enclosure, but maybe it had something to do with Garden Street as well. The properties created a triangular lot of about one and a half acres, and it was here that their library was to be built. But it was a doomed project. Cambridge is very particular about its historic preservation regulations, and records show that in his haste to build his "sacred city," O'More did not secure proper permits in tearing down several old buildings protected by the Cambridge Historical Commission.

O'More's efforts to proceed met with strong neighborhood opposition. One resident, Albion T. Sawyer, led a 1978 petition drive called the Arsenal Square Moratorium to prevent construction. Rumors swirled that Dolphin Realty Trust was a front for Harvard University, crudely seeking to expand its territory, a sensitive issue in a city where Harvard and Massachusetts Institute of Technology already own major parcels of tax-exempt real estate. The Planning Board became involved, the City Council was drawn in, meetings and hearings were held, votes were taken, orders made and renewed. The project was put on indefinite hold, and never got beyond the planning stage.

"There was a feeling out there that Haven O'More was a straw for Harvard," Dr. Owen Gingerich, professor of astronomy and the history of science at the nearby Harvard-Smithsonian Center for Astrophysics, recalled many years later. An ardent bibliophile in his own right, Dr. Gingerich is the world authority on the publishing history of Nicolaus Copernicus's *De Revolutionibus Orbium Coelestium,* a circumstance that first brought him in contact with O'More. He knew O'More as well as anyone at Harvard during the 1970s and 1980s, and followed the Arsenal Square controversy closely. "Of course it wasn't true at all, it was quite preposterous; Haven had nothing at all to do with Harvard, but the people in the neighborhood wouldn't believe it." Finally, O'More abandoned his dream. If his great library was going to go up, it would not do so in Cambridge. Gingerich said he heard stories that O'More "actually talked about putting the library into a space capsule and putting it into orbit," and failing that, "he would move everything down to Arkansas," where Lorea O'More is from, and where the couple maintained a second home.

In 1988, while *Davis vs. O'More* was being argued in Judge Izzo's court, an "unrestricted" grant of $221,142 was made by the Institute of Traditional Science to the Leonard and Sophie Davis Foundation of West Palm Beach, Florida, an entity of considerable assets and numerous philanthropic activities, chartered in New York State in 1961 for the purpose of helping Jewish charitable, religious, and educational organizations. Mr. and Mrs. Davis, and their son, Michael Davis, are officers. No doubt the transfer was part of some overall settlement between the Davis family and O'More. In 1991, the Institute of Traditional Science elected new officers. That year, too, properties owned by the Dolphin Realty Trust in Cambridge were offered at a public auction, and the large lot of open land once intended as the site of O'More's "great research library" was sold for $1.2 million. Michael Davis was permitted to withdraw from the Garden Ltd. partnership, and was replaced by Lorea O'More. The fabulous Garden sale would be just one intermediate act in the severing of the financial, if not the spiritual, bonds between Michael Davis and Haven O'More.

Haven O'More craved books in the most flawless condition, books of the greatest consequence. But just as much, according to the people who came to know him, he craved recognition. For many, it was his least endearing characteristic, even to his closest bookseller friends— his insistence on being recognized as the greatest book collector alive. He had declared as much, often, in the company of collectors who were undeniably great, people like William H. Scheide, Arthur Houghton, Jr., and Sir Geoffrey Keynes. "That is precisely why Arthur Houghton found him so insufferable," Stephen Massey said.

O'More routinely sought the company of the rich, the famous, and the eminent. Nicolas Barker, longtime editor of *The Book Collector* and recently retired as deputy keeper of rare books at the British Library, wrote in a four-page foreword to the Garden Ltd. catalogue that he was introduced to O'More at the house of Sir Geoffrey Keynes sometime around 1979. The late Sir Geoffrey Keynes (1887–1982), the younger brother of John Maynard Keynes and an honorary fellow of the British Academy, was the son of a Cambridge don, a bibliographer, and the world's leading authority on William Blake.

He was also a great collector, with a library, now at the University Library, Cambridge, that is "matchless in the history of science and medicine," according to Barker. Both O'More and Keynes "were excited" by their common interests, Barker wrote. "It was as if they had been conversing, without knowing it, for a long time, and . . . their first [meeting] had released a fund of enthusiasm that both found compulsive." O'More's "excitement was almost tangible, . . . the idea of the collection itself, the idea of a reliquary, a shrine, that should preserve and at the same time divulgate all that these writers had stood for and brought about by their words—this clearly electrified him."

During the first of two interviews I had with Barker, I asked him to elaborate on this published statement. "I met O'More just that one time, at the home of Keynes," he said, and explained that he wrote the foreword not as a gesture of friendship, but after being telephoned in England by Sotheby's officials with an urgent plea for help. "The essence of the conversation was that they couldn't send out a catalogue of some of the greatest books in the world without an introduction that their customers could understand. They asked if I could do it, and I agreed. Everything I know about the man is in that catalogue." I asked Barker to rank the Garden Library. After some thought, he said, "It's a collection of great books. I don't think it's a great collection. It doesn't seem to me to have anything that I would call a focus at all other than this vague concept of greatness, which obviously means something to Mr. O'More. It's what's called 'high-spot' collecting."

The New York bookseller Justin G. Schiller was introduced to O'More during the first Arthur Houghton sale after they had competed for a hand-colored copy of William Blake's *Songs of Innocence and of Experience,* one of only three copies known. "Blake is my passion," Schiller explained. "As a child, I learned many of the songs of innocence, and it was a book I never dreamed of owning." Schiller had gone to England in June 1979 to operate a booth at the London Book Fair, not to buy at the auction. "I did go to the viewing a few days before the sale, though, and came across the Blake quite by accident. I didn't want to look at it because I have this internal passion that drives me, and I can be a very possessive book person. So I resisted looking at it, but when I did, I went bonkers. When I got back to my hotel room, I began to reconstruct on paper all the rare books I own, and to put them under the categories of certain customers. Then I started making transatlantic telephone calls. I was able to get pledges from three of my customers against things that I own. I figured my absolute top bid could be sixty-five thousand pounds, one hundred sixty thousand dollars, which is more than I ever spent on anything."

The estimate for the lot was £30,000, which gave Schiller what he thought was adequate breathing room. He engaged the services of Quaritch Ltd. to bid for him, and stayed away from the gallery. "I was manning my booth at the fair when I was told it went for £70,000. First, they told me we didn't get the book; second, that they now had a terrible situation that had developed because there was this man Haven O'More who was the buyer of the book, and he was outraged at being pushed to pay £70,000. He was a good customer of theirs, and he was demanding an explanation. He wanted to know why they were bidding him up. He would not believe there was an underbidder, and Quaritch needed permission to tell Haven my name." Because Schiller agreed to this, he was invited to a cocktail party, where he met O'More. "By then, he was all gusto and bluster. Now he was saying he would have paid anything to get the book."

Their mutual interest in William Blake brought both Schiller and O'More in contact with Keynes. Schiller said he learned that O'More had "ingratiated himself" with the aging bibliographer by offering to underwrite the publication of some Blake facsimiles, which in fact took place. That statement is corroborated by Keynes himself in his 1981 autobiography, in which "Dr. Haven O'More, founder of the Institute of Traditional Science in Boston," is identified as the "main benefactor" of the Blake project. There is no hint of warmth or friendship in either of the two references Keynes makes to "Dr. Haven O'More." The last time Schiller saw Keynes, Keynes said to him, "Let me show you something special," and led him to "a couple of Blake oil paintings on copper that left me speechless. Then he said, 'Your Dr. O'More will *never* see these.' It turned out that he despised Haven. Geoffrey couldn't stand a braggart, particularly a braggart who tried to outbrag him."

Another New York City bookseller, Fred Schreiber, a dealer in early printed books, recalls an April day in 1979 when Haven O'More called to ask if he could see two items that were listed in his recent catalogue. "I was working out of my house in the Bronx at the time," Schreiber recalled in an interview. "Everyone in the business was talking about this man, and I agreed to meet with him."

About six hours after O'More said he would arrive, the doorbell rang at Schreiber's house. A woman said, "Dr. O'More is outside in the limousine. Can he come in and see the books?" Schreiber said he could, and the woman, O'More's wife, Lorca, returned to get him. "O'More came into the house holding my catalogue, rolled up, and slapping it in his palm. He then started jabbing me in the chest with it. 'Do you know who I am?' he said, 'I am Dr. O'More,' and he was emphasizing the *Dr.* 'Do you know what I do?' he went on. 'You are a book collector,' I answered. 'I am not just a book collector, I am *the* book collector.' "

Schreiber then showed O'More the books he had requested. One was the first printed edition of Aristotle's works in Greek, 1495, which he had listed in his catalogue for $4,500; the other was a second edition of Plato, 1534, printed in Basel, for $1,500. O'More said he wanted them, but insisted on a 40-percent discount. Schreiber refused and reached out to retrieve the books from O'More. "It was like a tug of war," he said. "I'm holding them, he's holding them, we're pulling back and forth. Then he said, 'All right, all right, 30 percent. Give me 30 percent, and you also get my good will.' I asked him what that meant. He said, 'I am the greatest book collector in the world. My good will is important to you.' Finally, against my better judgment, I agreed to give him 10 percent."

When their business was concluded, O'More asked to see Schreiber's stock of books, which was kept in a converted attic. The Ph.D. diploma in classical philology Schreiber received from Harvard in 1970 was hanging on the wall. " 'Oh, Harvard,' O'More said when he saw it. 'I've gone beyond Harvard; I've got three Ph.D.s myself.' I was mildly curious about this, and I asked him what his degrees were in. He said the classics, physics, and some other field that I can't remember. Then he said that he spoke twenty languages fluently. Being a philologist, I was interested in this as well, and I asked him which languages. 'Which ones do *you* know?' he said. When I replied, 'Naturally I know Greek and

Latin,' he interrupted me and said, 'I never studied *those*,' and changed the subject. When I heard that, I knew something wasn't quite right because a Ph.D. in classics presupposes fluency in Greek and Latin."

Ten years later, when Schreiber read O'More's preface to the Garden Ltd. catalogue, he was amused to see his suspicions confirmed. O'More's opening sentence involves a "contemplation of three words"—the Latin phrase *magnae mentis opera*—which he translated as "great or supreme works of the mind." O'More called it the "underlying principle controlling the inception and guiding of the formation" of the Garden collection. The only problem is that he got the Latin wrong. "What the phrase actually means is 'works of a great mind,' " Schreiber said.

Sacrificial Bone Inscriptions, a slim book of poetry written by Haven O'More, was published by SADEV, the imprint of the Garden Ltd., in 1987, and distributed by the Aperture Foundation. (The Aperture Foundation was established in 1952 by a group of leading photographers, Minor White, Edward Weston, and Ansel Adams among them, to publish their works and to serve as a forum of ideas.) It amounts to a preface, seventeen compact poems, and a coda. It has been offered for sale and in several Aperture catalogues as a SADEV book under a New Age category. Printed in Verona, Italy, by the noted firm Stamperia Valdonega, and with type designed by Giovanni Mardersteig in an edition of 750, O'More's modest collection of verse is a handsome production, flush with revealing, if rather disturbing, poetic sentiments.

Man, he declares in his preface, "must submit to sacrifice" to have "existence in the first place." Elsewhere, he asserts that to "taste death's full sweetness" there "must be life's fire on blood and flesh." In the coda, he declares that only "by **killing** all that is appearance and **dying** to it is **death** fully tasted." Life, he insists, must "be chewed to the limit" in order to "possess **death**—the gateway to eternal life."

When SADEV published the poems, it also issued a nineteen-page pamphlet entitled *Delighting All Who Pay: An Essay on Haven O'More's "Sacrificial Bone Inscriptions,"* by David Waxman. The essay gushes with praise for O'More the poet. "It is hard to resist poetry of such sinuous elegance," Waxman wrote. "We are dealing with a mystery: poetry at once dense and fluid, a synaesthetic breath-canvas flashing with the spectrum of tone and mood and color—but focusing to what?" The collection is "deeply pensive," "nobly high-minded," *"thoroughly oracular,"* "totally original," filled with "charm and genius," "triumphant," and "transcendent." It is, Waxman asserted, a "textbook of Sacrifice" in which "we are necessarily forced to energy." Understanding the message is difficult but challenging nonetheless: "If you would really get at *Sacrificial Bone Inscriptions, then memorize it!* Inscribe its pattern in your bone; let its poetry dwell and speak within you." Extracts from the essay were printed in Aperture catalogues and on the dustjacket of the book.

The other SADEV publications mentioned in Aperture's New Age backlist are two books of photographs. One, by Marilyn Silverstone, is described as "visions of India and the Himalayan Kingdom." Titled *Ocean of Life,* it was issued in 1985 with the help of a grant from the Institute of Traditional Science. *Markings,* published the following year, features "sacred landscapes from the air" by the noted aerial photographer Marilyn Bridges. Haven O'More wrote prefaces for both.

David G. Waxman is a bookseller in Great Neck, New York, whose business card once stated his specialty as "the best minds in the best editions." He acknowledged in an interview that he wrote the essay at the request of O'More, but his "only regret is that I didn't make it stronger, that I might not have done the work sufficient justice." Waxman's friendship with O'More began in the early 1970s, when he was a student at Brandeis. He said he knew Michael Davis during that time as well, having "had some interaction with him," but knew nothing of his partnership in the Garden Ltd. "One should not think that O'More was a man without accomplishment prior to this partnership," Waxman stressed. "It was my understanding that he was an accomplished man, that he had his own money. He was a man of accomplishment, and he was a book buyer in advance of this partnership." He said he believed O'More lived "somewhere in the Midwest" before moving to Massachusetts in the late 1960s or early 1970s.

Waxman acknowledged that SADEV is *vedas*—the ancient ritual and philosophical treatises of India written between 1500 and 500 B.C.—spelled backward. Regarding the given name of Haven O'More, Waxman said: "I would say that what is essential here is not the personal details; what is essential is what he tried to do in forming this library, and the great intellectuality which lies behind it. Now, you can get caught up in gossip mongering, but all that is basically irrelevant. What is important is the fact of his collection, the fact that he was trying to set an example for the book-collecting public and what it means to be a book collector, the kinds of things it is important to get involved in."

Despite all the unexplained contradictions that have surfaced about O'More, Waxman said he still "cannot emphasize too much that I consider him a very great writer," even though O'More has published only one book and written a few forewords for photography collections that have been underwritten by the Institute of Traditional Science. "People apparently don't really understand where he is coming from, what he is trying to do. *Sacrificial Bone Inscriptions,* let me say, for those who will work with it, evidences the very highest level of intelligence. It is not what it may seem on first reading. It is really exquisite, and poetry of the highest intelligence."

Waxman wasn't the only one who regarded O'More as a man of brilliance and accomplishment. Arthur Freeman, an American who taught for fifteen years at Boston University and Harvard before moving to London to work as a bookseller for Quaritch Ltd. in the 1970s, had been acquainted with O'More in both the United States and England. The first he heard of O'More's financial partner was at the announcement of the Garden sale. As for O'More's background, he said, "There *is* a 'Dr.' before his name, you know, and it was earned." Where had O'More earned his doctorate? "It could have been Brandeis or Berkeley, or maybe Oklahoma," he suggested. But officials at these schools—as well as universities in Arkansas, North Carolina, and Texas—carry no record of a Haven Moore or Haven O'More.

The whiff of New Age guru in O'More's available writings was also confirmed in part by a native New Yorker who is now working for an antiquarian bookseller in London and from 1977 to 1987 was office manager for the bookseller John Fleming. She agreed to discuss what she knows of the man on condition that her name be withheld from this work. She recalled frequent visits at the shop from O'More. "Haven was quite a character," she said. "We always kept a bottle of his favorite Greek brandy on hand, and whenever he came, he'd drink the whole thing. There were times when he'd spend the night, but that was no big deal, because we were used to putting up with a lot of eccentric people. John Fleming's place was famous for that."

O'More wore an unusual ring, "a big chunky ring, like a class ring," the woman said. "I asked him what it was, and he said it was the symbol of his Institute of Traditional Science. I asked him what traditional science was, and he didn't say anything." Whenever O'More spent the night, he would begin each morning with elaborate yoga exercises. "He had this dark blue robe he would wear, and he'd sit in the middle of the floor. John had the kind of place where all kinds of people were always passing through, people coming and going. One time Benny Goodman came in and began to rehearse. He was playing the clarinet while Haven was doing his yoga, and it was like Haven didn't even know he was there. I also remember that when he wasn't doing yoga, he was staring at himself in the mirror. The guy was a real kook."

Around 1984, O'More gave the woman instructions to send all future invoices for book purchases to the Garden Ltd. in Cambridge. "We were buying a lot of books for him and he was paying enormous prices," she said. "And that was when I saw Michael Davis's name on something he gave us about the Garden for the billing. I couldn't believe it because I knew Michael back in the sixties. We were both in our late teens then, early twenties, and we moved around in the same group, a Park Avenue crowd." The woman recalled that Davis was "quite the party animal" in those days, so "amazing" that his friends gave him the nickname Falstaff. "He was a pretty stocky guy, and he loved parties. I remember him as very shy, but he loved to party."

Sometime early in the 1970s Michael Davis "dropped out of sight. It wasn't unusual for people in the group to move around, but he didn't call anyone. Then we heard he had gone completely straight; people said he had lost a lot of weight, he was into macrobiotics and meditation, and he wasn't going to parties anymore." After John Fleming's death in 1987, the woman lived in Italy for a year, then moved to England, and "lost touch with a lot of what was going on."

Michael E. Hoffman, executive director of the Aperture Foundation, told me that he allowed the Garden Ltd. to use Aperture's address in Millerton, New York, as a "courtesy" to O'More. Though now based in New York City, Aperture was formed in the small upstate town, and still maintains an office there on Elm Street. Hoffman made the oblique comment that the nature of O'More's business in Millerton probably was "a banking interest." In addition, "Mr. O'More supported several extraordinary Aperture books and wrote a text for one or two of them." But there was "no formal relationship" between the two groups. The foundation depends to some extent on contributions, and by financially supporting some of its projects, O'More was able to get his SADEV books distributed by Aperture.

Hoffman added that he had known O'More for at least twenty-five years, and he had "a remarkable record of doing some rather significant work, and we certainly knew about him and his collecting, and we knew about some of his accomplishments." For example, through the Institute, O'More had supported the scholar J. A. B. van Buitenen's new translations of the Mahābhārata and the Bhagavad-gītā, later published by the University of Chicago Press, and had appeared in a film about Transcendental Meditation, *Hatha Yoga Darshana*. "These are some of the most important things that have been done anywhere," Hoffman said, though he was unable to say where a copy of the film could be located.

Though Hoffman said he was familiar with O'More's "incredible background," he declined to describe it. "I'm not sure what he's willing to put into print. He's an extremely discreet person and is not very happy with notoriety. This of course has led to misunderstandings regarding him in the past," he added mysteriously. "You're going to find yourself getting into things that may surprise you, and are over most people's heads, frankly," he warned. "And that's one of the reasons he doesn't explain himself."

What about his autobiographical statement to Sotheby's? "I think that Sotheby's thing was a smoke screen," he replied. "I don't think he has any interest in exposing himself. I can't say that's a good thing to do, but that's how he did it. But if you are able to find his actual work, and if you look at the books he supported of Aperture's alone, the text he wrote, you'll see you're dealing with some person of considerable ability." O'More is the "kind of person who just hates gossip and hates rumors and doesn't particularly want to be talked about," especially since he is "involved in a lot of esoteric work" that consumes most of his time. "It's not ordinary work. And it has taken him outside the realm of ordinary life. So he operates in a very different way than most people. And it's very hard to comprehend it partially for that reason." He added that anyone unfamiliar with hatha yoga "can't deal with O'More on any level, you can't comprehend what he is doing." Haven O'More "is one of the most accomplished yogis in the West."

Thus, trying to explain O'More's professional activity in straightforward terms is a pointless exercise. Hoffman said, "Certain works are there and available for people who understand them and not available for people who don't. It's that simple. He's not out looking for the press. He's not out looking for praise. He's not out looking for students or disciples. He's doing a very special kind of work which requires his full attention. And that's a very traditional way of working in the higher areas of certain esoteric practices."

Hoffman suggested that Leonard Davis, the father of Michael Davis, was behind the breakup of the Davis-O'More partnership. "He was attempting to really blaspheme O'More and destroy his credibility and character in order to win the allegiance of his son, who had become allied with O'More over a multiyear period. There was a great deal of money involved and the father decided that he was going to try to destroy O'More, who had become a sort of father figure for his son. It was a very outrageous suit without any justification which was eventually settled and that was the end of it. But O'More was totally blameless in this and there was never any proof of wrongdoing whatsoever."

I mentioned to Hoffman that Michael Davis had executed a power of attorney to Haven O'More that turned over complete authority of a family fortune that totaled more than $17 million. "I don't know all that," he said. "But Michael Davis was a free agent and O'More literally saved his life many years ago. This guy would have been on the street somewhere." Michael Davis would have been on the street, homeless, even though he is worth millions? I asked.

"That's right. His whole life was given purpose by his work with O'More."

The final key to unlocking the mystery of Haven O'More came to me in the form of a response to a Freedom of Information Act request from the National Personnel Records Center in St. Louis, Missouri. O'More had asserted in his Sotheby's statement that he had served two tours in the Army, one in Europe the other in Asia. Moreover, he had told acquaintances that he had served on General Douglas MacArthur's staff during the Korean War. My inquiries revealed otherwise.

Brigadier General Thomas J. Kilmartin, commanding officer of the center, unequivocally confirmed that the name Haven O'More used while serving in the United States Army was Haven Moore. Unfortunately, most of Haven Moore's military records were destroyed in a fire that swept through the personnel center on July 12, 1973, though a partial record was put together from a W.D.A.G.O. (War Department Adjutant General's Office) Form 100 that survived the disaster. The reconstructed record shows that Haven Moore was inducted on March 12, 1944, at Fort Bragg, North Carolina, and was discharged five months later, on August 17, 1944. He received no special education or training, and the highest rank he achieved was private.

Under "civilian education," Moore stated that he had attended no college or university, received no degrees, and left public school in 1938 after completing the second grade. The last school he attended is listed simply as Beaufort County, North Carolina. Under the category of "civilian occupations" was the information that from 1939 to May 1944 Moore had worked for M.U. Hodge of Washington, North Carolina, as a "general farmer" charged with a number of responsibilities: "Used mules to plant, cultivate, and harvest cotton, corn, tobacco, hay, peanuts and garden vegetables on 30 acre farm. Also raised poultry and livestock." As a secondary occupation, Moore listed a year of employment as a "faller" for Mack Bessel, also of Washington, North Carolina, in 1944. In this job Moore "cut down trees with ax and crosscut saw. Also cut them into log lengths and trimmed branches."

Why Moore was sent home after five months of military service just ten weeks after the Normandy invasion and a year before the end of World War II is not explained. There is no indication, moreover, that Moore served any time in Europe, as he asserted in the biographical statement published by Sotheby's, and no records exist to support his claim of a second tour later in Asia.

A more detailed statement of honorable discharge recorded in the Beaufort County Registry of Deeds on November 19, 1946, in Washington, North Carolina, discloses a bit more about Haven Moore. At the time of his induction on March 12, 1944, Haven Moore's age was given as "20%12 years." So he had probably been born in January or February 1924. Moore stated that he was a native of Beaufort County, that he had been a farmer prior to being drafted, and that he was single. He also certified that he participated in no battles, engagements, skirmishes, or expeditions, and had received no decorations, service medals, or citations. There is a notation that he had been "issued a discharge lapel button" at Fort McPherson in Georgia.

The nature of Haven Moore's discharge is listed as honorable by reason of "A.R. 615-369." An official of the Adjutant General's War Records Office said that Army Regulation 615-369 was a classified category in 1944, but that it mandated release from active duty for any one, or all, of three specific reasons: "ineptness," "lack of adaptability," and "enuresis," or bed-wetting. Haven Moore's certificate of honorable discharge asserts that his "character" was "not readable," and in a closing section set aside for "remarks," the soldier was "not recommended for reenlistment, induction or re-induction."

On the "signature of soldier" line is a prominent X in parentheses, the notation "his mark," and the sworn certification of two witnesses.

Not only is Moore's military record dramatically different from the biographical statement in the Sotheby's catalogue, but the scope of his education is decidedly different as well. In the catalogue, Haven O'More claimed "early readings" of Shakespeare, Milton, and the Bible "before starting to school." Military records show that when Haven Moore was drafted in 1944 at the age of twenty, he had not attended school since the age of thirteen and his highest level of achievement was the second grade. When released five months later on grounds that may have involved "ineptness" or "lack of adaptability," he made "his mark" with an X.

Twenty-five years elapsed between Haven Moore's release from active military duty and his spectacular metamorphosis into flamboyant guru, autodidact, and eccentric owner of great books. How Haven O'More came so close to building a great library on Garden Street a stone's throw from Harvard Yard with somebody else's money is still a mystery, and as long as the Commonwealth of Massachusetts keeps the contents of *Davis vs. O'More* sealed, it will remain so.

In the end, Haven O'More was to "have no more" of his "spiritual children." The "universal treasures" he once hoped to place at the "heart-core" of a "sacred city" finally did move on to other places and to new owners. It was a sad turn for this strange man who wanted so keenly to be proclaimed the world's greatest book collector.

7

Infinite Riches

And thus me thinkes should men of judgement frame
Their meanes of traffique from the vulgar trade,
And as their wealthe increaseth, so inclose
Infinite riches in a little roome.

> —Christopher Marlowe,
> *The Jew of Malta* (1.1.34–7)

The third-generation bibliophile slid a clamshell box, a special container for preserving fragile documents, out of a steel vault and carried it carefully over to a reading table in the middle of his library. There, he opened the case to reveal a bulky folio with hand-tooled ornamentation and brass clasps on the outside. "That's the original binding," William H. Scheide said softly, and rapped his knuckles on the precious book. "Pigskin on an oak board." Tucked inside the front cover, a yellowed sheet of paper dated February 10, 1873, carried the heading "Invoice of Merchandise Shipped by Steamer from Liverpool." Written beautifully in longhand by the famous expatriate American bookseller Henry Stevens, it documented the sale of a Biblia Latina to George Brinley of Hartford, Connecticut, for £600, plus £37 15*s*. for commission and insurance. Stevens also had written a postscript for the benefit of customs inspectors in New York; and a few of the curious are privileged enough to get a peek at it now:

Pray ponder for a moment to fully appreciate the rarity and importance of this precious consignment from the Old to the New World. It is not only the first *Bible,* but a fine copy of the *First Book ever printed.* It was read in Europe nearly half a century before America was discovered. Therefore, in view of these considerations, please to suggest to your Deputy at the Seat of Customs to uncover his head while in the presence of this First Book, and never for a moment to turn his back upon it while the case is open. Let no ungodly or thieving politician lay eyes or hands upon it. The sight can *now* do him no good, while the Bible may suffer. Let none of Uncle Samuel's Custom House officials, or other men in or out of authority, see it without first reverentially lifting their hats.

If there is a Holy Grail among collectors, it is without question this book. The volume containing the first printed text of the Old Testament lay open before me, and its owner was inviting me to touch it. William Scheide brought forth many treasures from his preserves that spring day, but the highlight of the visit was the half hour we spent discussing the finer points of his Gutenberg Bible.

A few months before his death in 1991, Edwin Wolf 2nd, the great Philadelphia librarian and noted biographer of A. S. W. Rosenbach, had told me unequivocally, "Bill Scheide owns the finest private library in North America and one of the finest in the world." The late John Carter once suggested that Scheide is not a book collector at all, "but an institution." Regardless of how the cognoscenti describe him, everyone agrees that Scheide represents the last of a classic breed, a bookman whose treasures rank with those of many nineteenth-century giants. And beyond mere possession is the expertise he brings to bear. Scheide knows his library intimately and with deep insight; he is familiar with every blemish, every detail, every nuance. "I couldn't have done it alone," he said, nodding to three portraits that hang over the door connecting his elegant chamber with the rare-book room of the Firestone Library at Princeton University. The likeness in the middle is his; to the left is a portrait of John H. Scheide, his father, and to the right is a painting of William T. Scheide, his grandfather.

When the Firestone Library is viewed from Nassau Street, there is nothing to indicate that the rectangular room built onto the roof exists apart from Princeton University. But in an unusual arrangement worked out in 1959, college officials allowed Scheide to build the addition at his expense, with no strings attached whatsoever. While the Scheide Library is routinely made available to scholars, the books remain an independent collection, curated by Scheide's personal librarian, William P. Stoneman. What will become of them after Scheide's death remains his decision, and he has chosen not to make that public. In the meantime, this remains very much a compact, carefully assembled private library where everything has a place.

The life spans of private collections usually can be measured by the life spans of the individuals who build them, which is why the collections of Sir Thomas Phillipps, George Brinley, and Robert Hoe III were especially impressive. Typically, final scores are tallied when the collectors die and catalogues are issued, or when their libraries are dispersed at auction or go off to institutions. The best-known American exceptions to that pattern are the John Carter Brown Library in Providence and the Pierpont Morgan Library in New York. In those cases, the succeeding generation not only continued collecting, but created independent research libraries to maintain the treasures that had been inherited. The Scheide Library also reflects the taste, energy, and sensibility of more than one person, but it remains privately owned after 130 years. "There were about four thousand items when I took it over," Scheide said, "and I have added perhaps a thousand."

The *Princeton University Library Chronicle* suggested in 1965, "The uniqueness of this collection as a continuing family tradition is that it is not a miscellaneous legacy of books handed down from one generation to another [but a] living and growing entity." Scheide once told a group of colleagues how he "grew up with a library which was already two generations old." His playroom was directly over copies of such works as John Foxe's *Book of Martyrs,* the folios of Muratori, and the Complutensian Polyglot Bible. "This was the air I breathed, and no one in the family ever thought to question it." Many years later, he reflected once again on his lifelong exposure to books: "Growing up with, inheriting, and developing such a collection has created for me feelings of humility, responsibility, and love."

After allowing me a few minutes to appreciate his Gutenberg Bible in silence, Scheide embarked on a detailed introduction to the book, beginning with the binding and the large margins, which have been preserved untouched for more than five centuries. "Because the binding is original, nothing has been trimmed off the sides," he explained, pointing between the leaves of the book to the fibers that fastened the signatures, or folded sheets of paper, into a "gathering." "There are threads down in there, string, and what they did was put this filament in so the string won't cut the paper." He proceeded deliberately, knowing exactly where he wanted to go.

"Now here," he said, "these may well be the most interesting pages in the volume. You ought to come closer if you want to. Look, there's a little more space between the lines on this page than there is in the others. Those others are slightly more crowded. Now, if you take the trouble to count—use the eraser end of your pencil—you're supposed to get forty-two lines. But what do you get there? You get *forty*. All these others, of course, have forty-two. But this has forty, and it's the same length as the pages with forty-two. Here, let's find a *Q* in this column. Look at this *Q*. Do you see a spike coming out of the top? How about over there. Now, you don't see a spike. It's been filed off. Let's take a look at a capital *P*, you see the same thing. See the spike up there? Filed down?

"This"—he pointed to the section with spikes—"has been thought to be the original form of the type. And this over here, this is from the second press. Gutenberg must have set up a second press, and he set it up to begin at *this* point in the Bible. What must have happened is that they printed for a while with this forty-line format, and then somebody said, 'Oh, we're getting a lot more orders, you've got to print more copies. This is wasting paper, we've got to get more type on a page.' Well, they tried hard, and they figured out a way to get two more lines on a page. And the way they did it was to file down the ascenders and descenders [parts of lower-case letters that rise above or descend below the main body of the letter (e.g., *h* or *y*)] of certain letters. Any copy you look at, there will be a mixture. Some are just forty-two, some of them have all pages with forty lines, some are forty and forty-two. My suspicion is that this is the oldest page in the book. Now, you see the pinholes?"

At the outside of every page, quite clearly once they have been pointed out, are the tiniest of punctures in the rag paper. "Go ahead, feel it," Scheide said. "That's where the pages were pinned down on the press. They pinned them right down on the press so they wouldn't wiggle. Look, here's another forty-line page.

"Let me show you something else. When they went to the forty-two-line page, they gave up red printing. This here is the only red printing you will see in the book. My guess is that it took up too much time to re-ink everything. Now, one of the fun things I enjoy about this book very much is the hyphens, though the margins are wonderful too. But I have yet to find a bottom line at the end of a column where a hyphenated word goes over from page to page, or column to column, for that matter. How they avoided that is just wonderful."

Having returned the Old Testament volume to the vault, he brought out a manuscript known as the Blickling Homilies. "This is the only Anglo-Saxon book to be found in this hemisphere," he said by way of introduction. "It's about a thousand years old." It was named for the hall in Norfolk, Blickling Hall, where it was kept for two centuries. In 1725 Humfrey Wanley wanted to buy it from William Pownall of Lincoln for the Harleian Library, but left empty-handed when the key to unlock it from a cabinet could not be found. Written almost a century before the Battle of Hastings in 1066, the Blickling Homilies is a collection of sermons and narratives and offers a rare look at life in England prior to the Norman Conquest. The book is in the United States and not England because a former owner, the marquess of Lothian, was pressed for cash and sold it to Anderson Galleries in 1932. Six years later, John Scheide bought the Blickling Homilies from Dr. A. S. W. Rosenbach for $38,000. After more than sixty years, the loss of this historic artifact still rankles British sensibilities. "It's a disgrace," Nicolas Barker said when I interviewed him at the British Library. "This is a piece of our national heritage that never should have been allowed out of the United Kingdom."

Next from the old vault came John Bunyan's *Pilgrim's Progress,* a copy so pristine that it traveled back to England on loan in 1963 for the "Printing and the Mind of Man" exhibition held at the British Library. It once belonged to Robert Stayner Holford, a great English collector whose choicest items were sold to Dr. Rosenbach in 1925, and has been described as "unquestionably the finest" copy in the world. As Scheide went off to fetch yet another treasure, he talked with amusement about a Coptic fragment of the Book of Acts he once examined at the Pierpont Morgan Library with the noted bookseller Hans P. Kraus. "They had it labeled 'a complete fragment.' What they have is about fifteen chapters, so they call it a 'complete fragment.' I asked Mr. Kraus what that means, how big does a fragment have to be in order to be complete. I was teasing him a little because that particular item had gone through his hands. He said, 'Bookseller's talk, bookseller's talk.' "

Scheide removed a tiny volume no more than four inches wide by five inches high from a compact box. With great care he located the title page of the ancient book, inscribed on parchment in a vaguely recognizable alphabet. "Well," he said, "this is not a fragment. This is a *complete* Gospel of Matthew. It is from the fifth century in Coptic, but it is written in a script that is very much like what you see in Greek codices of the same period." Remarkably, the delicate manuscript has managed to survive almost sixteen centuries in its original binding of beveled wooden boards, with bits of the original leather thongs still remaining. Scholars have determined that this codex is one of the four oldest known copies of the entire text of Matthew. Scheide began by discussing each letter in a note at the end known as the colophon or "finishing stroke" because it often includes such invaluable information as the title, author, printer, and place of printing.

"Imagine that is an *M* right there. The letter next to it is an *a*. And then this circle with a line through it, that's a theta, which sounds like 'th.' Then there's an *a, i, o,* and that *c* would be used as an *s*. So what that says is Mathios—Matthew, you see. And before that comes the word *kata,* which means 'according to Matthew.' And this word up here is the word for "gospel," *evangeleion,* 'the evangel,' where the word *evangelist* comes from. So what you have here is a complete fifth-century Coptic manuscript of the Gospel According to Matthew, an unusually early copy. In fact it has some things in it that were left out of later versions."

After returning the codex to its proper space, Scheide came back with "something really remarkable," a 1,100-year-old Carolingian manuscript with breathtaking calligraphic script, a book "about a hundred years older than the Blickling Homilies." When he was done discussing that treasure, he went to the vault and got yet another rare and marvelous book.

◆ ◆ ◆

In 1947, the librarian of Princeton University, Julian P. Boyd, wrote a "summary view" of the Scheide library, then housed in a remote region of northwest Pennsylvania near the Allegheny River that once played a prominent role in the emerging oil industry. "Some of the greatest of the world's books are to be found in the Scheide library, but all of them, even the greatest, have assumed new dignity and meaning because of the manner in which they were assembled and because of the purposes for which this was done." When Boyd wrote that, the library had been in private hands through two full generations. It would become even greater during the third.

William Taylor Scheide, the founder, was born in Philadelphia in 1847 and went "west" twenty years later to seek his fortune in the Pennsylvania oilfields. While others got rich drilling wells, he determined that money was to be made by transporting petroleum to major depots and refineries through pipelines. By the time he was thirty-three, Scheide was general manager of a system that had consolidated the whole network of oil pipelines, and at the age of forty-two he retired, even though John D. Rockefeller urged him to reconsider. He decided instead to augment his library, which for many years contained the only books to be found for miles around Titusville. As a service to his neighbors he maintained an open-shelf policy. He had forms printed up for borrowers with spaces for date, title, and signature, along with an admonition at the bottom: "To be returned in good order in one week from date."

On May 1, 1889, Scheide left for four months of book buying in Europe. Among his purchases were hundreds of medieval documents, including contracts, papal bulls, invoices, indulgences, deeds, and wills. Toward the end of his life, he cited his coming of age "amid the passions of the Civil War" as the reason he undertook the study of history. What resulted from his curiosity was a library that, Boyd wrote, "would have done credit to any professional scholar, but for William T. Scheide to create it in the time and place and circumstances was evidence enough that, whatever else he was, he was first and foremost a student." More significant was that Scheide wrote "one of the most interesting chapters in the annals of American book-collecting" and "laid the foundation for an even greater library." Once, he chided his son John for telling Mrs. Scheide how much money he had spent for an acquisition. "Your dear Mother absolutely cannot understand the value of books, although at times she tries, and so feels hurt when the subject of their cost arises. She *knows* their purchase is a wicked folly and fears the inevitable consequences for us."

When John Scheide received that letter in 1904, he was twenty-nine years old and living at a sanitorium in Saranac Lake in the Adirondacks recovering from tuberculosis. Though only eight years out of Princeton University, John Scheide had been forced by illness to quit the oil business. At his father's death in 1907, he not only took on the management of the family estate but also assumed responsibility for the Titusville library and conducted a thorough inventory. There were about 2,500 volumes in all, most of them acquired for the knowledge they possessed, though a number were rare, including some early manuscript material and several incunabula, among them Thomas Aquinas's *De Veritate,* printed by Nicholas Jenson in Venice in 1480; Euclid's *Elementa Geometriae,* Venice, 1482; Justinian's *Institutiones,* Basel, 1476; and a Nuremberg Chronicle.

It is uncertain when John Scheide began to collect in earnest, though Lathrop C. Harper recalled selling him a Bible in 1910. Great editions of the Bible would be represented, but the overall scheme was constantly refined. John Scheide once credited a Princeton professor's comment that modern history had been shaped by the invention of printing and the discovery of America with setting his overall theme. He came to know books with the soul of a connoisseur and the eye of a bibliographer, yet he never spent frivolously. Before long, he was buying books from Dr. Rosenbach. Their first transaction came in 1914, when Scheide wrote to authorize bids for four titles being offered in an upcoming session of the Huth sale in London, to be attended by Dr. Rosenbach's brother, Philip Rosenbach. "I am quite anxious to secure these items," John Scheide wrote Rosenbach. "I assume of course that your brother will endeavor to secure them as cheaply as he can."

On July 29, 1914, Rosenbach replied that only one of the four lots, a tract by Martin Luther, had been obtained. "Books that are desirable are selling high at auction despite the hard times and the threatened wars," he explained. "It is curious that while other securities are dropping, books and other literary property are selling higher than ever before." Scheide remained frugal, as a letter from Rosenbach four and a half years later demonstrates. "I have just returned from the Jones Sale, and certainly regret that I was unable to secure any of the items for which you kindly sent us the bids." Rosenbach itemized what the lots went for, and in several cases identified the buyers.

Despite these setbacks, spirited bargaining continued between Scheide and Rosenbach. After receiving a copy of the Icelandic Bible on approval in 1923, Scheide wrote that he would be pleased to purchase it "if we can agree on the price." After examining the book, he noted how it not only "lacks the blank leaf between the first and second parts," but that about one and a quarter inches had "been cropped off its height" and another five eighths of an inch trimmed "from the side margins." He also found evidence of repairs and the absence of some text. "On these accounts, it does seem to me that the price you quoted of $485 is high, and I shall be glad to hear what figure you are willing to place on it." The answer that came back acknowledged the "imperfections," but noted that a copy "with no repairs and all the blanks would fetch considerably more." As a consequence, the price was firm, and Scheide relented.

Another friendly exchange developed a few months later, when Rosenbach wrote Scheide that he was sending to Titusville "by express today the famous copy of the first edition of Homer, 1488," one of "the finest examples in existence," altogether a "perfect" copy. Rosenbach said that though he had listed the book at $2,200, "I am making you a special price of $1,950." Scheide wrote back that it "is indeed a delicious copy, one that delights the heart to handle, but is not the matchless copy that your enthusiasm paints it." Indeed, he found that the copy, far from being perfect, "lacks the famous blank leaf EX just before the text begins, which both the Hoe and Huth had, the presence of which was noted with some care in the sale catalogues." He also reported a height discrepancy of a quarter inch. Those reservations notwithstanding, Scheide allowed nevertheless that he was "glad to have it," and asked for a statement so "I may send my check."

Banter over an editio princeps of Homer and an Icelandic Bible were one matter, but when the prospect of installing a Gutenberg Bible in Titusville presented itself a few months later, the stakes were raised. Writing to Rosenbach on January 3, 1924, Scheide mentioned a recent conversation and recalled, almost as an afterthought, how "we had a hurried word together" on the subject of the Ellsworth-Brinley copy of the Gutenberg Bible, which Rosenbach had acquired a few months earlier. "I happen just now to be in funds, and in a position to talk with you on a strictly cash basis," Scheide continued, "and I am wondering whether you have anything you care to say to me in this connection."

The two men already had been doing business for ten years, mostly through the mails. Scheide now suggested that perhaps this was a good time for Rosenbach to make his first trip to Titusville, an invitation that was readily accepted. "I shall, of course, bring with me the Gutenberg Bible," Rosenbach wrote on February 5, 1924. Scheide replied that if the volumes were too cumbersome to bring along as baggage, he "might care to send them on in advance" by express. "My library is supposed to be as nearly fireproof as modern structural methods can make it, and in addition, I have a fireproof safe inside of it"—the same safe that is still used today in Princeton by his son. There is no discussion in these letters of money. Apparently Rosenbach took a train to Titusville, showed Scheide the two volumes, and stated a firm price of $46,000. That, according to the Rosenbach Company sales book, is how much Scheide paid.

In 1932 Rosenbach offered Scheide a copy of *Rationale divinorum officiorum,* a handbook prepared in the fifteenth century by Guillielmus Durandus for the clergy in celebrating the Mass and known commonly as the Durandus. It was printed in Mainz by Johann Fust and Peter Schöffer on October 6, 1459. "This magnificent copy is printed on vellum and is usually regarded as one of the greatest pieces of printing after the Gutenberg Bible," Rosenbach wrote. "It is the earliest procurable book from the press of Gutenberg's co-workers and successors. It is the third book printed with a date, the other two both being unprocurable." Scheide wrote back that even though the Durandus "makes my mouth water to think of it," the continuing poor economic situation of the Depression forced him to decline. Several decades later, Scheide's son William not only secured a copy of the Durandus, he obtained the "other two" books Dr. Rosenbach had maintained were "unprocurable," the Mainz Psalters of 1457 and 1459. William Scheide was trained as a musicologist, and his acquisitions also include autograph scores by Ludwig van Beethoven and Johann Sebastian Bach.

In 1990, the Grolier Club marked "125 years of growth" of the Scheide family library with a major exhibition of selected items. Among Bibles were Martin Luther's September Testament and a twelfth-century French manuscript of the Gospel of Matthew once owned by Sir Thomas Phillipps. The Aldine Aristotle, 1494, the pages "completely untrimmed" and once the property of a sixteenth-century king of France, was among the incunabula. Americana included an uncut copy of the Treaty of Paris, which ended the American Revolution, and a letter book kept by General Ulysses S. Grant during the Civil War. A 1549 Book of Common Prayer and three texts printed in Mexico eighty years before the production of the Bay Psalm Book, formerly owned by Robert Hoe, were displayed as well.

Paul Needham, formerly curator of rare books at the Pierpont Morgan Library and now head of the Rare Books Division of Sotheby's, wrote in 1976 that the Scheide Library "is one of only five libraries where those three greatest monuments of the first years of printing, the Gutenberg Bible, the 1457 Psalter and the 1459 Psalter, keep company together. Its associates in this honor are the British Library, the Rylands Library, the Bibliothèque Nationale, and the Deutsche Staatsbibliothek. . . . Those who have witnessed the unerring ease with which the present owner finds his way through the 42-line Bible or the Psalters quickly understands that this tradition is still alive; the books are used and read."

Another book frequently attributed to Gutenberg's press, the *Catholicon* of Johannes Balbus, is represented in the Scheide Library as well. Of particular interest here is the note inserted in the colophon. Translated in 1936 by Margaret Stillwell, the colophon for this book reads:

> With the help of Omnipotent God, at Whose very nod the tongues of infants are made eloquent, and Who often reveals to the humble what He withholds from the wise—this excellent book, Catholicon, has been printed in the goodly city of Mainz, in the glorious German nation (which, by the Grace of God, the Almighty has deigned to prefer and exalt above other nations of the earth by gracious gift and so lofty a light of genius), and it has been brought to completion in the year of our Lord's incar-

nation, 1460—not by means of reed, stylus, or quill, but with the miraculous and harmonious concurrence of punches and types cast in moulds. Hence to Thee, O Holy Father, Son, and Holy Ghost, let praise and honour be given Thee, Three Persons in One God, Holy Trinity. To the single glory of the Church let universal praise be given for this book, and let all tongues laud the Blessed Virgin Mary, henceforth, and forevermore. TO GOD BE THE THANKS.

When I first interviewed William Scheide, he said that the 1457 Psalter was his "favorite" book in the collection, not only because it was something that had been considered "unprocurable," but also because of what it contributed to his collection of early printing. A few months later, on November 27, 1991, he took another major step. Barely a month shy of his seventy-eighth birthday, he authorized his agent, Roland Folter, of H. P. Kraus, to bid a little under $2 million at Christie's in London for the first 36-line Bible printed with Gutenberg type to be sold in more than two hundred years. The identity of the new owner was not announced, but news moved quickly through the book world that the volume known as the Liverpool Copy of the 36-line Bible was coming to North America—the first time that any copy of the book had ever crossed the Atlantic Ocean—and that it would have a new home in the Scheide Library.

Now gathered under one roof are the five primary incunabula (the 42-line Gutenberg Bible, the two Mainz Psalters, the Durandus, and the 36-line Gutenberg Bible), only the third time ever that a private collector has owned them all; the other collectors were King George III of England and George John, second earl of Spencer. Four of these books—each for many years considered unobtainable—were added by the current owner. "I had always maintained that the Scheide Library was the finest private library anywhere," Paul Needham said. "But this acquisition made it absolutely extraordinary. What a marvelous way to climax a life in collecting."

8

Mirror Images

"Friend and fellow bibliophile, remember your library is the mirror of your personality," the French collector Maurice Robert cautioned in 1936 as Nazi mobs across the border made bonfires of "offensive" literature. "Tell me what you read," an old proverb states, "and I shall tell you what you are." Heartbroken at the loss of his eyesight in old age, the poet, scholar, and scientist Eratosthenes of Alexandria starved himself to death rather than live any longer without the companionship of his books. John Hill Burton told of a retired archdeacon who became so distraught at the dispersal of his library that he left the auction in a panic, returned in the uniform of an army officer, and bought back every lot that remained. Asked once how he possibly could know one title from another in a house weighted down with volumes that looked alike, Charles Lamb responded with a question of his own: "How does a shepherd know his sheep?"

There is pain to collecting. There is pleasure to collecting. Earlier this century, the English essayist Solomon Eagle wrote a short article

275

titled "Moving a Library" that described the dreaded exercise of relocating to new quarters.

> Night after night I have spent carting down two flights of stairs
> more books than I ever thought I possessed. Journey after jour-
> ney, as monotonously regular as the progresses of a train round
> the Inner Circle; upstairs empty-handed, and downstairs creep-
> ing with a decrepit crouch, a tall, crazy, dangerously bulging
> column of books wedged between my two hands and the
> indomitable point of my chin. The job simply has to be done;
> once it is started there is no escape from it; but at times during
> the process one hates books as the slaves who built the Pyra-
> mids must have hated public monuments. A strong and bitter
> book-sickness floods one's soul. How ignominious to be
> strapped to this ponderous mass of paper, print, and dead
> men's sentiments! Would it not be better, finer, braver, to leave
> the rubbish where it lies and walk out into the world a free,
> untrammelled, illiterate Superman?

Even more intimidating than mere physical exertion are the "complications of getting one's library straight" in a new setting, especially if the rooms are "totally different in shape and arrangement," since knowing where everything is located is what distinguishes the true collector from the hoarder. "That is where I am at this moment," Eagle concluded, "sitting in the midst of a large floor covered with sawdust, white distemper, nails, tobacco-ash, burnt matches, and the Greatest Works of the World's Greatest Masters. Fortunately, in Ruskin's words, 'I don't suppose I shall do it again for months and months and months.' "

New York City investor Carter Burden thrilled antiquarian booksellers throughout America by declaring, "You can never be too thin, too rich, or have too many books." When he made that statement in 1987, he was well into a ten-year mission to gather the full sweep of modern American literature. At that time, some six thousand authors were represented in his collection of books, manuscripts, unpublished screenplays, first appearances in magazines, criticism, ephemera—the entire spectrum. By one estimate, he already had acquired more than seventy thousand volumes. He boasted that books "do not merely furnish my rooms, they engulf them. They are everywhere—in my study, the library, the kitchen, the corridors, the bathrooms, the children's rooms."

Two years later, Burden sold his fourteen-room condominium overlooking the East River and commissioned the architect Mark Hampton to renovate a smaller apartment on Fifth Avenue, overlooking Central Park. Burden placed his library into storage and stopped buying books, an abrupt withdrawal that caused considerable anxiety throughout the trade. Some dealers suggested that his sudden inactivity marked the end of an era. "Not having the books around is distressing," Burden told me at the time. "I love to read my books, but I also enjoy them as objects. I like living with them. I like holding them. I make all my own glassine covers, and I like putting books where they belong. It's manual therapy for me, and to collect abstractly from a catalogue, without being able to handle them, is not collecting. So now I am in a hiatus."

A great-great-great grandson of Commodore Cornelius Vanderbilt on his father's side, Carter Burden works actively in the family investment firm of William A. M. Burden Company and has the means to collect virtually anything he wants, world classics among them. But from the start he wanted to form a collection of twentieth-century American first editions that would be in a class by itself.

"I decided that it could be done for a reasonable amount of money," he said. "I was buying paintings long before I was collecting books. I started collecting American contemporary art in the sixties, when you could buy a Frank Stella for two thousand and a Jasper Johns for ten thousand dollars. I never paid more than ten thousand for a single picture, but then that quickly got out of my league." When Burden decided he could build a library of the first magnitude with about the same money it would take to form a middle-level art collection, he began to sell his paintings. "The truth of the matter is that I basically paid for my books with the profits I made on the paintings. But I never considered them investments when I bought them. My family thought I was nuts at the time. Now they think I'm a genius. The whole point is that I wasn't nuts, and I'm not a genius."

Burden grew up in Beverly Hills, California, where his mother, Flo-belle Fairbanks, a niece of Douglas Fairbanks, was an actress. Accord-ing to one account, Burden arrived in Manhattan society in the mid-1960s as a "tall, blond, handsome, rich, and glamorous" man whose "background of great wealth and privilege" placed him "among the ranks of New York's social elite." His first marriage, in 1964, to Amanda Jay Mortimer, daughter of the second wife of CBS chairman William S. Paley, Babe Cushing Mortimer Paley, was a highly publi-cized social event. Carter and Amanda Burden were variously described as the "young locomotives" and "New York's number-one fun couple." *Vogue* promoted the radiant image with a ten-page spread about their life in the Dakota under the headline "The Young-Joyous Life." By 1972, though, the "young-joyous life" was over, and so was the marriage. "We were just too young," Burden said. He and Susan Burden were married in 1977. She is a family therapist who respects her husband's passion to collect but does not share it.

"I am convinced that the urge to collect is innate," he said. "It is not inherited—my kids have no real interest in collecting—but you either have the bug or you don't. I started collecting toy soldiers and baseball cards when I was six years old. That's not especially significant, but I think the fact that I have kept the toy soldiers all these years probably is."

A graduate of Harvard College and Columbia Law School, Burden worked as an aide to Senator Robert Kennedy before successfully run-ning for a seat on the New York City Council in 1968, where he served for eight years. Burden's political ambitions ended in 1978 when he sought the congressional seat vacated by Ed Koch, who resigned to run for mayor of New York. Despite spending $1 million of his own money on the campaign, he lost the general election and joined the family investment firm.

About the time Burden was approaching his fortieth birthday, in 1981, the idea for a great library took hold. Burden explained why he decided to go after American literature. "Prime material was readily available, prices were reasonably cheap," and serious competition, with a few exceptions, "was relatively weak." Having established the scope, he defined his expectations: "I wanted my entire collection to meet the highest bibliographic standards. I insisted on first editions, pristine condition, original dust jackets. I wanted all the rarities and high spots, but more than anything, I sought comprehensiveness and depth."

In addition to acknowledged masters like William Faulkner and Ernest Hemingway, he would collect authors such as Booth Tarkington and Pearl S. Buck that "nobody has paid attention to in years," and along with novelists, poets, and dramatists, his shelves would welcome "critics, humorists, detective writers, science fiction writers, Western writers, black writers, political writers. Moreover, I was committed to collecting the work of every important writer in depth—proofs, limited editions, variant issues, pamphlets, broadsides, English editions, magazine appearances." Before long, his large apartment on the East Side was filled with books. They were in every room and hall, in every corner and on every end table, and they shared space with all the other items he had been gathering for most of his life, a samelsurium that included Indian miniatures, drawings, bronzes, glass bells, wooden snuffboxes, even antique English ballot boxes with "Yea" and "Nay" painted above the appropriate slots.

Toward the end of the 1980s, there was an abrupt slowdown. Talk spread that Burden had quit collecting, and he was rumored to be selling his books. He gave a considerable collection of science fiction material to the New York Public Library and consigned an entire run of W. H. Auden material to the book dealer Ralph B. Sipper, owner of Joseph the Provider, Inc., in Santa Barbara, California. There were other murmurs that despite an enormous family fortune, Burden had gone broke buying books and he was being forced to sell not only his collections but his East Side apartment as well.

A few other insiders, however, saw the situation differently. "I believe Carter stopped buying because he pretty much has everything he wants," Peter B. Howard, owner of Serendipity Books in Berkeley, California, said. "People don't understand the Carter Burden phenomenon—and it most definitely was a phenomenon—because there has never been anything else like it. I have been in the business since 1965, and it is unique in my experience."

When Burden and I first talked, in 1990, he had just moved out of his East Side apartment. He said the move had been suggested by his wife, who wanted to live closer to the Metropolitan Museum of Art.

Even though the newer quarters on Fifth Avenue were smaller, a slow-down in the collecting would have resulted even if they had decided to stay where they were. "I was afraid the floor was going to collapse into the next apartment," he said. "The fact is that I made a manful effort, but what you quickly learn is that no collection is ever complete. So, yes, I was defeated. The point, I guess, is that I tried. If I were starting today, I certainly would never attempt to be as broad as I was in the beginning. Six thousand authors, in every issue of every book? Period-ical appearances and signed limited editions? And uncorrected proofs? That was a mistake, trying to collect all those proofs."

An uncorrected proof is a book that has already been set in type from the author's manuscript but has not been approved for final production. Only a hundred copies or so are produced at this stage of production, sometimes more, sometimes less, and they represent an intermediate phase between what has been written and what is being prepared for gen-eral release. Proofs are circulated within publishing houses, and some are sent out to critics in the hope that sufficient lead time will encourage a timely notice. Usually they are bound in plain paper and distributed with a standard caveat stamped inside or on the cover that reads something like "These are uncorrected advance proofs bound for your reviewing conve-nience. In quoting from this book for reviews or any other purpose, it is essential that the final printed book be referred to, since the author may make changes on these proofs before the book goes to press."

Publisher's proofs have been around for at least sixty years, and as the demand for modern literature has grown, collecting them has become fashionable, primarily because they represent a "state" that is earlier than the first edition, and in some cases actually can be consid-ered a "variant" form of the text. Many authors—John Updike, Anne Tyler, Philip Roth, and the late Bernard Malamud, to name just four—have revised novels right up to the final typesetting. Changes of such consequence were made in *The Witches of Eastwick, Dinner at the Homesick Restaurant,* and National Book Award winner Tim O'Brien's 1994 book, *In the Lake of the Woods,* that new proofs had to be printed, producing what amounted to two sets of galleys. The earlier versions were of course more desirable. Less dramatic modifications take place all the time; Henry Holt advised critics in 1986 that the names of several minor characters in Louise Erdrich's second novel, *The Beet Queen,* had been changed, and to avoid using them in any review.

Something small like this, prompted perhaps by a publisher's concern for legal propriety more than a novelist's sense of artistic purpose, is probably not worth paying a lot of money to own. But consider the matter of a "sampler" prepared in 1988 by a small Midwestern publisher, Academy Chicago, to promote the forthcoming publication of *The Uncollected Stories of John Cheever.* The sampler contained three of Cheever's early magazine pieces—"Bayonne," "Town House," and "The Habit." Several hundred copies of the twenty-three-page booklet were passed out at an American Booksellers Association convention in Anaheim, California, over the Memorial Day weekend in anticipation of the book's scheduled release in the fall. Publication was halted indefinitely, however, when an Illinois judge ruled in favor of the late author's estate, which had sued Academy Chicago to block the project, and for six years the samplers represented the only appearance of any part of the book. When a sharply truncated edition of *The Uncollected Stories of John Cheever* finally was released in 1994, only thirteen stories from the original sixty-eight were included, and just one from the sampler, "Bayonne," was among them. A prophetic disclaimer affixed to the booklet makes it especially attractive to collectors: "This sampler is not authorized by the family of John Cheever." The few reviewers fortunate enough to receive full sets of the uncorrected proofs before the project was halted possessed an even greater rarity.

Because proofs are not intended for general circulation, scarcity is guaranteed, intensifying demand. The Viking Press may elect to run off half a million copies of the latest Stephen King horror thriller in the first printing, but the number of proofs it produces will remain fairly constant, thus placing a premium value on copies that make their way into the marketplace.

Because he was trying to document every phase of the publishing process, Burden bought proofs by the score. He now believes this was a mistake; he also wishes he had not paid as much attention as he did to signed and numbered "fine-press" editions, books that typically take a story by a well-known author that has not appeared in a hardcover edition and print an attractive little booklet in limited numbers. "Man-

ufactured rarity" and "artificial rarity" are the phrases some collectors
use to describe the practice. Many prefer to collect only the first trade
editions of books, which more accurately reflect a work's publishing
history. "The only author I'm still collecting in limited editions is John
Updike," Burden said. "And that's because I already have five hundred
or so items; I can't afford to quit on him now."

Peter Howard described Burden's original "notion" as audacious
but nonetheless quite simple: "Carter had set about collecting all of
American literature from Waller Barrett on." The Clifton Waller Barrett Library, given to the University of Virginia in Charlottesville in
1960, spanned the full range of writing produced in the United States
prior to the twentieth century. A founding partner of the North
Atlantic and Gulf Steamship Company, Barrett once said that as he
became acquainted with such neglected writers as Charles Brockden
Brown, John Neal, William Gilmore Simms, Robert Montgomery Bird,
and James K. Paulding, he "became fired with the ambition to collect
complete sets of their original editions so that this authentic American
literature might be preserved for posterity." He gathered five hundred
major authors in depth during a half century of collecting; another five
hundred, including many nineteenth-century writers known only by
copies of their books in his library, were sought out as well. He selectively included a number of twentieth-century writers, but his collection through 1900 is comprehensive and without equal. At his death in
1991 at the age of ninety, Barrett's bequest totaled 112,000 manuscripts and 35,000 books. "I do not know how many writers and
scholars owe debts of gratitude to Clifton Waller Barrett," Leon Edel,
the biographer of Henry James, marveled in tribute. "He has been a
kind of twentieth-century literary Maecenas."

Peter Howard said that Burden "overlapped with Barrett slightly,"
but that he utilized the same style. "He collected the primary editions,
he collected significant inscribed and biographical editions, and he collected representative autograph material. The joy was that Carter
wanted one of every book by every serious twentieth-century American
author." This was possible for several reasons, not least of which was
Burden's willingness to commit a significant amount of money to the
effort. "This lit up the eyes of booksellers everywhere," Howard said.
"After a while he worked mostly with three or four dealers who were

most capable of finding what he wanted in a penetrating way." In addition to Howard, Burden's other primary suppliers were Ralph B. "Joe the Pro" Sipper of Santa Barbara, California, Glenn Horowitz of New York City, and the late Marguerite A. "Margie" Cohn, owner for many years of House of Books in New York and a pioneer dealer in modern first editions.

Though Howard does not speak for his colleagues, he is a past president of the American Antiquarian Booksellers Association and knows the trade well. "What happened was that this notion developed that Carter Burden was collecting all of American literature, and that all of American literature would be made available to him," he said. "What is truly extraordinary is that all of American literature *was* made available to him. And those books didn't just get born in the basements of those three or four primary booksellers. They had to come from somewhere, and the effort involved the whole of the book world. Just about everyone supplied those books, and they were repaid handsomely for their efforts."

The problem with most of his colleagues, Howard suggested, is that "today is only a way they use to get to tomorrow, and once Carter stopped buying, he ceased to be a part of their plans. But he put millions of dollars into the modern first edition book trade, and that money became a free-floating cannonball." As a consequence, Howard believes Burden gave modern first editions "ten, twenty, or thirty more years" of boundless activity and that the "trade ought to be everlastingly thankful" to him.

The result for Burden, Howard said, was that "in ten years and however many millions of dollars—how many millions, maybe ten million, maybe twenty million; I doubt if it was more than twenty million—he built a fabulous collection. And he brought it up to the point that he stopped. None of us have a clue as to why he stopped buying, or why he stopped collecting. It seems inconceivable that it was money that stopped him from buying, so I have to feel that the collection, in his view, for the most part, was done. But it was absolutely wonderful while it lasted."

Howard said that Burden, during the height of his activity, "represented more than twenty-five percent of my accounts receivable, which banks are inclined to tell you is a bad business practice. But I would not have my half-million-dollar building in Berkeley if Carter Burden had not come along when he did. So in truth and in memory, the Carter Burden phenomenon was a wonderful thing for the trade." Ralph Sipper, who provided Burden with a large number of books and has since taken a number of smaller collections back as part of the winnowing process, said, "What happened simply is that Carter ran out of room."

But was it really over?

The February 1992 issue of *Vogue* published a stunning feature of a Manhattan apartment, newly designed by Mark Hampton and conceived entirely around the theme of books. Though the owner was not named in John Russell's article, there was no doubt about the collector's identity. Only one person in the world has the books Russell described: "The authors in question are all modern American, from Mark Twain more or less to the present." Later, Russell noted that "this collector also delights in drafts (preferably unpublished) and will tackle movie scripts and diaries and rehearsal scripts, story lines and television plays and every other kind of memorabilia."

Burden and I met again over a glass of wine late one afternoon that summer. My first reaction was that Burden's Upper West Side apartment is more striking than the photographs reproduced so lavishly in *Vogue* were able to show, and later in *House & Garden,* which published a similar spread. While neither of these articles identified Carter and Susan Burden as the owners, the Burdens' taste is apparent. The objects from the old house are everywhere, the George III writing table, the William IV armchairs, the sculptures, bronzes, porcelain, drawings, and clocks. And throughout the apartment the prevailing motif is, in Mark Hampton's words, "books, books, books." Because the ceiling in the living room is fourteen feet high, the dark cabinets have room for ten shelves. The arrangement there is alphabetical by author, starting from the left, James Agee to John Steinbeck, and picking up in the next room with Peter Taylor and continuing through Kurt Vonnegut, Jr., Robert Penn Warren, William Carlos Williams, Eudora Welty, and Richard Wright. On one exterior wall, twelve clamshell boxes lie flat, each containing "special" John Updike material. Seventeen others, green with black labels, contain more than fifty "first draft playscripts" by Tennessee Williams.

It was an impressive sight, but there was still a small problem to be resolved. "I'm an old newspaper reporter who's pretty good at estimating crowds," I said, "and I figure something between ten and fifteen thousand books altogether in here." Burden laughed. "About twelve thousand, maybe a little less. The rest are still in storage. It's expensive, but I have access." So was it true what people were saying after all, that he had stopped buying books? "I will never stop collecting," he answered. "But the original scheme is finished. Six thousand authors is impossible. I finally realized that I can't do it all. I can't keep up with everything. It's absurd."

That he is still collecting, and collecting with purpose, was evident by his disclosure that Glenn Horowitz had recently bought for him a copy of Sinclair Lewis's first book, *Hike and the Aeroplane,* at the Swann Galleries auction of Charles Epstein's library. Published in 1912 under the pseudonym Tom Graham, the book was written for a juvenile audience that for the most part had "read the book to death." As a result, very few of the one thousand books have survived with jackets intact, making complete copies exceedingly scarce. The presale estimate was $3,000 to $5,000; Burden paid $19,250.

"With everything you've got, I would have figured you to have Sinclair Lewis pretty much covered," I said.

"I already had a copy of the book," Burden replied. "It was the dust jacket I needed."

When two people collect in tandem, a dynamic comes into play that may create a product greater than its parts. The best-known twentieth-century example is the shared passion of Henry Clay Folger (1857–1930) and his wife, Emily Jordan Folger (1858–1936), who created the Folger Shakespeare Library in the nation's capital. Their ashes are deposited behind a stone marker off the main reading room, with their legacy "for eternity."

There are approximately thirty thousand books in the large eighteenth-century house Leonard and Lisa Baskin own in western Massachusetts, but numbers are irrelevant, the artist said one Sunday afternoon while moving purposefully through the large library that adjoins his studio.

Baskin is one of the world's foremost printmakers, proficient in creating woodcuts, wood engravings, etchings, aquatints, and lithographs.

He also is one of America's most respected artists and sculptors, considered a maverick by some during the 1950s for his opposition to Abstract Expressionism, choosing instead to develop new images and forms that have attracted a devoted following for his work, which is represented in the permanent collections of more than fifty institutions. Baskin also has owned a fine press for more than fifty years.

"One book can be so fantastic that it makes numbers meaningless," Baskin said, and showed me a book titled *Les Bouquets des Bergeres* (*Bouquet of the Shepherdesses*). The large volume was published in Amsterdam in 1640 and features engravings by Crispin van De Pass, a man Baskin identified as one of the great Flemish engravers of the late sixteenth and early seventeenth centuries. "What you see here are Flemish and Dutch ladies of the aristocratic and upper middle class dressed as shepherds. Well, this is an incredibly scarce book. So what do numbers have to do with it? I could buy a thousand books for what this book is worth."

Baskin has been collecting since he was a child growing up in Brooklyn during the Depression, and he becomes especially animated when he recalls finding books he never knew existed until the moment of discovery. "It is a thrill when you see something that you know in an instant is important. And it is just as exciting when you have the perception to connect it with something else of equal importance." Leonard has been collecting with Lisa, his second wife, since the mid-1960s; she said that her "really passionate collecting" of books, pamphlets, letters, broadsides, almanacs, and ephemeral items relating to the political, social, and intellectual history of women from the sixteenth century on parallels her involvement with the revival of the women's movement.

"I would say that we collect some books in concert and that we pursue others independently," Baskin said. "Being older than Lisa, I've been doing it far longer, so there was a collection into which she merged. Then her own instincts had a way to express themselves. They were sharpened and intensified once our relationship was established."

Baskin established the Gehenna Press while a student at Yale School of Art during World War II. In 1992 a commemorative exhibition, curated by Lisa Baskin, was mounted in honor of the press's fiftieth anniversary. The Baskins' son, Hosea, prepared the bibliography, and

Colin Franklin, a British antiquarian bookman, contributed a lengthy essay to the exhibition catalogue. In it he compares Leonard Baskin's work as a printer favorably with that of William Morris and the Kelmscott Press. Both Morris and Baskin produced fine printing "against the background of typographic reform, bibliophile taste, [and] artistic work, bearing in mind always that for Baskin these books display just one facet of an artist's life." Franklin found Baskin's "chronic addiction as collector of books and prints" to be relevant to "any account of books he has printed, for they also grew within traditions. It is a commonplace of collecting, rare of attainment now, that no form of life in libraries compares with the intimacy of owning. The point has to be made, because the books and prints surrounding him are also within the soul of that art which informs this exhibition."

Franklin has known Baskin for more than twenty-five years, not only as a provider of books for his library, but also as a leading authority on fine press printing, the "peripheral, though splendid, activity" Baskin took up when he founded the Gehenna Press and which he has continued to master ever since. "Leonard is quite exceptional among collectors in that he has an artist's eye for things which other people are ignoring," Franklin said during an interview in his Oxford home. "He doesn't buy the fashionable things. He's a thoroughly original man. His knowledge of early color printing, for instance, or those seventeenth-century etchers and engravers he has uncovered, have demonstrated great perception. I would guess he feels something like contempt for people who collect middle-of-the-road things."

After Baskin returned *Les Bouquets des Bergeres* to its shelf, he brought out what he described as a "great new addition" to the collection that he "never knew existed" until the moment he laid eyes on it a few weeks earlier. "At first glance it's a rather common book of the life of St. Thomas Aquinas, which was published in 1610," he said. "This copy, as you can see, was owned by a cardinal, and part of the original covering is rather nicely preserved in a nineteenth-century binding, which has surrounded the original central portion. That is all very nice; but look further, and you will see there are thirty engravings after a man named Otto van Veen, whom I knew to be the teacher of Peter Paul Rubens. Now, what makes this copy very special is that the engravings have been gilded and colored by a very talented artist. It's breathtaking, actually. It's the sort of book I never dreamed we could possibly ever own, yet here it is. It absolutely takes my breath away."

What makes the book especially meaningful is Baskin's considered belief that the engravings were colored by someone closely related to the artist who drew them. "I knew Otto van Veen was a great theoretician and artist in his own right. And the quality of the painting here is unmistakable; this book was colored by a very fine artist. That is what was immediately apparent to me. I've been looking at books critically since I was thirteen years old, so call it instinct if you want, but it's a little more than that."

"We were still pretty lucky," Lisa added, and Leonard laughed.

"We were, indeed," he said. "We got it from a bookseller who didn't understand; he thought that because someone had colored in the engravings, they were worth less."

While discoveries of such magnitude are infrequent, the Baskins go out constantly to hunt for fresh material, and they both insist they find good books wherever they go.

"I can find good books anywhere," Lisa said.

"I just got a wonderful book at the Boston Book Fair that I had never seen or heard of before," Leonard said. "It's on the movement of water." He located *Les Raisons des forces mouvantes,* a scientific work published in Paris in 1624 that explains the mechanics necessary to move water through fountains.

"This man Salomon de Caus, I knew that man, he is famous for having done a perspective book which I could never find," Leonard said. "So this is fundamentally a book about machinery, about the movement of water, about waterwheels."

"Fundamentally a boring book," Lisa said.

"It's not *really* a boring book," Leonard said.

"It's boring," Lisa insisted.

"Yeah, maybe—*until* you get to these wonderful etchings. Look at this, this is like a tableau vivant, only in this case the animations are created with water. This is a musical instrument, a player piano, maybe, who knows? But look—here—this is a grotto, with fountains. *Look* at this plate. Here is a ball coming up out of the fountain, and all around it are chameleons, monsters, fairies, creatures, making a star of waterjets, and the creatures are keeping the ball in the air. It's a fabulous plate. It really knocked me for a loop when I saw it."

Another plate pictured a kind of seventeenth-century automaton, "worked by music, worked by water, and meanwhile the animals are charmed. You see the animals? In every nook and cranny there are animals. These are copper engravings or etchings, it's hard to say which, but look, you see these animals everywhere. I even know where most of them are copied from. You see this alligator hiding there? The owl up there? It's just gorgeous." He paused, considered a question, and continued almost in a whisper. "It hits me on every level, as an artist, as a collector, as a printer, on all levels, because it's a book of vast interest. And it's so peculiar. So unknown."

Baskin feels that the illustrated material he and his wife have assembled as a couple "should go out again, to collectors," but he believes her archive belongs in an institution. "What Lisa has done is put together diverse materials and made a new whole out of them. The ephemeral material, the journal material, the manuscript material, and the printed books together create a new entity which has never existed before. And as a result, it instructs us, it informs us, it delights us, it educates us, and it transforms us, and it won't ever be put together in that way again. It can't be, because the material is too ephemeral. To break that up, it seems to me, would be to betray its essential quality. Whereas to break up the collection of old books, you're not breaking anything up, that's just a very nice collection of miscellaneous early books."

A recent focus in the Baskin library is portrait books, books that feature likenesses of people, which Leonard finds desirable because "nobody else is interested" in them. "There are a half-dozen great portrait books that everybody knows and all the great libraries have, but beyond that there are hundreds and hundreds that nobody knows anything about. It's totally unknown because portrait collections tend to be boring, so they become a drag on the market. The booksellers don't like them. But since I have started this collection, the market has been rising slowly. I've had a direct influence on that to the point that every portrait book that comes along is offered to me."

The Baskins also collect a wide variety of other unusual items, Renaissance medals, bronzes, and casts among them. "I collect something called memorial jewelry, which nobody was interested in when I was buying it in the early sixties," Lisa said. Memorial jewelry, also known as commemorative jewelry, came into vogue during the Renaissance and was crafted to observe family milestones such as weddings, birthdays, and deaths. Because the pieces often bear personal inscriptions, they have the potential to "tell a story," a quality Lisa finds especially attractive. "We used to collect old master prints, too. We sold many of them and now we have begun only recently to collect them again."

"Do you know what watch papers are?" Leonard asked. "When people had those great big watches and they brought them in for repairs, the watchmaker made a note on a piece of paper explaining what work he did. The piece of paper was engraved with his name and locus. From that commercial interest, which was started in the eighteenth century, a device grew where lovers would give to sailors, or someone going off on a long trip, or just generally, a token of affection to keep inside their watch. It was a little watercolor. Well, we have the largest collection in the world of those. Whenever one comes on the market, it comes to us."

He noted that the American Antiquarian Society has "a very nice collection" of watch papers, though the one he and Lisa have assembled is stronger. "The Antiquarian Society also has an excellent collection of ferry tickets, which I admire. Things like ferry tickets are very important because that's how history takes on a graphic side. If you have an 1812 ferry ticket, that ferry becomes palpable in your imagination instead of just being a figment of your imagination. The presence of the ticket lends reality to the idea. Isn't that true?"

Because he has been a printer for more than half a century, Baskin enjoys documenting various aspects of that craft as well. "We don't collect bookplates because everybody collects bookplates, but we do collect booksellers' and bookbinders' tickets," he said. "Those are the little tickets they put in books, bound by so and so, sold by so and so. We have a vast collection of them. And we also have a large collection of circulating-library tickets. Why? Because they're part of the book trade and they're interesting typographically. There was a time for twenty-five or thirty years when I actually had a plant and a full-time pressman. I had to give that end of it up because I make my living as an artist. I'm not a rich dilettante who pokes around all day with this and that. I work all day. But I work at collecting too."

The Baskins don't keep everything they have collected. Among the items they have sold was "a great collection" of early colored engraved books. "We also had a great collection of perspective books," Leonard said. "We had a great collection of emblem books," Lisa added. "One of our goals was to get every sixteenth-century emblem book that was available," Leonard explained. "That's a hard thing to do. Today you can't even get any from the seventeenth century."

The Baskins agreed that parting with books, paintings, and artifacts can be traumatic, but they find ways to justify the decision. "We took the emblem books as far as they could go," Leonard said. "It was a finished collection; we couldn't acquire any more, so we sold them. We had a wonderful collection of Thomas Eakins paintings that today would be worth an incalculable fortune. That was probably the toughest thing we had to do, because that was like opening the bank. Anything was possible after that. Then the color engravings went. We had a collection of eighteenth- and nineteenth-century English pottery called Mocha ware, three hundred pieces; we sold those in the early seventies. They're getting colossal prices now. It's awful, it's painful, it can be unbearable, but what are you going to do?"

"It's terrible, that's all," Lisa said. "But with two kids in school and tuition to pay, this is how we do it."

I asked Leonard whether the collections have in any way influenced his own creative activity. "I am sure it is there, though it would be hard to find any direct relationship. I am unable to give you anything specific, but there can be no question but that there is a relationship."

He pointed out that through history virtually no artists have been serious collectors. "The most striking exception to that rule, of course, is Rembrandt. He collected paintings, he collected prints, he collected armor, he collected bronzes, he collected Renaissance medals, he collected drawings—he collected everything. Let me refine that: He collected anything that was beautiful. But he pauperized himself in the process. The control of his business and money ultimately was taken out of his hands by his wife and son and creditors. He was profligate, and it was because of his collecting." The Pop artist Andy Warhol gained additional celebrity after his death when enormous collections of antiques and knick-knacks were found among his possessions, though Baskin said the material gathered by Rembrandt was of "a much higher level; it was truly superior stuff."

Toward the end of our interview, I asked the Baskins if picking out favorite items and showing them to interested visitors is one way they enjoy their collections. "It's fun sharing it with people who love books, but most of the time when we're in here, we're by ourselves. We play," Lisa said.

"If ever I am bored with anything else, which I never could imagine happening, I would come into this library and start looking at stuff, and I would be enchanted," Leonard said. "I just love this stuff that we've got here."

"It's a madness," Lisa said.

"It is, indeed," Leonard agreed.

It was six o'clock on a weekday morning, and we had just left St. Louis, Missouri, for Cape Girardeau, a small elbow-shaped town 120 miles to the southeast that gets its marine-sounding name from a spit of sand that juts sharply into the Mississippi River. We had a whole day ahead of us, so I asked the book collector Louis Daniel Brodsky to start at the beginning, and he chose to start almost thirty years earlier, in 1963, when he failed to win an undergraduate book-collecting prize at Yale University.

"I'll never forget the trauma," the man rare-book aficionados know as "L.D." said in complete earnestness. He told how he had assembled two hundred books by and about William Faulkner, and how he was "shattered" when his entry was awarded second place in the contest. As a member of the soccer and crew teams at Yale—he captained both sports during his freshman year—Brodsky appreciates the vagaries of competition.

"What upset me was not that I had lost," he insisted, "but how I felt when I learned that first prize went to a collection of railroad time-tables. *That's* what hurt. This was supposed to be a book-collecting contest. The emphasis is on literature—on books—and I get beat out by a guy with timetables. That's what stung me." An even greater indignity followed when Brodsky received his runner-up prize. "They gave me a second printing of *A Farewell to Arms,* and it didn't even have a dust jacket," he said. "First place gets a cash prize, I get this crummy little reading copy of a Hemingway novel. I always had the feeling they were trying to tell me something, that maybe I was a jerk for collecting Faulkner, and *here's* the guy I ought to be interested in. Who knows? But the whole thing seemed ironic, and I guess it still rankles me after all these years."

The Adrian Van Sinderen Award is the oldest undergraduate book-collecting competition in the United States and by far the most prestigious. It was established in 1957 by Adrian Van Sinderen, class of 1910, to encourage students to build their own libraries. Cash prizes are given to first-place entries. Winners over the years have included William S. Reese and W. Graham Arader III, two booksellers with national reputations, and T. Kimball Brooker of Illinois, a noted collector of sixteenth-century books and the sponsor of a similar competition at the University of Chicago.

For Brodsky, his loss only redoubled the intensity of his collecting of the slighted Faulkner. The result is an archive of books, manuscripts, photographs, journals, letters, and assorted documents so comprehensive that it ranks among the finest collections in America put together by one person devoted to a single author. "I read Faulkner for the first time when I was a freshman at Yale, and I was moved beyond words. I read *The Sound and the Fury,* and I was Quentin Compson. So on that account I owe my intellectual awakening to Yale. My mind came alive there, and for that I will always be grateful."

Though he insists he bears no grudge against Yale, it is Cape Girardeau's Southeast Missouri State University that since 1988 has been the permanent home of the Louis Daniel Brodsky Faulkner Collection. During a visit to Yale's Beinecke Library several months after my trip to Missouri, I mentioned Brodsky's failure to win the award to Stephen Parks, a curator who now supervises the Van Sinderen Award competition. He shrugged and offered a mild observation: "I know of that railroad collection. It was very clever and it showed a lot of originality."

In later years, certainly Brodsky too showed much cleverness and originality in his collecting strategy. His vigorous approach in time brought him exclusive access to primary materials long before they had a chance to appear on the open market. "I hate buying from catalogues," he said. "It bores me, to tell you the truth, because by and large it's too static and too sedentary, and half the time when you see something nice in a catalogue, it's always gone when you call to get it, no matter how quickly you pick up the phone. So I've learned not to get all worked up about what you might see in a dealer's list. I'm a person who likes being in contact with people anyway. I care about collecting on a personal level. What I enjoy most of all is the fieldwork."

Though a number of interesting books came to Brodsky from dealers, his most triumphant acquisitions resulted from locating major pockets of primary material that were still in private hands. Sometimes he drove, sometimes he took the earliest flight out of St. Louis; what mattered was getting there first. But that approach would not take shape until 1975. After Yale, Brodsky did graduate work at Washington University in St. Louis and San Francisco State University, earning master's degrees in literature and creative writing. Disillusioned by several teaching assignments, in 1968 he moved to Farmington, Missouri, and took over the management of a plant that manufactured men's clothing for Biltwell, which his father, Saul Brodsky, had founded in 1929.

Brodsky's passion for collecting returned in 1974, when Margie Cohn of the House of Books, Ltd., offered him nine books inscribed by Faulkner during the 1930s to Hubert Starr, a close friend of Faulkner's in Hollywood. "It was like putting a glass of Chivas Regal under the nose of an alcoholic," he said. "I took out my first bank loan to get them. I borrowed eleven thousand, which worked out to something like a thousand to fifteen hundred a book."

Later that year Brodsky bought at a Swann Galleries sale two titles that had eluded him from the beginning, *The Marble Faun* and one of the hundred signed limited edition copies of *Go Down, Moses*. "At that point I had a complete run of the printed books," a circumstance that led Washington University in St. Louis to suggest he put on an exhibition. The publicity from that 1976 show brought a letter from Vance Carter Broach of Tulsa, Oklahoma, a second cousin of Faulkner's who had inherited a sizable cache of presentation copies, correspondence, juvenilia in typescript, and a railroad ledger that had belonged to Colonel W. C. Falkner, the author's great-grandfather and the prototype of John Sartoris. (William later added the *u* to his family name.) "When

I heard from Vance Broach, I took off and drove straight to Tulsa," Brodsky said. He had already borrowed money to buy the nine books from Margie Cohn, so he could not offer Broach cash for the collection.

"Vance Broach loved literature, and he wanted books. So I traded him hundreds of books that we agreed had an equivalent value to his material. Because I had many duplicates, I was able to outfit him with a massive Faulkner collection. What I did not have at that time was a second copy of the one book he wanted most of all, *The Marble Faun*. Since the whole deal hinged on that, I let him have it, and it was the best judgment I ever made. The beautiful thing is that Vance knew what I was doing. He knew I wasn't going to sell any of this stuff. He understood that my interest was in scholarship. So we were able to make the deal without any money changing hands."

From this experience the scope of Brodsky's collecting was altered forever. "What I realized was that William Faulkner was not just a great writer, he was a human being. There was a whole network of people out there who had known him—family, associates, Hollywood people, New York people, literary people—and all of them had a piece of the puzzle."

Two books influenced Brodsky's thinking. The first, *Each in Its Ordered Place: A Faulkner Collector's Notebook,* compiled in 1975 by Carl Petersen, another St. Louis resident who had spent four decades assembling an exceptional Faulkner collection, listed "in one place the sum of a single collection and the direction taken in its assembly." Petersen hoped to suggest to "younger collectors the varieties of collecting available to unorderly acquisitiveness. Or, more accurately, that some orderliness can be superimposed after the acquisitiveness has gotten out of hand." Brodsky said he memorized Petersen's book not only because it was a guide to what Faulkner had published, but for the challenge it presented. "Carl's book showed me what one man could do, and it told me that if my dreams were high enough, I could do the same thing."

Brodsky came to know Petersen, and they were friends for a number of years, though a falling-out left them not speaking with each other. I got together with Petersen the night before I drove to Cape Girardeau with Brodsky—Petersen was willing to see me only on condition that we meet alone. "If you talk to L.D., that's your business," he said. "But I will have nothing further to do with the man." There are any number of theories to explain what happened—the most plausible is that each craved recognition as the most accomplished Faulkner collector in the world—but neither man would say how their once close friendship had broken.

Petersen provided a model for Brodsky, but the new collector still wanted to know where he could find fresh material. He got it from Joseph Blotner's landmark biography of William Faulkner, published in 1974, the second book that influenced him strongly. "Blotner was my road map," Brodsky said. "His book told me who was alive and where I had to go to find them. William Faulkner was a very private man, an elusive man, and what I did was bring the pieces together. I traveled all over the country and met tons and tons of people, and they all had artifacts. I was getting in touch with Faulkner the human being. It was tension that always drove this collection; Carl Petersen was a friend, but I wanted to surpass him. And I did."

Brodsky's travels took him to Alabama, West Virginia, Florida, Tennessee, New York, South Carolina, New Jersey, California, and Oklahoma, as well as Faulkner's home state of Mississippi. His first major score was material once owned by Phil Stone, an Oxford, Mississippi, lawyer who played an important role in young Bill Faulkner's literary development and to whom all three volumes of the Snopes trilogy are dedicated. From Stone's widow, Emily, Brodsky acquired fifteen inscribed books and an archive of unique manuscript material. "She wanted fifty thousand, and I said, 'Oh Emily, that's an awful lot of money.' She was living in Birmingham, Alabama, at that time, and I flew back and forth a couple times, and finally we reached an agreement of thirty-five thousand dollars. I borrowed eighteen thousand dollars and I sold a bunch of antiques for another twenty thousand. My wife and I had some old slot machines that were pretty valuable, and that's where I got the rest of the money to do it. But I knew what I was getting. 'Brodsky,' I said, 'you're making a hell of a deal here.' "

Soon thereafter, Brodsky read in Blotner's biography that a woman named Myrtle Ramey Demarest had been Faulkner's high school sweetheart. "It turned out Faulkner had given her sketches for a 1913 yearbook that never got made, along with some manuscript poems and drawings, some inscribed books. Blotner mentioned that she had put on a little exhibition of this material in New Jersey. Well, it took me two and a half years to trace the woman down. I looked all through New Jersey, I went through newspaper files there, all sorts of records, and I couldn't find her. Finally I located some other Rameys back in Mississippi, and they directed me to White Sulphur Springs, West Virginia, where I tracked her down. She was ninety years old and in a nursing home; I negotiated with her daughter. You'll see the stuff when we get to Cape Girardeau. It's fabulous."

Brodsky said that when he explained what he was trying to accomplish, the woman was pleased to help. "This was 1978, and it was all the money I had. The whole thing cost me sixteen thousand dollars. I got ten inscribed books, including a *Marble Faun*, I got typescripts, manuscripts, drawings. Today, that *Marble Faun* alone is about a fifty-thousand-dollar book, but I never looked at it that way. I only offered them sixteen thousand because that was all I could put together. But they were absolutely thrilled to get the sixteen thousand."

From Dorothy B. Commins, the widow of Saxe Commins, Faulkner's editor at Random House from 1936 to 1958, Brodsky acquired an exceptional run of association copies. Among them was a presentation copy of *Big Woods,* which Faulkner had dedicated to Saxe Commins.

In 1927, Faulkner wrote a fairy tale about children who have the power to shrink and return to normal size, a light amusement he typed, bound by hand, then presented to Victoria (Cho-Cho) Franklin, the eight-year-old daughter of Estelle Oldham, the woman he would marry two years later when her divorce was final. *The Wishing Tree*—with the inscription "Bill he made this Book"—was placed on long-term deposit at the University of Virginia, but it remained the property of Victoria's daughter, a Florida resident also named Victoria, from whom Brodsky acquired a considerable body of material.

"She had sold me virtually everything else she had—family letters, photographs, everything except that one book that was at the University of Virginia. I told her, 'Victoria, this is extremely important; it needs to be with the rest of the collection.' She had some qualms, but then she became aware that if the University of Virginia had really wanted the book, why hadn't they made her an offer? I had offered her five thousand dollars, you see. So Victoria wrote them a letter, and said simply, 'I would like the book that my mother put on deposit, please send it back.' For three weeks she heard nothing. Finally she called them and said she wanted the book, that she was planning to sell it to a collector. I said, 'Awwhh, Victoria, I wish you hadn't told them that.' "

The University of Virginia made a counteroffer but went no higher than the $5,000 Brodsky had put on the table. "She called me back, and I doubled the ante to ten thousand," Brodsky said. To his "profound relief," Victoria accepted. "I flew down to Florida and was there when the package arrived special delivery. She started to cry and I started to cry. I couldn't believe I got it, because I was convinced they were going to come up with twenty-five, thirty, fifty grand, who knows; a unique item like that is worth a lot of money. Faulkner typed each page, bound it by hand, stapled it, inscribed it to his step-daughter-to-be. I borrowed five thousand dollars and my mother gave me the other five as a present."

Brodsky estimated he has acquired about twenty collections directly from people who were close to Faulkner. "The people who owned these artifacts would never have thought of them as a collection. A lot of this stuff was keepsakes, souvenirs, whatever, kept by the people who knew Faulkner best. So I would go to these people and acquire from them a collection that *they* had unconsciously collected."

We arrived at Southeast Missouri State University about midmorning. There we were joined by Robert W. Hamblin, a professor of English and Faulkner scholar who has worked with Brodsky's collection since 1979 and has coauthored with him eight comprehensive volumes of bibliography, seven of which have been published by the University Press of Mississippi.

The book Brodsky and Hamblin agree may contain the single most important Faulkner inscription is not a first edition, but a later copy of *The Sound and the Fury* presented to Malcolm Cowley, the editor who brought out a popular anthology of Faulkner's fiction in 1946 titled *The Portable Faulkner*. The inscription reads, "To Malcolm Cowley, Who beat me to what was to have been the leisurely pleasure of my old age. William Faulkner." Hamblin said the book's importance as an artifact lies in its context. "Cowley revived Faulkner's reputation when it was at its lowest. Cowley had rendered him a great service. What you have here is Faulkner paying tribute to this man who gave his career a new life."

After we sampled a few more items, the conversation returned to Brodsky's sale of the collection. "I offered it twice to Yale, and I got the impression that what I had to offer wasn't all that important," he said. But indifference and bruised feelings weighed little in his decision compared to Yale's unwillingness to allow him any say in how the collection would be handled. "That collection is a testimony to enormous passion, and they felt I should just turn everything over to them. And then they didn't want to pay me anything for it. They buy things all the time at Yale, and here is a collection that would have brought them great distinction."

In the end, Brodsky sold part of the collection to Southeast Missouri State University for $1 million and donated the rest, though he insisted that money was not the only reason he placed the collection in what he called a "no-name" school. "The short of it all is that I am now an employee of the state. I am curator of the Louis Daniel Brodsky Collection. The contract is good for twenty years and my curatorial powers are all-inclusive. I may deaccession and accession anything that I choose during that period. At the end of that time, there is an option to renegotiate. When I forgo my position, my successor will not have any power to deaccession anything, not one item." Proximity to Brodsky's home—and the apparent approbation it would bring from his family—weighed just as heavily with him.

A prevailing belief in antiquarian book circles is that Brodsky was able to go off wherever he wished on a moment's notice because a vast family fortune was available to support his collecting passion. When Carl Petersen sold his Faulkner collection in 1989 to a consortium of booksellers for $445,000, the dealer who arranged the purchase, Peter Howard of Berkeley, California, thought he could sell it en bloc to Brodsky through Glenn Horowitz of New York.

"It was my intention to sell the collection intact the day after I bought it," Howard said, "and the idea basically was to move it across the same town" to Brodsky. The asking price was $670,000. "He and his dealer were not interested in buying the collection at my price, so I determined that the next responsible thing that I could do was to catalogue the collection properly."

Howard acknowledged that Brodsky's collection is superior in its holdings of inscribed books, letters, and movie scripts, and little duplication would have resulted from the addition of Petersen's collection. "Carl had the most comprehensive *book* collection in private hands, and by far the best 'condition' collection." Petersen's collection encompassed Faulkner in all languages and in all printed forms, including appearances in periodicals, and was rich in secondary material.

When Petersen talked to me about his collecting over dinner in St. Louis, there were no words of remorse and no second thoughts. He had collected Faulkner for more than forty years, and then had let the collection go. A chemical engineer and lifelong bachelor, Petersen said he was comfortable but not wealthy. "I was able to put money into something like this without ever having to worry that I was depriving anyone of anything."

But as he approached his sixtieth birthday in the late 1980s, he began to reflect. "The major items in the collection—the *Marble Faun* typescript, for instance—were all in a bank vault, all out of sight. So what was I supposed to do, go down to the bank once a week and play with them? I never got bored with the collection, but once the decision was made, I had no problems living with it." He tried placing the collection with an institution, but gave up after a year. "Everyone wanted it—the Library of Congress was very interested—but they all wanted me to give it to them." Finally, he sold the books to Peter Howard of Serendipity and his group of investors in 1989.

"I was getting to the point where maybe the money began to mean more than the collection," Petersen admitted. "It had served a very useful purpose, and now it is serving another useful purpose. So now let somebody else enjoy them. William Faulkner has served a purpose at both ends of my life." Sadly, two and a half years after he sold the collection to secure a comfortable retirement, Carl Petersen died at the age of sixty-two.

When asked why he passed on the Petersen collection, Brodsky took pains to point out that he did not have unlimited funds to work with. "That was more money than everything I had put into my collection combined," he said. "In thirty years of collecting, the Brodsky Collection has cost six hundred thousand dollars, that's all. So let me tell you another trick about collecting. You size up what's there and you decide,

I'm either going to go for it or I'm not, because I'm either in this for the long haul, or I'm not, but you have to live by your decisions, and there's no looking back. You have to develop a sense of balance so that if you blow it on one, it'll wash out the next time around."

As for family wealth, Brodsky said that his father is "an enormously prosperous man," but he vigorously denied any suggestion that Saul Brodsky blindly underwrote his son's collecting. "My father put three hundred thousand dollars into the collection, but those were loans over a twenty-five-year period, and every nickel he put in he got back. The reality is that I scraped for everything I got. My father is a very pragmatic businessman who didn't think collecting Faulkner was very important, certainly not as good as stocks or real estate. I always tried to persuade him that what I was doing was a great investment, even though that was never my purpose at all."

Brodsky said that his most consuming goal has always been to gain recognition as a writer, and that collecting the manuscripts and books of William Faulkner fed that ambition in a stimulating way. Since 1963, he has written thirty-three volumes of poetry, twelve published by Time Being Books of St. Louis, a small press that specializes in poetry by American writers.

"You must understand, above all, that I am a poet, and that Faulkner was a poet, even though his poetry was prose. Looking back, I can say that the reason I collected Faulkner so hungrily all those years was because he fired my desire to emulate him. There is no question that he inspired me to be a writer, and I did write seven novels when I was a much younger man. Unfortunately, they all came out sounding like William Faulkner, and none of them has been published. What I finally realized is that if I were ever going to succeed as a writer, it would have to be in poetry, the medium Faulkner wanted so desperately to master, and the one in which he failed. So the truth of the matter is that I wasn't collecting just one great American author, I was collecting two, one of whom had already succeeded splendidly. The other—Louis Daniel Brodsky—is still striving to make his mark. It may well be my reason for being."

Michael Zinman was trying to explain why the old wooden three-decker house he owns outside Ardsley, New York, is filled with several hundred crates of American imprints, and why his home a few miles away and the building where he operates his business nearby contain almost as much material again. "I've always wanted action as opposed to quality," he said. "I have always collected indiscriminately. If you do that, the good stuff takes care of itself."

Experts around the country agree that Zinman has put together what is by far the most comprehensive private collection of material printed before the year 1800 in what is now the United States. He collects "imprints," a word that essentially means anything that came off a printing press in a certain place within a specific period of time. Books are imprints—so are pamphlets, agricultural tracts, sermons, broadsides, and almanacs. The Bay Psalm Book is the most famous and most precious of all because it is the oldest surviving document produced in British North America.

Because of their ephemeral nature—and because they were not, for the most part, produced to endure as hallmarks of the craft—the importance of imprints was recognized only after many of them had disappeared. Isaiah Thomas and George Brinley collected them with a passion. Significant institutional collections of American imprints are in the American Antiquarian Society, the Library of Congress, the Library Company of Philadelphia, the Massachusetts Historical Society, and the Huntington Library, but relatively few remain in private hands. Prevailing wisdom holds that interest has waned because most of the "good stuff" already has been accounted for and that only "imperfect" material remains. What Michael Zinman decided to do in the early 1970s was to gather all the early American material he could find, regardless of quality or condition.

Zinman is a businessman who lives and works about thirty minutes outside of New York City. His company, Earthworm, Inc., buys and sells heavy construction machinery on an international basis, and a lot of what he does requires intense negotiations. "Yes, my business is a form of action as well," he agreed, noting that a good deal of his activity is in the "energy area," which involves "dealing with major utilities" around the world. He started Earthworm in 1968, and with its success has come the freedom to collect on his own terms. "That doesn't mean I no longer owe money to the booksellers; it only means I now owe them more than I ever did," he said. "Most people collect for different reasons than I do. One of the things I did was always to collect objects

in multiples. Let me also say that for whatever compelling reason I have
to collect, it is not to possess. Possessing is irrelevant to me; it's the
action. Being a collector, accumulating, and having the fun, that's what
drives me; the pleasure that I always got was in the *act* of collecting.
The possessing of the book, as pleasurable as it is, is transferred. Most
of all, I believe collecting is an educative process. You have to handle
the goods. If you handle the goods objectively, then after a while you
learn to discriminate."

Zinman said that before he embarked on his American imprint
odyssey, he collected United States Revenue Stamps, stamps affixed to
documents to certify the payment of taxes. "I had a very formidable
collection, probably the best collection of tax-paid beer stamps around.
I loved them. But when I decided that books were overwhelming this
area of my interests, I didn't pack the stamps away; I dumped them
because they weren't alive anymore for me. I wasn't about to lock them
up and put them away."

William S. Reese of New Haven, Connecticut, the leading dealer in
Americana, described Zinman as the "earl of Ardsley" in a speech given
to mark the opening of an exhibition at the American Antiquarian Society in 1989 and later said, "Michael Zinman is in a class by himself."
Stephen Massey of Christie's in New York said, "Michael Zinman has
an extraordinary collection of Americana, and what makes it remarkable is that he has no reservations about acquiring imperfect copies."

Zinman agreed, though he does have some criteria. "What I have is
certainly the largest, certainly the most important, though not necessarily the *finest* collection, because I look at fine in terms of quality,
condition, and significance. I don't own many of the great high spots of
American imprints. I own three complete Eliot Bibles, for example, but
they are second editions. I do own half of a first edition. I can buy one
tomorrow, but I don't want to spend a quarter of a million dollars for
it. It's a premium that I'm not prepared to pay, because I have limited
sums of money to spend in a universe that would consume my money.
Having said all that, however, it is probably true that I have formed the
most comprehensive collection of American imprints in private hands
since George Brinley, and he collected more than a hundred years ago.
My feeling was that there had to be enough material out there for one
more serious player."

Zinman gravitated toward imprints "because they had been forgotten by the private collector, because supposedly all the good stuff was accounted for. Nobody had collected this material for fifty years. It was no longer being sold. When I started buying these things, an imperfect book was considered less than garbage. It wasn't even listed in catalogues. So I just started taking what nobody else wanted. My collecting mentality is that I acquire anything. I do it without discrimination. As you accumulate, all of a sudden this material reaches a critical mass, and soon it becomes a collection. The junk is absolutely essential. Some of the rarest books in my collection had been lying in the desk drawers of dealers' shops for thirty or forty years. By taking everything in, you see the difference. You have the goods. You put everything on the table side by side, and you compare."

What develops from handling the "goods" is a sense of connoisseurship, a clear sense of worth, not just value. When a document said to be a long-lost copy of *The Oath of a Freeman* surfaced in 1985, Michael Zinman was the first person to challenge its authenticity. Such a broadside is known to have been produced between 1638 and 1639 in Cambridge, Massachusetts, and is regarded as the first document to be printed in British North America, predating the Bay Psalm Book. Though no copies of it are known to survive, its contents—the oath colonial freemen swore before assuming citizenship—are well documented. "It was too good to be true," Zinman said, trying to explain why, unlike so many professional experts who believed it to be authentic, he advised every institution that sought his advice not to buy it. The Library of Congress passed on the $1.5 million asking price. The American Antiquarian Society made a firm offer of $250,000, which was rejected as too low by the owner, a Salt Lake City collector named Mark Hofmann.

That Hofmann was a master forger became dramatically clear only after several people who suspected his activities were killed by homemade pipe bombs. In 1987, Hofmann pleaded guilty to murder and fraud and was sentenced to life imprisonment. His activities, including many spectacular forgeries produced and sold to the Mormon church that accounted for more than $3 million in sales, have been the subject of at least four books, but from a bibliographical standpoint, the most authoritative by far is *The Judgment of Experts,* a series of essays and documents published by the American Antiquarian Society in 1991.

Zinman's name appears throughout as a voice of disbelief. "It just didn't settle right, not in any way," he said. "I can't explain it better than that. When I first saw it, it was so appealing it was seductive, but I had this feeling in my gut that something was wrong."

In the process of gathering material, Zinman has acquired copies or fragments of every imaginable kind of Bible printed in America, the 1663 Eliot Indian Bible being the most prominent. He has multiple copies of the first German Bible printed in Pennsylvania, by Christopher Saur in 1743; the first American Bible printed in English, by Robert Aitken in 1782; Matthew Carey's Roman Catholic Bible, known as the Douay Bible, published in 1790; first American Bibles in Hebrew, Greek, Spanish, Portuguese, Dutch, and French; the first Bible for the blind; the first children's Bible; and the first with illustrations.

"I have twenty copies of *Kometographia,* which is a great seventeenth-century scientific tract by the Massachusetts minister and author Increase Mather. I will buy any seventeenth-century book I can get my hands on, without exception. This is a very distinctive collection, and it grew out of accumulation. What I did was arrive on the scene, walk inside every bookstore I could find, and buy everything that was around. I wheeled and I dealed, and most of the time these people were thrilled simply to get rid of the stuff. I was fortunate in being in the right place at the right time. I bought it indiscriminately, and I wound up having a very great holding of this material. There is no holding like this that could be duplicated today."

Because he does not hesitate to part with books that no longer interest him, Zinman often sells material or gives it away to institutions. "Before I collected Americana, I was collecting natural history, so there was a time when I would go to one side of Quaritch and sell my natural history, and then go to the other and buy my Americana."

The question of why Zinman collects with such enthusiasm does not have a thoroughly clear answer. "It's the action, but there also is an *inter*action, a link with some mechanism of history that strikes a responsive chord for me. I'm doing something that has some meaning. I like having these imprints, but I'm just the caretaker, and when I'm done with them, they will be dispersed. There will still be five institutional collections that are better than mine. I don't think the world needs a sixth, or something clumped between five and ten."

Among the otherwise unknown items displayed in his exhibition at the American Antiquarian Society was a 1670 copy of the *Laws of Massachusetts,* a previously unrecorded eighteenth-century sermon given at a Boston execution, several early collections of church music, and an anthology of "meditations" that contains the only known published poem of Edward Taylor, a Colonial poet whose other work survived only in manuscript. Zinman said that he would like to follow the examples of George Brinley in the late 1800s and Thomas Streeter in the 1960s, collectors who ordered the sale of their libraries but also gave money to various institutions to bid for material at their auctions. "I like that," Zinman said. "You help the institutions you want to help; they can go after the specific things they want, and what's left goes out for everyone else to enjoy."

Every book collector has at least one "great story" to share, and Zinman's is unusually germane to his concept of unconditional accumulation. "About 1980 or so I got a call from a dealer by the name of Jim Rizik, a wonderful guy, and he says, 'Do you want to buy a collection of pornography?' It's a huge collection, he says, one of a kind. 'No way, I don't want it,' I tell him. But he's practically giving it to me, so I say, okay, fine. Why do I do this? Who knows, but probably because the quantity and the dollars were reasonable at the time. So I send a couple of my employees out in a truck to pick it up, and they come back and they say, 'You have no idea what you bought. You bought a house full of dirty books.' By the time they finish unpacking, I have two hundred and sixty-eight cartons. What I bought was essentially an example of the entire world of pornographic literature from 1950 to 1975. There were twenty thousand paperbacks, ten thousand magazines, fifty thousand pictures— God knows what. I put it in the basement of my office, and it began to grate on me. You have to understand that this is trash, irredeemable trash, absolutely the worst things. Anything you can think of is there. It is a tumor in my cellar and I don't know what to do with it."

The material was so offensive that sending it to the dump was out of the question. "I am a known person in my village," Zinman said. "I couldn't pile it up on the street, it was too much stuff. I couldn't burn it. I could not dispose of this material. The word would have gotten out and I didn't want the notoriety." Zinman called the Kinsey Institute in Indiana and found no interest. "I called Johnny Jenkins in Texas, but he didn't want any part of it either." Finally he persuaded the book-seller Terry Halladay, then working in Texas with another bookseller, Ray Walton, to take the material on speculation. "The deal was that I ship it down to him, I never see it again, and we split whatever he can get for it. It may be trash, I tell him, but it *is* comprehensive."

A year went by, and finally Halladay called Zinman with the news. "I can get rid of it," the bookseller told him. "Are you willing to give the collection to the University of Texas?" Zinman agreed, and the material was dispatched to the Harry Ransom Humanities Research Center in Austin. "Lyndon Johnson had formed something called the President's Commission on Pornography and Obscenity in 1968, and all the records are in Texas, all the notes, all the hearings, everything, but they had no examples of American pornography."

The collection was appraised, and Zinman was able to claim a sub-stantial deduction. "The upshot is that in May of 1990 I got a letter from the Dean of the University of Texas Law School. 'Dear Mr. Zin-man,' he writes, 'We are now in possession of the Zinman Collection of Pornography. And we are in the process of cataloguing it and we would like you to give us a curriculum vita on yourself and the history of the collection.' I call this guy up right away, and I say, 'What the hell is going on?' He tells me that the Law Library found this collection very interesting, and they have it. He was very serious. So I said, 'Do you have to call it the Zinman Collection?' He said when it came to the uni-versity, it came as the Zinman Collection, a gift from Michael Zinman. So I call up Terry Halladay and I tell him the story. Terry says to me, 'Did you ask him about a bookplate?' "

Might it be ironic, I asked, if a hundred years from now the only Zinman collection that endures is the Zinman Collection of Pornogra-phy at the University of Texas Law School?

"I love it," Zinman said. "I love it."

Anyone who has ever met Irwin T. "Toby" Holtzman inevitably agrees that the man is an unusually "intense" collector, an admitted fanatic so single-minded in his devotion to the printed word that after two days spent in his company, I was astonished to learn that he also makes room in his pantheon of passions for the Detroit Tigers. "Toby definitely can wear you down," Peter Howard said when he recommended that I travel to Michigan and talk with Holtzman, "but he has a native feeling for books that you really have to experience first hand to appreciate."

Though he has had time to become one of the most successful home builders in the state, Holtzman is totally focused when the subject is literature. Holtzman speaks of nearly nothing but books and collection creation. At the time of my visit, he and his wife, Shirley, were living in a beautiful home of Irish-Georgian design in Grosse Pointe Farms, an exclusive suburb on the shores of Lake St. Clair, where automobile industry executives have resided in quiet luxury for decades. Behind the red-brick house was a lovely herb garden. Inside, everything was precise and tasteful. Yet somehow, something seemed missing, something that became apparent only after I had followed my host to his impressive book room, an area quite separate from the family library and detached from the living quarters.

There were no pictures on the walls.

"You noticed," Holtzman replied, obviously pleased. "Good. I'm glad. If you understand nothing else, you must understand that this is a house of books. We have some wonderful pictures, but they are not framed and hanging on the walls. I've thought this through quite thoroughly. There can be no competition in this house between books and art. Part of the reason I have been successful as a collector is because I am a fanatic about it." He then pointed out that there was only one chair in the book room, the one behind his desk, where he did his work. "This is not a place for idle conversation. We can sit and talk in the library. You come in here to deal with books."

There were several exhibition cases in the center of the room where various collections were in the process of being categorized and prepared for presentation to institutions. During my visit, Holtzman was working on a collection of Israeli literature that he is planning to give to the Israel National and Hebrew University Library in Jerusalem when he feels it is complete. Expected to number about four thousand volumes, the collection has been forming since 1973 and will encompass all of Israeli literature from the founding of the state in 1948 to the present. Holtzman believes that releasing books from his custody is every bit as much a part of collecting as gathering them, and involves just as much thought and effort. "I'm in the process of divesting all my collections," he said. "That doesn't mean I have lost any of my fanaticism, because dispersal is just one aspect of the process."

Holtzman said he will install the Holtzman Family Collection of Israeli Writers in Jerusalem the same way he installed the Irwin T. and Shirley Holtzman Collection of William Faulkner at his alma mater, the University of Michigan, in 1989. Holtzman collected not only all of Faulkner's works in various editions, but also translations, biographies, and criticism. "I moved fourteen hundred Faulkner items by myself, in my station wagon, and nobody handled them in between. I had the shelves built to my specifications, and the books are arranged according to the order I have established. That was part of the agreement of the gift. I call it utilization," Holtzman said. "I created this collection. I paid for these books. I wept for them. You saw how I have the Faulkner shelved. The life. The work. The meaning. Collection. Study. You couldn't talk to anybody and have the author explained any better. That's what makes it a library: the comprehensiveness."

At one time, Holtzman collected the works of 350 American authors with similar thoroughness. "I build homes, I create dwellings, so the first books I bought dealt with housing, design, style, and architecture," he said. Though the collection of writings by and about architects was formidable—Frank Lloyd Wright, Buckminster Fuller, and Louis Sullivan among them—Holtzman's reputation as a collector was established mainly by his enthusiasm for modern first editions, arbitrarily selecting 1927 as his starting point. "The year of my birth," he explained. "The compass for my American literature collection was my own time," and the books were shelved in two sections, one for writers who were living, the other for those who were dead. "When an author died, I moved those works up to the top shelves, above the living authors, as soon as I heard the news, on the very same day. I am partial to the living, to the future. I can always pick up on what was written yesterday. I am more interested in what will be published tomorrow. I think that is the challenge of being a contemporary collector."

Unlike most collectors, who wait until books achieve a patina of scarcity, Holtzman has always tried to decide in advance what works will be important. When he began collecting fiction seriously in 1950, he took out a subscription to *Publishers Weekly*, the trade magazine noted for its concise forecasts of forthcoming books, and he has faithfully studied the periodical ever since. When he spots items of interest, he routinely calls bookstores such as the Strand in New York that acquire review books and uncorrected proofs in order to locate advance copies. Holtzman's insistence that he collects authors, not just books, makes him well known among writers throughout the country as the persistent man from Michigan who keeps asking them to inscribe copies of their works. "I have never pestered authors through the mails," Holtzman said. "I am an in-your-face kind of guy. I would chase them around, but always in public places. I am the collector who appears in front of them at airports." Holtzman estimated that he obtained book inscriptions from about five hundred authors during the thirty years he actively collected modern first editions.

Holtzman was always particular as to where authors inscribed the books. "Most writers instinctively gravitate to the title page because it looks pretty. But I believe that violates the book, so I like them to sign on the first blank page. My feeling is that somehow the first edition of a book should be as it appeared in the stores. This, for me, is paying proper respect to the book."

Because of his scouting techniques, Holtzman said that about forty percent of his books were acquired at their original prices, or in the case of remainders and secondhand books, even less. In 1979, Peter Howard estimated Holtzman's investment in American literature at a modest $150,000, yet still called his collection of ten thousand books "the finest assembly of its kind in one private room in the country," and compared it favorably with similar holdings in large university libraries.

"Most collectors wait until a book is 'collectible,' and then they pay seventy-five or a hundred dollars to buy it because by then it is rare. For me the idea is to get it fresh off the press. I know what will be collectible because I have always tried to be involved with every aspect of book culture." Holtzman not only collected the material written by his selected authors, but acquired secondary material as well. "I have the greatest respect for critics. I try as a reader and as a collector to get the whole body of opinion, and then I make my own decisions. I am a person who will not go to a movie unless I have read a couple of reviews. I never want to be surprised, I never want to be entertained; I want to know."

The decision to dispose of his modern first editions came after Holtzman made his first trip to Israel in 1973, when he decided to pursue a "new direction" that could make him "a great international collector." In 1980, he sold most of his contemporary literature to Peter Howard. "I decided to get rid of everything except the major-major and the major-minor writers," he said, explaining why he held on to the William Faulkner and Nathanael West material.

When we spoke, his book room was filled with close to four thousand books written by Israeli authors. "By the way, I decide who is an Israeli author and who is not," he said. "There is no reliable bibliography. What I am doing here will be the standard bibliography when it is complete. There are books here in Hebrew and Arabic. The key point is the date, May 15, 1948." He selected a volume of short stories by Nathan Shaham, the title of which translates as *Crops and Metal*, and opened it to the copyright page. The year 1948 appears under the words "State of Israel." Holtzman said he learned from the author that the book was published in the spring of that year. "I have not been able to determine yet whether any books came out the week of May 15, so for now this is the first book of literature published in the State of Israel. If it had been published in Jerusalem before that date, it would say Palestine."

When the collection is presented to Israel, Holtzman plans to install each book himself. "There will be nothing else like this anyplace else," he said. And once that project is in place, there is still the matter of the Russian literature collection he has put together that is strong in Boris Pasternak and Isaac Babel, and the collection of American Indian literature he has been assembling for a number of years.

"You have to be acquisitive to be a collector. But at some point along the line the acquisitiveness is the first thing that goes. You'll find that every single person at a certain age is not as frantic about releasing a book, or placing a collection, or even selling some parts of their library," Holtzman said. "I never had the equipment to become an architect, but I collected architects, and I came as close to being one as possible. There is an analogy there with my book collecting, I think, because even though I am not a writer, my attachment to writing and my love of writing is as close as a person can get to being a writer. As you see, living vicariously is just part of my makeup."

9

Instant Ivy

There was a time during the late 1950s and early '60s when crates filled with rare books and documents were arriving at the University of Texas campus in Austin so quickly that nobody knew where to put them, let alone say how soon any of the material would be catalogued or when it would be made available to scholars. But those were minor details that could be resolved once the buying spree ended; what mattered most during those peak oil years was that money was available and the spirit was willing.

When Harry Huntt Ransom, the provost of the University of Texas, called for the creation of a Humanities Research Center on the booming Austin campus in 1957, there was a sense of moment and consequence, a feeling that anything was possible. Texans frequently use the word "vision" to describe the passion Ransom had to build a library in the Southwest that would hold its own with those at Harvard, Yale, Columbia, or Princeton; others, less impressed, called it a crude attempt to create "instant ivy." Shortly after being named provost, in

312

1957, Ransom outlined his daring goal to the state philosophical society. "I propose that there be established somewhere in Texas—let's say in the capital city—a center of cultural compass, a research center to be the Bibliothèque Nationale of the only state that started out as an independent nation." For those who needed further convincing, Ransom spelled it out. "Texas, which now ranks high in private income among all the other states within the Union, has the material power to fulfill its intellectual obligations in practical ways." Put another way, the cash was flowing, and it would not flow forever.

Outsiders who stereotype Texas as a wild frontier populated by uncultured cowboys and football fanatics often forget that striving to be the biggest and the best at everything is very much a part of the region's persona. "Twenty-five years of reporting on the place and I still can't account for that lunatic quality of exaggeration, of being slightly larger than life, in a pie-eyed way, that afflicts the entire state," journalist Molly Ivins, a native of Lubbock, wrote in a best-selling collection of her audacious Texas commentary. "I just know it's there, and I'd be lying if I tried to pretend it isn't."

The path to realizing the idea that Texas could gather a collection of rare books and manuscripts that would compare with the best in the world was fraught with obstacles. Ransom realized that regardless of what he was willing to spend, the university would always be several generations behind established institutions in traditional areas, and that the only way to achieve dominance was to concentrate on fields neglected by the competition. With this in mind, he announced that people did not have to be dead or famous before they were collectible. If other libraries wanted to continue sifting through the cinders of history, that was fine, because Ransom was laying claim to the twentieth century while the fires of creation still burned. Some critics argued that the pursuit of immediacy can be impulsive, and therefore transitory, but the point was moot. Cast your net wide, Ransom seemed to say, and all sorts of interesting things will come your way.

"It is an obvious law of nature that collections of living men, however wise, constitute highly perishable collections of knowledge," Ransom explained. "Enlightened human minds almost invariably outmode themselves by encouraging a continual search for new knowledge, new synthesis. Furthermore, no matter how great their undertaking or how

vast their accomplishment, all knowing men are sooner or later over-
taken by death. So the collection of permanent records has always been
essential to civilization." Figuring out what is significant would take
care of itself later. What was important in the meantime was to embark
on a program of massive acquisitions.

In time, Ransom would welcome familiar names like James Joyce,
Oscar Wilde, T. E. Lawrence, Tennessee Williams, Graham Greene,
and Evelyn Waugh, but he also sought out a whole range of figures,
many of them unknown then, many of them still obscure to this day.
While writers would constitute the core of the collection, the full scope
of human accomplishment, be it theater, art, music, architecture, photography, cinema, journalism, broadcasting, or politics, was part of the
scheme as well. Printed books certainly were included, but they were
viewed as the logical conclusion of the creative process, not its beginning. Primary documents—manuscripts, letters, journals—were the
quarry.

The most important Texas holdings at that time were nineteenth-
century British materials acquired in the 1930s from John Wrenn, the
Chicago collector best known as a wealthy American targeted by
Thomas J. Wise as a purchaser of his forgeries of literary pamphlets.
"The Texas library was a good library," the current director of the
Humanities Research Center, Thomas F. Staley, commented, "but it
was not a great library. Harry Ransom understood what a great library
was." Within thirteen years, in 1970, the British bibliographer
Anthony Hobson would include the Humanities Research Center in his
respected survey, *Great Libraries,* and in 1975 the *New York Times*
ranked the library of the University of Texas with Harvard's, Yale's, the
New York Public Library, and the Huntington Library.

Ransom's most impressive triumph, however, was not that he
achieved respectability so quickly, but that he did it with the spirited
backing of a political machine that managed the flow of public money
with fierce, often ruthless, authority. To describe Texas state government as "rough and tumble" is to dance with euphemisms. "Actually,"
Molly Ivins wrote, "the criterion of being considered an honest politician in Texas is as follows: If you can't take their money, drink their
whiskey, screw their women, and vote against 'em anyway, you don't
belong in Texas politics."

Harry Ransom was not a politician, yet his dream depended on how skillfully he could manipulate the Board of Regents and the State legislature. Amazingly enough, he always got the money he wanted, and he usually got it on the strength of his word. "There was something about the man that made people believe anything was possible, even if it wasn't," said Warren Roberts, the administrator who served as Ransom's principal HRC executive for fifteen years, one Saturday morning in his home near the Austin campus. "Harry Ransom had a God-given talent for getting money out of the Board of Regents," Roberts added with a shake of his head. "I don't know how he did it year after year, but he did it every time."

Born in Galveston, Ransom spent most of his adult life at the University of Texas, starting as an assistant in the English Department in 1935 and becoming a full professor in 1947. He was named dean of the College of Arts and Sciences in 1954, vice president and provost in 1957, president of the University of Texas at Austin in 1960, and chancellor of the statewide system the following year. Warren Roberts researched his doctoral dissertation on D. H. Lawrence under the supervision of Dr. Harry Ransom and was appointed director of the Humanities Research Center in 1961, a position he held until 1976. As point man for Ransom's acquisitions program, Roberts often absorbed attacks that belittled the university's aggressive tactics. "They all thought we were a bunch of pirates, hayseed millionaires with no taste in anything," he said. "It didn't improve our reputation with the old guard very much that we were buying everyone we could find, *everyone,* and that we were doing it *intentionally* and as quickly as possible."

Roberts shrugged at the suggestion that this aggressive strategy inflated the value of twentieth-century material, and that other institutions were unable to compete in the face of such activity. "I admit that we probably were responsible for driving the prices up to higher levels," he said. "But I also knew that there wasn't enough money in the world to build a collection that would be the equal of Harvard's or Yale's. It didn't matter how rich you were thirty years ago or how rich you are now, that kind of material wasn't available then and it isn't available today. But there sure was enough money to build a better twentieth-century library. Once we decided that we were willing to pay good money for it, it became valuable overnight. That was inevitable. It's the nature of the marketplace."

Twelve years elapsed between Ransom's articulation of his proposal to the opening, in 1970, of the huge limestone citadel known as the HRC at Twenty-first and Guadalupe Streets; during these years, while the acquisitions program was proceeding at full speed, no permanent facility was available for storage. "The stuff was housed everywhere, all over the place," Roberts said. "We kept things in the main building, up in the tower, over where the president's office is now. Despite everything some people would have you believe, though, we did not buy indiscriminately, and regardless of where we put it, we had everything pretty well cared for."

But the image of rare documents gushing like so many rogue oil wells into Austin elicited ridicule and contempt, and lingered in some quarters for years. The New York manuscript dealer Charles Hamilton, without offering any specifics, alleged in print that the university spent millions of dollars for "virtually worthless" material, while the esteemed John Carter of Great Britain snorted in a self-serving letter to the widow of a noted Chicago collector that Texas was "the most bibliophilically unpopular institution in the entire United States."

More reliable evaluations, though, have come from people with no personal agendas. "Anyone who says Texas bought junk doesn't know what they are talking about, it's as simple as that," Roger E. Stoddard, curator of rare books at the Houghton Library at Harvard University, said. Robert L. Nikirk, for twenty years librarian of the Grolier Club, agreed: "You hear that whining every so often, and it's nothing but sour grapes." The British bookseller Colin Franklin reasoned that acquisition on the Texas scale "almost guarantees that you'll get some inferior material along the way. But they also bought a massive amount of genuinely useful things." Roger G. Kennedy, the former director of the National Museum of American History in Washington, D.C., and the author of many books on social and architectural history, asked, "What is junk anyway? Who makes those decisions? I believe that the only way to appreciate a masterpiece is to understand what created it. You can't just look at the end product, the polished work. If you want to understand something properly, you have to see the things that led to its creation."

Nicolas Barker, speaking in his office at the British Library, agreed with Kennedy's essential premise, and provided a comparison. "Just because someone is unknown does not mean they should not be collected. We have scholars in this building at this moment who are looking at the work of several obscure sixteenth-century poets. Who knows what they will find? What is important is that the material has survived, and it is here to be studied." G. Thomas Tanselle, the noted bibliographer and vice president of the Guggenheim Foundation, pointed out that fashion is always fickle and agreed that preservation should always take precedence over whether an author is in vogue or not.

Harry Ransom made his first great acquisition in 1958 when he purchased an enormous collection of literary material from Thomas Edward Hanley, a Bradford, Pennsylvania, brick manufacturer who had filled his house with many important paintings and thousands of books and manuscripts. "I found out about Hanley in an odd way," Roberts said. "I had gone to New Mexico in 1954 to do some research on my D. H. Lawrence bibliography, and I got to know Frieda Lawrence pretty well. She told me how this man in Pennsylvania had bought up a lot of her husband's manuscripts, some of them through Jake Zeitlin out in Los Angeles, some directly from her on the installment plan. She told me who he was, and I wrote him a letter, which began a correspondence that went on for some time."

Ransom opened negotiations with Hanley through Jacob Schwartz, a former Brooklyn dentist who operated the Ulysses Bookshop in London during the 1920s and was noted for his ability to acquire primary material from writers in need of cash. Indeed, on his stationery "Jake" Schwartz listed his specialty as "First Editions and Manuscripts of Esteemed Authors." Hanley bought thousands of manuscripts, letters, and memorabilia by such writers as George Bernard Shaw, Oscar Wilde, James Joyce, Dylan Thomas, Ezra Pound, T. S. Eliot, and T. E. Lawrence from Schwartz. Samuel Beckett called Schwartz the "Great Extractor" for his uncanny ability to separate authors from their literary material.

Hanley was a man of means, but his obsessive buying had gotten so far out of hand that in 1958 he owed Jake Schwartz $128,000, and that was just one dealer; he had been buying books and paintings for three decades, and his debts were numerous. What finally persuaded Hanley to divest himself of his books was not unpaid accounts, but the visit he received one day from his insurance company. "Hanley lived in an old Victorian frame house in Bradford," Roberts said, "and the underwriters flat out refused to give him another policy. They told him the place was a firetrap, there was no security, and it was filled with priceless things. The walls were completely covered with paintings—Renoir, Cézanne, Monet, Van Gogh, Gauguin—you name it. He decided to keep the art and sell everything on paper. We got there at just the right time."

Though Roberts does not remember the precise amount Texas paid Hanley for the 155,000 books and manuscript leaves that came to the university in several installments, Carlton Lake, the executive curator of the Humanities Research Center, wrote in a 1987 essay that the acquisition was "a seven-figure deal." In return, Texas acquired a collection that Anthony Hobson judged to be of "international importance." Roberts said he returned from Italy "just in time" to open the first boxes. "You would not believe the stuff that came out of that shipment. I don't think anybody knew what he had or what was going to come out next. It was one of the most exciting things that ever happened."

Among the prizes were Lawrence's manuscripts for *Kangaroo, The Lost Girl, The Rainbow, Women in Love,* and *The Virgin and the Gipsy*—more than twenty-five hundred pages in the writer's hand. The Samuel Beckett material included manuscript copies of *Waiting for Godot, Watt, Molloy, Malone Dies, The Unnamable,* and the heavily revised text of a work-in-progress titled *Beckett's Bums.* Among the hundreds of T. E. Lawrence items was the earliest surviving manuscript version of *Seven Pillars of Wisdom.* "The list was endless," Roberts said, and reaffirmed a point he made in a 1986 essay for *The Library Chronicle:* "Thomas Edward Hanley was an astute collector and an extraordinary man; although not a scholar himself, he had an uncanny instinct for buying the right manuscript or book, a distinction rare even among collectors. Scholars must always be grateful to Hanley because much of surpassing importance would have disappeared had it not been for his drive to collect in the contemporary field."

Hanley sold his personal books and manuscripts to Texas for cash because he needed the money, but the zest for giving had inspired him to help others who were less fortunate. The University of Arizona considers him the most important book donor in its history, a commitment that began with an impromptu visit he made during the Depression and continued for more than twenty-five years. Hanley's custom had been to spend three months during the winter in California buying books. While traveling by train to Los Angeles in 1936, he stopped briefly in Tucson to look up a Harvard classmate at the university, and discovered to his dismay that research and reference material in virtually every area of the humanities and fine arts was lacking. Arizona had fewer than half a million residents then, and the state university was struggling for survival, so book purchases were not a high priority.

Starting then, and continuing well into the 1960s, Hanley bought hundreds of rare and important books throughout the United States for the university, which he routinely shipped to Tucson with eccentric instructions for cataloguing, shelving, and possible function. "His passion for acquiring was so great that it usually exceeded even his own substantial resources," Lee Sorenson wrote in a commemorative booklet published by the Friends of the University of Arizona Library. "Shipments of books from Hanley appeared in all forms from all sources and at all times." When Hanley died in 1969, his book gifts were calculated to total 91,500 volumes, 38,550 to Arizona alone; other recipients included St. Bonaventure University in New York State, Albright College in Reading, Pennsylvania, and the Carnegie Library in Bradford, Pennsylvania.

For Texas, the Hanley acquisition represented a new way of doing business. As Warren Roberts pointed out, getting other archives now involved "visits to heirs and executors of estates, the cultivation of friendly and amiable relations with writers themselves, their kinsmen, booksellers, literary agents, and assorted friends, landlords, and hangers-on." Authors, moreover, were delighted with what they perceived as a lucrative new market for their material.

In an essay for the London *Sunday Times* of April 15, 1962, Cyril Connolly reported how a certain unnamed American university was willing not only "to pay for what an author has written but what he has tried to throw away; his note-books, correspondence, false starts; they will sort it all out for him and accept material which is never to be shown and provide him with copies and even resident facilities for writing his autobiography." The development, he concluded, was "probably the best thing that has happened to writers for many years."

Not surprisingly, Connolly's manuscripts and notebooks were among those that soon made the migration across the Atlantic to Austin. Exactly two years after the appearance of his article, another view was expressed in the same newspaper by William Rees-Moog, owner of Pickering & Chatto, one of the most respected booksellers in England. He warned that the steadily rising prices of contemporary books and manuscripts, very few of which were going to English institutions or universities, probably meant that "this is the last decade in which it is at all possible to form any sort of proper university collection of English literature. [The] opportunity is already slipping fast away. The University of Texas has been taking it—we have not."

What people were saying in confidence about the trend raised even greater alarms, not only in England but also in the United States. In one documentable case, a blatant appeal to regional loyalty helped terminate a deal that would have sent a major private American collection of English books to Austin in 1964 for $2.75 million; the sudden change of mind led to a civil suit to recover the lost commission. The New York bookseller John Fleming filed the court action in Illinois on August 6, 1964; he had negotiated to everyone's apparent satisfaction the sale of the Chicago hotel owner Louis H. Silver's library to the University of Texas. On the very day that Texas officials were expected in Chicago to close the deal, the arrangement was rescinded and the books were sold instead to the Newberry Library. In his suit Fleming claimed that because he had found a legitimate buyer, as directed by Silver's estate, he was still owed a commission of $200,000.

On December 17, 1968, after more than four years of depositions, hearings, and oral arguments before Judge James B. Parsons, Fleming accepted an offer of $92,000 from Silver's estate to settle out of court. Beyond validating the merits of Fleming's personal claim, the case also shed light on the bitterness Ransom's acquisitions program had engendered among his rivals. "This is an action for commissions due and owing to plaintiff for procuring a ready, willing and able purchaser for the Silver rare book collection," Fleming had stated in his complaint. "The sale was not completed because of defendants' wrongful refusal to consummate the transaction after reaching complete agreement upon all terms of sale."

In a lengthy brief filed with the court, Fleming explained how he spent sixteen years helping Louis Silver, a Chicago lawyer and president of Gold Coast Hotels, build "one of the most famous privately owned rare-book collections in the world." He recalled that he was in London in June 1963 when he received an urgent message to meet with Silver in New York. He returned immediately, and Silver told him that he had terminal cancer and wanted to arrange the sale of his books.

Though Silver had no misgivings about selling his library, he was adamant that it be sold en bloc and that it realize at least $2.2 million. During the four months that followed, Fleming offered the books to Paul Mellon, Arthur A. Houghton Jr., and Yale University. With Silver's authorization, he also asked Parke-Bernet of New York and Sotheby's of London to submit proposals for auctions. After Silver's death on October 27, 1963, Fleming met in Silver's home with John Carter, the British rare-book expert who had gained fame thirty years earlier with his exposé of the Thomas J. Wise forgeries. By that time Carter was working as a Sotheby's consultant, and he submitted a proposal to the Silver family for an auction.

Amy Silver remained committed to her husband's wishes, however, and insisted that the library be sold as a unit rather than piecemeal at auction. "Accordingly," the court papers state, "Fleming continued to search for an en bloc purchaser." On November 15, 1963, he received a call from a member of the Board of Regents in Texas. The next day, Harry Ransom was on the phone with Fleming, and the chancellor got right to the point: What would it cost Texas to acquire the Silver library? Fleming replied that a bid of $2.5 million to $3 million probably would be received favorably. Ransom then asked if $2.75 million "would do it." Fleming said he thought that figure "would be adequate."

Within a month Ransom had the money he needed from the Board of Regents, and a good-faith offer was submitted. Problems began to develop with the Silvers, however, when Fleming told them that he expected a commission of "at least two hundred thousand dollars" for arranging the deal. "The defendants rejected out of hand" such a commission, he asserted, but agreed to give him "something" for his efforts. The heirs expressed delight with the Texas offer, especially since Ransom had assured them that the books would be kept in Silver's name "in perpetuity."

Word about the imminent sale to Texas got out quickly, prompting John Carter to write an impassioned letter to Mrs. Silver, dated January 2, 1964. It was obtained by Fleming's lawyers during the discovery process and was included as an exhibit in the court documents. "Dear Amy," it began, "I won't say, because you know, how deeply disconcerted and distressed and disheartened I am that, after all the weeks of work and thought (and delay after delay at the Chicago end) since the evening you and I and Bob made our agreement for the sale of the library at Sotheby's, we now hear that John Fleming has negotiated its sale to Texas." He beseeched her to "think hard before the executors require you to sign any contract." After all, he stressed, "*you* are concerned, and rightly, not only with the money but with Lou's memory." It would be one thing if the books were going to the Newberry Library, the University of Chicago, Harvard, "or even Illinois," maybe then he could understand. "But what did Lou, what do you, care about Texas? It just has a lot of money, some empty shelves, and an overweening appetite."

Beyond the implied indignity of sending the books off to a university with an "overweening appetite" was the more delicate issue of what Mrs. Silver stood to earn from the sale. Carter disdained subtlety on that point as well. "John Fleming knows perfectly well that we shall get the estate more money than they are offering." On the matter of assuring Silver's place in history, Carter promised a magnificent catalogue, "the best and truest memorial in the eyes of future bookcollectors." A Sotheby's auction would give "collectors and scholars and libraries all over the world" a chance to buy some splendid books and to enjoy "the pleasure of keen competition" that "Lou himself so relished when he was collecting." That would be a far more fitting tribute, he argued, than to put the collection "behind glass thousands of miles away."

Once again, Carter appealed to whatever misgivings Mrs. Silver might harbor about Texas: instead of being "carted off as a captive to the most bibliophilically unpopular institution in the entire United States," the Silver Library could "culminate in a blaze of national glory." He ended with a plea that was personal and to the point: "Amy, I beg of you, think of all these things, and think hard, before you are persuaded to sign any contract. Don't let them close the door in our face." He closed the letter "Affectionately," and signed his name.

Whether Mrs. Silver was moved by Carter's plea cannot be determined from the court papers, but there is no doubt she knew that more than one prospect was now hovering in the wings. Two days after Carter's letter to Mrs. Silver was received, the deal with Texas began to waver, and negotiations with Sotheby's started—but the implied threat of legal action revived talks with Ransom. Fleming alleged in court documents that John Carter began to "spread the word" that the deal with Ransom had "fallen through," even though it had not, and that he hoped the University of Texas would "fall on its face." But on May 13, 1964, the Silver family did reach an agreement with the Newberry Library for $2.75 million—the same figure offered six months earlier by Ransom—and on the very day that HRC officials were expected in Chicago to conclude the sale. "Unknown to the University of Texas, back in Chicago the Silver group was busily rushing the Newberry Library through all the procedures necessary for the Library to consummate the purchase of the collection before the University's representatives could come to Chicago to claim it," alleged Fleming's complaint.

On May 16, Ransom wired Herman Smith, the director of the Newberry Library:

CONGRATULATIONS UPON THE ADDITION OF A GREAT COLLECTION OF BOOKS TO A VERY GREAT LIBRARY STOP AT THE UNIVERSITY OF TEXAS THE HIGH OPINION OF THE LOUIS SILVER COLLECTION WAS MANIFESTED BY UNANIMOUS APPROVAL OF ALL UNIVERSITY OFFICIALS, THE BOARD OF REGENTS AND EVERY STATE AGENCY CONCERNED TO OFFER TWO MILLION SEVEN HUNDRED AND FIFTY THOUSAND DOLLARS IN CASH FOR THE COLLECTION STOP THIS SUM WAS IMMEDIATELY AVAILABLE AND PLANS

FOR THE INSTALLATION OF THE LIBRARY HERE WERE COMPLETED STOP BUT GREAT COLLECTIONS OF BOOKS ARE NOT A MATTER OF MERE LOCAL CONCERN SO ALL MY COLLEAGUES JOIN IN THESE GOOD WISHES TO NEWBERRY STOP

As gracious as Ransom's words were, they emphasized in capital letters the fact that $2.75 million "in cash" had been "immediately available," and that provisions to keep the collection intact had been made. Meanwhile, officials at the Newberry Library were not nearly as flexible. While they had matched the Texas offer of $2.75 million, it soon became clear that the money was not "immediately available," and it was not "in cash." Indeed, the library mounted the first fund drive in its seventy-eight-year history to underwrite the purchase, and negotiated a series of bank loans. To raise more money, the trustees then announced that they would sell titles from the Silver collection that were duplicated by their own holdings, as well as other materials they considered "inappropriate" to their "collecting priorities."

Of the nine hundred items acquired from the Silver estate, fully three hundred were declared surplus. Among them were books said to be far superior to the copies already owned by the Newberry, including examples from the nineteenth-century English fine-press and -binding tradition: a Doves Bible, a Kelmscott *Chaucer* in pigskin, an exceptional Ashendene Malory on vellum, and a Kilmarnock Burns in original wrappers. Fanny Burney's 1778 novel *Evelina,* uncut in original boards, a Gutenberg tract from 1450, and the editio princeps of Homer were also among "rejects." On January 22, 1965, the Newberry Library Subcommittee on Books had a meeting. It was attended by George B. Young, the chairman, James M. Wells, associate director of the library, and John Carter of Sotheby's, London. Among the decisions reached, according to a memorandum in the Newberry Library files, was that a sale "of duplicate rare and scarce books and other works extraneous to the Library's holdings" which had been "created by the Silver Collection" should be sold at auction, and that the books be consigned to Sotheby's. John Carter, then, would be mounting a sale of Silver material after all.

Over the following year, two critical commentaries that appeared in *The Book Collector* raised more than a few eyebrows in the world of rare-book collecting. John Carter had not only written regularly for the London-based quarterly since its founding in 1951, but also served on its editorial board. In a commentary in its summer 1964 issue, well before any decision to sell off "surplus" Silver items had been reached, the quarterly termed the Newberry purchase an exercise in "gulosity"—greediness. The magazine's editors, John Carter among them, declared the "in toto" sale of Silver's books to the Newberry Library "a great pity."

A little more than a year later, however, in its fall 1965 issue, *The Book Collector* expressed a decidedly different attitude, occasioned, curiously enough, by the Newberry Library's startling decision to consign more than a third of the Silver material to Sotheby's, precisely the kind of dispersal the magazine seemed to be calling for four issues earlier. It was significant that John Carter's name did not appear on the masthead of this issue. John Hayward, the widely respected founding editor, signed this commentary alone. He began by noting how Sotheby's had "saved something from the wreckage of their hopes of acquiring for sale the Louis H. Silver collection," a "salvage operation" made possible by his colleague John Carter, "whose persistence in the face of progressive frustration and disappointment has at length been rewarded" by the Newberry Library trustees.

At that point, Hayward's commentary took on a sharper edge. The "salvage operation," he declared, "turns out to be far more important and valuable than anyone could have anticipated"; when studied closely, the items being sold were "by no means the throw-outs from an extremely choice cabinet." In addition to the printed books being dispersed were autograph letters and manuscript material by Castiglione, Machiavelli, Galileo, Harvey, and Chesterfield, and the holograph copy of *John Bull's Other Island,* one of the few remaining longhand manuscripts of Bernard Shaw available for sale.

"While all collectors, dealers, and libraries will welcome Newberry's decision to get rid of what they consider superfluous to their needs," Hayward wrote, "it does seem very odd that much of the material now to be thrown on the market should be the very stuff of which great research libraries (and Newberry justly pride themselves on being one of the foremost) are made." How, he wondered "in bewilderment," could they

afford to sell from a collection, purchased in order to fill specific gaps and generally to increase their research resources,
manuscripts and autograph letters which, being unique, cannot
conceivably be classed as "duplicates" and rare printed books
which may be loosely described as duplicates but which no
experienced bibliographer could say were "surplus" to his
needs—the Mainz *Cicero,* for example, with its mixed leaves,
or the Block Books with the possible inferences to be made
from the condition of the blocks? Maybe the answer is simply
that they could not afford not to, or in other words that they
had to pay more than they could really afford for something
they did not altogether want.

Hayward did not mention anything about how the materials could
have improved the Humanities Research Center in Texas, or whether
sufficient funds had been a problem there, or that the collection was
something Harry Ransom did "altogether want" and had intended to
preserve as a unit.

The sale catalogue itself opened with a lengthy preface, signed anonymously by "Sotheby and Co." and closed with an unusually defensive
paragraph:

We venture to think that the international fraternity of book-
collectors, rare book librarians and antiquarian booksellers will
join us in saluting the addition of the Newberry Library to the
roster of those enlightened institutions who have come to
believe, in the words of Dr. Louis B. Wright, Director of the Folger Library, Washington, D.C., that "if all libraries would take
stock of their possessions and sell books that have no predictable use, they would improve their cash position, gain space
that they need, and serve the public interest"; concluding that
"a vast shuffling of books by way of the sales rooms would help
libraries, stimulate collectors, and advance learning."

The consequent sale of books that had "no predictable use" was
held on November 8 and 9, 1965, in London, and the Newberry realized $800,000 for its "inappropriate" holdings.

Harry Ransom, meanwhile, had gone about the business of buying other material. Having lost in Chicago, he looked elsewhere, and he did not brood about what might have been. Four months after the Chicago agreement fell through, the $2.75 million given him by the Board of Regents "was fully used" to purchase "a number of archives, collections and libraries in lieu of the Silver Library."

Kathleen G. Hjerter, curator of art at the Harry Ransom Humanities Research Center from 1972 to 1992, was walking me through the Alfred A. Knopf Room when she paused at a portrait of Chancellor Ransom. "Look at his eyes," she said softly, whispering so she would not disturb a university function that was in progress nearby. "Tell me what you see."

"Tell me what *you* see," I replied.

"I see eyes that capture you," she said. "You can't say they pierce you or anything, but they *do* stick on you, and once you get into those eyes, you don't get out. He had a very melodious voice, too. It was not soft, but very full and mellow, and he had such beautiful diction. It didn't really matter what he said, he just said it all so exquisitely. You could have been the janitor or the governor, it didn't matter, he made you feel like you were the most important person in the world. You felt he had something he wanted to say just to you, and nobody else."

A few minutes later, as we stood in a corner where selected articles of Art Deco furniture from the Manhattan apartment of Alfred A. and Blanche Knopf repose as museum pieces, she told the story of Frances Hudspeth, a devoted secretary "who worked every night until midnight" for Harry Ransom. "She had a heart attack while Ransom's dream building was being finished, and her doctor told her that if she didn't quit work she had a year to live. And she said, 'Well, I just want to live long enough to see Dr. Ransom in his building.' So they finished the building, and she came over one day to my office to pick out some paintings for the new offices, and then Dr. Ransom moved in. Three days later they took her off to the hospital. She'd been in that building just three days when she died. I remember a painting she picked, too, it was 'Offering for the Day of the Dead,' by Jaime Flores, a Mexican artist. She never saw it hanging in there. She worked herself to death. But that's the way people felt about Harry Ransom."

Part of Ransom's appeal was an almost transcendent quality military officers call "command presence," something a person either has or does not have. "He walked into a room and everything stopped," Hjerter said. "And if there was anything that people liked to do it was to give him things. A famous story about Dr. Ransom is that one day a man came out of his office and somebody who had been waiting outside said, 'What did he say?' And the man said, 'I don't know, but I just gave him twenty thousand dollars for his program.' " Most important was Ransom's ability to make others share his enthusiasm. "The Board of Regents just adored him. All he had to do was go down and stand before them once a year and say, 'I want two million dollars.' They didn't even ask him what for; they totally trusted him."

Until her retirement Hjerter was responsible for a comprehensive collection of 100,000 works by a wide variety of artists, many of them with literary connections. In 1986, Harry N. Abrams published *Doubly Gifted,* Hjerter's examination of visual art produced by noted writers, a work based largely on the holdings she oversaw in Austin. There are pencil sketches by T. E. Lawrence, caricatures by Jean Cocteau, watercolors by e. e. cummings, drawings by G. K. Chesterton, cartoons by O. Henry, landscapes by Edward Lear, hand-colored engravings by William Blake, and oils by D. H. Lawrence. Some are curiosities that say something about a writer's impulses, others are strikingly beautiful in their own right.

Most of the artworks were acquired in tandem with the literary material Ransom was buying in great volume, many of them as peripheral afterthoughts to the manuscripts. But with so many paintings at his disposal, Ransom was pleased to lend some of them around. "That was one of my duties," Hjerter said during a walk through the huge room that is home to the works. "I would let people come and select paintings for any university facility, and also for the governor's office. These were Dr. Ransom's calling cards. They were a way of introducing us to these people and of doing them a favor, which might help later on."

Today, everything is neat and orderly in the Humanities Research Center, and though some 30 percent of the ten million pages of manuscript material is still uncatalogued, all of it is at least stored in protective clamshell cases and shelved sensibly in the seven-floor building. Hjerter recalled a time, though, when the situation approached chaos. "As the boxes began to appear in the early sixties, they were just stuffed into the tower. I remember going in to see Dr. Ransom's assistant once, right around the time they were moving into the new building. I walked down the hall to her office, and it was stacked to the ceiling with so many cardboard boxes that you had to walk sideways to get around. It was coming in so fast that they could barely keep up with it."

Dave Oliphant, editor of the *Texas Library Chronicle* since graduating from the University of Texas in 1971, remembers getting an unexpected telephone call one day from Ransom to congratulate him on a job particularly well done. "It was like hearing from God Himself," Oliphant said. "That's the way people felt about Harry Ransom. He was larger than life."

Dave Oliphant suggested that Ransom was like "God Himself," and Kathleen Hjerter called him a "royal presence." But for every Prince Hal, there usually is a Falstaff, and the quintessential foil for Harry Huntt Ransom was Lew David Feldman, the flamboyant owner of the House of El Dieff, Inc., for years a high-profile bookseller in Manhattan and the agent of choice for the Humanities Research Center during its frenzied years of creation. "Lew Feldman wanted to be known as the man behind the man who built the collection," Warren Roberts said. "He saw Texas as his moment in history. We were pleased to work with him because he got us the books and manuscripts we wanted, and he gave us time to pay. That is very important. He would buy stuff for us and hold it until we got more money from the Board of Regents, which often meant waiting a year or more. We did not pay him any interest, just his 10 percent commission, though there was a point, I don't remember exactly when, that he went up to fifteen percent. Still, there aren't any other dealers, so far as I know, who would do that for you. There were times when we owed him two or three million dollars, and we were always buying more."

Roberts said he frequently traveled to New York to reassure financial institutions that these unusual arrangements were valid. "One of the things I had to do was go to the bank with Lew Feldman and say,

'How do you do, Mr. Banker, yes, we are the University of Texas, and we do owe this man a lot of money for this material.' He borrowed money from the bank and he put up the books he was buying as security. Not many people know this. In effect, he was our banker. Only we weren't paying him any interest, just his commission."

A seven-paragraph obituary in the *New York Times* in 1976 described Feldman as "an imaginative and tenacious dealer who was willing to back his judgments with great amounts of cash," and who "was probably the only man who ever bid on fifty-six successive items at Sotheby's London while dressed in pajamas, a robe and a raincoat," an odd circumstance prompted by a case of sleeping late on the morning of an important sale. What the article did not mention was that Feldman bought just about everything he wanted on that November day sixteen years earlier, including 173 letters of Robert Southey for £1,950, five others written by Oscar Wilde for £220, and the autograph manuscript of D. H. Lawrence's *Etruscan Places* for £2,000. Five months earlier, at another Sotheby's sale, he accounted for half the money spent; among his purchases was every lot of a T. E. Lawrence collection. A few days after that triumph, he swept for Texas every important item offered at a Christie's sale, including the holograph copy of E. M. Forster's *A Passage to India* for £6,500, more than tripling the previous English record for a modern manuscript.

In a private purchase Feldman bought and sold to Texas material that came from the home of William Faulkner's mother: letters, manuscripts, and documents that more than two decades later still remain sealed in red boxes in the Humanities Research Center. One day, of course—presumably when all the parties to the transaction are dead—Faulkner scholars will be granted full access to this material. Similarly, in 1972 Feldman sold to Texas for $125,000 a collection of four hundred love letters of the nineteenth-century emperor of Mexico, Maximilian, and Empress Carlotta. Press accounts were vague about the source of the material, reporting only that the letters had been hidden for more than a century by Carlotta's relatives, the Belgian royal family.

"How Dr. Ransom got the letters, widely coveted in Europe as well as North America, is not exactly clear," Martin Waldron wrote in the *New York Times*. "Dr. Ransom is guarded about revealing his methods of knowing when and where rare books and papers will become available." Waldron then quoted Ransom directly: " 'We learned that the Belgian royal family was about to release the letters and an alumnus got an option. The existence of these letters was not commonly known.' " Waldron then wrote how in 1960, "only two years after he set about to upgrade the research files of the University of Texas library, Dr. Ransom began to anger collectors who were used to getting private libraries and collections of papers for small sums. But, as Dr. Ransom said, the University of Texas did not have the drawing power of Harvard or Yale, and if it was to get the materials, it had to buy them."

Warren Roberts said that Texas bought the Maximilian letters through Feldman, not some anonymous university alumnus. Thomas F. Staley, the current director, confirmed that detail, and furnished a document that clearly indicates "L.D.F." as the source. "Looking back, to tell you the truth, I don't recall that as being any big mystery," Roberts said. "That was something that Lew Feldman got and wanted us to have, and we were pleased to get it from him." Whatever the reason for vagueness—perhaps Feldman wanted to keep his European source confidential—the mystique that surrounded Harry Ransom was enhanced by news accounts lauding his ability to know "when and where rare books and papers will become available." His commitment to education got an endorsement as well. "Collecting," Ransom told Waldron, "is an empty vanity unless it's useful."

David Kirschenbaum, the founder of the Carnegie Bookstore in 1928 and for many years the undisputed dean of New York booksellers (he died in January 1994 a week after observing his ninety-ninth birthday), described to me a time in the late 1950s when Lew Feldman proposed that the two of them join forces and sell books to Texas. Kirschenbaum was a legend among his colleagues for having attended every major book auction over an eighty-year period, starting with the Robert Hoe sale in 1911, where he worked as a runner, and continuing without interruption through the Richard Manney sale in October 1991. One of Kirschenbaum's best-known clients was the late H. Bradley Martin, for whom he acquired George Washington's autographed copy of *The Federalist*, which fetched $1.43 million at auction in 1990; fifty years earlier, it cost Martin $5,000.

I talked with Kirschenbaum about his eight decades in the book trade over lunch at one of his favorite East Side restaurants. Inevitably, Feldman's name came up. "We were sitting down in a place just like this when all of a sudden, right out of the blue, Lew said he had a 'live one' lined up," Kirschenbaum said. "He was talking about the University of Texas, and from what he had to say it was pretty clear that he had the account all to himself. I have always been my own boss, so I told him I wasn't interested. But it turned out that Lew did some serious business with Texas, very serious indeed."

Bart Auerbach, who worked at the House of El Dieff from January of 1973 to July of 1976, said he could remember Feldman saying several times that he had tried to join forces with Kirschenbaum; Auerbach added that a phrase such as "a live one" would not have been out of character for Feldman. "That sounds just like Lew," Auerbach said. "I asked him once why he hadn't been paying any attention to a particular customer we had done business with in the past, and he said something like, 'Why bother with a bunch of roosters when you've got the golden goose laying eggs in your lap?' " An alliance with Kirschenbaum would have been especially attractive, Auerbach said, "because Dave was well known for having built a lot of important collections. He knew where everything was, and his contacts were tremendous. Lew felt that Dave could have opened the doors to some fresh material which they could have offered to Harry Ransom. It made a lot of sense for Lew to try and bring Dave into the operation."

A perfect example of why such a proposal made sense is underscored by an event that took place about the same time Texas was embarking on its great acquisitions program, and about the same time the two booksellers had their lunch. "It's a cute story," Kirschenbaum said, recalling the morning when one of his best customers asked him to find a new home for an exceptional private library he had spent many years building. "The man's name was DeCoursey Fales and he was the president of a big bank here in New York. He had a great collection of English literature, just wonderful material. He collected everything—first editions, translations, criticism, pamphlets, broadsides, hundreds of letters. If something had anything at all to do with the people he liked, he bought it. And he loved the stuff, he was nuts about it. So one day he came into my office—I was still up on Fifty-ninth Street at the time—and says he needs to talk to me. You have to understand that he had thousands of things in his house, thousands and thousands, the place was just splitting apart. And he says, 'Dave, I have a problem; my wife tells me she can't take it anymore. Either the books go or I go. What am I going to do?' "

Such domestic dilemmas are common among book collectors. "I am booked out of one wing and ratted out of the other," the exasperated wife of Sir Thomas Phillipps wrote to a friend about the congestion at Thirlestaine House in Cheltenham. A. N. L. Munby, the biographer of Sir Thomas Phillipps and a considerable collector in his own right, wrote how two of his friends routinely bought books they "dared not bring home" for fear of angering their spouses, and opted instead to leave their new acquisitions in the shops where they had bought them. "Such a compromise between retaining one's books or one's wife seems to me a dubious solution, but I have the problem continually in mind," Munby added.

Faced with similar opposition, DeCoursey Fales sought a solution that would satisfy his wife's demand for a bit of uncluttered living space and his wish to be near his beloved material. Kirschenbaum proposed finding a local institution willing to accept his collection, with the stipulation that adequate quarters be provided to keep it intact. "Everybody in New York wanted the collection, but nobody wanted to give him a room of his own," Kirschenbaum said. "I finally went over to New York University and the president there told me on the spot that he wanted the collection. 'I think we can do something,' he said. We got three rooms on Fifth Avenue and Eighth Street. We moved the stuff in there, and later we moved it to a bigger place in Washington Square. Ask them over at NYU what they had in special collections before DeCoursey Fales came along. They didn't have anything."

Frank Walker, curator of rare books at the Fales Library at New York University, confirmed the story. "DeCoursey Fales is remembered as a totally selfless man around here," Walker said. "He named the library in memory of his father, Haliburton Fales, not himself, and when he gave us the books, he came along with them as the unpaid librarian. He worked here without compensation until he died in 1966, and he single-handedly built the collection up to where it was four times larger than when he brought it in. And once the Fales material was here, other people began giving us material. Before he came along, NYU did not have much of anything in special collections. We were never able to compete with the New York Public Library or the Pierpont Morgan or Columbia or the New-York Historical Society. A university could not ask for a better benefactor than DeCoursey Fales."

Another collection that subsequently went to New York University was the Robert Berol Collection of Lewis Carroll material, and Kirschenbaum was instrumental in arranging this transfer as well. "I always got the greatest satisfaction out of bringing the right people together," Kirschenbaum said, explaining that he saw his role in such cases as matchmaker, not agent, which may explain why he never found Lew Feldman's offer attractive. "You like to see things go where they belong."

Kirschenbaum agreed that Lew Feldman was an authentic character, a crude and flamboyant philistine to some, a sensitive and knowledgeable connoisseur to others. How Feldman managed to line up what amounted to an exclusive arrangement with a state university has remained a matter of great curiosity to this day. Bart Auerbach said he recalled Feldman telling him how he met Harry Ransom. "Lew had bought some letters from Bertram Rota in London sometime in the late fifties that Harry Ransom wanted but missed getting by a telephone call. Ransom called Lew, and Lew agreed to sell the correspondence at his cost plus ten percent. They got together shortly after that, and apparently they developed a simpatico kind of relationship at their very first meeting."

Auerbach confirmed the unusual financial relationship Warren Roberts said that Texas established with Lew Feldman, and suggested that this may have been a key reason no other dealers were able to do major business with Texas. "I don't know many other dealers who would be able to extend that kind of credit over such a long period of time," Auerbach said. "It was an interesting procedure Lew had. He would factor the invoices at Banker's Trust as collateral for the loan. He would be able to demonstrate that he had firm accounts receivable, then would get the loan to buy the material. They would give him the money, some of which he would turn around and put into certificates of deposit to earn interest. It was a pretty clever way of doing business, and as far as I know it worked as a gentleman's agreement between Lew Feldman and Harry Ransom. I don't think there was ever anything to document it."

Ellen S. Dunlap worked in the HRC from 1971 to 1983 in a variety of capacities before becoming director of the Rosenbach Museum and Library in Philadelphia, a position she held for nine years before succeeding Marcus A. McCorison as director of the American Antiquarian Society in 1992. "I had various titles, but eventually I became the research librarian, and it was my job to help people who were using the manuscripts," Dunlap recalled. "I spent lots of time trying to sort out the history of the acquisitions and figure out when we got what and who we got it from. What is particularly amazing is that there are no proceedings whatsoever in any kind of ledger book. I can't speak for what it is like down there now, but the record keeping was never very straightforward while I was there. The only time I ever went in to see Dr. Ransom was when I was trying to untangle something, and every time I asked him a question, he always said the same thing: 'Well, my child, that's a very complex matter.' "

Auerbach agreed that the arrangements between Ransom and Feldman were unusual, but they worked. "Virtually nothing so far as I can recall was written down. Lew used to say that Harry would come up to New York and they would do most of their business in a limousine driving back and forth from the airport." Though productive for the most part, this informality occasionally led to some misunderstandings. "In 1971, Lew took an option for one hundred thousand dollars on Arthur Houghton's Gutenberg Bible that Kraus had bought, expecting to sell it to Texas. This was one of those rare cases where Lew guessed wrong, that this was something Ransom would want, but it fell through, and it cost him the hundred thousand. I remember Lew saying, 'Well, let's see what's in the files on that.' It gnawed at him, but it wasn't there. There was nothing at all in writing."

Possibly because the Ransom-Feldman files at the HRC are "complex" at best, or vague, superficial, and inconclusive at worst, Thomas F. Staley, the current director of the HRC, denied my request to examine them.

Finding a range of opinions about Lew Feldman is not difficult. The British bookseller Colin Franklin recalls doing several "quite major things" with Feldman, and judged him "perfectly correct" in all of their transactions. "I admired Lew Feldman," Franklin said. "He trusted me and I trusted him. He was a man of his word." Formerly vice chairman of the British publisher Routledge & Kegal Paul, Franklin left London publishing in 1967 and took up the life of an antiquarian bookman outside Oxford.

"Like many booksellers, he put up a tough front to the world," Franklin said. "But he was devoted to his books. And he knew his books. There were times when he couldn't sleep that he got up in the middle of the night and roamed around among his books. I don't know what was going through his head, whether it was dollars or literature, but he liked the presence of his books." Franklin believes Feldman "was wonderful" for Texas. "I think it was a great moment. Buying all sorts of things and complete archives of living people was an originality."

Dr. Haskell F. Norman, a San Francisco psychoanalyst who built an internationally respected collection of science and medicine, said flatly, "Despite his arrogance, I rather liked the man. I'd meet him in New York and we'd go out to dinner. He liked to have airs. He wore this lovely fur coat with a big collar, and he carried a gold cane. He had this beautiful apartment. And he had carte blanche because Harry Ransom was bankrolling him. I am certain that he was the source of great envy in the book trade."

The Hollywood television producer William Self, a prominent collector for more than thirty years, carries a decidedly different memory of Feldman. "The night before the Stockhausen sale in 1974, we had dinner and we talked about the *Tamerlane* that was going to be sold the next day. He told me he was pretty sure it would go for fifty thousand. He said he had heard there was a reserve on it for forty-five thousand, that the universities couldn't afford it at that price, so he was pretty sure the very next bid over that would probably get the book. I said fine, if it goes for that, I'll take it, and if it starts to go any higher, I'll be right there and we'll make a decision before we drop out." Self arrived at the Sotheby Parke-Bernet salesroom the next morning "all excited" with the prospect of finally owning one of the most coveted titles in American literature. "But then Lew came over and said, 'Another party has come to me.' He said, 'I have dealt with this man before, and he is a very reputable fellow. He's an old customer, and he's willing to bid more than we discussed.' I was a little upset because I had told him the night before I hadn't decided how far I was willing to go. He said, 'Well, Bill, very honestly, I don't think you can meet what this man is going to bid.' So I said, 'Well, fine,' and then I proceeded to drive Feldman out of the bidding at a hundred five thousand dollars."

Satisfaction was sweet, but like so many book stories, this one does not end with that little victory. "When I drove Feldman out," Self continued, "I was thinking, 'Oh boy, I am actually going to get this book,' because when he dropped out, I was the only one left. Well, right there is where John Fleming spoke up for the first time and said one hundred six thousand. I stayed with him for a few more bids, but John finally got it at one hundred twenty-three thousand. John and I talked a little later and he said he wished he had known I was interested, because he was going to get the *Tamerlane* at any cost. So I wouldn't have gotten it. But that was what ended it with me and Lew Feldman." A month later, the Baltimore *Sun* reported that Fleming had bought the *Tamerlane* for the Joseph and Helen Regenstein Foundation in Chicago, where the acquisition "will complete the collection of Poe first editions at the Joseph Regenstein Library at the University of Chicago."

Charles Hamilton, the New York authority on autographs who has made headlines over the years for his role in uncovering several frauds—including the purported diary of Adolf Hitler in 1983—wasted few words when asked about Feldman. "A pompous thief," he said one morning in a telephone interview. "I never liked the man," a repugnance he made bitingly clear in his 1981 book, *Auction Madness*. He wrote there:

> The ability to bilk one's clients at auction is a fine art, make no mistake about it. To succeed for a lifetime without detection or exposure, the auction-buying crook must have the cunning of a polecat, the ethics of a Gabon viper, and the acquisitive drive of a dung-beetle. All these feral qualities were uniquely fused in the late Lew David Feldman, a rare-book and manuscript dealer who operated under a firm name devised from his cutely bastardized initials—The House of El Dieff. Feldman's consuming ambition, like that of several contemporary rare-book czars, was to dominate the auction world by his spectacular purchases and grandiose catalogs. In 1974 Lew published at a cost of $15,000 his Fortieth Anniversary catalog, a collection of forty rare and costly books and manuscripts. In a colophon

he proudly announced the total buck value of the forty items ($1,925,077), a slip into bad taste that offended even his most vulgar competitors.

Aside from his personal attacks, Hamilton made a serious allegation, one that probably would have prompted a lawsuit if either Ransom or Feldman had still been alive when *Auction Madness* was published. Citing no specific instances and providing no substantiation of his charges, Hamilton stated outright that Ransom and Feldman had enriched themselves by selling the state of Texas thousands of worthless documents for tremendous sums of money. "The best deal Lew ever worked out was with the University of Texas where his 'arrangement' with the chancellor, Harry Ransom, blew in a gusher for both men," Hamilton wrote. "They made millions by bilking the University Library. They bought virtually worthless collections privately, then sold them to the university at an immense profit. Lew cut the chancellor in for a percentage of the take and Ransom made sure Lew's bills were quickly approved and promptly paid. Both men died rich, another proof of the old truism that crime pays."

Nine years after the publication of *Auction Madness,* I asked Charles Hamilton what information he had to support those allegations. "While a person is alive you cannot attack him in the way I attacked Lew D. Feldman," Hamilton pointed out. "You cannot libel the dead, and therefore, I felt free to use the information I possessed, which I got from Feldman's former private secretary, who is a close friend of mine." He would not name the secretary, but he did say that he saw her "every few days," that the woman knew "a lot about" Feldman, and that she had "speculations, which are numerous." He would not, however, detail any of the information he maintained he received from the former secretary. "Ransom and Feldman made a lot of money," he insisted, and they did it, he stressed, by trading in "tons of junk."

I asked Bart Auerbach, who worked with Lew Feldman during the final three years of his life, what he knew about this "former private secretary" and whatever "speculations" she might have shared with Charles Hamilton. "That explains it," Auerbach said. "All these years, I've been wondering what the hell Hamilton was trying to say there, and now I know." The "private secretary," Auerbach explained—and he named her—"was actually more of a companion in Lew's later years. Lew's wife had died sometime earlier, and this woman, who lived in the YWCA, came to work as what you would call his companion. She expected to be taken care of in Lew's will and she wasn't. I can't imagine what she could have told Hamilton about the business, because she never had anything to do with it. So she is the source of those charges? It's an outrage."

In addition to his indictment of Feldman's ethics, Hamilton unleashed a character assessment that ridiculed Feldman's famous one-word slogan, QVALITY. "My wife Diane could never decide whether Lew intended this word to be pronounced with a Yiddish accent or merely hoped that it would give a classic flavor to his vulgarity by incorporating the Roman *u*." Further on, Hamilton wondered why such clients as the New York Public Library "employed as an agent this exquisitely tasteless man who limped about with Mark Twain's silver-headed cane and a supercilious sneer on his fat upper lip."

Other people teased Feldman about the QVALITY slogan, "but they did it good-naturedly," Auerbach said. "One time after he swept everything he wanted at a Sotheby's sale, Herb Cahoon of the Morgan Library said to him, 'Well, Lew, now you've got QVANTITY to go along with the QVALITY.'"

John Maggs, a fourth-generation London bookseller, said during an interview in his office at 50 Berkeley Square that he knew Lew Feldman very well, but that he had no idea how Feldman became exclusive agent for Texas. "He was no scholar, that was my viewpoint, but he and Ransom certainly worked that oil well until it was nearly dry, I will say that. The result was that they may have paid too much at the time, but they got the books. I have been to and seen these great roomfuls of books in Austin, Texas, and it is a sight to see. They bought far beyond their capacity to absorb. But on the other hand, that's when the books were thick on the ground, and they are the ones who have them now. That certainly has to stand for something."

That Texas bought "far beyond its capacity to absorb" is evident by the fact that thirty-seven years after the program started, 30 percent of the manuscript holdings and 50 percent of the books remained to be catalogued. According to Mary Beth Bigger, assistant director in charge of cataloguing, there are about a million books in the HRC, along with thirty million leaves of manuscript, and five million photographs. "We are progressing," Bigger said, noting that in 1989, "we changed over from item-level cataloguing to collection-level cataloguing on the man- uscripts, which means we will get that job done a whole lot quicker." She said that strict "prioritization" guidelines are being observed as well, with the most important materials processed first. "I have three people working full time on cataloguing," she said, and was pleased to report that all of the Gloria Swanson and David O. Selznick material, two vast archives acquired in the 1980s, were "fully on line" by 1993. Meanwhile, new acquisitions continued to augment the existing work- load. In January 1994, the papers of Isaac Bashevis Singer, including correspondence in four languages, manuscripts of all the published books, and several unpublished and untranslated works, were being processed in Austin after a combination purchase-gift had been worked out with the Nobel laureate's estate the previous month. Thousands of documents spanning five decades came with the archive.

Clearly, Harry Ransom's enthusiasm for twentieth-century material such as this is part of a continuing legacy, but it did not prevent him from going after what combat pilots call targets of opportunity, as his pursuit of the Louis Silver library of English literature demonstrated in 1964. Considerably greater sums were at stake in 1965 when, sight unseen, he tried to buy the "residue" of the Sir Thomas Phillipps library, then in the possession of Robinson Brothers, noted British booksellers. The source for this anecdote is Lew Feldman himself, who recalled the pertinent details during an interview he gave on December 18, 1973, as part of an oral history project commissioned by Columbia University to document the New York antiquarian book scene. Though only twenty typewritten pages in length—Feldman was suffering then from Lou Gehrig's disease—the interview offers valuable insight into the man's sense of himself and his accomplishments as a bookseller.

By Feldman's reckoning, some 450 medieval and Renaissance man- uscripts on vellum, along with "hundreds of thousands of manuscripts on paper," were being offered. Feldman's celebrated bent for grand description and strained phrasing is very much in evidence throughout the interview: he called the Robinson brothers' London office their "sanctum" and the discussion they had a "colloquy." After describing the Phillipps material, which was then being stored in a house outside London, the Robinsons asked Feldman if he wanted to make an offer, even though he had not yet handled a single document.

I said they would find that I did not mince words nor matters, that I was candid and blunt to the point of hurting myself, but that I would take a calculated risk and tell them that I was talking in terms of ten million dollars cash. I assure you that as skilled as they were in arcane negotiations, this took them aback, and they both reported to me their interest, and could they be excused from the study for a few minutes to talk about it, and they would come back and give me their answer as to how we could proceed in this matter.

Fifteen minutes later the Robinson brothers reported they were "very much interested" in Feldman's offer, but they had a question: "Their query was, how could I possibly arrive at the figure of ten million dollars which I so freely gave them without having any knowledge of the contents of the collection. Surely a good question, but hardly one to faze me, since my eye was on such a magnificent goal that I brushed aside these questions and said, 'Well, I am quite sure that we'll cover that situation when we get to see the entire collection all at one time.' "

Arrangements were made to view the Phillipps material the following week, but in the meantime the Robinsons asked Feldman "to come around with them and talk to their solicitor," who quickly drew up a formal option that would hold the material for six months in return for a deposit of £10,000. "I remember standing up, and I said, 'Sir, as you may have already been informed, I represent the sovereign State of Texas in this matter, and I can assure you that the State of Texas does not pay for options.' " After another private "colloquy," the brothers and their solicitor declared that "it would be best to drop" the matter of a paid option.

The following week Feldman had a chance to examine some of the material before returning to America and placing the matter before Ransom. What happened next, Feldman told his interviewer, is "on the record" and "confirmed by correspondence." The Board of Regents and Governor John B. Connolly approved an appropriation "to the extent of the ten million dollars that was required" for the purchase, sight unseen and without any kind of professional evaluation. "Now, to understand the wheels that started to turn after I returned to America, you have to understand the very close and confidential relationship that existed between myself and my firm and the people in Austin, Texas," Feldman explained. He praised Harry Ransom for having "perseverance and utter prescience in the destiny" of the collections, and for entrusting him with the kind of confidence that "permitted me to accomplish the manifold achievements that transpired between us from 1956 through 1972." Without Ransom, he added, the acquisitions "would never have gotten off the ground, and I would never have had the opportunity for achieving the marvelous acts that were part of the program that developed between us."

Unfortunately for both Ransom and Feldman, those "marvelous acts" did not include acquiring the Phillipps manuscript material, because shortly after the $10 million had been authorized, "out of the blue" came an announcement that Lyndon Baines Johnson would be sending his presidential papers to Austin after he left office, and that the university would be building "a great library" to receive them. A choice had to be made, Lyndon Johnson or Sir Thomas Phillipps, and it came as no surprise to anyone in Texas when LBJ carried the day. "To go into further detail would really be harrowing," Feldman told his interviewer eight years later, "and as tragic as it might seem to me at this moment, I cannot blame anyone in the picture for deciding the way they apparently had to in order to keep faith with the President."

John Silber, the outspoken president of Boston University whose controversial political views brought him within 76,000 votes of the Massachusetts governorship in 1990, began his career in public life as a professor at the University of Texas in 1957. Silber's keen mind and unorthodox demeanor quickly attracted the attention of Harry Ransom, and by 1967 Silber had advanced through the history department to become dean of the College of Arts and Sciences. This highly influential position made him the odds-on favorite to become the next president of the College of Arts and Sciences. "Yes, I was one of Harry's boys," Silber said with a lingering Texas twang one morning in the

Boston office he has occupied since leaving Austin in 1971. He had been the victim a few months earlier of a summary firing at the hands of Frank C. Erwin, Jr., chairman of the University of Texas Board of Regents. "That's what everyone called me and a few other people Harry brought in as well, people like Norman Hackerman, Roger Shattuck and a few others; we were Harry's boys."

Silber not only confirmed that he was being groomed by Ransom to take over direction of the university, but also quickly added that he had intended to make it "the finest university in the United States." One reason he felt this would have happened was because "it had no excuse not to be. It had the money; all it needed was guidance. By now it would have been recognized as the greatest university in the world. I firmly believe that. The reason this has not happened is that it did not have the direction, and the direction that it did have, it was given first by Logan Wilson and then especially by Harry Ransom, and was muted in the last years of Harry Ransom's chancellorship by Frank Erwin, and then terminated when Frank Erwin proceeded to get rid of Norman Hackerman and me."

Silber said Texas was "a desert" when he arrived there. "When I went to Texas the only things I could find in the library were those damn Thomas Wise forgeries. That's a slight exaggeration, of course, but Harry Ransom did transform the place. When I left Texas after having been there for thirteen years, all those manuscripts he brought in were there, and that was no small achievement." He agreed that Ransom was a man who dreamed of greatness. "Extraordinary vision," he said, "and extraordinary daring. His strength was in his ignorance of the human modalities. He didn't know the difference between what was necessary, what was possible, or what was impossible, and consequently he would do things that reasonable people would have concluded were impossible and not worth trying to do, because he just didn't understand those modal relationships. And he was imaginative. If he liked an idea, he would usually stick his neck out for it." Silber recalled the first major report he wrote for Ransom on a proposed revision of the curriculum. "He read it, and his comment was, 'This is a splendid report with an engaging touch of the totally impossible.' "

Silber said that Ransom was not a "con man," as Charles Hamilton charged, because "there was never anything personal in it for him, of that I am absolutely certain. If Harry Ransom made millions, nobody ever found him spending it, and his wife certainly didn't become rich on his death." He agreed there is a "great deal of truth" to the frequent criticism that Ransom "was always breaking his promises," but quickly added that that was because "Harry would promise anything to damn near anybody. He was a man who had difficulty saying no to any idea that had any merit whatsoever."

One rumor that has circulated in Austin for two decades is that Ransom made what amounts to a "devil's deal" in 1970 with Frank Erwin over the fate of John Silber. As chairman of the Board of Regents, Erwin controlled the flow of money needed to build the Humanities Research Center, and when he determined, for a variety of reasons, that Silber had to go, Ransom never came forward to defend his protégé. Some people have suggested that Ransom remained silent because Erwin threatened to terminate support of the HRC if he interfered.

"It went much deeper than that," Silber said. "It is true that Harry *was* forced to make a choice, and he chose not to support me. He could have saved me if he wanted to, but he just lay low during the whole thing." Silber believes that what happened is that Erwin "made it very clear to Harry that if he tried to defend me, *he* was gone, and that he had the means to do it." Silber was not specific about what might have made Ransom vulnerable to such a threat, but his conviction is based on "something I know, and I think I will leave it at that. But let me say this. I knew Harry Ransom very well, and I knew Frank Erwin very well. And I know that Frank Erwin always looked for people's weaknesses so that he could exploit them. Frank Erwin was a very intelligent, very ambitious man, with a very limited education, who knew almost nothing about what was required to have a great university, but he was very, very smart, and he was politically astute. His idea for a university was a whole lot of buildings, a great football team, a great stadium, a great basketball team, a great baseball team, and if Harry Ransom wanted a great research center, well, that was all right, he liked that idea, too, because there was plenty of money for everything. Frank Erwin was a lot like Lyndon Johnson in many respects. He trusted no one that he could not control. And if Harry Ransom had not been controllable, Harry would not have been allowed to stick around."

Silber said that one reason Erwin demanded his own dismissal was because "I could not be controlled." Silber said that when he was named dean of the College of Arts and Sciences, he divested himself of an interest in a high-rise Austin dormitory bought at the invitation of a developer. "When I became dean, I immediately sold my interest, instantly, because then I was in a position to create residential colleges on the part of the university. I felt it would be a conflict of interest and I decided to divest. And I think that when Frank Erwin found out that I had divested, that was a bad mark against me, as far as he was concerned, because it meant that Silber was squeaky clean."

At that time, the College of Arts and Sciences accounted for 22,000 students, more than half of the total enrollment on the Austin campus. One of Silber's first acts was to propose a reorganization that would have placed even greater emphasis on liberal arts. Silber said he knew his days were numbered in the fall of 1969 when he told Erwin the Austin enrollment should be maintained at 35,000 students, and strive for quality, not constantly increasing numbers. "When that happens, I think it's time to fire the dean and break up the college," Silber recalled Erwin saying.

Eight months later, on a hot Friday afternoon in July, Silber was fired and the College of Arts and Sciences was dissolved; three smaller schools were created in its stead. Frank Erwin later said that the College of Arts and Sciences had become "an administrative monstrosity" that gave Silber "disproportionate control" of "more than half of everything at the university." Erwin told reporters that the character of students then enrolled in Arts and Sciences was another reason he wanted to form three smaller colleges. "A lot of students during this period went to college that might not have gone to college before," Erwin charged. "Many were people who went for fear of being drafted and going to Vietnam. And so, they signed up for the College of Arts and Sciences because they really didn't know what to major in."

A feature published in the magazine section of the Dallas *Morning News* in 1977 described Frank Erwin as "an unbroken power broker" known as "Chairman Frank" to some, "Frank Vermin" and "Emperor of the University" to others. Erwin was a former lobbyist and lawyer whose political influence began growing in the 1960s as he became a member of John Connally's inner circle. In 1963, Governor Connally

appointed him a regent at the same time he was named state Democratic chairman and Democratic national committeeman. With John
Connally in the state house and Lyndon Johnson in the White House,
Erwin's power to decide how huge dividends from state-owned oil and
natural gas leases would be spent was enormous. During Erwin's
tenure the Austin campus grew from 26,000 to 42,000 students. He
served as chairman of the Board of Regents from 1966 to 1971, left the
board in 1975, and died of a heart attack in 1980 at the age of sixty.
Lady Bird Johnson offered a special tribute. "He was a rare human
being who leaves a lonesome place in the world and the hearts of all
who knew and loved him. Most people have ideas. Frank Erwin had
ideas and ran with them."

In January 1971 Silber accepted an offer to become president of
Boston University. About the same time, Harry Ransom retired to
become chancellor emeritus and moved his offices into the recently
completed Humanities Research Center. In 1974, two years before he
died, the building was named the Harry Ransom Humanities Research
Center, an honor Kathleen Hjerter said was inevitable. "Why do you
think Dr. Ransom called it the HRC in the first place?" she asked. "He
was going to get his initials on that building whether they named it for
him or not."

No fewer than nineteen rooms at the Humanities Research Center are
named for notable people, and each one contains materials entrusted
by an important public figure. The Erle Stanley Gardner Room contains not only the mystery writer's personal library and curiosities but
also a redwood replica of the California study where most of the Perry
Mason stories were written. There is a John Foster Dulles Room, a
J. Frank Dobie Room and a Karl and Esther Hoblitzelle Room. This
appeal to a person's vanity is frequently the ultimate card the university
can play. "They always say, 'I'll give you my material, but give me a
room,'" Kathleen Hjerter said. "When Alfred Knopf was thinking
about where he would send his books, it didn't hurt our chances at all
when he found out we had this big, enormous room we were willing to
put aside just for him. He used to come down here once a year, too, just
to check things out and make sure everything was in the right place."

People need to be assured "that you really want them," Ellen Dunlap said, "and it takes more than words to convince them." Evelyn Waugh's books came along with his actual library, including shelves and furniture, shipped carefully from England to Texas. Before Gloria Swanson agreed to send her papers to Austin in 1982, she received assurances that her curator would be hired to watch over them. "I was part of the deal," Raymond S. Daum said.

One librarian distressed to hear that Miss Swanson's material was going to Austin was Howard B. Gotlieb at Boston University. Gotlieb is widely respected for having built a major twentieth-century archive with little more than charm, eloquent letters, and gentle persuasion. "I tried absolutely everything I knew," Gotlieb recalled with a wry smile. "I sent her flowers, I wrote her beautiful letters, I visited her, I ate macrobiotic food until it was coming out of my ears. But in the end I couldn't give her the kind of space she was demanding, and most of all I couldn't give her any money."

In 1971, James A. Michener and his wife were considering where they wanted to deposit their collection of 375 paintings, including works by Thomas Hart Benton, Helen Frankenthaler, Marsden Hartley, Hans Hofmann, Larry Rivers, and Max Weber. "We always intended to give it to a twentieth-century teaching institution where it would be used," the novelist recalled in an interview. "By a process of elimination, it had come down to Syracuse, Michigan, Nebraska, and Texas." Getting a large room and having it named for him was not what he wanted, but keeping the paintings together as a collection was.

"I spend my life trying to keep from having things named for me, but I do like to see good things done. So the work Harry Ransom had already accomplished was crucial, and the presentation he made was decisive. My wife was absolutely enchanted by the man." Though Michener did not give his papers, only his art, Ransom committed himself to setting aside the ground floor and part of the second floor at the HRC for the Archer M. Huntington Art Gallery, then housed elsewhere on campus. (Archer M. Huntington, the son of Collis Huntington and later the stepson of Henry E. Huntington, gave money to the University of Texas in 1927 to establish an art gallery.) The Mari and James A. Michener Collection of Twentieth-Century American Art was installed in the building and has been housed there ever since, a circumstance that caused some unusually graceless remarks by Decherd Turner during his tenure as director of the research center from 1981 to 1988.

"My feeling has always been that if the paintings are an imposition on the Harry Ransom Center, they shouldn't be there," Michener said. "Now, the situation is such that anytime I go in there I feel apologetic. It's a lovely place, and I agree it ought to be for books, not paintings. So there has been a basic conflict, a contradiction, and I recognize that, and I've advised them to get the collection out of there. I never made a point of keeping the paintings where they are." The problem is that if the paintings are removed from the HRC, they have to go to someplace else, and no other building on the Austin campus is equipped to display and care for them properly. As 1994 drew to a close, a move to other quarters was being discussed, though no definite plans had been made. "Our hope is alive to get a new building built on campus as quickly as possible, and to move all our staff and all our paintings there," Patricia D. Hendricks, curator of the Archer M. Huntington Art Gallery, said.

In his conversation with me, Michener made clear that he was never angered by the suggestion that his paintings might be taking up so much space, but by the crude manner in which it had been expressed. Bruised feelings and misunderstandings were a continuing problem during the eight-year tenure of Decherd Turner, an ordained Methodist minister whose retirement in 1988 was met with glee and relief by many people, including a number of unnamed "insiders" who were reported by the freelance writer Clifford Endres in a May 1988 article in *Texas Monthly* to have "sniped" that the "eccentric" director's departure was coming "none too soon."

Though Turner brought a number of important collections to Texas, he had a "feisty" and "confrontational" disposition that alienated colleagues and created enemies. In an effort to fill what he called "incredible gaps" in the Texas collection, he significantly underrated the importance of twentieth-century archival material and pursued instead such items as fine French bindings and *livres d'artiste*, books illustrated by prominent artists such as Matisse, Picasso, Chagall, and Rouault. For $2.6 million, he bought former Harvard professor

Robert Lee Wolff's collection of 17,000 Victorian best-sellers, and in 1986 he arranged the acquisition of the Carl and Lily Pforzheimer Library of English literature with a $15 million loan from H. Ross Perot.

Turner's most grievous offense, however, was that he criticized Harry Ransom, and he did it openly, flippantly sometimes, in a newsletter called *HRC Notes*. One issue, written in 1981 on Bloomsday—June 16, the day in which all the action of James Joyce's novel *Ulysses* takes place—is a parody of Joyce's style: "the trade took his name Ransom seriously for the most insignificant manuscript scrap is priced on a ransom level how grotesque it is that anything coming before the finished product commands so much more money than the published book I just cannot believe that a pre-publication uncased review copy is worth $500 more than a copy of the first published. . . ." and so on, without sentence breaks or punctuation, for three full, single-space, typewritten pages. In another newsletter, he warned against returning to the days of the "Ransom syndrome."

Six months before his retirement, Endres quoted Turner in the *Texas Monthly* article as saying he could "hardly wait" to leave. "In the forty-two years that I've been a director of libraries—at Vanderbilt, SMU, and here—for forty-one years and six months, I have lived in the presence of my immediate, disapproving predecessors. Now, I'll go down the street waving my hands and shouting, 'Free at last.' "

Turner was succeeded by Dr. Thomas F. Staley, the former director of special collections at the University of Tulsa and a noted James Joyce scholar and collector. One of his immediate aims was to restore morale and steady the course, and by all accounts he has succeeded. "Finally, we have our first true leader in over a decade," one senior staff member said in 1992. "We have a vision once again. He is creative, innovative, and willing to work with people. He does not have a hostile relationship with anyone."

Any reservations Staley might have about keeping the Michener Collection in the HRC have not been shared with anyone outside the building. For his part, Michener is sanguine about the situation. "My experience in quite a few of these things has always been that promises are made but never kept. All arrangements are made with the institution as it is then, and it's not going to continue that way for very long.

You deal with the people who are in control at a particular time, and they do not have the power to commit other people in the future. The minute Harry Ransom died, he was dead. It's as simple as that."

Carlton Lake has held the title of executive curator at the Harry Ransom Humanities Research Center since 1980, a position that pays him a respectable salary and confers considerable stature in the academic world. Originally, though, when he moved to Austin from Massachusetts in 1969, he was working on a pro bono basis. "Actually, I got paid a dollar a year back then," Lake said one February morning in his office, a cozy cubicle dominated by a bronze head of Picasso.

Though he had pursued a number of promising careers—he had written for several magazines, including the *New Yorker* and the *Atlantic Monthly* and from 1950 to 1965 was the Paris art critic for the *Christian Science Monitor*—Lake's primary interest in life was always his collecting. "You enter that world, and once you're in it, you can't get out," he said. "The truth is that you don't want to get out. I am convinced that it gets into your bloodstream."

Born into a family of New England merchants, Lake graduated from Boston University in 1936 with the idea of teaching Romance languages and literature at some small but respectable college. With the help of an "indulgent grandmother," Lake began collecting nineteenth-century French writers, Charles Baudelaire, Paul Verlaine, Arthur Rimbaud, and Stéphane Mallarmé among them. His first major purchase came in 1934 when he was nineteen and browsing through the catalogue of a forthcoming auction in New York of the library of Harry B. Smith, the American composer of popular musical comedies. Baudelaire's *Les Fleurs du mal* (specifically a presentation copy from the poet to his friend Nadar) caught his eye. "I had to have that book," he said. It also included several letters written by Baudelaire, and the original proof sheet of one of the poems in the book, "Les Litanies de Satan," with corrections in the author's hand. He paid $210 to get it; in 1957, when he lent the item to the Bibliothèque Nationale for an exhibition, a Paris dealer offered him $15,000, which he summarily declined. "My first great book," he recalled with pleasure. "It is the one book I always carried with me wherever I went. I could never bear to leave it behind."

Lake wrote a memoir of his collecting titled *Confessions of a Literary Archaeologist* in which he frequently discussed the ecstatic moment of discovery. He recalled the time he examined 4,200 folio pages of manuscript by Louis-Ferdinand Céline, comprising two complete versions of his novel *Guignol's Band,* and three of its sequel, *Le Pont de Londres,* in the shop of a Paris bookseller.

> I sat down and began to look through the piles of paper. How long that process went on, I don't know. One thing I do know is that by the time you have spent thirty-five or forty years digging out rare books and manuscripts in half the civilized countries of the world, when you pick up a book or a manuscript and you turn the pages and you palpate them and you fondle them, at some point there are vibrations that begin to pass out of the book or the manuscript into your fingers and your hands and up your arms and into your brain, and then, suddenly and very clearly, you get the message: right or not right, good or not good, and if good—how good.

After more than thirty years of collecting, Lake finally found himself in a quandary. "I gradually came to the idea that because so much of my material was unique—the volume of correspondence and manuscripts was just tremendous—that it should be kept together somewhere as a resource for scholars," he wrote. At the same time, "the sheer quantity of the whole thing was becoming impossible to deal with. Not only was my apartment in Paris full, I had a large safe at the Place Vendôme where I kept some of the more precious pieces. And it was no different back in Massachusetts. My house in Chestnut Hill had every room overflowing, and I had a walk-in vault in Boston. A few things, like the Baudelaire, I kept with me and wouldn't let out of my sight. It was pretty obvious that something had to be done."

Stories about the Humanities Research Center continued to be the talk of book circles, and even though Lake was a Massachusetts native, Boston University graduate, and self-confessed "Eastern snob," he looked toward Austin as a possible home for his collection of a quarter million pieces. "Texas was very strong in modern British and American material, but their French holdings for the same period were nothing to shout about," he said. "It seemed like a natural place for my collection to go." A friend then teaching at Texas put Lake in touch with Harry Ransom, and an agreement was quickly reached in 1969. Money was involved, but Lake said he agreed to sell the collection for a fraction of its market value because he was happy to see it get a permanent home.

Once Lake agreed to the deal, Ransom wrote with another offer. "I hope you will not consider my further suggestion as either an impertinence or an imposition. I should like to nominate you as lifetime Curator of these collections. The University would benefit by your advice; and both Dr. Roberts and I would be heartened by your personal association with the new Center. More important, perhaps, is the fact that visibility of a wise and agile collector is educative among both young students and mature scholars who use the Center."

From 1969 to 1975 Lake worked as a "dollar-a-year" consultant, and in 1975 he assumed the position of "lifetime executive curator" at the HRC. "The job was not part of the agreement," he said. "I had made no stipulations. I was trusting. I did not even demand that it be called the Carlton Lake Collection. I just wanted it to be kept together. At the same time, I must say in all candor that Harry Ransom was like nobody else. He could charm a bird right off the branch. He made people feel wonderful. If you want the truth, he made people feel greater than they really were."

Beyond securing the inestimable services of the person who knew the collection best, Ransom also ensured that there would be continued growth. "I have been accused of acting as if the collection is still mine," Lake said, partly because he has continued adding to it at his own expense long after turning it over to the University of Texas.

How important is the Carlton Lake Collection? Florence de Lussy, conservateur en chef de manuscrits at the Bibliothèque Nationale in Paris, had a straightforward answer to that question one chilly April day in 1990. "Remarkable," she said in heavily accented English. "Monsieur Lake is what we call 'un homme de goût'—a man of taste. In certain areas, for example Paul Valéry, the most important writer in twentieth-century France, you must go to Texas if you wish to study the man thoroughly. There are sheafs of manuscript there dealing with Valéry's last love that are unknown in France. I personally did not know this text existed. Consequently, the Carlton Lake Collection is essential, and very well known here in France. I wish it were here and not there."

Madame de Lussy paused for a moment, seeking a precise word. "He is not our enemy," she said. "But he is our rival. He looks for the same things we do, and there are times when he fights us at the auctions. Together, let me say, we are friends. Of course we are interested here in all of French history—letters, literature, and science. He is a specialist in the twentieth century. He is very clever; he has exceptional instinct."

Lake is unqualified in his admiration for Harry Ransom. "I would never say anything negative about him, nothing, because what he did was create the HRC, and if that is how he goes down in history, that is quite an achievement. It really doesn't matter what people went through to bring things here, or what it all cost, even though the cost was considerable, because I truly believe that what we have here is the Alexandria of the twentieth century."

Just how much Texas spent for books and manuscripts during the first fifteen years is uncertain. Some observers say as much as $50 million, others suggest even more. Nobody can say for sure because the money came not only from the state but also from private benefactors whom Ransom wooed, and the purchasing procedures he used were decidedly unorthodox. "I would be very surprised, to tell you the truth, if it's as much as twenty million," Warren Roberts said when pressed for a figure. "But whatever it is, my theory has always been that money is only money, and you can't believe the way people spend money for other things. You know how much money they spend over there for scientific research without even thinking about it? They'll spend five million for a machine that is obsolete before they even get it operating. What has gone into the humanities is practically nothing by comparison—nothing. And everything we bought will increase in value."

The current director, Thomas F. Staley, believes that a myth has grown around Harry Ransom. "The reason it's a myth is because you can get thirty people to talk about Ransom, and what they thought was Ransom's real mission and purpose, and it's amazing how various the stories can be." Staley explained how difficult it is to "demythologize" Harry Ransom in a speech at Cambridge University in 1989:

Like many brilliant leaders of institutions, Ransom was given
to both candor and secrecy, depending upon how he judged the
situation. Ransom created an aura of optimism that was compelling, even though this feeling could lead to expectations
beyond those that he could deliver. Many book dealers felt the
same way, I am sure, especially when they waited for final com-
mitments, and waited, too, for payment. Like many collectors,
his eyes were larger than his purse. Given the length of his
purse you can imagine the size of his eyes. Furthermore, even if
other institutional buyers had as large a purse, they would not
have had the same freedom to open it.

Colin Franklin, considering the changes at Texas several thousand
miles away at his book barn in England, called Staley "the right person
to be at the HRC" during a time of stabilization. "He's a decent person, he's probably diplomatic, and he's not going to continue the procedures of the past. He's interested in modern writers, and women
writers, and in filling the essential deficiencies. He's the man they need
for now, I think, because they've had their adventures. What they need
is to settle down a bit and live with it."

10

Obsessed
Amateurs

On June 1, 1983, the *New York Times* reported the discovery of an obscure but significant narrative, "Father Abraham," written around 1925 by William Faulkner, a fragment of fiction that is believed to have shaped themes and characters later embodied in the Snopes family trilogy. Described as "the brilliant beginning" of an unfinished novel, the twenty-four pages of handwritten manuscript had been overlooked by literary scholars for years, largely because they were not in any of the primary Faulkner repositories maintained at several American universities, nor were they owned by any of the leading private collectors who specialize in the life and works of the great Mississippi writer.

Instead, "Father Abraham" turned up in the Arents Collection at the New York Public Library. The reason for this is a reference to tobacco: early in the manuscript, Faulkner describes Uncle Flem as a man who "chews tobacco constantly and steadily and slowly, and no one ever saw his eyelids closed." The only known etching ever made by

Vincent Van Gogh is in the Arents Collection for the same reason: because the subject, Dr. Gachet, is pictured smoking a pipe. Oscar Wilde's manuscript for *The Importance of Being Earnest* was acquired because a key turn in the plot revolves around a cigarette case. Another item in the collection, a late sixteenth-century poem in manuscript by Robert Devereux, earl of Essex, includes the line, "It was not tobacco stupified my braine."

George Arents Jr. (1885–1960) was a prominent New Yorker whose personal fortune derived from his family's substantial interest in the American Tobacco Company. In 1900, Arents obtained a patent for a machine that manufactured cigars, an invention that led to the formation of the American Machine and Foundry Company, now called AMF, and a subsidiary known as International Cigar Machinery Company. As a collector, Arents sought to document every conceivable aspect of his lucrative livelihood, including the history, folklore, and literature of the tobacco plant. He gathered material that detailed cultivation of the crop and the marketing of its products, and he included every published argument he could find that favored or opposed its use. In addition to books, manuscripts, periodicals, pamphlets, drawings, prints, and sketches, Arents also acquired more than 125,000 cigarette cards; he turned over all this material to the New York Public Library in 1943, along with a generous endowment that provided for special rooms, a permanent staff, preparation of bibliographies, and continued additions to the holdings. In fact, The "Father Abraham" manuscript was purchased by the fund from the New York bookseller Philip C. Duschenes in 1953, ten years after Arents deposited the collection.

Bernard McTigue, former keeper of rare books at the New York Public Library and now chairman of the Department of Special Collections at the University of Florida, said the Arents Collection is something that "only an obsessed amateur" could ever possibly have imagined, let alone assembled. "Institutional libraries would not exist as we know them if it were not for private collectors like George Arents, James Lenox, the Berg brothers, Arthur Alfonso Schomburg, Mary Stillman Harkness, Florence Blumenthal, and all the others you see represented here," McTigue explained one afternoon as he guided me through an exhibition he curated in the fall of 1990 called "In Praise of Collectors: Historic Gifts to the New York Public Library."

"Private collectors have always been the people who put the pieces together," McTigue said. "It is their passion that builds these collections, along with their energy, their resources, and their expertise. They do all the work, and when everything is complete—and if we're lucky—they turn it over to us intact. Carter Burden's science fiction collection is a very recent case in point. That was a great addition for us because we never collected science fiction, certainly not as fastidiously as he did. Yet he made up for our past omission with a single gift, and he did it better than we might have ever done by ourselves."

Shortly after observing his seventieth birthday in 1989, the chef and restaurateur Louis I. Szathmary II closed his popular restaurant on Chicago's Near North Side. The time had come, he decided, to "take care of the books." Since several hundred thousand items were involved, completing the massive series of benefactions he had started a few years earlier to half a dozen institutions scattered throughout the United States was a task that demanded his full attention.

For twenty-six years, Szathmary (pronounced ZATH-ma-ree), a Hungarian who came to the United States in 1951, owned the Bakery restaurant, an unpretentious storefront eatery that *Gourmet* magazine declared a "gastronomic landmark" when it closed for good. "Chef Louis is not cooking anymore," the magazine lamented, "and too soon all traces of the Bakery will be gone from Lincoln Park when its sign comes down and the restaurant is replaced with office space." Szathmary was renowned for his exceptional Continental menu, but the most popular dish by far was his beef Wellington. "The food writers joke about beef Wellington now, but they all raved about it once, and I know that after twenty-six years, fifty percent of our sales is still beef Wellington," he told a reporter as the closing drew near. He grossed more than $1 million a year for much of the time he was in business. "And that's only five dinners a week—no lunch, no bar and no 'early birds.' "

Szathmary, a heavyset man with a generous face and large bushy mustache, has written five cookbooks, including one, *The Chef's Secret Cookbook,* that made the *Time* magazine best-seller list. He also served as general editor for *Cookery Americana,* an encyclopedic effort published by Arno Press that was issued in fifteen volumes. Chef

Louis, as he prefers to be called, speaks in accented but precisely phrased English, and his publicity photographs invariably picture him wearing a crisp white apron and a high chef's hat with a billowing flare at the top.

When I first met Chef Louis, he was neither in a kitchen nor wearing a big white hat, and seemed completely at ease and very much at home puttering about a cavernous warehouse in Providence, Rhode Island. Sitting behind the same old wooden desk he used in Chicago and surrounded by many familiar books and trinkets, Szathmary was supervising the installation of 200,000 assorted items from a culinary collection he recently had shipped to Johnson & Wales University, the world's largest school devoted to the food and service industry, where he has been given the title of chef laureate. "This will be a museum," he said with pride. "And it will be the best of its kind anywhere."

Thirteen hundred miles away, another segment of his collection, some 22,000 items comprising rare cookbooks, scarce pamphlets, and unique manuscripts spanning five centuries of culinary art, already was installed at the University of Iowa Library, while in his adopted city, Chicago, twelve thousand volumes devoted entirely to what is called Hungarology were being accessioned at the University of Chicago's Joseph Regenstein Library. Gifts to other institutions were being finalized as well: a collection of several thousand menus to the University of Nevada at Las Vegas, ten thousand books of Hungarian literature to Indiana University, and a small collection of Franz Liszt letters to Boston University—offerings from a man who forty years earlier left Europe with nothing more than loose change in his pocket and a few words of English in his vocabulary.

The Johnson & Wales warehouse, a temporary home for the culinary collection, is in an old industrial neighborhood on Providence Harbor. Some eighteen thousand square feet of floor space is available inside for the Szathmary Culinary Arts Collection, and the day I arrived much of it was crammed from stanchion to stanchion with fully loaded bookcases and cabinets, all recent arrivals from Chicago. Sixteen trailer trucks were used to make the transfer, and the cargo had been reunited here. Scattered around the floor were crates loosely packed with antique kitchen implements, a panorama of cheese graters, meat grinders, nutcrackers, raisin seeders, chocolate molds, fruit choppers, cherry pitters, coffee mills, and ice cream scoops. Wedged in between them were stacks of ephemera from all over the country, plus every manner of almanac and magazine related to food and cooking that one could imagine. And this, the chef said, was just the tip of the iceberg.

Where in the world, I asked, had he *stored* all this material?

"My restaurant was very small, just one hundred and seventeen chairs downstairs for the customers to sit," Chef Louis said, and there was a twinkle in his hazel-brown eyes. "But I owned the whole building, you see, and upstairs there were thirty-one rooms in seventeen apartments. That's where I kept all the books."

I learned about Chef Louis Szathmary in an unexpected way. Shortly after Stephen Blumberg was arrested in Ottumwa, Iowa, and charged with plundering libraries all over the United States, the curator of rare books at the University of Iowa, David Schoonover, was asked by the FBI to make a preliminary evaluation of what Blumberg had taken. As a consequence, Schoonover was among the first people I contacted for information on the intriguing Blumberg case. After telling me what he knew about the book thief, Schoonover mentioned an "amazing collector from Chicago" who recently had presented the University of Iowa library with "one of the very finest cookbook collections you are going to find anywhere." Overnight, the library had "become a major research center in the culinary arts."

The collection had many wonderful things, some of them going back several centuries. Schoonover mentioned the first printed tableside trencherbooks, or guides to cutting meat, in Spanish, Italian, German, and French as four examples. There was a cookbook in typescript that the novelist Nelson Algren had written for the Federal Writers Project during the Depression. The University of Iowa Press published it in 1992 as part of a new project called the Iowa Szathmary Culinary Series. Another curiosity in the collection is the handwritten cookbook of Katharina Schratt, the official mistress of Franz Joseph, emperor of Austria from 1849 to 1916 and king of Hungary from 1886 to 1916, who recorded recipes of interest from the royal kitchen.

Schoonover noted that the archive has many scholarly applications. The evolution of food and culture is anthropology; types of foods and where they are grown is agriculture; the importing and exporting of foodstuffs is economic history; how people have perceived food is folklore; how food is dealt with by artists and composers is cultural history; food as remedies is the history of medicine. "The Szathmary Collection of Culinary Arts provides excellent source material in all of these areas," he said. "And it came to us as a one hundred percent gift."

After service in the Hungarian army during World War II, Louis Szathmary spent time in a succession of German and Soviet prison camps, and thereafter was a "displaced person" confined to the American occupation zone in Austria. Even though he holds a Ph.D. in psychology from the University of Budapest, his education was little help when he was looking for meaningful work in postwar Europe. "My family in Hungary were book collectors for many generations," he said. "We had a standing account with one dealer going back to the 1790s. But then came the war, and when it was over, it was all gone; everything was destroyed or stolen. When I came to America in 1951, I had one dollar and ten cents in my pocket and fourteen books in my bag."

The chef paused, taking care to shape exactly what he wanted to say, and then continued. "We have this attitude in the old country, which is enforced by history and by nature, that says there are times when we must look in the mirror to make sure there are no eyes in the back of our heads. We feel that if God wants us to keep looking back, He would give us at least one eye for that purpose. But we have both of our eyes, and they are not looking behind us or to the sides, but to the front. That is the message—that we should look forward, not backward. Instead of crying about what we lost, we learn what to do for the future. So the books I give away now, they stay in my heart, just like all the others. I don't have to see them to love them."

There was silence for a few seconds, and then I asked what happened to the fourteen books he brought over with him from Europe. "They go nowhere," he said, "not until I meet my demise." The books Chef Louis carried with him to America included a Bible he received as a child, three books on Mozart, several volumes of Hungarian poetry, "and three or four things that I bought from other emigrants in Austria" before boarding the U.S.S. *General Hersey* in Bremerhaven, Germany, for New York. "I decided that this is what I wanted with me in America. I have my books on Mozart, the greatest Hungarian poets, and my Bible."

Before moving to Chicago in 1959, Szathmary worked at a variety of jobs in New York and New England. "When I got my first paycheck, I went to Marlboro Books at the corner of Forty-second Street and Broadway and bought a cookbook by Ludwig Bemelmans for nineteen cents. I had lots of time then, so I was able to pass whole days in a Salvation Army basement with secondhand books, and after sitting there for six or seven hours, I could come out with some books for five cents each. Later on, I had some very good jobs and I was highly paid. After I left my job in the day, I would work a second job in the evening, and on the seventh day, I spent all the money I made on books."

Before opening the Bakery with his wife, Sadako, in 1962, Szathmary worked as product development manager for Armour, coming up with ideas for new foods and ways to prepare them. He is credited with improving the freeze-drying process that is used by many food manufacturers today, and he designed a kitchen for military field hospitals that could be dropped by parachute and assembled quickly in combat zones. Once the Bakery was a success, Chef Louis formed his own consulting company, which he has continued to operate since closing the restaurant.

Szathmary explained that he has always bought books for various reasons. "When you bet on the horse race, you bet for win, for place, for show. When you buy books, you buy some to read, some to own, and some for reference. You want to possess the books, you want to own them, you want to hold them. Perhaps you even hope that you will read them. But I will say that most of the books I have ever had, I know what is inside. Many of our recipes at the restaurant came from the collection, and I have used them in my lectures and for my own cookbooks. So this was a living library." One reason the culinary materials were divided among several universities is that "some things were more appropriate to certain collections; but Iowa, I must tell you, only wanted the best books, they were very selective. So I said, 'You know, you want to collect the cream and leave me the skim milk.' So we made a very amicable, very friendly agreement, that we stop with the cookbooks I already gave them."

Included in the gift to Johnson & Wales is a "collection within the collection," a presidential autograph archive that includes documents dealing in one way or another with food, drink, or entertainment, written or signed by every American chief executive. In George Washington's handwriting is a list of table china he inherited from a relative. A handwritten letter from Mary Todd Lincoln invites a friend from Baltimore to the White House for an evening of relaxation. In a penciled note to his wife, Julia, Ulysses S. Grant asks that two bottles of champagne be sent to the Oval Office for a reception with congressional leaders. A family recipe for beef stew bears Dwight D. Eisenhower's signature. "I am interested in the presidents as eaters," the chef explained. "I intend to write a book on this subject, which I will call *The First Stomach*. That is my next project." The autograph collection includes items written by other historic figures, from Napoleon Bonaparte to Charles Dickens, as well as a note from the fourth earl of Sandwich, inventor of the most frequently ordered food item in the world.

For all the passion Chef Louis has invested in his books, he shows little anxiety about passing them along to institutions. "I still cry a little bit at night," he said, "but that is all part of love." When we spoke again several years later, the Johnson & Wales materials were being used by students, while plans were afoot for a move from the warehouse by the harbor to permanent quarters. "I am still buying books," Chef Louis confessed. "It is like getting pregnant after the menopause; it's not supposed to happen."

When the Watergate Apartments were being built in the 1960s, one split-level suite in the East Wing was reinforced with extra steel and concrete to accommodate the exacting requirements of a methodical book collector who worked a half hour's drive outside the nation's capital, in Langley, Virginia, and whose ten thousand–volume library, as a consequence, is divided in two distinct sections. One part of Walter L. Pforzheimer's library contains an elegant selection of French bindings and dramatic works that he received as a gift from his father several decades earlier; the other is a collection of books, manuscripts, and curiosities that illuminate the history of his veiled profession. Pforzheimer's former colleagues at the Central Intelligence Agency know these books as the "spy collection."

On the walls of Pforzheimer's apartment are four silk-screen prints produced by the KGB spy Colonel Rudolph Abel while he was imprisoned in the Atlanta Federal Penitentiary. "Colonel Abel was what we call an 'illegal,' a Soviet agent here without official cover," Pforzheimer said. "Part of his cover was that he worked as a commercial artist, which accounts for the excellence of the drawings you see here. He was a top Soviet agent in this country, and he never broke. We don't really know what he did here."

The library is on the second floor of the apartment, and entry must be made through a wrought-iron door that is always locked and equipped with a sophisticated security system. On the grille is an insert with the laced initials WP. Inside, two oversized plaques take up equal space on the walls, one the familiar seal of the CIA, the other the insignia of Yale University. "My father's library door was always open to me, because he saw that I could handle books. I liked being in his library. On my twenty-first birthday, he called me over and said, 'Well, son, you don't need another car, so I'm giving you this library as a present. Here it is.' It was quite a shock, but after all these years, it's still with me, and it stays with me along with all the other material."

Pforzheimer received his bachelor of arts degree in 1935 and his law degree in 1938, both from Yale. When World War II began, he attended officer candidate school and got a commission in the Army Air Force in 1942. "About a week before my graduation from OCS, an officer I had never seen before and have never seen since tapped me on the shoulder and asked me whether I would be interested in intelligence. I said that sounds great, and I've been in it every day since then. Even now, though I'm supposed to be retired." During the war, Pforzheimer was on the intelligence staff of the United States Strategic Air Forces in Europe, and in July of 1945 he entered Berlin with a team of American officers. "Once in a while you get a chance to collect, even in wartime," he said, as he pulled a book from one of the shelves. "Some people have books that they aren't going to need anymore. I was in this fellow's office in Berlin, and a few of these were lying around. So I took five out with me."

On the inside cover of an obscure German novel from the 1930s titled *Kamts Battle um Thurant* is a bookplate that features an eagle in profile, a swastika underneath, and the name Adolf Hitler. The author, a man named Robert Allmers, wrote an inscription, dated March 1933, to the Führer. "I was in the Reich Chancellery, and there they were," Pforzheimer said. "I didn't think the Führer was going to be needing them anymore. I gave one to the guy who cut my orders for Berlin, I gave one to the Grolier Club, I gave one to Yale, and I kept the other two."

When Pforzheimer took the five books from Hitler's shelves, he did not consider them as additions for any future collection, however. "I was acting instinctively, that's all," he said. The decision to collect intelligence material came after he joined the newly established Central Intelligence Group as legislative counsel and helped draft the legislation that formed the CIA in 1947. He continued in that position until 1956 and performed a variety of other assignments until he retired in 1974.

The decisive moment for Pforzheimer as a collector came when he was in New York on agency business in 1950. "I had been getting relevant things along the way, but they were to read, not collect. There is a fundamental difference, as you know. So I had been buying a few books, nothing terribly serious, though my bookseller friends had started pushing me back in time. For example, I bought one book by Alan Pinkerton from Dave Randall at Scribner's, *Spy of the Rebellion,* which brought me back to the Civil War. But anyway, one day I stopped into Rosenbach's branch office in New York to see my old friend Bill McCarthy about some little document he had, and he said, 'Walter, I think I have something else you might be interested in.' He then laid on a table a letter from Washington dated July 26, 1777, to Colonel Elias Dayton, who was Washington's intelligence chief in New Jersey. The letter's last paragraph has been quoted occasionally on Capitol Hill, and has been misquoted by many other people over the years."

Though the letter was lying in his lap, Pforzheimer recited the passage from memory: " 'The necessities of procuring good Intelligence is apparent and need not be further urged. All that remains for me to add is, that you keep the whole matter as secret as possible. For upon Secrecy Success depends in most Enterprises of the kind, and for want of it, they are generally defeated, however well planned and promising a favourable issue. I am, sir, your most obedient servant, G. Washington.' "

Pforzheimer said he looked at the letter lying on the bookstore table in green baize, and he gave the implications of what was about to happen deep consideration. "We were now at what you call the make or break point. Do you or don't you collect? I had not considered myself a collector of intelligence material until I was faced with this document, and what do you do? Well, there's no question of what you do; you just cannot let something like that go by. So obviously I got it, and at that point I was committed. What you see around here is the logical extension of what happened that day in New York." Pforzheimer owns three other George Washington letters, but this by far is the most important.

Among the curiosities Pforzheimer owns is a visa application requesting entry to France submitted by a Dutch woman named Margarethe Geertruida Zelle McLeod in 1916. "She never made it out of the country," Pforzheimer said. "As we say in the trade, it's signed in her 'true name,' and her 'pseudonym.' " The woman's pseudonym was Mata Hari. "That's an unhappy group of books down there," Pforzheimer continued, pointing to seventy-one volumes of bound documents lying in a pile. They contain classified material seized by the Iranians who captured the American embassy in 1979. Much of the material had been shredded, but was reconstructed by the intruders and printed in English and Iranian versions.

Pforzheimer considers the "cornerstone book of the collection" to be *The Memoirs of Secret Service,* published in 1699, "and from my standpoint the first book in English completely devoted to intelligence operations." His copy is inscribed by Matthew Smith, the author, to the Lord High Chancellor of England. Pforzheimer considers the "foundation book" of American intelligence to be a monograph dated September 29, 1780, which bears the title *Proceedings of a Board of General Officers, Held by Order of His Excellency Gen. Washington, Commander in Chief of the Army of the United States of America, Respecting Major John Andre, Adjutant General of the British Army.* John Andre was the case officer in the defection of Benedict Arnold at West Point, and the sentence imposed was "death by hanging at high noon." Pforzheimer also has "countless" memoirs written by contemporary intelligence people, many of them inscribed to him by the authors.

Though retired, Pforzheimer lectures at the Defense Intelligence College and edits the college's bibliography on intelligence literature. Some five thousand items are represented in the Walter Pforzheimer Collection on Intelligence Service, and new material is continually added. "When I was at Langley, Allen Dulles told me to start up the agency's book collection. He wanted a library on all aspects of the intelligence profession since the beginning of time to the latest book, in all languages, and he gave me a nice budget. So I established the Historical Intelligence Collection at the agency, and I was curator for many years, in addition to my other duties. After ten years as legislative counsel, that became my title. Collateral duties required me to travel the world from time to time, and I was able to collect books for the agency. When I left, they had twenty-one thousand volumes. It's a lot larger now."

Pforzheimer stressed that what he created at the CIA was a reference library. "What I have here for myself is a collector's collection. What they have at the agency is material in all languages. My stuff is primarily in English. And the agency doesn't collect rarities." Pforzheimer said his job as "head bookman" for the CIA provided the model for James Grady's novel *Six Days of the Condor;* it was adapted into a 1975 movie titled *Three Days of the Condor,* in which a CIA "reader" played by Robert Redford becomes drawn into a deadly internecine conflict. While the CIA would love to own his collection, Pforzheimer's decision to send everything to his alma mater is firm. "The agency makes noise every now and then, but they get their hands slapped. A lot of people make noises. The Hoover Institute made noise. They can't have it either. It's going to Yale, period, the end. Everything goes to Yale, including my ashes, if they want them."

As a lawyer skilled in negotiating detailed agreements with committees of Congress, Pforzheimer made sure the terms of his bequest to Yale were "clear as a bell." When he dies—and not a day before—the university gets his collection on intelligence along with the five thousand books he received from his father as a twenty-first birthday present. "They can't have one without the other. I know they're salivating to get the Molière stuff and the bindings, and the money of course, but I made it explicitly clear that everything goes together, or nothing goes at all."

The Molière collection assembled by his father "is probably the finest in this country in private hands. Father knew his books. It's an interesting collection. That last shelf of books on the left there, those are all plays by famous British playwrights. Now, why are they there? Because in every one, there are parts that were stolen from Molière."

His father's collection of exquisite royal French bindings, including one fashioned for Jean Grolier in the sixteenth century, is superb as well, and there is a sizable collection of royal French autographs. "I added a few things to the Molière collection, but did nothing with the bindings. If you're going to collect rare bindings, you do that to the exclusion of everything else."

How Pforzheimer's father, also named Walter, came to collect French authors, autographs, and elegant bindings is an interesting story in its own right. It relates to the collecting interests of Walter Jr.'s uncle, Carl H. Pforzheimer, whose collection of English literature, the Carl and Lily Pforzheimer collection, occasioned publication of one of the great bibliographies of the twentieth century and was sold in 1988 to the Humanities Research Center at the University of Texas for $15 million. In a separate purchase, Texas also bought from the Pforzheimer collection a Gutenberg Bible in 1978 for $2.4 million. Another segment of the collection, arguably the finest gathering of materials outside the British Library relating to Percy Bysshe Shelley and the Romantic poets, was given to the New York Public Library.

Three Pforzheimer brothers, Carl, Walter, and Arthur, were hugely successful Wall Street brokers who specialized in oil company stock, but in the mid-1920s, for a variety of personal reasons, they went their separate ways. "After Arthur and my father left the firm, Arthur set up his own rare-book business," said Walter Pforzheimer. "It was not a great success, but I'm devoted to his memory because when he and Father were together, he would always ask what I was studying, and whatever it was, some perfectly appropriate book would end up on my desk the next day. These were not rare books, but he was interested in young people, and he knew I was interested in reading."

Relations between Walter's father and his uncle Carl, on the other hand, were strained, and affected the course each man followed as collectors. Basically they stayed out of each other's way. Carl Pforzheimer continued to form his comprehensive collections of English literature while Walter Pforzheimer, Sr., concentrated on France. "My father was a very quiet, sensitive, lovely guy who would die at the mere mention of his name," Pforzheimer said. "Every charitable gift he ever made was anonymous. He didn't want any conflicts with anyone. Carl and

Lily, on the other hand, would never do anything unless their names were on it in lights. So that kind of limited where their great library could go. Harvard wouldn't build Carl a building—they already had the Houghton and he wanted to be sure the marquee over the door said, 'This is the Carl H. and Lily Pforzheimer Library,' so nothing much happened. Then he died in 1957. By the time the deal with Texas came together, Carl Senior was long gone."

In that regard, at least, there is a similarity between Walter Pforzheimer and his uncle Carl. "I go out the door feet first, then my library can go up to New Haven," he said. "I call it the Walter Pforzheimer Collection on Intelligence Service. But when it gets to Yale, I'm sure it will always be known as 'the spy collection.' "

Staff members at the University of Florida recall a warm spring day in 1990 when a nervous undergraduate appeared in the rare-book room on the second floor of the main library and asked to speak with Ruth M. Baldwin, who had built an enormous collection of children's literature that was named in her honor. When told that she had recently died, the student expressed profound relief, not sadness, a peculiar reaction that warranted an explanation. It turned out that as part of his initiation into a fraternity, the young man had been required to ask Dr. Baldwin if he could borrow some of her books.

"Her reputation was legendary on campus," said Rita Smith, the project cataloguer for the Baldwin Library. "Ruth Baldwin controlled her collection with an iron hand, and if she didn't think your reason for wanting to see something was good enough, you were gone. She even got angry with professors who sent students over here for what she thought were frivolous requests to use her books. She had her desk right by the entrance over there. She wanted to see everyone who came in, and everyone who went out, and when she wasn't at her desk, there was an alarm on the door that let out a high-pitched scream whenever the door was opened. She may have turned the books over to the university in 1978, but she came along as the curator, and she watched over her collection right up until the day she died."

Barely five feet tall, stout but by no means overweight, and gray-haired with glasses, Ruth Baldwin did not project a stereotypically intimidating image, but her books had become the guiding force in her life, and since possessiveness is not uncommon among book collectors, her unyielding attitude was accepted as part of the agreement she had struck with school officials. After all, she had put the University of Florida on the map as far as special collections are concerned, and if it took twelve years from the time she gave the books to the time she let them loose, that was all right too, because when she died in 1990 at the age of seventy-two, her distinguished collection of 100,000 nineteenth- and twentieth-century children's books became a full-service library, ready at last to serve the interests of scholarship.

"It's extraordinary," Bernard McTigue said shortly after moving to Gainesville from New York to become director of special collections at the University of Florida. "I really am in awe of what this woman did. In some areas the collection has no equal. What makes it very special is that Ruth Baldwin wanted books that children had used. She liked the fact that these specific books—these actual objects—had touched children's lives."

The Baldwin Library occupies much of the south end of the second floor of Library East at the University of Florida Gainesville campus, including four large rooms with connecting balconies, high cathedral ceilings, handsome wood shelving, and elegant walnut paneling. The collection is divided more or less equally into British and American children's books from the eighteenth, nineteenth, and twentieth centuries.

Ruth Baldwin began collecting children's books in her mid-thirties almost as a challenge from her father, a professor of English at the University of Illinois who was renowned for his own collection of sixteenth- and seventeenth-century books. In 1953, during one of many book-hunting trips to England, Dr. Thomas W. Baldwin and his wife, Elisabeth, bought about twenty old chapbooks and sent them to their daughter in Urbana, Illinois, where she was working toward her doctorate in library science. Along with the gift went the suggestion that children's books "might be a nice little hobby for a woman to pursue." She took up the challenge with unexpected enthusiasm.

"I was always a reader, but it never occurred to me to collect books," Ruth Baldwin told Jacob L. Chernofsky, the editor of *AB Bookman's Weekly*, a periodical published for the antiquarian trade, shortly after her retirement in 1988. "In high school, I was not allowed to go to games or dances or anything else like that, because of my parents' background—they just didn't think I should do those things. My father was a Southerner and he wouldn't let me go out after dark." She described her father as a man "driven" in his collecting, but interested only in material "that he thought might give him clues to the education and the writing of Shakespeare." There is no suggestion in Chernofsky's article as to whether or not Ruth Baldwin may have been trying to surpass her father as a collector, though Rita Smith thinks such a wish could have motivated her will to acquire.

Born in South Carolina in 1918, Ruth was a precocious child whose early ambition was to attend medical school. She told Chernovsky that one reason she transferred from the University of Illinois to Muskingum College, a Presbyterian school in New Concord, Ohio, was to distance herself from her parents, though the "atmosphere" at the college was "not much different from home." After graduating in 1939, she returned to the University of Illinois, where she would earn three more degrees.

A succession of interesting jobs followed in various sections of the country, leading finally to Louisiana State University in Baton Rouge in 1956, where she remained for two decades, retiring in 1977 as a professor emeritus. At that point, barely a year shy of her sixtieth birthday, the pivotal moment in her life as a book collector developed when a visiting professor from the University of Florida happened to see the enormous library she maintained in her home. A University of Florida delegation visited her shortly thereafter and issued her an invitation to move everything to Gainesville, which she accepted, with the understanding that she would go along as curator. Not only would her books have a permanent home, but she would be the full-time custodian, and she would have a free hand in shaping the collection's future. Retiring as professor emeritus at one university, Dr. Baldwin assumed an exciting new position at another; in 1988, at the age of seventy, she retired once again, this time with the title of university librarian emeritus.

"Ruth and I talked often in the afternoons," Smith said. "I grew up in Michigan, her family had a cottage in the Indian River Valley in Michigan, and we both studied library science at the University of Illinois. So we had a few things in common we could chat about. Her personality was extremely forceful, but she was not without a sense of humor. There were times when she talked about her childhood and her family when I wished there had been a tape recorder going. As to whether or not she was offended by her father's suggestion that children's books would be a nice thing for a woman to collect, I cannot say. But I do know that she certainly took him up on it, and from then on it became the total focus of her life."

Thomas Whitfield Baldwin was collecting what were regarded as the far more serious books, and his collection of about 5,500 titles is now in the University of Illinois at Urbana. "It's an extremely imaginative collection of sixteenth- and seventeenth-century books," according to Frederick Nash, curator of rare books there. "It includes Bibles, classical texts, colloquies, homilies, chapbooks, catechisms, logic, prayer books, all kinds of things that were available during Shakespeare's lifetime, and that might very well have influenced his thought and his writing."

Dr. Thomas Baldwin was a respected scholar and author of no fewer than seven books, several of which drew on this intelligently conceived collection. His best-known work is *William Shakespeare's small Latine & lesse Greeke,* which focused on knowledge, learning, and education during Elizabethan times. An earlier book, *William Shakspere's Petty School,* reproduced facsimiles of prayer books, catechisms, and devotions from Baldwin's collection.

Thomas Baldwin's books are an important part of the University of Illinois' special collections, but they are by no means the centerpiece. In fact, they are integrated with all the other books—including some important Carl Sandburg and Mark Twain archives—and listed in the eleven-volume catalogue with the rest of the holdings. Ruth Baldwin, on the other hand, produced a library that has its own wing in a major university and its own three-volume catalogue that currently is being updated and that is ranked among the best in the United States.

Even though Ruth Baldwin never expressed any bitterness about her father, Smith agreed there "could have been a competition" with him. "She did mention once to me that her father managed to run off any man that was brave enough to darken their front doorway. That's pretty much a direct quotation. I think she revered her father, but she was, I sensed, also sort of bitter. There were two other sisters, incidentally, and neither of them ever married either. What I also found interesting is that one of her sisters worked at an orphanage in England, the other taught kindergarten in Illinois. None of Dr. Baldwin's daughters ever married or had families, but all three were involved in one way or another with children."

The New York bookseller Justin G. Schiller, internationally regarded as the leading dealer in children's books and a collector of note in his own right, recalls trying without success to arrange a meeting with Ruth Baldwin for close to two years during the middle 1960s after finding out repeatedly that she was beating him to dozens of bookstores in England and cleaning out the stocks.

"Ruth had been a frequent visitor to England, and she would usually spend about three or four weeks, if not longer, visiting all the bookshops," he said. "There were times I discovered her only as a phantom. I would turn up at bookstores and I would ask for children's books, and they would look at me in shock, partly because Dr. Baldwin had just been there. Ruth's tactic was that she never selected one book at a time. She had an overall scheme, which was to build a collection of English-language children's books that would cover all editions and variations. Children's books in those days were not generally expensive, and condition was never an important consideration with her. She would walk in, look over the general stock, get a sense of the pricing, and then offer a block price for everything. I would show up a week or two later on my own tour of the provinces, and invariably they would have just finished wrapping these things for her and had taken them to the post office. They would then point to a series of empty shelves where the children's books had been stacked and inform me that Dr. Baldwin had already been through. This went on with such regularity for a number of years that I actually began to get paranoid about it."

Ruth Baldwin at that time was teaching at Louisiana State University, and all the books she had been acquiring were stored in her Baton Rouge house. Schiller said he finally wrote Baldwin a letter of introduction and asked to meet her, but the letter was never answered. "We finally met at the children's book sale they have every year at Sotheby's in London," Schiller said. A British bookseller they both did business with pointed "the phantom" Dr. Baldwin out, and Schiller walked over to where she was jotting notes in a sale catalogue.

"I waited for a pause in her scribbling, and finally she looked up as if she had known all along who I was and that I was in the room. She did not smile. There was a very sharp hello, a proper response to my handshake, and an abrupt dismissal. I had no opportunity to talk. She had a very stern face, as if I were the enemy. She had a mission, and her mission was to build one of the most remarkable libraries of English-language children's books in the world. And the fact is that she succeeded. She molded and formed a base by which children's literature can be traced through all its development."

Schiller, as it happened, knew Thomas W. Baldwin by reputation before he ever heard of the daughter. "My academic background was in Shakespeare, so I knew of his work. He was on the periphery of being very highly respected, and by this I do not mean to denigrate his scholarship in any way, but his approach was so blunt that I suspect he frightened people. His greatest achievement was in reconstructing what would have been Shakespeare's reference library. And like his daughter Ruth, he was not terribly concerned with condition. He just wanted the physical books, the objects."

As the 1960s became the 1970s, Schiller said that he "gradually persuaded Dr. Ruth Baldwin" that he "was not a threat," and they began a business relationship that developed into a friendship. She never "articulated" her purpose, he said, beyond a few words: "You must see it to understand what I am doing." And sometime in the early 1980s, Schiller went to Gainesville. "I didn't know what she meant until I did see it. That magnificent setting they have with the cathedral ceiling is part of the aura, but to see one hundred thousand books, all organized in various categories, was a moving experience." Schiller said his response was immediate. "I wanted to help her. To my mind, the goal of a good antiquarian dealer is to provide the right books to the right clients. That's my purpose. If you can do this at a margin of profit, well, so much the better."

Though Ruth Baldwin "never went for rarities," and quite pointedly did not issue want lists for specific titles, Schiller said there are some extremely valuable books in the collection. "The value of her collection is in the collection itself, in assembling this library of books that were published for people who were just learning to read, people who couldn't afford expensive books. Nobody would ever believe that she paid five figures for one title, but she did. It is *The Poetic Garland,* and I brought it down for her in my briefcase. It is one of her crowning titles."

Issued in London about 1808 by publisher John Harris, *The Poetic Garland* consists of thirty early chapbooks gathered into four volumes, including many original copperplate engravings, some of them hand-colored. "She couldn't believe it existed," Schiller said. They agreed on a price of $10,000, and he gave her "very liberal" payment terms spread out over a period of years. "I really wanted to see it in her collection, and it pleases me to this day that it is there."

Rita Smith was hired in 1989 as a cataloguer for the library; even though Dr. Baldwin had retired the previous year, she was still a powerful presence. "I worked with her for six months until she died," Smith said. "I was hired and began working almost immediately, so quickly that I didn't even have time that first week to arrange day care for my daughter Rachel, who was ten at the time and very well behaved. One afternoon I had to bring her in with me, and Ruth would not let her sit at a table inside the library. She had to sit at a table in the outside reading room. This wasn't a question of Rachel looking at the books, or even getting close to them. She just did not want children anywhere near her books."

What it came down to, Smith said, is that Dr. Baldwin "never saw herself as building a library for anyone other than herself. She gave the feeling that she really didn't want anybody to use these books. It was always pretty obvious to me that all these books were hers. She never really said that, but actions speak louder than words. It was a library of books that had been used by children, and that was important, but it was not for children."

Another apparent contradiction was that Dr. Baldwin's greatest satisfaction seemed to be in finding the books, not in enjoying them once they entered her collection. "It is a difficult thing to explain, because I don't want to sound like she didn't like them, or that she didn't love having them, but her interest in a particular book would drop once it arrived," Smith said.

"The hunt was everything for her. It was the excitement of finding it and getting it. Every trip she made was a book-scouting trip. She and her family had a cabin up by the Indian River in Michigan and they'd go up there every year, and in every city along the way they would stop and visit the bookstores. When she went to England to visit her sister, it would be the same thing. And even after she retired, she would still get up every Saturday morning and do garage sales. Every Monday morning she would bring in a pile of books that she had just purchased over the weekend and turn them over to us for cataloguing."

"She wouldn't let it go," I said, and Smith corrected me.

"She *couldn't* let it go. It was just a total commitment for her. It was the one consuming passion in her life. Let me also say that she was a wonderful person, and that she was not without a sense of humor. The way she focused and went after these books was an inspiration to me. I liked Dr. Baldwin to the core of her feisty little being."

As we pulled books at random from the shelves, it was plain that just about every item we examined had two stories, the one printed between the hard covers, the other suggested by the telltale evidence left by a former owner. Many volumes had worn edges, frayed corners, cracked spines, and loose hinges, others bear innocent doodlings, some had little fingerprints that were smeared on the pages with jam and hot chocolate. "Tiny little hands opened these books a hundred years ago and found something worthwhile in them," Smith said. "Most of them have an inscription too," she added, and a spot sampling soon showed that to be the case as well. "To Doris Knox from Mama, in the summer, 1896," reads a tattered, well-read book titled *Stories Children Love*. She picked up one with the inscription "Raymond Lovins from Miss Garsive, Christmas, 1880," in all likelihood a student's gift from a teacher. "Santa Claus, his friend, St. Nicholas," we saw inside another.

"So many books have unexpected treasures in them," Smith said. "I am so pleased you are writing about Ruth. She labored so long in obscurity, and I think that what she did was a masterful thing, and I don't think it can ever be duplicated again. It would just take a fortune to buy something like this today. When she was getting these books, she was paying fifty cents or a dollar for them. She would go into a store and tell the dealer, you have two thousand books there, I'll take them all off your hands for a thousand dollars, and he would think that was just great. Fifty years from now, who's going to have five hundred Golden Books from the mid-twentieth century? Nobody but us."

◆ ◆ ◆

The Beinecke Library of Rare Books and Manuscripts at Yale University is built around a central core of several hundred thousand volumes, a spire of collected wisdom that rises six tiers above the ground to make a powerfully dramatic statement about the majesty of the written word. Shelved behind glass walls and illuminated softly by diffused light, the rarities provide a striking background for exhibitions, especially one mounted in 1991 with the inviting title "Read Me a Story, Show Me a Book."

If books are beautiful objects to behold—and so many of them *are* exquisite—it is only incidental to their purpose, which is to instruct, inform, inspire, and entertain. Children's literature not only performs these tasks admirably, but it also involves the added dimensions of innocence, joy, and wonder. In every literate society, and in every generation, hopeful youngsters have made the same appeal: "Read me a story, show me a book."

The children's books displayed in the Beinecke exhibition—comprehensive in scope, depth, and sophistication—were not drawn from the university's own holdings of rare material, but were gathered entirely by a woman from New Jersey who not only selected the items for display, but supervised the installation, prepared the catalogue descriptions, wrote the introduction, and thought up the title. Betsy B. Shirley called an earlier show of her material, at the Brandywine River Museum in Chadds Ford, Pennsylvania, "A Child's Garden of Dreams," and one that ran in early 1993 at the High Museum in Atlanta, "Dream Makers: American Children's Book Illustrators."

Of Betsy B. Shirley, Justin Schiller said, "For all her energy, she is such a modest woman, yet everything that surrounds her demands respect and attention. Her collection is the best group of American juveniles in private hands."

Because the middle initial in Betsy B. Shirley's name stands for Beinecke, it is tempting to assume that her interest in book collecting is hereditary. Opened in 1963, the Beinecke Library was given to Yale by Edwin, Frederick, and Walter Beinecke, owners of the Sperry and Hutchinson Company, which makes S&H Green Stamps. Of the three brothers, Edwin was by far the most active bibliophile, a collector of

Samuel Johnson, Robert Louis Stevenson, papyri, early illuminated manuscripts, and incunabula, all of which he gave to his alma mater. Frederick Beinecke did not begin collecting until well into his sixties, but once he became interested in Western Americana, he gathered maps, manuscripts, books, pamphlets, and broadsides with great energy. This archive also was turned over to Yale, along with an endowment that guaranteed continued growth. Walter, Mrs. Shirley's father, did not collect books, but he participated generously in the great gift of the library.

"The love of books does run in the family," she said one summer afternoon in the course of giving me an enchanting introduction to her collection, "but I actually started to collect when our daughters were grown up and I was bored. Carl was busy making Kentucky rifles in the cellar, and I wanted to find something worthwhile to do with my spare time." Carl Shirley, who had been following the discussion closely, left the living room and returned with a long flintlock rifle, intricately carved and decorated on the stock, finely polished and oiled, fully functional—altogether an impressive example of the handicraft he had mastered more than twenty-five years earlier.

"I thought it would be fun to find an illustrated book about Daniel Boone or Davy Crockett for Carl that had pictures of Kentucky flintlock rifles," Mrs. Shirley said, "and that is how I happened to go into Justin Schiller's shop in New York sometime around 1970, and that is how I became fascinated with the world of children's books. Carl did get his Daniel Boone book, but I got hopelessly involved as a collector."

Because the earliest children's books were "very religious, moralizing, and didactic" tracts, Mrs. Shirley thought at first she would begin her collection around 1815 "because I knew they had color illustrations, they were fun, and they were interesting. But then I realized that all the others were interesting too, and that I should be collecting them as well. Not many people were collecting them at that time, so the prices were pretty good. Other collectors were going after the English, French, and German first editions, not the American. So I was ahead on that one."

There are easily four thousand books in Betsy Shirley's basement library, and perhaps another thousand or so placed in rooms throughout her house. Mrs. Shirley personally catalogues, categorizes, and shelves everything she acquires, but the size of the collection is "anybody's guess." What is relevant is the scope and breadth of what she has assembled. "The only way I can know the collection is to catalogue it myself," she said, explaining why she does not have a professional curator or librarian to help.

Glazed cabinets lined three exterior walls and both sides of a center partition in the converted basement of her home. "I don't collect schoolbooks, really, but there they are," she began, indicating several shelves of old primers. "This over here is all hobbies, things like astronomy, how to put on a circus, books for boys, books for girls, that kind of thing. Over here we have Christmas. Over there is ABCs, alphabet books. These are all, let's call them modern, 1920 on up to the present." Other cabinets held full selections of American history, geography, science, gift books, nonsense books. "I have all the Caldecott and Newbery winners over here," she said, indicating books that have won the most prestigious awards in children's literature, one named for the artist Randolph Caldecott, the other for the eighteenth-century publisher of children's books John Newbery. "Here I keep all of my Charles Dickens; yes, he is English, but that's not cheating, because these are all the first American editions. This over here is my Mother Goose, which I must admit is a really good collection."

Included among the first editions are familiar titles that need little introduction, books such as Mabel C. Bragg's *The Little Engine That Could,* Dr. Seuss's *Horton Hatches the Egg,* Hugh Lofting's *The Story of Dr. Dolittle,* Frances Hodgson Burnett's *The Secret Garden,* James Fenimore Cooper's *The Spy,* Maurice Sendak's *Where the Wild Things Are,* E. B. White's *Charlotte's Web.* They go on and on, one after another: *Pat the Bunny, Madeleine, Tom Swift and his Motor-Cycle, The Wizard of Oz, The Yearling*—"all the fun books," Mrs. Shirley said.

There also are eighteenth-century primers shaped like paddles known as hornbooks, one fashioned from leather, another from silver. To make a hornbook, a sheet of paper containing the alphabet, the Lord's Prayer, and the Invocation to the Trinity is covered with a thin strip of transparent material peeled from the horn of a cow. Such study aids remained popular for two and a half centuries. An example of the most popular workbook of all in Colonial America, *The New-England Primer,* is in Mrs. Shirley's collection as well.

Among early alphabet books are *The Young Child's ABC* and *The New Picture Primer*. Storybooks include such favorites as Nathaniel Hawthorne's *Wonder-Book for Girls and Boys*, Samuel Griswold Goodrich's *Tales of Peter Parley About America*, Lucy Montgomery's *Anne of Green Gables*, and Booth Tarkington's *Penrod*. The range of nursery rhymes, the Mother Goose collection, extends from a 1794 edition published by Isaiah Thomas to Frederick Winsor's *Space Child's Mother Goose* of 1958.

Other aspects of the collection include poetry, hand-colored chapbooks, religious books, women writers, etiquette, and works about the North and the South such as Charles D. McKenzie's *The Little Drummer Boy*, 1861, and Joel Chandler Harris's *Uncle Remus, His Songs and His Sayings: The Folk-Lore of the Old Plantation*, 1881. In three of the letters Mrs. Shirley has acquired, George Washington cautions a nephew to "quit the trifling amusements of a boy and assume the more dignified manners of a man," twelve-year-old John Quincy Adams writes a younger brother from a Spanish port, and Andrew Jackson implores his adopted son to attend his lessons and accustom himself to letter writing.

Censorship in juvenile literature is represented by works frequently banned by "protective" adults, books like J. D. Salinger's *The Catcher in the Rye* and Robert Cormier's *The Chocolate War*. A 1983 edition of *Little Red Riding Hood* was condemned because one of artist Trina Schart Hyman's illustrations shows Grandma enjoying a glass of wine with her lunch. A particularly scarce item in Mrs. Shirley's collection is writer and illustrator Garth Williams's 1958 tale, *The Rabbits' Wedding*, widely suppressed because in it a white bunny marries a black bunny.

Betsy Shirley's collection embraces every aspect of American children's literature, and in the area of illustrated books, an additional facet of her collection is evident in every room of her house—the kitchen, pantry, den, hallways, bedrooms, even the bathrooms. Wherever there is wall space can be seen original work created for children's books by such artists as Maxfield Parrish, Howard Pyle, Maurice Sendak, Felix O. C. Darley, A. B. Frost, E. W. Kemble, Edwin Abbey, Winslow Homer, Childe Hassam, Ludwig Bemelmans, Rockwell Kent, Johnny Gruelle, Justin Howard, Jessie Willcox Smith, all of the giants.

Some of the pictures are variants of what was published, others are working sketches, all of them are artifacts that clarify the creative process. The original oil painting executed by N. C. Wyeth in 1911 for *Treasure Island* that hangs in Mrs. Shirley's living room is an image of three pirates, one holding two muskets, another brandishing a saber, the third hoisting a skull and crossbones, and is known by millions of readers. Palmer Cox's 1891 painting of several dozen "brownies" seated at long tables, called "The Christmas Dinner," was a favorite at the High Museum exhibition in Atlanta.

Like virtually every other university in the United States, Yale never made any effort to collect children's literature, partly because the subject was not taken seriously by scholars until well into the present century. Mrs. Shirley's decision to place her collection in the Beinecke Library has filled that void with a single gesture. A gift of similar stature was presented to the Lilly Library at Indiana University in 1983 by the estate of Elisabeth W. Ball, who with her father, George A. Ball of Muncie, Indiana, had put together a comprehensive collection of historically important children's books. Most of the great institutional collections of children's books, in fact, exist because of collectors like Betsy Shirley, Elisabeth Ball, and Ruth Baldwin at the University of Florida. The Toronto Public Library's premier collection of British children's literature in North America, extending from 1566 to 1910, is the 1949 gift of an English couple, Edgar and Mabel Osborne, who wanted to establish an important repository in Canada, where they felt treasures of the scope and quality they had assembled might otherwise never be available. The Osborne Collection of Early Children's Books includes a number of historically important books known nowhere else.

Edgar Osborne's recollections of how the collection got started bear notice. In the introduction to a two-volume catalogue of the collection, he wrote: "It began on one of those all too rare occasions when I was able to return to my old home in Hampshire, England. There I found the nursery books I loved so much were lying neglected in the lumber room. The discovery also interested my wife, who wondered if she would be able to rescue the books from her early childhood from her home in the north of England. [Thus] began a partnership in collecting which continues to interest me, and which was of absorbing interest to my wife until her death in 1946."

"When the books came to Toronto it was realized that a unique gift had been placed in our hands," Jean Thompson wrote in the 1958 catalogue of the Osborne Collection. "Here were hundreds of books representing all types and phases of writing for children of the English-speaking world. And here this collection was to remain and grow, housed side by side with a large and active children's library. This priceless gift makes it possible for us in Canada, whose history began late, to establish a collection which will benefit all students of children's literature and to lay before them a wealth of material unavailable otherwise in this country."

In the United Kingdom, the Iona and Peter Opie Collection of Children's Literature was purchased with £1 million raised through a national appeal conducted under the patronage of the Prince of Wales, and was presented to the Bodleian Library at Oxford University in 1988. The Opies had gathered twenty thousand rare books, comics, and other ephemera for more than forty years as primary source material for their anthologies and scholarly writings, including *The Oxford Dictionary of Nursery Rhymes, The Lore and Language of Schoolchildren, The Classic Fairy Tales,* and *Children's Games in Street and Playground.*

The Betsy B. Shirley Collection is noteworthy for its emphasis on American children's literature, and the tradition of illustration that is so fundamentally related to its history over the past three centuries. "I wanted American things from the beginning, even if they were copies of the English," she said. "I figured that if you could document what young Americans read throughout our history, you could sort of tell what was going on in society. How people treated the young, what they produced for the young, what the taboos were, the attitudes on both sides around the time of the Civil War, all sorts of things like that."

She pointed out that a 1947 exhibition at the Grolier Club, "One Hundred Influential American Books Printed Before 1900," included twenty-nine titles written for children, or read by them. At first she thought she would apply a cut-off date of 1900, "but then I would not have been able to include *The Wizard of Oz,* which is 1912, and how could I avoid going after that?" The collection, which will go to Yale, will cover the full thrust of the American experience up to the present, as reflected by the books that children read and enjoyed.

"What Mrs. Shirley has done is extend the limits of a children's literature collection," Vincent Giroud, curator of modern books at the Beinecke Library, explained. "The Shirley Collection is an extraordinary record of the production of children's books from their origins in this country. In some cases Mrs. Shirley was able to acquire the only known copies of certain books. She acquired variant issues which are extremely important, but she also went beyond the books. Her collection includes original art, manuscripts, letters, even some material written by future writers when they were children. She has a remarkable command of the field." Giroud said that a popular course of children's literature is taught in the English Department, "so the collection already supports the curriculum. But it is so rich, there are limitless possibilities for research."

11

Destiny

To me the Yiddish language and the conduct of those who spoke it are identical. One can find in the Yiddish tongue and the Yiddish style expressions of pious joy, lust for life, longing for the Messiah, patience, and deep appreciation of human individuality. There is a quiet humor in Yiddish and a gratitude for every day of life, every crumb of success, each encounter of love. The Yiddish mentality is not haughty. It does not take victory for granted. It does not demand and command but it muddles through, sneaks by, smuggles itself amid the powers of destruction, knowing somewhere that God's plan for Creation is still at the very beginning.

—Isaac Bashevis Singer,
Nobel Lecture, 1978

Not long after he graduated from college and began working toward an advanced degree at McGill University in Montreal, an idealistic young man from New Bedford, Massachusetts, determined that his mission in life was to rescue books and preserve a culture that was threatened with extinction. "Yiddish is a dead language," Aaron Lansky was told when he sought help from major Jewish organizations. "Why waste your time? Go back to school. Go to Israel."

That was in 1979. I learned about Lansky's activities ten years later when a brief wire service story reported how this resourceful optimist who snatched books from the jaws of paper shredders and landfills had been given a $225,000 "genius grant" from the John D. and Catherine MacArthur Foundation. Other recipients of the prestigious award since its inception in 1981 have included poets, artists, novelists, archaeologists, paleontologists, scientists, musicians, filmmakers, even a clown and a carpenter—but only one recipient has been committed to preserving the books that document a vanishing way of life.

383

"It started out as a two-year project," Lansky said the first time we met in an old brick schoolhouse in downtown Amherst, Massachusetts, where his National Yiddish Book Center maintained offices for the first decade of its existence, and only four blocks from the house where Emily Dickinson spent her adult life composing brilliant poetry. "Prevailing wisdom then was that there were maybe seventy-five thousand volumes all together in Yiddish kicking around out there in the United States, and that it would take me that long to track them down. When I was done, I would finish my graduate work in Jewish studies and become a teacher." Three years later, Lansky had gathered 350,000—he had passed seventy-five thousand in the first eight months of his adventure—and volumes were still coming in at the rate of a thousand a week.

By the end of the 1980s, Lansky's collecting continued unabated, and close to a million books had been sorted and shelved on the fourth floor of an old paper factory in Holyoke, Massachusetts. As the new decade began, thousands of the rescued volumes had been placed in the libraries of 150 institutions on five continents, Yale and Oxford universities among them. Because texts now were available for classroom use, comprehensive courses in Yiddish began to be taught at about fifty universities all together, and plans were afoot to publish new editions of important Yiddish works.

"I grew up in a home in which books were valued," Lansky said. "My mother and my grandmother were great readers, but books in general have always been central to Jewish culture. If you drop a book, you pick it up and you kiss it. Originally this was done because they were prayer books, but it developed that you treat every book with respect, regardless of the content."

Politically active during the 1970s, Lansky considered following his father into the legal profession, but he remembers being mostly undecided about how he wanted to spend his life when he entered Hampshire College in 1972. "I took a course on the Holocaust my first semester, and it wasn't long before I understood just how much of Jewish culture had been destroyed. I also discovered that I was less interested in how all this was accomplished than I was in the rich culture itself. How the Nazis did what they did was a matter of mechanics applied to an evil purpose;

what I wanted to know was who these people were they wanted to exterminate, and what their world was all about."

A nontraditional college near Amherst that encourages "free-intellectual exploration," Hampshire College allowed Lansky to discover Jewish history alongside a professor who was equally interested in acquiring the same knowledge. Together, they discovered that for about a thousand years, between 900 and 1900, approximately 90 percent of all Jews had used Yiddish as their primary spoken language. "The more I studied, the more I realized that if I was to understand who these people were, I needed to understand their experiences, and that meant I had to learn Yiddish. It had been the vernacular of the Jewish masses in Eastern Europe, but as an assimilated American, I only knew it from a distance. I heard Yiddish around the house when I was a kid only when 'di eyniklekh zoln nisht farshteyn,' 'the grandchildren shouldn't understand.' "

Because the language was taught in only three American colleges at the time, and because at Hampshire he had an open curriculum, Lansky "went off in search of a teacher," finally finding one across town at the University of Massachusetts in Amherst. Dr. Jules Piccus, "a dynamic man with bushy white hair and a full white beard," taught Medieval Spanish Literature and was renowned in academic circles for his grasp of twenty languages, Yiddish foremost among them. "He agreed to teach a small group of students on an informal basis with the single condition that we work hard. In place of tuition, we brought a bottle of wine and a loaf of homemade bread to every class. We met one night a week for two years, and the sessions ran from three to five hours."

After graduating from Hampshire College in 1976, Lansky began graduate work at McGill University in Montreal under Dr. Ruth M. Wisse. For his master's thesis, he decided to write about Sholem Yankev Abramovitch (1836–1917), who published under the pen name Mendele Moykher Sforim, which means, literally, Mendele the Itinerant Book Peddler. Mendele's novel *Dos Kleyne Mentschele* (*The Little Man*), published in 1864, is considered the first work of modern Yiddish literature. "Mendele shared the contemporary prejudice that Yiddish was ugly, illegitimate, or at least undesirable," nothing more than a "necessary evil" to reach a wider audience, Lansky wrote several years later in his master's thesis. Yet once the author "made the break" and began to write in Yiddish, there was no turning back. "He came to regard Yiddish less as a tool for propaganda and more as an artistic medium in its own right."

At about this time, as Lansky was beginning to research his thesis, he received a letter from a friend in Ohio who told of a rabbi who had died and left nine hundred Yiddish books. "Nobody knew what to do with them, so they went off to the paper shredder. Not long after that, I went down to New Bedford to visit my parents, and while I was there I went over to our synagogue to talk with the rabbi. I walked into his office and on the floor was a fruit basket filled with a lot of old Yiddish books, and among them was the collected works of Mendele Moykher Sforim. So I said, 'Excuse me, Rabbi, what is Mendele doing on the floor in a fruit basket?' "

The rabbi replied that the books were going to be buried with some tattered Hebrew prayer books in a funeral service. "They were going to bury them with prayer books that were no longer usable. This is a very old Jewish tradition, that you give worn-out books that can no longer be used a proper burial. He said he didn't know what else to do with them, nobody wanted them. 'You want the books, you can have them.' So I put the fruit basket on my shoulder, and I said, 'Rabbi, if you have more books, I know dozens of people who can read them. Call my parents and they will be happy to pick them up.' Meantime, I went back to McGill, and I thought, if I could find books like this in New Bedford, imagine what I could find in Montreal."

Scouting missions were inevitable, and his first explorations in Canada were conducted on a bicycle, later on a moped. "People were calling me, and I was racing around from one end of the city to the other. Before I knew it, my apartment was filling up with books. The kitchen, the bathroom, everywhere you looked, it was completely out of hand. I was inundated." Before long the inevitable telephone call from New Bedford arrived. "It was my mother. 'Aaron,' she said, 'I think you better come down here pretty soon, because the rabbi has given us so many books we're afraid the second floor of the house is about to collapse.' "

It was at this point, as the books "were piling up and piling up," that Lansky was struck with a paradox. "I can remember the exact day.

I was sitting in class, a cold winter day, and we're arguing once again where we are going to find the books we need for our studies, and I'm thinking, this is ridiculous. Here we can't find the books we want for college and books are out there being destroyed. Something needs to be done." He decided he had to undertake a far-reaching initiative to preserve Yiddish-language books in a center established for that purpose. Thus was born the National Yiddish Book Center.

Dr. Ruth M. Wisse, then professor of Jewish Studies at McGill University, now at Harvard University, encouraged Lansky. "I thought it was a fantastic idea," she said. "I remember saying this would be one of the great desiderata of Jewish communal life, to have someone collect these books. This was a very particular situation, particular in the sense that here you have a culture of the most bookish people in the world, and suddenly, because they are such a culturally vital people, they leave their language behind and don't pass it on."

She recalled her early impressions of young Aaron Lansky. "He had the quality about him of what was then called a 'flower child,' a very gentle young man. But I also saw an entrepreneurial quality in him, a really American spirit. And I think that is why he has been so successful with his book center. He has a very down-to-earth approach. He is a realist who doesn't wallow in sentimentality. He makes things happen. And he doesn't focus on the past but on the future."

Before getting started, Lansky sought financial support from "every major Jewish organization" in the United States. "I put on a nice suit, I took the train to New York, and they all told me the same thing: 'Yiddish is dead. What are you wasting your time on this for?' That was the general attitude, and there was no money they could spare for the books. Well, I couldn't sit around and argue with these guys for the next ten years, I just had to go out and do something. I knew books were being destroyed."

He explained what forces were causing so much inexorable loss. "A grandparent dies and the kids come to clean out the apartment. They find a bunch of old books in a language they can't understand, and they throw them in the garbage. This has been happening for years." Especially distressing is how apathy like that runs counter to the historic attachment Jews have for books. "Jews are 'am hamsefer,' " he explained. "The people of the book."

Yiddish is a language with borrowings from German, Hebrew, and Slavic that is written in Hebrew characters; like Hebrew, it reads from right to left. For the better part of a millennium, Yiddish was the principal tongue of Ashkenazi Jews (broadly speaking, the Jews of Central and Eastern Europe), who by the end of the nineteenth century represented about ninety percent of the world's Jews. Unlike virtually every other language, Yiddish does not now have a clearly defined homeland, though it developed in Central Europe and is defined by linguistic historians as a west Germanic language. According to the sociolinguist Joshua A. Fishman in his essay "The Sociology of Yiddish," 10.7 million people spoke Yiddish as their primary language in 1940; forty years later that number had been reduced to 3.7 million, and most of these people were elderly and did not pass the tradition on to their children. Hasidic Jews, however, continue to use the language, leading Fishman to believe the number of people speaking Yiddish will stabilize at about two million by the turn of the century.

"As long as the traditional world remained intact, Jews wrote in Hebrew," Lansky explained. "Yiddish was the vernacular. When the old world began to break down, Jews suddenly had to figure out what it meant to live in the modern world, and they drew upon this vernacular which represented everyday Jewish experiences to create a whole new literature."

By far the most prominent contemporary Yiddish voice was the late Isaac Bashevis Singer. Though he spent most of his adult life in New York City, Singer always wrote in the language he learned as a child in the Warsaw home of his father, a rabbi. Singer's early support of the National Yiddish Book Center brought immediate credibility and needed viability, and he remained an honorary trustee until his death in 1991. When Singer accepted the Nobel Prize for Literature in 1978, he offered a moving tribute—to his native tongue. He started in Yiddish, declaring:

"The high honor bestowed upon me by the Swedish Academy is also a recognition of the Yiddish language—a language of exile, without a land, without frontiers, not supported by any government; a language which possesses no words for weapons, ammunition, military exercises, war tactics; a language that was despised by both Gentiles and emancipated Jews." He then spoke in English: "There are some who call Yiddish a dead language, but so was Hebrew called for two thousand years." But the language "has not said its last word," he insisted; it "contains treasures that have not been revealed to the eyes of the world." Yiddish, he concluded, is "the wise and humble language of us all, the idiom of frightened and hopeful humanity."

Singer's eloquence notwithstanding, the reality is that few writers outside of Israel still use the language as their principal medium of expression. About one hundred new works of fiction, poetry, and non-fiction are published each year in Yiddish, most of them in Israel, according to Zachary M. Baker, librarian of the YIVO Institute for Jewish Research in New York City. During the period between World War I and World War II, new releases averaged about a thousand titles a year. "There were eleven million people who spoke Yiddish in 1939, and by 1945 one out of every two had been murdered," Lansky explained. "So there was this culture that literally was ripped out of its roots in Europe. That is why I say the last thousand years of Jewish history resides in those books. They are the repository of the whole culture."

Benjamin Harshav, Blaustein Professor of Hebrew and Comparative Literature at Yale University, is equally blunt in his study, *The Meaning of Yiddish*. "It is true that Hitler and Stalin destroyed Yiddish culture in its European stronghold. The Jewish people lost a third of their numbers but nonetheless survived; the destruction of Yiddish, however, was total. Stalin killed the Yiddish writers, Hitler killed the writers and their readers alike. The Yiddish-speaking masses are no more." Yet even before the Holocaust, Harshav acknowledges, the trend of assimilation was "overpowering everywhere." In North America, for the children of immigrants English was the language of choice. During the 1920s, an attempt to teach Yiddish in New York public schools was a dismal failure. Later, in Israel, Hebrew emerged as the official tongue, while Yiddish, "with its mass newspapers and millions of readers," began to disappear. "The attempt to create a modern, cosmopolitan culture in a separate Jewish language, culturally autonomous and steeped in historical values and associations, was doomed to failure. For the writers sensing the loss of their readership, this was an indescribable tragedy."

Lansky's mission, then, went far beyond saving books to preserving a record of the way of life that they documented. Because most of his activities would be in the United States, he decided not to establish his organization in Montreal. "I decided against New York as well, because there were a lot of old Jewish organizations there, and a lot of politics that I wanted to avoid. I did not want to fight any of the old battles. It was essential that there be something grand about what we were about to do. My goal was to deliver books to the next generation."

With encouragement from Hampshire College, Amherst College, Mount Holyoke College, Smith College, and the University of Massachusetts—five schools within a twenty-mile radius of Amherst that allowed him to use their names for the project—Lansky established the National Yiddish Book Exchange in 1979, which was incorporated as the National Yiddish Book Center the following year. Getting three months deferred rent, Lansky set up shop in the loft of an old factory two miles from the Smith College campus in Northampton in June 1980. Office furniture consisted of a picnic table and two jury-rigged bookcases, and to defray costs, he shared space with a weaver, a potter, and a woman who sold goat's milk.

Working at a government-surplus typewriter, the twenty-four-year-old executive director issued a spate of press releases. In July, a letter arrived from the eighty-six-year-old father of the novelist Leon Uris. "I have three hundred Yiddish books," William Uris wrote. "These volumes are not yet scattered in attics and cellars, but are well preserved in my home. My question is, how do I get them to you?" Two months later, a letter came in from Marjorie Guthrie, widow of the folksinger Woody Guthrie. "I am writing to inquire if you would be interested in a collection of books which came from my family. My mother was a Yiddish poet, Aliza Greenblatt, who was friends with many outstanding Yiddish writers."

From the beginning, Lansky established several rules, foremost among them that anything printed in Yiddish is welcome. "It is too early in the history of the literature to judge what is important and what is not," Lansky explained. "Another policy is that we only accept contributions. We have never bought a book." For the first five years, primary emphasis was placed on collecting, Lansky often going out on solitary runs in vans he rented or was able to borrow from the neighboring colleges. "Someone would tell me there were books outside in the garbage, and I would find a way to go and get them," he said. "In

1981, I got a call from a friend in New York who had learned that some workers fixing up a building on Sixteenth Street had come across a library of eight thousand Yiddish books. They were all outside in a Dumpster, and it was the middle of winter." Rushing to New York, Lansky and some hastily enlisted helpers worked through the night in sleet and freezing rain to load a rented truck with the discarded books and bring them back to Massachusetts.

As books piled up, word began to spread, and in February 1981 the *New York Times* published a brief feature that prompted several hundred inquiries. More people gave books, others offered money, some came forward as volunteers. Three months later, the town of Amherst allowed the National Yiddish Book Center free use of the Old East Street School. By the end of 1983, that building was crammed with 300,000 books, while others continued to arrive. An urgent appeal for funds for further storage facilities was issued in 1984, and contributions came in from around the world, enabling Lansky to lease the fourth floor of an enormous old paper factory in downtown Holyoke, an aging industrial city on the Connecticut River in western Massachusetts. Called the Yiddish Book Annex, the facility is about as long as a football field and has 25,000 square feet of space available, enough to house the whole collection. When the center celebrated its tenth birthday in 1990, the repository held a million volumes.

Obviously, Lansky was not able to gather all those books by himself; he needed help, and for that he recruited a band of volunteers called *zamlers,* Yiddish for collectors. He was inspired by the example of Simon Dubnow, a twentieth-century Jewish historian who had used similar methods to acquire primary material for his research. "When I started the book center, Dubnow was my intellectual mentor, and I figured we could revive his concept of the *zamler,* which was to find people who were willing to go out and preserve these documents. In Dubnow's case the material was archival. Here, it was books we were after. But what I did was re-create Dubnow's *zamler* network in North America."

Within a decade, Lansky had more than two hundred *zamlers* working for him throughout the United States and Canada, many of them older people who shared his sense of urgency. For example, Sorell and Nathan Skolnik, who live about an hour's drive north of New York City, began gathering books while in their late seventies, and continued actively into their eighties. Lansky credits Sorell Skolnik—a social activist during the 1920s who once explained that she "didn't want to be a part [of any] melting pot if it meant losing my language"—with locating more than five thousand volumes by herself. Jacob Schaefer of Los Angeles is a survivor of Auschwitz who "ranks as our most active *zamler* ever," Lansky said. "He is tireless. He drives around in an old Chevy Nova and he will go anywhere in California to get books. We figure he has rounded up about forty thousand books for us." Morris and Sarah Willdorf of Brooklyn are equally committed. Lansky said that every time someone from the center goes to New York, there are books to pick up in the Willdorfs' garage.

Lansky estimated that only about one half of one percent of all Yiddish books have been translated into English, and for most works, the first edition is the only edition. Because Yiddish flourished as a literary language for less than a century, it is possible to estimate how many titles were printed. As more and more older Jews die or move into nursing homes, the dramatic scenes of the early years, in which extensive libraries were discovered, become fewer and fewer. "But it's still a steady fifty thousand books a year, about a thousand books a week, that we have coming in," he said.

The center has begun a program of transferring books to other institutions. Lansky said, "The best part is that we now have ten thousand books going out, and each year we place twice as many as we did the year before." Before books can be placed, of course, somebody has to want them, so creating a demand became Lansky's second priority. "When we started, nobody wanted these books; they were throwing them away. It became our job to educate the world as to why they are important."

Placements began almost immediately, but the major break came in 1989 when Yale University announced it would acquire ten thousand books from the center, the funding coming from Josalyn and Joseph Newman of New York City. "What Yale did was announce that anyone who wishes to pursue modern Jewish scholarship must deal with the Yiddish language," Lansky said. "It was a vindication of everything we set out to do."

As more institutions take books and introduce courses in Yiddish, Lansky sees his mission changing. "Ten years from now, twenty years from now, I'll be spending a lot less time rescuing books, but I'll have more work to do," he predicted. "One of my pet projects is to start reissuing works of Yiddish literature. Facsimiles aren't really satisfactory, because in any given Yiddish book, you find that between fifteen and twenty percent of the words do not appear in any Yiddish dictionary. There are words that come from Russia and Lithuania, Ukraine, where there were different concepts. So we will develop a database; maybe we'll even enter entire novels into the computer, run them against the database, and identify the words that are not in the dictionaries." The new editions will be annotated. Once undocumented material is recorded, "we will work with scholars and the older Jews who are still around to identify these words and phrases and cultural oddities that are no longer recognizable to modern readers. In the books we reprint, there will be English-language footnotes at the bottom of each Yiddish text that give these new translations and explanations."

When we first met, in 1990, Aaron Lansky was thirty-four years old and was putting in sixteen-hour days on his reclamation project. He traveled constantly to give lectures and raise money, he organized summer internships, he developed new programs, and he worked on the center's news magazine, *The Book Peddler*. "My mother keeps telling me I should slow down, find a good Jewish wife, and start a family," the young bachelor said with a shy shrug. There was no shortage of matchmakers trying to nudge him in the right direction.

Two and a half years later, it was time for another visit to the National Yiddish Book Center. The *Wall Street Journal* had recently published a story telling how Lansky had brought an old Linotype machine up from New York and reassembled it in the Holyoke annex, making it the only apparatus in the country still producing metal type in Yiddish. Also, Lansky had accepted a dollar-a-year offer from Mount Holyoke College to use a gracious old mansion that looks out on a range of western Massachusetts foothills, and had moved his headquarters from Amherst to South Hadley. Even though the arrangement is not permanent, it does allow time to move into a new home just off the campus of Hampshire College. Construction of a $4 million book center began in the fall of 1994 on the site of a onetime apple orchard; it is expected to open in 1996.

As we brought each other up to date, I was pleased to notice a wedding ring on Lansky's left hand. "We have a baby girl," he said, beaming, and showed me a photograph of Sarah Rayzel Lansky. "That doesn't mean things have slowed down," he quickly added, "it just means that I have my wife, Gail, to help me now."

Still, there are nights when Aaron Lansky goes into Holyoke by himself to make sure everything is all right at the annex. "I don't go to the factory in search of a religious experience, I go probably because the alarm is ringing," he said. But when his business is finished, and the lights are turned off, he invariably pauses for a moment before locking up and leaving for home.

"The life and the vitality and the culture of a thousand years is on those shelves, and I never take it for granted," he said. "Even in the dark, I can feel the weight of a million books. As I get older, and since I've had a child, my perception of all this becomes much deeper, because now that child validates everything that I do in my life. She reminds me all the more for whom I am saving those books."

Arthur Alfonso Schomburg was born in Puerto Rico in 1874, the son of Mary Joseph, an unwed laundress from the Virgin Islands, and Carlos Féderico Schomburg, a German-born merchant of mixed parentage then living in San Juan. Although Arthur took his father's surname, there is no evidence to suggest that he was raised as an heir of the Schomburgs, a family well known in Puerto Rico. Arthur Schomburg moved to New York in 1911, where he lived until his death in 1938. His biographer, Elinor Des Verney Sinnette, points out that like many other early black book collectors, Schomburg was not motivated by the prospect of indulging in a "delightful diversion," but as a mission "to document the history of their race." He was not the first black collector, but he devoted his greatest energy to the task, and his legacy is the Schomburg Center for Research in Black Culture (a division of the New York Public Library), a library in Harlem that is ranked among the world's best.

The need to document black history has been recognized by many individuals, especially that of the period from the end of the Civil War through the turn of the century. One such individual was William

Dorsey of Philadelphia, the custodian of the American Negro Historical Society and a dedicated compiler of 388 scrapbooks filled with thousands of clippings from newspapers published between 1873 and 1903. Most of the articles he preserved reported daily events in the lives of black people, including many obituaries, invitations to social events, and political broadsides. Deposited after Dorsey's death in 1923 at Cheyney State University in Pennsylvania, the scrapbooks were ignored and forgotten for half a century, only to be rediscovered in a library basement behind a movable wall by a graduate student in 1976. They have since provided the raw material for a detailed history of black urban life during this critical period of transition.

Unlike Dorsey, Arthur Alfonso Schomburg made sure his efforts would not be ignored. At a Howard University seminar on "Black Bibliophiles and Collectors: Preservers of Black History" in 1983, Dr. Sinnette told how during her research she found two typewritten sheets among Schomburg's papers that quoted the California book collector Hubert Howe Bancroft. On one piece of paper, "the Negro" was described as being an "incompetent and unreliable" citizen, "an unmitigated nuisance" who in all likelihood "will remain so." And on the other, Schomburg had copied this excerpt: "However learned he may become, however lofty his ideals or his aspirations, he must wear the badge of ignorance and servitude, he and his children, forever. God hath made him so. We do not need the Negro for any purpose and never shall." At the bottom of the second sheet, Schomburg had written in bold letters, "Where are our Negro historians, our defenders who have let Bancroft commit such a dastardly crime against the Negro race?"

Not only did early black collectors like Dorsey, Schomburg, Jesse E. Moorland, and Marcus Garvey seek out material that would refute such mindless pedantry, they collected the slanderous material itself. "These pioneer black collectors existed in a society that not only denied their humanity but seemed skeptical about their ability to achieve," Dr. Sinnette wrote. It is not surprising, therefore, to see such "scientific" works as Charles H. McCord's *The American Negro as a Dependant, Defective and Delinquent*, 1914, or Robert Bean's 1906 essay in the *American Journal of Anatomy*, "Some Racial Peculiarities of the Negro Brain," represented in their collections.

Schomburg became an active figure in what is known as the Harlem Renaissance, and included among his friends Langston Hughes and Paul Robeson. "We need in the coming dawn the man who will give us the background for our future; it matters not whether he comes from the Cloisters of the University or from the rank and file of the fields," he wrote in 1913. Three years later, he helped establish the Negro Book Collectors Exchange, which committed itself to contacting "all Negro book collectors throughout the United States, Africa, the West Indies, South America and Europe," and asking them to register the titles of books in their libraries. "They were drawn together by a common cause and shared a common passion for searching out evidence of the historical accomplishments of black people," Dr. Sinnette writes. "Theirs was a close, friendly network of men who corresponded with each other, visited each other's libraries, went book hunting together, and enjoyed the camaraderie of mutual interests."

Schomburg was by far the most driven of the group, and though he worked as a clerk for Bankers Trust on Wall Street for twenty-three years, collecting was his first priority. He developed a friendly rivalry with Arthur Spingarn, a wealthy white lawyer who shifted his collecting focus from English literature to the works of black authors as he became more involved in combating racism. Shortly after he became legal counsel for the National Association for the Advancement of Colored People in 1911, Spingarn began assembling a reference library, which evolved into a collection. A 1962 article in *Negro Digest* described him as a "White Warrior" for Civil Rights. He served as NAACP president from 1940 to 1965.

Spingarn's collection of five thousand books, journals, playbills, speeches, letters, and ephemera was purchased by Howard University in 1946 and was combined with the library of Jesse E. Moorland to form the Moorland-Spingarn Research Center. Spingarn's holdings were particularly strong in Afro-Cuban, Afro-Brazilian, and Haitian writers, and included many scarce titles. In an unpublished memoir on deposit at Howard University, Spingarn recalled that he met Schomburg "long before the First World War," and though the lawyer acknowledged having the means to travel more readily than his rival, he often found himself being beaten to the prey. "Whenever I discovered an interesting trail leading to Negro books I invariably found that

Schomburg had either been on it before me or else was following very close behind." Spingarn recalled occasions when he saw Schomburg "approach an immense pile of apparently worthless material and unerringly find in its huge mass one or two treasures which would have been lost to a less inspired collector; how he found them I never could discover unless he smelled them out." The best explanation for this uncanny success was the "infinite patience" Schomburg combined with a "sixth sense for rarities."

Though Schomburg's ability to travel was limited by a modest income, the scope of his collecting was not. He nurtured a correspondence with dealers throughout the United States and abroad, and he left no doubt that he was collecting materials "relating to Negroes everywhere." And he built up a network of friends and acquaintances around the world who were constantly on the alert. For instance, a schoolteacher in Haiti who wrote Schomburg hoping to find a pen pal soon was reporting on efforts to locate Haitian material. Similarly, a pianist planning a vacation in Bermuda was asked to look there for musical scores composed by blacks. Schomburg's good friend Alain Locke was routinely given lists of desiderata to seek out on his frequent trips to Europe, and James Weldon Johnson was asked to do the same in Central and South America. Langston Hughes found items relating to the black mother of the Russian writer Alexander Pushkin and the black Shakespearean actor Ira Aldridge in the Soviet Union, and sent them on to his friend in New York. Schomburg asked the United States envoy to Liberia, the Honorable A. Lester Walton, to acquire the papers of the African educator and statesman Edward Wilmot Blyden, which Schomburg understood to be in the possession of a certain Liberian woman. "Rather than have the termites make a meal of them," he wrote Walton in 1937, perhaps "a few" of the papers could be secured for the Schomburg collection.

Though his collection included rare items from all over the world, Schomburg only made one trip abroad. Shortly after his collection was purchased by the New York Public Library with $10,000 provided by the Carnegie Corporation, Schomburg sailed to Spain in the summer of 1926 on the steamer *Manuel Arnus*. "On the eve of my departure," he wrote a friend, "I express my sincere regards for the many years we have labored in the vineyards of usefulness to the race. I depart now on a mission of love to recapture my lost heritage."

Schomburg retired from Bankers Trust in 1929 at the age of fifty-nine, and promptly accepted an offer to develop a black history archive at Fisk University in Nashville, Tennessee. He returned to New York in 1932, became curator of the collection he had sold to the New York Public Library six years earlier, and tirelessly oversaw its fortunes until his death in 1938. With some backing from the Carnegie Corporation, Schomburg enhanced the holdings and continued to seek help from his friends. There were times during those lean Depression years when he ordered books without the approval of his superiors at the New York Public Library, hoping that satisfactory arrangements somehow would be worked out later. Sometimes the library would pay, most of the time it would not, but Schomburg always scraped money together, often from his own pocket.

Schomburg lectured widely on black heritage and culture, and though he had little formal education, he learned from his books and used what he had taught himself to write penetrating pieces for such journals and periodicals as *Crisis* and *Opportunity*. His best-known essay, "The Negro Digs Up His Past," was published in the March 1925 issue of *Survey Graphic,* which was devoted to the Harlem Renaissance of the 1920s. Schomburg's article was reprinted later that year in *The New Negro,* an important anthology edited by Alain Locke. "History must restore what slavery took away, for it is the social damage of slavery that the present generations must repair and offset," Schomburg wrote. "The Negro has been a man without a history because he has been considered a man without a worthy culture."

Charles L. Blockson was once described by his football coach at Pennsylvania State University as the kind of young man "who renews your faith in mankind." An opposing coach equally impressed by the running back's exemplary character said of Blockson's prowess on the field: "Blockson just runs right over people. He doesn't believe in being fancy."

During four years at Penn State, Charley "the Blockbuster" Blockson, as he was known in the 1950s, earned a varsity letter on three outstanding Nittany Lion teams, playing alongside Lenny Moore in the backfield and behind Roosevelt Grier at tackle. Their record for

1953–1955 was 21–9. As a college track star, Blockson threw the shot put and the discus; earlier competing for Norristown High School in Pennsylvania, he also ran the half mile, 440 relay, and 880 relay. "I would have considered the decathlon," Blockson said years later as he was flipping through some of his old scrapbooks, "but I couldn't do very much with the pole vault."

In 1956, after accepting an invitation to try out with the New York Giants, Blockson received a firm offer to join the team but declined. After close to forty years, the contract remains in his personal files, unsigned. "It really wasn't that hard a decision for me to make. I love athletics and I respect what they did for me. But I knew there were other things I could do with my life. I gave my body to sports from the time I was in junior high school. I wanted to keep my mind for myself."

As most sports fans know, Lenny Moore and Rosey Grier went on to standout professional careers. Pro Football Hall of Fame running back Moore recalled being "shocked" when he heard that his 6-foot-3, 215-pound college teammate had "walked away" from that offer. Moore was just beginning his own career with the Baltimore Colts, and remembers getting a telephone call from Roosevelt Grier, who had made the Giants squad a year earlier. "Charles and I go all the way back to high school," Moore said. "I played for Reading and he played for Norristown, and he was without question the best athlete in the state of Pennsylvania, and he did everything. Take a look at his track stats, you'll see what I mean. He was so much bigger than everyone else, he didn't have to worry about going around anyone. When he ran into you, it was like getting popped by a linebacker."

Moore said that after being rivals in high school, he and Blockson became close friends and roommates during their freshman year at Penn State. "When Rosey told me Charles had left the Giants training camp, I couldn't believe my ears. Rosey said Charles had the team made, but he just walked away from it. You don't find many black kids who would turn their backs on a career in pro sports, then or now. We had very few black heroes to look up to in those days, and if you wanted to advance, you took your first shot, if you were fortunate enough to get one."

What Lenny Moore did not know then, but what he learned many years later, was that what his friend wanted most of all was to become a "black bibliophile." In 1984, the Charles L. Blockson Afro-American Collection of twenty thousand books, pamphlets, prints, manuscripts, narratives, posters, photographs, sheet music, and broadsides was dedicated at Temple University in Philadelphia, rich testimony that he succeeded admirably in that pursuit. Under Blockson's uninterrupted direction, the collection's holdings quadrupled to more than eighty thousand items ten years later.

"The most important element in the Charles Blockson Collection is Charles Blockson himself," Peter J. Liacouras, president of Temple University, said categorically in an interview. When the material was presented to the university, the understanding was that the man who had assembled it would come along as curator. Equally important was that he would have a free hand in directing its continued growth, and that he serve as the university's link to the scholarly community on ways to use the material most effectively.

"The beauty of Charles is that he crosses all demographic boundaries," Liacouras said. "He relates beautifully with scholars, teachers, students, children at all levels of sophistication. That is one of the reasons I placed his collection right here with me in the most prestigious building in the university. I did not want him to be isolated over in special collections because his appeal goes beyond scholarship, and it is contagious. He came to Temple at a time when we were trying to assert ourselves as a university that serves all the people. Children can come into the same building that houses the president of the university and study their antecedents with Charles Blockson right by their side."

Liacouras explained that the Blockson Collection is something that a professional staff would never assemble on its own initiative. "Building an institutional collection is a lot like getting approval for a research project. The most funded programs require peer review, so you don't take tremendous risks, you play it safe. It is the people who are free from that sort of process who develop the most novel resources. It's no secret that mavericks are the innovators of society. Charles is not a businessperson or a professional scholar; he is an artist and a collector. My job is to give him a lot of freedom and allow him to flourish."

Blockson explained that the collection "is an extension of my soul," and emphasized that it has provided the raw source material for his own writing, which includes many magazine articles and seven books. *Pennsylvania's Black History* was published in 1975, followed in 1977 by *Black Genealogy,* now recognized as an essential reference for African-Americans interested in finding their roots. In July of 1984, *National Geographic* magazine devoted thirty-six pages to Blockson's essay "Escape from Slavery: The Underground Railroad" and featured it on the cover. Three years later, Blockson's expanded work on the subject, *The Underground Railroad,* presented first-person narratives of former slaves who had escaped bondage. These projects were inspired by stories Blockson had heard as a child about his great-grandfather's flight to freedom in 1856.

The oldest of nine children, Blockson remembers listening in awe as his grandfather told how *his* father, James Blockson, ran away from servitude in Delaware and fled to Canada, and how he and "tens of thousands of other black slaves who fled north along its invisible rails and hid in its clandestine stations in the years before the Civil War" kept the secrets of the Underground Railroad "locked in his heart until he died." Blockson credited these family stories with inspiring him "at an early age to begin collecting information on Afro-Americans in general and the Underground Railroad in particular."

The decision to become not just a writer but a bibliophile of black history and literature was reinforced by yet another childhood experience, one that Blockson relates without rancor, but offers as further explanation for the forces that drove him to gather the chronicles of his ancestors. "When I was eight years old and in the fourth grade, I asked my teacher if negroes have a history," he said. "There were maybe three black faces in the class then, and that's exactly what I said: 'Do negroes have a history of their own?' I knew of course about Booker T. Washington and George Washington Carver, and Jesse Owens and Paul Robeson were my idols, but aside from those obvious exceptions, it always seemed as though black people had never participated in the making of America. 'No,' she answered. 'Negroes have no history. They were born to serve white people.' "

The timing was coincidental, but exactly fifty years later, in 1991, the city of Norristown honored Charles L. Blockson with an Appreciation Day that included proclamations from the mayor, governor, both houses of the state legislature, and the Philadelphia City Council. By then, this driven bibliophile also had received honorary degrees from Villanova and Lincoln Universities, and he was constantly being asked to lecture on black history. Yet for all this recognition, Blockson said one of the most meaningful tributes he has received came when his former teacher, by then retired, sought him out and apologized for her thoughtless words of long ago. "Charles, you have taught us all something about ourselves and our place in history," the woman told him.

"I assured her I was never angry with her, because she only said what she had been taught," Blockson said. "I did not believe there had ever been any malice. She just didn't know any better. But looking back, I have to say I was stunned by what she said, and I was embarrassed. More than that, I was confused, because I knew about my grandfather, and I knew there were thousands of other people just like him. She was telling me they passed on no history? They had no background? No culture? It became very important for me to prove that what she said was false. That is when the collector in me was born, I think, that day in the fourth grade. I was a collector before I ever knew I was a collector."

Blockson began going to church bazaars, rummage sales, thrift shops, and used-book stores. "I picked up things that nobody was interested in. I have books in the collection today that I found before I ever got to high school, good things, too, things that cost me no more than a few pennies each." Fruitful sources were Salvation Army and Goodwill stores. "They had books for ten cents each. There were times when I buried books I wanted beneath others and waited until they had their half-price sales."

The youthful collector began with a simple focus. Any items that mentioned the words *black, Negro, African,* or *colored* were singled out and marked for acquisition. Among those early finds were two books by Carter G. Woodson—the author of several studies of black accomplishment and the originator of African-American History Month—*Negro Makers of History,* 1945, and *African Heroes and Heroines,* 1939, which provided an early refutation of the teacher's remarks. By the time he got to Penn State in 1953, Blockson had been acquiring material for ten years and had become more sophisticated in his quest. "The first thing Lenny and Rosey would do whenever we went somewhere for a road game was go check out the sorority houses.

I always started out at the used-book stores, even if I didn't buy anything. Just being among books was therapy enough for me."

While in New York City for a Madison Square Garden track meet, Blockson decided to spend some free time one afternoon in Upper Manhattan. "I took the 'A' Train to Harlem," he said melodically, and hummed a few off-key notes from Duke Ellington's famous theme song of the same name. "I got off at the One Hundred Thirty-fifth Street Station, went over to the Schomburg Center on Lenox Avenue, and walked into what I knew right away was the most important moment of my life. I looked around and I discovered that I wasn't alone. I saw what another black man had done, and what Arthur Schomburg had done became my model. I had found my purpose in life. And I have never looked back." In time Charles Blockson would be described as a modern-day Arthur Alfonso Schomburg; like Schomburg, he not only would entrust his cherished collection to a repository, but also would personally guide people in search of knowledge along its many pathways.

After spending two years in the Army, Blockson returned to Norristown in 1958 and started a janitorial business. "I made an adequate income," he said. "But my mind was on collecting, collecting, collecting." In 1970, he was appointed specialist in human relations and cultural affairs for the Norristown Area School District, an ideal position for a man whose goal in life was to promote pride and understanding among younger people. He taught ethnic and local history, conducted seminars and workshops for teachers, and acted as a liaison between the schools and the community. Meanwhile, he began to use the material he had been gathering for most of his life to write about black genealogy and history.

Blockson has a saying that he uses frequently in his lectures: "The hand that holds the pen, the quill, and the pencil controls history," and he is quick to point out that when he was growing up in the 1940s and 1950s, "the people who controlled the pens and the pencils did not present a proper history of African-Americans." But then, he added, "it wasn't so long before that when teaching slaves how to read was a criminal offense. It was against the law for black people to read. They were denied the right to learn anything about their history and their heritage. So it should come as no surprise that blacks used to be ashamed of their color."

Lenny Moore and Charles Blockson have remained close through five decades and keep tabs on each other's fortunes. "There are so many things I could say about Charles," Moore said. "What stands out is how he was always more focused than the rest of us. I thought he was crazy when he left the Giants camp, but I didn't know what he had in mind for his life. The amazing thing is that he knew so much earlier than any of us what he wanted to accomplish. I'm very fortunate that we have known each other all these years, because I love the man. I'm proud to call him my friend."

Fred J. Board of Stamford, Connecticut, has a house full of books, some devoted to individual authors, others to themes; some are fine-press books, thousands are miniatures no larger than a matchbook, hundreds are guidebooks published by the Federal Writers Project during the Depression. He has books shaped like circles, books printed on purple paper, one held together with steel bolts, another made of concrete. He has a book that moos like a cow, another that pulls open like an accordion.

"This one here is actually pretty rare," he said while showing me through his various collections. "It's French; it was made in 1799, and it's called a 'dos-à-dos' book, back-to-back. See. Three covers." He also has a tête-à-tête book, which allows two people to read the same volume while seated and facing each other, and another called an "upside-down" book, with two short stories printed on opposite pages, one aligned top to bottom, the other bottom to top. "Every time I open this one, I hope I don't see moths flying out," he said, and handed over a beautiful volume printed on Scottish woolen tartan. "Some people worry about book worms," he continued, picking up a book printed on large strips of pasta. "This one will probably get eaten by mice."

Board has many unusual book collections, but he keeps the ones that got him started fifty years ago in a small office on the first floor of the house. Several shelves there are devoted entirely to lakes—Huron, Superior, Winnipesaukee, Great Salt, and the like. "The rivers are over here, the mountains are over there," he said. "Up on top is my Frank Stockton collection. I have every darn thing the guy ever wrote except one obscure little pamphlet called *Northern Voice Toward Dissolution of the Union* that I'm never going to find. It took me five years to buy the Cracker Jack company, and I've spent fifty years on Frank Stockton, and I haven't completed him yet."

For thirty years, Board worked in marketing for Borden Company in New York. "When I retired a couple years ago I was vice president of corporate development. I did Borden's planning and acquisition work. I bought companies like Wise potato chips, ReaLemon, Sacramento tomato juice, and Snow's clam chowder." Before he went to Borden, Board did similar work for Procter & Gamble and Standard Brands. "I started off with P and G in the early forties, and I traveled all over the place. One day, I got to thinking, I know absolutely nothing about first editions, so I said I'd like to learn. I picked an author that nobody collected, Frank Stockton. He wrote a lot of books, perhaps fifty, and there were juveniles, which are very hard to get in good condition. I picked him because nobody else wanted him and they were cheap. I was only making a hundred fifty dollars a month at the time, Jane and I were newly married, so how much money do you have for books?"

A lot of Board's early work involved travel, and because his expense account was meager, he often stayed in dreary hotel rooms that all resembled each other. "I'd find myself in Bluefield, West Virginia, running a couponing test, or setting up a soap display in Mason City, Iowa. I can still see the rooms. Every one is in a concrete building two stories high, there's an old iron bed with a bare lightbulb dangling over it, a big black radiator hissing in the corner, and if you had your own bathroom, the toilet wasn't running and the tub was stained with rust from a leaky faucet. Well, in those days I didn't drink, and the only other place besides a bar in these towns was the used-book store. They were all over the country, and I'll bet I've been in ninety percent of them. Most of them are gone now, but they were wonderful. Every book dealer I met was an interesting person. I'd talk to them until they closed, and at the end of the night I'd buy a book."

Once Board began taking his wife with him on business trips, he began buying secondhand guides to cities and regions of the country that had been produced by the Federal Writers Project under the sponsorship of the Works Progress Administration from 1935 to 1939. Though most of the 6,600 unemployed writers, journalists, editors, and researchers who worked on the WPA American Guide Series were unknown at the time, their ranks included such names as John Cheever, Studs Terkel, Ralph Ellison, Saul Bellow, Richard Wright, Conrad Aiken, Samuel Putnam, Katherine Dunham, Frank Yerby, Loren Eiseley, Nelson Algren, and Margaret Walker. First editions of the books they produced have become increasingly collectible in recent years (Pantheon Books published new editions of several WPA guides during the 1980s).

"We were buying them because we used them," Board said. "I don't know if I have all of them or not, but I've got at least five hundred different titles, a lot of them in multiple copies. This Idaho guide here, I paid seven-fifty for it; I just saw it at a book fair for one hundred fifty dollars. There's an unopened box out in the garage that has twenty-five copies of *The Minnesota Arrowhead Country* guide in it."

But why would he buy twenty-five copies of the same book?

"Why else? It was a good deal. They were remaindered. I only paid a dollar apiece for them."

When Board went to work for Standard Brands in the early 1950s, he began working in New York City. "I did a lot of advertising and public relations, and for a time there I was trying to get a powdered milk business off the ground, and nobody was interested. So one of the things I had to do was make my case to the newspaper writers, and I met the food editor of the *New York Times,* a woman named Edith Asbury. Well, I found out she was married to an author named Herbert Asbury, so I started collecting him. Nobody collects Herbert Asbury. Not then. Not today. I ended up with about twenty books by Herbert Asbury, and one day Edith said to me, 'Gee, you know, Herbert would love to sign them for you.' So he came up to my office one day, and I had them all there under my desk, and he signed every one."

Board walked over to a shelf and pointed out books with such titles as *Carry Nation, Sucker's Progress, The Gangs of New York, Up from Methodism, The Barbary Coast, Ye Olde Fire Laddies, The Tick of the Clock,* and *The Devil of Pei-ling.* Every one is signed by Herbert Asbury and dated March 30, 1954. A few carry warm inscriptions, others just bear the man's name. "He ran out of juice after a while," Board explained.

Other author collections were started and pursued with similar vigor—Lafcadio Hearn, Norman Douglas, Mary Webb among them.

"I don't buy books to read," he admitted. "I don't read any of them, really, it's the chase I enjoy, the challenge. That's what I was doing in business, I was chasing these companies. Then I got interested in a private press in Portland, Maine, Mosher Press. They did about five hundred books, and I have all but three or four. And then I kind of got interested in epitaph books."

About the same time he put together the definitive Herbert Asbury collection, Board bought a copy of Dante's *Inferno* printed in white ink on purple paper. The book, in Italian, was published in the early 1800s. "I got it because it was different," he said. "And I guess that's when I started buying unusual things. Then I found a book that was purple on green, then I got a book shaped like a buffalo head. Here's one over here in the shape of a shield." He picked up a book written in a totally unfamiliar language. "You ever heard of the Deseret Alphabet? It was an alphabet invented by the Mormons in the 1860s. They printed four books in this language. Some lawyer found this in the basement of a temple in Salt Lake City. Can anybody read that language today? I'd love to find out."

In 1954, a book written by Walter Hart Blumenthal titled *Bookmen's Bedlam* showcased the same kind of "oddities" Board was collecting. A book shaped like the state of Georgia, a heart-shaped volume, an atlas five feet nine inches tall, books salvaged from sunken ships, books bound in skin, all sorts of bizarre books. Blumenthal, a Philadelphia writer and collector, had exhibited his oddities in libraries and had even appeared on television. Board was impressed and wrote the man asking if he wanted to sell the collection. He promptly received an itemized list and replied with an offer; two years later he acquired the books. "The man was getting along in years, and he was keeping them in a bank vault, so I guess I came along at the right time." In tribute, Board has collected all the known writings of Walter Hart Blumenthal.

As his two hundred–year-old house began groaning under the weight of so many books, Board began to worry about dwindling storage space and the possibility of structural damage, perhaps even personal injury to himself or to his wife. "You probably aren't old enough to remember anything about the Collyer brothers," he said with a laugh. "But I'll bet their place in New York didn't look a whole lot different than this."

Homer Lusk Collyer and Langley Collyer were urban hermits who lived in a dilapidated brownstone at 2078 Fifth Avenue in Harlem during the first four decades of this century. They were quintessential hoarders who surrounded themselves with books, newspapers, magazines, and a cache of "junk" that included seventeen pianos, an engine block from a Model T Ford, and the jawbone of a horse. The windows were boarded up and there were no electric, gas, water, or sewer connections operating in the house. The Collyer brothers were said to have withdrawn from society in the 1930s when Homer, a lawyer, lost his sight and became paralyzed. Langley, a courtly man who once aspired to be a concert pianist, went out at night to get food and reading material for the two of them.

The Collyer brothers became front-page news on March 21, 1947, when police responded to an anonymous telephone call and found Homer seated in a chair on the second floor, dead of starvation. Langley was nowhere to be found, and for a time it was feared he might be wandering the streets in a daze. As a room-by-room search of the building entered its third week, hundreds of people crowded the street outside. "He's right up there, looking out of the window and laughing at you," a spectator joked. But on April 8, Langley was found in a "mazelike tunnel" beneath an avalanche of newspaper bundles, wedged in a booby trap. He died, apparently, while carrying food to his brother.

A month after the Collyer brothers were buried, city health officials condemned their house as a hazard to public safety and issued a demolition order. By that time, more than 150 tons of debris had been hauled off to the municipal dump. Asked once by a neighbor during one of his nighttime walks why he was filling the house with so much reading material, Langley Collyer explained that he was collecting newspapers, magazines, and books for the day when Homer might regain his sight.

"I certainly like to think I have a little more focus than they did," Board said. "I also believe that unlike them, I have figured out a way to ease the space problem." He paused by an old bureau with three large drawers, and opened one. "There are three thousand miniature books in here." He pulled out a handful of volumes, then headed into another room that contained ten thousand more.

Board said he has several ideas about the disposition of his various collections, but hasn't made up his mind. A short-term solution is to sell off the duplicates, especially the WPA Guides, which have a devoted following among other collectors. Yale has expressed a keen interest in acquiring the oddities, but Board said he is having too much fun with them to consider anything that drastic.

"The beautiful thing about my specialty is that it's endless. There's no bibliography, there are hundreds of curious things in the world, and I'm the one who decides what is strange and unusual. I'm also the one who says when it's complete. I probably am the only person in America who collects these things, which is a plus. The only problem is that I have an awful time getting dealers to give me some quotes. I have written letters all over the United States explaining what I am looking for, and very seldom does anyone respond. One of them did write back a few years ago and said, 'I don't deal much in nutty books.' "

12

Continental
Drift

Ask any book dealer in the United States which antiquarian book fair is the most successful, and unhesitatingly you will be told the three-day extravaganza put on every February in California. Other fairs are held frequently throughout the nation, but this is the big one, so big that Los Angeles and San Francisco alternate as host city. As many as ten thousand collectors—most of them paying fifteen dollars each just to get in the door—routinely attend, and they go to buy, not merely to browse.

"California is where the new money plays," is one theory put forth by Marcia McGhee Carter, a partner with author Larry McMurtry in Booked Up, an antiquarian bookstore in Washington, D.C. She was expressing a mild complaint heard often among some booksellers and collectors that a major chunk of the rare-book action has moved away from the traditional power centers on the East Coast. "New money is happy money," Carter explained, "and happy money is more free."

Regardless of whether the money is "new" or "old," California has been the home of many distinguished collectors for most of the twentieth century. Henry Huntington's determination to build a great library on the West Coast began an unbroken tradition of major acquisitions that continues quietly but quite effectively today at the J. Paul Getty Center for the History of Art and the Humanities in Santa Monica, where millions of dollars are spent annually for important manuscripts. Harvard University is home to 12.8 million volumes, more by far than any other university library system anywhere, but the combined holdings of the University of California at Los Angeles and Berkeley are close. Nicolas Barker, retired keeper of rare books at the British Library, has suggested that Lawrence Clark Powell, the great developer of special collections at UCLA during the 1940s and 1950s who is now retired and living in Arizona, is "the greatest living American institutional collector." The East Coast may claim Dr. A. S. W. Rosenbach, Hans P. Kraus, and John Fleming as twentieth-century booksellers of distinction, but Californians can point without embarrassment to the late Jake Zeitlin of Los Angeles and the late Warren Howell of San Francisco. Significantly, the two monumental book auctions of the 1980s, those offering the libraries of H. Bradley Martin and Estelle Doheny, featured collections built over many years on a grand scale in New York City and Los Angeles. Each realized more than $35 million in sales, with the Doheny actually getting the edge by $1.7 million.

Just a few blocks from Rodeo Drive and Beverly Hills in Los Angeles is the Heritage Book Shop, a flashy enterprise at 8540 Melrose Avenue perfectly suited to its surroundings. A Rolls-Royce is often parked in the driveway, and the mock Tudor building itself, once a fashionable funeral home for the film colony, makes an emphatic statement about the clientele it serves. When the current owners acquired the property in 1986, they installed a stained-glass window that pictures a Renaissance printer at his press, attended by two smiling assistants. A close look shows the helpers to be none other than Lou and Ben Weinstein, who moved to California from Brooklyn in 1963 and started out in business as "junk dealers" (their phrase) in another part of town. The brothers can joke now about their humble beginnings because they are acknowledged to be the highest-grossing antiquarian booksellers in the United States.

Lou Weinstein has vivid memories of his first uncertain months in business, and he becomes especially sentimental when he tells about the day Peter Howard of Serendipity Books came into his shop and asked if there were any works around by William Faulkner. Neither Lou nor Ben had ever heard of the writer before, which seemed to please Howard enormously. For the next three hours, the savvy dealer from Berkeley carefully sifted through their stock of four thousand volumes, finally setting aside fourteen novels. "He left our complete run of *Reader's Digest* condensed books behind, all our cookbooks, and all our fix-it books, but he did give us twenty-seven dollars for the things he took," Lou said. "We thought that was pretty good, because it was twenty-six thirty more than what we paid for everything, and he didn't even ask for a discount. We decided right then and there we were in the book business to stay."

A few months later, another customer came in and looked through four boxes Lou Weinstein had "weeded" out that morning to discard with the trash. "New arrivals," he muttered to the man, who selected eight titles and paid the asking price without murmur or hesitation. "This experience somewhat unnerved me," Weinstein recalled, "because he had just purchased my garbage. I quickly and quietly returned the balance of the four boxes to the shelves."

All that, Lou Weinstein quickly emphasized, was in 1963, his first year in business "in another part of town." Three decades later, he and his brother routinely publish handsome catalogues, they have shelves filled with exceptional books, they operate a bindery, and they employ a large professional staff. During the Richard Manney sale at Sotheby's in October 1991, Heritage accounted for more than $1 million worth of purchases; within two and a half years, Weinstein had spent at least that much to acquire privately from Manney the two principal lots that had not met their reserves at the sale, the Eliot Indian Bible and the first four folios of Shakespeare. Concerning the handful of cynics who suggest that he needs to learn more about bibliography, Weinstein shrugged. "I have professional cataloguers working for me. I have a complete reference library. What we don't know we look up. This is a business just like any other."

For its thirtieth anniversary catalogue, issued in October 1994, Heritage Book Shop offered fifty-two impressive items, every one a high spot of world literature, including works by Joyce, Shakespeare, Shelley, Proust, and Blake. Prices ranged from $4,500 for a 1643 English Bible to $135,000 for an incunabulum printed by William Caxton, England's first printer. "In our early years of book selling, we only dreamed of trading in items such as A. S. W. Rosenbach, H. P. Kraus, and others discussed in their memoirs," Ben and Lou Weinstein wrote in the foreword.

Beverly Hills and Bel Air, two compact communities nearby, feature an arresting variety of opulent residences, many set snugly behind high fences and monitored closely by complex security systems. These people collect with quiet aggressiveness, and many of them do their business with the Weinstein brothers. During a stroll through the Weinsteins' elegantly appointed shop, which in its earlier role as a mortuary hosted the funerals of Rudolph Valentino, Spencer Tracy, and Clark Gable, Lou Weinstein was particularly proud of an upstairs room set aside for what he calls "collection development." "This is for people who have an interest in a particular author or a particular field, but have no time to pursue it." He indicated a shelf that featured a number of important Joseph Conrad first editions, including *Lord Jim, The Children of the Sea,* and *Nostromo.* "I started this a while ago for a customer who came in and said, 'I want the first editions of Conrad. Call me when you have them all.' This kind of arrangement represents a small percentage of my business, but it probably is the wealthiest. You could say it takes the fun out of collecting, but I'm in business to sell books. I am not foolish enough to tell someone, 'I am not going to do this.' What I am going to say is, 'I will help you in any way that I can. I wish to accommodate you.'"

Weinstein then pointed to another collection in various stages of "development," one that was being assembled for a client "who is suddenly one of the wealthiest people in the world," a client so important and so well known that "believe it or not, we cannot even use his name in the shop. I have about six customers like this whom I can only refer to by code. I cannot even use their initials. We have some people who actually say, 'You do not have permission to say my name, not ever.' This man is one of those people."

This collection-in-progress consisted of twenty-one authors, Charles Dickens, John Steinbeck, Jane Austen, George Eliot, and Edith Wharton among them. "The man came in one day with his wife. They said they had been married for twenty-one years, and they gave me a different author to mark each year of their marriage; they asked me to do a complete collection of first editions for each of these authors. There are no restrictions on the budget, which is the only way to do something like this. It may be two or three years before I get it all done. When it is finished, I will get in touch with them and arrange for the delivery. This man has never collected anything before. He has only been in my shop that one time, and I am sure that I will never see him again." There are other customers who call and say they are building new libraries in their homes. "They want some nice rare books they can put up on the shelves. They give me the funds, I earn a profit, and sometimes I even keep the books for a while because it may be several years before they can come pick them up." In 1994, Weinstein was said to be representing yet another "coded customer," a "high-spot" collector whose acquisitions were believed to include the Eliot Indian Bible and the Shakespeare folios bought privately by Heritage from Richard Manney of New York.

Weinstein was unfazed by the suggestion that some of his procedures sound more like interior decorating than book collecting. "In some cases it probably is," he agreed. "Let me also say there is no disgrace in being an interior decorator, especially when so many of your customers live in Beverly Hills and Bel Air." Indeed, ambience is as important an element in the Heritage Book Shop as the books that are offered for sale. "People would be uncomfortable walking into most used-book shops and spending five hundred dollars for a book. But they walk in here and they don't feel uneasy at all because they expect to spend that kind of money in a nice place like this." Lou Weinstein's brother, Ben, pointed out that they keep the front door to the shop locked for a reason. "You have to ring the bell to come in," he said. "It is intimidating in a way to ring that bell and have somebody come to the door. Once you're inside, you almost feel obligated to buy something."

A couple of miles away, at 535 North Larchmont Boulevard, is Dawson's Book Shop, possibly the nation's oldest antiquarian operation still owned by the founding family. Opened by Ernest Dawson in 1905, the store is an institution, a place bibliophiles from throughout the world call on routinely when visiting Southern California. Though outwardly modest—the building is partially obscured from the street and easy to drive by without seeing—the Dawsons have counted among their customers Estelle Doheny, William Andrews Clark (1877–1934), and Thomas W. Streeter (1883–1965). For more than fifty years, Dawson's has been operated by Glen and Muir Dawson, the founder's sons, bookmen who are widely respected for their knowledge and expertise and are called on often for their advice and guidance. When the FBI needed someone to help sort out Stephen Blumberg's book thefts, Glen Dawson testified as an expert witness at the Iowa trial.

There is no lock on the front door during business hours at Dawson's Book Shop, where poking through odd shelves is as much fun as making an unexpected find. There are fifty thousand books on view, in dozens of different categories. "I grew up wanting to be a bookseller," Glen Dawson said one morning over instant coffee in his second-floor office. "It's always been my life, it's what I enjoy doing. I got started when I was a kid. When my father died in 1945, my brother and I inherited the business as equal partners. It never occurred to us to do anything else."

Dawson recalled the first time he met the countess, Estelle Doheny. "One of my earliest book-selling recollections is delivering a book to her on Christmas Eve, and because I was a delivery boy, she gave me a silver dollar." Years later, he often acted as her agent at auctions. "She made it very clear that when she wanted something, she wanted it no matter what."

Dawson said that Thomas W. Streeter only visited his shop once, but that they did business together for many years. "He was a very satisfactory collector. If I wrote him by air mail, he wrote back by air mail. If I telegraphed him, he telegraphed me right back. And he would either say 'I'll buy the book,' or 'I want it on approval,' or he would say, 'I think your price is too high,' or 'I think your price is very fair but I just bought a copy two weeks ago.' He would buy from me promptly, and he would pay promptly. If he wasn't going to buy the book, he would tell me what he thought about it. He was just a perfect gentleman to do business with in every respect. He was interested in the first books printed in every state, and about every state in the country."

Of all the collectors he has known, though, Dawson's candidate for most memorable is an obscure postal clerk named Michael D. Hurley. "He never married, he never owned a car, he wore the same suit year in and year out, he lived in a small house that was rented, and the only furniture he had was bookcases," Dawson said. "All his energy and all his resources went into buying books. He never once sold a book and he never stopped buying them." A native of Cedar Rapids, Iowa, Hurley moved to California in 1930 when he was twenty-three. Because he had a secure job during the Depression, he was able to build his collection.

"He volunteered to work Sundays and the night shift, which was just fine with all the other postal workers," Dawson said. "He got a little more money that way, and he had the days free to look for books. He bought at auction and from dealers all over the place, people like Rosenbach, Maggs, and Quaritch. There were times he even did a little work for us as a shipping clerk. We would pay him something, but what he really wanted was to be here when private libraries came in so he could get first crack at them."

Though Hurley was guilty of hoarding, Dawson said he did collect with some purpose and direction. "He was a great reader of English literature, and there were authors he liked tremendously: P. G. Wodehouse, A. A. Milne, the Romantic poets. It's true that toward the end of his life he was filling his place with lots of junk, and he had no plans to do anything with any of it. One of my people here used to kid him along a little about leaving the collection to him, but as far as Hurley was concerned they could bury him and the books together in the city dump. He died without a will and the books all went to the county administrator for sale at auction. We found out through his sisters that he had died, and we were able to pick out a couple hundred interesting things from the house and list them in a catalogue."

Dawson's 477th catalogue, issued in August 1984, was devoted to the Hurley books they were able to acquire from the county administrator and sell on consignment. Among the items listed were an 1886 facsimile of the manuscript for *Alice's Adventures Under Ground* that

Lewis Carroll had inscribed to his sister, and an exceedingly rare 1820 volume in original boards of John Keats's poems, including "Lamia" and "The Eve of St. Agnes." Other titles included a fine copy of the 1846 edition of Herman Melville's first book, *Typee*, the two-volume first printing of James Boswell's *Life of Samuel Johnson*, and a "very pleasing large copy" of the 1632 Second Folio of Shakespeare's works.

A biographical sketch in the catalogue describes the condition of Hurley's house when he was found dead of natural causes. "One room was abandoned when the piles neared the ceiling, and at some point a subsidence of books blocked the door from the inside, sealing the room off. He established an annex in the garage, where piles of loose books mingled with unopened purchases from local shops and parcels from overseas." Stephen Tabor, Dawson's cataloguer, who wrote the brief piece, concluded that Michael D. Hurley, postal clerk, had died alone among his stacks of books, apparently "having done all he could to take them with him."

Below Griffith Park Observatory in Hollywood Hills, not far from the string of giant letters that have been a landmark on the horizon for half a century, Forrest J. Ackerman keeps his garish collection of memorabilia and fifty-odd thousand books dedicated entirely to the greater glory of science fiction. A visit to the onetime film agent's home is greeted with recorded monster messages, and inside, hundreds of old movie props, ranging from dinosaurs and mummies to vampires and flying saucers, stand in odd alignment among the bookshelves.

Ackerman has gathered these materials diligently for more than forty years, and his holdings are comprehensive. Paperbacks and pulp occupy equal space with hardcovers, and while rarity undoubtedly is present in abundance, the worth of the collection is in its scope. As Ackerman was pointing out curiosities in this unlikely sanctum in his vast basement, he stopped to withdraw an early book written by L. Ron Hubbard and inscribed to Ackerman. I saw that the page was a photocopy, and when I asked whether the original is kept in a vault for safekeeping, his eyebrows rose in amused disbelief. "Are you kidding? A collector offered me ten thousand dollars for it. The check cleared, and I got to make a copy for myself."

Ackerman said he would like to see his books kept together some-where as a collection in the United States, and added that he has turned down serious offers from Europe. As bizarre as his collection may seem, it commands the respect of some professional librarians. "What Forrest Ackerman has amassed rivals the collection that we have, and our collection of science fiction and fantasy is considered the very best in any institution," said Sidney E. Berger, curator of special collections at the University of California, Riverside, and editor of *Rare Books and Manuscripts Librarianship,* a publication issued by the American Library Association. "Our collection began in 1969 with the purchase of seventy-five hundred volumes from a collector named J. Lloyd Eaton. Since then, it has grown by ten times that number. I know some academics will turn up their noses when I say this, but it is the most fre-quently used collection in our library, not just by students, but by scholars from all over the world."

While Berger would like to add Ackerman's books to the univer-sity's collection, negotiations to acquire them have failed. "The prob-lem is that Forrest Ackerman's library comes with a lot of baggage. He wants all the artifacts to go with the books, and he wants us to build a museum to house them. It is extremely difficult for any institution to accept something like that. Not only will you pay a lot of money to acquire the skeletons and the monsters and the coffins, you will pay even more to take care of them properly year after year. We would very much like to work a deal for the books and documents, but we have to pass on the museum."

An additional difficulty was Ackerman's insistence that a device for projecting three-dimensional holograms similar to the one used in the Haunted Mansion attraction at Disneyland be installed. Here, it would be used to cast a lifelike image of the collector himself. "What Mr. Ack-erman wants is to give guided tours of his collection through perpetu-ity," Berger explained. Eccentric perhaps, but Forrest Ackerman in the flesh still welcomes visitors to his home to view the icons of fantasy, horror, and wonder, often by the busload.

Many spooky tales have emerged from California's movie studios over the years, but few can match the real-life horror story of the savings and loan scandal. One West Coast failure at least provided a tiny measure of comic relief when it was learned that a major book collection bought with depositors' funds for the personal amusement of the bank president was worth much more than it cost.

When the First Network Savings Bank of Los Angeles collapsed in 1990 with losses of more than $100 million, one of the assets seized by the federal government was the bank president's private "toy"—the world's preeminent collection of books, artifacts, and artwork on magic meticulously assembled earlier this century by John Mulholland, a distinguished magician, historian, writer, and close friend of Harry Houdini. Upon Mulholland's death in 1970, the collection became the property of The Players Club in New York. Fourteen years later, the material he had gathered with consummate taste was consigned to Swann Galleries for sale.

When Carl M. Rheuban anonymously acquired the Mulholland Library of Conjuring and the Allied Arts the following year for $575,000, he moved it to a section of Los Angeles known as Century City, and used bank funds to hire Ricky Jay, a well-known professional magician and respected bibliophile, as curator. Jay was given an office in Rheuban's building, a staff of three assistants, and a generous budget with which he was expected to augment the archive. A long-range plan to move the library to new quarters in downtown Los Angeles was abandoned abruptly in April of 1990 when California banking regulators closed First Network.

In its efforts to recoup some of the billions in losses brought on by the savings and loan failures, the Resolution Trust Company (RTC), the federal agency empowered to deal with the disaster, sold thousands of seized properties for a fraction of their cost. The case of the Mulholland Library, in an odd way, demonstrates how books not only retained their value during the worst recession to hit the country since the Depression, but in many cases appreciated dramatically. Early in 1992, the RTC sold the collection to Las Vegas magician David Copperfield for $2.2 million, more than twice the $850,000 Rheuban was reported to have put into it.

Six months before news of the scandal broke, I talked with Ricky Jay in Boston. Our discussion focused largely on his own magic collecting, which is considerable and widely respected, and his writing.

Learned Pigs and Fireproof Women, his lively survey of "unique, eccentric and amazing" entertainers, "stone eaters, mind readers, poison resisters, daredevils, and singing mice" among them, was based in great measure on the collection he began forming in the 1960s when he was a youngster growing up in New York. In 1991, the William Andrews Clark Library mounted an exhibition that featured some rarities from Jay's private library.

Though the Mulholland Library was a matter of peripheral interest at the time of our meeting, the identity of the "anonymous owner" did pique my curiosity. "Let me say that the man is an amateur magician, and he loves magic," was all Jay would say. The owner had never collected before, "but he does now; in an instant he acquired one of the major collections in the field." Jay explained that the man bought the library shortly before it was scheduled to be sold at auction by Swann Galleries in New York.

"It is one of the most famous magic collections in the world. The Players Club had tried to sell the collection quietly for a while, and when they couldn't do that, they consigned it for sale, at which point I was brought in as a consultant. One day a man called from out of nowhere and said he would very much like to keep this collection together. After I met with him several times in L.A., he said he would buy it provided I become his curator. I wanted to make sure that I could continue to perform and write, and he said that was no problem. What is important is that this absolutely amazing collection was going to be broken up, and possibly even taken out of the country. That would have been tragic. And we prevented that from happening."

William Self's graceful bookplate features his initials in elegant script, and the distinctive border that encloses the letters—a television screen—suggests what has enabled the veteran film producer to assemble what is arguably the world's leading collection of Charles Dickens books to be found in private hands. A native of Dayton, Ohio, Self moved to Hollywood in the early 1940s to act, and for seven years he appeared in such films as *I Was a Male War Bride* with Cary Grant, *Red River* and *Sands of Iwo Jima* with John Wayne, and *Pat and Mike* with Katharine Hepburn and Spencer Tracy. A close friendship with Tracy and Hepburn developed, and it was honest advice from the great actor that persuaded Self to seek a career change. "Spence said that unless you were a star, acting was a lousy job." Promptly turning to the production end of the business, Self put together a pilot for a series he proposed to CBS, called *The Twilight Zone*. That unqualified success led to many others, including numerous episodes of *M*A*S*H*, *Peyton Place*, *Batman*, *Daniel Boone*, and *Voyage to the Bottom of the Sea*, plus several hundred "made-for-TV movies" and miniseries. Later projects included an adaptation of Graham Greene's *The Tenth Man* for the Hallmark Hall of Fame, and an enormously successful production with the actress Glenn Close for television, *Sarah Plain and Tall*.

"I owe it all to television," Self said. From this brief discussion of his professional life the conversation turned to the extraordinary collection of Dickens titles his good fortune has enabled him to form. The condition is superb and the provenance is matchless, but what distinguishes these copies of *A Tale of Two Cities*, *Bleak House*, *A Christmas Carol*, and all the others, twenty-three in all, is that each is a presentation copy; every one is inscribed and signed by the author. Self's copy of *The Posthumous Papers of the Pickwick Club* bears this inscription at the top of the title page:

> Hans Christian Andersen
> From his friend and admirer
> Charles Dickens
> London July 1847

That book entered Self's library at a 1985 sale of the library of Paul Francis Webster, a Los Angeles lyricist who had died the previous year. Webster is best known for such Academy Award–winning songs as "Secret Love," "Love Is a Many Splendored Thing," and "The Shadow of Your Smile," and he had built what he described in 1971 as a "small, select library" of 180 items that spanned six hundred years of Western thought and culture. "I visited Paul in his house once and saw that book," Self said. "Never in my wildest dreams did I think I would one day own it." Self never thought he would own copies of Edgar Allan Poe's *Tamerlane* or the 1865 suppressed edition of *Alice's Adventures in Wonderland* either, but those two rarities are among his more notable possessions. "The *Tamerlane* in particular is a book I tried to get two earlier times," Self said.

Peggy Self travels to auctions with her husband and admits she encourages him to buy the books he wants, though she is not a collector herself. "I enjoy being on the fringe," she said. "I am exposed to it. I am part of it. But I am not the collector, Bill is the collector, even though I have always been in full agreement with what he was doing. Bill sometimes will hesitate to buy, and I will encourage him to go ahead and do it. But I honestly have to say that at that particular point in our lives, had Bill bought that book for one hundred twenty thousand dollars, we would have had to put a mortgage on the house to get it." Bill Self quickly added that even though he did not have the money when he first tried to buy a *Tamerlane,* "we had the assets; we could have done it. But we weren't about to deny our children's college education." So, in that case, the decision was made to stop bidding. "The proof is that I didn't buy it. I knew when it was time to quit."

After an hour of talk, Self got up and led the way to a long table he had prepared for this visit. "This afternoon I took a few things out of the vault I keep downtown," he said, and carefully picked up a fragile little book with paper covers and two wedge-shaped holes snipped out of the side. The book's author is not named; it is simply "By a Bostonian," and the date is 1827. "Well, this is my *Tamerlane,*" he said, and handed me the little book I had seen him spend $165,000 to get at the H. Bradley Martin sale in New York, an impressive victory that had persuaded me to learn his identity and request an interview. "You can say you have a good Poe collection," he was now saying, "but I don't think that you can say you have a *great* Poe collection unless you have a *Tamerlane,* just as I don't think you can say you have a *great* Lewis Carroll collection unless you have an 1865 *Alice.*"

Unlike the *Tamerlane,* which they bought at auction, Bill and Peggy Self bought their *Alice* in 1970 from Chicago booksellers Frances Hamill and Margery Barker. Only nineteen copies of the book are known to exist, and only three of these are privately owned. "Peggy wanted to give me a book as a birthday present, and what she tells me now is that she had only about five hundred or a thousand dollars in mind. I called Miss Hamill to see if she had anything special, and it turned out that I called her at the right time," he said. "She told me she had that item you are holding in your hands right now about to come in, and I told her she had to be mistaken, she couldn't be getting a '65 *Alice*. I had a census of all the copies, I knew where they all were, and none of them, so far as I knew, was up for sale. She said, 'Well, Bill, yes, there is one, and we're getting it.' "

Miss Hamill explained to Self that the book about to arrive in her store formerly had been in the celebrated library gathered by Carl and Lily Pforzheimer, most of which would later be sold to the University of Texas. "It seems that every once in a while the Pforzheimer estate pruned a few things out of the library and deaccessioned them," Self said. "A few years earlier, they had sold the *Alice* to a certain woman, and when I called Chicago, that woman apparently had just decided it was time for her to sell it. We wound up spending twenty-five thousand dollars. Actually, we spent a little more, because there was an 1866 *Alice* there too, the finest copy I have ever seen, and that was another two thousand dollars."

Self emphasized that he and his wife "didn't just snap these things up," they did "some serious soul-searching, because up to that time it was the most money we had ever spent for a book. And the reason we bought it, I guess, was the same reason we bought the *Tamerlane* twenty years after that; we felt we would never get another chance. I recently turned down a very substantial offer for the *Alice*. We have never bought for investment, but it is nice to know we haven't been throwing our money away all these years."

A diary Emily Brontë kept for several years in her youth came next from Self's table, followed by an eight-stanza fragment of poetry in Poe's hand, and then by some love letters written by Dylan Thomas. Self then picked up an octavo volume from the table and opened it to the title page. "This is one of my favorite books," he said. "This is Dickens's own copy of *David Copperfield*, presented to a man named J. L. Rickards, with an exceptional inscription. Here is what it says: 'Dear Sir, I wish to preserve between us some little outward and visible remembrance of your generous Mexican adventure, the adventure for which I was unconsciously responsible.' I will interject here that nobody I know has any idea what *that's* all about. But anyway, Dickens continues: 'Will you do me the favor to accept my own copy of a book, for which I have a particular affection, in the assurance that you will like it none the worse for coming from my own study shelves. I beg you to accept it with my thanks and good wishes. Charles Dickens.' ''

Inside the dark green cloth cover, on what is known as the front pastedown, are two bookplates, one belonging to William Self, the other bearing a design that combines the silhouette of a small bird with the initials KS. "This was a book that Charles Dickens took from his own library and gave to someone as a gift," Self said. "Many years later, after it had passed through the hands of several owners, a very dear friend of ours gave it to me as a gift. The man's name was Kenyon Starling, and he and I collected Dickens together for a number of years. It is a very special book."

Private book collecting is uncommon as a collaborative exercise, and when it is practiced, it is usually by husbands and wives such as Henry Clay and Emily Folger, who created the great Shakespeare library in Washington, D.C., that bears their name. It is not often that rival collectors suddenly combine their efforts and pool their trophies, yet the reason Bill Self believes he has the world's finest Dickens collection in private hands is because he happened by chance to meet a rival from his hometown named Kenyon Starling.

In November of 1971, Bill and Peggy Self went to England intending to buy a number of lots in the two-day Sotheby's sale of the Comte Alain de Suzannet Dickens Collection. "We had figured out in advance what we wanted and what we were willing to spend. I got a few small things, but we did not get a single lot that was a first-choice item. Every time I went after something especially nice, I kept getting outbid by someone."

"It was the House of El Dieff," Peggy Self said.

"Exactly," Bill Self continued. "So I finally said to someone, 'Who's Lew Feldman bidding for?' And the man, I forget who it was, said, 'He's bidding for a guy from Dayton, Ohio.' I said, 'Hey, I'm from Dayton, Ohio, I don't know anybody from Dayton who collects Dickens.' And he said, 'Well, this guy's a recluse, not many people know him,' and I thought he said the fellow's name was Sterling. So I remembered that name. And we came back home, and a little later we were going to Chicago for a television convention, and I said to Peggy, 'Why don't we go over to Dayton and see some friends, and I'll try to find this guy Sterling who outbid us, and maybe he'll show us his collection.' The only problem is, I didn't know how to contact him. I didn't call Lew Feldman because I was sure he would not want me getting together with one of his top clients. So I called John Fleming in New York, and I asked him if he knew this collector from Dayton named Sterling. John Fleming said, 'The gentleman's name is Starling, Kenyon Starling, not Sterling, and he's standing right here by my side. Let me put him on the phone.' And that is how I got together with Kenyon Starling."

Starling loved showing people his books, and he invited Bill and Peggy Self to visit him in Dayton when they were in Chicago. "It was a library to put mine to shame," Self said. About a year later, Starling visited the Selfs in California. "Another year went by and I ran into him in a New York bookstore. There he was, smoking his pipe, and I asked him what he was doing in New York. 'Buying some books,' he said. So I took him out to dinner—we went to a theatrical hangout called the Palm, which he got a great kick out of—and our friendship developed from there."

Bill and Peggy Self traveled to Paris with Starling, they took a cruise off Alaska together, they were always choosing and acquiring books together. Soon, Bill Self was asking Starling's opinion of certain Dickens titles that were coming up at auction, and he began receiving odd advice. "He would say, 'I wouldn't buy that.' And I said, 'Well, I know you wouldn't buy it, because you're such a stickler for condition, you won't buy anything unless it's terrific, but I haven't got it.' And he said, 'Yes, but it's not a very good copy, I wouldn't buy it.' So I said okay. Then another Dickens item would come around, and it would look pretty decent to me, but he would say the same thing. Once again I asked him why not, and he said, 'Well, you're forcing me to tell you something.' I said, 'What is that?' He said, 'I've willed my Dickens collection to you. You're from Dayton, I'm from Dayton. I haven't got any heirs and most of my books are going to universities. But I want you to have my Dickens collection.' "

Robert Liska, owner of Colophon Books in Exeter, New Hampshire, remembers dealing with both men, particularly Kenyon Starling, in the late 1970s. "It was right after my wife and I began our business, and we were doing our first New York Book Fair. I wanted to make a good impression, so I had brought along the cream of my own John Steinbeck collection, which let me say was second to none. Everything I had was in perfect condition—I even had a mint copy of *Cup of Gold* in dust jacket—and I put them off by themselves in a glass case, maybe twenty or twenty-five titles all together. I priced them high because deep down I guess I really didn't want to lose them, but hey, I was in business. Well, right after the fair opened, this awfully nice fellow came by and asked me if the Steinbecks were for sale. I told him they were, which one would he like to look at. He said, 'I'll take them all.' I said, 'Excuse me?' He said, 'I would like to buy all of them.' He didn't ask the price, he didn't even handle them. He saw they were perfect and he bought them on the spot." Liska recalls being paid about $17,000 for the books.

After Starling's death in 1983, the Dickens books went to Self. About ten thousand other titles were given to Stanford University, where Starling had received a bachelor of arts degree in 1927. According to the rare-book librarian at Stanford, David Sullivan, "He gave us an extraordinary batch of first editions for Joseph Conrad, W. Somerset Maugham, Anthony Trollope, Wilkie Collins, and Thomas Hardy," along with some "very fine holdings in many of the other major novelists of the nineteenth and twentieth centuries. Starling was a fanatic for quality, and our copies show it." Sullivan said university officials had no idea that such a gift was forthcoming. "Our file on the collection begins with a letter from his estate, and then we have a copy of the will that splits the book collections. Prior to that letter, there is nothing. We had no idea whatsoever that these wonderful books were coming."

When Louise Taper decided early in the 1980s to document the life and times of Abraham Lincoln, she confined herself to acquiring unique objects like letters, deeds, certificates, journals, and precious family artifacts. Once begun, the quest grew into a competition between herself and the great collectors of all time, living and dead. "I will do it, sooner or later," the Beverly Hills collector predicted, and she believes that when "it" happens—when she owns more material than any of her competitors—the only standard she will have to exceed is her own.

Louise Taper's days are long and intense, but fairly easy to describe. It is Lincoln in the morning, Lincoln in the afternoon, Lincoln at night. "Yes, I work at it all the time," she acknowledged with a bright smile.

"But I enjoy it. I love it, actually; I am driven by it." When asked whether she collects simply because she wants to know Lincoln and his family, or because she wants the finest collection ever put together by one person on the subject, she answered without hesitation. "It is everything that you're saying, and more. Once you get an area going, you start doing your research, and then you find yourself working on something else. That's how I got into John Wilkes Booth. When you've been around buying the way I have, people hear about you, and they offer you things. It just takes off, and you can't control it. You don't want to control it. You don't even try."

On those rare occasions that she needs to get remotivated, Taper will glance through a catalogue assembled more than a half century ago by the late Oliver R. Barrett and figure how many documents she needs to surpass his holdings. Barrett was a Chicago lawyer whose zeal for collecting began as a child. In 1880, President Rutherford B. Hayes received a form letter from Barrett, then seven years old, which said: "I enclose you a portion of my autograph book and would be very much obliged if you would sign your name on one page and then address an envelope to the next person after you on the opposite page, enclosing this letter and the book."

In addition to President Hayes, Barrett included the names and addresses of Oliver Wendell Holmes, Samuel Clemens, Charles Dudley Warner, Harriet Beecher Stowe, and General William T. Sherman. Everyone on the list complied with the request, and the book came back to Barrett with handwritten responses from everyone. Samuel Clemens (Mark Twain) signed, and wrote instructions on the envelope to pass "the damn piece of impudence" on to the next name on the boy's list.

When Carl Sandburg came to know Barrett, his Lincoln collection was without equal. Sandburg was given unlimited access to the material, much of which he used to write his six-volume biography of the sixteenth president, a monumental effort that earned him a Pulitzer Prize in 1940. Barrett's archive was so essential to the research that Sandburg later wrote a respectful biography about him entitled *The Lincoln Collector.* "Where would history and biography be unless there were collectors?" Sandburg asked, and paid the ultimate tribute: "The collector's flair leading Barrett since he was a boy has resulted in a mass of source materials wherein are many items that would have probably been lost for historical purposes but for the sagacity and method by which they were sought out."

Sandburg told how Barrett had filled his house in the suburbs with so many items that he began sneaking new acquisitions inside through a cellar window so as not to aggravate his wife. After Barrett's death in 1950, the collection was sold and "scattered to the four winds," according to Paul Gehl of the Newberry Library. Ralph G. Newman of Chicago, widely renowned as the world's leading dealer in Lincoln material, said that he bought "eighty percent of the Barrett sale" at Parke-Bernet Galleries in 1950, and that he originally had wanted to buy the collection en bloc from the family. "As a matter of fact, I offered them more than what they finally got in the auction, but they thought they could do better at a public sale, so that's the way it went." Newman added, though, that even if he had bought the collection privately, he still would have broken it up and sold the material piecemeal.

Because of his specialty, Newman also knows Louise Taper well, and with more than sixty years' experience as a bookseller, he is able to place her accomplishment in perspective. He ranked her among the foremost collectors of Lincoln of all time. "What I like is that even though Louise can make up her mind in a hurry, everything she buys fits in with everything else she has. It isn't random material, it's selected, and that's because she does her research. Louise never plays it by ear. Her collection on Booth is exceptional, and she certainly has the finest private collection of Mary Lincoln material you're going to find anywhere. She's very competitive—you don't collect if you're not competitive—but she isn't foolish. If she wants something, she's willing to go for it, and maybe even stretch a bit, but she never loses sight of where it is she's trying to go with her collection."

Taper's competitiveness shows in how she went about establishing her goals. "I looked up all of the leading Lincoln collectors, not just Barrett, and I counted how many letters each of them had," she said. Before her 1985 marriage to the Los Angeles investor and developer Barry Taper, who is the son of the prominent Southern California banker and philanthropist Mark Taper, Louise worked for the noted Lincoln scholar Justin Turner, who had a major Lincoln collection of his own. "I sat with Justin and I actually counted with him how many letters he had," she said during our first interview. "Once I passed him, I got pretty excited. But what he really had was the greatest Mary Lincoln collection ever, so that was another goal I set for myself, and I am now within five of catching up with him there." Ten months later, Taper was pleased to report that she had passed her mentor in that category as well. A year after that, the purchase of a Lincoln dinner plate was the beginning of a china, flatware, and crystal collection to include all American Presidents.

"When I read Carl Sandburg's book and saw what Oliver Barrett had done, how obsessed he was, how he competed with people, and how he went about getting things, I said, 'Oh God, that's just like me. I'm doing that now,' " Taper said. "And it's so much harder as a woman."

I asked how it is harder as a woman.

"You don't get the proper respect," she replied. "My husband and I had been married about three years when we had some of his friends over to the house. I had a lot of my Lincoln things out and they came in, and a couple of them said to Barry, 'Gee, I didn't know you collect Lincoln.' I said, 'Hey, wait a minute, *I'm* the Lincoln collector.' And a lot of his tennis friends, they looked at me like I was just, you know— because he's older than me—like I'm just some empty-headed girlfriend of his. This went on until one day my husband missed a match, and they said, 'Where were you?' And he said, 'I went with Louise to buy some John Wilkes Booth letters.' Well, that was very nice."

The next time Barry Taper showed up at the Beverly Hills Tennis Club, one of the members gave him a small black box to take home and show Louise. Inside was a pardon Abraham Lincoln had written on a bandage for a dying soldier, dated May 28, 1864. "I looked at it, it was absolutely authentic, and I said, 'Well, so what? What does he want? Is he just showing it off?' It turns out the man is a lawyer who has been keeping it for a client of his. I called the man and said, 'I have to have it.' " The lawyer replied he doubted his client would sell it. "I said, 'Let your client name a price. It is cruel to keep this from history, because people should know about it.' And so he told his client, and I bought it. I took it to Springfield, where they photographed it at the Illinois State Historical Library; it is absolutely authentic." Taper has since determined that Lincoln probably wrote the unusual "document" while visiting a hospital. "This boy must have been dying and Lincoln wanted to pardon him, and there was no paper nearby, so he picked up this piece of bandage and wrote on it." Because it is dated, she was able to research it in the War Records Office in Washington.

After putting the "bandage" safely away, Taper brought out a succession of other documents. "I have most all the Lincoln ancestors going back five generations," she said. "I have the great-grandfather. I have the uncles, the great-uncles. I have almost all of them. I've got all the descendants, every single one. I have the grandsons. I have them all." She explained that when she says "I have," she not only means "documents they wrote," but related material like a watercolor one of the granddaughters painted, or, most impressive of all, the only stovepipe hat worn by Lincoln known to be privately owned. "I feel like I have every phase of Abraham Lincoln's life before and after, right down to Robert Todd Lincoln Beckwith, who was the last in the line. He's the one that owned that deed on the table over there. A lot of the artifacts I have came through him. I guess what I like the best are family and all the happy parts."

Having the money to buy these objects is essential, of course, but it by no means guarantees a superior collection. "If you don't have a collector's mentality, and you are not focused, you cannot acquire a collection like this," she said. "You have to have the knowledge and the direction. I have met accumulators who have advisers come into their homes and put their collections together for them; they do the whole thing. I fly wherever I have to go, I pick up the new pieces myself, then I bring them back here. Then we catalogue them. We get them deacidified and properly protected. Then we do all the research. And then they enter the collection."

She is particularly pleased to own the earliest surviving piece of writing known to have been done by Abraham Lincoln. Dated 1824–1826, it is the first of ten leaves from a homemade notebook Lincoln used as a teenager to practice his mathematics. It has three signatures, and a pair of rhyming couplets:

> *Abraham Lincoln is my nam[e]*
> *And with my pen I wrote the same*
> *I wrote in both hast[e] and speed*
> *and left it here for fools to read.*

ABOVE: The Harry Elkins Widener Library at Harvard, a mother's gift to honor her son, a bibliophile who went down with the *Titanic*.

BELOW: The Harry Ransom Humanities Research Center at the University of Texas.

The Exhibition Hall of the Huntington Library, San Marino, California.

A collector paid $66,000 at the Garden Ltd. sale for a two-volume copy of Samuel Johnson's *A Dictionary of the English Language* (1755), untrimmed in the original marbled boards.

To the Reader.

This Figure, that thou here seeft put,
    It was for gentle Shakefpeare cut;
Wherein the Grauer had a ftrife
    with Nature, to out-doo the life :
O, could he but haue drawne his wit
    As well in braffe, as he hath hit
His face ; the Print would then furpaffe
    All, that was euer writ in braffe.
But, fince he cannot, Reader, looke
    Not on his Picture, but his Booke.

                                        B. I.

Mr. WILLIAM
SHAKESPEARES
COMEDIES,
HISTORIES, &
TRAGEDIES.

Publifhed according to the True Originall Copies.

LONDON
Printed by Ifaac Iaggard, and Ed. Blount. 1623

ABOVE: Title page of the First Folio of Shakespeare's works (1623), which sold with the Second, Third, and Fourth folios as one lot at the Garden Ltd. sale in 1989 for $2.1 million to Richard Manney. Two years later, the same set failed to meet its reserve at Manney's sale, and has since been acquired by a California collector.

LEFT: A first-edition copy of William Blake's *Songs of Innocence and of Experience* (1794), including numerous engravings hand colored by Blake in delicate watercolors, sold for $1.32 million at the Garden Ltd. sale.

riverrun brings us back to
Howth Castle & Environs. Sir Tristram, violer d'amores,
fr' over the short sea, had passencore rearrived from
North Armorica on this side the scraggy isthmus of Europe
Minor to wielderfight his penisolate war; nor had topsawyer's
rocks by the stream Oconee exaggerated themselse to Laurens
County's gorgios, while they went doublin their mumper all
the time; nor avoice from afire bellowsed mishe mishe to
tauftauf thuartpeatrick: not yet, though venissoon after,
had a kidscad buttended a bland old isaac; not yet, though
all's fair in vanessy, were sosie sesthers wroth with twone
nathandjoe. Rot a peck of pa's malt had Jhem or Shen
brewed by arclight and rory end to the reggimbrow was to be
seen ringsome on the waterface.

The fall (badalgharaghtakammimarrounkotmbrowntonnerrount-
Mounthunntrovarrhounawnskawntoohoohoordenenthunnuck!) of a once
wallstrait oldparr is retaled early in bed and later on
life down through all christian minstrelsy. The great fall
of the offwall entailed at such short notice the schute of
Finnigan, erse solid man, that the humptyhillhead of humself
promptly sends an unquiring one well to the west in quest of
his tumptytumtoes: and their upturnpikepoint and place is
at the knock out in the park where oranges have been laid

A page from the corrected typescript for the opening episode of
Finnegans Wake, signed and dated December 16, 1926 by James
Joyce; it was sold for $99,000 at the Garden Ltd. sale.

RIGHT: Arthur Alfonso Schomburg
(1874–1938), who dedicated his life
to the documentation of black history
and culture.

ABOVE AND RIGHT: Charles L.
Blockson, a star fullback at
Pennsylvania State University in
1955, and as curator of the
Charles L. Blockson Afro-
American Collection at Temple
University in Philadelphia.

RIGHT: The Holyoke, Massachusetts, annex of the National Yiddish Book Center in the early 1980s.

BELOW: Summer interns working at the National Yiddish Book Center.

Aaron Lansky, founder of the National Yiddish Book Center.

LEFT AND BELOW: Chef Louis Szathmary II in chef's attire, and in his Chicago library.

Ruth Baldwin (1918–1990), whose 100,000-volume library of eighteenth-, nineteenth-, and twentieth-century children's books is installed at the University of Florida, Gainesville.

LEFT: Louise Taper of Beverly Hills, California, at a Huntington Library exhibition in 1994 that featured many of her Abraham Lincoln items.

RIGHT: Harry Huntt Ransom, creator of the Humanities Research Center at the University of Texas, Austin, which today bears his name. Portrait by Robert Joy.

BELOW: William H. Scheide of Princeton, New Jersey, with his copy of the 36-line Bible printed at Bamberg by Albrecht Pfister.

THE
FEDERALIST:
A COLLECTION
OF
ESSAYS,
WRITTEN IN FAVOUR OF THE
NEW CONSTITUTION,
AS AGREED UPON BY THE FEDERAL CONVENTION,
SEPTEMBER 17, 1787.

IN TWO VOLUMES.

VOL. I.

NEW-YORK;
PRINTED AND SOLD BY J. AND A. M'LEAN,
No. 41, HANOVER-SQUARE,
M, DCC, LXXXVIII,

The Federalist, with George Washington's autograph, which sold for $1.43 million at the sale of H. Bradley Martin's library in 1990.

H. Bradley Martin's copy of the Declaration of Independence, which sold for $1.59 million in 1990.

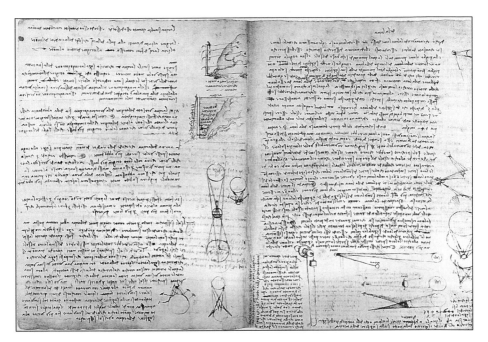

ABOVE: A page from Leonardo da Vinci's seventy-two-page manuscript, which was bought by William Gates for $30.8 million at auction in November 1994.

BELOW: First page of the handwritten copy of the Constitution of the Confederate States of America, owned by David Karpeles of Santa Barbara, California.

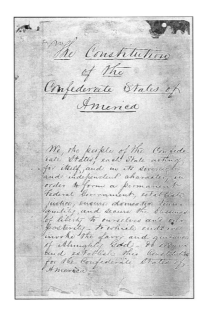

Four-time Emmy award winner John Larroquette, collector of modern first editions.

LEFT: Dr. Haskell F. Norman of Marin County, California, with the dedication copy of Vesalius's *De Humani, Corporis Fabrica Libri Septem* (Basel, 1543), bound in purple velvet for presentation to Emperor Charles V.

BELOW: David Karpeles of Santa Barbara, California, owner of more than one million manuscripts.

William Self, California collector.

The bibliokleptomaniac enjoys a moment in the "California Room" of his Ottumwa house, now empty of his treasured acquisitions.

Four days before a verdict was reached in his 1991 trial, Stephen C. Blumberg gave the author a guided tour of the Ottumwa, Iowa, house he used as a library to store his collection of stolen books.

ABOVE: Blumberg peruses a book he found lying among doorknobs, stained-glass windows, and old records stored in his Ottumwa warehouse.

BELOW: "Dumpster diving," one of Blumberg's favorite pastimes, often enabled him to "rescue a treasure" from other people's garbage.

The Library of Richard Manney, which was sold at a Sotheby's auction in 1991.

Another document represents the only instance in which Lincoln is known to have borrowed money for a professional enterprise. Dated October 19, 1833, it is a promissory note for debts incurred when Lincoln entered a partnership to open a general store in New Salem, Illinois. It is written entirely in Lincoln's hand and is signed by him. On February 1, 1988, Taper was the "anonymous" collector who spent $71,500 at the Estelle Doheny sale for the first California printing of the Emancipation Proclamation, one of three signed by Lincoln; the presale estimate was between $10,000 and $15,000. A year later, in Session V of the same sale, with Ralph Newman bidding in her behalf, she spent $19,800 for a first printing of the political debates between Lincoln and Stephen A. Douglas, signed and presented by Lincoln to R. M. Elder, a friend.

In 1990, she went to Kennebunk, Maine, with her secretary to attend an auction at the nearby Boothbay Theater Museum. Her modest intention at first was to buy some letters and manuscripts relating to the Booth family that she knew were being offered. "It turned out that not many people showed up, so I wound up buying about half of the auction." An article in *Maine Antique Digest* credited whatever success the disappointing sale realized to "the presence of a single buyer from California who bought virtually every major item in the Booth collection, including a collection of forty-five holograph letters from Edwin Booth to American landscape painter Jervis McEntee, for $13,200, the sale's top price."

I wondered whether there has ever been anything she really wanted that she failed to get. "No," she replied after a thoughtful pause, "not really, no. I guess I haven't, have I? Because if you really want something, you'll pay anything for it, if you have to. I decided from the beginning that I wanted to have the greatest Lincoln collection ever, not just now, but the best private collection in history, and that I wanted every phase. I want it to be the one by which all others are measured."

That she is making progress toward that goal is reflected by an exhibition mounted in the fall of 1993 by the Huntington Library. The library has an excellent Lincoln collection of its own, which for the exhibition was supplemented with additional material supplied by the Illinois State Historical Library, and one private collection—the one owned by Barry and Louise Taper of Beverly Hills. Mark E. Neely, Jr., a Pulitzer

Prize–winning historian, wrote the text for *The Last Best Hope of Earth: Abraham Lincoln and the Promise of America,* a critical study that Harvard University Press published to complement the exhibition. When it closed in October of 1994, more than 300,000 people had come calling at the San Marino library.

Because she figures she has at least twenty-five more years of productive collecting ahead of her, Louise Taper has given little thought to the final disposition of her collection. "You're the first one to ask," she said with a light laugh. "There are certain pieces right now, just off the top of my head, pieces like the sculptures, this piece here that Robert Todd Lincoln owned for instance, I would say the artifacts probably should be broken up. But the manuscripts and the letters? I don't know what I'll do with them."

One possible solution might be to make sure that certain categories are kept intact. "I see it all as a number of separate collections. There is a Mary Lincoln collection, an Abraham Lincoln collection, and then a Lincoln Family collection. I see it as a John Wilkes Booth collection, and I also see it as a Booth Family collection. That's how I got on the board of the Hampden Booth Theater Library in The Players Club in New York, as a matter of fact. The Players Club was once the home of Edwin Booth, the great Shakespearean actor and the older brother of John Wilkes Booth. Maybe a lot of my Booth stuff should go there."

But all those decisions, she quickly pointed out, will not be made for many years. "At the moment, I don't know," she said. "Right now, I'm just enjoying my collection."

Before taking me in to see his library of about two thousand modern first editions, the man known to millions of television viewers as the outrageously libidinous lawyer Dan Fielding on the long-running comedy series *Night Court* made a pot of strong Louisiana coffee, a rich brew cut with chicory and served piping hot. As we sat in his kitchen, John Larroquette spoke with the same good humor that energized the characterization that won him four successive Emmy Awards from 1983 to 1987.

"I can tell you exactly when I became a book collector," he said, recalling the leaner times of just a decade earlier when he performed in a variety of odd theater jobs. "I had just gotten the part of Ham in a local production of *Endgame*, which was quite a thrill because I had always loved reading Beckett, going back to the time when I was about fourteen and growing up in New Orleans."

A few days before the play opened, Larroquette was browsing through a shop in Venice, California, that specialized in seashells. "In the back was a little shelf with some books on it, and among them was this sixteen-volume collection of Beckett's collected works that Grove Press published in 1970. There was a signed limited set of the same thing there for four hundred dollars, which was too much money for me. The sixteen volumes were a hundred twenty-five. They weren't first editions, of course, but they were all of Beckett's plays. I bit my tongue and paid the money for these books. It gave me such a wonderful feeling to know that in one fell swoop I had gotten all of these books. It just gave me a feeling of fulfillment."

When he was offered the Dan Fielding part on *Night Court* in 1980, Larroquette's fortunes improved dramatically, and the level of his book-collecting activity picked up accordingly. A few weeks before we met he had acquired an exceptional collection of eight hundred Beckett items that were formerly the property of an actor who Larroquette said was "one of the best interpreters of Beckett" ever. Understandably, those books were given a choice location in Larroquette's handsome library. But pride of place is still assigned to those first sixteen volumes he bought in a seashell shop.

Larroquette collects what are known as modern first editions, but his books more appropriately are called contemporary first editions, books written by authors who not only are still alive, but are still writing. In this pursuit his focus parallels those of most other American book collectors. He is particularly proud of his Anne Tyler books, especially the Baltimore author's first two novels, *If Morning Ever Comes* and *The Tin Can Tree*, which regularly sell at fairs and in catalogues for $750 to $1,000. "I don't know why, but it matters to me that when I read the books of my favorite authors, I want to read the first editions," he said, and pointed to titles by John Fowles, Anthony Burgess, and Barry Hannah.

Once Larroquette was buying rare books, he learned the subtleties that every serious collector must master: how to identify first editions, how to look for points, the importance of dust jackets, the essence of good condition. "That became an end in itself, being able to pick up a book and to know something about it," he said. "What really excites me the most now is signed copies, the fact that an author I admire so greatly actually had possession of it, for a moment anyway."

At first Larroquette bought just the individual titles that he wanted, but in time he appreciated the wisdom of assembling comprehensive author collections. "I will still get single works by authors. I recently got a nice copy of *A Streetcar Named Desire*. I don't collect Tennessee Williams, but I bought it because it was published the year I was born and I used to ride that streetcar in New Orleans when I was a kid."

Larroquette's passion for book collecting became so well known around Los Angeles that he was duped into attending a mock auction set up at a Hollywood antiques store for a television program hosted by Dick Clark called *Bloopers and Practical Jokes*. "They set up a fake auction, and my wife worked right along with them," he said. "I got an invitation in the mail, and just put it on my dresser. My wife said nothing, she just played dumb. They were offering precisely the kinds of things I collect, so the day came around, and I said to my wife, 'I think I'm going to go to this, do you mind?' She said, 'No, I'll go with you.' "

When they arrived at the shop, Larroquette's wife excused herself while he went into the sales room. As soon as he sat down, the action turned immediately from paintings to books. "They had talked to people I do a lot of business with, and the idea of the joke was to sell books they knew I already had at a fraction of what I had paid for my copies. They were counting on my staying out of the bidding because these were things I already owned. But I'm not stupid; when I saw a book I knew was worth eighty dollars, I would get in when it was five. When it got to eighty or eighty-five, I would stop. So they couldn't get me on that. What they did next was go to the other extreme. People started bidding a thousand and two thousand for books that I knew were worth one hundred. By that time, of course, my wife Liz was sitting next to me wired with a microphone, and they were able to pick up my reactions. They had to bleep out a lot of what I was saying because I was pretty astounded, to say the least, about how insane some of the prices were going. Finally, they pulled the rug out from under me. They walked over, just like that, and gave me a book. I looked up, I saw the mirrors on the wall, and then I saw the camera lenses. I had fallen for it, hook, line, and sinker. But it shows you, doesn't it? When a man has greed for books, he will believe anything."

One of the booksellers who had been alerted to the television prank was Ralph B. Sipper, owner of Joseph the Provider Books in Santa Barbara, California. Known as "Joe the Pro" throughout the antiquarian book world, Sipper formed the business in 1970 with the clear intention of "providing" nothing but the best books he could find; Joseph was the name of a beloved grandfather, and the resonance of a Thomas Mann character from the biblical tetralogy *Joseph and His Brothers* (1933–1942) made the choice all the more appropriate. Though he loves books, Sipper said being a professional dealer makes it difficult for him to collect. "I get my satisfaction in knowing that certain beautiful books pass through my hands, and that they help build nice collections."

Sipper cited John Larroquette as an example of the kind of collector he particularly enjoys working with. "I take pride in having gained John's confidence and having been able to pass along some nice things to him," he said. "The way I met him was, he came around to book fairs very quietly for two or three years, not just out here in California, but others. I remember, for instance, that he came over to our booth in Boston once. I didn't know who he was because I don't really have time to watch much television. But I recognized that this was somebody who was asking the right questions, even though he was a novice. And I could see not only a genuine interest, but a pragmatic intelligence. Then after he started buying some books, I realized he also had the ability to buy. And we have become very good friends."

The Samuel Beckett collection he acquired for Larroquette is a good example of matching books with customers. "If you want to collect Beckett today, and you came to me with five or ten times the amount of money that John paid for that collection, I could not produce those books. I probably could over a period of time, but my point is that it's not only the money, but having the right copies available at a given time. Things of this caliber usually disappear into institutional collections."

Another writer who has a special place in Larroquette's library is the poet Charles Bukowski, who died in 1994. "I discovered him around 1980," Larroquette said. "I was drinking pretty heavily at the time when I found him, very heavily. That first-person voyage he goes through, I identified with it. I look at it all as a man living in the under-belly of life, but a man who still has the strength to push one hand out and type. I thought this is not a bad way to go if you have to live in this pain, to be able to communicate what it is like and how horrible it is. I could never do that."

A shelf on one of the library walls holds two of the four Emmys Lar-roquette won in successive years from 1983 to 1987, an unequaled accomplishment. Between those two gold statuettes, in mute counter-point, stands an unusual sculpture depicting two grizzled men sitting on a bench, waiting for a bus that may never come. "I keep that right there to remind myself of who I am and where I was headed with my life," he said quietly.

Larroquette agreed that he collects books obsessively, but he does not see it as a healthy substitute for alcohol. "When there are lots of books around me, I feel safe, I feel secure, I feel in the company of others even though I may be sitting in my study all alone. Drinking is just drinking, that's all, it has nothing to do with books. I am an alco-holic and there are only two ways for an alcoholic to go, and that is either continue or stop. One night I decided to stop. That is why I keep that statue by the Emmys, just to remind myself not to feel too self-important about any kind of achievement, because everything we have is all so very fragile."

The actor looked around his library, nodded at the four Emmy Awards, and with a sweeping arm motion took in his superb collection of modern first editions. "If I walked in here off the street, I suppose I might say this fellow must be pretty important," he said. "It may sound like false modesty, but I really try to take no credit whatsoever for what has happened to me. I show up for work and I try to take care of my responsibilities and I hope that whatever happens is pleasant. But I can't just say I did it, because it just doesn't mean anything when I say that to myself. It's all been wonderful, but so much of it is luck."

In just fifteen years of determined collecting, a Santa Barbara real estate investor has acquired about a million pages of historic manu-scripts, an archive so vast it requires a reinforced steel vault ten feet wide by thirty feet long to assure safe storage. Driven by a passion that approaches missionary zeal, David Karpeles has gathered original material in virtually every conceivable field—history, exploration, cartography, religion, art, music, politics, science, literature, and medicine among them. "Whatever I get must make sense to a fifth-grade student, that is the only limitation I have," he said when interviewed one August afternoon in his spacious home. "Finding a great document is better than cotton candy, watermelon, and sex."

Two documents were displayed as centerpieces for his daughter Cheryl's wedding reception, held in one of five private museums Karpeles maintains in various parts of the country to showcase his treasures. Richard Wagner's manuscript copy of the Wedding March, from the opera *Lohengrin*, a composition synonymous with the joyful lyric "Here comes the bride," was featured in one cabinet, while Felix Mendelssohn's original score of the sixth number of his incidental music to *A Midsummer Night's Dream*, the lively melody bridal parties everywhere know as the recessional, was lying in the other. A string quartet entertained the guests with memorable renditions of the two pieces.

"We like celebrating important events with manuscripts from our collection," Karpeles said. To honor the bicentennial of the American Constitution in 1987, he mounted an exhibition that displayed five documents: the report of the Committee to Implement the Articles of Confederation, the announcement by Congress of the election of the first president of the United States, New York's ratification of the Constitution, the Emancipation Proclamation Amendment to the Constitution signed by Abraham Lincoln and the full Senate, and the original constitution of the French monarchy proposed and submitted to King Louis XVI.

In 1989, Karpeles marked the fiftieth anniversary of the death of Sigmund Freud by exhibiting a number of papers in which the father of psychoanalysis discussed headaches, dreams, and self-analysis. The following year, the invention of electronic communications was marked with an exhibition of pertinent Samuel Morse, Alexander Graham Bell, and Guglielmo Marconi materials, including the first pencil sketch of the radio. A 1991 music exhibition featured the original manuscript for Mozart's *Marriage of Figaro*, Beethoven's "Emperor" Concerto, Stravinsky's *Rite of Spring*, Puccini's *Madama Butterfly*, and Paderewski's Minuet in G.

Karpeles explained that his fervor was inspired by nothing less than a midlife epiphany, a revelation that came in 1978 when he was forty-two years old and visiting the Huntington Library in San Marino with his wife, Marsha. "We looked in an exhibit case and we saw something that we could not believe was there, something we felt belonged in the Smithsonian Institution," he said. "It was a pass that President Lincoln had given to one of his bodyguards the night he was killed. We asked some questions and we found out that this little pass is nothing, that there are documents changing hands all the time that would make you faint. Right there, I decided I would go into this, and I would go into it with a vengeance. I would see how many of these great documents I could get before people realized what they were selling."

Karpeles began to pore over catalogues from dealers and auction houses, and before long he had agents bidding for him at sales all over the United States and Europe. "What we saw were documents like the Emancipation Proclamation and the Declaration of Independence of Peru, original, handwritten drafts of great documents, and people were selling them!" If people were willing to sell, Karpeles was willing to buy, and he emerged as a buyer who competed successfully with the most conspicuous manuscript collector of the 1980s, Malcolm Forbes, the New York publisher who died in 1990.

The Karpeles strategy was remarkable for its simplicity. "We went out and we tried to purchase every single thing that looked important to us. We looked at the catalogues and marked off everything we wanted, and if there was something we wanted, we kept on bidding, no matter what. For four years, we bought every major document that came up, every single one. We just kept on bidding until everybody else dropped out. We figured that if other knowledgeable people were bidding, then the document must be worth at least the amount of money they were willing to spend. All we had to do was outlast these other people, and it would be ours."

Often called the "underbidder principle," this method assumes that true value is established by an open competition in which several people bid on an item that only one of them can get. The underbidder is the last person who drops out, thereby determining what price the victor will pay. There are a number of pitfalls to this tactic, as Karpeles readily admits. One is that several people who do not know very much about a particular item can find themselves blindly following each other's lead. A more serious danger is that when someone is willing to buy an article "at all costs," word often gets out, encouraging others to "run up" the tally out of spite or self-interest. "I don't doubt for a second that my purchases affected the market," Karpeles said. "There came a point when I had to impose limits on what I was willing to spend. I do not buy everything that comes up anymore. My competitors have to know now there are times when I will drop out, and they will be left with things they might not want at the prices they will have to pay."

Though the number of documents he has bought is immense, Karpeles stressed he is not overly interested in "getting every piece of paper that is put up for sale." Instead, he concentrates on "anything that is important," a flexible guideline that gives him tremendous latitude. The day we talked, he had brought a selection of manuscripts from his downtown vault to illustrate his point. There was a draft copy of the Bill of Rights, a papal decree signed in 1183 by Pope Lucius III proclaiming the sacred duties of the Knights Templar in the Holy Crusades, a proclamation signed by George Washington on October 3, 1789, declaring the fourth Thursday of the following month to be a day of Thanksgiving, and a document signed by Martin Luther in 1532 approving terms offered by Emperor Charles V that recognized the Protestant movement.

When Karpeles finished with those items, he left and brought back a few more. First, he handed over one of the most quoted documents of the American Revolution, a letter written by General George Washington at his headquarters in Valley Forge, Pennsylvania, on December 29, 1777. Starting with the simple address "Gentlemen," the commander asks the Congress for aid, saying that his soldiers "are barefoot and otherwise naked." It is a quotation now found in countless history books.

"I got this at a small auction at Swann Galleries," Karpeles said. "I told Bart Auerbach, my agent, to just go over there and don't even look at the thing, just act dumb, I don't even care if it's fake or not, just keep cool. There was a low estimate on it and I didn't think anybody else knew what it was. But then all of a sudden in comes the secretary of Malcolm Forbes. Forbes usually went to these sales himself, but I guess this time he didn't want to arouse any suspicion. It starts off around two thousand dollars, something real low, and it goes up, and up, and up. Around thirty thousand the secretary starts to hesitate, and it was there that Bart said he felt he had her. She finally gave up around fifty-five thousand dollars." Karpeles was vague about the limit he gave Auerbach—"under one hundred thousand or something"—but quickly added that he would have been "heartbroken" if he had failed to get the letter.

The next document Karpeles showed me was the constitution of the Confederate States of America, not one of the hundred copies initially printed from the original version, but the actual holograph copy written by General Thomas R. R. Cobb of Georgia on forty-one leaves of light-blue paper and dated February 27, 1861. "Isn't that something that should be in the National Archives?" I asked after a long silence. Karpeles smiled. "You would think so," he said. "But it is here."

For almost three quarters of a century, this draft of the Confederate constitution had been on deposit at the University of Georgia in Athens, placed there in 1908 by Cobb's descendants, who had retained ownership of the document. "We assumed, after so many years, that it had been given to us," Mary Ellen Brooks, curator of rare books at the university, told me later in a telephone interview. "The heirs were the true owners, and it turned out we had it all that time on loan. We still have the permanent constitution of the Confederacy. The one in California is the provisional constitution. Needless to say, we would very much prefer to still have both."

Karpeles heard about the availability of the document through a bookseller. "I was told that the owner walked into the university one day and said, 'I'm afraid my family would like our constitution back.' And they said, 'What do you mean, *your* constitution?' He told them, 'Look in your file, it's only on loan. It's been on loan all these years from our family.' So then they asked him, 'Well, why do you want it back?' And the man said, 'We need the money.' "

The owner agreed to give the university time to raise money to purchase the document, either from the state or private subscription, but those efforts fell short. "That's how I heard about it," Karpeles said. "I heard through a dealer that they were looking for donations. I didn't think about donating it, but what I did tell them was, 'Listen, why not just sell it to me. I will take very good care of it, and we will let you exhibit it every so many years.' " Karpeles declined to disclose how much he paid for the Confederate constitution or to identify the individual who offered the document for sale. "I agreed to keep those details confidential," he explained. Other sources did reveal, however, that the document had been consigned to the Wilmington, North Carolina, bookseller Thomas Broadfoot, who offered it for sale in 1982. General Cobb's descendants were named in a three-page catalogue description of the item as owners, and an asking price of $200,000 was listed.

The constitution that remains at the University of Georgia, dated two weeks later than the one owned by Karpeles, also has a history of uncertain custodianship. According to the National Archives, the document known as the Permanent Constitution of the Confederate States of America, written in script on vellum and ratified on March 11, 1861, became the property of the federal government at the end of the Civil War, but never reached Washington. When approached by Union troops in April 1865 at a railroad depot in Chester, South Carolina, the Southern officials charged with turning the document over took fright and fled, leaving it and other records behind. Felix G. De Fontaine, a local newspaper publisher, rescued some of the abandoned papers and kept them for eighteen years. In debt and strapped for money, he sold the Permanent Constitution to a woman named Mrs. George W. J. De Renne in 1883. The document remained the property of her family until 1939, when the University of Georgia bought it for $25,000.

Because public comment about the sale of the Cobb family constitution was kept at a minimum, the transfer took place with little fanfare. "The president of the American Manuscript Society brought it here on an airplane from Georgia," Karpeles said. "It was in a briefcase strapped to his wrist. I was shaking with excitement. I was dizzy for several days after that." The idea of giving the document to the state of Georgia as a gesture of goodwill was never considered. "If they really wanted to keep it, they could have bought it," he said. "I'm not that type of a philanthropist."

On December 7, 1990—Pearl Harbor Day—a matter of similar delicacy arose when Karpeles bought a two-page letter written in 1787 by Ethan Allen, the Vermont patriot who commanded the Green Mountain Boys during the American Revolution and captured Fort Ticonderoga from the British. Addressed to Guy Carleton, the lord governor of Quebec, Allen's letter boldly hints that Vermont might consider becoming a Canadian province if denied statehood in the recently formed American Union. "I belong to this Republic, which is not connected with the United States of America," Allen wrote.

Four years later, Vermont became the fourteenth state admitted to the Union, but some observers have suggested that Colonel Allen's northern inquiries may have bordered on treason. Though not conclusive either way, the letter nevertheless is a primary document of considerable historic significance. Before the sale, Christie's estimated a value of $15,000 to $20,000 on the lot, but competition was stiff, and Karpeles had to pay $41,800 before he was able to get the letter for his library. A year later, he confided that he had been willing to go as high as $80,000 if necessary.

Shortly after Karpeles was identified as the new owner of the Ethan Allen letter, he received a telephone call from Madeleine M. Kunin, then the governor of Vermont. "I didn't know who she was," Karpeles said, "but she had met my wife at some function for Brandeis University," an institution whose fund-raising activities both women actively support. "The governor informed me that Vermont was the underbidder on the Allen letter, and she asked if I would consider giving it to her state as a gift." While he was sympathetic to Governor Kunin's request, Karpeles said he felt the item belonged in his comprehensive collection of Early American documents, and opted to keep it in California.

Karpeles owns a substantial number of items relating to his native state as well, a collection he calls the California archive. It includes more than twenty letters written by Fra Junípero Serra, founder of many California missions during the eighteenth century. "You can feel the presence of these great minds," he said. "We've got documents that actually have fingerprints on them. They have spilled ink on the paper, and you can see their fingerprints. I have a document where George Washington was writing something, and his fingerprint is right there. But what you really see on things like these are the ideas, which give you an even closer tie, and sometimes you can see where people changed their minds. They will cross out one thing and write in something else, so you can get an idea of what their first thoughts were. Because so many of these manuscripts are drafts, you can see how they changed from the time they were written to the time they were printed."

Karpeles explained that he likes "to stick with the monumental documents, though sometimes I fill in around them." To illustrate his point, he picked up a draft copy of the Bill of Rights, which guarantees every American "life, liberty, and property." "Well, as I'm sure you know, the issue of slave ownership came up, and the whole idea of property became pretty sticky, so they changed 'property' to 'the pursuit of happiness.' You can see history right there on that piece of paper."

David Karpeles is the largest owner of single-family housing in Santa Barbara County, most of it property he bought during the 1960s with the idea of renting and selling to the Baby Boom generation that was about to come of age. "I am first and foremost a mathematician," he explained, noting that before he became a businessman he taught at Westmont College and Santa Barbara City College nearby, and worked in the computer industry. "You could just see the huge classes in the schools, from the ninth grade down, and before long you knew this whole mass of young people would be graduating and inundating the housing stock. I just knew the prices were going to go up, and that this was the time to get into it. It seemed pretty straightforward to me at the time. So I kept investing in houses. I couldn't buy them any faster than I did because I knew where they were going. Pretty soon I had so many houses that I had no time to teach."

By the end of the 1980s, Karpeles said that buildings he paid $10,000 and $20,000 for were worth upward of $250,000 each. Though the recession of the early 1990s did not stop his collecting, economic conditions did force him to sell about fifty houses to generate the capital he needed to continue nourishing his library. "It's no different from buying the houses," he said. "The prices I have to pay for some of these things may sound high, but in a few years they'll be considered cheap. The Ferdinand and Isabella letter we got a few years ago? We paid Hans Kraus fifty or seventy thousand for it, I don't remember exactly, but when the five hundredth anniversary of the Columbus voyage was coming up, I felt that whatever it was they were asking, it was a bargain."

What happens to all this material is of course the salient question. "The Karpeles Manuscript Library will exist in perpetuity," he said. "I am a mathematician, and I have it figured out precisely." A Santa Barbara institution bearing that name was established in 1983, and has since expanded to include exhibition halls in New York, Tacoma, Washington, D.C., and Jacksonville, Florida.

"You ask is this an obsession? Yes. I'm sure this is an obsession," Karpeles said. "But is that bad? You have to be obsessive, I think, or it just doesn't work."

Exactly when a person becomes a book collector has been debated often through the decades, usually without any consensus being reached. One theory holds that the defining moment occurs when a person buys a book with the prior certainty that he will never read it, though other views are less cynical. "So subtile [*sic*] and so infectious is this grand passion that one is hardly aware of its presence before it has complete possession of him," Eugene Field explained a century ago, which suggests that he had no idea whatsoever when he crossed the line.

For a Northern California couple whose shared passion to own beautiful objects was once confined to furniture and decorative-art works, the motivation to acquire books can be traced to a day in 1965 when they bought an inexpensive facsimile of the most celebrated fine-press volume ever published, the Kelmscott *Works of Geoffrey Chaucer,* a product of the Kelmscott Press, founded in 1890 by the English poet and designer William Morris. "It was a modest copy, not even full size, but there was something totally magnetic about it," Sanford L. Berger recalled one summer morning in his retirement home, a comfortable house on the Monterey Peninsula with a sweeping view of the Pacific Ocean.

"What I noticed right away was the striking similarity the artistic designs had to the drawings and carvings my father used to make, especially the detailed borders and the flowing decorations. My father just loved doing that kind of relief work, and this is what I saw when I opened that book." Sandy Berger's father, Samuel Berger, moved to California from Romania in 1904 at the age of nineteen, to become the most successful wood carver in San Francisco, producing decorative works that still adorn some of the better-known landmarks in the city, such as Mission Dolores, Grace Cathedral, and the Bohemian Club. "As far back as I can remember, my father had me sitting on the bench watching him carve. My three sisters and I got to do all the stencil markings for him, and he taught me to draw. But he always said, 'Don't be a carver, be the architect; the architect decides where the carvings are going to go."

Berger not only became an architect, he married one, an alliance that nurtured aesthetic interests that have been maintained for more than half a century. Sandy and Helen Berger met in 1941 at the Harvard Graduate School of Design. "We both went there to study under Walter Gropius, who had founded the Bauhaus School, and his associate, Marcel Breuer. They were in the United States as refugees from Nazi Germany. It was largely through their influence that our first apartment was furnished in pure International Style furniture, the modern things that were just becoming popular, and that got us started as collectors." Before long, they were buying Art Nouveau pieces as well.

Though the Bergers assembled an excellent reference library to document their holdings, they never considered themselves book collectors until Sandy Berger decided one December day in 1965 to skip lunch and visit Warren Howell's bookshop on 434 Post Street in downtown San Francisco. "My intention was to go out and find a single Kelmscott Press book that was authentic," he said. "I had no idea what would be in there; I just knew the place by reputation and went in to look around." What happened in Howell's shop that day was the first of several encounters Berger would experience over the years that have reinforced his belief in the magic of serendipity. "This collection is more than luck," he said, and recalled a detailed exhibition catalogue published by the University of California Press in 1984. In the preface to that catalogue, Berger wrote that at the risk of being judged "mystical or superstitious," he often feels "as if the collection willed itself" into existence.

"Warren Howell wasn't around the day I showed up, but when I asked if there were any Kelmscott Press books around, the fellow who was minding the store opened a door to this collection that had just come in on consignment. Nothing had been put out on display yet." Of the sixty-six volumes comprising fifty-three titles printed at the Kelmscott Press, Howell had obtained fifty-one of them from the library of the late Templeton Crocker, a wealthy San Francisco collector best known for a remarkable archive of California imprints, travel accounts, Gold Rush diaries, maps, and newspapers that was sold to the University of California, Los Angeles, in 1961. Crocker also loved fine printing, and his collection included many of the books produced by the legendary fifteenth-century Venetian printer Aldus Manutius and known as Aldines. All of the William Morris books Crocker had gathered were in superb condition, all had flawless provenance, and most had important inscriptions. During three "successive extended lunch hours" spent in Howell's shop, Berger examined each one before finally selecting *The Life and Death of Jason,* presented to the artist Sir Edward Burne-Jones by his lifelong friend and colleague William Morris on June 30, 1895. "It's an extraordinary association copy, and it was mint, so fine," Berger said. "It was just one book, a large quarto, but it was the one I felt I had to have."

Instead of providing gratification, though, the acquisition produced what Berger called "a severe case of anticipation syndrome," which he described as "the reverse of withdrawal symptoms." The syndrome went away only when he returned and bought the remaining fifty books three weeks later. "I brought home three cardboard boxes, and those three cardboard boxes started it all," he said. "What I had experienced was something uncontainable; handling so many Kelmscott Press books in so short a period of time was like handling a marble figurine. There was some sort of transference, a realization that these are jewels, these are important. I get chills just remembering it."

Over the next few years, Warren Howell found the remaining items the Bergers needed to complete their run of Kelmscott Press titles. One came from the library of an elderly American expatriate who was living in Montevideo. "Warren bought a number of things down there, but he carried *this* back in his lap," Berger said as he brought forth a genuine copy of the book that had so captivated him twenty-five years earlier in a facsimile version. The Kelmscott *Chaucer* is a masterpiece of typography, ornamentation, and design that William Butler Yeats once declared to be "the most beautiful of all printed books." William Morris produced 425 paper copies of the *Chaucer* in 1896, 379 of which were issued in quarter-linen binding and blue paper-covered boards, with linen spines and pasted labels. The remaining forty-six—

bound in white pigskin, blind-stamped with a design drawn by Morris himself, and bound at the Doves Bindery—are the rarest of all; the *Chaucer* Warren Howell brought back from Uruguay was one of these. (When decorations or lettering are said to be *blind-stamped* this means that an impression has been made in the leather or cloth binding by a tool without the addition of gold or color.) "Go ahead," Berger offered. "Feel it for yourself. It's like ivory."

Within three years, the Bergers' Kelmscott Press collection was largely complete, yet their serious collecting of William Morris had just begun. "What followed from there was a natural development," Berger said, pointing out that anyone who wants to appreciate the full measure of Morris must also take into account not only the man's work as a fine-press typographic designer, but his notable accomplishments as a writer, poet, translator, publisher, painter, weaver, illuminator, designer, businessman, embroiderer, and social activist. In 1892, Morris declined an opportunity to succeed Alfred, Lord Tennyson, as poet laureate; he was too busy doing other things. Politically, Morris was passionately committed to socialist causes and published a number of controversial tracts and pamphlets, most of which Berger has acquired. Moreover, Morris & Company (which from 1861 to 1875 was Morris, Marshall, Faulkner & Company), manufactured wallpaper, textiles, furniture, stained-glass, metalwork, tiles, and carpets, and produced patterns that have been in production for over a century.

"His work in the field of the applied arts inspired an entire generation of designers and architects; his concern with decorative honesty and truth to materials had a direct bearing on the principles of what was to be the Modern Movement," Elizabeth Wilhide wrote in a monograph on Morris's enormous influence, and stressed how he "transformed the whole status of decorative art" by challenging the "mass-produced mediocrity of the nineteenth century and re-establishing the value of handcrafted work."

In an 1877 lecture, Morris said that everything manufactured by human hands

> has a form, which must be either beautiful or ugly; beautiful if it is in accord with Nature, and helps her; ugly if it is discordant with Nature, and thwarts her; it cannot be indifferent.

[The] one great office of decoration [is to] give people pleasure in the things they must perforce *use,* [while nothing] can be a work of art which is not useful; that is to say, which does not minister to the body when well under command of the mind, or which does not amuse, soothe, or elevate the mind in a healthy state. What tons upon tons of unutterable rubbish pretending to be works of art in some degree would this maxim clear out of our London houses, if it were understood and acted upon!

A number of Morris collections are maintained in several American and British institutions, but most of them focus only on individual aspects of the complete work. "You must not forget that Helen and I are architects," Berger emphasized. "So it wasn't long before we wanted to document all the sequences that take place in the design process, from the first concept, to the preliminary development, to everything that goes on before the final stage. It's so easy to look at a finished product and forget what went into creating it."

In order to appreciate the creative phases of book production, Berger bought an Albion press and mastered the craft of hand-printing. "Morris inspired me to do good calligraphy. I am a very good calligrapher. And because he printed, I have to print. When you've tried it yourself, it becomes a marvel when you look at the real thing. You are able to see where all the pieces fit. You can grasp the full scope of the design process."

As Berger spoke, the afternoon sun passed through five stained-glass panels that once graced the Unitarian church in Haywood, Lancashire, filling his living room with glorious beams of colored light. Five other figures from the same ensemble are in another room of the house, and a rose window that once surmounted the two rows—three angels with trumpets—is in a third. "I was buying some Morris ceramic tiles from an antiques dealer in London when the saleswoman asked if I might be interested in a Morris stained-glass window," he said. Because the glass panels were too large for display, they had been gathering dust in a back storeroom for two years. Berger borrowed from the dealer a photograph that showed how the windows appeared in situ in the church, which had been condemned and demolished.

"The whole thing, taken together, was eleven feet wide by eighteen feet high, absolutely enormous," Berger said. "When I showed the picture to my wife, I told her this was our latest acquisition. She thought I meant the photograph. 'Not the picture,' I told her. 'We bought the entire window.' "

The stained-glass window is the largest individual item in the Berger collection, but was by no means the Bergers' most significant acquisition. That distinction belongs to two crates, "each one the size of an automobile, each weighing about half a ton," containing a vast jumble of watercolors, letters, files, notes, tiles, pots, books, drawings, hundreds of designs for wallpaper and tapestries, detailed dye books, instructions and formulas for printed fabrics, textile samples, and precise full-size drawings for stained-glass windows called cartoons. It was the archives of Morris & Company in London, bought en bloc by Berger in 1968.

The manner of the archives' acquisition provides yet another example of what Berger means when he suggests that the collection was "willed into being." David Magee, for five decades a prominent San Francisco bookseller, routinely traveled through Britain to make what he called his "rounds" of reliable sources. While chatting one day in 1968 with the London bookseller Anthony Rota, he noticed a watercolor by Edward Burne-Jones propped against a wall that was part of a huge lot just purchased from the estate of Duncan Dearle, managing director of Morris & Company when it ceased operations in 1940. In his memoirs Magee recalled buying "the William Morris lot" on the spot knowing that a valued customer was about to be offered something "which he had never dreamed he might possess." That "valued customer" was of course Sandy Berger.

When the crates arrived from England, Berger drove immediately from Berkeley to San Francisco for what would be three thrilling hours of discovery, oblivious to the "sacred dust" that layered the cache. At one point, Magee dropped some rolled-up cartoons of stained-glass window designs on the floor. "Now, watch out," Berger scolded gently. "You may not realize it, but these don't belong to you anymore." Without making a formal offer or discussing terms, Berger had made clear he was buying the entire archive. Magee recalled that even though he had no misgivings about Berger's "financial ability" to handle the purchase, what he "could not imagine" was how his friend planned to store such a formidable mass of material. Berger's solution was succinct. "I just won't be able to show everything at one time."

During my visit, Berger was unable to contain his enthusiasm for the items he kept producing from the archive. "Feel the quality of that," he said, handing over a hand-knotted sample of carpet. "Look," he continued, "these are the early proofs of initials and ornaments from the original woodblocks of the Kelmscott Press. There were three sets of these proofs pulled when the press closed. The British Library has one, the Pierpont Morgan Library has another, this is the third. Over here, this is all wallpaper." From wallpaper and textiles we moved to yet another storage area. "This is Morris's own drawing," he said, unrolling a full-size cartoon for a stained-glass window. "Talk about economy of line, look at what he achieved here," he continued, bringing forth yet another. "This is the figure for a tapestry. We have seven hundred watercolor drawings for stained-glass, another hundred and fifty for textiles and carpets. One hundred and forty of these are figure studies drawn by Morris himself. I think the Victoria and Albert Museum in London has the next most; they have seven I know of."

Though Berger admitted to overextending himself to obtain some material, his only regrets involve items he failed to buy when he had the opportunity. "I have a nice list of 'should'ves,' things I should have bought and didn't." In 1968, for example, he was offered a 1638 copy of Gerarde's *Herbal,* the book that influenced many of Morris's early floral designs. "It was three hundred dollars and I didn't get it because in 1968 I was focusing only on Kelmscott Press items. Now that I'm deep into the decorative arts, I realize how nice it would be to have that book. I see it every once in a while in a catalogue, but now it goes for four thousand dollars. I don't care to have it that much. But I 'should've' bought it for three hundred dollars when I had the chance." Obviously, then, there are limits to what he will spend. "It depends on the item and whether or not we can afford it. I have never let myself get into debt. As soon as a book arrives, I write the check. I don't order something if I can't pay for it."

The Bergers' archive has cartoons for panels that are even larger than the stained-glass windows in their house. Three are exquisite designs for windows twenty-five feet high. "The only time we've seen them unrolled was when the museum in Monterey had an exhibition, and they got the fire department to bring in their ladders. The firemen climbed up and mounted them from the ceiling and hung them from the peak."

Marjorie Wynne, formerly a rare-books librarian at Yale, explained in her 1987 Sol M. Malkin lecture at Columbia University the ultimate reason for collecting. "To *use* rare books and manuscripts is to justify the process of collecting and preserving them." In the preface to a catalogue of a William Morris exhibition at the University of California, Berkeley, in 1984, Berger wrote of his "particular joy to see a growing shelf of master's theses, doctoral dissertations, monographs, catalogues, and books produced by scholars" using his collection.

A close examination indicates just how indebted these scholars are to the Bergers. Norman Kelvin, a professor of English at the City College of New York and editor of a comprehensive edition of Morris's letters, wrote how it is collectors like Berger "who locate and make accessible the material essential for scholarship." William S. Peterson's recent history of Morris and his "typographical adventure" of the 1890s, *The Kelmscott Press*, thanks the Bergers for assistance "in ways too numerous to describe," while Charles Sewter, author of a two-volume reference work on the stained-glass windows produced by the William Morris Company, had to amend his book when he learned of material in the Berger collection. "I sent Sewter two cardboard cartons of photocopies of all seven hundred drawings in the archive, and all one hundred forty of the drapery studies," Berger said. "He was totally unaware of this material, and he had to revise the book from the galleys. Can you imagine the scholarly disaster if this material had not been included?" Sewter's book, *The Stained Glass of William Morris*, lists three full columns of credits to "S. L. Berger."

The variety of these studies makes clear that the Bergers have great depth in all of Morris's activities. "You can go to many institutions that might have more in any one of them, but I don't know of any one place that will save you a lot of travel as we can," Berger said. "And that brings me to the question of where I want this collection to end up. My hope is that it can be placed in an institution that will house it all in one place for the use of scholars, so that you can look at the drawing, then go see it in the illuminated page, or in the window, or in the drawing of the tapestry, and not send the drawings over to the art department and all the socialist pamphlets over to the history department and so on. It's got to be kept in one place."

Before any decision on the future of the collection is made, however, the Bergers intend to enjoy it to the fullest. An ongoing project is to photograph windows throughout the world that were produced by Morris & Company "When I'm about eighty-eight, that's going to be my Ph.D. dissertation, to compare the sketch designs with the actual windows that were executed," Berger said. "A day doesn't go by that William Morris doesn't somehow command my full attention. He has made every day of my retirement a joy. Those books I snuck into the house twenty years ago? I'm not only cataloguing them in the computer, I've finally gotten around to reading them."

In 1985, Sanford L. Berger was the eighteenth recipient of the Sir Thomas More Medal for book collecting, the only award of its kind given in the United States. It was the brainchild of a resourceful Jesuit priest who has been called the "penniless de Medici" of San Francisco for the creative methods he has devised to build a respectable collection of rare books and manuscripts.

The Reverend William J. Monihan, S.J., was named director of special collections at the Gleeson Library of the University of San Francisco in 1947. Over the next four decades, he acquired more than forty notable collections, including half a dozen from one of the great bibliophiles of the past half century, Norman H. Strouse, the former chairman of the board of the J. Walter Thompson advertising agency, who died in January 1993.

"I got the idea for the Sir Thomas More Medal when I was visiting Europe with the Grolier Club in 1967," Father Monihan said. "I discovered that the Royal Library of Sweden gives such an award, and I was impressed by the concept. I even borrowed their motto, which translates 'private book collecting—a public benefit.' I came back and talked to our library associates and said, 'Why can't we do this?' "

He named the medal for Sir Thomas More, who was the focus of his first major acquisition; the collection now includes about a thousand items, foremost among them a volume of the martyr's writings

annotated in the hand of John Donne. The first person Father Monihan wanted to receive the honor was Norman Strouse. "In 1968 Norman was approaching retirement. We had lunch together in New York,
and he said, 'I'd like to help your library.' After we gave him the first
medal he said to me, 'When I move back out to California, I am going
to help make your library great.' And he has done exactly that. I can
immediately name at least seven or eight important collections that
are identified with his name, and not just here. There's a marvelous
Thomas Carlyle collection he gave to the University of California at
Santa Cruz when they were just getting started. And the Bancroft
Library over at Berkeley named a room for him, he has helped them so
significantly."

Though the Sir Thomas More Medal is sponsored by a university,
all but two of the first twenty-five recipients—Frederick R. Goff in
1974, then chief of rare books at the Library of Congress, and
Lawrence Clark Powell, former director of libraries at the University of
California, Los Angeles—have been private collectors. Other recipients
have included Wilmarth S. Lewis, Clifton Waller Barrett, Lessing J.
Rosenwald, Mary Hyde Eccles, William H. Scheide, Otto Schäfer of
West Germany, and Dr. Mitsuo Kodama of Japan, who represents yet
another trend in collecting. The scholar's Shakespeare and Shake-
speareana collection of more than ten thousand items, now housed at
Tokyo's Meisei University Library, ranks second only to the Folger
Library in Washington, D.C., and his Abraham Lincoln collection is
the largest and most comprehensive outside the United States.

"I am a Jesuit, and I took a vow of poverty," Father Monihan
explained in our interview. "I have no interest at all in owning anything
for myself. But I love books, and I collect them. The difference is that I
collect them for an institution, not myself. Early on I knew that I could
never have a strong library if I depended upon university funds. They
would say, 'We would love to help you, Will, but we just can't do it.' So
when I became head of the library in 1947, I went outside. I went out
to meet people. And I've been doing it ever since. I have created enthusiasm among friends to support us. Now we have an endowment fund
of some size, and I'm always getting gifts. So what you are seeing here
is largely from friends, with no university funds used at all. This is all
outside money doing this."

Father Monihan has a warm smile, silver hair, and a gentle demeanor. His blue eyes sparkle when he talks about books, and he is unshakably persuasive about his mission. The ability to get so much "outside help," as he put it, has been his gift. "I love people and they love me," he explained. "And that's all that counts." On May 9, 1993, the University of San Francisco expressed its gratitude to this kindly man who has "devoted his life to libraries and to books" by naming him the twenty-sixth recipient of the Sir Thomas More Medal.

Any literary tour of the West Coast must include visits to the Huntington Library, the Getty Museum, the William Andrews Clark Library, and the Karpeles Manuscript Library in Southern California, and certainly the Bancroft Library at the University of California, Berkeley. If the Reverend Thomas Frognall Dibdin were making such an excursion today, he would also surely stop at the Silverado Museum in Napa Valley, where the late Norman H. Strouse created a bibliographical oasis at the foot of Mount St. Helena. Set tastefully among vineyards in the state's wine country, the museum is devoted entirely to the life and works of Robert Louis Stevenson, who spent his honeymoon in 1880 in an abandoned bunkhouse at the old Silverado Mine on the slope of that very mountain.

When he was a young man living in the state of Washington, Strouse acquired a copy of John Henry Nash's fine-press edition of *The Silverado Squatters,* Stevenson's account of his stay at the mine, and later visited the site. When Strouse retired in 1968, he and his wife moved to St. Helena and immediately established the Valima Foundation with the express purpose of creating a museum that would house his distinguished collection of Robert Louis Stevenson material. Before moving into permanent quarters adjacent to the St. Helena Public Library Center in 1979, the museum occupied space in a handsome old stone building downtown. Strouse's initial gift of eight hundred items has grown over the years to more than eight thousand, many acquired directly from heirs and friends of the Stevenson family. Original letters, manuscripts, first and variant editions, sculptures, photographs, and memorabilia form the core of the collection, which is presented in a "jewel box" setting.

High spots include Stevenson's own copy of his first book, *An Inland Voyage,* the copy of *A Child's Garden of Verses* that he presented to his wife, manuscript notes for *The Master of Ballantrae,* and more than a hundred volumes from the author's library on Samoa. Artifacts include Stevenson's lead soldier collection, his working desk, and his wedding ring. Nineteenth-century paintings by such artists as Thomas Hill, H. R. Bloomer, and Virgil Williams, and sculptures by Saint-Gaudens and John Tweed—all with Stevenson associations—are on display as well.

Norman Strouse died in January 1993 after a long bout with Parkinson's disease, and was unable to grant any interviews during the final years of his life. Ellen Shaffer, a nationally respected bookwoman for more than sixty years and curator of the Silverado Museum from the time it opened in 1969 until her retirement twenty-three years later, was delighted to talk about books and collecting. She was sixty-six years old when she left her job as rare-books librarian at the Free Library of Philadelphia for a new job in California, where she had begun her life among rare books several decades earlier. She recalled these experiences one morning in her office off the main floor of the Silverado Museum.

A native of Leadville, Colorado, Miss Shaffer moved to California in 1924 and got a job working for Ernest Dawson in Los Angeles. Norman Strouse, meanwhile, had spent a lot of time on the West Coast as a senior executive with the J. Walter Thompson advertising agency. "Norman and I got to know each other sometime around 1930," Miss Shaffer said. "He was just getting started in advertising and I was working in Los Angeles. He has always haunted bookshops. I used to sell him books, though later it was mostly by mail. Then he finally got promoted over eighty vice presidents into the presidency of the biggest advertising agency in the world, and he moved to New York, where he lived for close to fifty years."

Miss Shaffer went to work in Philadelphia in 1953 and began teaching a rare-books seminar at Columbia University in New York. "I would go up once a week in the fall semester, and I would take my students over to see Norman. This was wonderful because students could get to libraries and they could get to antiquarian shops, but they couldn't get to the private collections unless somebody took them. So I used to take them in to see Norman, who always regretted never going to college and was always delighted to help students and universities in every way that he could."

Strouse gave books and money to institutions all over the United States. "When I was rare-books librarian in Philadelphia, he gave us a wonderful collection of presidential letters. I had somebody come in here one time and say, 'I'm sorry Mr. Strouse isn't around, because I'd like to tell him how much I appreciate the collection on the Panama Canal that he gave to the Stanford Public Library.' I knew him all these years, and that was the first I'd heard of that one."

For all his generosity, Miss Shaffer said Strouse manifested "a sort of a ruthless quality" in his book collecting. "He was the ultimate browser in bookshops, he could tell you every book he ever had. He could tell you where he bought it, what he paid for it. But he always established a firm personal limit. He kept his inventory at a very specific figure, and if he saw something that he really wanted, then he would give something else away. But he never let his heart run away with his head. He figured that what he was giving was going to just the right place."

Miss Shaffer was always a bibliophile, "even when I was growing up in Colorado. I used to go around hunting up these old books, and when I got home, I'd put them in a cupboard with a saucer of water and a sponge to combat the dryness, because at ten thousand feet you have a very dry atmosphere. I always cared for books."

Among the many people she met at Dawson's, Miss Shaffer had very warm memories of Estelle Doheny. "She was a wonderful person. I was in the Air Corps in the Philippines for two years during the war, and when I got out, I decided to use my G.I. Bill and go down to Mexico and study for a while. And so she gave a luncheon for me. And there was a lovely big card at each table in an envelope, a wonderful handkerchief in it, and inside my envelope was a check for one hundred dollars. And she said, very privately, 'Each month that you're in Mexico, you will get one of these checks, and I'll pray for you too.' That was the countess. She was a wonderful woman. And despite everything people said about her being an accumulator and not a collector, she knew her books. They sure found out how much she knew when the archbishop sold them off and got something like forty million dollars."

Miss Shaffer retired as curator of the Silverado Museum in November 1992, and died fourteen months later at the age of ninety.

The issue at hand was the phrase "a gentle madness." Dr. Haskell F. Norman, a San Francisco psychiatrist, wanted to know if we were talking about *actual* madness, or just a harmless hobby? He thought for a moment before framing his response with a question of his own:

"All right, why *does* one collect books?"

He paused once again, then continued at a measured pace.

"Assuming you have the means to collect, why would you collect books rather than something else? That's the big question to begin with, I think, because if you're wealthy enough, you can collect anything you want. People who collect books have a certain intellectual curiosity, I think, about books, period, and what books represent to them. The transition between collecting books as objects and collecting books for information is to differentiate, if you will, between work and play."

Dr. Norman has dedicated his professional life to understanding the quirks of human emotion. His livelihood and reputation depend on how successfully he can gauge motivation, purpose, and passion. In addition to building a successful Bay Area practice over the past forty-five years, he has assembled a major collection of books in science, medicine, and psychiatry, and now he was being asked to diagnose his own fascination for rare books. "We take madness *very* seriously in my line of work," he joked, but his point had been made. "In the first place, you have to have an interest in acquisition, and that's the psychological factor. Now, if it remains within certain bounds, just like any other part of your personality, if your personality has adapted in terms of society, that is considered reasonably normal. If it's maladapted, then you can start talking about madness."

With that, the conversation lightened up considerably because it was time to look at his books, which was the purpose of my visit to San Francisco that morning. We were meeting in the downtown offices of Dr. Norman's son, Jeremy Norman, an antiquarian bookseller who was putting the finishing touches on a two-volume catalogue of his father's collection, a project that had taken the better part of seven years to complete. Some of Dr. Norman's most impressive possessions were there for our examination.

"Every collector wants to have at least one *great* book," Dr. Norman said. "Here, I submit, is what any reasonable person would have to agree is a great book." Lying flat on a nearby Bible stand was his copy of the physician and anatomist Andreas Vesalius's *De Humani corporis fabrica,* printed at Basel in 1543, and bound in imperial purple silk velvet. Known commonly as the *Fabrica,* the landmark work provided the first detailed description of human anatomy and includes drawings of bones and the nervous system of such accuracy that Vesalius was accused by his enemies of body snatching for the evil purpose of dissection. A death sentence imposed upon the physician by the Inquisition was commuted, provided he make a pilgrimage to Jerusalem; this atonement Vesalius undertook, but he died on the return journey in 1564. What makes Dr. Norman's copy of this prize truly great is that it is the dedication copy presented by the author to the Holy Roman Emperor, Charles V.

"This book represents the beginning of the study of human anatomy in the Western world," Dr. Norman said, now glowing with pride. "And if you can believe it, I found it offered for sale in a French dealer's catalogue." One reason the book was on the open market in 1963 is because the association between Vesalius and the Holy Roman emperor had not yet been determined. "A few people thought that because the plates are colored, it was an inferior copy. The fact is that this is the only copy, so far as we can determine, that has contemporary colored plates, and that is because it was intended for presentation."

All other documented copies of the first edition have woodcut engravings, which are reproduced in black and white. "When woodcut books are colored in, they are usually very crudely done. The first tipoff was that these are not colored in any conventional sense; they were executed by a miniaturist and illuminated in silver and gold. Just look at what we're talking about," he said, and he opened the sixteenth-century folio to the title page, which pictures Vesalius performing an autopsy before an audience of horrified onlookers; it has the freshness and precision of a master painting.

Dr. Norman conducted extensive research on the history of the book before traveling to Paris to buy it. "I knew when I got there that

Vesalius had delivered a copy to Charles V, that the copy had been bound in imperial purple velvet, and that it was hand-illuminated." He also learned that the dedication copy did not remain in the emperor's possession, that it had been presented as a gift to the French ambassador, Jacques Mesnae. Where it went subsequently had remained a mystery. "When I picked up the book, I was convinced I was holding in my hands the long-lost dedication copy of the *Fabrica.*"

By the time Dr. Norman acquired his first "great book," he had been collecting actively for ten years. "It was at that point that I decided to concentrate on presentation copies and dedication copies," he said. "Because they are so hard to find, I usually acquired a regular copy of what I was looking for, and when something more interesting came along, I would either sell off the inferior copy or trade it up for something else." The search for association copies developed into an "important aspect" of his collection. "It adds an extra dimension to the experience. The books expose you to the minds of the great pioneers, but the associations give you a glimpse into their biography. Admittedly, a great deal of the pleasure comes with the knowledge that you have something unique."

Dr. Norman's copy of Robert Hooke's 1665 folio, *Micrographia,* the first book devoted entirely to descriptions of microscopic observations, is the only known presentation copy extant of the first edition. His 1628 copy of William Harvey's report on the circulation of the blood—the cornerstone of modern physiology—was once owned by Johann Friedrich Blumenbach, the founder of modern anthropology. A collection of John Locke's essays, published posthumously for the first time in 1720, bears the bookplate of Sir Isaac Newton. An 1847 dissertation on stereochemistry by Louis Pasteur, which predates his work in microbiology, was a presentation copy to the scientist's most intimate friend, Charles Chappuis. The first modern textbook on chemistry, a two-volume work by Antoine-Laurent Lavoisier published in 1789, was presented by the author to Michel Adanson, a noted natural historian whose annotations appear throughout the work. Marie Curie's doctoral dissertation on radioactivity, published in 1903, bears an inscription to Ernest Rutherford, who hypothesized the existence of the atomic nucleus. A first edition of Charles Darwin's 1839 narrative account of several "surveying voyages" made on the

Beagle was a gift to Dr. Andrew Smith, a British surgeon the author visited in South Africa.

Dr. Norman's books on the history of psychiatry, his initial focus, are without equal in private hands. "That's how it began," he said. "When I started out in 1950 or so, I wasn't really interested in first editions, I was interested in getting things that I could use, and at some point along the way I felt that since I was in training as a psychoanalyst, I should get a first edition of Freud's *Die Traumdeutung,* which is *The Interpretation of Dreams.* You have to remember that I could still read German then. So I acquired a copy of that book, and it seemed like something that was interesting, then after I bought that, I felt maybe I should collect a few others. Once I was well on my way to getting all of Freud, the idea came that maybe I should collect a few of these other people, his colleagues, and the people who came before him."

By then, Dr. Norman had accepted that he no longer was acquiring these materials because they helped him in his work. "When I started teaching psychoanalysis at the University of California, I rationalized that I was getting books I could use in my class. Of course I didn't really need first editions, copies were perfectly adequate. But I had become interested in rarity, I was interested in price, I was interested in condition. My feeling was, well, this is kind of fun. Let's see if I can collect more."

The decision to transform a good collection into a major collection was occasioned by Jeremy Norman's decision to become a professional bookseller. "It always concerned me that I had a collection of valuable books, and that there was nobody I could depend on to disperse them if anything happened to me. When my son first went to work for Warren Howell in 1964, I began to feel reassured. Once Jeremy was interested, I had more freedom to feel that it wouldn't be lost. This was such an incentive because the books are an important asset to my family. I knew very well how collections frequently get inherited by people who don't know what they are worth. This made it possible for me to continue collecting comfortably, because otherwise it wasn't fair to my wife."

With the support of his family, Dr. Norman's enthusiasm quickened. "I had made some money in investments, and I felt it was time to get a great book," he said. "The book I decided I really wanted to have was a first edition of Copernicus's *De Revolutionibus Orbium Coelestium*, and I came very close to getting the most important copy." He had learned from a London bookseller that the copy inscribed to Andreas Goldschmidt on April 20, 1543, by Rheticus, the astronomer's disciple who was responsible for the book's publication, was available from another dealer, possibly for $12,000. "I said get it for me, but by then it was already gone. It had just been bought by Harrison Horblit."

On a subsequent trip to New York, Dr. Norman met Horblit, a celebrated collector, and saw the great private collection that had inspired a major exhibition at the Grolier Club in 1958, "One Hundred Books Famous in the History of Science." "That was a great thrill for me, to see that extraordinary collection of books that he had been building since the 1940s." Horblit showed Dr. Norman the Copernicus that had almost been his, bound in blind-stamped contemporary pigskin, and many other superb titles, including Kepler's *Astronomia nova* of 1698. "We became friends, and I became a regular visitor to his home in New York. Every time I saw him, he taught me something new about bibliography. He is also the reason why I have been so concerned about getting a catalogue of my own collection produced."

The late Harrison D. Horblit—a New York carpet manufacturer who had given many wonderful things to several institutions over the years, Harvard University quite prominent among them—decided in 1974 to stop collecting and sell his library. Two elegant volumes detailing part of his library were issued by Sotheby's under the title *The Celebrated Library of Harrison D. Horblit, Esq.*, and encompassed the first two parts of what was expected to be an extended auction to take place in multiple sessions in London. Part 1 was held in June 1974, part 2 five months later. As in most major sales, the books were listed alphabetically by author; part 1 covered A through C, part 2 went from D to G, leaving nineteen letters to be catalogued and sold at later dates. For reasons never fully explained, the sales ended abruptly at the end of part 2, and no catalogues were issued for the remaining titles. Horblit gave some items to Harvard, and sold most of what remained to Hans P. Kraus.

Owen Gingerich, professor of astronomy and the history of science at the Harvard-Smithsonian Center for Astrophysics in Cambridge,

Massachusetts, was a close friend of Horblit's and was instrumental in securing a number of the items for the university. I interviewed Dr. Gingerich to talk about his extraordinary quest to document the history of every known first and second edition of Copernicus, and to talk about another book collector he had known for many years, Haven O'More. Harrison Horblit's name came up, and I asked if he could explain why the man stopped collecting so abruptly, and what he knew about the unfinished catalogue.

"What I believe happened is that Harrison stopped collecting because he just couldn't cope with the fact that the books were rising so dramatically in price. He was still collecting at the time, but he was pursuing another field, which was early photography. He had bought, sight unseen, all the early photographs acquired in the nineteenth century by Sir Thomas Phillipps; so he was actively going after other things. But he had dropped out of the history of science."

The reason Gingerich gave for the Horblit catalogue's ending at the letter G is especially ironic. "Harrison wanted the catalogue to be the monument to his collection. He also had promised a lot of institutions various favors, but because he wanted his books written up in a catalogue, he was reluctant to give them away outright. So he consigned his library to Sotheby's, and they agreed to prepare a beautiful series of catalogues. What Harrison then proceeded to do was give a number of institutions a lot of money to bid on his books. He urged them to go through John Fleming, with the result that John bought nearly half of the books in the first part of the sale. Well, when this story got out and spread around, it created quite a stir, because a lot of people felt Harrison really shouldn't be handing out money to people so they could buy books at his own auction. So along came the second part of the sale, and all the other dealers deliberately sat on their hands. They bought for their customers, but they refused to buy for stock. The second sale flopped so badly that Sotheby's said, 'We can't have this.' As I understand it, there was some sort of falling out, and Harrison took back the rest of his books and sold most of them to Hans Kraus. And that is why there are only two catalogues, going from A to C and D to G, and why H through the rest of the alphabet never appeared."

Appearing as a frontispiece to part 1 of the Horblit catalogue is a full-color photo of Lot 240, a large folio bound in blind-stamped contemporary pigskin, dated 1543 with the initials AG on the cover. "This superb presentation copy of the first edition is without doubt the most important copy extant of one of the greatest landmarks in the history of scientific thought," the caption reads, and in the preface to the catalogue is a further discussion of the same item and its place in the Horblit Library: "The pinnacle of the collection is, of course, the magnificent presentation copy of Copernicus's *De Revolutionibus*, 1543, which has the closest associations with the great astronomer's most intimate circle." The book was sold for $100,000 to Lew David Feldman and the House of El Dieff, where it passed into the hands of Haven O'More; it was sold in 1989 at the Garden Ltd. auction for $473,000 to an Italian dealer.

For Dr. Norman it was the "great book" that got away. But unlike Horblit, he did get a complete catalogue of his collection, and that means so much more. "Harrison built one of the great libraries of our time, and there is no complete record available of what he put together," Dr. Norman said. "I have always considered that a great tragedy." The preparation of his own catalogue, as a consequence, became a "very significant" project, "and not just for what it means to me personally, but because of the information it contains. Catalogues are essential tools in bibliography, and no science catalogue has ever been produced that has all the descriptions and the detail we have put in ours."

Unlike Horblit, Dr. Norman was "blessed" by having a son actively involved in the rare-book trade. When Jeremy was establishing his own company in 1970, Dr. Norman offered to help. "We sort of had an agreement" he said. "I lent him books for his business with the idea that he would one day catalogue my library."

Jeremy Norman acknowledged that his own love for books developed at an early age, largely due to the example set by his father. In gratitude, he was pleased to honor his father with a catalogue. The project occupied seven years of "almost continuous" attention by Jeremy Norman and Diana H. Hook, a graduate of the Columbia University School of Library Service who was hired in 1984 to work on the catalogue. Printed on acid-free paper and bound durably in three-piece red and black cloth, *The Haskell F. Norman Library of Science and Medicine* was published in 1992 in two volumes and includes full descriptions of 2,597 works. There are more than three hundred illustrations, thirty-two of them, including the plate from the Vesalius dedication copy, in color.

Completing the catalogue also means that for all intents and purposes the collection is finished. "I still would very much like to have a Copernicus; but once you issue the catalogue of your collection, it all becomes a moot point, because you can't put any more in it. And on that account, I have no plans to compile an addendum."

As for the future of his library, Dr. Norman said, with evident relief, "I am not going to decide that. Whatever is decided will be by a unanimous vote of my family. It probably either will be dispersed at auction or it could be sold en bloc, depending on whatever arrangement they want to make. But I thought about this very seriously, and I just decided that if I'm gone, what difference does it make if they have a wing somewhere named for me? I will let my heirs choose what they want to do with the collection. Maybe some will keep books, maybe some will take money. It's their decision." He paused for a moment, then added, "The catalogue will be sufficient to satisfy my ego."

13

The Blumberg Collection

"I really don't know why you want to come out here," FBI Special Agent W. Dennis Aiken said with an edge of exasperation. "All you're going to see is seven rooms stacked to the ceiling with old books." Perhaps he was right; maybe it was foolish to fly all the way to Omaha for what would be no more than twenty minutes inside a secret government warehouse. But the Blumberg collection was about to be dissolved, and if I was going to see these nineteen tons of books together in one place, I had to do it soon. Aiken relented, and agreed to see me the following week.

Nine months earlier, as his trial in the United States District Court for the Southern District of Iowa reached the halfway point, Stephen Carrie Blumberg had invited me to spend a Saturday with him in Ottumwa, the city where he had been arrested by a squad of federal agents. We spent nine hours together, and for much of that time he talked passionately about why he had looted scores of libraries and institutions throughout North America during two decades of uncontrollable collecting. "You are about to see the skeleton of my life," he said as we walked toward the big brick house on North Jefferson Street. "Twenty years' worth of work and knowledge and accumulation," he said bitterly, "and it's stripped bare. It's just a shell."

Two hours after arriving in Nebraska, I took a taxi to a McDonald's off Interstate 80 and waited by the flagpole as Aiken had instructed. After picking me up, he drove to a nondescript brick building with opaque windows and the number 8631F in the front. No other journalist had been admitted to the warehouse, and its whereabouts had been hidden from everyone except the professional librarians who had helped identify the stolen books. Inside, past a bank of glowing security devices, Jerry Tucker, an agent who had been working full time on the case for nineteen months, was typing data into a computer terminal. Because Blumberg had removed identifying marks from most of the books, determining who owned what had caused monumental problems. Tucker's job turned out to be nothing less than forensic bibliography, and he had become very good at it. The delicate way Tucker handled each volume suggested as well that he had become a bibliophile in his own right. "Isn't *this* something," he said quietly as he picked up a miniature book "about the size of a dime" taken from Claremont College outside Los Angeles. He pointed with special admiration to a large atlas in a green clamshell box stolen from the University of Southern California, and he marveled at the decorated leather spines of some eighteenth-century books that soon would be returning to Connecticut.

As Aiken had said, the building was stacked top to bottom with books, though the most striking image was not one of mass, but of neatly stenciled signs secured to the 3,500 feet of plain metal shelving the government had purchased for the unprecedented task. I scribbled some of the names in my notebook: University of California at Los Angeles, University of California at Riverside, Duke University, Harvard University, University of Minnesota, Colorado College, University of Cincinnati, University of New Mexico, Connecticut State Library, University of Oregon, Wisconsin State Historical Society, Washington State University, University of Southern California, Dartmouth College, Zamorano Club, University of Michigan, University of Wisconsin, Wayne State University.

"Coast to coast," Jerry Tucker said. Blumberg had taken about 23,600 books from 268 libraries in forty-five states, two Canadian provinces, and the District of Columbia. Aiken said that a forty-foot tractor-trailer was rented from North American Van Lines to haul the books from Ottumwa to Omaha, and another was needed to remove a mass of seized antiques. "None of us knew how big this was going to be until the day we walked into that house," he said. "Eight hundred and seventy-nine cardboard packing boxes. It took seventeen people two days to get them all out of there. We had twenty-three thousand books, and we had no earthly idea where any of them came from."

Making the dilemma doubly difficult was that very few of the books had ever been known to be missing. "Every institution we called, without exception, either had no idea what they lost, or didn't understand the extent of their losses," Aiken said. "I couldn't tell you how many people came in here and said the very same thing: 'I know the shelf this is supposed to be on.'"

Roger E. Stoddard, the curator of rare books at the Houghton Library of Harvard University, spoke for many of his colleagues when he explained the problem institutions face. "We have twelve and a half million books at Harvard. As a practical matter, you discover that a book is missing when someone wants it, because until you check your records and determine that a book is not signed out, you have no reason to suspect it has been stolen. Harvard alone has one hundred separate libraries. There is no way to monitor every book in a large institution and provide access for students at the same time. That is why libraries are such vulnerable places."

Though Blumberg removed most traces of identification from the volumes, he kept a selection of bookplates in several scrapbooks, a little collection of mementos he had gathered during his travels. "It basically was a list of the libraries where he had been," Aiken said. "What it gave us was a place to start. It told us whom we had to start calling." In his interview with me, Blumberg confirmed that he had kept bookplates as souvenirs, though he said he did not steal from all the institutions represented in the scrapbooks. "That became a collection in its own right. You'll see there's a bookplate in there from the New York Public Library; I have never been in the New York Public Library."

Because these crimes went largely unnoticed, Blumberg was not captured because of any alarm that had been sounded throughout the country. Though he had been detained at the University of California at Riverside in 1988 after being arrested with burglary tools in his possession, and though an alert security officer at Washington State University had matched Blumberg's fingerprints with those of an alias he was using and had passed the information along to the authorities, Blumberg's arrest in Ottumwa at two A.M. on March 20, 1990, came after Kenneth J. Rhodes, a friend of Blumberg's of fifteen years, turned the book thief in for a $56,000 bounty negotiated with the Justice Department.

Coincidentally, Stephen Blumberg's telephone call to my room that Saturday morning during his trial came a half hour after I had spotted Rhodes in the hotel lobby and had asked him for an interview. "What's in it for me?" he wanted to know. Nothing, I said, just an opportunity to give a more balanced version of his story. Rhodes had admitted during pretrial proceedings to extensive criminal activity, including a contract offer he received once from drug dealers to kill a school official in California, and he had described three other occasions where he worked as a paid government informant. "If all I have to go on is your testimony," I told him, "you come out looking like a pretty bad guy." Rhodes squared his shoulders and squinted his eyes. "We don't need to talk," he said evenly. "I *am* a bad guy."

The evening before our hotel-lobby encounter, though, the solidly built Rhodes had been all charm. He had dined in the hotel atrium with a group of university librarians who had testified earlier in the day, and he was the center of attention. Dressed smartly in a salt-and-pepper sports jacket and sipping appreciatively from a straight-up martini, he was an able conversationalist, the kind of amusing rogue rarely met in faculty clubs. He even made a flourish about signing for the check, leading his table companions to assume that dinner and drinks were on Kenny Rhodes, when in fact the United States government was covering its star witness's expenses.

Despite his checkered past, Rhodes provided some of the most damaging testimony against Stephen Blumberg. Yes, Rhodes admitted, he had committed felonies, he had been involved in drug dealing, he had in the past bartered information with federal agencies for money and immunity. But he also described a friendship with Blumberg that went back to the mid-1970s, and his detailed accounts of their nomadic adventures were unshakable. Where appropriate, Rhodes also paid tribute to the defendant's expertise.

"Was Mr. Blumberg, from your conversations, knowledgeable, fairly knowledgeable, about antiques and stained glass?" Assistant United States Attorney Linda R. Reade asked him. "Expert," Rhodes replied, "absolutely one of the tops in the country." During cross-examination, he went further. "He could identify any window, what time period it was from," as well as "tell you what city it was from" and "what studio made it." Blumberg, he marveled, "was just walking knowledge and information." Later, he even admitted to admiring the book thief's independence, made possible by a generous family trust that gave him about $72,000 a year in unencumbered funds for living expenses. "At one point I was quite envious of him. He had a very carefree life. He could come and go. He could travel anywhere he wanted at any time and do anything he wanted to do, and he chose to do what he wanted to do."

Rhodes described numerous exploits: driving from Detroit to Cincinnati, from Cincinnati to Blumberg's hometown of St. Paul, out again to the Southwest and Texas, often spending several months on the road. Detained once by snow in Ohio, "Stephen managed to get into the library and obtain some books" at the University of Cincinnati. Their travels usually featured excursions into abandoned buildings to gather cast-iron gates, stained-glass windows, chimney pots, doorknobs. On one trip they spent about a week in Houston, "and Stephen would make a nightly run over to Rice University, because they didn't have an alarm system in their libraries, and he'd go over every night for about a week and bring out as many books as he could."

Rhodes said Blumberg gained access to Rice by claiming he was a scholar doing research; once he was alone with the books he had selected, he would prepare them for removal. "He'd take the card pocket out, and he would also take the library sticker off the inside of the binding. He'd search for any little metal alarm devices. And he'd sand the edges of the page off [to eradicate library stamp marks], and he'd restaple [the pages] and then reglue. He had a little container of glue and a razor blade, and he'd cut out a page that might be embossed with 'Rice University' on it, hide that in his briefcase and do that to each book, and it would take a considerable amount of time. He would actually have to physically lick the bookplate until the glue loosened and he could peel it off. And then he'd put the new [bookplate] on and out through the security he'd go."

When this particular disclosure was reported by the Associated Press the following day, officials at Rice University said that they had no knowledge of stolen books, and that an inventory would be undertaken immediately. "This is news to me," Associate University Librarian Jennifer Cargill told the *Houston Post*. She acknowledged that there had been no alarms in the general stacks during the period of Blumberg's admitted thefts. "I was unaware that we were one of the sites," Cargill said, "and I'm interested in learning more about this." In due course she would learn that one of Blumberg's most prized acquisitions—a beautiful sixteenth-century volume known as the Bishop's Bible—had come from Rice.

Rhodes said that the agenda was similar everywhere they went. Sometimes Blumberg would wear an oversized coat with large pockets sewn inside to hide books; other times, when larger removals were planned, he would go in after hours. Rhodes described a week they spent in Tucson. Every night Blumberg would go over to the University of Arizona library, find the books he wanted, lick stickers off the pastedowns, and use sandpaper to remove embossed stamp marks off the edges. Because there were security systems, Blumberg had to be more careful.

"So he would go in at different hours," Rhodes explained. "I would have to come pick him up." And when Rhodes arrived there would be so many books that Blumberg would have to make several trips inside, each entry timed to coincide with the point when guards were being relieved. "He'd go in during one shift, leave, hide some books in the bushes and go back in and get some more books and come back out, and I was to pick him up at a certain spot at a certain time every night, which I did."

From Arizona they moved through a "dozen different states," perpetually gathering antiques, perpetually stealing books. "We crossed back through Texas, Louisiana, and we collected things all the way coming up through the South, through Kentucky, Tennessee. We went to Nashville, Knoxville, Memphis, Louisville." Rhodes said that Blumberg always kept an eye out for "slum areas" with empty and boarded-up houses where they could go in and take all the hardware, stained glass, and fixtures.

Some of the house fixtures would be sold to dealers, and many items would be stored in Cincinnati or shipped back by United Parcel Service to the Twin Cities, where other friends placed the booty in a leased warehouse. "We'd sell it to some big buyers, people that were restoring old buildings, you know, restaurants and things of that nature." And in the evenings, invariably, Blumberg went out alone to the libraries. "Every time he came back, he had books," Rhodes said, and when Blumberg returned to whatever inexpensive motel they had rented, he would spend much of the night customizing his newest trophies. "He'd clean them up again, constantly licking the books until he made himself sick," working to get the stickers off and "make them look like normal books." Inside each volume he would write a little code in pencil to suggest they had been bought from secondhand dealers at prices of "anywhere from five cents to a dollar."

After going on several of these trips, one of which lasted for six months, Rhodes said he got a job in 1978 repairing stained-glass windows with a Michigan antiques dealer, while Blumberg continued on his travels, always going to Texas, but alternating the routes he took so he could visit different sections of the country. Rhodes said they remained in touch over the next two years, and Blumberg continually boasted about the "universities he went into and what books he had got." Reade wanted to know if Blumberg had formulated any clear ideas in advance, and whether he was familiar with what he was stealing. "He did extensive research on what books were rare and valuable and that he wanted," Rhodes said, "and if it was a collection or a whole run, he'd spend extra time in that city, that town, and keep going back because you couldn't get the whole set of books out at one time."

About 1980, Rhodes said, Blumberg looked him up in Kalamazoo and brought him up to date on his activities. Blumberg had continued his pattern of "traveling, buying, selling, stealing, and acquiring books at libraries." Reade asked how Blumberg got into areas that were off-limits to all outsiders, including qualified researchers. "There were a dozen different ways that he described," Rhodes answered, "from pushing up a panel from one side of the wall, wherever he could crawl through over the ceiling, get through ductwork. There was a steel grating around one rare-book section, but he said whoever built it didn't do a very good job because they left six or eight inches from the ceiling, and he could climb up. It would be like venting material. He could climb up the metal grating and slip over it, and get in and pick much finer, better, higher-quality, more expensive, rarer books."

Rhodes said Blumberg showed him keys that allowed access to other libraries. "He would wait until the staff left, and he's quite, quite clever with locks, and I consider him a locksmith, and he would pick some locks and get in and get into the librarian's room and go through their key chains, their key rings. If he could find the key that would fit [the secure book storage area], he would slip it off and go get a copy of it made, and the next day he would slip the original key back on the key ring, and then he would have his own passkey." Reade entered into evidence several dozen keys found in Blumberg's house that fit locks in many of the institutions that were robbed.

Rhodes said the plunder continued through much of the 1980s, though he and Blumberg lost contact once again. The next time they spoke, Blumberg reported that he had been spending a lot of time on the West Coast. "He always wanted to go out there because of the universities, and he finally got out there and fell in love with the 'easy pickings,' as he called it, in California." Reade asked Rhodes to explain that phrase. "He said he would get pickup-truck loads of books out of there," so many that he had to get a larger vehicle. Blumberg was able to take so many "because he could pick the locks" to "certain floors," and because he knew how to "stop an elevator on any floor, and most people couldn't do that, couldn't stop on the rare-book floors." Often, Blumberg would "go in after hours and get book carts and pick dozens and dozens of rare books and put them in the elevator, take them down and box them up and set them on the shipping dock and come back and pick them up later." Because there were so many books, help was necessary to load the truck, and Rhodes said Blumberg enlisted the assistance of several young men.

In 1988, Blumberg was apprehended in a restricted area of the University of California at Riverside library. Along with the identity card of a University of Minnesota faculty member, Blumberg was caught carrying a bag of dental picks, sandpaper, and other tools, along with a pouch containing about a pound of gold. Blumberg later told Rhodes that in the moments before his arrest, he frantically "ate a rubber stamp" that was with his burglary equipment. Another witness, Brian Teeuwe, also recalled the incident with the rubber-stamp, which said "University of Minnesota." While posing as a professor from the University of Minnesota, Matthew McGue, Blumberg often used the stamp on targeted books to suggest that he had brought them in with him. I asked Blumberg if he in fact ate a rubber stamp at Riverside. He said he did, and I asked why. "How else was I supposed to get rid of it?" he answered.

Teeuwe testified that he went to the University of Southern California about seven times and helped Blumberg remove books. "Stephen would go into the special-collections room, which was on the seventh floor, and he would pick out the books that he wanted and then bring them down to the sixth floor, where there was a study area; and he would use his razor blades, sandpaper, and he would even lick to get the catalog pockets out of the book to remove the markings and put his own in. Then I would take the books out of the library." Teeuwe said that Blumberg joked about "how easy" it was to remove books from Claremont College and that he bragged how he had been to "almost every university in the country."

At Riverside, however, Blumberg's mood changed from amusement to fear. He had been caught, and even though he was using an alias, he was frightened about the possible consequences. Charged with trespassing, he was fingerprinted, released on $100 bond, and given a date to appear on the misdemeanor charge. He hired a lawyer, pled guilty to the misdemeanor, and was given three years' probation. Shaken by the incident, he gathered up whatever books he had stored in California, returned to Minnesota, and stopped raiding libraries for about two years. Meanwhile, he found a house in Iowa—it was in the middle of the country and "on the way to Texas," he explained to me later—and bought it for $16,000 cash.

Shortly after Blumberg moved to Ottumwa in 1989, Rhodes contacted his old traveling buddy and asked if he could come live with him. Blumberg agreed. Once there, Rhodes started gathering information that documented the book thefts, then initiated discussions with the FBI. He said he was paid $56,000 by the government for his information, and under cross-examination admitted that he tried to get more money from various universities in the form of a 10 percent "finder's fee." Though the issue of what the books were worth came up frequently during the trial, an early figure suggested the value might be as high as $20 million. Rhodes said he used that figure in his discussions, and was disappointed when he received no more money.

Rhodes described how Blumberg carried out his thefts, but it was the victims—in this instance a succession of librarians and curators from all over the country—who explained what the thefts meant to their institutions. At the University of Washington the loss of crucial papers relating to settlement of the Southwest was discovered when librarians were asked by the State Department to furnish material for an exhibition that was being planned in Mexico. Fraser Cocks, the curator of special collections at the University of Oregon, told how twenty linear feet of manuscript material was discovered missing in January 1987 when a donor's relative asked to see a particular item. All of the papers related to the early years of settlement and statehood in Oregon, roughly spanning the period from the early 1840s through the late 1870s, were gone.

"It was an enormous loss," Cocks said, noting that a prominent autograph dealer, Kenneth Rendell of Massachusetts, New York, and Beverly Hills, had placed a value of $645,940 on the material. Some thirty-six boxes finally were determined to have been taken, and they included the papers of several historic Oregon pioneers. Cocks said the documents were kept in a secure area of the special collections department, which occupies the fourth, fifth, and sixth floors of the university library; researchers are allowed to see only a few documents at a time. He stressed that access to the rooms is granted only to staff members and is possible only with keys.

"These materials constitute the information from which histories are written," Cocks told the jury. "Histories don't just appear. The people who write them get their insights from archives like this." Cocks began his job at the University of Oregon in 1990, just a few weeks before Blumberg's arrest. "This whole thing fell in my lap the minute I got here," he said several months after the trial. "I have no doubt that there was a time back then when Stephen Blumberg knew more about my collection than I did."

Susan E. Allen, the head of special collections for the six Claremont Colleges located in Claremont, California, described the disappearance of 684 books estimated by Los Angeles book dealer Glen Dawson to have a total value of $644,038, including several unusually scarce items of Western Americana. She also explained the meaning of the word *incunabula* for the Iowa jury, using as a visual aide the exquisite Nuremberg Chronicle, printed by Hartmann Schedel, and bound in ivory calfskin, that Blumberg had taken from the Claremont collection. "It is the cradle period of printing," she said, "which means any book printed between 1450 and 1500." Allen held the folio up for the jury to see and pointed out that Schedel's book was the last major history of the world that failed to account for the discovery of the New World; it first went to press in 1493. Among its six hundred illustrations, she added, were a few executed by Albrecht Dürer when he was a teenager. Her feeling for the objects she described was palpable. "I could go on forever," she said finally, "but I think that's probably enough."

During a short recess, a group of courthouse employees were allowed to look at some of the rare books that had been brought in as exhibits. Don C. Nickerson, one of Blumberg's lawyers, was standing by the evidence table, holding a cup of coffee, when someone cautioned him to be careful not to spill anything on any of the books. "God," he said in mock horror, looking quickly over at the defense table, "Stephen will kill me." Blumberg had not left the courtroom and was watching intently from his chair at the table. During our drive to Ottumwa the next day, I asked Blumberg what he felt as he watched these people flip through the pages of "his" books. "I wanted to go over and explain what they were looking at," he said, and insisted that he had come to terms with the "loss" several months earlier when he visited the warehouse in Nebraska during pretrial proceedings. "I said good-bye to the books in Omaha."

After the recess, Lynne Newell, director of preservation for the Connecticut State Library, explained that all materials under her supervision are kept in vaults like bank vaults, "one of which is six stories high." She recalled being asked by the FBI if anything from the noncirculating collection of state archives was missing. "They showed me some bookplates, which I identified as ours." Most of the 271 items later determined to be theirs had been shelved "in a vault specifically built to hold them." One of the books, an octavo titled *A Confession of Faith*, published in 1710, is the state library's own copy of the first book published in Connecticut. Another was the first book of poetry published in the state. The total value was estimated by Glen Dawson at $225,280, though Newell said, "We believe they are worth more than that, especially in New England."

As devastating as that discovery was, though, the image of an Oregon scholar learning that irreplaceable materials deposited in a secure archive by her family in 1960 were nowhere to be found was intriguing, because in this instance, a person's life—not just the raw fabric of history—had been tampered with by a book thief. Shannon Applegate's name was never mentioned at the Blumberg trial, but when we talked many months afterward, she recalled what happened on January 2, 1988, when she decided to celebrate the completion of a book that had taken her twenty years to write.

Her book, published by William Morrow in 1988, is titled *Skookum: An Oregon Primer of a Family's History and Lore*. The family Shannon Applegate wrote about is her own, and the title refers to a Chinook word used by an old chief to describe her descendants when they asked if they could settle in the Yancola Valley. "The chief said they were 'skookum, hia skookum,' which means very full of spirit," the great-great-granddaughter of Charles and Melinda Applegate said. "The letters in the Oliver Cromwell Applegate Collection represented the Charles Applegate branch, the Lindsey Applegate branch, and the Jesse Applegate branch, these three families, three brothers who married two sisters, and came to Oregon" in the nineteenth century. Jesse Applegate "led the major part of the 1843 migration, which was the first migration into the state, and tripled the population of settlers overnight. So this is really significant material."

Because reliable typescripts were available, Applegate was able to conduct her research without having to handle the original documents. "These things belong to everyone and you do not touch them if you can avoid it," she said. "Many of the Applegate letters have exquisite drawings in their margins, things like bear traps from the Siskeel Mountains. We're not just talking about a few letters, we're talking about this extraordinary collection. These materials have a real richness."

Research for *Skookum* began in 1967, was interrupted periodically by the birth of several children, and continued with unbroken enthusiasm thereafter. "People didn't think I was ever going to finish, but in

1987, it was done, and there I was at last, in the library, going over the card catalog to make sure all my citations were in order." Accompanied by her cousin Susan Applegate, an artist who designed the book jacket for *Skookum*, Shannon suggested a celebration. "We had gone through this as cousins, so it seemed there had to be some way to observe this journey, which in some ways felt every bit as long as going across the country in a covered wagon." She decided to mark the moment by calling for the Webfoot Diary, a journal named for the early settlers of Oregon who had worked in the southern gold mines. "I had made extensive use of this material in my book," she said, "but I had never actually held it in my hands."

Hilary Cummings, then the curator of manuscripts at the University of Oregon, went off to get the diary. "Well, we waited and we waited and we waited. About forty-five minutes went by, and then I just said, 'This is ridiculous, what are they doing, rewriting it?' Finally, Hilary came out, with this sort of ashen face, and this worried look, and she mumbled, 'I have to apologize, Ms. Applegate, we are unable to lay our hands on the document at this time.' Well, I live in Roseburg, it takes me an hour and a half to get to the library. So I said, 'Fine. But I certainly will be asking you the next time I come in to see it.' I wasn't anxious at this point, I was annoyed. If someone had told me at that moment the diary was missing, I would have found it unbelievable."

On January 22, Susan Applegate made an urgent telephone call to her cousin in Roseburg. "My God, Shannon," she shouted. "Have you seen the *Register-Guard?*" On the front page of the Eugene newspaper that morning was a major story under a four-column headline in forty-eight-point type: "UO Documents Missing." A "slice of Oregon's history" was gone, the article declared: "Thousands of letters, diaries, Indian treaties, railroad records and stock certificates disappeared from the Special Collections section of the University of Oregon Library sometime last fall, library officials revealed Thursday."

Though the theft had been reported three weeks earlier—in fact, right after Shannon Applegate asked to see the Webfoot Diary—the police had delayed public disclosure in the hope that the robber would return for more material. A sidebar to the main story outlined the extent of the losses. "This is how I found out," Shannon Applegate said. "I was flabbergasted. Susan and I just cried over the telephone. I cannot tell you how personal this was. As I look back, I really did go through all this self-denial with that material, and here it had just disappeared, and nobody had even noticed that it was gone. I felt physically sick."

On April 23, 1988, another story in the Eugene *Register-Guard* raised a flurry of hope with the report that a man had been arrested inside a special collections room at the University of California at Riverside, and that he was a "strong suspect" in a number of other library thefts, including the one reported two months earlier at the University of Oregon. Officials from the University of Oregon, the Claremont Colleges, and Washington State University were said to be "requesting information" about the Riverside arrest. But the man claiming to be Matthew McGue had been released on his own recognizance; the promising lead hit a dead-end when the suspect was allowed to go free.

In Oregon, meanwhile, sadness turned to outrage, and outrage led to suspicion. "There was this sense of powerlessness," Applegate recalled. "But I was also furious with the university. I felt there had been an incredible betrayal. Scholars aren't even allowed inside those special collections stacks. It seemed that it had to be an inside job. We all agreed that was the only way it could have happened. How was it possible to remove what they said amounted to a truckload of documents?"

Several university employees were questioned, even a member of the Applegate family was suspected. Two years went by and nothing happened. On March 21, 1990, Applegate was seated in an airplane, preparing to take off on a regional flight, when she glanced at the front page of a *Register-Guard* lying in the lap of a passenger in the next seat. Once again, there was a large headline: "Man Arrested in Theft of Rare UO Books." Though information was still fragmentary, the Applegate family collection was among thousands of items that had been recovered in a small Iowa community by the FBI.

Stephen Blumberg picked me up in front of the Embassy Suites Hotel. His trial was at the halfway point, court was in recess for the weekend, and he remained free on a $50,000 bail, provided he did not travel outside the state of Iowa without his attorney, or "enter any museum or library." A day trip to Ottumwa would not violate any of these restrictions.

I had been talking with Blumberg throughout the trial, though unlike other journalists who asked how he felt about his prospects, I talked about books. "I'll bet you and I are the only people in this building who know anything about points," he quipped during one recess, referring to the various ways rare books are identified. "I wish you could have seen the incunabula I had," he said another time as we paced through the second-floor corridor. I gave him my card, told him where I was staying, and expressed the hope that we could get together sometime before the trial ended.

When Blumberg called that Saturday morning, most of the prosecution's case had been heard. I had listened to Kenny Rhodes, Brian Teeuwe, Dwaine G. Olson, Kenneth Broden, and Howard Bergstrom, and a parade of librarians and curators who told of how their institutions had been ransacked. The defense lawyers had yet to present their case but had already made known that the prosecution's facts were correct. There was no doubt that Blumberg had committed the crimes. The only question was why.

Fifteen minutes after Blumberg's telephone call, we were driving past the five-domed capitol building into East Des Moines, a little side trip to a run-down section of town before we headed for Ottumwa. We visited for about a half hour with a middle-aged woman named Gerry Madison and an extended family of nine young men and women, most of whom were watching wrestling matches on television when we arrived. Later he told me he had met one of the young men "under the bridge," a place where many of the area's homeless residents congregate. "These are my kind of people," he explained.

Once outside the city, Blumberg's mood improved, but a sense of gloom was still apparent. Even though his defense would begin in a few days, acquittal was not an option available to the jury. The verdict would be either guilty or not guilty by reason of insanity. In the latter case, Blumberg would be remanded to the custody of Judge Harold D. Vietor, who would commit him to a mental-health facility.

For that strategy to succeed, the defense had to demonstrate that Blumberg was consumed by delusional fantasies. While Blumberg seemed totally sincere about the need to protect fragile American artifacts from destruction, he wanted no part of being declared insane. "It's Catch-22," he said. "If I lose, I wind up in prison. If I win, I wind up in the grin bin, and they can keep you in there for the rest of your life. If I win, then that also means I'm crazy and that I'm a danger to society. So to tell you the truth, I'd rather be locked up, do my time, and get out. What's victory here for me? What's defeat? It doesn't look good either way."

Regardless of the outcome, *United States vs. Steven* [Stephen] *Carrie Blumberg* was unique in that it marked the only time a "not guilty by reason of insanity" defense has ever been used in an American court to explain the consequences of criminal bibliomania.

"Let's talk about books," I said finally. "Tell me about the Blumberg Collection."

Blumberg confirmed what the librarians had made clear the day before, that he had a special passion for Americana. That focus developed because he wanted to know more about the antiques he had been gathering for most of his life. "It started as a reference library," he explained. "Generally, I knew about a book before I acquired it. I knew its significance, and it didn't matter if it was in a library or at the bottom of a box in a junk store. I knew instantly what it was and how it could help me." He developed a "want list" but kept his desiderata "pretty much" in his head. "Some things I'd write down, but very little, because I knew what I wanted. I also saw the books as a form of security in that they were a form of knowledge, or a form of art, to be enjoyed."

Though reluctant to describe the specific methods he used to get into libraries, Blumberg did say that he often found himself crawling through ventilation ducts and squirming over partitions to penetrate secure areas. "I almost got crushed to death once out in California," he said. "There was an elevator they used in one of the colleges to haul books back and forth, and I was inside the shaft climbing up. I didn't think anybody was still in the building, but about halfway up there I heard a terrific noise, and above me I saw this thing coming straight down. I was able to squeeze myself into one of the nooks they have at each of the floors where the elevator stops, but it was pretty tight."

Despite the close calls, Blumberg said he never had much fear for his safety. "I didn't figure the librarians were going to shoot me or anything, but there were some tense moments. I was consumed by the passion to collect. Seeing something like the Miguel Costansó diary they had in court yesterday was enough to take my mind off everything else. I'd be so wrapped up in that, I wouldn't really think about the whys or the wheres of what else was happening."

Blumberg raised the question of respect several times while we were together. Not only does he crave recognition as the greatest book thief of the twentieth century, he wants to be recognized for his taste in books. At one point, he jokingly suggested that "one day when all this is gone and forgotten" he might like to give a talk at the Grolier Club in New York about the "true hazards" of book collecting. And he was pleased when he learned that Glen Dawson, the Los Angeles dealer who appraised the cache for the government, had said that "other than the fact that I don't like 'ex libris' books [books that bear traces of prior library ownership], it was an excellent collection of Americana."

Curiously, Blumberg does not entirely agree with librarians who have complained about their security systems. "I never saw it so much as a matter of poor security. To me it was a matter of opportunity. I'm not bragging or anything, but I'm pretty ingenious with resources, if you know what I mean. If one way isn't amenable, I can figure out three or four other ways to get inside."

On that, at least, Special Agent Aiken is in complete agreement with Blumberg. "My conviction is that Steve Blumberg was going to get this stuff no matter what he had to do. He did nighttime burglaries. He defeated sophisticated alarm systems. He threw books out windows. He knew what was going on in the life of the libraries, and he picked their weakest moments. I suppose if these people were willing to dig a fifty-foot hole in the ground and encase everything in concrete, he might not have been able to get in, but I wouldn't bet on that either. This is a very clever man. Book theft was his life."

The consequential moment in Blumberg's "growth" as a collector did not come in an elevator shaft or a ventilation tube, but through a stroke of happenstance. One day in 1980, while leaving the University of Minnesota library, a bright plastic card on the circulation desk caught his eye. "It was instantaneous," he said. "I saw that, and I thought, 'You know, I understand how these things are made,' and it was in my pocket."

He had just stolen the identification card of an associate professor of psychology named Matthew McGue. As an added stroke of luck, McGue bore a distinct similarity to Stephen Blumberg. "But I wanted to do this right. I wanted to get all the proper identification, and I knew I couldn't do it in Minneapolis, it was too close to my own home. So I went out to California and got established there. I got a driver's license and other things."

One of the prosecution's most dramatic witnesses was Matthew McGue, who identified a faculty identification card entered into evidence as being his, and another that was not, even though it carried his name; the photograph on the bogus ID pictured Stephen Blumberg. McGue described the difficulties he had been through, as time after time he was queried about research he was supposed to be doing. He said that he had never had a California driver's license, that he had never been arrested in Riverside, and that he had never applied for reading privileges at Boston University, Harvard University, the Clements Library at the University of Michigan, or the Ohio Historical Society. Looking at another card that had his name on it, he declared, "This is accurate in every way. But it is not mine."

By assuming McGue's professional persona, Blumberg was able to elevate the level of his collecting. Kenny Rhodes testified that up to that point Blumberg had been gathering material from the general stacks. Now, by impersonating a legitimate academician, "Professor McGue," he had access to the buildings where special collections are kept, and he relished the role he was able to play. Whenever a "research trip" was planned, he washed, wore eccentric but presentable clothes, and carried a briefcase. Once inside the libraries, he spoke with authority to presumed peers. "I went around to schools, and I was accepted. Even though I've done a lot of reading, I barely made it through high school. All my education has come from books and talking to people and observing what's around me, and speculating and analyzing. Here I was, a visiting professor, there to do research, a scholar. And they accepted me."

The Oregon manuscript cache notwithstanding, Blumberg said he was primarily interested in printed books: "The truth is that I touched very lightly on manuscripts." He took the archive because he recognized an opportunity when he saw one. "They were there," he said simply. "But mainly, my general interests were architecture and views of cities and American history."

So why, then, did he take a Nuremberg Chronicle?

"Well, okay, so I got into printing history too, and I managed to put together a collection of one hundred incunabula in just three years. So I suppose those were books I enjoyed because they were important artifacts." He thought about that for a moment, laughed, and added, "That's quite an impressive assemblage of incunabula being brought together in the late twentieth century, don't you think?"

The scope of Blumberg's foraging came into sharper focus when we arrived at the Ottumwa house. No books had been shelved on the first floor, which Blumberg kept for an old man from Cincinnati named Jim Hall whom he brought in to live with him. Upstairs, however, were nine rooms, all stacked high with plain pine boards. Because the ceilings were thirteen feet high, there was room for eleven shelves on most of the walls. FBI evidence tags were still stuck here and there, but otherwise the place was empty.

"This is where I had my desk. Over there were my books on numismatics, and I had some nice bindings over here." I asked him to point out the California Room, named for the state where he made his most dramatic acquisitions and reserved strictly for those books. "We're in it now," he said. "This is where I had the one hundred incunabula. The Nuremberg Chronicle was on the lower shelf to the right. The Zamorano Club books were in that cabinet over there. This is where I slept." He smiled while I snapped a couple of photographs. The only trace of the Golden State left in the room was a University of California pennant he picked up in Berkeley; it was still tacked to a large cabinet.

Elsewhere, Blumberg had separate spaces devoted to architecture, periodicals, and photographic portfolios, as well as a special sorting room and a book repair and classification area. "I was working on my own catalogue system," he said. "I based it on the Dewey Decimal System, which I had memorized. It helped me locate things when I was on the road, and I was using it as a model for what I was putting together here." Near the processing area was a music room where Blumberg said he had set up a line of old horn Victrolas. "I've got one hundred twenty thousand old seventy-eight records down at the warehouse along with a lot of other stuff."

◆ ◆ ◆

For much of the preceding week, Assistant United States Attorney Linda R. Reade had done a thorough job of characterizing Blumberg's life on the road. A number of young men befriended by Blumberg were given reduced sentences on conspiracy charges in return for their testimony. Dwaine Olson and Brian Teeuwe told how they accompanied Blumberg on trips to flea markets and how on numerous occasions they loaded stained-glass windows, chandeliers, light fixtures, hand-tooled fireplaces, and crates of doorknobs into a van and helped him move them around between various states, often ending up in Texas.

While everyone agreed that the vast majority of antique windows and fixtures he gathered were taken from condemned buildings about to be demolished, apparently Blumberg also practiced something called "combing the obits." Brian Teeuwe and Howard Bergstrom told how Blumberg would scan newspaper obituary pages for the names of old people who had just died and left no apparent survivors. Locating the homes where these recently deceased people lived, Blumberg and his associates would break in and burgle whatever antiques he found appealing.

One accomplice in the obit burglaries, Howard Bergstrom, testified that between 1980 and 1983 alone he committed about one hundred of these crimes with Blumberg. "We traveled to Ohio, Kentucky, Pennsylvania, New York, Vermont, Massachusetts," he said; the object was always the same: stained-glass windows, doorknobs, mantelpieces. "Some of the places we just ran into, some we'd find in the obit columns."

Every witness testified to the disarray in Blumberg's personal hygiene. He rarely bathed or changed his clothes, a pattern he followed for at least twenty years. Throughout the ten-day trial, he wore the same blue jeans, plaid shirt, and cardigan sweater, though he appeared to be bathed and to be wearing clean clothes. Later he told me that when he was on the road and needed fresh clothes, he followed a standard routine. "I used to go inside a Goodwill box, take off my dirty pants and shirt, leave them in there, put on some clean ones, and pop right out."

One item the FBI recovered in Ottumwa was a spiral-bound booklet titled *The Shinn Lists,* a compilation of books stolen over a period of years, presumably to be sold for profit by a man known as James Shinn.

That information was gathered in 1982 by William A. Moffett, then director of libraries at Oberlin College in Oberlin, Ohio. Moffett was the first not only to suspect Shinn's activities, but to gather the information that would eventually lead to his arrest, prosecution, and imprisonment.

Shinn's "want list" was not like Blumberg's, but his career, and his reputation, were. The first sentence of the 144-page booklet explains: "The Shinn lists are being shared as part of an effort to document the career of a man *The American Book Collector* has called 'the most accomplished book thief' of our time, and to assist dealers, librarians, and law enforcement agencies in the process of replevin."

Kenny Rhodes testified that Blumberg mentioned several times how Shinn was said to be the "greatest book thief the world had ever known," and that this claim seemed to rankle him immensely. When I asked Blumberg about it, he not only admitted to being "fascinated" by the notoriety of his rival but also added that he had investigated Shinn's exploits carefully. "I had a real good collection of news clippings," he said. "I even went to Oberlin College to their school newspaper and went through the files there one night. I even looked up Bill Moffett's house. I was sort of a fanatic about it. I just wanted to see where Moffett lived. It was in a brick Victorian house."

Why did he want to see where Bill Moffett lived?

"I wanted to see what the guy who undid Shinn lived like. I thought I would probably like him. I would really like to have met him. I would still like to meet him."

So did Blumberg admire Shinn?

"I was just fascinated—sort of like a moth being drawn to a flame. I was fascinated by Shinn's undoing, but I didn't admire him. I thought he violated the books. He was in it for the money. He sold them."

Shinn first attracted national attention when he was arrested in the Oberlin College Library on April 23, 1981, after behaving suspiciously in the library stacks. A search of his motel room led to the discovery of sixty books stolen from Oberlin, the University of Pennsylvania, and the Lutheran Theological Seminary in Philadelphia, as well as an impressive variety of false identification papers, burglary tools, and counterfeiting implements. Released after posting a $4,000 bond, Shinn disappeared and continued his library thefts for eight more months before being arrested again in Allentown, Pennsylvania, on December 16, 1981.

Once in custody, further investigation showed that Shinn had an extensive criminal record and had used several aliases—he would later tell Moffett that his identity of choice was George V. Allen—and that many of the books he stole were sold to unsuspecting dealers on the basis of want lists routinely published in *AB Bookman's Weekly,* a leading trade journal. "Shinn is clearly not only an accomplished thief but also possesses considerable ability at altering his books to remove shelf marks, endpapers with bookplates and card pockets, and perforations, stamps, and similarly obvious marks," William Burton reported.

Moffett's interest in what we might call bibliopathology began with his work on Shinn. "I spent an awful lot of time trying to find out who he was, what he had stolen, how he had managed it, which libraries had been his victims, whether they were aware of having been robbed, and whether they were interested in trying to recover their property," he said. A few institutions were not interested at all. "Some people are obsessed about collecting books; I collect book thieves. They are my obsession. I have hundreds of folders documenting cases of book theft, probably the most extensive file of its kind anywhere."

What Moffett found most fascinating about Shinn was that "such a dubious character had been able to find such ready buyers for stolen property within the trade, and for a time I suspected all antiquarian book dealers. Above all, I began to see how vulnerable academic and research libraries were to determined thieves, and how unprepared most of them seemed to be, not only in how to recover their property, but simply in how to catch or prosecute the people who were ripping them off. Overnight, it seemed I found a completely new field of inquiry that had suddenly opened up to me. I've never managed to escape its fascination."

Shinn's thefts ended when a librarian recognized him from a photograph Moffett had distributed. "Patricia Sacks of Muhlenburg/Cedar Crest Libraries called me, and I arranged for the FBI to stake out the motel where he was holed up. Ultimately, Shinn was tried in U.S. District Court in Philadelphia. He pled guilty and received two consecutive ten-year terms in federal prison."

Though he took books from institutions on both coasts "and everywhere in between," Shinn, like Blumberg, was not prosecuted for theft, but for possession and transportation of stolen goods, which are much easier charges to prove. Moffett said that estimating a dollar value of the material Shinn stole is difficult. "Just as in the Blumberg case, you can never really know how much a cache of books is worth unless you actually put it up for sale and see what it would go for. For that matter, we still can't be sure exactly how many books Shinn stole because some of the libraries he looted never knew they had been hit, and he sold a lot before we put him out of business. We did come up with a general figure of about three quarters of a million dollars, and until Stephen came along, Shinn was regarded as the number one American book thief of all time."

As Moffett saw it, Blumberg's accomplishment was this: "Statistically, there has not been anyone who stole more books of such obviously high quality from more libraries than Stephen Blumberg. There have been other thieves, perhaps, with higher profiles—Charles Merrill Mount's spectacular manuscript thefts from the National Archives come to mind—but for sheer quantity and for total value, everyone else is quite insignificant when stacked up against what Stephen brought together."

Moffett left Oberlin College in 1990 to become director of the Huntington Library in California, and hardly a year had gone by before he made headlines once again. On September 22, 1991, the *New York Times* led its front page with Moffett's announcement that researchers could have unlimited access to photographic copies of the Dead Sea Scrolls owned by his institution, a move that ended a forty-year monopoly imposed on biblical scholarship by a group of textual editors approved by the Israeli Antiquities Authority. The scrolls, some eight hundred manuscripts in Hebrew and Aramaic dating from 200 B.C., were discovered in caves east of Jerusalem near the ruins of Qumran on the Dead Sea between 1947 and 1956. Since taking custody of them, the Antiquities Authority has been accused of selectively denying access to the scrolls from some researchers while arbitrarily granting permission to others. In the early 1980s, the scrolls were photographed, and negatives were placed in four repositories, the Huntington Library among them. By deciding to make the copies under his control available without restriction, Moffett effectively ended the monopoly. Moffett's death on February 20, 1995, occasioned a tribute from Dr. James H. Charlesworth, editor of the Dead Sea Scrolls Project at Princeton Theological Seminary. Moffett, Charlesworth said, had "risked his reputation and career to do what he thought was right," and his decision to release the ancient documents had resulted in an "explosion of interest in scrolls scholarship."

Moffett's opinions on the factors that produce the most serious book theft were similarly fraught with potential for controversy, and unlike some of his colleagues, who would like to see Blumberg drawn and quartered, he expressed a measure of compassion for the man. "What Blumberg did is reprehensible and inexcusable, but in a very real way he and Shinn performed a valuable service by demonstrating how vulnerable libraries are to theft. Blumberg succeeded in doing something no librarian had been able to do: he got the attention of the FBI about the magnitude of the problem."

Moffett said that it is not the "occasional rogue collector like Blumberg who poses the most persistent threat, but dishonest students and faculty. And they in turn are less of a problem, historically, than librarians themselves. In the case of rare books and manuscripts, our most serious threat is from 'insider theft.' "

In fact, seventeen months before Blumberg was captured, the former head of special collections at the University of Georgia, Robert M. "Skeet" Willingham, Jr., was found guilty in Clarke County Superior Court in Athens, Georgia, on thirteen counts of theft; he had stolen rare manuscripts, prints, and books from the Hargrett Rare Book Room, which he had supervised for ten years prior to his arrest in 1986. Like Blumberg, Willingham was forty-one years old at the time of his conviction, but unlike Blumberg, his crimes generated no national attention and were not explored in any detail by any professional or trade periodicals. Because Willingham stole for profit, the full extent of what he took may never be determined.

Evidence presented in the two-week trial showed that "Skeet" Willingham not only took valuable items from the rare-book room he supervised but removed, and apparently destroyed, university records that documented their accession. By all accounts, Willingham was a refined country gentleman respected not only for his good manners but for his knowledge of Confederate imprints, an area in which the University of Georgia is remarkably strong. With Michael T. Parrish of Austin, Texas, "Skeet" Willingham compiled an authoritative bibliography of "Southern publications from secession to surrender" titled, appropriately enough, *Confederate Imprints*. It was published in 1987, a year after his arrest by Georgia authorities.

People who knew Willingham well were incredulous at the charges. Defense witnesses told how he taught Sunday school, sang in the church choir, served on the Washington, Georgia, city council, and was basically "a hometown boy" who did well. "He's a wonderful guy," a lifelong friend asserted. "I cannot say enough about his integrity. I never even played golf with him where he cheated on a shot." Among others who appeared in his behalf was former U.S. Representative Robert D. Stephens, Jr., of Georgia.

"Mr. Willingham is not on trial for being a nice, gregarious person, but for being a thief," Assistant District Attorney Rick Weaver said. The prosecution produced testimony from an Atlanta rare-book dealer with the unlikely name of Gary Zippidy Duda; Duda said he and his partner had misled police over how they acquired a rare letter written by Nathanael Greene, an American general in the Revolutionary War. "We both lied to the officers," Duda admitted. "We were concerned about getting Skeet in trouble."

Georgia authorities began an investigation in 1985 when W. Graham Arader, a well-known manuscript and print dealer with offices in Philadelphia and New York, informed officials he had been offered a letter written by General Nathanael Greene that he was certain belonged to the University of Georgia. A year later, a Hargrett staff member noticed that a rare map of South Carolina was missing, and further investigation showed that many others were gone as well, including twenty-eight maps once owned by George Washington. Several searches of Willingham's home turned up more than five thousand maps, books, and other antiquarian documents, some of which were believed to be university property.

An indictment was issued in 1987, and testimony began the following year; Willingham insisted he was innocent. The principal charge was that he stole the University of Georgia's copy of *Les Liliacées,* an eight-volume collection of nineteenth-century floral prints by Pierre-Joseph Redouté that one witness estimated could be worth as much as $1 million if broken up and sold individually. Only two volumes were ever recovered, and several prints from them were missing. Willingham had sold those books to a physician for $40,000 after removing all library records that might have established university ownership. The prosecution, however, found a photocopy of a library card that had been cross-referenced in the Science Department. It matched nearly word for word a letter Willingham wrote offering the Redouté prints to an Atlanta dealer, including matching lists of misnumbered pages that one art expert told the jury were unique.

Willingham had insisted that he acquired the prints from the estate of a dead relative, but crime laboratory tests showed evidence of a signature, "H. Jackson," on the front page of the first volume. The prosecution asserted it was the signature of Henry Jackson, the nineteenth-century professor of natural history who brought a set of the prints home to Georgia after visiting France and later presented it to the university. The state crime lab technician James Kelly said that even though the name had been erased, he was able to pick it up with an infrared light. Evidence was presented that Willingham demanded cash for the prints, and that he received his money in paper bags, $27,000 as a down payment in 1984, and the remaining $13,000 on delivery.

Kelly also identified a blurred oval ink stain on the back of an oversize map taken from Willingham's home as a university library stamp. A portion of the map's cloth backing had been cut away, but enough of the ink had bled through to allow an identification. Kelly testified that twelve Indian prints traced to Willingham had been torn out of rare books in the university library. He was able to determine that the prints came from the university's set of McKenney and Hall's *History of the Indian Tribes of North America* by matching tear patterns and stains.

On September 8, 1988, Willingham was found guilty on thirteen counts and sentenced to fifteen years in prison and fined $45,000. The jury acquitted him of one charge: that he stole a collection of Civil War orders by the Union admiral John Dahlgren, then gave the material back to the university in return for a $3,600 credit toward membership in the prestigious President's Club. On July 8, 1991, the book thief who sang in the church choir and never cheated at golf lost his final appeal and was ordered back to jail, where he had been off and on since his conviction. On September 1, 1993, after serving a total of thirty months behind bars, Willingham was released on parole with the condition that he not live within forty miles of the University of Georgia.

◆   ◆   ◆

I asked Blumberg if that is what he really thought he was doing, rescuing these things. "Yes, in all of it I was doing that—not only the
books, but the doorknobs and the windows, the old house, and even
the old people like Mr. Hall; yes, I believe I was."

But how is taking books out of secure repositories an act of rescue?

"Well, maybe that's a rationalization on my part. I was sort of—
okay, let's put it this way: they were sort of on an interlibrary loan to
me. That's what I figure. I don't know if that's how they would consider it, but that's the way I look at it. Because I always intended to give
everything back. I don't regret putting the collection together, but I
regret my inconsideration of others. So in that respect, I wouldn't do it
again."

At another point he was talking about Canadian imprints, and the
title of a certain bibliography had escaped him. "Damn," he said, "if
we could go through my books, I'd show it to you. It'll come to me
eventually." That thought jogged his memory about conditions in the
Omaha warehouse where the books were being kept by the FBI. "What
bothered me as much as anything is that the books were not in order,"
he complained. "All my organization was gone. I had everything in
perfect order; I could put my hands on anything I wanted, instantly. I
had the incunabula categorized by year. I had the Americana by states
and regions. And I had little special collections within the collections.
Everything had its place. When they took me out to Omaha, it was no
longer a collection." I pointed out that the books were "out of order"
in Omaha because shelving had been arranged according to actual
owner, not his classification scheme. "I guess that's true," he agreed.
"They are more interested in provenance out there than they are with
subjects. But I'd still like to break it down by categories so we could
make some comparisons."

Blumberg said he has the greatest respect for George Brinley and
Thomas W. Streeter among other collectors of Americana. "Brinley
was the obvious goal, but that would have been impossible because of
the time frame. He's more than a hundred years ago. But I think I could
have caught up with Streeter, and in some areas I actually was getting
there, especially in imprints. He was really strong in imprints, and I had

a feeling I was getting close to the magnitude of Streeter in the Americana. I just loved to look at his bibliography and see how I was doing."

Then, with a sign of nostalgia, he observed, "The chase really is something, isn't it? It just gets worse, especially when you get close to achieving the ultimate. It's agonizing. Sometimes you wish you hadn't started."

When Blumberg learned that the FBI had produced a rudimentary catalogue of the books found in his home, he expressed great interest in getting a set. The *FBI Omaha Book List* consists of five bulky volumes fastened with spiral bindings and carries the identification code 87G-OM-36172. Everything is listed alphabetically by author, or in cases where authors are not known, alphabetically by title, and each includes a physical description and place of publication. Blumberg's displeasure that the books had been "out of order" is reflected by two other pieces of information furnished for each title, "current location" in the warehouse, and "seizure location" in Ottumwa.

A seizure location of "2B," for instance, would have been the California Room. One book recovered from that sector is *Cosmographia Siue De Situ Orbis,* by the first-century geographer Pomponius Mela, an incunabulum published in Venice in 1482, thirty years after the invention of printing, with a value conservatively estimated by Glen Dawson to be $5,000. The Zamorano Club titles—the essential books on California history—were removed from the 2B location as well, and Blumberg's pride in having come so close to getting all eighty of them is demonstrated by another item recovered there: the Zamorano Coat of Arms.

This, as it turned out, was Blumberg's one vigorous attempt to succeed at what is known popularly as "list collecting," when a collector goes after, say, every novel that has won a Pulitzer Prize, or every book that has been adapted for the screen and won an Academy Award, or every book on the Grolier Club list of one hundred classic works of Western Literature, or every one of the one hundred books that Cyril Connolly declared in 1966 to be the most influential works of the twentieth century. Science fiction collectors will try and get first editions of every book that has won a Nebula Award, while mystery fans will seek out Edgar Allan Poe Award recipients.

For Blumberg, the goal was to get one copy of every book on a list established in 1945 by a group of prominent book collectors who were members of the Zamorano Club of Los Angeles, an organization founded in 1928 and named for Don Augustin Zamorano, California's first printer. Initially, the idea was to identify one hundred books central to the history of California, but the six men who compiled the list could agree only on eighty, and that is where it remained. Even then, a degree of political maneuvering was evident. Henry R. Wagner of Los Angeles, a former mining executive who helped make the selections, insisted that *The Life and Adventures of Joaquin Murieta, the Celebrated California Bandit* by John Rollin Ridge, published in San Francisco in 1854, be included, possibly because he owned the only known first edition of the book. As happens so often with "unique" items, however, two more copies came to light after the list was circulated. Most of Wagner's library, including his Zamorano books, went to Yale, his alma mater, which explains why an East Coast university is the only institution in the world to own a complete run of books that illuminate the history of California. Even the Huntington Library, which is particularly strong in Western Americana, lacks a *Joaquin Murieta*.

Blumberg found many of the items he needed to complete his Zamorano list in the rich preserves of the Claremont Colleges' Honnold Library. Others he took from the Zamorano Club library itself, conveniently housed at the University of Southern California for many years. One mystery never resolved at the trial was which college Blumberg had robbed to get the Zamorano 80 titles owned by the club. Tyrus G. Harmsen, the Occidental College rare-books librarian, said in his testimony that the first he knew about the loss was when he received a telephone call from the FBI in 1990. Prior to that, the assumption had been that the Zamorano Club's collection of books from its own list had been secure. Harmsen said that in 1989 the club's entire library had been moved to Occidental College, and the prevailing belief was that the Zamorano 80 books went with them. "They were moved from one locked storage area to another locked storage area, and there was no particular reason why they should have been inventoried at that point," Harmsen explained.

Since the club itself did not have every book on its list either, Blumberg had to look elsewhere if he wanted a definitive collection. What he learned is that only two complete Zamorano 80 collections are known. One is at the Beinecke Library at Yale University in Connecticut; the other was owned privately by a retired investment broker and collector of Californiana, Henry H. Clifford of Pasadena.

Three prosecution witnesses testified as to how Blumberg became so fixed on the idea of filling out "his" Zamorano 80 collection that he not only initiated a surveillance of Henry Clifford's house but devised various schemes to get inside. Testimony on hundreds of felonious entries and thefts was given during the trial, but this was the only instance where Blumberg was said to have considered taking books forcibly from an individual, a suggestion he told me was made idly by his young friends, not himself. "I have never hurt anybody," he said. "I am not a violent person." He stressed that the theft never went beyond the planning stage.

Brian Teeuwe testified that he and Dwaine Olson not only "staked out" Clifford's home but also "walked around the house looking for a way in past the security system" and that finally "we did find a way." He and Olson went beneath the house through the crawl space where they found the warning devices, complete with instruction manual. Blumberg copied the material, and Teeuwe returned it to the house the next night, pausing to take pictures of the layout. They discussed either "finding somebody who knew the alarm system" or taking a more direct approach, like "showing up at the door as pizza delivery men and putting a gun on [the Cliffords] and tying them up." They never tried it, and nothing more was said about the idea after Blumberg was arrested in Riverside and "had to leave town." Once Kenny Rhodes decided to turn Blumberg over to the authorities, he called Henry Clifford to warn him of the plot. Clifford confirmed this to me several months afterward. "What I would have liked to say to the man if I had a chance was that I also have a nice collection of guns," he said, "and I keep a few of them loaded."

In his frenzied attempt to gather information about the Pasadena house and its occupant, Blumberg went so far as to root through Clifford's trash, a detail he brought up after I remarked on a practice he called "Dumpster diving." During our drive he abruptly stopped the car in Ottumwa, got out without saying a word, and bounded quickly through the top hatch of a large refuse receptacle to see if anything valuable was inside. He came back stinking of garbage but also exuding triumph, for he had "rescued" several items from the scrap heap. "That's how I got the Clifford material," he explained. "You can learn almost as much about a person by his trash as by talking to him."

Henry Clifford died on February 21, 1994, eleven days after observing his eighty-fourth birthday. The books Stephen Blumberg had schemed so zealously to steal from him were consigned to the Austin, Texas, rare-book dealer Dorothy Sloan for dispersal at auction. On October 23, 1994, during the first of three sales held in Los Angeles, Clifford's Zamorano 80 collection went on the block. *The Life and Adventures of Joaquín Murieta, the Celebrated California Bandit,* the only copy privately owned and the one book of Clifford's particularly coveted by Blumberg, was bought for $69,000 by a collector, who chose to remain anonymous. Sloan reported total receipts of $1.17 million for Clifford's library.

After leaving the "library" on Jefferson Street, Blumberg took me to his warehouse downtown. The facility was searched thoroughly by the FBI, but since the government was only looking for books, virtually everything else was left behind. Blumberg had not been inside since his arrest ten months earlier and was giddy with excitement when we got there. I took about twenty photographs of him as he went through these possessions, and he is radiant in every one.

"Oh, look at that," Blumberg shouted at one point, howling with delight. "A prefire Chicago imprint." Finding an oversize illustrated book titled *Ornamental Art,* he quickly opened it and began looking carefully at the pages. I guessed out loud that there must be about two hundred books in the room. "Wasn't it nice of them to leave me something," Blumberg said. A few minutes later, he was looking at doorknobs packed in about a hundred neatly stacked plastic milk cases, perhaps, as he said earlier, as many as fifty thousand of them. In another area, dozens of old suitcases were piled to the ceiling, some of them empty, others filled with assorted items. Stained-glass windows stood upright throughout the building, at least a hundred, possibly more. And in a far corner were crates upon crates of old seventy-eight r.p.m. records.

"I didn't know everything that I had in here myself," he said in wonder. "I'm alive," he said several times, "I'm living."

♦ ♦ ♦

The bibliokleptomaniac's crimes were outlined in painstaking detail by Linda Reade. The defense lawyers, Don C. Nickerson and Raymond Rosenberg, did not deny that Blumberg had stolen the books. Sanity was the issue, and Judge Harold D. Vietor would make clear in his instructions that the defense had the "burden of proving, by clear and convincing evidence," that Blumberg was insane when he stole books and transported them across state lines into Iowa.

On Tuesday morning, January 29, 1991, Nickerson and Rosenberg called their first witness, a seventy-three-year-old antiques dealer from St. Paul, Minnesota. Emily Augustine Fredericksen testified she met Blumberg about 1960, when the boy was twelve. "A skinny little guy," dirty like "dry old soot" but "very gentle," came into her shop one day on a "rickety bicycle" outfitted with an unusual trailer to carry around items he had removed from old houses. "I can remember his eyes. His eyes were very prominent," she said, but what impressed her most of all was the youngster's knowledge. "Can you imagine a twelve-year-old boy interested in the design of hardware on a door, door hinges, window openings?" An immediate rapport was established. Mrs. Fredericksen asserted that she and young Stephen were "two of a kind," but there was a fundamental difference: "I collected because I was doing it for the profits to live on; he didn't sell, he just collected to preserve."

This was about the time, she continued, when many elegant old houses were being taken by eminent domain to make way for a new freeway being built between St. Paul and Minneapolis. "These were some beautiful old homes, just gorgeous," she said. "It was just something that you'd walk in and be back there." Because the houses were condemned, vandalism was rampant, and the things Blumberg took were things no one wanted. "This was just going to be crushed under the ground and bulldozed over."

Occasionally Mrs. Fredericksen went out with Blumberg to some of these buildings. "Steve had no fear that I could see. If he saw something that he wanted to preserve or have, it didn't matter if he was going to break his neck or back, he would go after it." She described one time when he had permission to take a weather vane from an old barn. "I wish you could have seen that young man climb that roof and go up. I was scared to death that I was going to pick him up, that he was going to slide down. He got it down, no damage."

Mrs. Fredericksen said she then drove the boy home and met his father, Dr. Henry Blumberg, in the driveway. Instead of complimenting Stephen on his latest acquisition, Dr. Blumberg "took it and threw it off the driveway." She said she later learned that Dr. Blumberg routinely destroyed many of the artifacts his son brought home. "Steve was a loner from the first time I met him. He didn't need anybody. He didn't need anything. He didn't need food. Food wasn't important. Dress, clothing, entertainment was not of any interest to him. His only interest was in the past." She judged him to be "brilliant," "honest," and "truthful," always a gentleman, with "no roughness" or "coarseness" about him. "Well, let's say I loved the kid. He just got to me. I just loved him."

A psychologist from the Menninger Clinic in Topeka, Kansas, where Dr. Blumberg sent his son in 1990, testified regarding ten tests he had given Blumberg. The Menninger Clinic was founded in the 1920s to treat people with chronic mental illness. Dr. Glen S. Lipson concluded that Blumberg "is someone who has an encapsulated delusional system pertaining to how he sees the world," and that he had "created his own world that motivates a lot of his actions." He defined a delusion as a "belief that is inconsistent with the way most people perceive reality." Dr. Lipson testified that an earlier evaluation of Blumberg done at the Menninger Clinic in 1965—twenty-four years before his arrest in Iowa—"noticed many of the same things." In fact, he said, "I was surprised by a lot of the consistencies," particularly Blumberg's "overconcern" then "with things of the past and that are old," and by his "inability to deal with what is going on" in the present. "What we see twenty-five years later is a man of complete absorption," he said. "He became an expert in the past," a person who "could talk to you about doorknobs and books, but who retreats when you ask him about himself."

The defense then called Dr. William S. Logan, at the time of the trial the director of the Law and Psychiatry Department at the Menninger Clinic (where he had been since 1985) and a nationally recognized authority in forensic psychiatry. Since credibility in such a case is essential, Nickerson devoted thirty minutes to having Dr. Logan present his qualifications. He said that he had given expert testimony in forty-five other federal cases, and had once been cited by the U.S. attorney general for meritorious service.

Dr. Logan reported that he spent 33.4 hours interviewing Blumberg and an additional 21.75 hours with relatives and acquaintances who knew the patient. He noted that while it is "quite unusual" for him to spend that much time on a single case, "I'm still not aware of all of Mr. Blumberg's delusional beliefs, many of which only come to light through various codes and symbols that he uses." One "code" Dr. Logan described was a fictitious institution called the Columbian Library. He had named it after the World's Columbian Exposition held in 1893 to commemorate the discovery of the New World four centuries earlier. Designed by a team of architects that included Charles F. McKim, Stanford White, Louis H. Sullivan, and Frederick Law Olmstead, the six-month extravaganza drew more than 27 million visitors to the banks of Lake Michigan and is viewed as an unqualified triumph of Victorian culture. Blumberg "so revered that era," Dr. Logan said, "that he relabeled his books after this particular exhibition," which is better known today as the Chicago Fair.

Of central importance to Blumberg's defense was the family history, which Dr. Logan outlined in detail, beginning with Moses "Mose" Zimmerman, Stephen's great-grandfather and the family patriarch, a "horse trader of some renown" who was born in Iowa and moved to what is now the Twin Cities area of St. Paul and Minneapolis in the mid-1800s. A true nineteenth-century entrepreneur, Mose Zimmerman supplied horses not only to the United States Cavalry, but to various European combatants in the Boer War as well. "The significant thing about Mose that I found interesting was that he was perhaps the first recorded collector in the family," Dr. Logan said. "He would collect junk, piles of it, huge storehouses of it. He at one point bought a whole twine factory for which there was no practical use. Some of the other things he collected were a hundred buffalo coats and ten thousand horse collars."

Much of what Blumberg's great-grandfather collected had "very little practical value," including large parcels of what were thought then to be "worthless pieces" of real estate in St. Paul, Minnesota. "Later, as the city expanded—and by 'later' I mean as much as a hundred years later—these portions of land became quite valuable and the basis for a considerable family fortune."

Today, the family fortune is managed under the company name of Zimmerman Realty, which is operated by Dr. Henry Blumberg, Stephen's father. Everyone Dr. Logan interviewed agreed that Mose Zimmerman "compulsively collected things, even things that others may not have particularly wanted," yet he "was very much adored by the rest of the family," and was even perceived by some "as the major figure or hero in the family."

Two people who exerted tremendous influence on young Stephen were his great-grandmother—Mose's wife, Carrie—and her daughter, also named Carrie, Stephen's grandmother. "Both of these women lived to be quite elderly, eighties and nineties, and both were present throughout all of Stephen's childhood and adolescence," Dr. Logan said. "They lived together in an old large home, very Victorian in nature, because they were quite elderly and liked that style. Stephen was extremely attached to both of these women, particularly to his Grandmother Carrie. In fact, Stephen's middle name is Carrie. His father intended that it be spelled in a more masculine way, C-a-r-y, but one of the first of many disagreements they had when they entered my office was they argued about Stephen's name." Blumberg insists on spelling his middle name "exactly the way his grandmother spelled it," Dr. Logan explained; he is "so attached to her memory, he stated he would like to be buried with her."

The family's history of mental illness also begins with Grandmother Carrie, Dr. Logan said. After the death of a child, she "suffered a major depression" from which she "never recovered," a condition that probably caused her "to drink heavily and abuse pills." Carrie's husband, Reuben Blumberg, also had a family history of mental illness, including a paternal grandmother "who had been hospitalized for a nervous breakdown."

Dr. Logan outlined other family problems, including the depression of Dr. Henry Blumberg. "He saw a psychiatrist while he was in medical school, [has] had suicidal thoughts, [and has even] considered killing Stephen as well." Henry Blumberg saw action in both the European and Pacific theaters during World War II "and had nightmares and some evidence of a post-traumatic stress disorder which occurred periodically."

With Blumberg's mother, Jeanne, there was "conclusive proof" of "demonstrated emotional instability," according to Dr. Logan, including "major psychiatric records" dating back to the early 1970s that diagnosed her as "schizophrenic or schizoaffective," for which she required "psychotropic medication." Dr. Logan described Jeanne Blumberg as a woman who "believes that the radio and TV have special messages for her." Blumberg had been a "frequent target" of his mother's "rage" since childhood. His mother sometimes expressed anger by burning her son's and husband's clothes, and once she attacked Henry Blumberg with a knife.

As an adolescent in grade school, Blumberg found he "could begin to escape some of the things around him" in books, and he grew particularly fond of an elderly teacher who encouraged his reading. "He was very isolated, very withdrawn, basically no peer relationships at all," Dr. Logan said. Enrolled in a private Catholic high school twelve miles from home, Blumberg saw his grades begin to decline. It was during this period when he found it necessary to "walk back and forth" that he began to develop an interest in antiques, Dr. Logan said. "Particularly, he had to walk around the construction of Interstate 94," which goes through Minneapolis and St. Paul and required the demolition of many old houses.

After a year in the Catholic school Blumberg transferred back to public school. He began to spend more time away from home and went out "looking at old buildings." His personal appearance began to decline, he was more hostile, and he seemed resentful of a younger sister. Dr. Blumberg was so concerned that in 1965 he took his sixteen-year-old son to a psychiatrist, who admitted him to St. Mary's Hospital in St. Paul. Shortly after his release, Stephen's continued "disturbing" behavior prompted his father to file a petition requesting that his son become a ward of the Ramsey County Juvenile Court. A judge ordered a second hospitalization at St. Mary's Hospital that lasted for six weeks. The psychiatrists who examined him diagnosed a "personality moving in a schizophrenic direction," and concluded that Blumberg's "thinking was unusual enough" already to support a characterization of "delusional." They recommended that he be "in a treatment program for the severely emotionally disturbed." A third evaluation in 1965 by "a whole team of people" at the Menninger

Clinic supported the finding of schizophrenia, and also recommended "inpatient hospitalization."

In 1966, Blumberg underwent another series of evaluations, beginning at the Ramsey County Hospital Psychiatric Unit in St. Paul, where he remained for eight weeks. Doctors described him as "an anxious, depressed kid who has an absolute obsession about collecting and going into old homes and getting things." Later that year, treatment at a state hospital was recommended, and Blumberg was admitted to the Minnesota State Hospital in Anoka for two and a half months in 1966. Dr. Logan said that at one point Dr. Henry Blumberg went to the hospital with his attorney and "confronted the psychiatrist" over reports that his son "had been locked in a seclusion room" for a period of time. "Stephen eventually wound up running away from the facility," said Dr. Logan, and fled to Chicago, where his father "eventually retrieved him."

In 1967, Blumberg was admitted to the Hardy Hospital for Psychiatry and Neurology in Worthington, Ohio. After six weeks of evaluation, he was judged to have an "adjustment reaction" consistent with a person who is "developing schizoid and compulsive tendencies," a diagnosis that Dr. Logan explained referred "once again" to an obsessive "accumulation of things." Blumberg spent another seven weeks at Harding Hospital in 1968 followed by two more weeks in 1969, producing further corroboration of the earlier examinations and resulting in a "guarded prognosis."

Dr. Henry Blumberg decided finally that perhaps the best course of action would be to set Stephen up in his own apartment in Minneapolis. Though his son agreed to attend Marshall High School in St. Paul, he participated in no activities, made no friends, and "remained very withdrawn and passive." Blumberg did graduate in 1968, but sat in the back of the auditorium with his father during ceremonies and would not go up on the stage to receive his diploma.

It was at about this time, Dr. Logan said, that Blumberg started "to create his own Victorian world" in his apartment. "In many ways, he felt discarded and unappreciated by his parents and other people," and began to identify with "these beautiful stained-glass windows or Victorian doorknobs or other objects, the lamp shades we find in these homes. His whole idea was to preserve or to rescue these materials from what he believed was destruction."

And it was also at about this time, said Dr. Logan, that Blumberg began his raids on libraries. "Basically he had begun to explore books about Victorian architecture. In the process of doing that, he went into the rare-book stacks at the University of Minnesota. His primary focus at the time was on architectural digests from the 1800s. How he would use these would be, say, to take an architectural digest relating to the City of St. Louis. He would go down there using the description of the building that he found in that book to locate which buildings had not been demolished and see if they were in the process of disrepair or abandonment. If so, he would then explore them."

Prior to his arrest in 1990, Blumberg had no further hospitalizations, though he did receive periodic inpatient treatment at the Central Medical Center in St. Paul between 1970 and 1990. In 1974 his doctor reported "a severe schizoid personality disorder and possibly a paranoid state," but by that time Blumberg was well into his travels through the backroads of America in search of antiques, stained-glass windows, doorknobs, seventy-eight–r.p.m. records, and rare books.

For his part, Henry Blumberg began to develop some pride in his son's collecting and stopped calling the items he gathered "junk." There came, too, a degree of outside attention. In 1972, two publications took note of Blumberg's activities, one of them a local newspaper, the other a national architectural magazine. "The Victorian World of Steve Blumberg" was the headline on a January 16, 1972, Sunday feature in the St. Paul *Pioneer Press;* a shorter article in the November 1972 issue of *Historic Preservation* had a similar title, "The World of Stephen Blumberg," and led with an unusually prescient paragraph:

"Stephen Blumberg lives in a paper world. The Victorian houses he loves, with their gingerbread decoration and stained-glass windows, exist only in the intricate drawings he has done of them. They are nearly real—buildings similar to them exist in cities around the country—but the real buildings are neglected in run-down parts of town." The article focused on a skill Blumberg had been developing since he was fourteen, "drawing picturesque old buildings" modeled on structures in Minneapolis–St. Paul and other cities he had driven to throughout the country in the "big, old limousines" he favored. His three-room Minneapolis apartment was described as "loaded with hundreds of relics from buildings that have been demolished or allowed to deteriorate." The article emphasized that he had located the actual buildings "by referring to old city guidebooks that feature engravings and vivid descriptions."

In order to make "completely realistic" sketches of the buildings, Blumberg told the reporter, he would have had to "add all the modernization" that had gone on around them, but that "by cheating a little" and creating idealized settings he called "architectural composites," he was able to "show the beauty of the city better." Dr. Logan believes that what Blumberg actually was doing in these sanitized drawings was to remove all evidence of the twentieth century. "I go to these cities and invariably wind up in the oldest and worst districts," Blumberg explained in the 1972 article. "But this, to me, is only an added incentive; I want all the more to salvage and preserve the structures, even if only graphically, because of the apparent imminence of their destruction."

"The Victorian World of Stephen Blumberg," in the St. Paul *Pioneer Press,* included what in retrospect are some unusually pertinent observations. "Stephen Blumberg stands amid the Victorian Americana he has created out of three rooms of an old building at 1605 Hennipen Avenue in Minneapolis and it is difficult to describe his life style," the article began. The writer was struck by the fact that despite Blumberg's youth—he was twenty-three—"he lives almost a solitary existence, completely absorbed in his passion for the 'gingerbread' period of American architecture and the accoutrements that complemented it." Blumberg was described even then as an "anachronism" who is "intense" and "in deep depression, not for himself, but for the terrible sins committed by Urban Renewal in demolishing the Victorian glory in the name of progress across America."

The reporter described some of the artifacts in Blumberg's apartment. "Stephen has amassed perhaps the most outstanding collection of stained glass from the condemned mansions, houses and public buildings of every major city," while his "piles of glazed ceramic tiles are enviable," and his "antique doorknob collection" numbered in the "hundreds." To get them, Blumberg had "haunted the once grand and then fading and now extinct old residential sections of Chicago's south and west sides, Cincinnati, Buffalo, Pittsburgh, St. Louis, Boston, New York and Philadelphia," even getting himself arrested once for "stealing ornamental doorknobs from an old Minneapolis mansion on the assumption he had not gotten the owner's permission. He had."

The reporter wanted to know why Blumberg had such a special fascination for stained glass:

" 'Stained glass,' he says, lovingly describing one of the pieces with which he has decorated his home, 'is the most beautiful part of Victorian America—even more lovely than the carved woodworking, the friezes, the balustrades, wood paneling and ceramic tiled walls, floors and fireplaces.' "

The reporter wondered how Blumberg knew where to find all these deteriorating mansions. "He takes old city guidebooks published before 1900 and follows those to the old neighborhoods. 'I have the pictures in the guidebooks of how some houses looked, or buildings, and I have found them in desolate, horrible run-down blocks.' "

Blumberg then told how he obtained his material: "I beg, buy—but never steal—anything from empty, about-to-be demolished buildings."

The reporter talked to Dr. Henry Blumberg for a final comment. "What bothers Stephen's father more than the son is where this youthful obsession with one age of American history will lead." The article concluded by quoting Dr. Blumberg directly:

"Here he's got all this talent for collecting, for drawing, for painting, this urge to get involved with preservation, he's got this fortune in 'gingerbread,' and he lives like a hermit."

These two stories offered rare early glimpses into the "Victorian world of Stephen Blumberg," and constitute the only outside attention this unusual young man's dogged preoccupation with the past received during the next eighteen years.

When Blumberg was showing me through the empty rooms of his Ottumwa house, I noticed a rectangular piece of soiled cotton cloth lying at the bottom of an empty pine shelf. The FBI had removed all the shelves' contents, but this little fragment had been left behind, most likely because it was not a book and had no apparent value. It was a print, embossed in red ink on a plain white background, of an old gingerbread house.

"It's something I made when I was in high school," Blumberg said sadly. "I carved it out of a piece of linoleum, and used the linoleum like a woodblock to pull a couple of prints. I did that in 1965 when I was sixteen." He gave the print to me as a "memento" of our day in Ottumwa, a gift I accepted with thanks after he inscribed and dated it in the lower-right-hand corner. Later, in the downtown warehouse, he also gave me a brass doorknob selected randomly from one of many plastic milk crates stacked in a corner. He looked intently at the fixture and quickly announced it was made in 1895 by the Reading Hardware Company of Reading, Pennsylvania. "Just soak it in a paint stripper or something, and then, if you want to polish it, polish it up nice. It's a beauty."

Though Stephen Blumberg had been stealing for most of his life, the element of revenge did not become a factor until the mid-1980s, according to Dr. Logan. One prosecution witness, Brian Teeuwe, came close to explaining what drove his friend to take so much material out of the Twin Cities and drive it south. "Steve used to say that his great goal in life was to steal all of Minneapolis and sell it to Texas." Dr. Logan testified that it was the loss of an old building Stephen called the Elliot House that had generated so much rage.

In 1978, using part of the $72,000 annual stipend he received from a trust established by his grandmother Carrie, Blumberg bought an old building at 1628 Elliot Avenue in Minneapolis "that was going to hold his Victorian collection," a thirty-six-room Romanesque structure built in 1888. It would be a "show place" where "he could create the world that he wanted to create." Almost immediately, however, "there were various building and zoning restrictions and various codes." His father, "for whatever reasons not entirely clear," argued strongly against the house and "urged" Stephen to sell it. In one instance, where Stephen had trouble evicting a destructive tenant, "his father actually paid the man's rent and came into court and testified for the tenant. Steve was absolutely astounded."

Difficulties with the city continued, until Blumberg was finally forced to sell the property. "He became virtually enraged," Dr. Logan said. "He really did not have a mission or goal in life. His ideas about the government conspiring against him and others like him really increased after this time, as did some of his activities in taking things." That was when he began the obituary burglaries. "He would talk about going through the drawers of these dead people, trying to figure out what kind of person this was, almost like an archaeologist." When Blumberg found photographs of "these elderly dead people," he would take them, "put them up in his home and tell people they were his relatives."

At this time Blumberg's fascination for books moved away from Americana to embrace "all old books," including the oldest of all, incunabula, though he had no interest in fiction, art, or much of anything that went into the twentieth century. Dr. Logan said Blumberg was convinced that the bureaucracy "was trying to prevent the ordinary man from having any access to seeing these rare works of beauty. . . . He would somehow liberate and preserve them, and sort of thwart this government plot. So he was focused more on taking books, and his travels began to increase."

Despite the value of the material, Dr. Logan stressed that the books "were not financially significant" to Blumberg. "They became an extension of his own delusional ideas, his feelings of what his worth, his value was. The more depressed or upset he was, the more angry he was about what was going on in his life, so the more he sought a release in either seeking revenge by getting the books or actually having the books, and the more he became fascinated and engulfed in these ideas, in this whole pursuit of taking these things."

One of the most striking exhibits Dr. Logan presented was a drawing Blumberg made of himself as part of a series of psychiatric tests in 1965 when he was sixteen years old. The picture shows an older man with a beard, dressed in nineteenth-century clothes. "The same test administered today looks virtually the same," said Dr. Logan.

He also described at length the other directions Blumberg's paranoia took, including his belief that a totalitarian state where the "government would control everybody" was imminent. One illustration of this fear—which had also been described earlier by several of the young men who testified for the prosecution—was Blumberg's grim prediction that everyone eventually will have "bar codes" tattooed on their foreheads "so they can be scanned" by optical computer devices like so many supermarket products. His conviction that major economic collapse was imminent is reflected as well by his massive hoarding of gold coins and pieces. "So it started out with simple ideas and grew more elaborate as time progressed," Dr. Logan said in summation. "The one manifestation of his fear of the world at large was that he tried to create this Victorian world much as a cocoon about him."

Finally, it came time for Dr. Logan's evaluation. Everyone had agreed that Blumberg stole millions of dollars worth of rare books, and nobody doubted that he was a collector out of control. But was he insane?

The lights inside the courtroom dimmed and Dr. Logan projected a slide on a screen. It showed an entry in a book known commonly as "DSM-III-R," the third edition of the *Diagnostic and Statistical Manual of Psychiatry*. Under entry 297.10, he indicated "Delusional (Paranoid) Disorder" as his basic diagnosis. Stephen Blumberg, he declared, suffered from "a very severe, very chronic disorder" that includes a "grandiose delusion." He explained further: "The content [of the delusion] involves an exaggerated sense of importance and power; in Stephen's case, his identity as a Victorian man, his importance in preserving Victorian artifacts and books, particularly historically valuable books. Secondly, a persecutory delusion [involves] a person or group [feeling] attacked, harassed, cheated, persecuted or conspired against; and this principally involves . . . ideas about how the government plans to control and manage and prevent [the person] from obtaining any wealth . . . anybody who is poor, disadvantaged, or members of minority groups. He includes himself among that group, feels he has been personally harassed at times."

With that, the defense rested its case.

Linda Reade's cross-examination focused initially not on Dr. Logan's diagnosis but on how much the Blumberg family paid the Menninger Clinic for the evaluation. Twenty minutes later he was excused, and the prosecution called its own psychiatrist, Dr. Michael Taylor of Des Moines, who said he had examined Blumberg in his office at the request of the government for "no more" than two hours, though possibly for as short a time period as forty-five minutes, as the defense later suggested.

Dr. Taylor said he had not interviewed any other Blumberg family members, though he did review the medical records that detailed Blumberg's previous "psychiatric difficulties." Dr. Taylor said, however, that mental health problems any other family members might have suffered were "of no relevance" to the case anyway. His purpose was to find "evidence of what Dr. Logan claimed existed," and his conclusion was a summary dismissal of all the defense psychiatrist's assertions as being "irrelevant" to Blumberg's state of mind.

As to the massive book thefts, Dr. Taylor said they represented an area where Blumberg felt he "could become important," nothing more. Dr. Taylor agreed that Blumberg had "a strong affinity" for the Victorian era, but said all it represented was a "romanticized period" for him. "He drew old Victorian houses. People who are interested in horses draw horses. I certainly don't think you can jump to the conclusion that because he draws these houses in precise detail, it's anything other than [that] he has an interest in this, and he said that."

While "well aware" that Blumberg "had hospitalization" in the past, Dr. Taylor concluded nevertheless that there was "no evidence to indicate anything that would qualify as a severe mental condition or defect." Finally, in his opinion, there was "no sense of delusional thinking or paranoid thinking." Asked under cross-examination to explain how two psychiatrists could come to such profoundly conflicting conclusions, Dr. Taylor said, "Mr. Blumberg told Dr. Logan a different story from the one he told me."

The next day, after closing arguments, detailed instructions to the jury from Judge Vietor, and a break for lunch, the jury came back with a swift verdict to convict Blumberg on all four counts. Following the advice of the judge, the jury chose not to discuss its verdict with reporters. In the eyes of the law, Stephen Blumberg was sane, guilty, and criminally accountable for his actions.

Sentencing was set for April 26, but was put off several times so that appraisals acceptable to both sides could be compiled. The books' worth was crucial because the length of Blumberg's prison term would be determined in large measure by the value of the material he had stolen. While the $20 million figure initially put out made for good news copy, everyone in the book world understood that the Blumberg collection was by no means in league with the Bradley Martin or Estelle Doheny libraries, each of which brought more than $30 million in highly publicized auctions held between 1987 and 1990, nor was it superior to the Garden Ltd., which sold for $16 million in 1989. It was an exceedingly valuable selection of books, but just how valuable was a crucial point of contention.

In her presentation to the jury, Linda Reade produced figures relating to 3,345 specific books and manuscripts from seventeen institutions that had been valued by Glen Dawson of Los Angeles and Kenneth Rendell of Massachusetts at $2,310,377. Some twenty thousand additional titles from more than two hundred other libraries remained to be valued, and they would be the subject of new appraisals prepared by experts for each side, though everyone agreed that much of what remained was bulk. In the end, Bart Auerbach of New York City and Ken Nyesbaum of New Haven, Connecticut, would submit separate appraisals that established a strong middle ground of about $5.3 million for the whole collection, a figure that Reade and Rosenberg ultimately accepted as realistic.

While he awaited sentencing, Blumberg was brought to the Omaha warehouse on a daily basis to assist in the book identifications, a voluntary gesture designed to demonstrate "acceptance of responsibility," another factor that Judge Vietor would consider when he decided how much time Blumberg must serve in prison. During the July 31 sentencing hearing, FBI agent David Oxler was asked if Blumberg happened to be in the warehouse while a librarian from Duke University was there to determine which titles might be his. Oxler said he was. And did Mr. Blumberg at one point go up to the librarian and apologize for his thefts? Yes, Oxler said, he did.

When I got back to Massachusetts, I called Duke University and asked John L. Sharpe III, the academic librarian there, to recall his meeting with the infamous book thief. "The agents were concerned that I not be offended by the presence of Blumberg in the warehouse," he said. "Would it bother me at all, they asked, if he were brought into the room with me. I said not at all; I actually was very curious to see what he looked like and what he sounded like. I wanted to see what kind of character had wormed his way into our libraries and taken so many of our books."

Sharpe said that some books already had been identified as having been taken from Duke but that he still had no idea how extensive the losses were. "The thing about Blumberg is that he didn't just go around removing materials haphazardly. He was quite selective. He had a bibliographical concern." Sharpe spent his first day in Omaha "working through the collections," trying to find books that had not yet been determined to be Duke's. "I kept finding pieces that were not listed in the FBI list, things that I could identify readily by means of the style of the markings on the spine."

Blumberg, meanwhile, was confined to a specific area of the warehouse. Books would be brought to him, and he would work at a table. "Somehow, it was mentioned that I was from Duke University, and he looked at me, and he said, 'Duke University?' I said, 'That's right.' He said, 'You have a beautiful campus.' I said, 'Yes, thank you very much.' " Blumberg then returned to his work, but sometime the next day, the two of them were left alone for a brief period. "The place was locked, of course, but the agents said jokingly, 'John, don't let Stephen go out the front door.' After a while, he came over to where I was working, stood with his feet kind of spread out and hunched back, and looked at me, and said, 'I didn't realize I was creating so much trouble for so many people. I didn't think it would matter if I took one or two books.' "

Sharpe responded that he had not taken just "one or two" from Duke, but dozens. "How many did you take from us anyway?" he wanted to know. Blumberg guessed five or six hundred, which stunned Sharpe, because "we had only identified about a hundred and fifty at that time." He then asked Blumberg if he "by chance" had taken a tapestry that was missing from the chapel, and Blumberg said he had not, "though I was in there many times." Blumberg then dropped a bombshell: "Well, I did steal Duke's one millionth volume. It had a little card in it that said one millionth volume, Duke University, Flowers Collection."

Sharpe said he could have been "tipped over" by the admission. "I knew that book was not where it was supposed to be, because I had brought it out and showed it from time to time, and I exhibited it along with the two millionth and the three millionth books. I had been looking for it and couldn't find it, though I didn't know what that meant. All I knew was that it was not on the shelf." Immediately, Sharpe called his assistant in Durham, North Carolina, and asked for the proper entry information of a book printed in 1711 in Bern, Switzerland, which, translated, is titled *A Guide for German Travelers from Switzerland to the Carolinas,* by Jonas Ochs. Presently, Sharpe's assistant came back on the line with the bibliographical data, which Special Agent Tucker typed into the FBI computer. "And there it was."

Blumberg, meanwhile, had been watching with unusual intensity. After the one millionth book had been retrieved, he offered another morsel. "I also took your John Smith narration of his voyage to the Carolinas," a 1624 work titled *Generall Historie of Virginia, New-England, and the Summer Isles*, and Sharpe thought, "Oh no, there goes that beautiful orange morocco volume." That book, too, he remembered not being able to find. "So we looked it up, and in the room where we found that, I saw some other pieces he had taken from the Flowers Collection as well."

While relieved to recover so many valuable items, Sharpe recalled feeling a profound sense of violation. "What I felt more than anything else was that we in libraries have to operate on a trust system every time we bring a book to someone's table. This is what I think is so sinister about the whole thing. This man chose to debase that, to debase that commodity that is so essential in gathering information in an open institution. And I think he betrayed everything that we try to represent in making information available as freely and as uninhibitedly as possible. And I think that's what really just enraged me, to think that this man took advantage of that kind of access."

Sharpe and his staff tried to reconstruct how Blumberg gained access to the secure areas at Duke. "I think he stole a set of our keys," Sharpe said, "but he didn't steal them and keep them, he stole them, made copies, and then returned the originals. I can remember once not being able to find my keys, and having to get a spare set that we keep in another part of the department, and then having them turn up again later."

Blumberg told Sharpe that he had "visited" Duke twice, and that each time he stayed for about two weeks. "What's fascinating about this is that I can remember getting up in the middle of the night a couple of times and going over to the library to check the department because the alarm system was signaling an entry. We thought something was wrong with the alarm system, because we could find absolutely no evidence of egress, yet all the sensors were working. All the sensors had been alerted and had picked up the movement, but when I got there everything appeared normal. He just walked right on through the security."

Blumberg's memory of the specific Duke titles he took corroborated something he told me during our trip to Ottumwa, when his fate was still uncertain, and when he still viewed his assistance in identifying stolen books as "a bargaining chip" he might use down the road with the authorities. "I know where everything came from; they don't," he said. At that point, Blumberg asked me to turn off my tape recorder, and then he said, "You know the *Uncle Tom's Cabin* they think I got from Harvard? Well, it belongs to USC." Like so many bargaining chips, though, that one lost its currency; investigators soon determined on their own which institution owned the exceedingly rare first edition of Harriet Beecher Stowe's landmark novel.

Much of what Blumberg did not tell me about his book thefts he outlined in a series of autobiographical statements prepared for the Menninger Clinic. These statements were mentioned during the trial by both Dr. Logan and Dr. Taylor, but were never entered into evidence. One is headed "Trips," another "Biography."

"Trips" is especially useful from the standpoint of establishing basic facts. Dr. Logan established a precise structure for Blumberg to follow in providing information on all of his "collecting" trips. Logan had him answer six specific questions on a month-by-month basis, starting in 1986:

Where did you go?
Whom were you with?
Did you take anything?
What did you take?
From which library?
Why did you take it?

The first entry is for the University of Colorado in April 1986. Blumberg records stealing twenty-five to thirty pamphlets and eight to ten books on Colorado history. Why? "They were in nice cases and I wanted to read on Colorado. Liked artwork of cases." On the same trip he removed four or five books on Western history from Colorado College because he "didn't have them in collection." Later, in September, he took between twenty-five and thirty pamphlets "bound in thin books" from the Connecticut State Library. He already "had taken some" from the same place in May of 1985 and "wanted to add to collection and study."

His 1987 adventures included no fewer than six visits to the flea markets of Canton, Texas, punctuated by thefts at numerous libraries in California, Montana, Idaho, Washington, Oregon, Utah, Nevada, and New Mexico. At the Claremont Colleges he removed as many as 170 volumes, mostly incunabula and books on bibliography and California history. At the University of Idaho he picked up five books on Western history. In December 1987—just a few weeks before Shannon Applegate asked to see the Webfoot Diary—Blumberg removed twenty to twenty-five boxes of manuscripts and pamphlets, and another fifteen to twenty containing "old stock certificates, ledgers, letter heads, pamphlet type things relating to Western history" at the University of Oregon. These materials made for "fascinating reading at leisure."

The Zamorano 80 collection was taken from the "restricted floor of USC Library" during a "solitary trip" in 1987. He used stolen keys at no fewer than nine institutions between 1986 and 1988. Only at Harvard, UCLA, and the University of Cincinnati was he unable during that period to penetrate restricted areas.

Other segments of Blumberg's written testimony describe his early fascination with condemned buildings. He explained the early formulation of his plan. "I would ride out the urban renewal crisis and look for vacant buildings to go in and salvage antiques. Back then they would leave them and kids or vandals would just break them up or sell them for scrap. There was an infinite supply as literally hundreds of buildings were vacant and were being wrecked in each city."

As his travels throughout the country continued, his knowledge expanded. "I was visiting out of town libraries as my interest in books had grown, and was looking at it as a reading resource and for research." He also justified his book thefts. The material he saw "was little used and I would never be there again, so I better avail myself of the opportunity." From the beginning, he never considered selling the books. "I felt I'd be doing a dishonest thing by selling ill-gotten books for money." As to what would happen to the books "after my passing," he felt that ultimately they "would get back to the proper hands," if not "the same location I took them from," at least to "someone who would use, share, and care for them. I looked at myself as a custodian of these things."

Blumberg repeated what he had explained in his talk with me, that he always had specific material in mind when he entered libraries. "I would take different books from different locations to fill in gaps of what I had," the ultimate goal being the creation of a repository. By "taking vital little slices" from libraries, he felt he could "complete and coordinate the ultimate collection in my field of interest, backed up by fixtures, and parts of these same buildings. I feel I pretty much accomplished this until my demise. I was interested in the nineteenth-century settlements and buildings of the U.S. and its architecture and locations. I used these books as one vast working reference library. I'd authenticate my architectural materials with the books and know the history of the part of the country they came from."

This "ultimate collection" was supposed to go in the Elliot House, and Blumberg recalled the joy and hope he felt when he bought that "fine old building" in 1978, and the profound anger that consumed him when he had to sell it three years later. "I had an immense amount of pride in myself in owning that place. I had preserved it and had a prospective use for my avocation. I just hated to sell it." Forced to move out in 1981, he "had to dispose of my stuff," including eight old cars he "literally gave away." He estimates that "fully" 30 percent of his time over the next seven years was "in transit," and notes that he "felt totally defeated" by the turn of events.

"I just burned and finally exploded. I crossed the line. I rationalized to myself. If for all my insight and hard work and ambition all I could get was city bureaucratical bullshit and deception, I was going to pay it back. I started knocking off everything and place I figured I could get away with." Teaming up with Howie Bergstrom and "some bikers" he knew, Blumberg "let loose" and intensified his raids. "I figured out the obit scam," he wrote. "I was beside myself with rage at the city of Minneapolis and my father. I told him I was breaking into places and his comment was 'Don't threaten me.'"

After a few years—he was not specific as to when—Blumberg "gave obits up," primarily because the young men he had befriended were then "breaking into businesses in the area," and he was not interested in becoming involved in that activity. "I told them I'd buy stained-glass windows, doors and fireplaces from condemned places. I was out of town a lot and they would accumulate things for me and

I'd purchase them when I got back." And he felt a sense of responsibility to them as well.

"Those kids were of great help to me as they gave me companionship and moral support. I was traveling a lot and my library thefts were increasing. I rationalized that by clearly opening the restricted areas of large libraries and museums, I'd have choice pickings. It also was a release to me of my anger and frustration of my failed past. My family had given me, in my mind, deception or stubborn resistance to my wishes. I wasn't asking for something for nothing, only an even chance."

It was during a trip to Texas in 1985 that he "started checking the Texas antique market and went up and discovered Canton, Texas." Canton was great, he exclaimed, more than six thousand dealers, "mostly antiques and high prices." Also at about this time he determined that the world economy would collapse and that he would be better off putting "every cent" into "rare gold coins." Consequently, he began to divest himself of antiques in Texas and at the huge flea market operated three weeks each year in Brimfield, Massachusetts. All the proceeds went into the purchase of gold. Acting reluctantly on his father's advice, he secured a safety deposit box in Minnesota, a decision he later came to regret when the contents were seized by the government and coins valued at more than $100,000 were taken into custody. "Something kept telling me to go into Mexico and bury it," he wrote ruefully.

"My only storage problem at this point, I was beginning to see, was in the books," he continued. "I used them as a reference library of knowledge. I would spend more and more time reading. I read of book collecting and learned how to spot value. I figured a book was a silent source of wisdom and if I illegitimately obtained it from neglect, of mainly the government, I was to use it. Guard it. Preserve it for others, which I did, plus shared with the underprivileged youths."

Finally, in 1988, he decided to buy another house, and he knew precisely what he was looking for. "Nestled in a lush green valley amidst the miles of corn fields lies Ottumwa, Iowa. Rural Iowa small town neighborly folk. Howdy neighbor! Welcome friend! Nice to meet you! Come far?"

That, however, was "not the general tone" he found.

"I envisioned a friendly small town neighborly attitude in smaller towns. The friendly farmer in bib overalls, the nice waitress in the restaurant. The cute freckle-faced girl with pigtails. The buck tooth boy with a cowlick. The kindly neighbor with a hot pie under a clean dish towel. The solemn and consoling minister with the welcome and 'the lord doth bless' who when he sees need sends over a kindly elderly lady from the church club. Where peril and suffering doesn't have to be spoken of to be addressed. I moved to Ottumwa, Iowa, to find this and for a while leave the big city and all its evils. All I found was ostracism in a more concentrated form."

After buying the brick house at 116 North Jefferson Street for $16,000 cash, he "took in an elderly man, also alone in a city," James Hall from Cincinnati. "I was trying by leaving Minneapolis to escape the bitterness I had to being screwed around in my living and collecting situation as well as gradually weed myself away from the criminal element. The bitterness I had made me want to commit crimes. The selling and on the road and the gold gave me a feel of accomplishment but added to the loneliness."

All this made him agreeable to the unexpected request from an old friend. "I was contacted by Ken Rhodes and moved him in as I was lonely. Mr. Hall needed a friend, Rhodes needed a place and wanted to open an art glass repair shop. He had the credentials, he did good work." Because they had known each other for fifteen years, he thought the man was sincere.

"Little did I know my assets in books and antiques would weigh on his mind until he conceived a way to lie and get me arrested, my stuff taken, and conveniently with me out of the way, he could simply state, 'Oh, that's mine,' or 'I lent Steve that.' The FBI wouldn't know about something that wasn't stolen even after the investigation. He was left there and he stole all the art glass out of the place and all the light fixtures, drapes, dishes, even the doorknobs. This is the kind of scoundrel the government calls a generally reliable informant."

Rhodes was asked during the trial if he took any of Blumberg's possessions out of the Ottumwa house, and Rhodes admitted that he had taken material to his home in Detroit and had intended to use whatever proceeds he could generate to establish a "trust fund" in

Blumberg's behalf, a disclosure that even had people at the prosecutor's table smiling.

Though a former specialist in internal medicine, Dr. Blumberg said that he gave up his practice in the 1970s for several reasons. Somebody had to manage Zimmerman Realty, but more important, "Stephen became a full-time concern and required most of my attention." He added that he often felt "helpless" trying to deal with his son's obsessions.

Dr. Blumberg was in Des Moines for all of the criminal proceedings, though he remained outside the courtroom while witnesses were being questioned. "It's just too much, too painful," he said at the time. "It is an appallingly sad situation, and it has been this way since Stephen was a child. He was always a little guy, a shrimp really, but he had the face of an angel. He never had a date, not once. He was always a loner, but he got along so well with older people. He was always introducing me to these elderly people he made friends with, and they all just loved him."

In addition to the family real estate holdings, Dr. Blumberg also administers the Carrie Blumberg Trust, and always made sure his son received the money he had coming from it. While he knew Stephen had gathered thousands of books, he said he always assumed they were bought legitimately. "They looked like plain old books to me," he said. "There was no reason, as far as I could see, why he would have to steal books." Once his son was arrested, Dr. Blumberg underwrote a defense that cost close to $500,000 and pursued a vigorous appeal. When that was denied in 1992, he paid the $200,000 fine that Judge Vietor had imposed. The judge handed down a prison sentence of five years and eleven months.

"No fewer than twelve psychiatrists have examined him over twenty-six years, and only Dr. Taylor found him sane," Dr. Logan told me on the day his patient was sentenced by Judge Vietor. "He was in and out of juvenile court on seventeen different occasions," beginning in 1965 when his father brought him in for incorrigibility. "He was sixteen years old and his father couldn't stop him from going into old buildings."

By 1969, Blumberg had been hospitalized three times, and by then he was traveling around the country "going into abandoned households, taking old doorknobs, scooping up Victorian junk," Dr. Logan said. "You don't take what a person says, you look at what the record shows. These people don't pop up like magic. What Stephen shares with a lot of criminals is the kick he gets out of getting away with what he does. He wasn't risking his life just to get the book, he was risking his life to get it out of the library. Stephen was going for the record. That is why he was so fixated on surpassing Shinn." Dr. Logan also found Blumberg's fondness for beautiful bindings marginally significant. "He dresses shabbily, but he likes the way certain books are 'clothed.' I haven't quite figured that one out just yet."

"The man is a thief," Linda Reade repeated in court and on the local television news shows. "Just like any cat burglar, he is a thief." She opposed all suggestions that Blumberg receive anything other than a long term in the penitentiary. "The federal prison system is fully equipped to offer appropriate medical care," she replied when asked about the professional attention Blumberg seemed to require, if not for his own benefit, then at least for that of the society he will rejoin in 1996 when he is scheduled to be released from a federal penitentiary in Rochester, Minnesota, still a relatively young man of forty-eight.

Six hours after Judge Vietor handed down his sentence, the late-July temperatures were still in the high nineties when Ray Cornell, a Des Moines private detective, took me to a local hangout called The Viking. Shortly after Blumberg's arrest, Cornell had been hired by Dr. Blumberg; his investigation had disclosed the government's frequent use of Kenny Rhodes as a paid informant. Blumberg also was released to Cornell's custody while awaiting trial, so they saw each other every day for more than a year.

We ordered a couple of beers and an Iowa specialty the detective had been insisting I try ever since we met at the trial in January: a deep-fried pork tenderloin sandwich lathered in spicy mustard and garnished with thickly sliced onions. Inevitably, the subject came around to Judge Vietor's sentence earlier in the day; we agreed that laws had been broken and people had been hurt, but the case still required some perspective.

"Nothing happens in a vacuum," Cornell pointed out. "Stephen is a clever thief and he deserves to pay a price for what he did. But I have a lot of trouble with those people who want to see him hang. Maybe I'm coming at it from a different direction, but then most of the cases I work on are murders, rapes, wife beatings, drugs, and child abuse, so I have a hard time making Steve out to be something that he isn't. He stole valuable books, but he treated them with respect, and they are going back to where they belong. Harm was done, but maybe now these libraries will pay a little more attention to their security. It may be true that he is one of the great cultural robbers of our time. But he is not an evil man."

Cornell paused for a deep pull from the long-necked bottle before offering one more thought. "Look, there was no violence, okay? There were no drugs and nobody was robbed of their life savings. Which makes me wonder: What kind of time is the savings and loan crowd doing? Those are federal cases too. How come I don't see any of those guys going off for six years with Steve Blumberg?"

With his left hand, the private detective placed the beer on the table in front of him and in a swift motion reached deftly under his right arm.

"See," he said, patting the empty space. "No gun. I haven't carried my little nine-millimeter in seven months. Come Monday, the shoulder holster gets strapped on and I go back to the real world."

14

Carpe Diem

Four large folios bound in crimson morocco spun into view on a revolving dais at the front of Sotheby's main auction gallery on Manhattan's Upper East Side. "Lot One Hundred, the Shakespeares," John L. Marion announced from the old mahogany pulpit he uses as a rostrum, and paused briefly before proceeding with what would become the most consequential book transaction of the 1980s.

The bidding opened at $500,000 and quickly advanced in $50,000 increments to $1 million. Paddles had been raised throughout the room, but at $1.5 million just two contestants were left, one of them— a wealthy Japanese businessman, it was later rumored—bidding on the telephone. The other, a man who had made a fortune by brokering advertising time on television during the 1970s and 1980s, was seated in the center of the hall next to his agent.

"One million five-fifty against you, sir," Marion said, and pointed at Richard Manney, the man in the center of the hall. Manney nodded yes.

"One million six-fifty at the desk," the auctioneer countered; Manney nodded once again. The telephone bidder affirmed $1.75 million and Manney raised the stakes to $1.8 million. When an attendant confirmed the telephone bidder's advance to $1.85 million, there were ten seconds of absolute silence.

"Think about it," Marion finally said in a soothing voice, and was rewarded by the nod that closed the contest. With the ten percent buyer's premium added, Richard Manney had just agreed to pay a little under $2.1 million for the First Folio of 1623, the Second Folio of 1632, the Third Folio of 1664, and the Fourth Folio of 1685, all bearing the same title, *Comedies, Histories, & Tragedies*. When the Garden Ltd. sale ended the next day, 308 books had found new owners, and $16.2 million, an average of $52,815 per lot, had been spent, 12 percent of that for the seventeenth-century books known collectively as the First Four Folios of Shakespeare. They had cost Haven O'More a mere $200,000 when he bought them from Hans P. Kraus in the late 1970s, but these were the freewheeling 1980s, and this turned out to be the last big sale of the decade.

"In my heart of hearts I knew I had to have them," Manney said on the telephone shortly after the sale, and when we met later in New York he explained his goals as a collector. "The great books of all time, okay? The 'high spots' if you want, call them what you will, but these are the greatest books in the world, and that is what I am after." Certainly he had paid more than twice the upper estimate, but he offered a bit of advice about what it takes to collect at his level. "When you are bidding on the best objects, I don't care what they are, you usually pay more than what everybody expects it will take. And you have to be prepared to do this. You have to go in with that understanding, because the best always commands a premium."

Ten seconds does not sound like such a long time, but that night in the gallery, with so much at stake, it felt like an eternity. "It wasn't the price," Manney insisted. "It was, 'Do I really want these books that badly?' Because, frankly, there were some other Shakespeares out there on the market, nice ones, for a lot less money. But my thinking was, these are the best copies we will see in my lifetime, and I either get them now or regret it forever."

Manney also was interested in acquiring an exceedingly rare copy of *Don Quixote* at the Garden sale, but dropped out of that contest at $650,000. "I knew the Shakespeares were coming along, so I decided to hang loose. The estimate on the Cervantes was two hundred thousand. I knew it would go higher than that, but when it passed six hundred fifty thousand, I figured, let the people who really want it that badly have it. There's always another day." After he withdrew, the bidding for that book kept on going for another $1 million before being hammered down to Arthur Freeman of Quaritch Ltd., representing an unidentified Spanish collector. A few months later, I asked Freeman how the presale estimates could have been so far off. "Two people wanted one book very badly," he explained. "It's as simple as that."

Not long after the sale, I asked John Marion about the clever way he had drawn one more $50,000 bid out of Dick Manney. "I looked down, and I could see him shaking his head, so essentially, he was done," the auctioneer recalled. "I was looking right at him, and he shook his head no, so for all intents and purposes, that was it. I looked away, and that's when I came back and said, 'Think about it.' I gave him that moment for himself. I just knew he was going to bid one more time. I had this other bid on the phone, and I was certain he would bid again. That's why I do what I do. It's my instinct."

A year before he bought the Shakespeares, Manney was the anonymous buyer of a previously unrecorded copy of Poe's *Tamerlane,* a little book that made headlines when a commercial fisherman found it buried beneath a pile of agricultural tracts in a New Hampshire antiques barn and bought it for $15. Manney had no serious competition that night, just the reserve established by Sotheby's as the minimum amount it would accept for the "black orchid" of American literature; he paid $198,000.

Before his marriage in 1963, Manney enjoyed trying his luck at various table games in Las Vegas. Once he and his wife, Gloria, became collectors, however, his casino play ended. "I just had no desire to shoot craps or play baccarat once I got involved in art, furnishings, antiques, and books," he said. "I found that the auctions satisfy my taste for gambling quite nicely. I get all the action I can handle at a big sale. The hunt is everything. I go in there ready to do battle, and my heart just starts to pound if there's something we want. The tension, the anxiety—I love it. I won't bid on something unless we're really going to own it, because I try to get what I go after, without being ridiculous. Up or down in the price range means nothing, because you have to have the object."

Once Dick and Gloria Manney began collecting in the 1960s, they fed each other's enthusiasm. Manney estimated that during the height of their activity they were spending between $5 million and $6 million a year on their various hobbies. "We're building several specific collections," he said during our first interview. "I'm building a major book collection of some of the great high spots in world literature. We're building a collection of American Federal furniture, and we're putting the finishing touches on our American paintings collection. Then we're always buying objets d'art. We're always buying little things, big things—just things that strike our fancy. If I'm not buying something, my wife is. We're always out, she's in the shops, I'm walking up and down Madison Avenue, we're both looking. Dealers call me up all the time, and a day of the week doesn't go by where we don't add something. We must buy four or five hundred things a year."

He described himself as an entrepreneur who started out "with sixty dollars in my pocket," a "kid from the streets of the Bronx" who made it big in the advertising business. A phrase in vogue during the 1980s was "disposable income," meaning money that people could spend on diversions like books, paintings, and antiques. "I detest that expression," Manney said. "As far as I'm concerned, there's no such thing as disposable income. Disposable means there's money that you don't really need and that you're willing to throw away, that what you are doing with it is unnecessary. I believe strongly that what my wife and I have done is necessary."

The downside to this passion for beautiful things, Manney added, is that "the collection owns us, we don't own the collection. There are times when we don't even leave the house. I have the most sophisticated security system imaginable, and yet there's always somebody there. It's a great responsibility. You have to worry about taking care of the objects, restoring the objects, conserving the objects. They must always be protected and insured, be taken care of by a curator. For the books at least, I am the curator."

♦ ♦ ♦

On May 17, 1991, a year and a half after Richard Manney bought the Shakespeares, I was in New York to attend the Stuart B. Schimmel Collection of Book Arts sale at Christie's. During a lull, the New York bookseller Bart Auerbach asked if I had heard the news: "Dick Manney is selling his library."

As we spoke, an impressive selection of Manney's books was on display a few blocks away at the Grolier Club. The members there would never allow an exhibition of material about to be sold, I said; it would give off an unfavorable impression of showcasing a person's goods. "Check it out," Auerbach replied, and returned to the sale. I asked around, and sure enough, not only was Manney selling his books, he had caused a minor uproar by announcing his plans at a dinner meeting of the Grolier Club when the books were already being exhibited. "I find it unspeakably vulgar," a woman who had been a member for many years said. "I feel used," a former club president added.

When next we met, Manney seemed genuinely sorry about the feelings he had bruised, but insisted that the timing of his announcement was coincidental. "The club invited me to exhibit the books a year ago. But a year is a long time and my decision to sell the books came quite suddenly." The decision, he went on to explain, was caused by the recession, which had been dragging on interminably and was "just killing" his business. "My profits from the business cannot sustain our collecting habit. I am selling my books because I'm afraid to sell anything else. There's no way I can get the value back on the antiques that I can get for the books. So if I have to sell anything, I've got to sell the books. I can always start another library."

I also learned from Manney that he had been given a line of credit for whatever purchases he might make before bidding at the Garden sale. "Never in the history of the world have I borrowed a nickel to buy anything for my antique and art collections," he said, "but I was given a year to pay for the folios. I had to give them so much money at certain periods during that twelve months. And that is the only deal that I ever made in my life to buy books."

Manney bought the Shakespeares on November 9, 1989. When he described for me his arrangement with Sotheby's, nineteen months had elapsed and he still owed the auction house "a million and change, a million one or a million two." Apparently, he had begun to suffer major cash-flow problems well before he decided to disperse his library. "I need money to pay Sotheby's back. That was my first motivation. But then I said, 'Things are tight. I can only draw so much out of the business, so I'll sell all of the books.' The collection's worth, I don't know, seven million bucks, take a number. I never intended to keep the books forever anyway, I already told you that."

Manney had in fact mentioned during our earlier interview that his wife and he felt that the library ultimately should return to the market-place. "I believe books should be circulated," he said. "Paintings are one of a kind, they're unique, and when they are really special, they belong in a place where people can see them. When a rare book goes into an institution, you have to be a scholar and you have to get special permission to go in and see it. Very rarely are they ever on display. Don't get me wrong, it is proper that certain books go into institutions. I just feel that because my wife and I give mostly everything else we collect away, I should return something to the people who are going to love them and enjoy them and visit with them the way I do."

Manney acknowledged he was allowing the auction house "to take the million two off the top" of the proceeds. But, he said, "this is very important, okay? Read my lips. I am not selling the library because this is the only way to satisfy Sotheby's. If that were the case, I'd pick a few items and just sell them, and that would take care of that. But I'm not going to cut the heart out of the collection and cheat the public. If you're going to sell something, let people come and buy and be offered the extent of what you put together."

Still, "the larger fact of the matter is that I could use some money right now. As collectors, we spent all our liquid income on our passion. I am selling the books because they have held their value. The paintings and the antiques, the way this economy is going, if we sold any of them right now, we'd take a real beating." Manney stressed over and over how he had "to get liquid" again. "What am I going to get liquid with? Something I'm going to take a major hit on, or something that will return its value? I'm a successful businessman. Since I was twenty-two years old, I've been in business for myself. I've got enough smarts to know that if I'm going to sell anything, I'm going to sell what has maintained the value. Should I go and sell my Childe Hassam, which is probably one of the three finest Childe Hassam paintings in the world? If I were to sell that now, I'd deserve to have my head examined."

The recession was not entirely to blame for his troubles, he admitted. "We all are in command of our own lives. I'm not a victim of any third party. I'm a victim of myself. I'm in command of my own life. I simply have to raise some money." Quoting Mike Todd, the late Hollywood producer, he said, " 'I am not poor. I am temporarily out of funds.' I feel the same way." He saw no contradiction in disposing of his library and keeping the art. "My wife and I give most of our art away. We have two collections with our names on them at the Metropolitan Museum of Art, another at the Art Institute of Chicago, our Rococo Revival furniture is at the Winterthur in Delaware. But as for the books, I have an obligation to the next generation of collectors. I have earned the right to make that statement."

In 1991, Harry N. Abrams published a book on the Gloria Manney Collection of Miniature Portraits on Ivory deposited at the Metropolitan. After an exhibition in New York, the paintings were shown at the National Museum of American Art in Washington, D.C. In 1986, the Manneys gave the Winterthur Museum in Odessa, Delaware, seventy-one pieces of furniture built by the nineteenth-century German-born cabinetmaker John Henry Belter and provided funds for their installation and conservation. "I admire the Manneys tremendously," Mrs. Pauline L. du Pont Harrison, honorary trustee and daughter of the museum's founder, Henry F. du Pont, said. "They have been very generous to our museum. The furniture they gave fits in perfectly here because it extended our coverage. I feel very strongly about them." As a member of the Winterthur board, Richard Manney offered "very wise vision and an intelligent viewpoint," she added. "I felt from the start that he would help us open our museum to the world. He knows a great deal about business, and he gave us sound advice on how we could get a commercial program for the museum started. Richard and Gloria have been tremendously helpful. I am devoted to both of them."

On October 11, 1991, the major players again gathered at Sotheby's. Richard Manney was in an upstairs booth at the back of the room, pacing; nearby stood Diana D. Brooks, president and chief executive officer of Sotheby's American operations. The books about to be sold were Manney's, and this time it was not the titles that were important, but the numbers. The library brought a little under $4 million for 314 lots, with high prices spent for important works of Jack London, Nathaniel Hawthorne, Arthur Conan Doyle, Ernest Hemingway, and Oscar Wilde, as well as the King James Bible and a copy of Bacon's *Essayes*. Lou Weinstein of Heritage Book Shop in Los Angeles accounted for $1 million of the $3.9 million spent, paying a third of that for Charles Dickens's autograph manuscript of *The Haunted Man* and *The Ghost's Bargain*. One gem of the collection, the dedication copy of *Huckleberry Finn*, sold for $99,000, well above the high estimate of $80,000. The inscription on the front free endpaper reads:

> *To*
> *Livy L. Clemens*
> *with the matured and perfect love of*
> *The Author*
> *Xmas, 1884.*

Manney's first-issue copy of *Paradise Lost*, one of a handful still in an original binding, went for the same figure. A copy of Dashiell Hammett's *The Maltese Falcon* sold for $29,700, and a copy of *Dracula* inscribed by Bram Stoker on its publication date went for $44,000. Disappointing was the interest in Manney's *Tamerlane*, which was bought by Stephan Loewentheil of the 19th Century Bookshop in Baltimore for $143,000. But overall the sale was a success. "Almost like the old days," Los Angeles dealer Mark Hime said afterward. "You'd never have known there was a recession going on outside the building."

Only two lots did not meet Sotheby's reserve, or were "bought in" by the house. The 1661 Eliot Indian Bible was "bought in" at $135,000 and the four Shakespeare folios, which had carried a daunting presale estimate of $1.5 million to $2.5 million, attracted tepid interest from the floor. Only a few paddles were raised during the early going, and the auctioneer, David Redden, stopped calling out numbers at $1.1 million. Thus, the very books whose purchase on credit had forced the dispersal remained unsold, providing a cautionary note about how tastes and trends can change.

A few weeks later, advertising trade journals were reporting another kind of activity, this time at the other end of Manhattan, in the United States Bankruptcy Court. Manney's company, The Mediators, Inc., owed more than $32 million to various networks and television stations throughout the United States. Soon, what had started as an involuntary proceeding became a reorganization under Chapter 11. Court papers showed that it was rapidly becoming a brawl. Frustrated by their attempts to secure what they felt was an acceptable settlement from Richard and Gloria Manney's company, the creditors had sought permission to attach the couple's art, which was itemized in a list of seven hundred works. Included among them was "Rain Shower on Rue Bonaparte," a Paris street scene painted by Childe Hassam, and originally purchased for $735,000. The Manneys had acquired Norman Rockwell's "The Right to Know" for $225,000 in 1982.

Court papers indicated that all the works on that list had been bought by The Mediators over a period of years, but had been sold on one day, June 30, 1988, to the Manneys, who were listed as one hundred percent owners of the company, for $12.6 million. Lawyers talked back and forth and resolved nothing, but representatives of both sides agreed that it would take many months to sort everything out. The Manneys, meanwhile, placed their large home in Irvington-on-Hudson up for sale.

In June 1993, Sotheby's featured a number of prize antiques from the Richard and Gloria Manney collection at a major spring sale of Americana. Among the items sold was a silver dining-table centerpiece made by John W. Forbes in 1825 and presented to the then governor of New York, De Witt Clinton, upon completion of the Erie Canal. When the Manneys bought it for $264,000 in 1982, they outbid the State Department. The price eleven years later was $266,500, and the buyer was the Metropolitan Museum of Art, where the couple had placed the intricately crafted piece known as a mirrored plateau on indefinite loan. "We had to have it, we've had it so long," Morrison Heckscher, curator of the American Wing at the museum, said. "It will go right back on display."

The bankruptcy hearings continued with little movement toward a settlement. After three years of legal maneuvering, nothing had been resolved. In June 1994 a plan of reorganization for The Mediators, Inc. drafted by the creditors committee included liquidation of the company. Hope was expressed that some form of settlement would be reached by the end of the year. Manney, meanwhile, had been named president of M.P.I. International Ltd. in 1993, a marketing and media company doing business with the motion picture industry.

Walking with Manney on Madison Avenue back to his office from lunch, I had once asked him what he thought about the talk going around that suggested he was the Donald Trump of the rare-book world, a mocking reference to the highly publicized adventures of the young wheeler-dealer who had enjoyed celebrity status for his successful exploits during the 1980s, but had become the butt of snide jokes afterward when he fell on hard times.

"Put on your tape recorder," Manney said, stopping in his tracks so abruptly that there was a mild flurry of curiosity among other pedestrians. "The people who really know me know that I am not a flash in the pan. For twenty-eight years my wife and I have put together collections and given them away." He smiled. "I'm flattered that I am able to make the kind of mark where some of my enemies are so jealous they want to compare me to Donald Trump. I take that as a compliment."

Epilogue

If the 1990s was to be a stripped-down version of the decade that preceded it, then no setting was more appropriate for a big book sale than Swann Galleries, the no-nonsense auction house at 104 East Twenty-fifth Street in New York. For two days in April 1992, the major dealers gathered in this turn-of-the-century loft building on Lower Manhattan, a structure of unadorned function that had been home to a prosperous printing shop before Swann owner George S. Lowry converted the sixth floor to an auction hall in 1980.

Instead of fancy plastic paddles, the registration numbers are marked on paper cards. Unlike the auction rooms at Christie's and Sotheby's farther uptown, Swann has no elegant paintings hanging on its walls, and no effort has been made to disguise the ventilation ducts that snake across the ceiling. But the seats are comfortable and the sound system works, and though the items put on the block are not Gutenberg Bibles or Audubon folios, they are the kinds of books gathered by the vast majority of collectors in the United States.

For this sale, mounted to mark the golden anniversary of Swann Galleries, 519 items covering a full range of categories—American, English, and Continental literature; Judaica, children's literature, detective fiction, fantasy, and science fiction among them—had been culled from a ten thousand–volume library consigned by Raymond Epstein of Chicago, a retired engineer and architect.

Sitting in the front row next to Epstein was Ralph Newman of Chicago. Lou Weinstein and Mark Hime were in from California, and Jim Cummins, Glenn Horowitz, Steve Weissman, Justin Schiller, and Bart Auerbach made up part of the New York contingent. Bill Reese was in from New Haven, Anne and David Bromer had driven down from Boston, Stephan Loewentheil had come up from Baltimore, Clarence Wolf was in from Philadelphia. Arthur Freeman flew over from London, and even Stephen Massey, head of the rare-book department at Christie's, dropped by to watch. Altogether an impressive crowd, and most dealers were carrying commissions from customers.

"I've been collecting for forty years, and now it's time for the books to go," Raymond Epstein explained before the sale. "I'm seventy-four years old, and my wife and my kids wouldn't know what to do if they were stuck with all these books. The truth is that I also can use the money in my retirement. I must say that when I got here this morning and saw them all laid out like this, I said to George Lowry, 'Pack them up, I'll take them home.' But I am very happy about the sale because a lot of people are getting books they want to own. They're going back into circulation."

Soon, a Kelmscott *Chaucer* sold for $35,200, $15,000 above the upper estimate. L. Frank Baum's *Wizard of Oz* brought $20,900, and Wilkie Collins's *The Queen of Hearts* in three volumes showed strength at $10,450. Patterns require repetition to take shape, so it was nothing particularly remarkable when on the second day of the sale a woman holding number 108 bought an inscribed copy of Jack London's *White Fang* for $5,500 and Peter Newell's 1908 illustrated work for children, *The Hole Book,* for $1,320. But when number 108 topped all comers for a fine limited edition of Beatrix Potter's *The Tale of Peter Rabbit* at $55,000, people began to pay attention. In the very next lot, she spent another $20,900 for the first trade edition of the same book, going ten times higher than the presale estimate to get it. As she continued to buy, more heads turned in her direction. Lot 417, Mary Wollstonecraft Shelley's *Frankenstein, or the Modern Prometheus,* for $30,800, and Lot 418, Adam Smith's *Wealth of Nations,* $26,400, then became her property; next, Lot 421, Gertrude Smith's *The Arabella and Araminta Stories,* one of fifteen large copies on Royal Japan paper, was knocked down to her number for $26,400.

As Lot 440 was being sold, a Swann employee held up a piece of paper with a scrawled note that read, "We just broke $1 million," the first time in Swann's fifty-year history that that magic number had been surpassed. Then, an 1855 edition of Walt Whitman's *Leaves of Grass,* one of just two hundred copies produced in a first issue binding of dark green cloth with gilt decorations, came up in Lot 500. When the bidding reached $15,000, the dark-haired woman in the middle of the room raised her number and held it high until the prize was hers; the price, with a 10 percent house commission known as a "buyer's premium" added, came to $30,800. Fifteen minutes later the sale was over, and no fewer than ten booksellers were introducing themselves to the woman most knew only as number 108.

"Joan Hill," she said with a bright smile, and offered her hand. She and her husband, Daryl, live in a suburb of Santa Barbara, California, and though they "dabble" in the trade of children's books, their purchases this day were for themselves. "We've just started putting together a high-spot collection," she said. After dropping all the new business cards she had just received in her purse, Hill walked over to Raymond Epstein and introduced herself.

Later, Epstein said wistfully before leaving the auction gallery, "The books you see here used to be stacked all over my house, but it was never enough. I used to read catalogues in bed at night, and I would say to my wife, 'Look at this, here's a book I paid fifty dollars for, a dealer wants thirty-five hundred for it.' And my wife would say, 'So sell it.' Well, today she finally got her wish."

Notes

Sources cited in the Notes by the author's last name or by a short form of the title are to be found in the "General Bibliography," pages 584–604.

Complete information on archives containing cited material can be found on page 583.

Prologue

Page

2   "accountable for anything": Edna Ferber, *A Peculiar Treasure* (New York: Literary Guild of America, 1939), 30–31.

5   "instinct to collect": Wroth, "The Chief End of Book Madness," 77.

Part One

1: "TOUCHING THE HAND"

9   "The bibliophile is": Lawrence S. Thompson, 42.

9   "A great library": Burton, 171.

| 10 | "O my darling books": Fitzgerald, 1. |

10 "My wish is that": Newton, *Amenities of Book Collecting*, 94.

11–12 "In the days that followed": The following from Uzanne: "In memory of the happy moments," 134; "perfect politeness," 133; "in his own image . . . customs of men," 135; "special costume . . . Paris bookstall men," 228–30.

12–13 "A child bearing the name": *John Carter Brown Library*, 65; "No one but the collector," Ibid., 41.

14 "They may some day": Stillwell, 13. For more on Hawkins, see also Cannon, 188–91, and Dickinson, 154–55.

14 "On my coffin when in the grave": Jackson, vol. 2, 265.

14 "I have given my friends to understand": Field, 170.

15 When Elizabeth Eleanor Siddal Rossetti: Dante Gabriel Rossetti's letters from Buck.

16 What undoubtedly qualifies: For more on the Gospel of St. John, see Olmert 9–10, and Hubert Chadwick, SJ, "Unfamiliar Libraries II: Stonyhurst College," *Book Collector*, Winter 1957, 343–49.

16 "disposition to collect books": Burton, v.

16–17 "It is, as you will observe": Ibid., 231.

17 "For all time these courts": Theodore Blegen, "A Glorious Court," in *Book Collecting and Scholarship*, 23.

17 "It is a wonderful and magnificent thing": Rosenbach, *Books and Bidders*, 254–55.

18 "I have known men": Ibid., 37; "are buzzards": Ibid., 17–18. Rosenbach also tells of the time his Uncle Moses Polock dropped a treasured copy of *Tom Jones* out of a horse-drawn wagon onto an icy Philadelphia bridge. "You should have let me get your book. You might have broken your leg!" young Abe, then thirteen, said when his mentor returned from retrieving the volume. "I would risk breaking two legs for this book," Polock grumbled. Ibid., 36–37.

18 "My main anxiety . . . Philobiblon Club?": Adelman, vii. See also Adelman, "Introducing the Collection," in *The Adelman Collection* (Bryn Mawr, Pa.: Bryn Mawr College Library, 1976), 7–11; see also Adelman obituary, *Philadelphia Inquirer*, April 27, 1985.

18 "First of all": Barrett, 18.

18–19 "It must be clearly understood": Taylor, "Battle Between Libraries," 232.

19 "The trouble with you": Ibid., 238.

19   "integrity of this library . . . serve the purpose?": Jameson, 11–14. See also Maxwell.

20   "Every item was purchased": Osborne, *Alfred Clark Chapin,* 12.

20   "With no disrespect": Hofer, 4; "he that hath a library": ibid., 2. For more on Hofer, see Hofer, "On Collecting Japanese Manuscript [MS] Scrolls," *Book Collector,* Winter 1958, 369–80; William A. Jackson, "Philip Hofer," *Book Collector,* Summer 1960, 151–64; Bond, *Philip Hofer Bequest,* vii–xiv (introduction).

20–23   Account of Ellis and Fitzpatrick: Vosper.

23   "with chiseled features": Hellmann, "Steward of Strawberry Hill—I," 26.

23   "The loyalty of collectors": Hellmann, "Farmington Revisited," 168. For books by Wilmarth Lewis, see bibliography.

24   "he had hardly any serious rival": Muir, *Talks on Book-Collecting,* 4. For more on Michael Sadleir, see Sadleir, "The Sadleir Library," *Book Collector,* Summer 1955, 115–21; John Carter, "Michael Sadleir: A Valediction," *Book Collector,* Spring 1958, 58–61.

24   In a 1951 essay: Sadleir, vol. 1, xii.

25   "the finest and most beautiful": Hobson, 273.

25   "It has raged": Dibdin, 11.

25   "ingenious views": For background on Dr. Ferriar, see entry in *Dictionary of National Biography.*

25–26   "What wild desires . . . mind engage": Ferriar, 139–40.

26   "pride, pleasure, and privileges . . . READING THEM": *Bibliosophia,* 1–4.

27   "Do you take care . . . bibliomanie": ed., Strachey, vol. 2, 40–41 (March 19, 1750). On the publishing history of the letters, see ibid., vol. 1, xlvii–xlviii.

27–28   "inordinate desire . . . instinctual drives": Weiner, 217; "literature of bibliomania . . . in Bohemia": Ibid., 220; "fetish . . . castration anxiety": Ibid., 231; "It has never": Quoted in Ibid., 217. For a more current evaluation by a psychoanalyst of collecting in general, see Muensterberger.

28   "It speaks rather well": Rosenbach, *Book Hunter's Holiday,* 106–7; "Let us forgive her": Ibid., 114.

29   Among history's more dogged: The account of Queen Christina's library is from Charles Elton, "Christina of Sweden and Her Books," in *Bibliographica,* vol. 1, 5–30; "Continue to send me" and "was arranged in four great halls": Ibid., 11.

30   "If Freud's helpless love": Gay, 170.

30   "Miss Lowell had a well-defined plan": Rosenbach, *Book Hunter's Holiday,* 126.

31   Regrettably, visitors: For more on Mrs. Pope, see Charles Ryskamp, "Abbie Pope," in *Book Collector,* Spring 1984, 39–52.

31   "Fifteen Women Book Collectors": See article by Marie E. Korey and Ruth Mortimer, 49–87. See also Frances Hamill, "Some Unconventional Women Before 1800: Printers, Booksellers, and Collectors," in *Papers of the Bibliographical Society of America,* 4th qtr., 1955, 300–14.

31–32   "origin of a new species . . . *unending pursuit*": Mary Hyde Eccles, 89–100. For more on the Hyde Collection, see Austin, *Four Oaks Farm* and *Four Oaks Library,* and Donald and Mary Hyde, "The Hyde Collection," *Book Collector,* Autumn 1955, 208–16.

32   "My mother died": Janny Scott, "Onassis Burial to Be Monday at Arlington," *New York Times,* May 21, 1994, 1.

33   "With the development of bibliomania": Sander, 155.

34   "I am not a thief. . . . My copy is not unique": Ibid., 157. For more on Don Vincente, see Rosenbach, *Books and Bidders,* 37–38; Flaubert, see Koch's "Postscript," 49–56; L. S. Thompson, 41–89, and Charles G. Roland, M.D., "Bibliomania," *Journal of the American Medical Association* 212, (April 6, 1970), 133–35.

34   "scarcely knew how . . . the only copy in Spain!": Flaubert, *Bibliomania: A Tale,* 47–48.

35   "For him that stealeth": Drogin, 88.

35   Historians agree: For more on *l'affaire Libri,* see De Ricci, 131–38; Sander, 158–60; L. S. Thompson, 53–54.

36–37   Throughout history: The following examples are from Cim: Emil Bessels, 663–64; Mr. Bryan, the American expatriate, 664; Henri de la Bédoyère, 667; Anquetil-Duperron, 672; Bordas-Demoulin, 674–75.

37   The nineteenth-century French pianist: Eric Blom, ed., *Grove's Dictionary of Music and Musicians,* 5th ed., vol. 1, 111–12, s.v. "Alkan."

37   Professor Theodor Mommsen: "Prof. Mommsen's Peril," *New York Times,* Jan. 27, 1903, 8; "Prof. Mommsen Is Dead," *New York Times,* Nov. 2, 1903, 1.

38   "He is in himself a great library": Anderton, 4.

38   "low and mean rank . . . luxury of book learning" and "The only copy of this work": Dibdin, *Bibliomania,* 86.

38   "indispensable condition": Cochrane, 267.

38   "lived on titles and indexes" and "dirty, ragged, and as happy as a king": Elton and Elton, 74–75.

39   "If I were the owner": Smith, *A Sentimental Library,* xii. See also Smith, *First Nights and First Editions.*

39–40   "I here refer not": Muir, *Talks on Book-Collecting* 9. For more on Wise, see Partington.

40   "way ahead of his time": Wolf and Fleming, 189. For more on Quinn, see Reid, "A Note by John Quinn" in *Complete Catalogue of the Library of John Quinn,* vol. 1, unpaginated; Cannon, 228–30; and Dickinson, 265–66.

41   "One of my high": Pierpont Morgan Library, 13.

41–42   Fields: "There is a sacredness," 3; "As I quote these lines," 7; "There is no Leigh Hunt," 15. Full text and critical commentary of "Sleep and Poetry," in Miriam Allott, ed., *Keats: The Complete Poems* (New York: Longman, 1970), 69–85; the lines quoted by Mrs. Fields are on 354–58. For more on the lure of association copies, see Robert Alan Shaddy, "A World of Sentimental Attachments: The Cult of Collecting, 1890–1938," *Book Collector,* Summer 1994, 186–200.

42–43   "What shall I do": "Hobbies," in Churchill, 300.

43   A century earlier: See Lamb. For more on Coleridge's book habits, see George Whalley, "Samuel Taylor Coleridge," *Book Collector,* Autumn 1961, 275–90: "He was interested first in what was written in a book; condition meant nothing; his instinct was not acquisitive. . . . Coleridge's library was that of an affectionate and myriad-minded scholar."

44   "like a great mansion": Goff, *The Lessing J. Rosenwald,* ix; "no collector or lover of books": Ibid., xii. See also *Vision of a Collector;* Frederick Goff, "The Rosenwald Library," *Book Collector,* Spring 1956, 28–37; Dickinson, 274–75.

45   "Prozess Gegen . . . Later investigation": Rosenwald, 30–33.

46   "If popularity be taken" and for publishing history of *Das Narrenschiff:* T. H. Jamieson in Brant, ix.

47   "I am the first foole": Brant, 18; "for to haue plenty": Ibid., 20.

47   In a fanciful story: Anthony Burgess, "A Meeting in Valladolid," in *The Devil's Mode* (New York: Random House: 1989), 3–21.

48   "Be it known": Cervantes, 28.

48   "The poet's eye": Shakespeare, *A Midsummer Night's Dream,* 5.1.12–17.

49   "As you from crimes": Shakespeare, *The Tempest*, epilogue, lines 19–20.

49   "My library": Ibid., 1.2.109–10; "seize . . . possess . . . burn his books": Ibid., 3.2.89–95; "potent art": Ibid., 5.1.50; "drown . . . fathoms in the earth": Ibid., 5.1.55–57.

49   "Our copy isn't": Author's interview with Julian Roberts.

50   "To the Great Variety of Readers": Evans, 63.

51   Book madness: The following quotations are from Canetti: "She is the heaven-sent instrument," 47; "Greatly daring," 89; "When the flames reached," 464.

51   Combustion is also: See Ray Bradbury, *Fahrenheit 451: 40th Anniversary Edition* (New York: Simon and Schuster, 1993), with a new foreword by Bradbury.

52   "Everything turns": Eco, 446; "It was the greatest library . . . hinder him any more": Ibid., 491.

52   The British author A. S. Byatt: Byatt, *Possession* (New York: Random House, 1990).

52   With the release: For theme of "falling books" in work of E. M. Forster, see Nicola Beauman, *E. M. Forster: A Biography* (New York: Knopf, 1994), 105, 116, 145–46.

53   "Moore was much flattered": Julian Symons, 42–43.

53–54   Conversely, the late Ian Fleming: For more on Fleming, see "Commentary," *Book Collector*, Winter 1964, 431–33; Percy Muir, "Ian Fleming: A Personal Memoir," *Book Collector*, Spring 1965, 24–33.

54   "because special signed editions: Blotner, 294.

54–55   "He had his friends": Updike, 4–11.

54–55   "I am older . . . doesn't anybody care?": Benchley's essay in Targ, *Carousel*, 31–36.

56   "It is impossible . . . betray their confidence": West, 18–19.

57   "People will drive": Author's interview with James A. Michener.

57   "Milton was in his early forties": Author's interview with Reynolds Price. For more on Reynolds Price, see his memoir, *A Whole New Life: An Illness and a Healing* (New York: Atheneum, 1994).

2: "BALM FOR THE SOUL"

58   "The house of healing": Lutz, *The Oldest Library*, 18.

59   "Pray tell me, Euthydemus": Socrates, quoted in Xenophon, vol. 3, Part 1, 135–36.

60   "Come! no more line for line!": Sandys, vol. 1, 54.

60   "The last great master": Mumby, 14.

60   "You think that by buying ... to their owner": Lucian of Samosata, vol. 3, 265–67.

61   "because with purchased books": Austin, *Library of Jean Grolier,* 3 (introduction by Colin Eisher).

61   "Of what use are books without number": Canfora, 57.

61   "Bibliophiles, an idiotic class": Carter, *Taste and Technique,* xii.

61   "All literature, all philosophy": Cicero, quoted in Watts, 21–25. Cicero's letters to Atticus requesting book purchases: Carcopino, vol. 2, 469. For more on publishing and bookselling in Rome, see full chapter in Carcopino, vol. 2, "Atticus as Publisher," 412–529.

62   Cleopatra of Egypt: See Lucy Hughes-Hallett, *Cleopatra* (New York: Harper & Row, 1990).

63   "to collect, if he could": Parsons, *Alexandrian Library,* 98.

63   "all the sovereigns": Canfora, 20.

63   Agents were sent out: Platthy writes in *Sources on the Earliest Greek Libraries,* "There were libraries in many small cities in ancient Greece, [and] there was almost no significant city without a library or archive" (2). He further documents how the tyrant Pisistratus established the first library devoted to the liberal arts in Athens in the fifth century B.C. (17). For a detailed explanation of library locations, organization, book manufacture, and bookselling in ancient times, see J. W. Thompson, *Ancient Libraries.*

64   "They are not written in Syriac": Canfora, 28.

64   "populous land of Egypt": Ibid., 28.

64   Just how keenly contested: For more on Pergamum, see ibid., chap. 9, "The Rival Library."

65   "At length, but not before the books": Edwards, *Memoirs of Libraries,* 18.

66   For centuries: For chronology involving Alexandrian Library (335 B.C. to A.D. 639), see Canfora, vii–ix.

67   *"Kai su, teknon"*: Howatson, 103.

67–68   "Caesar, for the nonce ... of the great collection": Parsons, *Alexandrian Library,* 284–85.

68   Within two years: Antony seizes 200,000 "distinct volumes" from Pergamum in "Antony," Plutarch, 1137.

68   Though the great rivalry: The story of the Roman patrician's "living library" is retold by Horatio Rogers, 20.

68   "Twenty-two acknowledged concubines": Gibbon, vol. 1, 312.
69   Quintilian was so pleased: Mumby, 21.
69   "You have sold my discourse": Ibid., 19.
69   "He composes an oration": Curwen, 11.
69   "I have conquered the great city": Canfora, 83.
69   "You have taken possession of them": Ibid., 83.
69   "As for the books you mention": Ibid., 98.
70   "The study of letters has perished": Deuel, 4.
71   "It was the hand of Cassiodorus": Putnam, vol. 1, 21.
71   "While the gaze of Boethius": Sandys, vol. 1, 255.
71   "throughout that period": Isaac Taylor, 72.
71   "Take the first one": Sandys, vol. 2, 4.
72   "For every illustrious name": Deuel, 7.
72   "Please, if you love me": Martz, 7.
73   "Your letters I sought": Deuel, 13.
74   "Ah, the prayers": Ibid., 9.
74   "Be reasonable": Bergin, 56.
75   "Boccaccio stepped . . . to sell to women.": Sandys, vol. 2, 13.
75   For more on Bracciolini and Niccoli, see Gordan.
76   "So then, O man of study": Symonds, vol. 2, 97–98.
76   "both of the luminaries": Sandys, vol. 2, 15.
76   "for the last seven centuries": Ibid., vol 2, 19–20.
77   "I verily believe": Symonds, vol. 2, 98–99.
78   "and in a single month . . . in the same way": Lowry, 50.
79   "written with the pen": Sandys, vol. 2, 96.
79   "stuffed with books": Ibid., 7.
79   *richissimo:* Ibid., 8.
80   "vulgarizing intellectual life": Ibid., 26.
80   Walk through book district: Ibid., 36–37.
81   "I shall buy my Hebrew books": Putnam, vol. 1, 436.
81   "real possibility that special orders": Lowry, 280.
81   "All subsequent achievements": Symonds, vol. 1, 18–19.

                          3: "RULE BRITANNIA"

84   "Ye are the tree": de Bury, vol. 2, 23.
85   "affairs became prosperous . . . dirt and sand": Ibid., 68–80.
85   "Are you not ashamed": Merryweather, 115.
85   "What leveret . . . loan for a time": De Bury, vol. 2, 70–74.

86   "He was a man . . . above the commonplace": Ibid., vol. 3, 26.
      For De Bury's bequest to Oxford, see vol. 2, 136–40.

86   "in our different . . . labour over books": Ibid., 79.

86   By all accounts: For more on Humfrey as collector, see Roberto
      Weiss, "Humfrey, Duke of Gloucester," *Book Collector*, Sum-
      mer 1964, 161–70. For more on history of Bodleian Library, see
      Macray and Rogers.

87   "It is incredible what a treasure": Merryweather, 75. For more
      on the destruction of the monasteries, see Cram. The systematic
      plunder of cultural treasure is by no means an isolated occur-
      rence; for more on a recent episode, see Lynn H. Nicholas, *The
      Rape of Europa* (New York: Alfred A. Knopf, 1994), a detailed
      study of the elaborate Nazi program to steal artworks, jewels,
      coins, tapestries, furniture, and books from occupied nations.
      For more on the lingering aftermath of that policy, see Michael
      Specter, "For Russians, Literary Loot Turns Awkward," *New
      York Times*, October 31, 1994, C13. The article details how at
      the end of World War II, victorious Soviet troops took ten mil-
      lion books out of Germany and distributed them among dozens
      of Russian libraries. The Nazis are believed to have destroyed
      nearly two hundred million Russian books during the war,
      prompting some officials to consider the act a form of justifiable
      retaliation. Others felt that the books, which included a Guten-
      berg Bible, should be returned. "This is Germany's culture, not
      ours," Yevgeny I. Kuzmin, director of the department of
      libraries for the Russian Ministry of Culture, said. "They have
      an absolute right to their own books. World War II ended fifty
      years ago, and the Cold War ended almost ten years ago. We
      have to decide are we going to spend the rest of time remember-
      ing that once the Germans were our enemies or are we ready to
      start thinking about what we can accomplish as friends?"

88   "Except for such altar books": Esdaile, 22; "laboryouse jour-
      ney," Ibid., 23.

88   "superstitious monasteries": Modernized version of Bale quota-
      tion in Edwards, *Memoirs of Libraries*, 360; sixteenth-century
      version in Merryweather, 22–23.

89   For more on King George III and his library: Willson, Beckles;
      Paintin. For more on the British Library, see Edwards; Esdaile;
      Barker et al.; Miller.

90   For more on Robert Cotton's imperial pressmarks, see C. G. C. Tite, "Early Catalogues of the Cottonian Library," *British Library Bulletin,* Autumn 1980, 144–57.

90   Nearby is Sir Gawain: For more on Cotton's associations with writers, see Sharpe, 34; Barker et al., 46.

91   "He seems to have persuaded": Sharpe, 59.

91   Dee buries his books: Aubrey, 95. For more on Dee as collector, see Roberts and Watson.

92   For more on Lord Hunsdon, see S. Schoenbaum, *William Shakespeare: A Documentary Life* (New York: Oxford University Press, 1975), 135–36, 145–46; Sharpe, 200–2.

93   "It is pleasant to fancy": Geoffrey Bullough, *Narrative and Dramatic Sources of Shakespeare* (London and New York: Routledge & Kegan Paul and Columbia University Press, 1960), vol. 3, 372.

93   "Dee is shadowed": Yates, 77–78; "defended in Prospero": Ibid., 160.

93   "lent to his Majesty": Ibid., 78–79.

94   "pestilent tractate": Quoted in Edwards, *Memoirs of Libraries,* 427.

94   "outworn in a few months": Ibid., 428

94   "Tell the Lord Privy Seal": Edwards, *Lives of the Founders,* 124.

94   "loss of such a character": Dibdin, 26.

94–95   The books remained: The extract of the Parliamentary Committee of Inquiry regarding the fire at Ashburnham House and damage to Cottonian library is from Edwards, *Memoirs of Libraries,* 431–34.

96   For a full account of George Thomason's collecting and quotations from broadsides, see Falconer Madan, "Notes on the Thomason Collection of Civil War Tracts," *Bibliographica,* vol. 3, 291–308.

98   For more on Thomas Hollis III, see Bond, *Thomas Hollis of Lincoln's Inn.*

99   "the most valuable set": Barker et al., 65.

99   "His achievement": Madan, 292.

100   For more on codicils to Pepys's will and a description of the library, see Sidgwick, and "The Pepysian" in Hartshorne, 217–29. See also Hobson, 212–21.

100   All Richard Luckett quotations are from the author's interview.

103   "with great pains": Latham, 634.

105	"I doubt I shall ever": Ibid., 1023.
106	"epidemical . . . cost and industry": Lawler, xx.
106	"learned idiot": Steele and Addison, 880–81 (April 13, 1710).
106	On March 12, 1688: For more on the recovered fragment of *Metamorphoses,* see W. Granger Blair, "A Caxton Work Breaks Price Record for MSS," *New York Times,* June 28, 1966, 49.
107	In 1715: For more on Wanley, see Wright and Wright, vol. 1, xi–lxxxiii (introduction). For more on Harley, see C. E. Wright, "Edward Harley, Earl of Oxford," *Book Collector,* Summer 1962, 158–74.
108	Osborne buys Harley's books: Marston, 48.
109	Even though Thomas Frognall Dibdin: For more on Osborne and *Paradise Lost,* see Bate, 225.
109	Pope: See *The Dunciad,* edited by James Sutherland, 2d. ed. (London: Metheun, 1953), 303–4.
109	"I have been in business": Marston, 50.
109	"If I have set a high value": Dibdin, *Bibliomania,* 348.
109	"lion in harness": Bate, 224.
109–10	"unnecessary delay . . . ignorance and obscurity": Marston, 50–52. This anecdote was first reported by John Hawkins in 1785 in his *Life of Samuel Johnson, LL.D.* In 1791 James Boswell quoted Samuel Johnson directly on the matter in his great biography: "Sir, he was impertinent to me, and I beat him. But it was not in his shop; it was in my own chamber." (Roger Ingpen, ed., *The Life of Samuel Johnson,* vol. 1, Boston: Charles E. Lauriat Co., 1921, 84.) Bate suggests that Johnson was working on the *Harleian Miscellany,* not on a translation, when the "knock-down" incident occurred. Accounts of precisely how many Harley library catalogue volumes Johnson worked on vary as well. See also Kaminski.
110	Munby estimates Heber's holdings at 150,000 books: See "Father and Son," in *Essays and Papers,* 233; de Ricci (p. 102) suggests 200,000 to 300,000.
110–11	"can comfortably do without three": Fletcher, 337.
111	"His name occurs": de Ricci, 102.
111	"awakening bibliomania": Munby, "Father and Son," 225.
111	All letters between Richard Heber and his father: Ibid., 226–34.
113	*"Thy volumes"*: Fletcher, 339.
113	"Poor man!": Fitzgerald, 230.

113   "I looked round me": Dibdin, *Reminiscences of a Literary Life,* vol. 1, 436–37.

113   Heber's relationship with protégé Hartshorne: Arnold Hunt, "A Study in Bibliomania: Charles Henry Hartshorne and Richard Heber," Part I, in *The Book Collector,* Spring 1993, 25–44; Part II, Summer 1993, 185–212. Miss Richardson Currer: Anne Lyon Haight, "Are Women the Natural Enemies of Books?" in Bennett, 107; De Ricci, 141–43.

114   "The market was absolutely glutted": de Ricci, 102.

115–16 "probably stirred up . . . the grand era of Bibliomania": Dibdin, *Bibliographical Decameron,* vol. 3, 49–69. For more on Napoleon, see J. W. Thompson, "Napoleon as a Booklover," in his *Byways in Bookland,* 53–73.

116   The Fortsas sale: Quotations from *The Fortsas Catalogue,* translations, and factual information are from Blades, "Bibliographical Hoaxing." A facsimile edition catalogue was published in 1970 in a limited edition of 250 copies by Lessing J. Rosenwald for the Philobiblon Club of Philadelphia.

120   "I wish to have one copy": Barker, *Portrait of an Obsession,* xvi.

120   "In amassing my collection . . . French Revolution": de Ricci, 119–20.

121   "vain, selfish, dogmatic . . . conception and execution": Munby, quoted in Barker, *Portrait of an Obsession,* 266.

121–22 "Altho' I greatly sympathize": Ibid., 259.

122   "pleased no one in life": Ibid., 263. See also "The Will and Testament of Thomas Phillipps," *Phillipps Studies,* vol. 2, 106–15.

123   "residue" of the Phillipps collection: Munby, *Phillipps Studies,* vol. 5, 104. Note: This concluding volume in Munby's series is titled *The Dispersal of the Phillipps Library* and offers considerable detail on where material went.

123   William A. Jackson, Harvard's Houghton librarian: Ibid., 102–3.

124   "many thousands": Ibid., 110–11.

124    $10 million for what remained: Lew David Feldman, interviewed by Gerald Gottlieb, Dec. 18, 1973. Quoted with permission. Transcript available at Oral History Research Office, Butler Library, Columbia University.

124   "I am confident": Kraus, 226.

124   "It is still like Christmas": *Bibliotheca Phillippica,* 5.

125   "disaster of dispersion": Guppy, 4. See also Hobson, 268–79.

126   "The library will be entitled": in Guppy, 6–7.

126   On April 14, 1988, Manchester University sold sixty-seven "duplicate" books from the Spencer Collection and twenty-three from another. Nicolas Barker, at that time deputy keeper of rare books at the British Library, argued in "The Rape of the Rylands" that the number of books, though comparatively small, was an "outrage" and "betrayal" nonetheless (*Book Collector,* Summer 1988, 169–84).

4: "AMERICA, AMERICANS, AMERICANA"

127   As he lay dying: For more on John Harvard, see Shelley. For more on Yale, see Herman W. Liebert and Marjorie G. Wynne, "The General Collection of Rare Books and Manuscripts," in *Beinecke Rare Book and Manuscript Library,* 7–26.

128   "Books were scarce": Marjorie Wynne, 7.

128   "It was inevitable": Lehmann-Haupt, Wroth, and Silver, 5. See also Wroth, *Colonial Printer.*

128   The first "great" book: On the Eliot Indian Bible, early owners, and copies in various collections, see John Wright, 1–27. "Beyold, ye Americans": Ibid., 16.

129   "slapping and pinching himself": Gray, 76.

130   "Books are my disease": Wolf, *The Library,* xvii.

130   "In many ways James Logan": Ibid., xviii.

130   "I confess a Book has from my Infancy": Ibid., xvii.

131   "I observe thy method": Ibid., xliii.

131   "I am under this great Disadvantage": Ibid., xxv.

131–32   "Thou may therefore": Ibid., xx.

133   "While from all sides": Translation from Latin in Tolles, 96–97.

133   "to a bookseller who lived . . . thou bought it of": Wolf, *The Library,* 402–3.

134   "base and lying lackeys": Gray, 3.

134   "was done by a Gentleman": Tolles, 212.

134   "Proposals Relating to the Education": In J. A. Leo Lemay, ed. *Franklin* (New York: The Library of America, 1987), 326–27.

135   "But the most noble Monument": Wolf, *The Library,* xlv.

135   "I here behold the portrait": Ibid., liii.

136   "After it was dark": James Green, 7. See also Jack Greene.

137   "I send you the catalogue . . . exhausted": Stern, 27–29.

138   Born to affluent parents: For Prince's background, see *The Prince Library*, v–xvi (introduction by Justin Winsor). See also Cannon, 1–15.

138   "Inquire of the Rev. Mr. Prince": Cannon, 4–13.

140   "mounted up to the balcony": Cannon, 11.

140   "a very ruinous situation": Ibid., 10.

140   For an annual census of the Bay Psalm Book, see Amory, 24–27.

141   "What is *that* worth, Madame?": Randall, 21.

141   "The suggestion that we sell": Author's interview with the Reverend James W. Crawford.

142   "inquisitive disposition": Louis L. Tucker, in Drumney, 15.

142   "The preservation of books . . . especially in the historical way": Whitehill, *Independent Historical Societies,* 8–9.

143   "There is nothing like having": Drumney, 16.

143   "In preference to a collegiate": Ibid., 17.

144   "with great satisfaction": Whitehill, *Independent Historical Societies,* 4.

144   "The art of printing affords": Drumney, 17.

144   "the preserver of all art": Shipton, 81.

145   Baskerville of America: Benjamin Franklin Thomas, "Memoir of Isaiah Thomas," Thomas, vol. 1, lxxvii. The reference is to John Baskerville (1706–1775), a noted English printer and publisher and the designer of several elegant typefaces that bear his name.

145   "He spread his products": Shipton, 1.

146   "old papers, Boston Evening Post": Cannon, 52–53.

146   "We cannot obtain": *Collections and Programs of the American Antiquarian Society,* 18.

147   "to show what articles" and "after advertising for another copy": Cannon, 55, 54.

147   A proposal to raise funds: Diary entries quoted in Whitehill, *Independent,* 70–71; Shipton, 76–77.

147   "touched early by that gentlest of infirmities": Thomas, lxxxii.

148   "dessicated mummy": Whitehill, *Independent Historical Society,* 69–70.

148   "better preservation": Ibid., 67.

148   "triumph of vandalism": Mearns, 28.

148–50   After reading about the disaster: Jefferson's letter proposing sale of his library to nation is quoted in Mearns, 28–30.

150   "It might be inferred": Randolph G. Adams, 86.

150   Though cost was an issue: On the formula to assess Jefferson's books, see ibid., 88–89.

151   "is such to render all valuation": Ibid., 88.

151   On the education of congressmen who voted on measure to buy Jefferson's books, see Adams, 90–92.

152   "So it was the South": Ibid., 91.

152   On the breakdown of the congressional vote on the "Act to Authorize the Purchase of the Library of Thomas Jefferson," see Mearns, 33–36.

152   On Webster's failure to pay Audubon, see Fries, 249–51.

152–53   "It is the choicest collection": Malone, 181.

153   "great hue and cry": Stevens, 82.

154   "You will find eventually": Ibid., 86.

154   "The idea was to get popular . . . all others are judged": Author's interview with John Lannon.

155   "We have been and still are": Walter Muir Whitehill in the introduction to Crandall, vol. 1, xvi. Introduction contains detailed history of the collection.

155   "This country is sadly in want": Farnham, 5. For similar surveys of the period, see James Wynne and Horatio Rogers. Of related interest, see also John Francis McDermott, "Private Libraries in Frontier St. Louis," in *Papers of the Bibliographical Society of America,* first quarter, 1957, 19–37.

156   "there were many things": Farnham, 7–8.

157   Roger E. Stoddard reports: Ibid., iii–vi, 81–98.

157   "has produced a few authors": Ibid., 7.

158   "it is probable": Knepper, 117.

158   "I was encouraged to undertake": Washington Irving, *A History of the Life and Voyages of Christopher Columbus* (New York: G. & C. Carvill, 1828), vol. 1, vii.

159   "I fear the Congress": Knepper, 121.

159   "He has uniformly executed": Ibid., 113.

160   armed with a "general commission to forage": On Stevens's shipping five hundred titles to Providence, see Danforth and Hintenlang, 37.

160   "Those were happy days": Stevens, 13.

160–61   "paid his taxes": Ibid., 5–7.

161   "He gave me his money" and "He had a mind of his own": Ibid., 9, 103.

161   "I am still of the opinion . . . withdrawal of a good Customer": Thomas R. Adams, "A Collection's Progress," in *Gazette of the Grolier Club,* vol. 8, October 1968, 2–13.

162   "find the five-pound notes": Stevens, 23. For more on Stevens, see Parker and Randolph G. Adams, chapter 3; on Brinley, 35–67.

162   "Don't buy too many": Letter from John Nicholas Brown to George Parker Winship, Jan. 28, 1897, quoted in Danforth, 51.

163   "Brinley strove to rescue": Randolph G. Adams, 39–40.

164   "By pursuing this method . . . in any subsequent sale.": George Watson Cole, "Book Collectors as Benefactors of Public Libraries," *Papers of the Bibliographical Society of America,* 1st qtr., 1915.

164   In an unpublished memoir: Carbon typescript of unpublished Charles Brinley memoir in Watkinson Library, Trinity College, Hartford, Conn. Original copy in William Clement's Library, University of Michigan, Ann Arbor.

164   "upon condition that": Randolph G. Adams, 43.

164   "What, do you mean to say": Stevens, 118–19.

165   "That goose is now a swan": Ibid., 119.

165   "greatest bibliographical rarity": Ibid., 125.

165   "I am glad to see": Randolph G. Adams, 51.

165   "the greatest library": Brigham, in his introduction to McKay, 17.

166   "the service rendered": J. Hammond Trumbull, in the preface to *Catalogue of the American Library of the Late Mr. George Brinley of Hartford, Conn.,* vol. 5, 3. See also Joseph Rosenblum, "George Brinley and His Sales," *American Book Collector* 6, no. 5, new ser., September/October 1985, 13–23.

167–68   Only three collections: For an account of John A. Rice, Edward G. Asay, and Ebenezer Lane, see Rosenthal. One of Chicago's great collectors and benefactors, John M. Wing (1844–1917), assembled at the turn of the century a folio-sized scrapbook containing several hundred newspaper clippings. He called it "Old Corner Library Scrapbook About Books, Bibliography, Book-Plates, Libraries, and Other Things, Picked Up Here and There, by a Philosopher. Chicago: Pasted at the Old Corner. 1899." Wing called the library in his house at 743 Congress Street the Old Corner Library, and he had a bookplate to that effect. His scrapbook is an excellent source of information and is in the Wing Collection at the Newberry Library.

168   "by the acre and sold it": Lawrence W. Towner, in Achilles, 17.

168   "Certain it is": *Chicago Inter-Ocean,* clipping from files of Newberry Library.

169   "I desire the books": Goodspeed, 55.

169   "In the unfoldings": Bancroft, 6.

169   "Bibliomaniac I was not": Ibid., 89.

170   "certain books I knew . . . separate them": Ibid., 90–91.

171   "From London I went": Ibid., 94.

171   "new light broke in": Ibid., 97.

172   "the largest collection": Ibid., 120.

172   "I trembled for its safety": Ibid., 109.

172   "In fact, there is probably": Burton, 180–81.

172   "prodigious accomplishment . . . agency involved": Boyd, 8.

5: "BRANDY FOR HEROES"

173   "If the great collections": Beverly Chew, in his foreword to the Hoe Sale catalogue, Part 1 (A–K), v.

173–74   "Donating the incunables": Sotheby's, *Incunables from the Shøyen Collection,* unpaginated.

174   "Without counting each": Bierstadt, 5. Commenting on James Wynne's book of 1860, *Private Libraries of New York,* Bierstadt wrote: "It is hardly a generation ago that this book was published, but it reads already like ancient history, so important have been the acquisitions made since then" (page 2). For more on Hoe as entrepreneur, see Comparato.

175   "I specifically authorize": Towner, 262.

175   "covered with dust": Chew's introduction to Bierstadt, v.

175   Though Robert Hoe: For more on E. Dwight Church, see Cannon, 142–43; *Grolier 75,* 12–14; Dickinson, 65–66; *New York Times,* April 8, 1911.

175–76   "hopeful . . . to private collections": Undated and unidentified newspaper clipping, "Big Sum for Old Books," Huntington Institutional Archives (hereafter referred to as HIA), 31.1.1.42.

176–78   "Mr. Pierpont Morgan's Library," *The Times* (London), Dec. 4, 1908, 12.

178   "The book that is arousing": *New York Times,* April 13, 1911.

179   "How Americans Get Private Libraries Worth Fortunes," *New York Times*, April 14, 1911.

180   "richly illuminated in gold": Hoe Sale catalogue, Part 1 (A–K), 23 (Lot 142).

180   "remarkably fine copy": Ibid., 43 (Lot 252).

180–81   Biblia Sacra Latina: Ibid., 47 (Lot 269).

180–81   Press reports of Hoe sale and clippings in Grolier Club Album.

181   "to the vanishing point": Ibid., *New York Herald,* April 26, 1911.

181   "bent upon getting the treasure": Ibid., *New York Times,*

181–82   "George D. Smith made": Ibid., New York *Tribune,* April 18, 1911.

182   "absurdly high . . . taller than your buildings": Ibid., *New York Times,* April 28, 1911.

182–84   "The Man Who Paid $50,000 for the Gutenberg Bible" and "J. P. Morgan's Librarian Says High Book Prices Are Harmful": Ibid., *New York Times,* April 30, 1911, v, 13.

184   "You may now have your reply": Cannon, 279.

184   "Her victory evoked": *New York Times,* May 2, 1911, 1.

184   "Shall I buy": *Grolier 75,* 20.

185   "I do not wish . . . everything will be gone": Newton, *Amenities,* 352.

186   "I think I'll take": Ibid., 354.

186   A few hours before: For more on Harry Widener's final purchases and final words, see Arthur Freeman, "Harry Widener's Last Books" in *Book Collector*, Summer 1977, 173–85.

186–87   "I think if Harry Elkins Widener": Rosenbach, *Books and Bidders,* 45.

187   "All joy of living": Letter from Eleanor Elkins Widener to Rosenbach, July 3, 1914, Rosenbach Company Archives (hereafter referred to as RCA), I:181:31.

187   "hurricane of buying": Wolf and Fleming, 79.

187   "the utter inadequacy": Bentinck-Smith, 10.

188   "in a state of suspended": Ibid., 53.

188   "WANTED—A MILLIONAIRE": Undated *Boston American* newspaper clipping from Harvard University Archives; reproduced in Carpenter, 135.

188   "Do you know anyone": Bentinck-Smith, 54.

188   "out of tragedy": Ibid., 54.

188   "we should have": Ibid., 55.

189   "I should not be surprised": Ibid., 56.

189   "When the Library": Letter from Eleanor Elkins Widener to Dr. Rosenbach, July 3, 1914, RCA, I:181:31.

189   "unremarkable but grateful": Parks, 3 (Alan Bell's introduction).

190   "shy and reticent . . . in his own right": Gilbert McCoy Troxell, "The Elizabethan Club: Its Origins and Its Books," *Yale University Library Gazette,* No. 27 (1952), 19–22.

191   "Little did I guess": Quoted in Bell's introduction to Parks, 11.

191   "welcome flood of gifts": Carpenter, 170.

192   "For, let it be said . . . carried away with enthusiasm": Boies Penrose, "George Parker Winship," in *Grolier 75,* 185–87. In a description for *The Book Collector* of his specialized collection of early books on geography (Autumn 1961, 301–10), Penrose noted that it was Winship who "encouraged my interests" by suggesting that he "cut [his] teeth by translating Breydenbach's Pilgrimage to the Holy Land—a project that came to naught, although it did result in my buying a copy of the Mainz 1486 *Breydenbach* from Lathrop Harper in March 1926, an event which may be taken as the start of my collecting career."

192   "This course is intended": Stoddard, "Teaching the History."

193   "Mr. Kilgour realized": William A. Jackson, preface to *The Kilgour Collection of Russian Literature 1750–1920,* unpaginated.

193   "grand acquisitor . . . club pin": Stoddard, "Teaching the History."

193   "perpetually in the lead": Hobson, 226.

194   "Men may come": Rosenbach, *Books and Bidders,* 252.

194   "When the rulers of kingdoms": Charles F. Heartman, "George D. Smith, 1870–1920: A Memorial Tribute to the Greatest Bookseller the World Has Ever Known" (privately printed, 1945), reprinted in *American Book Collector,* May–June 1973, 3–26. See also Donald C. Dickinson, "Mr. Huntington and Mr. Smith," *Book Collector,* Autumn 1988, 376–93.

194–95   "It cannot be stated too often": George Sherburn, *Huntington Library Bulletin,* No. 1 (May 1931), 33.

195   "I have not slept a wink": Thorpe, *Henry Edwards Huntington,* 279.

195   "I had the satisfaction": Bruccoli, "George D. Smith," 2524.

196   "I am very glad to see": Letter from Henry Huntington to
      George Smith, Sept. 25, 1918, HIA, 31.1.1.42.1.

196   "neglected to tell": Richard S. Wormser, "George D. Smith," in
      Grolier 75, 184.

196   "purchased for stock": Telegram, Aug. 1, 1919, RCA, I:93:01.

197   "all for the special price": Handwritten memo, Aug. 19, 1919,
      initialed "HEH," RCA, I:93:01.

197   "One day I was talking": Brigham, 48. A framed photograph of
      Marsden J. Perry hangs in the treasure room of the Folger
      Shakespeare Library in Washington, D.C., near the shelves
      where many of the books he collected are now stored, a modest
      but meaningful tribute to a respected bibliophile.

198   "At this time": Letter from Dr. Rosenbach to Henry C. Folger,
      July 23, 1919, RCA, I:62:17.

198   "I do not hesitate": Rosenbach, *Books and Bidders,* 88.

198   "Henry, I see from the papers": Wolf and Fleming, *Rosenbach,*
      122.

199   "Very Confidential": Letter from Rosenbach to Folger, June 27,
      1922, RCA, I:62:23.

199   "It makes quite a reduction": Letter from Huntington to George
      Watson Cole, Aug. 21, 1919, HIA, 31.1.1.42.1.

200   "the greatest collection": Letter from Brigham to Huntington,
      April 17, 1920, HIA, 31.1.1.1.6.2.

200   "kind offer to get": Letter from Huntington to Brigham, May
      18, 1920, HIA, 31.1.1.6.2.

200   "Absolutely no one has suspected": Letter from Brigham to
      Huntington, July 27, 1920, HIA, 31.1.1.6.2.

201   "A dealer would charge $20,000": Letter from Brigham to
      Huntington, Aug. 17, 1920, HIA, 31.1.1.6.2.

201   "spending most of my evenings": Letter from Brigham to Hun-
      tington, Sept. 21, 1920, from the Henry E. Huntington file in the
      American Antiquarian Society Institutional Archives (hereafter
      referred to as AAS).

201   "I am delighted to know": Letter from Cole to Brigham, Nov.
      27, 1920, AAS.

201   "and as I plan": Letter from Huntington to Brigham, Dec. 13,
      1920, AAS.

201   "you have at the present time": Letter from Brigham to Hun-
      tington, Jan. 19, 1921, AAS.

201   "Mr. Huntington after reading": Letter from Cole to Brigham, April 6, 1921, AAS.

201   "We can readily see": Letter from Cole to Brigham, June 10, 1921, AAS.

202   "Because of the approaching . . . purchasing for myself": Letter from Brigham to Huntington, May 13, 1921, AAS.

202   "The books go forward . . . buying for you": Letter from Brigham to Huntington, Dec. 19, 1921, AAS.

203   "I note with interest": Letter from Huntington to Brigham, Dec. 21, 1924, HIA, 31.1.1.6.2.

203   "I have made three foreign trips": Letter from Brigham to Huntington, Jan. 7, 1924, HIA, 31.1.1.6.2.

203   "the years 1921–1925": *Huntington Library Bulletin,* No. 1 (May 1931), 85.

203–4   "Mr. Huntington never 'employed' ": Letter from Brigham to Max Farrand, July 10, 1931, AAS.

205   "I think that I have spent": Clarence Brigham, in Percy Lawler, ed., 53. See also Donald C. Dickinson, "Mr. Huntington and Mr. Brigham," *Book Collector,* Winter 1993, 507–22.

205   "Mr. Huntington was an opportunist": Schad, 13.

205   "we most emphatically do not": Letter from Leslie E. Bliss to Rosenbach, Jan. 25, 1923, RCA, I:93:03.

206   "You buy the collection": Letter from Bliss to Rosenbach, Jan. 25, 1923, RCA, I:93:03

206   "keep the matter confidential": Letter from Rosenbach to Huntington, Feb. 6, 1923, RCA, I:93:03.

206   "rather clumsily altered": Letter from Huntington to Rosenbach, Feb. 6, 1923, RCA, I:93:03.

206   "I note that you purchased": Letter from Huntington to Rosenbach, May 14, 1923, RCA, I:93:04.

206   "concerning this item": Letter from Rosenbach to Huntington, May 22, 1923, RCA, I:93:04.

207   "It may interest you to know": Letter from Rosenbach to Huntington, July 13, 1923, RCA, I:93:04. For more on Rosenbach's "private treaty" purchases in Europe, see Morris, *Rosenbach Abroad* and *Rosenbach Redux.*

207   The volumes, all bought: The bill of sale for $36,500, dated Aug. 3, 1923, RCA, I:93:05.

207   Muniments of Battle Abbey: Aug. 9, 1923, RCA, I:93:05.

207   "It is unlikely that a collection": Schad, 12.

208 "above the spot where": Letter from Huntington to Rosenbach, Dec. 18, 1924, RCA, I:93:09.

208 "were not at all flexible": Letter from Rosenbach to Huntington, May 27, 1926, RCA, I:94:02.

209 "I have received": Letter from Huntington to Rosenbach, June 4, 1926, RCA, I:94:02.

209 "You will pardon us": Letter from Bliss to Rosenbach, June 5, 1926, RCA, I:94:02.

209 "Mr. Hapgood": Letter from Huntington to Philip Rosenbach, June 5, 1926, RCA, I:95:04.

210 "Two boxes are in from you": Letter from Bliss to Rosenbach, May 24, 1927, RCA, I:95:04.

210 "I should like to buy it": Letter from Belle da Costa Greene to Rosenbach, March 21, 1928, RCA, I:126:03.

211 "It is now dawning upon us": Wolf and Fleming, 169.

211 "As my collection has grown": "Noted Kern Library Will Be Auctioned," *New York Times,* Oct. 18, 1928, 19.

212 "MY GOD WHATS": Quoted in Bruccoli, *The Fortunes,* 204.

212 "For many of the volumes": "Kern Sees Prices of Books Mounting," *New York Times,* January 28, 1929, 24.

213 "I am obliged to confess . . . to other volunteers": Case and Case, 411–15. See "Young Collection of Rare Volumes Is Gift to Library," *New York Times,* May 5, 1941, 1.

213 "the greatest trial lawyer": *Washington Daily News,* May 16, 1944.

214 "In September I promise": Letter from Frank J. Hogan to Rosenbach, July 18, 1931, RCA, I:088:33.

215 "our four recent catalogues": Letter from Rosenbach to Hogan, July 29, 1931, RCA, I:088:33.

215 "untimely death": Letter from Hogan to Rosenbach, Aug. 3, 1931, RCA, I:088:33.

215 "BEST WISHES": Telegram, Dec. 30, 1931, RCA, I:088:33.

215 "For the sleep I lost": Letter from Hogan to Rosenbach, Jan. 19, 1932, RCA, I:088:34.

215 "I speak of temporarily": Letter from Hogan to Rosenbach, Jan. 28, 1932, RCA, I:088:34.

216 "Come to the house . . . BRANDY FOR HEROES!!": Letter from Rosenbach to Hogan, March 21, 1932, RCA, I:088:34.

216 "I do not want to tempt you": Letter from Rosenbach to Hogan, July 12, 1932, RCA, I:088:34.

216   "Well, I hope I can pay you": Wolf and Fleming, 434.

216   "I am as hard up as the devil": Letter from Rosenbach to Hogan, April 21, 1933, RCA, I:088:35.

216   "appropriate to myself": Letter from Hogan to Rosenbach, April 22, 1933, RCA, I:088:35.

216   "which involves more money than": Letter from Hogan to Rosenbach, May 19, 1933, RCA, I:088:35.

217   "Folger has no copy as fine": Telegram, June 15, 1933, RCA, I:088:35.

217   "It gave me a real thrill": Letter from Rosenbach to Hogan, July 11, 1933, RCA, I:088:35.

217   "I am still thrilled beyond": Letter from Hogan to Rosenbach, Aug. 22, 1933, RCA, I:088:35.

218   "Fate, and the traveling man's": Letter from Hogan to Arthur E. Houghton, Jr., Oct. 20, 1938; carbon copy in RCA, I:089:01.

218   "I was just casting around": Letter from Hogan to Rosenbach, Dec. 18, 1934, RCA, I:088:37.

219   "I am sure you will enjoy . . . as they appear in the press": Letter from Rosenbach to Hogan, July 2, 1934, RCA, I:088:37.

219   "Manifestly Pollard and Carter": Letter from Hogan to Rosenbach, Aug. 8, 1934, RCA, I:088:37.

220   "I have known Thomas J. Wise": Letter from Rosenbach to Hogan, Aug. 15, 1934, RCA, I:088:37.

220   "the possession of a complete run . . . great collector of books": Letter from Hogan to Rosenbach, Aug. 17, 1934, RCA, I:088:37.

221   "my dear friend Frank J. Hogan": Rosenbach, *Book Hunter's Holiday*, 15.

221   "I had thought of bequeathing": Copy of Frank J. Hogan's will, RCA, I:089:07.

222   "This is no time": Jordan-Smith, 13.

Part Two

6: "TO HAVE AND TO HAVE NO MORE"

This chapter draws on the author's interviews with David Redden, Bart Auerbach, Stephen Massey, George S. Lowry, Priscilla Juvelis, Justin G. Schiller, Fred Schreiber, Robert L. Nikirk, Colin Franklin, Owen Gingerich, Nicolas Barker, David Waxman, Arthur Freeman, and Michael Hoffman. See Bibliography, "Author's Interviews" (pp. 575–82), for further details.

227   For more on Codex Hammer, see Carol Vogel, "Leonardo Note-
        book Sells for $30.8 Million," *The New York Times,* November
        12, 1994, 1; Christie's, *The Leonardo da Vinci.*

227   When Carrie Estelle Betzold Doheny: For further information
        on Estelle Doheny's collection, see Christie's, *The Estelle
        Doheny Collection,* and Ellen Shaffer, "Reminiscences of a Cal-
        ifornia Collector: Mrs. Edward Doheny 1875–1958," *Book
        Collector,* Spring 1965, 49–59.

228   While that sale was taking place: For further information on the
        Martin sale, see Sotheby's, *The Library of H. Bradley Martin*;
        Robert H. Taylor, "H. Bradley Martin," *Book Collector,* Sum-
        mer 1963, 184–93; C. W. Cottrell, Jr., "H. Bradley Martin; The
        Ornithological Collection," *Book Collector,* Autumn 1963,
        316–32.

235   "Michael Davis is a private investor": Sotheby's, *Collection of
        the Garden Ltd.*

235–37 "Haven O'More was inspired . . . reality or essence": Ibid.

244   The week after the sale: The docket sheet—Middlesex Superior
        Court, case no. 88-635, *Michael Davis, Indiv., & as Trustee vs.
        Haven O'More, Indiv., & as Trustee, et als. & Trustees.* Com-
        plaint entered Jan. 29, 1988, discharged July 5, 1989; eighty-five
        separate entries listed.

244   On December 14, 1989: Letter from Brian T. Mulcahy, adminis-
        trative attorney to the chief administrative justice of the Com-
        monwealth of Massachusetts, to author, Jan. 17, 1990, reporting
        that *Davis vs. O'More* "has been impounded and is not available
        for public inspection."

245–46 Michael Davis is the son of: Biographical material on Leonard
        Davis from clips in libraries of the *New York Times* (July 7, 1961;
        March 17, 1965; March 31, 1974; May 13, 1975; Dec. 1, 1975;
        May 14, 1983) and the *Philadelphia Inquirer* (Oct. 17, 1967; May
        13, 1976; May 7, 1978, July 2, 1978).

246   "a New York limited partnership": Middlesex County Registry
        of Deeds, Cambridge, Mass., Feb. 1, 1985, Book 16002, p. 452.

246–47 Michael Davis, the certificate discloses: Certificate of Limited
        Partnership for the Garden Ltd., with power of attorney
        attached, recorded in Dutchess County Clerk's Office, Pough-
        keepsie, New York; notarized Nov. 17, 1983; amendment nota-
        rized Oct. 10, 1984; Michael Davis allowed to withdraw,
        received Dec. 27, 1990.

248   Most states have laws: *Poughkeepsie Journal* and *Millbrook Round Table*, legal notices on the filing of limited-partnership papers.

248   "to explore the knowledge": Articles of Organization, Institute of Traditional Science, Inc. (federal identification no. 14642), Commonwealth of Massachusetts, Secretary of State, Corporation Division, recorded Sept. 27, 1974.

249   At about the same time: Dolphin Realty Trust, Haven O'More, Lorea Honeycutt O'More, and Michael Davis, trustees. See Massachusetts, Commonwealth of, Middlesex County Registry of Deeds, Cambridge, Book 12758, p. 634.

249   O'More's efforts: Documents relating to Arsenal Square Moratorium, Cambridge, Mass. City Council Order no. 10, September 25, 1978, filed in city clerk's office. Motion approved by 7–2 vote on Jan. 29, 1979.

250   In 1988: Unrestricted grant of $221,142 from Institute of Traditional Science (04-2577162) to Leonard and Sophie Davis Foundation, recorded with 1988 IRS Return of Private Foundation, Form 990-PF, copy filed in Massachusetts State Attorney General's Office, Boston, Division of Public Charities. Similar form for Leonard and Sophie Davis Foundation (13-6062579), filed with Florida State Attorney General's Office, Tallahassee, shows receipt of that amount during overlapping reporting period.

251   "matchless in the history . . . clearly electrified him": Nicolas Barker, in his foreword to Sotheby's, *Garden Ltd.*

252   "Dr. Haven O'More": Keynes, 327, 328.

254   "must submit to sacrifice": O'More, 4.

254–55   "It is hard": Waxman, *Delighting All Who Pay* (Millerton, N.Y.: SADEV, 1988), 5–16.

260   Brigadier General Thomas J. Kilmartin: Letter from Kilmartin, commanding officer, U.S. Army Reserve Personnel Center, to author, Oct. 1, 1991: "This is a final reply to your Freedom of Information Act request pertaining to a Haven O'More. The name he used while serving in the United States Army was Haven Moore." A Social Security number for O'More, obtained legally from the Massachusetts Registry of Motor Vehicles, was furnished by the author to help make a positive identification.

261   Honorable discharge for Haven Moore, Beaufort County, North Carolina, Registry of Deeds, Book 7, 44, recorded Nov. 19, 1946.

7: "INFINITE RICHES"

This chapter draws on the author's interviews with Edwin Wolf 2nd, William H. Scheide, William P. Stoneman, Nicolas Barker, and Paul Needham. See Bibliography, "Author's Interviews," (pp. 575–82), for further details.

264   "Pray ponder": Invoice dated Feb. 10, 1873, for Gutenberg Bible now in Scheide Library.

264   "an institution": William H. Scheide, "Anecdotes from a Family Library," speech given March 16, 1992, transcript in Grolier Club archive, 15.

265   "the uniqueness of this collection": Julian P. Boyd, "A Toast to Happy Alliance," *The Princeton University Library Chronicle* 27, 1965–66, 22.

265   "grew up with a library": William Scheide, "Love for the Printed Word as Expressed in the Scheide Library," *Papers of the Bibliographical Society of America* 51, 217.

265   "Growing up with": Book Club of California *Quarterly News-Letter* 51, no. 3 (1986), 76.

267   Humfrey Wanley wanted to buy Blickling Homilies: See Wright and Wright, vol. 2., 458–59.

268   "unquestionably the finest": Boyd, 126.

269   "Some of the greatest": Boyd, 9.

269   "To be returned": Boyd, 24.

269   "amid the passions": William T. Scheide, unpublished memoir, quoted in Boyd, 13. Copy of the memoir on file in the Scheide Library.

269–70 "that would have done credit . . . greater library": Ibid., 31.

270   "The dear Mother": Ibid., 23.

270   "I am quite anxious": Letter from John Scheide to Rosenbach, June 20, 1914, Rosenbach Company Archives (hereafter cited as RCA), I:152:20.

270   "Books that are desirable": Letter from Rosenbach to John Scheide, July 29, 1914, RCA, I:152:20.

271   "I have just returned: Letter from Rosenbach to John Scheide, Dec. 6, 1918, RCA, I:152:20.

271   "if we can agree": Letter from John Scheide to Rosenbach, June 15, 1923, RCA, I:152:20.

271   "imperfections": Letter from Rosenbach to John Scheide, June 19, 1923, RCA, I:152:20.

271   "by express today": Letter from Rosenbach to John Scheide, Aug. 31, 1923, RCA, I:152:20.

271   "is indeed a delicious copy": Letter from John Scheide to Rosenbach, Sept. 5, 1923, RCA, I:152:20.

272   "we had a hurried word": Letter from John Scheide to Rosenbach, Jan. 3, 1924, RCA, I:152:21.

272   "I shall, of course": Letter from Rosenbach to John Scheide, Feb. 5, 1924, RCA, I:152:21.

272   "My library is supposed": Letter from John Scheide to Rosenbach, Feb. 7, 1924, RCA, I:152:21.

272   "This magnificent copy": Letter from Rosenbach to John Scheide, RCA, I:152:26.

272   "makes my mouth water": Letter from John Scheide to Rosenbach, RCA, I:152:26.

273   "is one of only five libraries": Needham, *Princeton University Library Chronicle* 37 (1976), 85.

273–74   Margaret Stillwell's translation of *Catholicon* colophon: In Frederick R. Goff, "Johann Gutenberg and the Scheide Library at Princeton," in *The Princeton University Library Chronicle*, 37, Winter 1976, 82.

274   Now gathered under one roof: For more on Scheide library Bibles, see Boyd, chaps. 5 and 6.

8: "MIRROR IMAGES"

This chapter draws on the author's interviews with Carter Burden, Peter B. Howard, Ralph B. Sipper, Leonard and Lisa Baskin, Colin Franklin, Louis Daniel Brodsky, Carl A. Petersen, Michael Zinman, William S. Reese, Stephen Massey, and Irwin T. Holtzman. See Bibliography, "Author's Interviews," (pp. 575–82), for further details.

275   "Friend and fellow bibliophile": Robert, xii–xiii. Eratosthenes of Alexandria's starving himself to death has been cited by numerous authorities. See Cim, 661–62.

275   Retired Archdeacon buys back his books: Burton, 12–16.

275   "How does a shepherd know his sheep?": Anecdote told by Leigh Hunt, cited by Irving Browne, "Famous Book Collectors," in Targ, *Carousel for Bibliophiles*, 85. See also Amy Cruse, "A Supper at Charles Lamb's," in Targ, *Bouillabaisse for Bibliophiles*, 163–72.

275–76   Earlier this century: Eagle, "Moving a Library," *Eagle,* 143–45.

276   "You can never be too thin": Burden, 126. See also Rhoda Koenig, "Baring the Burdens," *Vogue,* August 1989, 318.

278   "tall, blond, handsome": David Grafton, *The Sisters* (New York: Random House, 1992), 185.

278   "young locomotives": Ibid., 186.

282   "I do not know": Leon Edel, *Happy Birthday to Waller: A Salute to Clifton Waller Barrett on His Eightieth Birthday from Friends and Admirers,* Charlottesville, Va., privately printed, June 1, 1981, unpaginated. For more on Clifton Waller Barrett, see Cahoon; see also C. Waller Barrett, "The Barrett Collection," *Book Collector,* Autumn 1956, 218–30.

283   Marguerite A. "Margie" Cohn founded the House of Books in Manhattan in 1930 with her husband, Louis Henry Cohn, who died shortly thereafter. She operated the business by herself for more than fifty years and established important relationships with numerous collectors, institutions, and writers such as Frost, Hemingway, Fitzgerald, and Thomas Wolfe. For more, see "Special Section in Honor of Marguerite A. Cohn," a collection of essays, in *American Book Collector* 1, no. 5, new ser., September/October 1980, 3–24; her death in 1984 is noticed by Jack W. C. Hagstrom in *American Book Collector* 6, no. 1, new ser., January/February 1985, 17–18.

284   February 1992 issue: See John Russell, "All Booked Up," *Vogue,* February 1992, 229–36; John Richardson, "Imprint of the Connoisseur," *House & Garden,* September 1992.

287   "against the background": Franklin, "Fifty Years of the Gehenna Press," in Baskin, 7; "must one day": Ibid., 26; "chronic addiction . . . informs this exhibition": Ibid., 8.

291–92   For more on pop artist Andy Warhol's obsessive collecting, see Paul Alexander, *Death and Disaster: The Rise of the Warhol Empire and the Race for Andy's Millions* (New York: Villard Books, 1994).

295   "in one place the sum": Petersen, 14.

304   Put another way: For more on Mark Hofmann forgeries, see Gilreath; Nicolas Barker, "A Scandal in America," parts 1 and 2, *Book Collector,* Winter 1987, 449–70, and Spring 1987, 9–28; and Kenneth W. Rendell, "The Mormon Forger, Con Man, and Murderer," in Rendell, 124–40.

310   "the finest assembly": Peter B. Howard, "American Fiction Since 1960," in Peters, 268–69.

9: "INSTANT IVY"

This chapter draws on the author's interviews with Thomas F. Staley, Roger E. Stoddard, Robert L. Nikirk, Roger G. Kennedy, Nicolas Barker, Warren Roberts, Kathleen G. Hjerter, Dave Oliphant, David Kirschenbaum, Bart Auerbach, Ellen S. Dunlap, Colin Franklin, William Self, John R. Silber, Charles Hamilton, John Maggs, Mary Beth Bigger, Raymond W. Daum, Howard B. Gotlieb, James A. Michener, Carlton Lake, and Florence de Lussy. See Bibliography, "Author's Interviews," (pp. 575–82), for further details.

313   "I propose": Ransom, viii–xiv. See also Hazel H. Ransom, ed., *The Conscience of the University* (Austin, Tx.: University of Texas Press, 1982).

313   "Twenty-five years": Molly Ivins, *Molly Ivins Can't Say That, Can She?* (New York: Random House, 1991), xiv.

313   "It is an obvious law": Ransom, 73.

314   "Actually," Ivins, 58.

318   "seven-figure deal": Carlton Lake, "Ed the Collector, Jake the Dentist and Beckett: A Tale That Ends in Texas," *New York Times Book Review,* Sept. 6, 1987, 3.

318   "Thomas Edward Hanley": Warren Roberts, "D. H. Lawrence," 31. See also Hobson, 307–10.

319   For Hanley's relationship with, and gifts to, the University of Arizona and other institutions, see Lee Sorenson, *Determined Donor* (Phoenix: Friends of the University of Arizona Library, 1989).

319   "visits to heirs": Warren Roberts, "D. H. Lawrence," 36.

319–20   "to pay for what an author": Hobson, 308.

320   "this is the last decade": William Rees-Moog, "Sellers' Market in Books," *The Sunday Times* (London), April 19, 1964.

320–21   "This is an action": *Fleming vs. Beutel*, 1. A copy of the documents relevant to the suit can be found in the Louis Silver file, box 7, at the Newberry Library. The full title of the complaint is: *John F. Fleming, Incorporated, a New York Corporation, Plaintiff, vs. Clarence A. Beutel, individually as Co-Executor of the Estate of Louis H. Silver, deceased, and AMERICAN NATIONAL BANK AND TRUST COMPANY OF CHICAGO, a national banking association, individually and as Co-Executor of the Estate of Louis H. Silver, deceased, Defendants.* Civil case no. 64-C-1372, in the United States District Court for the Northern District of Illinois, Eastern Division, Chicago, Illinois. (Hereafter cited as *Fleming vs. Beutel.*)

322–23   "Dear Amy . . . Affectionately": Letter from John Carter to Amy Silver, Jan. 2, 1964, reproduced in ibid., 25–27. The perception in some quarters that Texas has an "overweening appetite" for rare material persists to this day. Early in 1994, the British Library announced it would pay £1 million for the sole surviving complete copy of William Tyndale's 1526 translation of the New Testament. The price, reached after nine months of negotiations between Bristol Baptist College, owner of the book since 1784, and the British Library, was described as a "remarkable bargain." Numerous "higher offers from abroad" had been made for the book, according to Roger Hayden, a college official, but the lower offer was accepted to make sure this "cornerstone of English Protestantism" remained in the United Kingdom. "We felt it might end up in a Texas vault," Hayden told the *Daily Telegraph* (London, April 27, 1994, 9). Only one complete copy of the book survives because most were destroyed in a wave of reactionary fervor that attended its publication. Tyndale's stated aim had been to produce a Bible that was accessible to the common man, but the result (90 percent of which was ultimately incorporated in the King James Bible of 1611) antagonized ecclesiastical authorities, including Sir Thomas More. Tyndale fled to the continent, where he was hunted down, strangled, and burned at the stake as a heretic in 1536. For more, see Ditchfield, and David Daniell, *William Tyndale: A Biography* (New Haven and London: Yale University Press, 1994).

323   "fall on its face": Ibid., 45.

323–24   "CONGRATULATIONS": *Fleming vs. Beutel,* 61 (telegram from Harry Ransom to Herman Dunlap Smith).

324   "duplicate rare and scarce": Report of Subcommittee on Books, Jan. 22, 1965, from Louis Silver files in the Newberry Library.

324   Of the nine hundred items: For full description of materials sold as surplus, see Sotheby's, *Catalogue of Rare First Editions. . . .* For more on Silver, see Dickinson, 285–87.

325   "gulosity . . . a great pity": "Commentary," in *Book Collector,* Summer 1964, 143–44.

325–26   "saved something . . . not altogether want": "Commentary," in *Book Collector,* Autumn 1965, 297–301.

326	"We venture to think": Sotheby's *Catalogue of Rare First Editions . . .* , 7.
327	"was fully used": *Fleming vs. Beutel,* 61.
330	"an imaginative and tenacious": "Lew D. Feldman, 70, Book Dealer, Dead," *New York Times,* Nov. 30, 1976, 42.
330	"How Dr. Ransom got the letters": Martin Waldron, "Books Rival Athletics at the U. of Texas," *New York Times,* Jan. 2, 1973, 42.
331	"when and where rare books": Ibid.
332–33	See Rita Reif, "David Kirschenbaum Dies at 99; A Leading Dealer in Rare Books," *New York Times,* Jan. 21, 1994, B8.
333	"I am booked": Quoted in Munby, "Floreat Bibliomania," in Barker, *Essays and Papers,* 39.
333	"Such a compromise": Ibid., 40.
333	For more on DeCoursey Fales, see John T. Winterich, *The Fales Collection: An Appreciation* (New York: New York University Press, 1959).
337	"will complete the collection": J. Wynn Rousuck, " 'Tamerlane': 15-cent bomb to $123,000 gem," Baltimore *Sunday Sun,* Dec. 1, 1974.
337–38	"The ability to bilk . . . crime pays": Hamilton, 19–21.
339	"My wife Diane": Hamilton, 20.
340–42	"hundreds of thousands . . . with the President": Gotlieb.
342–45	"Yes, I was one . . . break up the college": Silber's dismissal was reported in the *Dallas Morning News,* July 26, 1970.
345	"an administrative monstrosity": John Yemma, "Erwin on Erwin," in *Scene* magazine (*Dallas Morning News*), Dec. 11, 1977, 2–9. Other biographical information on Erwin from news clippings in library of the *Dallas Morning News.*
346	"He was a rare human being": Quoted by Joan Cook in "Frank C. Erwin Jr., Ex-Texas U. Regent," *New York Times,* Oct. 3, 1980, D-15.
348–49	"insiders . . . 'Free at last' ": Clifford Endres, "Paying the Price," *Texas Monthly,* May 1988, 124–27. Turner used the phrase "Ransom syndrome" not only in the newsletter but also in interviews with the press. See "HRC—UT's Cultural Treasury," *Dallas Morning News,* July 4, 1982. For Ross Perot's decision to "give" $15 million (later disclosed to be a loan) for a key purchase, see "Rare Pforzheimer Books Bought for U. of Texas," *New York Times,* Jan. 22, 1986, C15.

351   "I sat down and began": Lake, 116–17.
352   "I hope you will not": Letter from Harry Ransom to Carlton
        Lake, March 20, 1969.
353   "I would never say": For more on Lake, see Clifford Endres,
        "Treasure Hunter," in *Third Coast,* March 1984.
354   "Like many brilliant leaders": Thomas F. Staley, "The Develop-
        ment of Twentieth Century Collections in American Research
        Institutions," speech delivered at Cambridge University, Sept. 8,
        1989. Transcript available at Harry Ransom Humanities
        Research Center.

10: "OBSESSED AMATEURS"

This chapter draws on the author's interviews with Louis I. Szathmary II,
David E. Schoonover, Walter L. Pforzheimer, Bernard McTigue, Rita Smith,
Frederick Nash, Justin G. Schiller, Betsy Beinecke Shirley, and Vincent Giroud.
See Bibliography, "Author's Interviews," (pp. 575–82), for further details.

355   "the brilliant beginning": William Faulkner, *Father Abraham,*
        ed. James Meriwether (New York: Random House, 1983), 3.
355   "chews tobacco constantly": Faulkner, *Father Abraham,* 14.
357   "Chef Louis is not cooking": Fred Ferretti, "A Gourmet at
        Large," in *Gourmet,* August 1989, 46.
357   "The food writers joke": Robert Cross, "The Godfather of
        Gourmet," in *Chicago Tribune,* May 4, 1989, sect. 7, 1.
369   "I was always a reader": Chernovsky, "Children's Books as a
        Source of Cultural History," *AB Bookman's Weekly,* Nov. 14,
        1988, 1905–8.
376   "Read Me a Story, Show Me a Book": See Shirley.
376   For more on the Beinecke brothers, see Dickinson, 31–33.
380   For more on the Elisabeth W. Ball Collection, see David War-
        rington, "Children's Literature," in *The Lilly Library,* 147–57;
        Dickinson, 25–26.
380   "It began on one of those": Edgar Osborne, introduction to St.
        John, xvii.
381   "When the books came . . . in this country": Ibid., v.
381   For more on the Iona and Peter Opie Collection, see Iona Opie,
        Peter Opie, and Brian Alderson, *The Treasures of Childhood*
        (New York: Arcade Publishing, 1989).

11: "DESTINY"

This chapter draws on the author's interviews with Aaron Lansky, Ruth M. Wisse, Charles L. Blockson, Lenny Moore, Peter J. Liacouras, and Fred J. Board. See Bibliography, "Author's Interviews," (pp. 575–82), for further details.

383 "To me the Yiddish Language": The text of Singer's speech is reprinted in Singer.

385–86 "Mendele shared": Aaron Lansky, "Artistic Voice and Implicit Social Theory in the Early Yiddish Fiction of Mendele Moykher Sforim," master's thesis, McGill University, 1980, 12.

388 According to sociolinguist Joshua A. Fishman: in Harshav, 85.

388 "The high honor": Singer, 6–9.

389 "It is true that Hitler": Harshav, 86.

390 Letters from William Uris and Marjorie Guthrie from files of National Yiddish Book Center.

394 "delightful diversion": Elinor Des Verney Sinnette, "Arthur Alfonso Schomburg," in Sinnette, Coates, and Battle, eds., 35.

395 "incompetent and unreliable": Sinnette, 40. Hubert Howe Bancroft (1832–1918), author of the offensive comments (in *Retrospection, Political and Personal*), is best remembered for his book collecting (see chapter 4), not his scholarship.

395 "However learned": Sinnette, Coates, and Battle, 35–36.

396 "We need in the coming dawn": Sinnette, 73.

396 Spingarn's collection: For more on Moorland and Spingarn, see Dickinson, 232–33 and 293.

396 "long before . . . to Negroes everywhere": Sinnette, 87.

397 "On the eve of my departure": Ibid., 145.

398 "History must restore": Schomburg, 231; "The Negro has been": Ibid., 237.

398 "who renews your faith" and "Blockson just runs": News clippings from scrapbook in Charles L. Blockson Collection.

401 "tens of thousands": Blockson, *National Geographic*, July 1984, 3. See also Blockson, *The Underground Railroad* (New York: Prentice-Hall, 1987).

405 Information on the Federal Writers Project from Alfred Kazin, introduction to Federal Writers Project's *New York Panorama* (New York: Pantheon, 1984), xiii–xxii.

408   For an account of the "hermit" Collyer Brothers: see *The New
           York Times* for Jan. 28, March 22, March 23, March 25, March
           26, March 30, April 2, April 5, April 6, April 9, April 12, May
           10, all 1947.

12: "CONTINENTAL DRIFT"

This chapter draws on the author's interviews with Marcia McGhee Carter,
Nicolas Barker, Lew and Ben Weinstein, Glen Dawson, Forrest J. Ackerman,
Sidney E. Berger, Ricky Jay, William and Peggy Self, David Sullivan, Louise
Taper, Paul Gehl, Ralph G. Newman, John Larroquette, Ralph B. Sipper,
David Karpeles, Mary Ellen Brooks, Sanford L. Berger, William J. Monihan,
Ellen Shaffer, Dr. Haskell F. Norman, Jeremy Norman, and Owen Gingerich.
See Bibliography, "Author's Interviews," (pp. 575–82), for further details.

410   For more detailed information on California bookselling, book
           collecting and book culture, see Bidwell and Briggs; and Warren
           R. Howell, "Exploring California Book-Trade History," *AB
           Bookman's Weekly,* Jan. 8, 1979, 240–65. Superb interviews have
           been compiled under the auspices of the Oral History Program,
           University of California at Los Angeles: James V. Mink, *Looking
           Back at Sixty: Recollections of Lawrence Clark Powell, Librarian,
           Teacher, and Writer* (2 vols., 1973); Joel Gardner, *Books and the
           Imagination: Fifty Years of Rare Books—Jake Zeitlin* (2 vols.,
           1980). Available at the Oral History Office, Bancroft Library,
           University of California at Berkeley is Ruth Teiser, *William J.
           Monihan, S.J., Librarian and Dedicated Bookman, University of
           San Francisco, 1947–1988* (1988).
412   "He left our complete run . . . boxes to the shelves": Lew Wein-
           stein, "Heritage Book-Shop—The First Year," *The Professional
           Rare Bookman,* Journal of the American Antiquarian Book-
           sellers of America, Inc., no. 4 (1982), 29–33.
417   "One room . . . take them with him": Stephen Tabor, profile of
           Michael D. Hurley in catalogue no. 477 of Dawson's Book-
           Shop, August 1984, unpaginated.
419   For more on Carl M. Rheuban, see "How One Savings Institu-
           tion Came Apart," *New York Times,* June 12, 1990, A1.
420   "Let me say . . . that from happening": For more on Ricky Jay
           as magician, scholar, writer, and obsessive collector, see Mark

Singer, "Secrets of the Magus," in *The New Yorker,* April 5, 1993, 54–73.

421–22 See William Self profiles and news articles in *Dayton Daily News:* Aug. 29, 1954; March 18, 1962; Oct. 18, 1964; Oct. 31, 1966; May 8, 1976.

426 Biographical background on Kenyon L. Starling from news clippings in the library of the *Dayton Daily News.* Obituary, Dec. 5, 1983.

427 "I enclose you a portion": Sandburg, 9–10.

427 "Where would history and biography be": Ibid., xv.

428 Sandburg told how Barrett: Ibid., 16.

431 "the presence of a single buyer": Mark Sisco, "The Boothbay Theatre Museum Collection," *Maine Antique Digest,* Sept. 1990, 1-B.

431–32 In 1990: See John Rhodehamel and Thomas F. Schwartz, *The Last Best Hope of Earth . . . Promise of America,* catalogue of exhibition at Huntington Library that featured Taper material. A 58-minute videocassette, *The Making of the Last Best Hope of America,* which dramatizes the formation of the exhibition and is narrated by Walter Matthau, with commentary by Louise Taper (Fido Productions, Beverly Hills), is available at the Huntington Library bookstore.

441 The constitution that remains: Details regarding Permanent Constitution of the Confederate States of America in *Archives of the Government of the Confederate States of America* (Washington, D.C.: National Archives of the United States, 1986), 4.

441–42 Description of Ethan Allen letter in Christie's catalogue *Printed Books and Manuscripts Including Americana,* Dec. 7, 1990, 93 (Lot 181).

444 "So subtile": Field, 50.

445 "mystical or superstitious": Berger, 6.

446 See Peterson for descriptions of books produced by William Morris.

447 "His work in the field": Wilhide, 9.

447–48 "has a form . . . acted upon!": Naylor, 206–7.

449–50 Sanford L. Berger's purchase of the "Morris Lot" from Anthony Rota is recalled by Magee, 209–13.

451 "To *use* rare books": Wynne, 22.

451   "particular joy": Berger, 7.
452   "penniless de Medici": Kevin Starr, "A Priest for All Seasons,"
           Image magazine (*San Francisco Examiner*), Aug. 7, 1988, 12–15.
452–54   For more on the Sir Thomas More Medal, see Jeremy Norman,
           "Private Book Collecting—A Public Benefit," in *AB Bookman's
           Weekly,* Sept. 8, 1986, 814–15.
461–62   See Owen Gingerich, *Collector's Choice: A Selection of Books
           and Manuscripts Given by Harrison D. Horblit to the Harvard
           College Library.* In a foreword Horblit wrote: "In the back of
           every collector's mind is the question of the ultimate fate of his
           beloved possession. The ideal solution, of course, when one
           passes from this earthly realm, is to 'take it with you.' Since this
           has its drawbacks, a second solution might be to 'stay with it,'
           which has been rather attractively accomplished in several
           instances. In my case, a third solution has proven most satisfac-
           tory and rewarding—many of my favorite books now reside at
           Harvard."
462–63   "This superb presentation . . . intimate circle": Sotheby's, *The
           Celebrated Library of Harrison D. Horblit, Esq. . . . ,* vol. 1,
           unpaginated (Lot 240). Additional history of this copy of the
           Copernicus is documented in Sotheby's, *The Collection of the
           Garden Ltd. . . . ,* unpaginated (Lot 51). For census, see also
           Gingerich, *Great Copernicus Chase,* 69–81.

                 13: "THE BLUMBERG COLLECTION"

This chapter draws on the author's interviews with W. Dennis Aiken, Stephen
C. Blumberg, Jerry Tucker, Roger E. Stoddard, Kenneth J. Rhodes, Shannon
Applegate, William A. Moffett, Henry H. Clifford, Glen Dawson, John L.
Sharpe III, Dr. Henry B. Blumberg, Dr. William S. Logan, and Raymond Cor-
nell. See Bibliography, "Author's Interviews," (pp. 575–82), for further details.

467   A volunteer force of librarians helped the FBI identify the most
           valuable books stolen by Stephen Blumberg. The unprecedented
           project was coordinated by the Online Computer Library Center,
           Inc., of Dublin, Ohio, which produced a twelve-minute videotape
           of the project, *The Omaha Project: A Rare Book Adventure.* It
           was distributed to libraries throughout the country, and includes a
           number of interior views of the warehouse. But not all of the books

removed from Blumberg's house could be identified, prompting the FBI to give three thousand volumes of undetermined ownership to Creighton University in Omaha, which had provided considerable staff assistance to its agents. The donated books included a Latin tragedy published in 1583, a postage stamp–sized copy of the New Testament printed about 1500, and an 1874 copy of *My Life on the Plains, or, Personal Experiences with Indians,* by General George Armstrong Custer. On April 5, 1994, Creighton officials received a letter from Stephen Blumberg. "He basically states that he feels he has some claim over the books," a Creighton spokesman reported. "He said that since they were seized from his house and the rightful owners could not be found, he should have possession of them." University officials nevertheless announced their determination to keep the books. See Kevin O'Hanlon, "C.U. Asked to Return Volumes to Convicted Iowa Book Thief," in the *Omaha-World Herald,* April 6, 1994, 13.

467   By June 30, 1994, the number of books at Harvard totaled 12,877,360 volumes, according to the university librarian's annual report for the year.

468   U.S. District Court for the Southern District of Iowa, Central Division. *United States of America vs. Steven* [sic] *Carrie Blumberg* (criminal case no. 90-63). Direct testimony and cross-examination of Kenneth J. Rhodes, trial transcript, vol. 2, 172–270 (hereafter cited as *U.S. vs. Blumberg*), supplemented by author's court room notes.

473   "Stephen would go": Testimony of Brian T. Teeuwe, ibid., vol. 4, 486–532.

474   "It was an enormous loss": Testimony of Fraser Cocks, ibid., 323–44.

475   "It is the cradle period": Testimony of Susan M. Allen, ibid., 354–69.

475   "one of which is six stories high": Testimony of Lynne Newell, *U.S. vs. Blumberg,* vol. 3, 375–84.

482   "This is accurate": Testimony of Matthew McGue, *U.S. vs. Blumberg,* vol. 3, 392–96.

484   "We traveled to Ohio": Testimony of Howard Bergstrom, *U.S. vs. Blumberg,* vol. 4, 533–54.

485   "The Shinn lists are being shared": Moffett, 1. In "Armed and Bibliographically Dangerous," *American Book Collector* 3, no. 1, new ser., January/February 1982, 38–41, William Burton lists

eight names known to have been used by James Shinn in 1981 alone, including James L. Coffman, his birth name.

487   Stephen Blumberg's nefarious accomplishment—that he probably stole more books of "obviously high quality" than anyone else this century—remains intact, although the exploits of one British bibliokleptomaniac, Duncan Charles Le Worsley Jevons, are sufficient to draw comparisons. On June 1, 1994, Jevons, a forty-nine-year-old turkey farm worker from Suffolk, England, was sentenced to fifteen months in prison after admitting that he had taken 42,000 books from libraries, churches, and colleges throughout Great Britain over a thirty-year period. Most of the books the onetime theology student removed from the institutions in a tattered old briefcase dealt with religion, philosophy, and history, although few were considered particularly rare. Officials computed losses at £500,000. That figure included costs for labor, storage, and shipment of the recovered books, as well as estimated replacement value. Jevons was arrested after he tried to sell a book bearing the logo of a library he had robbed to a suspicious buyer at a "car boot sale" in Cumbria. A search of the run-down eighteenth-century house in Suffolk where Jevons lived alone turned up thirty-five tons of purloined books. "Perhaps I do not have much sense of self-worth—or maybe I have the subconscious belief that if I surround myself with all these books, the knowledge within them will somehow seep into me," Jevons told Suzanne O'Shea, for a story in the *Daily Mail* (London), "Jail for the Magpie Man Who Was Brought to Book," June 2, 1994, 33. "The day of reckoning has come," Ipswich Crown Court Judge John Turner declared prior to imposing sentence. "You are not mentally ill, you have just got a personality which is like a magpie to steal these kinds of books." See also *The Daily Telegraph* (London), "Aspiring Philosopher Stole 42,000 Books," June 2, 1994, 3.

488   Moffett's death: See John Noble Wilford, "William A. Moffett, 62, Is Dead; Opened Door to Dead Sea Scrolls," *New York Times,* February 22, 1995, B8.

488   "Insider theft" was suspected in the disappearance of twenty-two medieval manuscripts valued at $1 million from Columbia University's Butler Library in the fall of 1994. Among the items reported missing were a papal bull written by Pope Innocent III

in 1202 and a French copy of the Book of Hours from the four-teenth century. All of the manuscripts were kept in a restricted area of the sixth floor of the rare-books and manuscripts library. "If it were just one or two manuscripts, they could have been stolen by a visitor, but when this number of items is missing, you figure the thief knew his way around," one expert said. The FBI was asked to investigate. See William H. Honan, "Manuscript Mystery," *New York Times*, October 8, 1994, 25.

488–90   Details and court proceedings of the trial of Robert M. "Skeet" Willingham, Jr., are based on reports in the Atlanta *Constitution* and Atlanta *Journal*. Computer printouts of the articles furnished to the author by the newspapers. January 1, 1988; March 13, 1988; August 22, 23, 24, 26, 27, 30, 31, 1988; September 3, 7, 8, 9, 1988. For more on W. Graham Arader III and his spirited deal-ings in paintings, maps, engravings, and imprints, particularly his strategy to purchase for $5.1 million at a November 20, 1985, auction the original watercolors Pierre-Joseph Redouté executed for *Les Liliaceés*, and then sell them individually to a syndicate of subscribers, see Mark Singer, "Wall Power," in *Mr. Personality: Profiles and Talk Pieces* (New York: Knopf, 1989), 318–61.

492   For more on the Zamorano 80, see *The Zamorano 80: Collec-tors' Books About California,* a checklist and brief history of the club issued in conduction with an exhibition held at the Hunt-ington Library in 1986–1987. Also see volume 1 of *The Collec-tion of Henry Clifford* ("The Zamorano Eighty").

496–97   "A skinny little guy . . . I just loved him": Testimony of Emily A. Fredericksen, *U.S. vs. Blumberg*, vol. 5, 579–601.

497   "is someone who has an encapsulated": Testimony of Glen S. Lipson, *U.S. vs. Blumberg*, 601–74.

498–502   "quite unusual . . . a paranoid state": Testimony of William S. Logan, *U.S. vs. Blumberg*, vol. 6, 686–829, 895–916.

505   "Steve used to say": Testimony of Brian Teeuwe, *U.S. vs. Blum-berg*, vol. 4, 486–532.

505–7   "that was going to hold . . . personally harassed at times": Tes-timony of William S. Logan, *U.S. vs. Blumberg*, vol. 6, 784.

507–8   "no more . . . the one he told me": Testimony of Michael Taylor, *U.S. vs. Blumberg*, vol. 6, 829–90.

509   Prosecutor Linda R. Reade's summation in *U.S. vs. Blumberg*, vol. 7, 922–35, 976–86; Defense Attorney Raymond Rosen-berg's closing remarks, 954–76.

14: "CARPE DIEM"

This chapter draws on the author's interviews with Richard Manney, John L. Marion, and Pauline L. du Pont Harrison. See Bibliography, "Author's Interviews," (pp. 575–82), for further details.

520   Four large folios: See Sotheby's, *The Collection of the Garden Ltd.* (Lot 100) for a description of the First Four Folios of Shakespeare (hereafter cited as *Garden Ltd.*).

522   Manney also was interested: *Garden Ltd.* (Lot 80), *Don Quixote.*

522   For more on this *Tamerlane* discovery, see Marion, 26.

526–28   For more on the sale of the Manney library, see Sotheby's, *The Library of Richard Manney.*

528   For more on the controversy surrounding The Mediators, see the following articles, all by Mike Reynolds, writing in *Inside Media:* "The Mediators Moves Toward Liquidation," Jan. 22, 1992, 8; "Barter breach stuns stations," Feb. 20, 1992, 1; "Where's the Art?" March 18, 1992, 24; "Mediators workings revealed in audit," April 17, 1992, 4; "Creditors press Mediators for better deal," May 1, 1992, 1. See also Lita Solis-Cohen, "Manneys Fight to Keep Collection," *Maine Antique Digest,* May 1992, 7-A.

　　For full details of the Mediators bankruptcy proceedings, see U.S. Bankruptcy Court, Southern District of New York, in the Matter of the *Mediators,* Inc., Debtor (case no. 91 B 12980). An itemized list of 700 artworks is part of the case file.

528   For full details of the sale featuring the silver and mirror plateau from the Manney collection, see Lita Solis-Cohen, "Americana Prices Roll Back a Decade," *Maine Antique Digest,* August 1993, 1-E.

EPILOGUE

The epilogue draws on the author's interviews with Raymond Epstein and Joan Hill. See Bibliography, "Author's Interviews," (pp. 575–82), for further details.

531   For this sale: See Swann Galleries.

Bibliography

Author's Interviews

Forrest J. Ackerman. Science fiction collector. Hollywood, California, June 12, 1991.

Thomas R. Adams. Retired librarian, John Carter Brown Library. Providence, R.I., September 6, 1990.

Allen Ahearn. Maryland bookseller and compiler of *Collected Books: The Guide to Values*. Telephone interview, March 21, 1991.

W. Dennis Aiken, Special agent, FBI Omaha, August 15, 1991.

Shannon Applegate. Writer whose family archive at University of Oregon was stolen by Stephen Blumberg. Telephone conversation, July 9, 1992.

Bart Auerbach. Bookseller, consultant to Christie's and former employee of Lew David Feldman. New York, June 17, 1990, and numerous telephone conversations.

Nicolas Barker. Editor of *The Book Collector* and retired keeper of rare books at the British Library. Worcester, Massachusetts, November 15, 1989; London, April 18, 1990.

Leonard and Lisa Baskin. Artist, printer, and collector, and his wife, also a collector. Leeds, Massachusetts, December 10, 1989.

Sanford L. Berger. Collector of William Morris material. Carmel, California, August 9, 1990.

Sidney Berger. Curator of rare books, University of California, Riverside, and editor of *Rare Books & Manuscripts Librarianship*. Numerous telephone conversations.

Charles L. Blockson. Collector, philanthropist, and curator of Charles L. Blockson Afro-American Collection, Temple University. Philadelphia, September 20, 1991.

Stephen Carrie Blumberg. Biblioklept. Des Moines and Ottumwa, Iowa, January 26, 1991, and private correspondence.

Henry B. Blumberg, M.D. Father of Stephen Blumberg. Des Moines, January 27, 1991.

Fred J. Board. Collector of oddities. Stamford, Connecticut, October 28, 1992.

Louis Daniel Brodsky. Collector of William Faulkner materials. St. Louis and Cape Girardeau, Missouri, October 3, 1990.

Carter Burden. Collector of American literature. New York, September 13, 1990, and May 7 and July 8, 1992.

William R. Cagle. Director of Lilly Library, Indiana University. Bloomington, October 6, 1990.

Marcia McGhee Carter. Partner with Larry McMurtry in Booked Up, Washington, D.C. Washington, D.C., July 11, 1990.

Henry H. Clifford. "Zamorano 80" collector from Pasadena targeted by Stephen Blumberg. Telephone conversation, July 5, 1992.

Fraser Cocks. Director of special collections, University of Oregon, and witness at trial of Stephen Blumberg. Telephone conversation, July 1, 1992.

Raymond Cornell. Private detective. Des Moines, Iowa, July 31, 1990, and January 27, and July 6, 1991.

The Rev. James W. Crawford. Pastor, Old South Church, Boston. Boston, October 22, 1991.

John Dann. Director and librarian, Clements Library, University of Michigan. Ann Arbor, August 2, 1991.

Raymond W. Daum. Retired curator of Gloria Swanson Archive, Harry Ransom Humanities Research Center, University of Texas. Austin, February 22, 1990.

Glen Dawson. Los Angeles bookseller and expert witness at Stephen Blumberg trial. Los Angeles, August 6, 1990.

Florence de Lussy. Conservator en chef de manuscrits, Bibliothèque Nationale, Paris. Paris, April 17, 1990.

Marie Devine. Curator, Lewis Walpole Library, Yale University. Farmington, Connecticut, April 14, 1991.

Ellen S. Dunlap. Staff member, Harry Ransom Humanities Research Center, University of Texas, Austin, 1971–1983; director of the Rosenbach Museum and Library, Philadelphia, 1983–1992; appointed director of American Antiquarian Society in 1992. Philadelphia, January 10, 1990.

J. M. Edelstein. Senior bibliographer and resource coordinator, Getty Center for the History of Art and the Humanities, Santa Monica. Santa Monica, August 6, 1990.

Raymond Epstein. Chicago collector. New York, April 30, 1992.

Norman Fiering. Librarian, John Carter Brown Library, Brown University. Providence, September 6, 1990.

W. George Fletcher. Astor Curator of Printed Books and Bindings, Pierpont Morgan Library. New York, March 19, 1992.

Mary Ann Kraus Folter. An owner of H. P. Kraus, New York booksellers. October 14, 1994.

Mirjam M. Foot. Curator, British Library. London, April 18, 1990.

Colin Franklin. Bookseller, Oxford, England. April 10, 1990.

Arthur Freeman. Quaritch Ltd. bookseller, friend of Haven O'More. London, April 19, 1990.

Paul F. Gehl. Custodian of John M. Wing Foundation, Newberry Library. Chicago, October 4, 1990.

Owen Gingerich. Professor of Astronomy and History of Science at Harvard-Smithsonian Center for Astrophysics; author and noted authority on publishing history of Copernicus; friend of Haven O'More and Harrison D. Horblit. Cambridge, Massachusetts, May 18, 1992.

Vincent Giroud. Curator of modern books, Beinecke Library, Yale University. Telephone conversation, December 16, 1992.

David R. Godine. Publisher and collector. Boston, August 27, 1991.

Howard B. Gotlieb. Director of special collections, Mugar Memorial Library, Boston University. Boston, October 22, 1990.

Robert W. Hamblin. Curator of Louis Daniel Brodsky Collection, Southeast Missouri State University, Cape Girardeau, Missouri. Cape Girardeau, October 3, 1990.

Charles Hamilton. New York handwriting expert and autograph dealer. Telephone conversation, March 26, 1990.

Pauline L. du Pont Harrison. Honorary trustee, Winterthur Museum, Odessa, Delaware, and friend of Richard and Gloria Manney. Telephone conversation, August 31, 1992.

Joan Hill. California bookseller and collector. New York, April 30, 1992.

Kathleen Gee Hjerter. Director of art, Harry Ransom Humanities Research Center, University of Texas, Austin, 1972–1992. Austin, February 22, 1990.

Michael E. Hoffman. Executive director of Aperture Foundation, Inc., and publishing colleague of Haven O'More. Telephone conversation, February 13, 1992.

Irwin T. Holtzman. Collector and philanthropist. Grosse Point Farms, Michigan, August 4–5, 1991.

Peter B. Howard. Owner of Serendipity Books, Berkeley, California, and past president of Antiquarian Booksellers Association of America. Hadley, Massachusetts, November 7, 1990.

Ricky Jay. Professional magician, author, and collector. Cambridge, Massachusetts, March 5, 1990.

William L. Joyce. Associate university librarian for rare books and special collections, Princeton University. Princeton, March 20,1992.

Alan Jutzi. Curator of rare books, Huntington Library. San Marino, California, June 10, 1990.

Priscilla Juvelis. Bookseller. Boston, April 4, 1990.

David Karpeles. Manuscript collector. Santa Barbara, August 8, 1990.

Roger G. Kennedy. Director emeritus of National Museum of American History. Telephone conversation, March 13, 1990.

David Kirschenbaum. Founder of Carnegie Book Shop and dean of New York booksellers. New York, December 28, 1989.

Thomas J. Kren. Curator of manuscripts, J. Paul Getty Museum, Santa Monica. Malibu, June 12, 1991.

Carlton Lake. Collector of twentieth-century French manuscripts and executive curator of Harry Ransom Humanities Research Center, University of Texas, Austin. Austin, February 25, 1990.

John Lannon. Head of acquisitions, Boston Athenæum. Boston, November 7, 1991.

Aaron Lansky. Founder of National Yiddish Book Center. Amherst, Massachusetts, February 20, 1990, and South Hadley, Massachusetts, July 15, 1992.

John Larroquette. Actor and collector of modern American literature. Malibu, California, August 6, 1990.

Peter J. Liacouras. President of Temple University, Philadelphia. Telephone conversation, October 6, 1992.

Robert Liska. Owner of Colophon, booksellers, Exeter, New Hampshire. Exeter, April 27, 1992.

William S. Logan, M.D. Director of Department of Law and Psychiatry, Menninger Clinic, Topeka, and Stephen Blumberg's psychiatrist. Des Moines, July 31, 1991.

George S. Lowry. President of Swann Galleries. New York, September 26, 1990.

Richard Luckett. Pepys librarian, Magdalene College, Cambridge University. Cambridge, April 21, 1990.

John Maggs. Director of Maggs Bros., Ltd., booksellers, London. London, April 18, 1990.

Richard Manney. Collector. New York, March 23, 1990, and June 27, 1991. Numerous telephone conversations.

John L. Marion. Chief auctioneer and chairman for Sotheby's in North America. Boston, November 28, 1989.

Stephen Massey. Director of the rare-books department, Christie's. New York, September 24, 1991.

Marcus A. McCorison. Former director and librarian of American Antiquarian Society. Worcester, July 16, 1990.

Matthew McGue. Minnesota professor impersonated by Stephen Blumberg. Telephone conversation, July 27, 1992.

Bernard McTigue. Former keeper of rare books, New York Public Library; currently chairman, Department of Special Collections, University of Florida, Gainesville. New York, September 26, 1990.

David R. Meeker. Collector of Ernest Hemingway material. Sacramento, August 11, 1990.

James A. Michener. Author and benefactor of art at Harry Ransom Humanities Research Center, University of Texas, Austin. Telephone conversation, April 1, 1992.

William A. Moffett. Director, Huntington Library. San Marino, California, June 10, 1991.

The Reverend William J. Monihan, S.J. Director of library relations, University of San Francisco. San Francisco, August 10, 1990.

Laura V. Monti. Keeper of rare books, Boston Public Library. Boston, October 15, 1991.

Lenny Moore. Retired professional football player and friend of Charles L. Blockson. Telephone conversation, August 13, 1992.

Paul Needham. Former curator of manuscripts at J. Pierpont Morgan Library; currently vice president and director of Rare Books Department, Sotheby's. New York, January 16, 1992.

Robert L. Nikirk. Librarian of the Grolier Club, 1970–1990. New York, November 9, 1989.

Haskell F. Norman, M.D. Collector of Freud, science, and medicine materials. San Francisco, June 14, 1991.

Jeremy M. Norman. San Francisco bookseller. Telephone conversation, May 4, 1992.

Stephen Parks. Curator of Elizabethan Club Library, Yale University. New Haven, April 14, 1991.

Carl A. Petersen. Collector of William Faulkner material. St. Louis, Missouri, October 3, 1990.

Walter Pforzheimer. Former C.I.A. general counsel and collector of espionage materials. Washington, D.C., July 11, 1990.

Irwin J. Pincus, M.D. Collector of books on the history of medicine. Beverly Hills, June 11, 1991.

Daniel Posnansky. Collector of Arthur Conan Doyle material. Boston, April 4, 1990.

Reynolds Price. Author and collector. Cambridge, Massachusetts, May 15, 1992.

Linda R. Reade. Prosecutor in Stephen Blumberg case. Des Moines, February 3, 1991.

David N. Redden. Senior vice president, head of Books and Manuscripts Division, Sotheby's. Telephone conversation, November 22, 1989; New York, June 7, 1991.

William S. Reese. Founder of William Reese Company, bookseller, New Haven. New York, November 9, 1989.

Kenneth W. Rendell. Massachusetts autograph dealer. Newton, Massachusetts, March 30, 1990.

Stephen T. Riley. Director emeritus, Massachusetts Historical Society. Boston, December 5, 1989.

Julian Roberts. Executive librarian, Bodleian Library, Oxford University. Oxford, April 20, 1990.

Warren Roberts. Director of Harry Ransom Humanities Research Center, University of Texas, Austin, 1961–1976. Austin, February 25, 1990.

Samuel Rosenthal. Collector of illustrated books and fine bindings and philanthropist. Chicago, October 7, 1990.

Leona Rostenberg and Madeleine B. Stern. New York booksellers and authors of numerous books. New York, May 5, 1990.

Christa Sammons. Curator of German literature, Beinecke Library, Yale University. New Haven, April 14, 1991.

William H. Scheide. Collector. Princeton, March 9, 1990, and March 20, 1992.

Justin G. Schiller. New York bookseller and collector. Telephone conversation, July 29, 1992.

David E. Schoonover. Curator of rare books, University of Iowa. Telephone conversation, August 23, 1990.

Fred Schreiber. New York City bookseller. Telephone conversation, October 16, 1994.

William Self. Hollywood producer, and collector of Dickens, Poe, and Melville material. Bel Air, June 10, 1991.

Ellen Shaffer. Founding director and curator of Silverado Museum, St. Helena, California. St. Helena, August 11, 1990.

John L. Sharpe III. Academic librarian, William R. Perkins Library, Duke University, Durham, North Carolina. Telephone conversation, November 4, 1991.

Betsy Beinecke Shirley. Collector of American children's literature and philanthropist. Bernardsville, New Jersey, August 3, 1992.

John Silber. President of Boston University since 1971 and dean of College of Arts and Sciences at University of Texas, 1967–1970, under then president Harry Ransom. Boston, August 8, 1991.

Joel Silver. Director of public services, Lilly Library, Indiana University, Bloomington. Bloomington, October 6, 1990.

Ralph B. Sipper. Founder of Joseph the Provider, booksellers, Santa Barbara. Santa Barbara, August 8, 1990; telephone conversation, June 6, 1992.

Rita Smith. Project cataloguer, Ruth Baldwin Library, University of Florida, Gainesville. Gainesville, December 14, 1990.

Thomas F. Staley. Director, Harry Ransom Humanities Research Center, University of Texas, Austin. Austin, February 22, 1990.

Roger E. Stoddard. Curator of rare books, Houghton Library, Harvard University. Cambridge, November 8, 1989, and November 8, 1990.

William P. Stoneman. Scheide librarian, Princeton University, and editor of *Gazette of the Grolier Club*. Princeton, March 9, 1990, and March 20, 1992.

Frank S. Streeter. Collector, son of Thomas W. Streeter. New York, June 7, 1991.

David Sullivan. Curator of rare books, Stanford University, Palo Alto. Telephone conversation, August 19, 1992.

Sem Sutter. Bibliographer for Western European Languages and Literatures, University of Chicago Library. Chicago, October 5, 1990.

Louis S. Szathmary II. Restaurateur, collector, philanthropist. Providence, September 6, 1990, and August 20, 1992.

G. Thomas Tanselle. Bibliographer, collector, vice president of Guggenheim Foundation and past president of the Grolier Club. New York, April 25, 1990.

Louise Taper. Collector of Lincolniana. Beverly Hills, June 12, 1991.

Jerry Tucker. F.B.I. special agent. Omaha, August 15, 1991.

John Van Horne. Librarian, Library Company of Philadelphia. Philadelphia, January 10, 1990.

Peter M. V an Wingen. Specialist for the Book Arts, Rare Books and Special Collections Division, Library of Congress. Washington, D.C., January 3, 1992.

Arthur E. Vershbow and Charlotte Vershbow. Collectors of illustrated books. Newton, Massachusetts, February 7, 1990.

Frank Walker. Director of special collections, New York University. Telephone conversation, March 27, 1992.

Elizabeth Walsh. Reading room supervisor, Folger Shakespeare Library. Washington, D.C., January 3, 1992.

David G. Waxman. Bookseller in Great Neck, New York, and friend of Haven O'More. Telephone conversation, October 28, 1991.

Louis Weinstein and Ben Weinstein. Founders of Heritage Book Shop, Los Angeles. Los Angeles, August 7, 1990.

Ruth M. Wisse. Professor of Yiddish at Harvard University, mentor to Aaron Lansky. Telephone conversation, August 6, 1992.

Edwin Wolf 2nd. Bookman and biographer of Dr. A. S. W. Rosenbach. Philadelphia, January 10, 1990.

David Zeidberg. Director of special collections, University of California at Los Angeles. Los Angeles, June 13, 1991.

Michael Zinman. Collector of American imprints. Ardsley, New York, August 5, 1990, and October 12, 1992.

Archives

American Antiquarian Society, Worcester, Massachusetts. Correspondence of Clarence S. Brigham and Henry E. Huntington.

Grolier Club, New York City. Three volumes of newspaper clippings concerning the Robert Hoe III auction in New York City, 1911–1912.

Huntington Library, San Marino, California. Documents pertaining to George D. Smith, Dr. A. S. W. Rosenbach, and Henry Huntington's acquisition of the E. Dwight Church Collection in 1911.

Newberry Library, Chicago. Files pertaining to formation of library and acquisition of Louis H. Silver library.

Rosenbach Museum and Library, Philadelphia. Rosenbach Company Archives. Correspondence of Dr. A. S. W. Rosenbach and Henry E. Huntington, Belle da Costa Greene, John H. Scheide, Frank Hogan, Estelle Doheny, Eleanor Elkins Widener, Henry Folger, and William Andrews Clark.

General Bibliography

Achilles, Rolf, ed. *Humanities' Mirror: Reading at the Newberry, 1887–1987*. Chicago: Newberry Library, 1987.

Adams, Randolph G. *Three Americanists*. Philadelphia: University of Pennsylvania Press, 1939.

Adams, Thomas R. "Chapin Library: An Idea." *Williams College Alumni Review,* May 1956, 23–26.

Adelman, Seymour. *The Moving Pageant*. Lititz, Pa.: Sutter House, 1977.

Ahearn, Allen, and Patricia Ahearn. *Collected Books: The Guide to Values*. New York: G. P. Putnam's Sons, 1991.

Allan, P. B. *The Book-Hunter at Home*. New York: G. P. Putnam's Sons, 1920.

Alsop, Joseph. *The Rare Art Traditions: The History of Art Collecting and Its Linked Phenomena*. Princeton: Princeton University Press; New York: Harper & Row, 1982.

Altick, Richard D. *The Scholar Adventurers*. New York: Macmillan, 1950.

Amory, Hugh. *First Impressions: Printing in Cambridge, 1639–1989: Catalogue of an Exhibition at the Houghton Library and at the Harvard Law School Library October 6 through October 27, 1989*. Cambridge, Mass.: Harvard University, 1989. Includes an annual census of the Bay Psalm Book.

Anderson Auction Co. *The Library of Robert Hoe of New York*. 8 vols. New York: Anderson Auction Co., 1911–1912. Foreword by Beverly Chew and bibliographical notes in "Part I: A to K."

Anderson Galleries. *The Library of Jerome Kern*. 2 vols. New York: Anderson Auction Co., 1929.

Anderton, Basil. *Fragrance Among Old Volumes: Essays and Idylls of a Book Lover*. London: Kegan Paul, Trench, Trübner, 1910.

Andrews, Irene Dwen. *Owners of Books: The Dissipations of a Collector*. Washington, D.C.: Bruin Press, 1936.

Arnold, Denis, ed. *The New Oxford Companion to Music*. 2 vols. Oxford and New York: Oxford University Press, 1983.

Arnold, William Harris. *Ventures in Book Collecting*. New York: Charles Scribner's Sons, 1923.

Aubrey, John. *Brief Lives.* Edited by Richard Barber. Totowa, N.J.: Barnes & Noble Books, 1983.

Auchincloss, Louis. *J. P. Morgan: The Financier as Collector.* New York: Harry N. Abrams, 1990.

Austin, Gabriel. *The Library of Jean Grolier.* With an introductory essay by Colin Eisler. New York: Grolier Club, 1971.

————, ed. *Four Oaks Farm.* Somerville, N.J.: Privately printed, 1967.

————, ed. *Four Oaks Library.* Somerville, N.J.: Privately printed, 1967.

Avrin, Leila. *Scribes, Script and Books: The Book Arts from Antiquity to the Renaissance.* Chicago: American Library Association; London: British Library, 1991.

Babb, James T. *A Bibliography of the Writings of William McFee.* Garden City, N.Y.: Doubleday, Doran, 1931. Introduction and notes by William McFee.

Baldwin, Ruth M. *100 Rhyming Nineteenth-Century Alphabets in English from the Library of Ruth M. Baldwin.* Carbondale and Edwardsville, Ill.: Southern Illinois University Press; London and Amsterdam: Feffer & Simmons, 1972.

Bancroft, Hubert Howe. *Literary Industries: A Memoir.* New York: Harper & Brothers, 1891.

Barker, Nicolas. *Portrait of an Obsession.* New York: G. P. Putnam's Sons, 1967. An adaptation of the five-volume *Phillipps Studies* by A. N. L. Munby.

Barker, Nicolas, and John Collins. *A Sequel to an Enquiry into the Nature of Certain XIXth Century Pamphlets by John Carter and Graham Pollard.* London: Scolar Press, 1983.

Barker, Nicolas, et al. *Treasures of the British Library.* New York: Harry N. Abrams, 1989.

Barrett, Clifton Waller. "Some Bibliographical Adventures in Americana." *Papers of the Bibliographical Society of America,* 1st quarter, 1950, 17–28.

Baskin, Lisa Unger. *The Gehenna Press: The Work of Fifty Years, 1942–1992.* Dallas: Bridwell Library and Gehenna Press, 1992. Catalogue of an exhibition curated by Lisa Unger Baskin. Essay by Colin Franklin. Bibliography by Hosea Baskin. Notes on the books by Leonard Baskin.

Bate, W. Jackson. *Samuel Johnson.* New York: Harcourt Brace Jovanovich, 1975.

The Bay Psalm Book. New York: New England Society, 1903. A facsimile reprint of the first edition printed by Stephen Daye at Cambridge, Massachusetts, in 1640, with an introduction and census by Wilberforce Eames.

The Beinecke Rare Book and Manuscript Library: A Guide to Its Collections. New Haven: Yale University Press, 1974. Introduction by Louis L. Martz.

Benjamin, Walter. "Unpacking My Library: A Talk About Book Collecting." In *Illuminations: Essays and Reflections.* Translated from the German by Harry Zohn. New York: Schocken Books, 1969.

Bennett, Paul A., ed. *Books and Printing: A Treasury for Typophiles.* Cleveland and New York: World Publishing, 1951.

Bentinck-Smith, William. *Building a Great Library: The Coolidge Years at Harvard.* Cambridge, Mass.: Harvard University Library, 1976.

Berger, Sanford. *William Morris: The Sanford and Helen Berger Collection.* Berkeley: The Bancroft Library and University Art Museum, 1984.

Bergin, Thomas G. *Boccaccio.* New York: Viking Press, 1981.

Bibliographica: Papers on Books, Their History and Art. 3 vols. London: Kegan Paul, Trench, Trübner, 1895–1897.

Bibliosophia; or Book-Wisdom: Containing Some Account of the Pride, Pleasure, and Privileges, of that Glorious Vocation, Book-Collecting. London: William Miller, 1810. A contemporary satire of Thomas Frognall Dibdin written pseudonymously "By an Aspirant," but attributed in 1965 by William A. Jackson to James Beresford.

Bibliotheca Phillippica: Manuscripts on Vellum and Paper from the 9th to the 18th Centuries from the Celebrated Collection formed by Sir Thomas Phillipps. New York: H. P. Kraus, 1979.

Bidwell, John, and Carol R. Briggs, eds. *A Bibliophile's Los Angeles: Essays for the International Association of Bibliophiles on the Occasion of Its XIVth Congress, 30 September–11 October, 1985.* Los Angeles: William Andrews Clark Memorial Library, 1985.

Bierstadt, O. A. *The Library of Robert Hoe.* New York: Privately printed, 1895.

Bishop, Morris. *Petrarch and His World*. Bloomington, Ind.: Indiana University Press, 1963.

Blades, William. "Bibliographical Hoaxing: Count De Fortsas's Library." *The Philobiblon* 2 (April 1863): 75–84.

———. *The Enemies of Books*. London: Elliot Stock, 1902.

Blockson, Charles L., ed. *Catalogue of the Charles L. Blockson Afro-American Collection*. Philadelphia: Temple University Press, 1990.

———. *The Underground Railroad: First Person Narratives of Escapes to Freedom in the North*. New York: Prentice Hall, 1987.

Blotner, Joseph. *Faulkner: A Biography*. 1974. Rev. ed. New York: Random House, 1984. A one-volume edition, revised, updated, and condensed by Blotner from the 1974, two-volume edition.

Blumberg, Stephen Carrie. "Biography." A 43-page autobiographical reflection, and "Trips," a 12-page summary of book theft. Both written at the Menninger Clinic, Topeka, Kansas, and used by permission of Dr. Henry B. Blumberg.

Blumenthal, Walter Hart. *Bookmen's Bedlam: An Olio of Literary Oddities*. New Brunswick, N.J.: Rutgers University Press, 1955.

Bond, William H. Introduction to *The Philip Hofer Bequest: A Catalogue of an Exhibition in the Department of Printing and Graphic Arts*. Cambridge, Mass.: Harvard College Library, 1988.

———. *Thomas Hollis of Lincoln's Inn: A Whig and His Books*. Cambridge, England: Cambridge University Press, 1990.

———, ed. *Records of a Bibliographer: Selected Papers of William Alexander Jackson*. Cambridge, Mass.: Harvard University Press, Belknap Press, 1967.

Bonnardot, Alfred. *The Mirror of the Parisian Bibliophile: A Satirical Tale*. Translated from the French and edited by Theodore Wesley Koch. Chicago: Privately printed, 1931.

Book Collecting and Scholarship: Essays by Theodore C. Blegen, James Ford Bell, Stanley Pargellis, Colton Storm and Louis B. Wright. Minneapolis: University of Minnesota Press, 1954.

The Book-Lover: A Magazine of Book Lore, Being a Miscellany of Curiously Interesting and Generally Unknown Facts about the World's Literature and Literary People; Now Newly Arranged, with Incidental Divertissement, and All Very Delightful to Read. San Francisco: The Book-Lover Press, 1900.

Boyd, Julian P. *The Scheide Library.* Princeton: Privately printed, 1947.

Boynton, Henry Walcott. *Annals of American Bookselling.* With an introduction by Joseph Rosenblum. 1932. Reprint. New Castle, Dela.: Oak Knoll Books, 1991.

Brant, Sebastian. *The Ship of Fools.* Translated from the German by Alexander Barclay. Edinburgh: William Paterson; New York: D. Appleton, 1874.

Brigham, Clarence S. *Fifty Years of Collecting Americana for the Library of the American Antiquarian Society, 1908–1958.* Worcester, Mass.: American Antiquarian Society, 1958.

Brinley, Charles A. "Recollections of Charles Brinley Written for His Great Grandchildren." Unpublished memoir dated September 13, 1910; includes information on his father, George Brinley. Typescript copy at Watkinson Library, Trinity College, Hartford, Connecticut.

Brodsky, Louis Daniel. *William Faulkner: Life Glimpses.* Austin, Tex.: University of Texas Press, 1990.

Bruccoli, Matthew J. *The Fortunes of Mitchell Kennerley, Bookman.* San Diego: Harcourt Brace Jovanovich, 1986.

———. "George D. Smith and the Anglo-American Book Migration." *AB Bookman's Weekly,* June 14, 1993, 2424–38.

Buck, Janet Camp. "Charles Augustus Howell and the Exhumation of Rossetti's Poems." *The Colophon,* part 15, 1933, unpaginated (12 pages).

Burden, Carter. "Voluminous Obsession." *House & Garden,* March 1987, 126.

Burton, John Hill. *The Book-Hunter.* New York: Sheldon, 1862.

Cahoon, Herbert. "The Clifton Waller Barrett Library," parts 1 and 2. *The University of Virginia News Letter* 38, no. 1 (September 15, 1961): 1–4, and no. 2 (October 15, 1961): 5–8.

Canetti, Elias. *Auto-da-Fé.* New York: The Noonday Press, 1984.

Canfora, Luciano. *The Vanished Library: A Wonder of the Ancient World.* Translated from the Italian by Martin Ryle. London: Hutchinson Radius, 1989.

Cannon, Carl L. *American Book Collectors and Collecting from Colonial Times to the Present.* New York: H. W. Wilson, 1941.

Carcopino, Jérôme. *Cicero: The Secrets of His Correspondence.* 2 vols. New Haven, Conn.: Yale University Press, 1951.

Carpenter, Kenneth E., ed. *Books and Society in History.* New York: R. R. Bowker, 1983.

———. *The First 350 Years of the Harvard University Library.* Cambridge, Mass.: Harvard University Library, 1986.

Carter, John. *ABC for Book Collectors.* 1952. 6th ed., revised by Nicolas Barker. London: Granada, 1980.

———. *Books and Book-Collectors.* Cleveland and New York: World Publishing, 1957.

———. *Taste and Technique in Book Collecting.* New York: R. R. Bowker, 1948.

———, ed. *New Paths in Book-Collecting.* London: Constable, 1934.

Carter, John, and Percy H. Muir, eds. *Printing and the Mind of Man.* London: Cassell; New York: Holt, Rinehart & Winston, 1967.

Carter, John, and Graham Pollard. *An Enquiry into the Nature of Certain Nineteenth Century Pamphlets.* London: Constable; New York: Charles Scribner's Sons, 1934.

Carter, Sebastian. *The Book Becomes: The Making of a Fine Edition.* London: Rampant Lions Press, 1984.

Case, Josephine Young, and Everett Needham Case. *Owen D. Young and American Enterprise.* Boston: David R. Godine, 1982.

Catalogue of the American Library of the Late Mr. George Brinley, of Hartford, Conn. 5 vols. Hartford: Geo. A. Leavitt, 1879–1893.

Catalogue of the Collection of Books and Manuscripts Belonging to Mr. Brayton Ives of New York. New York: De Vinne Press, 1891.

Cervantes, Miguel de. *The Adventures of Don Quixote de la Mancha.* Translated by Tobias Smollett, with an introduction by Carlos Fuentes. New York: Farrar Straus & Giroux, 1986.

Chappell, Warren. *A Short History of the Printed Word.* New York: Alfred A. Knopf, 1970.

Chernow, Ron. *The House of Morgan: An American Dynasty and the Rise of Modern Finance.* New York: Atlantic Monthly Press, 1990.

Christie's. *The Estelle Doheny Collection.* 5 vols. New York: 1987–1989.

————. *Books and Manuscripts from the Library of Arthur A. Houghton, Jr.* 2 vols. London: 1979–1980.

————. *The Leonardo da Vinci Codex Hammer.* New York: Christie's, 1994.

Churchill, Winston S. *Thoughts and Adventures.* London: Thornton Butterworth, 1932.

Cim, Albert. "Les Victimes du livre." *La Revue,* no. 5 (March 1, 1911), 660–83.

Clair, Colin. *A History of European Printing.* London, New York, San Francisco: Academic Press, 1976.

Clark, Ronald W. *Benjamin Franklin: A Biography.* New York: Random House, 1983.

Clements, William L., and George Parker Winship. *The William L. Clements Library of Americana at the University of Michigan.* Ann Arbor: University of Michigan Press, 1923.

Cochrane, Eric. *Florence in the Forgotten Centuries 1527–1800: A History of Florence and the Florentines in the Age of the Grand Dukes.* Chicago and London: University of Chicago Press, 1973.

The Collection of Henry H. Clifford. 3 vols. Austin, Tex.: Dorothy Sloan Rare Books, 1994. Includes the Zamorano 80.

The Collections and Programs of the American Antiquarian Society: A 175th Anniversary Guide. Worcester, Mass.: American Antiquarian Society, 1987. By the staff of the society.

Comparato, Frank E. *Chronicles of Genius and Folly: R. Hoe & Company and the Printing Press as a Service to Democracy.* Culver City, Calif.: Labyrinthos, 1979.

Complete Catalogue of the Library of John Quinn Sold by Auction in Five Parts. 1923–1924. Reprint (2 vols). New York: Lemma, 1969.

Connolly, Cyril. *The Modern Movement: A Discussion of 100 Key Books from England, France and America, 1800–1950.* New York: Atheneum, 1966.

Conway, William E., and Robert Stevenson. *William Andrews Clark, Jr.: His Cultural Legacy.* Los Angeles: William Andrews Clark Memorial Library, University of California at Los Angeles, 1985.

Cram, Ralph Adams. *The Ruined Abbeys of Great Britain.* Boston: Marshall Jones, 1927.

Crandall, Marjorie Lyle. *Confederate Imprints: A Check List on the Collection of the Boston Athenæum.* 2 vols. Boston: Boston Athenæum, 1955. With an introduction by Walter Muir Whitehill.

Curle, Richard. *Collecting American First Editions, Its Pitfalls and Its Pleasures.* Indianapolis: Bobbs-Merrill, 1930.

Currie, Barton. *Fishers of Books.* Boston: Little, Brown, 1931.

Curwen, Henry. *A History of Booksellers: The Old and the New.* London: Chatto & Windus, 1873.

Dain, Phyllis. *The New York Public Library: A History of Its Founding and Early Years.* New York: New York Public Library, Astor, Lenox and Tilden foundations, 1972.

Danforth, Susan L., and Anne Hintenlang. "The 'Great Subject,' 'La Grande Bibliothèque,' and the John Carter Brown Library of Today." Commentary and notes prepared for an exhibition mounted for the 39th annual meeting of the Associates of the John Carter Brown Library, Providence, Rhode Island, April 30, 1982. Typescript available at John Carter Brown Library, Providence, R.I.

Darling, Will Y. *The Bankrupt Bookseller.* Edinburgh: Robert Grant & Son, 1947.

Davidson, James West, and Mark Hamilton Lytle. *After the Fact: The Art of Historical Detection.* New York: Alfred A. Knopf, 1982.

Davidson, Marshall B., and Bernard McTigue. *Treasures of the New York Public Library.* New York: Harry N. Abrams, 1988.

Davie, Michael. *Titanic: The Death and Life of a Legend.* New York: Alfred A. Knopf, 1987.

De Bury, Richard. *Philobiblon.* Translated by E. C. Thomas, edited with a foreword by Michael Maclagan. Oxford: Basil Blackwell, 1960.

De Ricci, Seymour. *English Collectors of Books and Manuscripts (1530–1930) and Their Marks of Ownership.* 1930. Facsimile reprint. New York: Burt Franklin, 1969.

Deuel, Leo. *Testaments of Time: The Search for Lost Manuscripts and Records.* New York: Alfred A. Knopf, 1965.

Dibdin, Thomas Frognall. *Bibliomania; or Book-Madness; A Bibliographical Romance.* 1809. 2d ed. London: Chatto & Windus, 1840.

————. *The Bibliographical Decameron.* 3 vols. London: Privately printed, 1817.

————. *Reminiscences of a Literary Life.* 2 vols. London: John Major, 1846.

Dibdin's Bibliomania. 4 vols. Boston: Bibliophile Society, 1903. With essays by Richard Garnett and William P. Cutter.

Dickinson, Donald C. *Dictionary of American Book Collectors.* Westport, Conn.: Greenwood Press, 1986.

Dictionary of American Biography. The American Council of Learned Societies. New York: Charles Scribner's Sons, 1933.

Dictionary of National Biography. Edited by Sir Leslie Stephen and Sir Sidney Lee. Oxford: Oxford University Press, 1959–1960.

Ditchfield, P. H. *Books Fatal to Their Authors.* London: Elliot Stock, 1895.

Drabble, Margaret, ed. *The Oxford Companion to English Literature.* 5th ed. Oxford: Oxford University Press, 1985.

Drogin, Marc. *Anathema! Medieval Scribes and the History of Book Curses.* Totowa, N.J.: Allanheld & Schram, 1983.

Drumney, Peter, et al. *Witness to America's Past: Two Centuries of Collecting by the Massachusetts Historical Society.* Boston: Massachusetts Historical Society and the Museum of Fine Arts, 1991.

Eagle, Solomon. *Books in General.* New York: Alfred A. Knopf, 1919.

Eccles, Mary Hyde. ". . . Unending Pursuit . . ." *Gazette of the Grolier Club,* no. 42 (1990): 89–100.

Eco, Umberto. *The Name of the Rose.* Translated from the Italian by William Weaver. San Diego: Harcourt Brace Jovanovich, 1983.

Edler, Florence. "The Monastic Scriptorium." *Thought* 6 (September 1931): 181–206.

Edwards, Edward. *Libraries and Founders of Libraries.* London: Trübner, 1865.

————. *Lives of the Founders of the British Museum with Notices of Its Chief Augmentors and Other Benefactors 1570–1870.* London: Trübner; New York: J. W. Bouton, 1870.

————. *Memoirs of Libraries; Including a Handbook of Library-Economy.* London: Trübner; Leipzig: F. A. Brockhaus, 1859.

The 1812 Catalogue of the Library of Congress: A Facsimile. Washington, D.C.: Library of Congress, 1982. Introduction by Robert A. Rutland.

Elsner, James, and Roger Cardinal, eds. *The Cultures of Collecting.* Cambridge: Harvard University Press, 1994.

Elton, Charles Isaac, and Mary Augusta Elton. *The Great Book-Collectors.* London: Kegan Paul, Trench, Trübner, 1893.

Esdaile, Arundell. *The British Museum Library: A Short History and Survey.* London: George Allen & Unwin, 1946.

Evans, G. Blakemore, ed. *The Riverside Shakespeare.* Boston: Houghton Mifflin, 1974.

Everitt, Charles P. *The Adventures of a Treasure Hunter: A Rare Bookman in Search of American History.* Boston: Little, Brown, 1951.

Farnham, Luther. *A Glance at Private Libraries.* 1855. Facsimile reprint. Weston, Mass.: M & S Books, 1991. With an introduction and annotated index by Roger E. Stoddard.

Farrer, J. A. *Literary Forgeries.* London: Longmans, Green, 1907.

Feather, John. *A Dictionary of Book History.* London: Croom Helm, 1986.

Fern, Alan, and Judith O'Sullivan. *The Complete Prints of Leonard Baskin: A Catalogue Raisonné 1948–1983.* Boston: New York Graphic Society, 1984. Introduction by Ted Hughes.

Ferriar, John. "The Bibliomania: An Epistle to Richard Heber, Esq." *The Philobiblon* 2 (June and July 1863): 139–42, and 162–63. First published in 1809.

Field, Eugene. *The Love Affairs of a Bibliomaniac.* New York: Charles Scribner's Sons, 1896.

Fields, Mrs. James T. *A Shelf of Old Books.* New York: Charles Scribner's Sons, 1894.

Fine, Ruth E. *Lessing J. Rosenwald: Tribute to a Collector.* Washington, D.C.: National Gallery of Art, 1982.

The First Quarter Century of the Pierpont Morgan Library: A Retrospective Exhibition in Honor of Belle da Costa Greene. New York: Pierpont Morgan Library, 1949. With a tribute to the library and its first director by Lawrence C. Wroth.

Fitzgerald, Percy. *The Book Fancier.* London, 1886. Philadelphia: J. B. Lippincott, n.d.

Flaubert, Gustave. *Bibliomania: A Tale.* Translated by Theodore Wesley Koch. Evanston, Ill.: Northwestern University Press, 1929.

Fletcher, William Younger. *English Book Collectors.* 1902. Facsimile reprint. New York: Burt Franklin, 1969.

Fortieth Anniversary Catalogue. New York: House of El Dieff, 1975.

The Fortsas Catalogue. Paris. Facsimile reprint. Philadelphia: Philobiblon Club, 1970. With an introduction by Lessing J. Rosenwald.

Franklin, Colin. *The Private Presses.* 2d ed. Hants, England: Scolar Press, 1991.

Sigmund Freud: An Exhibition of Original Editions, Autographed Letters, and Portraits from the Library of Haskell F. Norman. With essays by Haskell F. Norman, M.D., Roy A. Ginsburg, M.D., and Paul A. Robinson. Palo Alto, Calif.: Stanford University Libraries, 1991.

Fries, Waldemar H. *The Double Elephant Folio: The Story of Audubon's "Birds of America."* Chicago: American Library Association, 1973.

From Witches to Wonder-Land: American Children's Books 1692–1947: An Exhibition in the Central Research Library, November 22, 1985 to January 11, 1986. From the Betsy Beinecke Shirley Collection. New York: The New York Public Library, Astor, Lenox, and Tilden foundations, 1985.

Gallup, Donald C. *Pigeons on the Granite: Memories of a Yale Librarian.* New Haven: Beinecke Rare Book and Manuscript Library, 1988.

Gay, Peter. *Freud: A Life for Our Time.* New York: W. W. Norton, 1988.

Gibbon, Edward. *The History of the Decline and Fall of the Roman Empire,* vol. 1, with notes by Dean Milman and M. Guizot. London: John Murray, 1862 (a new edition with additional notes by William Smith).

Gilreath, James, ed. *The Judgment of Experts: Essays and Documents About the Investigation of the Forging of the "Oath of a Freeman."* Worcester, Mass.: American Antiquarian Society, 1991.

Gilreath, James, and Douglas L. Wilson, eds. *Thomas Jefferson's Library: A Catalog with the Entries in His Own Order.* Washington, D.C.: Library of Congress, 1989.

Gingerich, Owen. *The Great Copernicus Chase and Other Adventures in Astronomical History.* Cambridge, Mass.: Sky Publishing; Cambridge, England: Cambridge University Press, 1992.

———, ed. *Collector's Choice: A Selection of Books and Manuscripts Given by Harrison D. Horblit to the Harvard College Library.* Cambridge, Mass.: Houghton Library, 1983. Catalogue of a commencement exhibition for the class of 1933. Foreword by Harrison D. Horblit. With an introduction by Gingerich.

Goff, Frederick R. *The Lessing J. Rosenwald Collection.* Washington, D.C.: Library of Congress, 1977.

———. "Peter Force." *The Papers of the Bibliographical Society of America* 44 (1st quarter, 1950): 1–17.

Goodrum, Charles A. *Treasures of the Library of Congress.* New York: Harry N. Abrams, 1980.

Goodspeed, Thomas W. *John Crerar and the Will of John Crerar.* Chicago: John Crerar Library, 1939.

Gordan, Phyllis Walter Goodhart. *Two Renaissance Book Hunters: The Letters of Poggius Bracciolini to Nicolaus de Niccolis.* New York: Columbia University Press, 1974.

Granniss, Ruth Shepard. "American Book Collecting and the Growth of Libraries." In Hellmut Lehmann-Haupt et al. *The Book in America.* New York: R. R. Bowker, 1939. This essay does not appear in the heavily revised 1951 second edition of the book.

Gray, Austin K. *Benjamin Franklin's Library.* New York: Macmillan, 1936.

Green, James. *Poor Richard's Books: An Exhibition of Books Owned by Benjamin Franklin Now on the Shelves of the Library Company of Philadelphia.* Philadelphia: Library Company of Philadelphia, 1990.

Greene, Jack P. *The Intellectual Heritage of the Constitutional Era: The Delegates' Library.* Philadelphia: Library Company of Philadelphia, 1986.

Grolier 75: A Biographical Retrospective to Celebrate the Seventy-Fifth Anniversary of the Grolier Club in New York. New York: Grolier Club, 1959.

Growoll, A. *American Book Clubs.* 1897. Facsimile reprint. New York: Burt Franklin, n.d.

Guppy, Henry. *The John Rylands Library, Manchester: A Brief Historical Description of the Library and Its Contents with Thirty-Seven Views and Facsimiles*. Manchester: University Press; London: Bernard Quaritch Ltd., and Sherratt & Hughes, 1914.

Hamilton, Charles. *Auction Madness*. New York: Everest House, 1981.

Harshav, Benjamin. *The Meaning of Yiddish*. Berkeley and Los Angeles: University of California Press, 1990.

Hart, James D., ed. *The Oxford Companion to American Literature*. 5th ed. New York: Oxford University Press, 1983.

Hartshorne, Rev. C. H., M.A. *The Book Rarities in the University of Cambridge Illustrated by Original Letters and Notes, Biographical, Literary, and Antiquarian*. London: Longman, Rees, Orme, Brown and Green; Cambridge, England: J. and J. J. Deighton, 1829.

Hazlitt, W. Carew. *The Book-Collector*. London: John Grant, 1904.

Hearsey, John. *Young Mr. Pepys*. New York: Charles Scribner's Sons, 1973.

Hellmann, Geoffrey T. "The Steward of Strawberry Hill," parts 1 and 2. *The New Yorker*, August 6, 1949, 26–37; August 13, 1949, 31–41.

———. "Farmington Revisited." *The New Yorker*, October 31, 1959, 156–72.

Hjerter, Kathleen G. *Doubly Gifted: The Author as Visual Artist*. New York: Harry N. Abrams, in association with the Harry Ransom Humanities Research Center at the University of Texas, Austin, 1986. Foreword by John Updike.

Hobson, Anthony. *Great Libraries*. New York: G. P. Putnam's Sons, 1970.

Hofer, Philip. *Mishaps of a Compulsive Collector*. Northampton, Mass.: Friends of the Smith College Library, 1970.

Honce, Charles. *Notes from a Bookman's Cuff: Some Beefs, Boasts, Bellyaches and Bouquets from a Practicing Newspaperman*. New York: Golden Eagle Press, 1949.

Howatson, M. C. *The Oxford Companion to Classical Literature*. 2nd ed. Oxford and New York: Oxford University Press, 1989.

Hsia, R. Po-chia. *Trent 1475*. New Haven: Yale University Press, 1992. A modern edition of the Yeshiva Manuscript, which was brought to the United States by Lessing J. Rosenwald in 1937.

Humphreys, A. L. *The Private Library*. London: Strangeways & Sons, 1907.

Hunter, Dard. *Papermaking Through Eighteen Centuries*. New York: William Edwin Rudge, 1930.

Huntington Library. "Huntington Library Collections." *The Huntington Library Bulletin*, no. 1 (May 1931): 33–106.

The Ian Fleming Collection of 19th–20th Century Source Material Concerning Western Civilization Together with the Originals of the James Bond 007 Tales. Lilly Library Publication no. 12. Bloomington, Ind: The Lilly Library, Indiana University, n.d.

Irwin, Raymond. *The Origins of the English Library*. London: George Allen & Unwin, 1958.

Jackson, Holbrook. *The Anatomy of Bibliomania*. 2 vols. London: Soncino Press, 1930, 1932.

———. *The Fear of Books*. New York: Charles Scribner's Sons, 1932.

Jameson, J. Franklin. *The American Historian's Raw Materials: An Address with the Presentation and Other Exercises at the Dedication of the William L. Clements Library of Americana*. Ann Arbor: University of Michigan, 1923.

The John Carter Brown Library: The Dedication of the Library Building, May the Seventeenth A.D. MDCCCCIIII. Providence: Privately printed, 1905. With addresses by William Vail Kellen, Ll.D. and Frederick Jackson Turner, Ph.D.

Jordan-Smith, Paul. *For the Love of Books: The Adventures of an Impecunious Collector*. New York: Oxford University Press, 1934.

Jutzi, Alan. "Early Americana at the Huntington Library." Speech given at the Huntington Library, 1991. Contains information on the acquisition of the E. Dwight Church Library and other early acquisitions.

Kaminski, Thomas. *The Early Career of Samuel Johnson*. Oxford and New York: Oxford University Press, 1987.

Kazin, Alfred. Introduction to *New York Panorama: The Best of 1930s New York: As Seen by the Federal Writers' Project*. New York: Pantheon Books, 1984.

Kearney, Patrick J. *The Private Case: An Annotated Bibliography of the Private Case Erotica Collection in the British (Museum) Library*. London: Jay Landesman, 1981.

Ker, Neil Ripley. *Books, Collectors and Libraries: Studies in the Medieval Heritage*. Edited by Andrew G. Watson. London and Ronceverte, W.V.: Hambledon Press, 1985.

Keynes, Geoffrey Kt. *The Gates of Memory*. Oxford: Oxford University Press, Clarendon Press, 1981.

The Kilgour Collection of Russian Literature 1750–1920. Cambridge, Mass.: Harvard College Library, 1959.

King, Stanley. *Recollections of the Folger Shakespeare Library*. Ithaca, N.Y.: Cornell University Press, 1950. Published for the Trustees of Amherst College.

Knepper, Adrian W. "Obadiah Rich: Bibliopole." *Papers of the Bibliographical Society of America* 49, 112–30.

Korey, Marie E., and Ruth Mortimer. "Fifteen Women Book Collectors." *Gazette of the Grolier Club,* no. 42 (1990), 49–88.

Kraus, Hans P. *A Rare Book Saga*. New York: G. P. Putnam's Sons, 1978.

Lake, Carlton. *Confessions of a Literary Archaeologist*. New York: New Directions, 1990.

Lake, Carlton, ed. *Baudelaire to Beckett: A Century of French Art and Literature*. Austin, Tex.: Harry Ransom Humanities Research Center, University of Texas, 1975.

Lamb, Charles. "The Two Races of Men." In *The Works of Charles Lamb*. Edited by Sir Thomas Noon Talfourd. Vol. 3, 44–51.New York: A. C. Armstrong & Son, 1880.

Lane, Roger. *William Dorsey's Philadelphia and Ours: On the Past and Future of the Black City in America*. New York: Oxford University Press, 1991.

Lang, Andrew. *Books and Bookmen*. New York: George J. Coombes, 1886.

———. *The Library*. London: Macmillan, 1881.

Latham, Robert, ed. *The Shorter Pepys*. Berkeley and Los Angeles: University of California Press, 1985.

Lawler, John. *Book Auctions in England in the Seventeenth Century (1676–1700)*. London: Elliot Stock, 1898.

Lawler, Percy E., ed. *To Doctor R.: Essays Here Collected and Published in Honor of the Seventieth Birthday of Dr. A. S. W. Rosenbach, July 22, 1946*. Philadelphia: Privately printed, 1946.

Lehmann-Haupt, Hellmut. *Gutenberg and the Master of the Playing Cards*. New Haven: Yale University Press, 1966. A study of the William Scheide copy of the 42-line Bible.

———, ed. *Homage to a Bookman: Essays on Manuscripts, Books and Printing Written for Hans P. Kraus on His 60th Birthday, Oct. 12, 1967*. Berlin: Gebr. Mann Verlag, 1967.

Lehmann-Haupt, Hellmut, Lawrence C. Wroth, and Rollo G. Silver. *The Book in America: A History of the Making and Selling of Books in the United States*. 2d ed. New York: R. R. Bowker, 1951.

Lewis, David Levering. *When Harlem Was in Vogue*. New York: Alfred A. Knopf, 1981.

Lewis, Roy Harley. *Antiquarian Books: An Insider's Account*. New York: Arco Publishing, 1978.

Lewis, Wilmarth Sheldon. *Collector's Progress*. New York: Alfred A. Knopf, 1951.

———. *Horace Walpole: The A. W. Mellon Lectures in the Fine Arts, 1960*. Bollingen Series 35, no. 9. Washington, D.C.: National Gallery of Art; New York: Pantheon Books, 1960.

———. *One Man's Education*. New York: Alfred A. Knopf, 1968.

———. *Horace Walpole's Library: The Sandars Lectures, 1957*. Cambridge, England: Cambridge University Press, 1958.

The Lilly Library: The First Quarter Century, 1960–1985. Bloomington, Ind.: Lilly Library, Indiana University, 1985.

Lowry, Martin. *The World of Aldus Manutius: Business and Scholarship in Renaissance Venice*. Ithaca, N.Y.: Cornell University Press, 1979.

Lucian of Samosata. "Remarks Addressed to an Illiterate Book-Fancier." In *The Works of Lucian of Samosata*, translated by H. W. Fowler and F. G. Fowler. Vol. 3, 265–78. Oxford: Clarendon Press, 1905.

Lutz, Cora E. *The Oldest Library Motto and Other Library Essays*. Hamden, Conn.: Archon Books, 1979.

———. *Essays on Manuscripts and Rare Books*. Hamden, Conn.: Archon Books, 1975.

Lydenberg, Harry Miller. *History of the New York Public Library: Astor, Lenox and Tilden Foundations*. New York: New York Public Library, 1923.

Macray, William Dunn. *Annals of the Bodleian Library*. Oxford: Oxford University Press, Clarendon Press, 1868 (2d ed., 1890).

Madan, Falconer. *Books in Manuscript*. London: Kegan Paul, Trench, Trübner, 1893.

Magee, David. *Infinite Riches: The Adventures of a Rare Book Dealer*. New York: Paul S. Eriksson, 1973.

Magnusson, Magnus, and Rosemary Goring, eds. *Cambridge Biographical Dictionary*. Cambridge, England: Cambridge University Press, 1990.

Malone, Dumas. *Jefferson and His Time: The Sage of Monticello*. New York: Little Brown, 1981.

Marion, John L., and Christopher Andersen. *The Best of Everything: The Insider's Guide to Collecting—for Every Taste and Every Budget*. New York: Simon & Schuster, 1989.

Marston, E. *Sketches of Some Booksellers of the Time of Dr. Samuel Johnson*. London: Sampson Low, Marston, 1902.

Maxwell, Margaret. *Shaping a Library: William L. Clements as Collector*. Amsterdam: Nico Israel, 1973.

McKay, George L. *American Book Auction Catalogues 1713–1934: A Union List*. New York: New York Public Library, 1937. Introduction by Clarence S. Brigham.

Mearns, David C. "The Story Up to Now." In *Annual Report of the Librarian of Congress for the Fiscal Year Ending June 30, 1946*. Washington, D.C.: Government Printing Office, 1947.

Merryweather, F. Somner. *Bibliomania in the Middle Ages*. 1849. Rev. ed. London: Woodstock Press, 1933.

Miller, Edward. *Prince of Librarians: The Life and Times of Antonio Panizzi of the British Museum*. London: British Library, 1988.

Miner, Dorothy, ed. *Studies in Art and Literature for Belle da Costa Greene*. Princeton: Princeton University Press, 1954.

Mirrlees, Hope. *A Fly in Amber*. London: Faber & Faber, 1962. A biography of Robert Cotton.

Moffett, William A. *The Shinn Lists*. Oberlin, Ohio: Oberlin College, 1982.

Morris, Leslie A. *Rosenbach Abroad: In Pursuit of Books in Private Collections*. Philadelphia: Rosenbach Museum and Library, 1988.

———. *Rosenbach Redux: Further Book Adventures in England and Ireland*. Philadelphia: Rosenbach Museum and Library, 1989.

Morris, William. *The Ideal Book: Essays and Lectures on the Art of the Book*. Edited by William S. Peterson. Berkeley and Los Angeles: University of California Press, 1982.

Muensterberger, Werner. *Collecting an Unruly Passion: Psychological Perspectives*. Princeton: Princeton University Press, 1994.

Muir, Percy H. *Minding My Own Business: An Autobiography*. London: Chatto & Windus, 1956.

———. *Book-Collecting as a Hobby: In a Series of Letters to Everyman*. New York: Alfred A. Knopf, 1974.

———, ed. *Talks on Book-Collecting*. London: Cassell, 1952.

Mumby, Frank Arthur. *Publishing and Bookselling: A History from the Earliest Times to the Present Day*. 4th ed. London: Jonathan Cape, 1956.

Munby, A. N. L. *The Cult of the Autograph Letter in England*. London: Athlone Press, 1962.

———. *Essays and Papers*. London: Scolar Press, 1978. Introduction by Nicolas Barker.

———. *Phillipps Studies*. 5 vols. Cambridge, England: Cambridge University Press, 1951–1960.

Naylor, Gillian, ed. *William Morris by Himself: Designs and Writings*. Boston: New York Graphic Society, 1988.

Neely, Mark E., Jr. *The Last Best Hope of Earth: Abraham Lincoln and the Promise of America*. Louise and Barry Taper Collection. Cambridge, Mass.: Harvard University Press; San Marino, Calif.: Huntington Library; Springfield, Ill.: Illinois State Historical Library, 1993.

Newton, A. Edward. *The Amenities of Book-Collecting and Kindred Affections*. Boston: Atlantic Monthly Press, 1918.

———. *The Greatest Book in the World and Other Papers*. Boston: Little, Brown, 1925.

———. *A Magnificent Farce and Other Diversions of a Book-Collector*. Boston: Atlantic Monthly Press, 1921.

O'Dwyer, E. J. *Thomas Frognall Dibdin: Bibliographer and Bibliomaniac Extraordinary, 1776–1847*. Pinner, England: Private Libraries Association, 1967.

O'More, Haven. *Sacrificial Bone Inscriptions*. Millerton, N.Y.: SADEV, 1987.

Olmert, Michael. *The Smithsonian Book of Books*. Washington, D.C.: Smithsonian Books, 1992.

Orcutt, William Dana. *The Kingdom of Books*. Boston: Little, Brown, 1927.

———. *The Magic of the Book: More Reminiscences and Adventures of a Bookman*. Boston: Little, Brown, 1930.

Osborne, Lucy Eugenia. *Alfred Clark Chapin: March 8, 1848–October 2, 1936*. Portland, Me.: Privately printed, 1937.

———, ed. *A Short Title List of the Books in the Chapin Library, Williams College*. Portland, Me.: Southworth-Anthoensen Press; London: Bernard Quaritch Ltd., 1939.

Painter, George D. *William Caxton: A Biography*. New York: G. P. Putnam's Sons, 1977.

Paintin, Elaine M. *The King's Library*. London: British Library, 1989.

Parke-Bernet Galleries. *The Celebrated Collection of Americana Formed by the Late Thomas Winthrop Streeter*. 8 vols. New York: Parke-Bernet Galleries, 1966–1970.

Parker, Wyman. *W. Henry Stevens of Vermont: An American Book Dealer in London, 1845–86*. Amsterdam: Nico Israel, 1963.

Parks, Stephen. *The Elizabethan Club of Yale University and Its Library*. New Haven: Yale University Press, 1986.

Parsons, Edward Alexander. *The Alexandrian Library: Glory of the Hellenic World*. Amsterdam: Elsevier Press, 1952.

———. *The Wonder and the Glory: Confessions of a Southern Bibliophile*. New York: Thistle Press, 1962.

Partington, Wilfred. *Thomas J. Wise in the Original Cloth: The Life and Record of the Forger of the Nineteenth-Century Pamphlets*. 1947. Reprint. London: Dawson's of Pall Mall, 1974. Published in the United States under the title *Forging Ahead*.

Peters, Jean, ed. *Collectible Books*. New York: R. R. Bowker, 1979.

Petersen, Carl. *Each in Its Ordered Place: A Faulkner Collector's Notebook*. Ann Arbor: Ardis Publishers, 1975.

Peterson, William S. *The Kelmscott Press: A History of William Morris's Typographical Adventure*. Berkeley and Los Angeles: University of California Press, 1991.

Pierpont Morgan Library. *In August Company: The Collections of the Pierpont Morgan Library*. New York: Pierpont Morgan Library, 1993.

Platthy, Jenö. *Sources on the Earliest Greek Libraries with the Testimonia*. Amsterdam: Adolf M. Hakkert, 1968.

Plomer, H. R., G. H. Bushnell, and E. R. McC. Dix. *A Dictionary of the Printers and Booksellers Who Were at Work in England, Scotland and Ireland from 1726 to 1775*. 1932. Reprint. London: Bibliographical Society, 1968.

Plutarch. *The Lives of the Noble Grecians and Romans*. Translated by John Dryden and revised by Arthur Hugh Clough. 1864. Reprint. New York: Modern Library, n.d.

Pollard, Alfred W. *Early Illustrated Books*. London: Kegan Paul, Trench, Trübner, 1893.

Powell, Lawrence Clark. *A Passion for Books*. Cleveland and New York: World Publishing, 1958.

The Prince Library: A Catalogue of the Collection of Books and Manuscripts Which Formerly Belonged to the Reverend Thomas Prince, and Was by Him Bequeathed to the Old South Church, and Is Now Deposited in the Public Library of the City of Boston. Boston: Alfred Mudge & Son, 1870. Introduction by Justin Winsor.

Putnam, George Haven. *Books and Their Makers During the Middle Ages*. 1896–1897. Reprint (2 vols.). New York: Hillary House, 1962.

Quaritch, Bernard, ed. *Contributions Towards a Dictionary of English Book-Collectors*. 1892. Facsimile reprint. New York: Burt Franklin, 1968.

Quayle, Eric. *The Collector's Book of Books*. New York: Clarkson N. Potter, 1971.

Randall, David A. *Dukedom Large Enough: Reminiscences of a Rare Book Dealer, 1929–1956*. New York: Random House, 1969.

Ransom, Harry Huntt. "The Collection of Knowledge in Texas." *Texas Quarterly* (Winter 1958): viii–xiv.

Rawlings, Gertrude Burford. *The Story of Books*. New York: D. Appleton, 1915.

Rees, J. Rogers. *The Diversions of a Bookworm*. New York: George J. Coombes, 1887.

Reese, William S. *The Printers' First Fruits: An Exhibition of American Imprints 1640–1742, from the Collections of the American Antiquarian Society.* Worcester, Mass.: American Antiquarian Society, 1989.

Rees-Moog, William. *How to Buy Rare Books: A Practical Guide to the Antiquarian Book Market.* Oxford: Phaidon·Christie's, 1985.

Regan, Mary Jane. *Echoes from the Past: Reminiscences of the Boston Athenæum, with a Memoir.* Boston: Boston Athenæum, 1927.

Reid, B. L. *The Man from New York: John Quinn and His Friends.* New York: Oxford University Press, 1968.

Rendell, Kenneth W. *Forging History: The Detection of Fake Letters and Documents.* Norman, Okla., and London: University of Oklahoma Press, 1994.

Richardson, John. "Imprint of the Connoisseur." *House & Garden,* September 1992, 166–72.

Ridley, Jasper. *Henry VIII: The Politics of Tyranny.* New York: Viking, 1985.

Robert, Maurice, and Frederic Warde. *A Code for the Collector of Beautiful Books.* Translated from the French by Jacques Le Clercq. New York: The Limited Editions Club, 1936.

Roberts, Julian, and Andrew G. Watson, eds. *John Dee's Library Catalogue.* London: Bibliographical Society, 1990.

Roberts, Warren. "Modern Research Materials at the University of Texas." *The Journal of Modern Literature* 2, no. 3, 1971.

———. "D. H. Lawrence at Texas: A Memoir," in *The Library Chronicle of the University of Texas,* Austin, Texas: University of Texas, 1986, new ser. no. 34, 23–38.

Roberts, William. *The Book-Hunter in London: Historical and Other Studies of Collectors and Collecting.* London: Elliot Stock, 1895.

Rogers, David. *The Bodleian Library and Its Treasures, 1320–1700.* Oxford, England: Aidan Ellis, 1991.

Rogers, Horatio. *Private Libraries of Providence with a Preliminary Essay on the Love of Books.* Providence: Sidney S. Rider, 1878.

Rosenbach, A. S. W. *A Book Hunter's Holiday.* Boston: Houghton Mifflin, 1936.

———. *Books and Bidders.* Boston: Little, Brown, 1927.

———. *Early American Children's Books: With Bibliographical Descriptions of the Books in His Private Collection*. Foreword by A. Edward Newton. Portland, Me.: The Southworth Press, 1933.

———. "Henry C. Folger as Collector." In *Henry C. Folger: 18 June 1857–11 June 1930*. New Haven: Privately printed, 1931, 75–105.

———. *The Unpublishable Memoirs*. New York: Mitchell Kennerley, 1917.

———. *The Collected Catalogues of Dr. A. S. W. Rosenbach, 1904–1951*. 10 vols. New York: Arno Press, 1967.

Rosenthal, Robert. "Three Early Book Collectors of Chicago." *Library Quarterly* 53 (1983): 371–83.

Rosenwald, Lessing J. *Recollections of a Collector*. Jenkintown, Pa.: Alverthorpe Gallery, 1976.

Rostenberg, Leona, and Madeleine B. Stern. *Between Boards: New Thoughts on Old Books*. Montclair, N.J.: Allanheld & Schram; London: George Prior, 1978.

———. *Old and Rare: Thirty Years in the Book Business*. New York: Abner Schram; London: George Prior, 1974.

Russell, John. "All Booked Up." *Vogue*, February 1992, 230–35.

Sadleir, Michael. *XIX Century Fiction: A Bibliographical Record Based on His Own Collection*. 2 vols. London: Constable & Co., Ltd.; and Berkeley, Calif.: University of California Press, 1951.

St. John, Judith. *The Osborne Collection of Early Children's Books*. 1958. Rev. ed. (2 vols.). Toronto: Toronto Public Library, 1966.

A Salute to Clifton Waller Barrett on His Eightieth from Friends and Admirers. Charlottesville, Va.: University of Virginia, 1981.

Sandburg, Carl. *Lincoln Collector: The Story of the Oliver R. Barrett Lincoln Collection*. 1949. Reprint. New York: Harcourt, Brace and Company, 1960.

Sander, Max. "Bibliomania." *Journal of Criminal Law and Criminology* 31 (1943): 155–61.

Sandys, John Edwin. *A History of Classical Scholarship*. 3 vols. Cambridge, England: Cambridge University Press, 1908.

Sawyer, Charles J., and F. J. Harvey Darton. *English Books, 1475–1900: A Signpost for Collectors*. 2 vols. London: Chas. J. Sawyer, 1927.

Schad, Robert O. "Henry Edwards Huntington: The Founder and the Library." *The Huntington Library Bulletin,* no. 1 (May 1931): 3–32.

Schomburg, Arthur A. "The Negro Digs Up His Past." In *The New Negro: An Interpretation.* Edited by Alain Locke. 1925. Reprint. New York: Arno Press and the New York Times, 1968.

Scoggin, G. C. *As to Bibliomania.* New York: Henry Holt, 1919.

Sharpe, Kevin. *Sir Robert Cotton, 1586–1631: History and Politics in Early Modern England.* Oxford: Oxford University Press, 1979.

Shellabarger, Samuel. *Lord Chesterfield and His World.* Boston: Little, Brown, 1951.

Shelley, Henry C. *John Harvard and His Times.* London: Smith, Elder, 1907.

Shipton, Clifford K. *Isaiah Thomas: Printer, Patriot and Philanthropist.* Rochester, N.Y.: Leo Hart, 1948.

Shirley, Betsy B. *Read Me a Story, Show Me a Book: American Children's Literature 1690–1988. From the Collection of Betsy Beinecke Shirley.* New Haven: Yale University, 1991. Catalogue of an exhibition at the Beinecke Rare Book and Manuscript Library, Yale University, October–December 1991, curated by Betsy B. Shirley.

Sidgwick, F. Introduction to part 2 of *A Descriptive Catalogue of the Library of Samuel Pepys.* London: Sidgwick & Jackson, Ltd. 1914.

Sims, George. *The Rare Book Game.* Philadelphia: Holmes Publishing, 1985.

———. *More of the Rare Book Game.* Philadelphia: Holmes Publishing, 1988.

Singer, Isaac Bashevis. *Nobel Lecture.* New York: Farrar, Straus & Giroux, 1978.

Sinnette, Elinor Des Verney. *Arthur Alfonso Schomburg: Black Bibliophile and Collector.* New York: New York Public Library; Detroit: Wayne State University Press, 1989.

Sinnette, Elinor Des Verney, Paul W. Coates, and Thomas C. Battle, eds. *Black Bibliophiles and Collectors: Preservers of Black History.* Washington, D.C.: Howard University Press, 1990.

Smith, Harry B. *A Sentimental Library: Comprising Books Formerly Owned by Famous Writers, Presentation Copies, Manuscripts, and Drawings.* Privately printed at the DeVinne Press, 1914.

————. *First Nights and First Editions.* Boston: Little, Brown, 1931.

Sotheby's. *Catalogue of Rare First Editions of English Literature of the 16th to the 20th Century, Blockbooks, Incunabula and Early Continental Printing, Important Scientific Books, Autograph Letters of the Renaissance and Literary Manuscripts, the Majority Deriving From the Celebrated Collection of the late Louis H. Silver of Chicago, the Property of The Newberry Library, Chicago (Sold by Order of the Trustees).* London: Sotheby's, 1965.

————. *The Celebrated Library of Harrison D. Horblit Esq., Removed from Ridgefield, Connecticut.* 2 vols. London: Sotheby's, 1974.

————. *The Collection of the Garden Ltd. Magnificent Books and Manuscripts: Conceived and Formed by Haven O'More, Funded by Michael Davis.* New York: Sotheby's, 1989.

————. *Incunables from the Schøyen Collection.* New York: Sotheby's, 1991.

————. *The Library of H. Bradley Martin.* 9 vols. New York: Sotheby's, 1989–1990.

————. *The Library of Richard Manney.* New York: Sotheby's, 1991.

Sowerby, E. Millicent. *Rare People and Rare Books.* London, 1967. Reprint. Williamsburg, Va.: The Bookpress, 1987.

Special Collections in College and University Libraries. With an introduction by Leona Rostenberg and Madeleine B. Stern. New York: Macmillan, 1989.

Staley, Thomas F. "The Development of Twentieth Century Collections in American Research Libraries." Speech given at Cambridge University, Cambridge, England, September 8, 1989. Typescript available at Harry Ransom Humanities Research Center, Austin, Texas.

Starr, Kevin. *Material Dreams: Southern California Through the 1920s.* New York: Oxford University Press, 1990. Deals with Jake Zeitlin and the Los Angeles rare-book trade.

Starrett, Vincent. *Penny Wise and Book Foolish.* New York: Covici Friede, 1929.

Steele, Sir Richard, and Joseph Addison. *The Tatler and Guardian.* New York: Bangs, 1852. With an account of the authors by Thomas Babbington Macaulay.

Stein, Susan R. *The Worlds of Thomas Jefferson at Monticello.* New York: Harry N. Abrams, 1993.

Stern, Madeleine B. *Nicholas Gouin Dufief of Philadelphia: Franco-American Bookseller, 1776–1834*. Philadelphia: Philobiblon Club, 1988.

Stevens, Henry. *Recollections of James Lenox and the Formation of His Library*. 1886. Revised and edited by Victor Hugo Paltsits. New York: New York Public Library, 1951.

Stillwell, Margaret Bingham. *The Annmary Brown Memorial: A Booklover's Shrine*. Providence: Privately printed, 1940.

Stoddard, Roger E. "A Talk for the Opening of the Fiftieth-Anniversary Exhibition of the Houghton Library, March 3, 1992." Speech given at the Houghton Library, Harvard University, March 3, 1992. Typescript available at Houghton Library, Cambridge, Massachucetts.

———. "Teaching the History of Books at Harvard, 1910–1987/88." Paper delivered at the American Antiquarian Society, Worcester, Massachusetts, June 13, 1987. Typescript available at Houghton Library. Includes detailed information on Fine Arts 5e, the book-collecting course taught by George Parker Winship, 1915–1931.

Storm, Colton, and Howard Peckham. *Invitation to Book Collecting, Its Pleasures and Practices: With Kindred Discussions of Manuscripts, Maps, and Prints*. New York: R. R. Bowker, 1947.

Strachey, Charles, ed. *The Letters of the Earl of Chesterfield to His Son*. 2 vols. London: Methuen, 1901.

Swann Galleries. *Highlights from the Epstein Family Collection*. New York: Swann Galleries, 1992.

Symonds, John Addington. *Renaissance in Italy*. 7 vols. London: Smith, Elder, & Co., 1904.

Symons, A. J. A. *The Quest for Corvo: An Experiment in Biography*. New York: Macmillan, 1934.

Symons, Julian. *A. J. A. Symons: His Life and Speculations*. London: Eyre & Spottiswoode, 1950.

Szladits, Lola L. *Brothers: The Origins of the Henry W. and Albert A. Berg Collection of English and American Literature*. New York: New York Public Library, 1985.

———. *Owen D. Young: Book Collector*. New York: New York Public Library, 1974. Introduction by Joseph Young Case.

Tanselle, G. Thomas. *Libraries, Museums, and Reading: The Sixth Solomon M. Malkin Lecture in Bibliography at the Columbia University School of Library Service, Dec. 17, 1990.* New York: Columbia University, 1991.

Targ, William, ed. *Bibliophile in the Nursery: A Bookman's Treasure of Collectors' Lore on Old and Rare Children's Books.* Cleveland and New York: World Publishing, 1957.

———, ed. *Bouillabaisse for Bibliophiles.* Cleveland and New York: World, 1955.

———, ed. *Carousel for Bibliophiles: A Treasury of Tales, Narratives, Songs, Epigrams and Sundry Curious Studies Relating to a Noble Theme.* New York: Philip C. Duschenes, 1947.

Taylor, Francis Henry. *The Taste of Angels: A History of Art Collecting from Rameses to Napoleon.* Boston: Atlantic Monthly Press, 1948.

Taylor, Isaac. *History of the Transmission of Ancient Books to Modern Times Together With the Process of Historical Proof.* 1859. Reprint. Liverpool: Edward Howell, 1889.

Taylor, Robert H. "Battle Between Libraries and Taylor." In *Papers of the Bibliographical Society of America* (Fall 1954).

———. *Certain Small Works.* Princeton: Princeton University Press, 1980.

Thomas, Alan G. *Great Books and Book Collectors.* New York: G. P. Putnam's Sons, 1975.

Thomas, Isaiah. *The History of Printing in America with a Biography of Printers, and an Account of Newspapers.* 2 vols. Albany: Joel Munsell, 1874. Includes a memoir of the author by his grandson, Benjamin Franklin Thomas.

Thompson, James Westfall. *Ancient Libraries.* Berkeley: University of California Press, 1940.

———. *Byways in Bookland.* Berkeley: Book Arts Club of California, 1935.

———. *The Medieval Library.* Chicago: The University of Chicago Press, 1939.

Thompson, Lawrence S. *Bibliologia Comica, or Humorous Aspects of the Caparisoning and Conservation of Books.* Hamden, Conn.: Archon Books, 1968.

Thorpe, James. *Gifts of Genius: Treasures of the Huntington Library.* San Marino, Calif.: Huntington Library, 1980.

———. *Henry Edwards Huntington: A Biography.* Berkeley, Los Angeles, London: University of California Press, 1994.

Tite, Colin G. C. "Early Catalogues of the Cottonian Library." *The British Library Journal* (Autumn 1980): 144–57.

Tolles, Frederick B. *James Logan and the Culture of Provincial America.* Boston: Little, Brown, 1957.

Towner, Wesley. *The Elegant Auctioneers.* New York: Hill & Wang, 1970. Completed by Stephen Varble.

Tryon, W. S. *Parnassus Corner: A Life of James T. Fields, Publisher to the Victorians.* Boston: Houghton Mifflin, 1963.

Turner, Decherd. *HRC Notes.* A series of newsletters written by the former director of the Humanities Research Center at the University of Texas, Austin, from 1981 to 1988. Available at Harry Ransom Humanities Research Center.

Updike, John. *Bech Is Back.* New York: Alfred A. Knopf, 1982.

Uzanne, Octave. *The Book-Hunter in Paris: Studies Among the Bookstalls and the Quays.* Chicago: A. C. McClurg, 1893.

Vision of a Collector: The Lessing J. Rosenwald Collection in the Library of Congress. Washington, D.C.: Library of Congress, 1991. Introduction by James H. Billington.

Vosper, Robert. "A Pair of Bibliomanes for Kansas: Ralph Ellis and Thomas Jefferson Fitzpatrick." *Papers of the Bibliographical Society of America* 55 (3rd quarter, 1961), 207–25.

Walden, Milton. *Americana: The Literature of American History.* New York: Henry Holt, 1925.

Watts, N. H. *Cicero: The Speeches with an English Translation.* Cambridge, Mass., and London: Harvard University Press/William Heinemann Ltd., 1961.

Webber, Winslow L. *Books About Books: A Bio-Bibliography for Collectors.* Boston: Hale, Cushman & Flint, 1937.

Weiner, Norman D., M.D. "On Bibliomania." *The Psychoanalytic Quarterly* 35 (1966), 217–32.

Weinstein, Louis. "Heritage Book Shop: The First Year." *The Professional Rare Bookman, Journal of the Antiquarian Booksellers of America,* no. 4 (1982): 29–33.

Weitzmann, Kurt, and Herbert L. Kessler. *The Cotton Genesis: British Library Codex Cotton OTHO B.VI.* Princeton: Princeton University Press, 1986.

Wendorf, Richard, ed. "Rare Book and Manuscript Libraries in the Twenty-First Century: An International Symposium," parts 1 and 2. *Harvard Library Bulletin* 4 (new series), nos. 1 and 2 (Summer 1993).

West, Andrew Fleming, ed. *The "Philobiblon" of Richard de Bury.* 3 vols. New York: Grolier Club, 1889. With an introduction, notes, original Latin text, and printing history.

West, Herbert Faulkner. *Modern Book Collecting for the Impecunious Amateur.* Boston: Little, Brown, 1936.

Whitehill, Walter Muir. *Boston Public Library: A Centennial History.* Cambridge, Mass.: Harvard University Press, 1956.

———. *Independent Historical Societies.* Boston: Boston Athenæum, 1962.

Widener, Harry E. *A Catalogue of Some of the More Important Books, Manuscripts and Drawings in the Library of Harry Elkins Widener.* Philadelphia: Privately printed, 1910.

Wilhide, Elizabeth. *William Morris: Decor and Design.* New York: Harry N. Abrams, 1991.

Williams, Alexander Whiteside. *Social History of the Club of Odd Volumes, 1887–1967.* Boston: Club of Odd Volumes, 1969.

Willson, Beckles. *George III as Man, Monarch and Statesman.* Philadelphia: George W. Jacobs, 1907.

Wilson, Robert A. *Modern Book Collecting: A Guide for the Beginner Who Is Buying First Editions for the First Time.* New York: Alfred A. Knopf, 1980.

Winks, Robin W., ed. *The Historian as Detective: Essays on Evidence.* New York: Harper & Row, 1969.

Winterich, John T. *Early American Books and Printing.* Boston: Houghton Mifflin, 1935.

Wolf, Edwin, 2nd. *The Library of James Logan of Philadelphia.* Philadelphia: Library Company of Philadelphia, 1974.

———, ed. *Legacies of Genius: A Celebration of Philadelphia Libraries.* Philadelphia: Philadelphia Area Consortium of Special Collections Libraries, 1988.

Wolf, Edwin, 2nd, and John Fleming. *Rosenbach: A Biography.* Cleveland and New York: World Publishing, 1960.

Wolf, Edwin, 2nd, and Marie Elena Korey. *Quarter of a Millennium: The Library Company of Philadelphia, 1731–1981.* Philadelphia: Library Company of Philadelphia, 1981.

Wright, C. E., and Ruth C. Wright. *Diary of Humfrey Wanley, 1715–1726.* 2 vols. London: Bibliographical Society, 1966.

Wright, Rev. John. *Early Bibles of America.* New York: Thomas Whittaker, 1892.

Wroth, Lawrence C. "The Chief End of Book Madness." *The Library of Congress Quarterly Journal of Current Acquisitions* 3 (October 1945): 69–77.

————. *The Colonial Printer.* New York: Grolier Club, 1931.

Wynne, James. *Private Libraries of New York.* New York: E. French, 1860.

Wynne, Marjorie G. *The Rare Book Collections at Yale: Recollections, 1942–1987. The Third Sol. M. Malkin Lecture in Bibliography at the Columbia University School of Library Service, 14 December 1987.* New York: Columbia University, 1988.

Xenophon. "Socrates and Euthydemus." In *The Works of Xenophon,* translated by H. G. Dakyns, vol. 3, part 1, 134–36. New York: Macmillan and Co., 1897.

Yates, Frances A. *The Occult Philosophy in the Elizabethan Age.* London, Boston, and Henley: Routledge & Kegan Paul, 1979.

The Zamorano 80: Collector's Books About California. Los Angeles: Zamorano Club, 1986. Describes itself as "an Annotated Check List Occasioned by the Exhibition of Famous and Notorious California Classics" at the Huntington Library.

Zeitlin, Jake. *Book Stalking at Home and Abroad.* Dallas: DeGoyler Library, Southern Methodist University, 1987.

Zempel, Edward N., and Linda A. Verkler. *First Editions: A Guide to Identification.* 2nd. ed. Peoria: Spoon River Press, 1984.

Zinsser, William K. *Search and Research: The Collections and Uses of the New York Public Library at Fifth Avenue and 42nd Street.* New York: New York Public Library, 1961.

Index

613